T0318739

PRINCIPLES OF CONTEMPORARY CORPORATE GOVERNANCE

FIFTH EDITION

Corporate governance plays a key role in ensuring that companies act responsibly and legally in the pursuit of long-term, sustainable growth. Now in its fifth edition, *Principles of Contemporary Corporate Governance* offers a comprehensive introduction to the rules and regulations of corporate governance systems. It takes an inclusive stakeholder approach to examine how companies apply corporate governance principles in the private sector.

The book's four-part structure has been consolidated and streamlined to provide logical coverage of fundamental contemporary themes and issues. These include basic concepts, board structures and company officers; corporate governance in Australia; shareholder activism and business ethics; and corporate governance in international and global contexts. The text has been comprehensively updated to include new case studies and discussion of recent developments, such as the impact of the COVID-19 pandemic and the destruction of a sacred rock shelter at Juukan Gorge. A new section on corporate governance in Singapore offers additional insight into corporate governance internationally.

Written by an expert author team, with contributions from international scholars, *Principles of Contemporary Corporate Governance* remains an indispensable resource for business and law students studying corporate governance.

Jean Jacques du Plessis is Professor of Corporate Law in the Deakin Law School at Deakin University and Extraordinary Professor at the Faculty of Law, University of the Western Cape (South Africa).

Anil Hargovan is an Associate Professor in the School of Management and Governance at the University of New South Wales.

Beth Nosworthy is an Associate Professor in the Adelaide Law School at the University of Adelaide.

Cambridge University Press acknowledges the Australian Aboriginal and Torres Strait Islander peoples of this nation. We acknowledge the traditional custodians of the lands on which our company is located and where we conduct our business. We pay our respects to ancestors and Elders, past and present. Cambridge University Press is committed to honouring Australian Aboriginal and Torres Strait Islander peoples' unique cultural and spiritual relationships to the land, waters and seas and their rich contribution to society.

Cambridge University Press acknowledges the Māori people as *tangata whenua* of Aotearoa New Zealand. We pay our respects to the First Nation Elders of New Zealand, past, present and emerging.

PRINCIPLES OF CONTEMPORARY CORPORATE GOVERNANCE

FIFTH EDITION

JEAN JACQUES DU PLESSIS
ANIL HARGOVAN
BETH NOSWORTHY

CONTRIBUTORS

MATTHEW BERKAHN, IRENE-MARIÉ ESSER, SUREN GOMTSIAN,
AKSHAYA KAMALNATH, HELEN KANG, SOUICHIROU KOZUKA,
TINEKE LAMBOOY, LUH LAN, LUKE NOTTAGE, POONAM PURI,
ALEXANDER SCHEUCH, ROSALIEN VAN 'T FOORT-DIEPEVEEN,
JEROEN VELDMAN, LÉCIA VICENTE, CHAO XI

CAMBRIDGE
UNIVERSITY PRESS

CAMBRIDGE
UNIVERSITY PRESS

Shaftesbury Road, Cambridge CB2 8EA, United Kingdom

One Liberty Plaza, 20th Floor, New York, NY 10006, USA

477 Williamstown Road, Port Melbourne, VIC 3207, Australia

314–321, 3rd Floor, Plot 3, Splendor Forum, Jasola District Centre, New Delhi – 110025, India

103 Penang Road, #05–06/07, Visioncrest Commercial, Singapore 238467

Cambridge University Press is part of Cambridge University Press & Assessment,
a department of the University of Cambridge.

We share the University's mission to contribute to society through the pursuit of
education, learning and research at the highest international levels of excellence.

www.cambridge.org
Information on this title: www.cambridge.org/highereducation/isbn/9781009287388

First edition © Jean Jacques du Plessis, James McConvill and Mirko Bagaric 2005
Second, third, fourth and fifth editions © Cambridge University Press & Assessment 2011, 2015, 2018, 2024

First published 2005
Second edition 2011
Third edition 2015
Fourth edition 2018
Fifth edition 2024

Cover designed by Simon Rattray, Squirt Creative
Typeset by Lumina Datamatics Ltd

A catalogue record for this publication is available from the British Library

A catalogue record for this book is available from the National Library of Australia

ISBN 978-1-009-28738-8 Paperback

Additional resources for this publication at www.cambridge.org/highereducation/
isbn/9781009287388/resources

Reproduction and communication for educational purposes
The Australian *Copyright Act 1968* (the Act) allows a maximum of one chapter or 10% of the pages
of this work, whichever is the greater, to be reproduced and/or communicated by any educational
institution for its educational purposes provided that the educational institution (or the body that
administers it) has given a remuneration notice to Copyright Agency Limited (CAL) under the Act.

For details of the CAL licence for educational institutions contact:

Copyright Agency Limited
Level 12, 66 Goulburn Street
Sydney NSW 2000
Telephone: (02) 9394 7600
Facsimile: (02) 9394 7601
E-mail: memberservices@copyright.com.au

*Please be aware that this publication may contain several variations of Aboriginal and Torres Strait Islander
terms and spellings; no disrespect is intended. Please note that the terms 'Indigenous Australians', 'Aboriginal
and Torres Strait Islander peoples' and 'First Nations peoples' may be used interchangeably in this publication.*

CONTENTS

AUTHORS AND CONTRIBUTORS

Authors

Jean Jacques du Plessis is Professor of Corporate Law in the Deakin Law School, Deakin University (Australia) and an Extraordinary Professor in the Faculty of Law, University the University of the Western Cape (South Africa). He developed and taught a one-year corporate governance graduate diploma in South Africa in 1998 (this was one of the first such courses in the world) at the University of Johannesburg. He also developed and established the Corporate Governance postgraduate unit (MLM706) for Deakin University in 2004 and redirected the content of that unit to reflect the content of the first edition of *Principles of Contemporary Corporate Governance*. Jean writes actively in the area of corporate governance, having more than 100 articles published in refereed Australian and international journals. He is co-author of several books, published in Australia, Germany and South Africa. He is an Alexander von Humboldt Scholar and received the Anneliese Maier Research Award from the Alexander von Humboldt Foundation for a five-year period (2013–18). He assisted the South African Government with its Corporate Law Reform Program. This resulted in the development of the South African *Companies Act 71 of 2008,* which became law in April 2012. He has been involved in that Reform Program since 2004. He was the Head of the Deakin Law School (2000–02) and President of the Corporate Law Teachers Association ('CLTA') (2008–09) and became a graduate of the Australian Institute of Company Directors ('AICD') in October 2011. Jean teaches in the areas of corporate governance, corporate law and business law.

Anil Hargovan is an Associate Professor in the School of Management and Governance at the University of New South Wales ('UNSW'). His research interests are in the area of corporate and insolvency law, a discipline in which he has presented many conference papers and published widely in refereed Australian and international law journals. His academic work, which includes over 110 publications, has been cited by the Corporations and Markets Advisory Committee and the judiciary. Anil has authored and co-authored several books, including *Australian Corporate Law* (LexisNexis, 2023). He was President of the Society of Corporate Law Scholars ('SCOLA', formerly Corporate Law Teachers Association) and is currently a member of the Executive Committee of SCOLA. Anil currently serves on the Corporate Governance Subject Advisory Committee and on the Applied Corporate Law Subject Advisory Committee at the Governance Institute of Australia. He has conducted the Corporate Governance course in the MBA program at the Australian Graduate School of Management at UNSW.

Beth Nosworthy is an Associate Professor in the University of Adelaide Law School who researches corporate law, with a focus on corporate structures and directors' duties. She worked as a judge's associate in the Supreme Court of South Australia and as a commercial lawyer with an Adelaide firm before commencing her career as an academic. Since joining the University of Adelaide, Beth has taught corporate law and equity at the under-graduate and postgraduate levels and is the Director of the Entrepreneur and Venture Advice Clinic, a pro bono service for startups and new ventures within the Clinical Legal Education program at the Adelaide Law School. Beth has presented many confer-ence papers and published widely in relation to directors' duties and corporate gover-nance, and co-authored several books, including *Contemporary Australian Corporate Law* (Cambridge University Press, 2nd ed, 2021). She sits on the Executive Committee of the Society of Corporate Law Academics and the Education Committee of the Governance Institute of Australia.

Contributors

Matthew Berkahn is an Associate Professor of Law at Massey Business School, Massey University, New Zealand. His doctoral thesis on corporate law was completed at Deakin University in 2003. His teaching focuses mainly on corporate law and he has published in that area (particularly shareholder remedies and directors' duties), as well as banking, competition and consumer law, in New Zealand and Australia. His recent publications include several chapters in a leading New Zealand corporate law treatise. Matt's work has been cited with approval by New Zealand, Australian and Singaporean courts, and by the OECD's Committee on Competition Law and Policy.

Irene-marié Esser is Professor of Corporate Law and Governance in the School of Law at the University of Glasgow and Dean of the Graduate School, College of Social Sciences. Since 2020 she has been an Extraordinary Professor at Stellenbosch University, South Africa, and since 2023, a Visiting Professor at the National Law University Jodhpur, India. She was admitted as an Attorney of the High Court of South Africa in 2005. She was the Company Law Convener for the UK Society of Legal Scholars for three years until 2021, and acted as external consultant to the King IV Committee on Corporate Governance in South Africa. She currently teaches corporate governance, corporate social responsibil-ity and company law at the University of Glasgow and supervises postgraduate research students in the United Kingdom and South Africa. Her research spans doctrinal and empirical approaches, covering the United Kingdom, European Union and South Africa in the field of corporate governance, company law and corporate social responsibility.

Suren Gomtsian is an Assistant Professor in the LSE Law School. He holds a PhD in Law (2016) and an LLM Research Master in Law (2012, cum laude) from Tilburg University. His research, which focuses on corporate law and private ordering, has been published in various journals, including *Modern Law Review, Journal of Corporation Law, Journal of Corporate Law Studies, Yale Journal of International Law, American Business Law Journal,* and *Delaware Journal of Corporate Law*. He has also been cited in the *Financial Times,* by the United States Court of Appeals (4th Circuit) and by the Delaware Court of Chancery.

Akshaya Kamalnath is an Associate Professor at the ANU College of Law. She has authored the book *The Corporate Diversity Jigsaw,* published by Cambridge University

Press in 2022, and numerous journal articles on corporate law and corporate insolvency. She blogs at *The Hitchhiker's Guide to Corporate Governance*.

Helen Kang is an Associate Professor in the School of Accounting, Auditing and Taxation, and Associate Dean Higher Degree Research UNSW Business School, at UNSW in Sydney. Helen's research interests are focused in the areas of international accounting, voluntary disclosures, and corporate governance. She has publications in leading international journals including *European Accounting Review, British Accounting Review, The International Journal of Accounting* and *Corporate Governance: An International Review*. Helen teaches undergraduate and postgraduate courses on international corporate governance and global financial reporting. She also supervises PhD students on topics including corporate governance and financial reporting practices of firms around the world.

Souichirou Kozuka (PhD, Tokyo) is Professor of Law at Gakushuin University, Tokyo. He specialises in commercial and corporate law. He has taught at Chiba University (Chiba), Sophia University (Tokyo), Keio University (Tokyo) and at Tokyo seminars annually sponsored by Ritsumeikan University and the Australian Network for Japanese Law ('ANJeL'). He has written extensively about corporate governance in Japan, including contributing to *The Cambridge Handbook of Corporate Law, Corporate Governance and Sustainability* (2020). Professor Kozuka is correspondent of UNIDROIT ('International Institute for the Unification of Private Law') and Associate Member of the International Academy of Comparative Law ('IACL').

Dr Tineke Lambooy LLM is full-time Professor of Corporate Law at Nyenrode Business Universiteit in the Netherlands. She also holds the position of Adjunct Professor at Airlangga University, Surabaya, Indonesia. Her research focuses on corporate law, corporate governance, corporate social responsibility, business and biodiversity and rights of nature.

Luh Lan is an Associate Professor at the Faculty of Law, National University of Singapore. She has a PhD (Business Policy) from the National University of Singapore (NUS) and an LLM (First Class) in Commercial Law from the University of Cambridge. She researches in the areas of company finance law and corporate governance and is the author of *Essentials of Corporate Law and Governance in Singapore* (Sweet & Maxwell, 2nd ed, 2022), an ECGI research member, Chairperson for the Global Corporate Governance Colloquia (2018–20) and a board member of the International Corporate Governance Society.

Luke Nottage (PhD, VUW; LLD, Kyoto) is Professor of Comparative and Transnational Business Law at the University of Sydney Law School, Associate Director (Japan) at its Centre for Asian and Pacific Law, founding Co-Director of the Australian Network for Japanese Law, and Special Counsel with Williams Trade Law. He specialises in commercial and consumer law, and has published hundreds of articles or chapters and 20 books, including Nottage, Wolff and Anderson (eds) *Corporate Governance in the*

21st Century: Japan's Gradual Transformation (Elgar, 2008) and Puchniak, Baum and Nottage (eds) *Independent Directors in Asia* (Cambridge University Press, 2017). Luke is qualified in New South Wales and New Zealand, has worked closely with law firms in Japan since 1990 and is a director of Japanese Law Links Pty Ltd. He has served as expert witness and consulted for many other law firms worldwide, as well as for ASEAN, the OECD, the European Commission, the UN Development Programme, and the governments of Japan and Saudi Arabia.

Poonam Puri is Full Professor of Law and the York Research Chair in Corporate Governance, Investor Protection and Financial Markets at Osgoode Hall Law School of York University in Toronto, Canada. Internationally recognised as a leading scholar of corporate law and governance and capital markets regulation, Professor Puri has been awarded the David Walter Mundell Medal for excellence in legal writing, the Law Society Medal for outstanding service to the profession and the Royal Society of Canada's Yvan Allaire Medal for exemplary contributions to the governance of public and private institutions in Canada.

Alexander Scheuch is Professor of Civil Law, Commercial, Corporate and Civil Procedural Law at the University of Bonn, Germany. His research areas include corporate governance, sustainability, and digitalisation of corporate law. He obtained his doctorate degree (Dr iur) from the University of Münster, Germany. After completing his legal clerkship at the Higher Regional Court of Cologne, Alexander worked as an in-house lawyer for a professional sports club before his return to the University of Münster as a lecturer at the Institute for International Business Law. He was named a Young Fellow of the North Rhine-Westphalian Academy of Sciences and Arts in 2017.

Dr Rosalien van 't Foort-Diepeveen LLM is an Assistant Professor at Nyenrode Business Universiteit. Her research and teaching mainly focuses on diversity on boards, corporate governance and corporate law.

Jeroen Veldman is Professor of Corporate Governance at Nyenrode Business Universiteit, Academic Director of the Nyenrode Board and Governance Executive Education Programs, Chairman of the Nyenrode Corporate Governance Institute and Associate Editor at the *Journal of Business Ethics,* Corporate Governance Section.

Lécia Vicente is a Visiting Professor at the University of Camerino, where she teaches comparative corporate governance. She is also the founder and principal of a global law observatory for business, where she analyses evolutionary trends in the law of the United States and around the world. She has advised government officials in the United Nations, held the Henry Plauché Dart Professorship at Louisiana State University, and was a lecturer at the University of Illinois. Her research focuses on market structures across jurisdictions and how those structures impact institutions and organisations. Her scholarship has been published or is forthcoming with Springer, Cambridge University Press, Wolters Kluwer, Hart Publishing, Intersentia, Oxford University Press and law reviews in the

United States. She holds a PhD from the European University Institute in Florence, Italy. Her expertise has been utilised in various research projects, including at the Institute of Social Sciences at the University of Lisbon and the UC Berkeley School of Law.

Chao Xi is Professor and Outstanding Fellow at the Faculty of Law, the Chinese University of Hong Kong ('CUHK LAW'), where he concurrently serves as Associate Dean (Research). He also chairs the CUHK LAW's CCTL Corporate Law and Governance Cluster. He is the author of *Corporate Governance and Legal Reform in China* (Widley, Simmons & Hill, 2009) and co-edits the *Cambridge Handbook of Shareholder Engagement and Voting* (2022).

PREFACE

The modern corporation knows few bounds – its widespread use in business and the corporatisation of essential services means that it permeates almost every aspect of our daily lives. It is companies, small and large, that drive economies and that can create economic prosperity for countries. However, all is not bright and shining; companies, especially large multinational corporations, have caused considerable harm to the environment and society generally by creating pollution, exploiting employees and not providing safe working environments.

Since the appearance of the first edition of *Principles of Contemporary Corporate Governance* in 2005, developments have gained velocity, and the volume of materials on corporate governance has grown exponentially. This made the appearance of a second edition in 2011 inevitable. The global financial crisis that emerged in 2007–08 and global financial uncertainties in the European Union (since 2008) made us predict in 2011 (in the Preface to the second edition of this book) that the discipline of corporate governance would retain its prominence in future. That has indeed been the case, and it was a main motivation for us to bring out the third edition (2015) and fourth edition (2018) of *Principles of Contemporary Corporate Governance*.

Many things have happened since 2018 that necessitated this updated fifth edition. Probably the three most significant developments that have impacted corporate governance since 2018 were the COVID-19 pandemic, a more prominent focus on all stakeholders (not only shareholders) (see Section 2.2), and the sharp focus, worldwide, on climate change. As far as climate change is concerned, the global trend has been to require corporations to report on non-financial matters. One particular issue, which we focus on in several parts of this book, is 'greenwashing' or 'greenscreening' (see Section 3.4.5). The way in which corporations are expected to report on climate change matters varies from jurisdiction to jurisdiction, with slightly different reporting framework applying (see Section 3.4), but the message is very clear: investors and other stakeholders want to ensure that corporations are good corporate citizens and that investments should only be made in corporations that are responsible as far as climate change matters and other non-financial issues, like human rights, are concerned. As well as recognising the impact that irresponsible corporate behaviour can have on investments in companies by investors, regulators are stepping in to hold corporations accountable for issuing misleading and deceptive information regarding non-financial matters. A good example is the Australian Securities and Investments Commission ('ASIC'), which since the end of 2022 has launched several court actions and issued several infringement notices against corporations, alleging they misled the markets regarding information pertaining to environmental, social and governance ('ESG') matters (see Section 3.4.5). We predict that strengthened regulation will be the global trend and that corporations will increasingly be very careful when reporting on and disclosing ESG matters.

After addressing the climate change issue, we looked at the book in its entirety and asked how we could keep it relevant and contemporary. Our response was to restructure the book. First, we expanded Chapters 1–2 to three chapters (now Chapters 1–3). Our aim was to provide a more comprehensive overview of the development of the concept of 'corporate governance', reflecting some of the most recent trends and developments. We have again refined our definition of 'corporate governance' and now present it much earlier in Chapter 1 (see Section 1.2). By working through the remaining parts of Chapter 1, as well as Chapters 2 and 3, the reader will be informed about how we derived at our current definition of 'corporate governance'. Second, we moved the important parts on shareholder activism and business ethics, from Chapters 13 and 14 to Part 3, now Chapters 9 and 10. Third, we now dedicate Part 4 to international perspectives (Chapters 11 and 12). A significant new approach was to present corporate governance in other jurisdictions and the OECD Principles of Corporate Governance, in a more consistent way – basically focusing on the same themes in all parts of these two chapters. We are of the opinion that this approach will enable readers to more easily compare the similarities and differences in corporate governance approaches as far as comparative corporate governance perspectives are concerned. Given our era of globalisation, we further expanded the coverage on comparative corporate governance by adding a section in Chapter 11 on corporate governance in Singapore. Those familiar with the first four editions will also note that there are several new scholars that have contributed to Chapters 11 and 12. Some of the previous contributors had other commitments and were substituted by new contributors. We are really pleased that all the sections in Chapters 11 and 12 are now written by scholars specialising in corporate governance in these jurisdictions.

- **Part 1** (Chapters 1–5) deals with basic concepts, board structures and company officers.
- **Part 2** (Chapters 6–8) focuses on corporate governance in Australia.
- **Part 3** (Chapters 9 and 10) deals with shareholder activism and business ethics.
- **Part 4** (Chapters 11 and 12) concludes the book with a discussion of corporate governance in international and global contexts.

As with all the previous four editions of this book (2005, 2011, 2015 and 2018), we trust that this edition will expose the reader to the most important principles of contemporary corporate governance. We also do not claim to present any in-depth discussion of the issues touched upon in this book as a very strict word limit prevents us from doing so. However, with comprehensive references to additional sources, like reports, court cases, academic articles and influential media pieces, we are confident that there is ample scope for the reader to delve deeper into the issues we cover.

We trust that this fifth edition will again broaden the perspectives and understanding of all people interested in corporate governance and corporate regulation and management, including company secretaries, compliance officers, judicial officers, lawyers, accountants, academics and students of law and business management.

Last, but not least, we would like to thank Professor Jason Harris (University of Sydney Law School) for his invaluable contribution to the third and fourth editions and for agreeing that we could still use some of the work he has done for these editions. Professor Harris had to focus on other commitments and stepped down as author, but we were very fortunate that Associate Professor Beth Nosworthy agreed to join us as an author. Professor Nosworthy played a major role in the restructuring of this fifth edition.

Jean Jacques du Plessis, Professor (Corporate Law),
Deakin University (Australia) and Extraordinary Professor,
Faculty of Law, University of the Western Cape (South Africa)
Anil Hargovan, University of New South Wales
Beth Nosworthy, Adelaide Law School, University of Adelaide
August 2023

ACKNOWLEDGEMENTS

Cambridge University Press and the authors would like to acknowledge the feedback provided by peer reviewers of the draft manuscript, including Jamie Ferrill, Hannah Harris, Ashoor Khan, Kelli Larson and Noel Tracey. Their feedback and comments were invaluable to the development of this edition.

The authors and Cambridge University Press would also like to thank the following for permission to reproduce material in this book.

Figures 4.1–4.6: reproduced with permission from Robert Tricker.

Extracts from ASX, *Corporate Governance Principles and Recommendations* (4th ed, 2019): © Copyright 2023 ASX Corporate Governance Council Association of Superannuation Funds of Australia Ltd, ACN 002 786 290, Australian Council of Superannuation Investors, Australian Financial Markets Association Limited ACN 119 827 904, Australian Institute of Company Directors ACN 008 484 197, Australian Institute of Superannuation Trustees ACN 123 284 275, Australasian Investor Relations Association Limited ACN 095 554 153, Australian Shareholders' Association Limited ACN 000 625 669, ASX Limited ABN 98 008 624 691 trading as Australian Securities Exchange, Business Council of Australia ACN 008 483 216, Chartered Accountants Australia and New Zealand, CPA Australia Ltd ACN 008 392 452, Financial Services Institute of Australasia ACN 066 027 389, Group of 100 Inc, The Institute of Actuaries of Australia ACN 000 423 656, ABN 50 084 642 571, The Institute of Internal Auditors – Australia ACN 001 797 557, Financial Services Council ACN 080 744 163, Governance Institute of Australia Ltd ACN 008 615 950, Law Council of Australia Limited ACN 005 260 622, National Institute of Accountants ACN 004 130 643, Property Council of Australia Limited ACN 008 474 422, Stockbrokers Association of Australia ACN 089 767 706. All rights reserved 2023.

Extracts from Paul Redmond, 'Directors' duties and corporate social responsiveness' (2012) 35(1) *University of New South Wales Law Journal* 317: © UNSW Law Journal, reproduced with permission.

Extracts from Organisation for Economic Co-operation and Development, *G20/OECD Principles of Corporate Governance* (2015): © OECD 2015, reproduced with permission.

Extract from *Royal Commission into the Casino Operator and Licence* (Report, October 2021) vol 1, ch 18 [43]–[47]: © Copyright State Government of Victoria. Reproduced under Creative Commons Attribution 4.0 International (CC BY 4.0): https://creativecommons.org/licenses/by/4.0/.

Extracts from Australian Corporations and Securities Reports: originally published by LexisNexis.

Extracts from Commonwealth legislation: sourced from the Federal Register of Legislation and reproduced under Creative Commons Attribution 4.0 International (CC

BY 4.0). For the latest information on Australian Government law please go to https://www.legislation.gov.au.

Every effort has been made to trace and acknowledge copyright. The publisher apologises for any accidental infringement and welcomes information that would redress this situation.

TABLE OF CASES

TABLE OF STATUTES

BASIC CONCEPTS, BOARD STRUCTURES AND COMPANY OFFICERS

THE EVOLUTION OF 'CORPORATE GOVERNANCE', CORPORATE THEORIES, CORPORATE GOVERNANCE PRINCIPLES AND SOME CONTEMPORARY DEBATES AND ISSUES

1

1.1 Introduction

1.1.1 Overview and structure of this book

Part 1 of this book deals with basic concepts, board structures and company officers. We trust that Chapter 1 (read in conjunction with Chapters 2 and 3) will enable the reader to better understand board functions and structures (Chapter 4) and the role and functions of different types of directors and officers (Chapter 5).

In Part 2 (Chapters 6–8) the focus is on corporate governance in Australia. However, many of the principles underpinning Australian corporate law and corporate governance, either derived from the United Kingdom, or were influenced in some other way by international corporate law and corporate governance developments globally. By analogy, this makes the book relevant for other jurisdictions.

In Part 3 (Chapters 9 and 10) we deal with shareholder activism and business ethics. The focus is on Australia, but these two aspects are of great importance internationally and most jurisdictions are converging to a similar approach regarding shareholder activism and business ethics, because the same underlying problems are addressed: the dominance of majority shareholders; poor corporate culture; and the evils associated with corruption, including aspects like bribery and modern slavery.

In Part 4 we conclude the book with a discussion of corporate governance in international and global contexts, exposing the reader to a basic overview of two principal approaches: in Chapter 11, adherence to a unitary (one-tier) board structure model (by the United States, the United Kingdom, New Zealand, Canada, South Africa, India and Singapore); and in Chapter 12, adoption of the two-tier board structure as the default legal model to corporate governance (by Germany, Japan and China) or recognition of this structure (as in the European Union and the *G20/OECD Principles of Corporate Governance*).

As with all the previous four editions of this book (2005, 2011, 2015 and 2018), we trust that it will expose the reader to the most important principles of contemporary corporate governance. This book does not claim to be based on 'black letter legal principles' and strict legal rules only – the principles of contemporary corporate governance simply do not lend themselves to such a strict and legalistic exposition.[1] We present different views and perspectives to stimulate debate and we provide what we hope will be 'food for thought', espousing an open-minded approach to corporate governance, not a dogmatic one. We also do not claim any in-depth discussion of any of the issues touched upon in this book as a very strict word limit prevents us from doing so. However, with comprehensive references to additional sources, like reports, court cases, academic articles and influential media pieces, we are confident that there is ample scope for the reader to delve deeper into the issues we cover.

1.1.2 Introduction to Chapter 1

In this chapter, on which Chapters 2 and 3 build, we establish the foundations for extracting principles of contemporary corporate governance. We begin the chapter by providing our own definition of the term 'corporate governance'. The reason for this is to enable the reader to gain a good understanding of how we approach the principles of contemporary corporate governance in this book. We have adjusted the definition in each of the previous four editions, as well as in this edition. The reason is that corporate governance is a dynamic concept and we strive to keep the definition updated to reflect contemporary principles.

1.2 Definition of 'corporate governance'

1.2.1 Our definition

We discuss the most significant trends and developments in the area of corporate governance in the remaining part of this chapter and in Chapters 2 and 3. Our definition of corporate governance is informed by all these trends and developments, but we consider it appropriate, different from the previous editions, to present our definition of corporate governance at the outset. It might be difficult for the reader to fully understand

---

1   Ronald J Gilson, 'From corporate law to corporate governance' in Jeffrey N Gordon and Wolf-Georg Ringe (eds), *Oxford Handbook of Corporate Law and Governance* (Oxford University Press, 2018) 3.

all the elements of our definition immediately. We trust that the reader will be stimulated by our definition to explore all elements of it in much greater detail in the rest of this book. We will also remind the reader regularly to revisit our definition of 'corporate governance' throughout the later parts of the book. We believe that 'corporate governance' could be defined as follows:[2]

> The system of regulating and overseeing corporate conduct and of balancing the interests of all internal parties (for example, shareholders and employees) and other parties (for example, external stakeholders, governments and local communities) who can be affected by the corporation's conduct, to ensure responsible behaviour by corporations, requiring of them to have regard to the corporation's corporate social responsibility ('CSR'), and to create long-term, sustainable growth for the corporation.

The most important elements of this definition are that corporate governance:

(1) is the system of regulating and overseeing corporate conduct
(2) takes into consideration the interests of internal stakeholders and other parties who can be affected by the corporation's conduct
(3) aims at ensuring responsible behaviour by corporations
(4) requires that corporations must have regard to their corporate social responsibilities
(5) aims at creating long-term, sustainable growth for the corporation.

1.2.2 Ultimate aim with a wide and all-inclusive definition

With our proposed definition of 'corporate governance', we essentially argue for a move away from 'short-termism' – the pressure to deliver quick results to the potential detriment of the longer-term and sustainable development of a company[3] and, as in the past, we promote an all-inclusive stakeholder approach to corporate governance, recognising the impact that corporations have on society and promoting responsible

---

2   For other useful definitions of corporate governance, see Ken Rushton, 'Introduction' in Ken Rushton (ed), *The Business Case for Corporate Governance* (Cambridge University Press, 2008) 2; Morten Huse, *Boards, Governance and Value Creation: The Human Side of Corporate Governance* (Cambridge University Press, 2007) 15, 18–24; Bob Garratt, *Thin on Top* (Nicholas Brealey Publishing, 2003) 12; John Farrar, 'Corporate governance and the judges' (2003) 15(1) *Bond Law Review* 65; and Güler Manisali Darman, *Corporate Governance Worldwide: A Guide to Best Practices and Managers* (ICC Publishing, 2004) 9–11.

3   Sir George Cox, *Overcoming Short-termism within British Business: The Key to Sustained Economic Growth: An independent review commissioned by the Labor Party* (March 2013) <www.yourbritain.org .uk/uploads/editor/files/Overcoming_Short-termism.pdf>. In 2015, Angel Gurría, OECD Secretary-General, stated the purpose of corporate governance as helping to 'build an environment of trust, transparency and accountability necessary for fostering long-term investment, financial stability and business integrity, thereby supporting stronger growth and more inclusive societies': Organization for Economic Cooperation and Development ('OECD'), *G20/OECD Principles of Corporate Governance* (2015) 7 <https://www.oecd.org/publications/g20-oecd-principles-of-corporate-governance-2015-9789264236882-en.htm>. See also Christopher Ansell, *Rethinking Theories of Governance* (Edward Elgar, 2023) 153.

behaviour by corporations. These goals are, of course, aspirational – we would hope that all companies would aspire to take all elements in our definition of corporate governance seriously. If short-termism remains the dominant focus for corporate management,[4] if companies keep on neglecting interests like those of employees – accentuated during the COVID-19 crisis – if they do not voluntarily strive to create long-term, sustainable growth, then more drastic measures, such as legislation, will be required to ensure companies observe good corporate governance. We hope this doesn't transpire, but it is conceivable that tough measures might be needed if self-regulation, soft law and voluntary market-based pressures do not have the desired effect. Evidence from the Interim and Final Hayne Reports[5] suggests that the soft law approach in Australia has done little to prevent poor and irresponsible behaviour by many corporations since the first adoption of a national corporate governance code in 2003 (see Section 1.4).

What we need to establish is how the principles of contemporary corporate governance contribute to ensuring better governance of companies, in particular large public companies. This will become clearer in the following chapters of this book.

1.3 Contextual background to corporate governance

Corporate governance is as old as the corporate form itself.[6] However, the phrase 'corporate governance' was scarcely used until the 1980s.[7] Issues related to poor corporate governance gained international prominence in the late 1990s and early 2000s in the wake of a series of corporate accounting scandals, most notably the BCCI and Maxwell scandals in the United Kingdom ('UK'), that in effect resulted in the Cadbury Report in 1992;[8] Enron in the United States ('US'); and HIH Insurance Ltd in Australia,

---

4   See David Millon, 'Enlightened shareholder value, social responsibility and the redefinition of corporate purpose without law' in PB Vasudev and Susan Watson (eds), *Corporate Governance after the Financial Crisis* (Edward Elgar, 2012) 68, 96–7.

5   *Royal Commission into Misconduct in the Banking Industry, Superannuation and Financial Services Industry* (Interim Report, September 2018) vol 1 ('Interim Hayne Report'); *Royal Commission into Misconduct in the Banking Industry, Superannuation and Financial Services Industry* (Final Report, February 2019) vol 1 ('Final Hayne Report').

6   Jean J du Plessis, 'Corporate law and corporate governance lessons from the past: Ebbs and flows, but far from "The end of history ...: Part 1"' (2009) 30(2) *Company Lawyer* 43, 44; Harwell Wells, 'The birth of corporate governance' (2010) 33(4) *Seattle University Law Review* 1247.

7   Bob Tricker, *Corporate Governance: Principles, Policies and Practices* (Oxford University Press, 4th ed, 2019) 4. See Corina Gavrea and Roxana Stegerean, 'Comparative study on corporate governance' (2011) 20(2) *Annals of the University of Oradea, Economic Science Series* 674 for a literature review and an analysis of the concept of 'corporate governance'. Note, however, that Cheffins points out that in the US, the term came into vogue during the 1970s: see Brian R Cheffins, 'The history of corporate governance' in Mike Wright et al (eds), *The Oxford Handbook of Corporate Governance* (Oxford University Press, 2013) 46. See also Gilson, 'From corporate law to corporate governance' in Gordon and Ringe (eds), *Oxford Handbook of Corporate Law and Governance* (2018) 3, 5.

8   Committee on the Financial Aspects of Corporate Governance, *The Financial Aspects of Corporate Governance* ('Cadbury Report') (Burgess Science Press, 1992): see Preface by Lord Cadbury and [4.60].

which was the trigger for the adoption of the first corporate governance principles and recommendations in Australia in 2003.[9] The focus on corporate governance intensified after 2008, in the aftermath of the Global Financial Crisis ('GFC').[10] And then there was again renewed interest in corporate governance issues during 2019–21 because of the COVID-19 pandemic. This pandemic exposed, probably more than ever since the 1970s, some of the most fundamental problems with a pure Milton Friedman form of capitalism (see Section 1.5.1.3). It was the neglect of the interests of employees, after years of financial prosperity for corporations, that caused serious concerns as employees were left in the cold when internationally COVID-19 lockdowns became the norm at the end of 2019 and for almost all of 2020.[11] The question was, how did we end up with this apparent neglect of employees who are core stakeholders of corporations?[12] The impact on supply chains was also considerable throughout the COVID-19 pandemic;[13] for example, significant disruptions of production supply chains were caused by the lockdowns in Shanghai, Beijing and other major cities in China in 2022, the effect of which were felt several months later in many countries dependent on Chinese imports.

In addition, climate change (global warming) became a prominent social and political issue from at least the early 2000s, culminating in the United Nations' climate change treaty, referred to as the *Paris Agreement*.[14] This brought the impact corporations have on the environment into play and resulted in a renewed focus on the importance of proper corporate governance. Again fundamental corporate governance questions were asked: Who is ultimately responsible for corporate conduct? How is corporate behaviour governed, and how do we ensure that corporations are responsible 'corporate citizens'?[15]

It is important to provide a final cautionary note about corporate governance codes. They became the topic of the day after the UK Cadbury Report in 1992. However, that was during the heyday of shareholder primacy and almost all corporate governance codes developed later were based on entrenching and promoting shareholder primacy. As will be seen in our later discussions,[16] things have changed a lot in recent times with the rise of an all-inclusive stakeholder approach. The problem with corporate governance codes

9   Du Plessis, 'Corporate law and corporate governance lessons from the past' (2009) 30(2) *Company Lawyer* 43. See also Gerry H Grant, 'The evolution of corporate governance and its impact on modern corporate America' (2003) 41(9) *Management Decision* 923–4.

10 Iilia Lupu, 'The indirect relation between corporate governance and financial stability' (2015) 22 *Procedia Economics and Finance* 538.

11 Leo E Strine and Dorothy S Lund, 'How to restore strength and fairness to our economy', *The New York Times* (10 April 2020).

12 It was a landmark win for Qantas workers when the High Court held that it was illegal to sack Qantas employees during the pandemic by outsourcing services: see *Qantas Airways Limited v Transport Workers Union of Australia* (2023) 412 ALR 134.

13 For an example of an affected industry, see Ninia Reza and Jean J du Plessis, 'The garment industry in Bangladesh, corporate social responsibility (CSR) of multinational corporations (MNCs) and the impact of COVID-19' (2022) 9(2) *Asian Journal of Law and Society* 255.

14 *Paris Agreement*, opened for signature 22 April 2016, [2016] ATS 24 (entered into force 4 November 2016) <https://unfccc.int/sites/default/files/english_paris_agreement.pdf>. For an overview of the aims with the *Paris Agreement*, see United Nations, 'The Paris Agreement' <https://unfccc.int/process-and-meetings/the-paris-agreement>.

15 Mervyn King, *The Corporate Citizen* (Penguin, 2006).

16 See remaining parts of this chapter, but also Chapters 2 and 3.

has been emphasised prominently.[17] Nowadays there are calls for abolishing corporate governance codes as they have reached their use-by date.[18]

1.4 Difficulties in defining 'corporate governance' precisely

While a discussion of the principles of contemporary governance requires a closer description of corporate governance, the concept remains one that does not lend itself to a single,[19] specific or narrow definition. Corporate governance, by its very nature, is organic and flexible, constantly evolving in response to a changing corporate environment.[20] In addition, as Christopher Ansell points out, different disciplines perceive the concept of corporate governance differently.[21]

A comparison of older definitions or descriptions of corporate governance, such as those used in the South African King I (1994) Report, and more recent definitions, such as those used in the King IV (2016) Report and others discussed in Section 1.2 and in this Section 1.4, reveal a change of focus. It has shifted from a narrow, inward-looking approach that primarily addresses internal director-related rules within the corporation to an outward-looking, more inclusive and multifaceted approach that recognises that corporate governance is about much more than managing the manner in which directors exercise and use their powers and fulfil their duties to corporations – it extends to 'the exercise of ethical and effective leadership by the governing body towards the achievement of ... governance outcomes' in relation to ethical culture, good performance, effective control and legitimacy.[22]

Early attempts at a definition focused on corporate governance as a 'system': the UK Cadbury Report (1992)[23] and the King I (1994) Report[24] both defined corporate governance as '*the system* by which companies are directed and controlled' (emphasis added). In 2003, the Report of the HIH Royal Commission on the collapse of HIH Insurance Ltd ('the Owen Report'), one of Australia's largest corporate collapses, emphasised that corporate governance extends beyond mere models and systems and includes the

17 Beate Sjåfjell, 'When the solution becomes the problem: The triple failure of Corporate Governance Codes' in Jean J du Plessis and Chee Keong Low (eds), *Corporate Governance Codes for the 21st Century* (Springer, 2017) 23.
18 Brian R Cheffins and Bobby V Reddy, 'Thirty Years and Done – Time to Abolish the UK Corporate Governance Code' (Working Paper No 654/2022, European Corporate Governance Institute, June 2022) <https://papers.ssrn.com/sol3/papers.cfm?abstract_id=4132617>.
19 See generally Janet Dine and Marios Koutsias, *The Nature of Corporate Governance: The Significance of National Cultural Identity* (Edward Elgar, 2013) 67–70.
20 The discussion of different corporate governance theories in Section 1.5.2 illustrates how changed perceptions and expectations of corporations impact on the concept and, ultimately, on how we define 'corporate governance' in Section 1.6. For an insightful review of the history of corporate governance that underscores its evolutionary nature, see Brian R Cheffins, 'The history of corporate governance' in Mike Wright et al (eds), *The Oxford Handbook of Corporate Governance* (Oxford University Press, 2013) 46. See also Gilson, 'From corporate law to corporate governance' in Gordon and Ringe (eds), *Oxford Handbook of Corporate Law and Governance* (2018) 3.
21 Ansell, *Rethinking Theories of Governance* (2023) 2.
22 *Report on Corporate Governance for South Africa 2016* ('King IV Report') (Institute of Directors in Southern Africa, 2016) 11 (definition of 'corporate governance').
23 Committee on the Financial Aspects of Corporate Governance, *The Financial Aspects of Corporate Governance* ('Cadbury Report') (Burgess Science Press, 1992).
24 *The King Report on Corporate Governance* ('King I Report') (Institute of Directors in Southern Africa, 1994).

'practices by which that exercise and control of authority is in fact effected'.[25] A narrow focus on corporate governance is no longer tenable, as Clarke points out.[26]

The Australian Securities Exchange ('ASX') Corporate Governance Council continued the trend to define corporate governance more precisely by including references to setting and achieving specific objectives, the monitoring of risk, and the optimisation of performance in the 2003 ASX *Principles of Good Corporate Governance and Best Practice Recommendations*.[27] The description used in the 2014 version (also adopted in the 2019 version[28]) of the ASX *Corporate Governance Principles and Recommendations* broadened the concept even further by adding another aspect, namely 'accountability', by adopting the definition of corporate governance stated by Justice Owen in the HIH Royal Commission Report (2003):[29]

> the framework of rules, relationships, systems and processes within and by which authority is exercised and controlled in corporations. It encompasses the mechanisms by which companies, and those in control, *are held to account* [emphasis added].[30]

The *G20/OECD Principles of Corporate Governance* (2015)[31] specifically included a reference to the relationships between the parties involved in corporations, describing corporate governance as:[32]

> a set of relationships between a company's management, its board, its shareholders and other stakeholders. Corporate governance also provides the structure through which the objectives of the company are set, and the means of attaining those objectives and monitoring performance are determined.

As was seen in Section 1.2 above, we attempt to define 'corporate governance' in wide terms. We approach the definition in a similar way as the OECD, referring to the interests of all parties and stakeholders that can be impacted by corporate behaviour and corporate conduct.

In the next section we consider the origins of both the corporate governance and the stakeholder debates.

25 Report of the HIH Royal Commission ('Owen Report'), *The Failure of HIH Insurance – Volume I: A Corporate Collapse and Its Lessons* (Commonwealth of Australia, 2003) xxxiii.
26 Thomas Clarke, *International Corporate Governance: A Comparative Approach* (Routledge, 2nd ed, 2017) 411.
27 ASX, *Principles of Good Corporate Governance and Best Practice Recommendations* (March 2003) 3 <www.asx.com.au/documents/asx-compliance/principles-and-recommendations-march-2003.pdf>.
28 ASX, *Corporate Governance Principles and Recommendations* (4th ed, 2019) 1 <https://www.asx.com.au/documents/asx-compliance/cgc-principles-and-recommendations-fourth-edn.pdf>.
29 Owen Report, *The Failure of HIH Insurance* (2003) vol 1, xxxiv.
30 ASX, *Corporate Governance Principles and Recommendations* (3rd ed, 2014) 3 <www.asx.com.au/documents/asx-compliance/cgc-principles-and-recommendations-3rd-edn.pdf>.
31 *G20/OECD Principles of Corporate Governance* (2015) <https://www.oecd.org/publications/g20-oecd-principles-of-corporate-governance-2015-9789264236882-en.htm>. In September 2023, the 2015 Principles were replaced by the 2023 *G20/OECD Principles of Corporate Governance* <https://doi.org/10.1787/ed750b30-en>. The *G20/OECD Principles of Corporate Governance* are set out in the Appendix to the OECD *Recommendation on Principles of Corporate Governance* (OECD/LEGAL/0413) adopted by the OECD Council on 8 July 2015 and revised on 8 June 2023. See discussions in Sections 12.2 and 12.3.
32 *G20/OECD Principles of Corporate Governance* (2015) 9.

1.5 Origins of the corporate governance debate and changing views

1.5.1 Origins and developments in the 1900s

1.5.1.1 Prominence of the corporate governance debate

It is difficult to determine exactly when the corporate governance debate started,[33] but in 2021 Lund and Pollman illustrated clearly that 'the concept of corporate governance developed alongside the shareholder primacy movement'.[34] However, there is little doubt that there were many factors that brought the debate to prominence: the separation of ownership and control (so pertinently illustrated in 1932 by Berle and Means in their book, *The Modern Corporation and Private Property*), which resulted in the so-called managerial revolution,[35] or 'managerialism';[36] the pivotal role of the corporate form in generating wealth and economic prosperity for nations;[37] the huge powers of corporations,[38] and the effects of these on our daily lives; the enormous consequences that flow from collapses of large public corporations;[39] and the practical reality of the almost unfettered powers of boards of directors. In most Australian corporations, directors will have the power to manage the business of the corporation themselves, or the power to manage the business of the corporation will be under the direction of the directors.[40] And, normally, these powers will only be restricted by specific provisions in corporate legislation, or specific provisions in Australian corporations' constitutions (if one has been adopted).[41] We are, indeed, as Allan Hutchinson describes it so appropriately, living in an age of 'corpocracy'.[42]

It is also beyond dispute that the corporate governance debate became particularly prominent when the basic perception of the company changed. At first the only real concern of a company was the maximisation of profits.[43] Profits for whom? – the

---

33   See John Farrar and Pamela Hanrahan, *Corporate Governance* (LexisNexis, 2017) 29–33. Gilson traces it back to the mid 1970s, when Jensen and Meckling reframed corporate law into something far broader than disputes over statutory language. See Michael C Jensen and William H Meckling, 'Theory of the firm: Managerial behavior, agency costs and the theory of the firm' (1976) 3(2) *Journal of Financial Economics* 305, cited in Ronald J Gilson, 'From Corporate Law to Corporate Governance' in Gordon and Wolf-Goerg (eds), *The Oxford Handbook of Corporate Law and Governance* (Oxford University Press, 2015) 3, 5.

34   Dorothy S Lund and Elizabeth Pollman, 'The corporate governance machine' (2021) 121(8) *Columbia Law Review* 2563, 2575–8.

35   See, eg, Klaus J Hopt, 'Preface' in Theodor Baums, Richard M Buxbaum and Klaus J Hopt (eds), *Institutional Investors and Corporate Governance* (W de Gruyter, 1994) 1; and OECD, *Principles of Corporate Governance* (April 2004) 12 <www.oecd.org/dataoecd/32/18/31557724.pdf>.

36   Stephen M Bainbridge, *The New Corporate Governance in Theory and Practice* (Oxford University Press, 2008) 9, 19–20, 155 *et seq*.

37   Colin Mayer, *Prosperity* (Oxford University Press, 2018) 34–5, 64.

38   Kent Greenfield, *The Failure of Corporate Law* (University of Chicago Press, 2006) 4–5; James E Post, Lee E Preston and Sybille Sachs, *Redefining the Corporation: Stakeholder Management and Organizational Wealth* (Stanford Business Books, 2002) 10–11; Robert C Hinkley, *Time to Change Corporations: Closing the Citizen Gap* (Robert C Hinkley, 2011) 9, 15.

39   See generally Roberta Romano, *The Genius of American Corporate Law* (AEI Press, 1993); and David SR Leighton and Donald H Thain, *Making Boards Work* (McGraw-Hill Ryerson, 1997) 9–10.

40   See, eg, *Corporations Act 2001* (Cth) s 198A(1).

41   *Corporations Act 2001* (Cth) s 198A(2).

42   Allan C Hutchinson, *The Companies We Keep* (Irwin Law, 2005) 8.

43   Adolf A Berle, 'The impact of the corporation on classical theory' in Thomas Clarke (ed), *Theories of Corporate Governance: The Philosophical Foundations of Corporate Governance* (Routledge, 2004) 45, 49 *et seq*.

shareholders.[44] This was confirmed in 1919 in the US case of *Dodge v Ford Motor*, decided in the State of Michigan:[45]

> A business corporation is organized and carried on primarily for the profit of the stockholders. The powers of the directors are to be employed for that end. The discretion of directors is to be exercised in the choice of means to attain that end, and does not extend to the change of the end itself, to the reduction of profits, or to the nondistribution of profits among stockholders in order to devote them to other purposes.

This has served as the guiding principle for American boards since 1919 and was confirmed as good law[46] in 1986 in the Delaware[47] case of *Katz v Oak Industries*,[48] only a year after the much discussed case of *Smith v Van Gorkom* where it was again confirmed that directors also owe fundamental duties to shareholders:[49]

> Under Delaware law, the business judgment rule is the offspring of the fundamental principle, codified in Del.C. § 141(a), that the business affairs of a Delaware corporation are managed by or under its board of directors ... In carrying out their managerial roles, directors are charged with an unyielding fiduciary duty to the corporation *and its shareholders* ... [emphasis added].

1.5.1.2 Myths exposed: Shareholders as 'owners' of the corporation and directors as 'agents' of the 'shareholder-principals'

Shareholders were previously considered to be the dominant stakeholders as far as directors' fiduciary duties were concerned.[50] Thus, they were described as the 'owners of the company'.[51] They were considered to be the providers of capital, which enabled

---

44 Margaret M Blair, 'Ownership and control: Rethinking corporate governance for the twenty-first century' in Thomas Clarke (ed), *Theories of Corporate Governance* (2004) 175, 181. See also Bainbridge, *The New Corporate Governance in Theory and Practice* (2008) 53.

45 *Dodge v Ford Motor Co*, 170 NW 668, 684 (Mich, 1919); (1919) 204 Mich 459, 507. For an overview of the *Dodge* case, see Leonard I Rothman, 'Re-evaluating the basis of corporate governance in the post-Enron era' in Vasudev and Watson (eds), *Corporate Governance after the Financial Crisis* (2012) 96, 101, 110–12.

46 For an overview of the impact and adoption of the Dodge principle in the US, see David G Yosifon, 'The law of corporate purpose' (2013) 10(2) *Berkeley Business Law Journal* 181. See also Lund and Pollman, 'The corporate governance machine' (2021) 121(8) *Columbia Law Review* 2563, 2581.

47 Delaware has been the dominant state, setting the tone for corporate law and corporate governance principles for a very long time. By far the largest number of public companies are listed in the State of Delaware, primarily because of the 'liberal' way in directors and officers are protected against personal liability (referred to 'the race to the bottom'), but also for tax reasons. See generally Lund and Pollman, 'The corporate governance machine' (2021) 121(8) *Columbia Law Review* 2563, 2579–88.

48 *Katz v Oak Industries Inc*, 508 A 2d 873, 879 (Del Ch, 1986).

49 *Smith v Van Gorkom*, 488 A 2d 858 (Del, 1985). For a summary of prevailing views of directors' fiduciary duties under US corporate law, see Haig Panossian, 'Workers vs shareholders under United States corporate law: Reforming corporate fiduciary law to protect worker interests' (2007) 10 *Journal of Law and Social Change* 81, 85.

50 For an important recent judicial decision on directors' duties, including their fiduciary duties, see the decision of the *Eastland Food Corporation v Mekhaya*, 486 Md 1 (Md, 2023).

51 See generally Greenfield, *The Failure of Corporate Law* (2006) 43, but also see his arguments dispelling this 'myth' (44–7). For various forms 'ownership' of enterprises, see Henry Hansmann, *The Ownership of Enterprises* (Belknap Press, 1996).

the company to conduct business with little or no regard to the vital role other stakeholders play in ensuring that corporations remain going concerns during their lifespan. The focus on shareholders resulted in what has become known as the 'shareholder primacy theory'.[52] The agency theory of the corporation, also called the contract, contractual or contractarian theory,[53] provided a justification for the shareholder primacy theory and was primarily inspired by economics,[54] later on inspired especially by the 'Friedman Doctrine', as will be seen in Section 1.5.1.3.

The notion that shareholders were the 'owners' of the corporation went unchallenged for many decades. However, the legal basis of the shareholders being the owners of the corporation came under intense scrutiny when in-depth historic research revealed that shareholders' 'company-ownership claim' was more based on the historic development of the corporate form, as influenced by the law of partnership, joint stock companies and unincorporated deed of settlement companies, rather than on sound legal grounds.[55] Post, Preston and Sachs sum up the fallacy of past perceptions well under the heading 'Inaccuracy of the "ownership" model and its implications':[56]

> Shareowners hold securities, but they do not own the corporation in any meaningful sense, nor are they the only constituents vital to its existence and success. The notion that shareowner interests should dominate those of all other corporate constituents is inconsistent with the observed behaviour of successful firms. Therefore, the conventional shareowner-dominant model of the corporation is unrealistic, as well as normatively unacceptable.

In fact, it was realised, inter alia because of the legal concept of 'ownership', that nobody can 'own' the company, as it is a separate 'legal person'. Thus, the question of ownership of the company is as irrelevant as the question of who are the 'owners' of natural persons. The questions of the proprietary rights of the corporation as a separate legal entity, the proprietary rights of shareholders in their shareholdings, and shareholders' rights during the existence of the company as a going concern and when a corporation is liquidated are relevant but not the focus of this book.

An aspect related to the myth of shareholders as the 'owners' of the corporation,[57] is that the 'shareholders' are also seen as the 'principals' and the 'directors (managers)' as

52 See generally, on the theory of 'shareholder primacy', Irene-marié Esser, *Recognition of Various Stakeholder Interests in the Company Management: Corporate Social Responsibility and Directors' Duties* (VDM Verlag Dr Müller, 2009) 19.

53 Henry N Butler, 'The contractual theory of the corporation' (1989) 11(4) *George Mason University Law Review* 99.

54 David Wishart, 'A reconfiguration of company and/or corporate law theory' (2010) 10(1) *Journal of Corporate Law Studies* 151, 169. See also Marc Moore and Martin Petrin, *Corporate Governance: Law Regulation and Theory* (Macmillan Educationl, 2017) 29.

55 Paddy Ireland, 'Company law and the myth of shareholder ownership' (1999) 62(1) *Modern Law Review* 32.

56 Post, Preston and Sachs, *Redefining the Corporation* (2002) 11. See also *BTI 2014 LLC v Sequana SA* [2022] 3 WLR 709, [20] per Lord Reed.

57 This section is mainly extracted from Jean J du Plessis, 'Some myths and fallacies regarding corporate law and corporate governance: Have they been debunked in South Africa?' in Hermie Coetzee and Carika Fritz (eds), *De Serie Legenda, Developments in Commercial Law, Entrepreneurial Law* (LexisNexis, 2019) vol III, 40, 44–5.

the 'agents' of the shareholders, their 'principals'.[58] It has been proven convincingly that this is also a myth in law – it has no legal underpinning.[59] Directors have just one 'principal' and that is the company as a separate legal entity. Furthermore, it is a weak argument to defend the shareholder primacy theory based on the fact that directors cannot serve more than one master[60] and that if they need to account to all stakeholders they will in fact be accountable to none as nobody will take responsibility to enforce directors' duties.[61] It is a reality that directors can and should consider competing interests of different corporate constituencies.[62]

The shareholder primacy theory has at times also been defended based on the fact that 'agency costs' would be much higher if it is not left to the shareholders, as 'principals,' to enforce directors' duties on behalf of the company. This argument stems from an article published in 1976 by Jensen and Meckling.[63] They defined 'agency costs' as 'the sum of ... (1) the monitoring expenditures by the principal [which they saw as the shareholders], (2) the bonding expenditure by the agent [which they saw as the managers of shareholder funds], and (3) residual loss'.[64] This article has been based on a very particular perception of the meaning of 'property rights' and a very particular view of the control of the 'principals' (shareholders/stockholders or 'outside equity and debts holders'[65]) over their 'agents' ('top management of the corporation'[66] or 'managers'[67] as stewards in control of shareholders' money)[68] However, in essence, the agency cost theory was solely developed as a tool to measure whether profits could be 'maximised to the maximum' for the shareholders as 'owners' as part of Milton Friedman's insistence that corporate officials should 'make as much money for their stockholders as possible'

58 John Armour, Henry Hansmann and Reinier Kraakman, 'Agency problems and legal strategies' in Reinier Kraakman et al, *The Anatomy of Corporate Law: A Comparative and Functional Approach* (Oxford University Press, 2nd ed, 2009) 35.

59 Margaret M Blair and Lynn A Stout, 'A team production theory of corporate law' (1999) 85(2) *Virginia Law Review* 247, 291: 'Because American law does not permit shareholders to command the board to action, describing directors as "agents" grossly misrepresents at least the legal nature of the relationship'. See also Daniel Attenborough, 'How directors should act when owing duties to the companies' shareholders: Why we need to stop applying Greenhalgh' (2009) 20(10) *International Company and Commercial Law Review* 340, fn 14; Lynn A Stout et al, 'The modern corporation statement on company law' (2016) [8] <https://papers.ssrn.com/sol3/papers.cfm?abstract_id=2848833>. See also Jean J du Plessis 'Directors' duty to act in the best interests of the corporation: "Hard cases make bad law"' (2019) 34(1) *Australian Journal of Corporate Law* 3, 20.

60 Lynn Stout, *The Shareholder Value Myth: How Putting Shareholders First Harms Investors, Corporations, and the Public* (Berrett-Koehler Publisher Inc, 2012) 108. Moore and Petrin, *Corporate Governance* (2017) 46 quoting WH Easterbrook and DR Fischel, *The Economic Structure of Corporate Law* (Harvard University Press, 1991) 38: 'a manager told to serve two masters ... has been freed of both and is answerable to neither'. However, Moore and Petrin correctly point out that this view is 'somewhat exaggerated'.

61 Adolf A Berle, 'For whom are corporate managers trustees: A note' (1932) 45(8) *Harvard Law Review* 1365, 1367–8. Sulette Lombard, 'Directors' duties to creditors' (LLD Thesis, University of Pretoria, 2006) 38–41 correctly, it is submitted, points out why shareholders are not in actual fact the most efficient monitors of managerial performance.

62 Blair and Stout, 'A team production theory of corporate law' (1999) 85(2) *Virginia Law Review* 247, 291.

63 Jensen and Meckling, 'Theory of the firm' (1976) 3(2) *Journal of Financial Economics* 305.

64 Ibid 309.

65 Ibid 310.

66 Ibid 308

67 Ibid 309.

68 Ibid 306–8.

(see quote and discussion in Section 1.5.1.3).[69] If the bases of these assumptions have been challenged and proven to be myths, as illustrated above, the traditional justification for reduction of 'agency costs' through enforcement of directors' duties by shareholders should also be viewed with circumspection.

There are other ways of reducing so-called 'agency costs' in the context of enforcing directors' duties. For instance, in Australia, the principal regulator, the Australian Securities and Investments Commission ('ASIC'), can bring actions for breaches of directors' statutory duties, if to do so would be in the public interest. Thus, the 'agency costs' are reduced considerably,[70] as not putting the burden of enforcement on the shareholders alone reduces so-called 'agency costs'. It is also noteworthy that in Australia funded class actions, although controversial and under regular law reform,[71] also play a significant role in diverting litigation costs away from companies by reducing the need to rely on statutory derivative actions by shareholders to enforce directors' duties. In Australia the number of class actions filed increased from 18 in 2012–13 to 64 in 2020–21, with a slight drop to 54 in 2021–22.[72] In total there were 433 class actions filed in Australia from 2012–13 to 2021–22.[73] In the majority of cases class actions are settled,[74] thereby allowing corporations to avoid the expensive process of having to institute actions against directors for a breach of their duties towards the company. In other words, even though the class actions as such are not linked to breaches of directors' duties directly, the fact is that there is always the possibility that shareholders might institute action against directors to recover the damages suffered by the corporations because of a successful class action against a corporation.

Taking into consideration how certain well-accepted principles were disposed of as 'myths', it could be argued that the days of shareholder primacy are numbered. This was basically the case made out by Lynn Stout, in her 2012 essay, 'New thinking on "shareholder primacy"'.[75] Although this piece did not break fresh ground, as there were others who had made the assertion before, it drove the point home very clearly – it

---

69 Moore and Petrin, *Corporate Governance* (2017) 36–7; Butler, 'The contractual theory of the corporation' (1989) 11(4) *George Mason University Law Review* 99, 116–17.

70 Du Plessis, 'Some myths and fallacies regarding corporate law and corporate governance' in Coetzee and Fritz (eds), *De Serie Legenda, Developments in Commercial Law, Entrepreneurial Law* (2019) 40, 45. See generally regarding legal strategies to reduce agency costs, Armour, Hansmann and Kraakman, 'Agency problems and legal strategies' in Kraakman et al, *The Anatomy of Corporate Law* (2009) 35, 37–45.

71 Alexander Morris et al, *The Review: Class Actions in Australia 2021/2022* (King & Wood/Mallesons, September 2022) 20–1. As class actions are often linked to corporations' contravention of the strict continuous disclosure rules under the *Corporations Act 2001* (Cth), the relevant provisions were amended in 2021 by way of sch 2 of the *Treasury Laws Amendment (2021 Measures No 1) Act 2021* (Cth) and again in 2022 by way of the *Treasury Laws Amendment (2022 Measures No 1) Act 2022* (Cth).

72 Morris at al, *The Review: Class Actions in Australia 2021/2022* (September 2022) 6. See generally, as far as 2021 is concerned, Cat Fredenburgh, 'Class action filing plummet as law firms, litigation funders regroup', *Lawyerly* (3 September 2021) <https://www.lawyerly.com.au/class-action-filings-plummet-as-law-firms-litigation-funders-regroup/>.

73 Morris et al, *The Review* (September 2022) 6.

74 Ibid 12, where Morris et al point out that '[a]t least 12 class action settlements were approved in 2021/2022, representing at least $475M in settlement funds'.

75 Lynn Stout, 'New thinking on "shareholder primacy"' in Vasudev and Watson (eds), *Corporate Governance after the Financial Crisis* (2012) 25.

helped the penny to drop. More recently, in a tribute to Lynn Stout and her book *The Shareholder Value Myth*,[76] several comprehensive and in-depth papers by leading scholars were published to expose the myth of shareholder ownership and shareholder primacy even further,[77] hammering in more nails into the coffins of these concepts. The scholar, practitioner and former judge nowadays most forcefully arguing against a shareholder primacy corporate law model is Justice Leo Strine Jnr, former Chief Justice of the Delaware Supreme Court. His arguments in favour of recognising other stakeholders are clear and convincing.[78] He has correctly been described as one of the 'all-time top-scoring stakeholderists',[79] albeit in a cynical way, as there are clearly two camps,[80] the 'shareholder primacy camp'[81] and the 'all-inclusive stakeholder camp'.[82] We make clear in this book that we associate ourselves with the latter camp.

1.5.1.3 The Friedman legacy: 'Shareholder capitalism'

Despite the above discussion, the impact of the idea that shareholders were considered to be the owners of the corporation should not be underestimated. It provided the impetus for what can generally be called 'shareholder capitalism'. This form of capitalism became

---

76 Lynn Stout, *The Shareholder Value Myth: How Putting Shareholders First Harms Investors, Corporations, and the Public* (Berrett-Koehler Publishers, 2012).

77 'The Corporate Issue: A tribute to Lynn Stout' (2020) 10(3) *Accounting, Economics and Law: A Convivium* <https://www.degruyter.com/journal/key/ael/10/3/html>.

78 Leo E Strine Jr, 'Good corporate citizenship we can all get behind?: Toward a principled, non-ideological approach to making money the right way' (2023) 78(2) *The Business Lawyer* 329; Leo E Strine Jr, 'Restoration: The role stakeholder governance must play in recreating a fair and sustainable American Economy: A reply to Professor Rock' (2020) *Faculty Scholarship at Penn Carey Law* 2238 <https://scholarship.law.upenn.edu/faculty_scholarship/2238>; Leo E Strine Jr, 'Toward fair and sustainable capitalism: A comprehensive proposal to help American workers, restore fair gainsharing between employees and shareholders, and increase American competitiveness by reorienting our corporate governance system toward sustainable long-term growth and encouraging investments in America's future' (2019) *Faculty Scholarship at Penn Carey Law* 2104 <https://scholarship.law.upenn.edu/faculty_scholarship/2104>.

79 David H Webber, 'The humanities strike back: (E)ESG and Justice Strine challenge gamer shareholder primacy' (2022) 24(4) *University of Pennsylvania Journal of Business Law* 875, 876.

80 David Millon, 'Looking back, looking forward: Personal reflections on a scholarly career' (2017) 74(2) *Washington and Lee Law Review* 699; Leo E Strine Jr, 'Corporate power is corporate purpose II: Future considerations from Professor Johnson and Millon' (2017) 74(2) *Washington and Lee Law Review* 1165.

81 Stephen M Bainbridge, *The Profit Motive: Defending Shareholder Value Maximization* (Cambridge University Press, 2023); Lucian A Bebchuk and Roberto Tallarita, 'The illusory promise of stakeholder governance' (2020–21) 106 *Cornell Law Review* 91; P M Vasudev 'The stakeholder principle, corporate governance, and theory: Evidence from the field and the path onward' (2014) 41(2) *Hofstra Law Review* 399. See also Lucian Bebchuk, 'Three Conceptions of Capitalism: 2023 Wallenberg Lecture', *ECGI Blog* (26 October 2023) <https://www.ecgi.global/blog/three-conceptions-capitalism-2023-wallenberg-lecture?mc_cid=73691d42ca&mc_eid=acacb5df5d>.

82 See our discussion in Chapter 2, Sections 2.2 and 2.3; and Chapter 3. See also Katharine V Jackson, 'Towards a stakeholder-shareholder theory of corporate governance: A comparative analysis' (2011) 7(2) *Hastings Business Law Journal* 309; Flore Bridoux and J W Stoelhorst, 'Stakeholder governance: On overcoming the problems in the traditional narrative of capitalism' in Till Talaulicar (ed), *Research Handbook on Corporate Governance* (Edward Elgar, 2023) 25; and Elizabeth Pollman, 'Corporate acceptance of stakeholderism: Will it hinder or boost government regulation of corporate externalities?', *ECGI Blog* (19 October 2023) <https://www.ecgi.global/blog/corporate-acceptance-stakeholderism-will-it-hinder-or-boost-government-regulation-corporate?mc_cid=73691d42ca&mc_eid=acacb5df5d>.

prominent following the publication of a short piece by Milton Friedman[83] in the *New York Times* on 13 September 1970. The article earned him the honour of being described as 'perhaps the most influential intellectual force in popularizing ... the idea of shareholder value maximization';[84] more recently he has been boldly described by Alex Edmans as the 'second most influential economist of all times after John Maynard Keynes'.[85] It was the title, 'The Social Responsibility of Business Is to Increase Its Profits', that caught the imagination of the world, with the piece cited thousands of times[86] and becoming the economic justification for 'unadulterated' capitalism in the Western World, also called the 'Friedman Doctrine'.[87] In later years this this line of thinking has been referred to as the 'Chicago School of Economics', Friedman being a Professor at the Chicago School of Economics,[88] a School that relentlessly spread the Friedman gospel for many years from 1972.

Friedman branded those not believing in profit maximisation for shareholders as the purpose of the corporation as believers in socialism:[89]

> [B]usinessmen (who speak eloquently about the 'social responsibilities of business in a free-enterprise system') believe that they are defending free enterprise when they declaim that business is not concerned 'merely' with profit but also with promoting desirable 'social' ends; that business has a 'social conscience' and takes seriously its responsibilities for providing employment, eliminating discrimination, avoiding pollution and whatever else may be the catchwords of the contemporary crop of reformers ... In fact they are – or would be if they or anyone else took them seriously – preaching pure and unadulterated socialism. Businessmen who talk this way are unwitting puppets of the intellectual forces that have been undermining the basis of a free society these past decades.

Friedman articulated this slightly differently in *Capitalism and Freedom,* published eight years earlier in 1962:[90]

> The view has been gaining widespread acceptance that corporate officials and labor leaders have a 'social responsibility' that goes beyond serving the interest

---

83 Friedman was Professor of Economics at the Chicago School of Economics during 1946–77, and during 1977–2006 was attached to the Hoover Institution, Stanford University: <https://en.wikipedia .org/wiki/Milton_Friedman>.

84 Rebecca Henderson, *Reimagining Capitalism in a World on Fire* (PublicAffairs, 2020) 12.

85 Alex Edmans, *Grow the Pie: How Great Companies Deliver Both Purpose and Profit* (Cambridge University Press, 2020) 38.

86 Ibid 38, where Edmans mentions exactly '17,000 times' (in 2020 when the book was published), which probably should have been qualified by 'approximately' or 'roughly'.

87 British Academy, *Future of the Corporation: Research Summaries* (2018) 7 <https://www .thebritishacademy.ac.uk/publications/future-corporation-research-summaries/>; Mayer, *Prosperity* (2018) 2, 138. However, it was the heading in the *New York Times Magazine* that was quoted most often: see, eg, Paul Redmond, *Corporations and Financial Markets Law* (Thomson Reuters, 6th ed, 2013) 80, fn 167.

88 Joseph E Stiglitz, *The Price of Inequality* (Penguin Books, 2013) 55–6.

89 Milton Friedman, 'A Friedman doctrine – The social responsibility of business is to increase its profits', *The New York Times* (13 September 1970).

90 Milton Friedman, *Capitalism and Freedom* (University of Chicago Press, 1962) 133. See also Hinkley, *Time to Change Corporations: Closing the Citizen Gap* (2011) 9, 15.

of their stockholders or members. This view shows a fundamental misconception of the character and nature of a free economy. In such an economy there is one and only one social responsibility of a business – to use its resources and engage in activities designed to increase its profits so long as it stays within the rules of the game, which is to say, *engages in open and free competition, without deception or fraud* ... [emphasis added].

Few trends could so thoroughly undermine the very foundation of our free society as the acceptance by corporate officials of a social responsibility other than *to make as much money for stockholders as possible* [emphasis added].

Those defending 'Friedman capitalism' are quick to point out his qualification in the last sentence of the first paragraph quoted above, but they hardly ever emphasise his disregard for corporations' responsibilities towards their employees, expressed in his 1970 declaration,[91] and his brushing off the significance of corporations' responsibilities as 'eliminating discrimination' and 'avoiding pollution'. History has illustrated that black letter law was required in almost all sophisticated economies to curb rampant problems such as 'misleading and deceptive' and 'unconscionable' conduct by corporations.[92] Often these representations are solely aimed at boosting the share price of corporations. And there is no lack of examples where corporations, specifically because of their unrelenting quest for profit maximisation for shareholders, have been involved in unfair, unconscionable, wrongful, fraudulent and illegal conduct.[93]

1.5.2 Changing views about shareholder primacy

1.5.2.1 New insights regarding the impact of corporations

Before examining the current wisdom in the US (see Section 2.2), it is worth pointing out that gradually the 'shareholder supremacy'[94] view changed, and the company, especially the large public company, came to be seen in a different light. It was observed more pertinently that there were other stakeholders in a company; that if the only purpose of a company was 'the maximisation of profits for the shareholders' (aligned with excessive executive remuneration),[95] society could suffer tremendously – poor working conditions for workers, exploitation of the environment, pollution and so on would lead to 'a world on fire'.[96] As John Coats expresses well, there are two sides of the coin in capitalism:

---

91 This was at exactly the same time that Japan and Germany embraced a more employee-orientated corporate law model: see Henderson, *Reimagining Capitalism in a World on Fire* (2020) 18.
92 Final Hayne Report (2019) 10, 95, 114, 424–42, 495.
93 Ibid 13, 204, 248, 279, 301, 394,
94 See generally Greenfield, *The Failure of Corporate Law* (2006) 2, 44–6.
95 Mayer, *Prosperity* (2018) 1.
96 Henderson, *Reimagining Capitalism in a World on Fire* (2020) 8. See also Kent H Baker and John R Nofsinger, 'Socially responsible finance and investing: An overview' in Kent H Baker and John R Nofsinger (eds), *Socially Responsible Finance and Investing: Financial Institutions, Corporations, Investors, and Activists – Robert W Kolb Series in Finance* (John Wiley & Sons, 2010–12) vol 612, 2; Mayer, *Prosperity* (2018) especially ch 1; Beate Sjåfjell and Christopher M Bruner, 'Corporations and sustainability' in Beate Sjåfjell and Christopher Bruner (eds), *The Cambridge Handbook of Corporate Law, Corporate Governance and Sustainability* (Cambridge University Press, 2019) 3.

it 'has created huge benefits for humanity – wealth, health, and much longer life spans – along with inequality, misery, and the existential threat of climate change'.[97]

Then came the realisation that corporations 'have rights and duties vis-à-vis that society in somewhat the same way as has an individual'.[98] It became clear that shareholder dominance was no longer acceptable since in the limited liability company other interests, namely those of investors, creditors, employees, consumers and the public, were also represented[99] These other interests were identified on the basis that the groups representing these interests could be affected significantly by how corporations conduct their business. In other words, these groups have vested interests in the wellbeing and sustainability of corporations (see discussion in Section 3.7.2). Collectively they started to be referred to as stakeholders, with the term including the shareholders, employees, creditors, customers, the community, the environment and government. The 'stakeholder theory' thereby emerged, countering the 'shareholder primacy theory'.[100] In Section 3.7 we focus on the various stakeholders in greater detail.

Already in the early 1960s the concept of 'managing the corporation' started to be expressed in terms of these other interests.[101] Thus, the concept of 'corporate governance' came to include this new articulation of 'managing the corporation', with a central focus on the relationships between internal groups and individuals – examples of both actors are the board of directors, the shareholders in general meetings, the employees, the managing directors, the executive directors, the non-executive directors, the managers, the audit committees and other committees of the board. External stakeholder relationships now also became more prominent.[102] However, the profit motive was still dominant and shareholder primacy was not challenged at that stage.

1.5.2.2 Shareholder primacy challenged

Over time the traditional position regarding shareholder primacy[103] began to be challenged more forcefully,[104] with statements such as 'managerial accountability to shareholders is corporate law's central problem';[105] 'corporate law is currently in

97 John Coats, *The Problem of Twelve: When a Few Financial Institutions Control Everything* (Columbia Global Reports New York, 2023) 1.
98 Charles de Hoghton (ed), *The Company: Law, Structure and Reform in Eleven Countries* (Allen & Unwin, 1970) 7.
99 John J Farrar et al, *Farrar's Company Law* (Butterworths, 1991) 13.
100 Wishart, 'A reconfiguration of company and/or corporate law theory' (2010) 10(1) *Journal of Corporate Law Studies* 151, 171.
101 George Goyder, *The Responsible Company* (Blackwell, 1961) 45.
102 Brian R Cheffins, *Company Law: Theory, Structure and Operation* (Clarendon Press, 1997) 47.
103 See Esser, *Recognition of Various Stakeholder Interests in the Company Management* (2009) 19–23.
104 See generally Edward Freeman and David L Reed, 'Stockholders and stakeholders: A new perspective on corporate governance' (1983) 26(1) *California Management Review* 88; Thomas Donaldson and Lee E Preston, 'The stakeholder theory of the corporation: Concepts, evidence, and implications' (1995) 20(1) *The Academy of Management Review* 65. See also Liliana Eraković, 'Board of directors and stakeholders: Building bridges of understanding (2017) 23 *New Zealand Business Law Quarterly* 202; Max B E Clarkson, 'Stakeholder framework of analyzing and evaluating corporate social performance' (1995) 20(1) *The Academy of Management Review* 92.
105 David Millon, 'New directions in corporate law: Communitarians, contractarians, and the crisis in corporate law' (1993) 50(4) *Washington and Lee Law Review* 1373, 1374.

the midst of crisis, because of the exhaustion of the shareholder primacy model';[106] 'shareholder dominance should be questioned';[107] and 'shareholder primacy theory is suffering a crisis of confidence'.[108] There were even stronger calls for urgent change to the shareholder primacy model on the basis that shareholder primacy was a barrier to sustainable companies[109] and the primary reason for the deepening of a crisis in capitalism.[110]

Although there is little doubt that the shareholder primacy theory of corporate law still underpins the corporate law models of many countries, including Australia,[111] calls ring loud for a rethinking of the true purpose of the corporation, which in Western understanding still relies on 18th- and 19th-century principles, concepts and notions.[112] The dominant role of shareholders has been embedded in Western corporate law models through some of the first modern corporate law legislation, such as the introduction of the English *Joint Stock Companies Act 1844*. Since then, there have been many significant expansions and refinements of shareholder rights, shareholder powers and shareholder remedies through the various Companies and Corporations Acts around the world, including the current legislation governing corporations and corporate governance models in all Western countries.[113] The statutory and regulatory neutering of shareholders makes it inevitable that shareholders still deserve a special place in any discussion on corporate stakeholders[114] and that is not disputed in this book. However, this shareholder-focused approach does not detract from the fact that in the 21st century the community's focus is indisputably wider – it is now on the purpose, role, function and impact of corporations as they operate *in society*, locally and

---

106 Ibid 1390.

107 Huse, *Boards, Governance and Value Creation* (2007) 29.

108 Lynn A Stout, 'The shareholder value myth', *European Financial Review* (11 June 2013; written 1 April 2013) <http://ssrn.com/abstract=2277141>. Despite these statements, the shareholder primacy model remains prominent in the UK and continues to be supported by a shareholder-centric company law framework. See Marc Moore, 'Shareholder primacy, labour and the historic ambivalence of UK company law' (Research Paper No 40/2016, University of Cambridge Faculty of Law, September 2016) 5 <https://papers.ssrn.com/sol3/papers.cfm?abstract_id=2835990>. However, Moore suggests that although most directors and senior managers of UK companies would likely regard shareholder supremacy as underpinning the current UK company law model, the notion of shareholder supremacy will increasingly be challenged in the future.

109 Beate Sjåfjell, 'Corporate governance for sustainability: The necessary reform of EU company law' in Beate Sjåfjell and Anja Wiesbrock (eds), *The Greening of European Business under EU Law: Taking Article 11 TFEU Seriously* (Routledge, 2015) 97.

110 Richard D Wolff, *Capitalism's Crisis Deepens* (Haymarket Books, 2016).

111 See Jean J du Plessis, 'Shareholder primacy and other stakeholder interests' (2016) 34(3) *Company and Securities Law Journal* 238, 241; and Jean J du Plessis 'Corporate social responsibility and "contemporary community expectations"' (2017) 35(1) *Company and Securities Law Journal* 30.

112 See in particular Tricker, *Corporate Governance* (2019) 500–2, 5–10, 159–62.

113 I Ramsay, 'Increased corporate governance powers of shareholders and regulators and the role of the corporate regulator in enforcing duties owed by corporate directors and managers' (2015) 26(1) *European Business Law Review* 49, 53; Ian M Ramsay and Benjamin B Saunders, 'Litigation by shareholders and directors: An empirical study of the Australian statutory derivative action' (2006) 6(2) *Journal of Corporate Law Studies* 397; Tim Bowley and Jennifer G Hill, *Shareholder Inspection Rights in Australia: Then and Now* (Working Paper No 652/2022, European Corporate Governance Institute, July 2022). See generally Du Plessis, 'Shareholder primacy and other stakeholder interests' (2016) 34(3) *Company and Securities Law Journal* 238.

114 Christine Mallin, *Corporate Governance* (Oxford University Press, 6th ed, 2019) 79.

globally, with shareholders being dragged into the ring with all other stakeholders.[115] Or to see it from the other perspective, shareholders are being pulled down from the top of the pecking order of stakeholders and are now being considered as part of the stakeholder pack.

1.6 Some contemporary theories and debates

1.6.1 Section 172 of the *Companies Act 2006* (UK): 'The enlightened shareholder value' theory

Based on the well-founded criticism of the pure shareholder primacy theory, an attempt was made in the UK to move to a slightly different framework, the 'enlightened shareholder value' theory. This theory, very generally, holds that productive relationships (with other stakeholders) can be achieved within the framework of existing corporate law and corporate governance concepts, in fact maintaining 'shareholder supremacy', but ensuring that directors pursue shareholders' interests in an enlightened and inclusive way. This 'enlightened' approach allowed directors *to have regard to* the interests of other stakeholders, *but no more than that.*[116] The principal manifestation of this theory is found in s 172 of the *Companies Act 2006* (UK). It is quoted in its entirety, with sub-s (1) setting the tone as to how, in exercising their duty to promote the success of the company, UK directors should perceive non-shareholder interests:[117]

172 Duty to promote the success of the company

(1) A director of a company must act in the way he considers, in good faith, would be most likely to promote the success of the company for the benefit of its members as a whole, and in doing so have regard (amongst other matters) to –

   (a) the likely consequences of any decision in the long term,

   (b) the interests of the company's employees,

   (c) the need to foster the company's business relationships with suppliers, customers and others,

   (d) the impact of the company's operations on the community and the environment,

---

115 See, eg, George Dallas, 'Who cares about corporate purpose?' (Responsible Capitalism Initiative and Copenhagen Business School, 31 July 2023) <http://eepurl.com/iwCbgo>.
116 See generally Millon, 'Enlightened shareholder value, social responsibility and the redefinition of corporate purpose without law' in Vasudev and Watson (eds), *Corporate Governance after the Financial Crisis* (2012) 68, 79–80; Andrew Keay, 'Tackling the issue of corporate objective: An analysis of the United Kingdom's "enlightened shareholder value approach"' (2007) 29(4) *Sydney Law Review* 577, 589–90; I Esser and JJ du Plessis, 'The stakeholder debate and directors' fiduciary duties' (2007) 19(3) *South African Mercantile Law Journal* 346, 351–2; and Luh Luh Lan and Walter Wan, 'ESG and Director's Duties: Defining and Advancing the Interests of the Company' (Law Working Paper No 737/2023, European Corporate Governance Institute, October 2023).
117 See Andrew Keay, 'Section 172(1) of the Companies Act 2006: An interpretation and assessment' (2007) 28(4) *Company Lawyer* 106; and Millon, 'Enlightened shareholder value, social responsibility and the redefinition of corporate purpose without law' in Vasudev and Watson (eds), *Corporate Governance after the Financial Crisis* (2012) 69, 79–80.

    (e) the desirability of the company maintaining a reputation for high standards of business conduct, and

    (f) the need to act fairly as between members of the company.

  (2) Where or to the extent that the purposes of the company consist of or include purposes other than the benefit of its members, subsection (1) has effect as if the reference to promoting the success of the company for the benefit of its members were to achieving those purposes.

  (3) The duty imposed by this section has effect subject to any enactment or rule of law requiring directors, in certain circumstances, to consider or act in the interests of creditors of the company.

Having already been adopted in 2006, one would have expected that the enlightened shareholder value theory would have provided an acceptable 'alternative' to the pure shareholder value theory in the UK, but that has not been the case.[118]

1.6.2 The British Academy: A fresh look at 'the purpose of the corporation'

1.6.2.1 Background

In 2017 the British Academy initiated a comprehensive rethinking of 'the purpose of the corporation' and it resulted in what it called 'one of the most ambitious programmes of research to have been undertaken to date on the current state and future prospects of business'.[119] It was undertaken by the British Academy as part of a project called 'Future of the Corporation'.[120] The project's Final Report was published in June 2021. It brought together 'the results of four years of in-depth research and extensive engagement with hundreds of business leaders, researchers, policymakers and other practitioners'.[121] One should, however, remember that this quest to determine the 'purpose' of the private business corporation is not new.[122] Apart from several other attempts to clarify the purpose of the corporation, an admirable attempt was made by Post, Preston and Sachs in

---

118 For example, Edmans, *Grow the Pie* (2020) does not include any in-depth or critical discussion of s 172 of the *Companies Act 2006* (UK), although he refers generously to the 'enlightened shareholder value theory', giving the impression that this theory underlies the 'Pieconomics' theory that seems to underpin the entire book (Edmans, 2020, 27). It is also disappointing that the work of Colin Mayer and the British Academy's significant work on the future and purpose of the corporation undertaken between 2017 and 2020 (before Edman's book was published) seem to have escaped the attention of Edman.

119 British Academy, *Reforming Business for the 21st Century: A Framework for the Future of the Corporation* (2018) 5 <https://www.thebritishacademy.ac.uk/publications/reforming-business-21st-century-framework-future-corporation/> per Colin Mayer, under the heading 'A *radical* reformulation of the concept of the firm' (emphasis added).

120 British Academy, 'Future of the corporation' (2017–21) <https://www.thebritishacademy.ac.uk/programmes/future-of-the-corporation/>.

121 British Academy, *Policy and Practice for Purposeful Business: The Final Report of the Future of the Corporation Programme* (2021) 5 <https://www.thebritishacademy.ac.uk/publications/policy-and-practice-for-purposeful-business/>.

122 See generally Brian R Cheffins, 'The past, present and future of corporate purpose' (2023) *Delaware Journal of Corporate Law* (University of Cambridge Faculty of Law Research Paper No 15/2023; European Corporate Governance Institute – Law Working Paper No 713/2023) <https://ssrn.com/abstract=4420800>.

their work *Redefining the Corporation: Stakeholder Management and Organizational Wealth* (2002). It aimed specifically 'to clarify [the private business organisation's] status and purpose within contemporary society and the global economy'.[123]

The urgency of the British Academy's project was initially driven by the realisation that businesses, and business models, were having several negative impacts, especially as far as people and the planet were concerned. Accordingly, the focus of this project became the exact role that businesses (especially large corporations) play *in society*. The entire Future of the Corporation project was almost exclusively focused on contemporary views of what is, or rather should be, the true *purpose of the corporation* in society.[124] In other words, it had a similar focus as Post, Preston and Sachs expressed in 2002, almost 20 years earlier than the publication of the British Academy's Final Report in 2021.

In the Final Report, the proposals for reform were based on the concepts of 'accountability' and 'implementation'.[125] A good summary of the underlying corporate governance problems, as relevant for other jurisdictions as for the UK, appears in the Executive Summary of the Final 2021 Report:[126]

> A permissive legal, regulatory, governance and reporting framework is required to enable and encourage purposeful business, and the UK has such a framework. But in the UK there is insufficient accountability for, and implementation of, purposeful business. Few companies take up the option that exists within the law to adopt purposes beyond promoting shareholder interests, and there is insufficient appreciation and enforcement of directors' duties under the law.

1.6.2.2 British Academy sidesteps fundamental problems with s 172

Probably the most surprising aspect of the British Academy's Final Report is that it does not focus more pertinently on the problems caused by embedding in legislation, through s 172 of the *Companies Act 2006* (UK), the 'enlightened shareholder value' approach. If it is a significant issue that '[f]ew companies take up the option that exists within the law to adopt purposes beyond promoting shareholder interests' (see quote immediately above), the question arises: is it not because of the fact that the core of s 172 is shareholder-focused? Section 172, only in a peripheral way, focuses on the interests of other stakeholders because ultimately directors need to consider what 'would be most likely to promote the success of the company *for the benefit of its members as a whole*' (s 172(1)) [emphasis added].

---

123 Post, Preston and Sachs, *Redefining the Corporation* (2002) 229.
124 See the publications preceding the 2021 Final Report: *Future of the Corporation: Research Summaries* (2018) <https://www.thebritishacademy.ac.uk/publications/future-corporation-research-summaries/>; *Reforming Business for the 21st Century* (2018) <https://www.thebritishacademy.ac.uk/publications/reforming-business-21st-century-framework-future-corporation/>; *Executive Summary* (2019) <https://www.thebritishacademy.ac.uk/publications/future-of-the-corporation-principles-purposeful-business-executive-summary/>; *Principles for Purposeful Business* (2019) <https://www.thebritishacademy.ac.uk/publications/future-of-the-corporation-principles-for-purposeful-business/>.
125 British Academy, *Policy and Practice for Purposeful Business* (2021) 6.
126 Ibid.

It hardly seems possible to hold directors 'accountable' for, and ensure proper 'implementation' of (the two core concepts underlying the proposed reforms of the British Academy), delivery of 'profitable solutions which benefit customers, the work-force, investors, communities, society and the environment'[127] if the duty to pro-mote the success of the company is codified in the way it is in s 172 of the *Companies Act 2006* (UK).

The actual impact of s 172 of the *Companies Act 2006* on how directors perceive and implement 'the purpose of the corporation' received scant attention in the Final Report of the British Academy. Professor Colin Mayer, a driving force behind the British Academy's Future of the Corporation project,[128] clearly envisaged a more fundamental change in the law by proposing formal law reform, directing corporations to align their 'corporate purpose' with their 'social purpose'.[129] He envisaged corporate law reform[130] to be the driving force behind the 'radical reinterpretation of the nature of the corpora-tion' he imagined.[131] In the Final Report of the British Academy Principle 1 of the Eight Principles for Purposeful Business identified in 2019 was restated:[132]

> **Corporate law** should place purpose at the heart of the corporation and require directors to state their purposes and demonstrate commitment to them.

1.6.2.3 Difficulty in moving away from the statutory shareholder model

The nature of the problem, a particular one for the UK as shareholder primacy has been *statutorily* entrenched by way of s 172 of the *Companies Act 2006* (UK), is summarised well in the British Academy's Final Report:[133]

> In the UK and countries with similar systems, the law requires that directors promote the interests of shareholders ('shareholder primacy') and those of other stakeholders only to the extent that they enhance long-term shareholder value ('enlightened shareholder value'). They should not promote the interests of other stakeholders in their own right. This view subordinates the interests of most stakeholders to those of shareholders, even in the long term.

That s 172 of the *Companies Act 2006* entrenches the common law shareholder pri-macy model in UK company law was also commented on in the recent case UK case of

127 British Academy, 'Future of the corporation' (2017–21) <https://www.thebritishacademy.ac.uk/programmes/future-of-the-corporation/>, under the 'Implementation' mechanism.
128 Mayer's interest in the project was fuelled by his research and the publication of his book *Prosperity* (2018).
129 Colin Mayer, 'The future of the corporation: Towards humane business' (2018) 6 *Journal of the British Academy* 1, 11–12. See also The Honourable Justice James Edelman, 'The future of the Australian business corporation: A legal perspective' (Conference Paper, Supreme Court of New South Wales: Annual Commercial Law Conference, 29 October 2019) 3 <https://az659834.vo.msecnd.net/eventsairaueprod/production-lawsociety-public/4efb653dbaf8476eaff1a845ff100b88>.
130 Mayer, 'The future of the corporation' (2018) 6 *Journal of the British Academy* 1, 11: '[C]orporate law should be the means by which companies make credible commitments to their purpose'.
131 Ibid 1, 11, 12.
132 British Academy, *Policy and Practice for Purposeful Business* (2021) 11.
133 Ibid.

BTI 2014 LLC v Sequana SA,[134] but the Supreme Court confirmed that s 172 in no way weakens the concept of the company as a separate legal entity (see Section 1.6.3.2).

The Final Report acknowledged that to move away from a shareholder primacy orientated model would require legislative reform, but that it might be 'a complex and drawn-out process'.[135] An interim solution was proposed in the Final Report by way of 'policy starting points'. Through these 'policy starting points' companies would only be encouraged to have a purpose statement in their articles of association and to issue 'explanatory guidance to encourage use of existing option to embed purpose' in these articles of association. Several questions arise from this soft-brush approach: How will this be enforced, and will companies state their 'purpose' so vaguely,[136] and so broadly, that it is in fact insignificant from an accountability, implementation and enforcement point of view? In a slightly different context, Kent Greenfield expresses the limits to this approach very well:[137]

> Law requires constraint. When voluntary codes become so 'soft' that they impose no genuine constraint on the regulated actors, then it is a misnomer to use the term 'law' to describe such codes. It is also possible for judicially-imposed rules to be so soft, either in the sense of imposition of a duty so low that it imposes no real constraint, or so vague that it can be evaded at will by courts overseeing it, that they, too, do not deserve the label of law.

Addressing some of the most fundamental problems in defining the purpose of the corporation and addressing 'the negative impacts that some businesses and business models have'[138] will require more significant law reform,[139] including a specific reflection on the wording of s 172 in the UK. To the credit of the British Academy, some interesting and constructive discussions took place at the Future of the Corporation – September 2021 Purpose Summit and Report Launch held in September 2021,[140] including how universities can integrate purposeful business into teaching and the student experience.[141]

---

134 *BTI 2014 LLC v Sequana SA* [2022] 3 WLR 709, [209] (Lord Briggs), [265], [332] (Lady Arden).

135 British Academy, *Policy and Practice for Purposeful Business* (2021) 22.

136 See Edelman, 'The future of the Australian business corporation' (Conference Paper, 29 October 2019) 8–9.

137 Kent Greenfield, 'No law?' in Jean J du Plessis and Chee Keong Low (eds), *Corporate Governance Codes for the 21st Century* (Springer, 2017) 57, 73.

138 British Academy, 'Future of the Corporation – September 2021 Purpose Summit and Reports Launch' (2021) <https://www.thebritishacademy.ac.uk/programmes/future-of-the-corporation/events/purpose-summit-and-report-launch-september-2021/>.

139 See generally on the necessity of fundamental corporate law reform Sjåfjell, 'When the solution becomes the problem: The triple failure of corporate governance codes' in *Corporate Governance Codes for the 21st Century,* in Du Plessis and Keong Low (eds) (Springer, 2017) 23, 24. See also Rosemary Teele Langford, 'Social licence to operate and directors' duties: Is there a need for change?' (2019) 37(3) *Company and Securities Law Journal* 200, 210, 212.

140 British Academy, 'Future of the Corporation – September 2021 Purpose Summit and Report Launch' (2021) <https://www.thebritishacademy.ac.uk/programmes/future-of-the-corporation/events/purpose-summit-and-report-launch-september-2021/>.

141 British Academy, 'How can universities integrate purposeful business into teaching and the student experience?' (2021) <https://www.thebritishacademy.ac.uk/programmes/future-of-the-corporation/events/purpose-summit-and-report-launch-september-2021/how-can-universities-integrate-purposeful-business-into-teaching-and-the-student-experience/>.

1.6.2.4 'Having regard to other interests' had little impact

That s 172 of the *Companies Act 2006* (UK) does not necessarily require directors to have 'regard to' non-shareholder interests in exercising their duty to promote the success of the company,[142] even in large public companies involved in significant government projects, was illustrated well by the collapse of Carillion plc in January 2018. Carillion plc, one of the largest UK corporations, was involved in some of the biggest government-funded projects in the country for several years before its collapse. The House of Commons, Business, Energy and Industrial Strategy and Work and Pensions Committees described Carillion plc's approach to business as a 'story of recklessness, hubris and greed' based on a 'business model of "a relentless dash for cash"'[143] – gains for the shareholders and executives were the focus with hardly any 'regard' for the interests of the other stakeholders mentioned in s 172 of the *Companies Act 2006* (UK):

> [Carillion] presented accounts that misrepresented the reality of the business, and increased its dividend every year, come what may. Long-term obligations, such as adequately funding its pension schemes, were treated with contempt. Even as the company very publicly began to unravel, the board was concerned with increasing and protecting generous executive bonuses. Carillion was unsustainable. The mystery is not that it collapsed, but that it lasted so long.[144]

The UK corporate law and corporate governance regime appears to be still squarely based on the shareholder primacy model, even though it has envisaged an 'enlightened shareholder value' model. It is, however, to be welcomed that in its Final Report the British Academy, in its depiction of accountability and implementation mechanisms 'to put purpose at the heart of business', identifies the most significant stakeholders as investors, government, regulators, business, communities, citizens, workforce, customers and suppliers.[145]

The 'enlightened shareholder value' tag notwithstanding, s 172 of the *Companies Act 2006* (UK) is undoubtedly a firm *statutory* entrenchment of the shareholder primacy model, in sharp contrast with Australia where there is no statutory provision comparable

---

142 See generally Julia Dreosti, Bimaya de Silva and Kate Walsh, 'A civil law solution to social licence to operate and directors' duties conundrum in Australia' (2021) 38(6) *Company and Securities Law Journal* 404, 423–4; Langford, 'Social licence to operate and directors' duties' (2019) 37(3) *Company and Securities Law Journal* 200, 208. See also *Coppage v Safety New Security Ltd* [2013] IRLR 970, [28] on the uncertainty as to how the statutory provisions in the UK and the existing common law principles are intended to coexist.

143 Business, Energy and Industrial Strategy and Work and Pensions Committees, *Carillion* (House of Commons Paper No 769, Session 2017–19) 3.

144 Ibid. In October 2023, KPMG was fined £21 million by the Financial Reporting Council ('FRC') following two investigations conducted by the regulator: FRC, 'Sanctions against KPMG LLP, KPMG Audit plc and two former partners' (12 October 2023) <https://www.frc.org.uk/news-and-events/news/2023/10/sanctions-against-kpmg-llp-kpmg-audit-plc-and-two-former-partners/>. See analysis by Thomas Parker, 'KPMG receives record fine over Carillion audit' (12 October 2024) <https://www.tristrategy.co.uk/home/home-page-news-tri-strategy/kpmg-receive-record-fine-over-carillion-audit>.

145 British Academy, *Policy and Practice for Purposeful Business* (2021) 17.

to s 172.[146] Moving away from this model will require statutory invention to repeal or reformulate s 172, but this could expected to be 'a complex and drawn-out process'.[147]

1.6.3 Some recent Australian and UK perspectives

1.6.3.1 Meaning of 'the best interests of the corporation'

As stated, in Australia there is no statutory provision comparable to s 172 of the *Companies Act 2006* (UK). The focus here has been on directors' duty 'to act in the best interests of the corporation'.[148] Unfortunately the word 'corporation' has been given a meaning that equates to 'the bests interests of *the shareholders* as a whole'. This view is based on Australian cases, using principles that were intended to guide *shareholders* when they voted on certain matters, but applying it to instances where the courts were expected to determine whether *directors* 'acted in the best interests of the corporation'.[149] In addition, this shareholder-orientated definition of a 'corporation' ignores the statutory meaning of 'corporation' as separate legal entity for purposes of the *Corporations Act 2001* (Cth).[150]

1.6.3.2 The corporation 'as separate legal entity'

Recognising the corporation as a separate legal entity, separated from shareholders and *not* defined in terms of 'the shareholders as a whole', is a well-established approach taken in several court cases in Australia and in other jurisdictions.[151] Furthermore, that director owe their duties to the separate legal entity has been analysed and affirmed by some commentators.[152] Justice Edelman, extrajudicially, put it succinctly in 2019: '[T]he ultimate statutory and equitable command has always been for the duties of the directors to *the corporation* [original emphasis]'.[153]

The most recent confirmation of this basic principle in the UK is the case of *BTI 2014 LLC v Sequana SA*.[154] The case concerned directors' fiduciary duties and the interests of

---

146 Jean J du Plessis, 'Directors' duty to act in the best interests of the corporation' (2019) 34(1) *Australian Journal of Corporate Law* 3, 11–12. In 2006 CAMAC specifically opposed the introduction of a provision similar to s 172 of the *Companies Act 2006* (UK), because it could be 'counterproductive' and because in the Committee's view 'there is a real danger that such a provision would blur rather than clarify the purpose that directors are expected to serve. In so doing, it could make directors less accountable to shareholders without significantly enhancing the rights of other parties': see CAMAC, *The Social Responsibility of Corporations Report* (2006) 111–12.
147 British Academy, *Policy and Practice for Purposeful Business* (2021) 22.
148 *Corporations Act 2001* (Cth) s 181.
149 See the reference to *Greenhalgh v Arderne Cinemas Ltd* [1951] Ch 286, applied in *Ngurli Ltd v McCann* (1953) 90 CLR 425 (and several later cases), in Du Plessis, 'Directors' duty to act in the best interests of the corporation' (2019) 34(1) *Australian Journal of Corporate Law* 3. For a recent explanation of this fallacy, see the recent UK case of *BTI 2014 LLC v Sequana SA* [2022] 3 WLR 709, [21] (Lord Reed).
150 Ibid 14–17. See also Edelman, 'The future of the Australian business corporation' (Conference Paper, 29 October 2019) 9.
151 *Walker v Wimborne* (1976) 137 CLR 1, 6–7; *Bell Group Ltd (in liq) v Westpac Banking Corporation (No 9)* (2008) 39 WAR 1; *Westpac Banking Corporation v Bell Group Ltd (in liq) (No 3)* (2012) 44 WAR 1, [2051]; *Australian Securities and Investments Commission v Cassimatis (No 8)* (2016) 336 ALR 209; *BCE Inc v 1976 Debentureholders* [2008] 3 SCR 560; *BTI 2014 LLC v Sequana SA* [2022] 3 WLR 709.
152 Esser and Du Plessis, 'The stakeholder debate and directors' fiduciary duties' (2007) 19(3) *South African Mercantile Law Journal* 346, 361, and this exposition of the law has been adopted by the South African corporate governance code since 2016: see King IV Report (2016).
153 Edelman, 'The future of the Australian business corporation' (Conference Paper, 29 October 2019) 9.
154 [2022] 3 WLR 709.

creditors,[155] but as a point of departure, the importance of the company as a separate legal entity, as dealt with extensively in *Salomon v A Salomon & Co Ltd* [1897] AC 22, was emphasised in numerous instances in this case.[156] Lord Briggs (with whom Lord Kitchin agreed) referred to the limited circumstance where 'shareholders could ... be equated with the company itself', but could not make clearer where the law now stands:[157]

> But the law has since moved on a long way from a view that the interests of oth-
> ers in relation to the company, and its relationships with others, are altogether
> irrelevant. Put shortly, of the two strands in the reasoning in the *Salomon* case,
> namely the company as a separate entity with its own interests and responsibil-
> ities and the company as an abstract equivalent of its shareholders, it is the first
> which has clearly prevailed over time.

1.6.3.3 Gradual recognition by the courts of non-shareholder interests

Fortunately, non-shareholder interests started to be recognised judicially in Australia when they were affected by corporate conduct. For instance, in the 2012 case of *Westpac Banking Corporation v Bell Group Ltd (in liq) (No 3)* Drummond AJA observed as follows:[158]

> The impacts of corporate decision-making on a wider range of interests than
> shareholders are now being given more recognition. The need to ensure pro-
> tection of those interests also I think serves to explain why modern company
> courts have become more interventionist, in reviewing the activities of direc-
> tors, than was traditionally the case.

One of the most recent judicial recognitions in Australia that there are several interests that can be harmed by the acts or omissions of directors is the case of *Australian Securities and Investments Commission v Cassimatis (No 8)*, where Justice Edelman referred specifi-cally to several interests, including the interest constituted by a company's reputation.[159] These observations were not rejected by the Full Court of the Federal Court of Australia in *Cassimatis v Australian Securities and Investments Commission*, but rather were quoted with approval by all the judges of the Full Federal Court.[160] The Full Federal Court also endorsed the rule that directors owe their duty of care and diligence only towards the company as separate legal entity.[161] Furthermore, the Court of Appeal held that when

---

155 The Court, very clearly, and correctly in our view, rejected the proposition that there is a 'self-standing creditor' duty imposed on directors: see ibid [277], [405], [435] (Lady Arden); [11] (Lord Reed).

156 Ibid [19], [21]–[22], [52] (Lord Reed); [136] (Lord Briggs, with whom Lord Kitchin agreed); [276], [332] (Lady Arden).

157 Ibid [139].

158 (2012) 44 WAR 1, [2049], [2051]. For a critical analysis of the majority decision of the Court of Appeal, see Jason Harris and Anil Hargovan, 'For whom the bell tolls: Directors' duties to creditors after *Bell*' (2013) 35(2) *Sydney Law Review* 433.

159 (2016) 336 ALR 209, [480]–[483]. For a more comprehensive overview of Edelman's judgment, see Rosemary Langford, '*Cassimatis v Australian Securities and Investments Commission* [2020] FCAFC 52 – "Dystopian accessorial liability" or the end of "stepping stones" as we know It?' (2020) 37(5) *Company and Securities Law Journal* 362, 363. See also Pamela Hanrahan, 'Corporate governance in these "exciting times"' (2017) 32(2) *Australian Journal of Corporate Law* 142, 147.

160 (2020) 275 FCR 533, [85]–[86], [245], [248], [426], [484].

161 Ibid [81] (as per Greenwood J) and [453] (as per Rares J).

directors acted in a way that caused, or would have been foreseen by a reasonable director to cause, serious harm (not only financial harm, but also reputational harm) to a corporation's interests, they would be liable for a breach of their duty of care and diligence towards the company.[162] The Court referred to 'a foreseeable risk of *serious harm* (original emphasis)'[163] or a 'reasonably foreseeable harm'.[164]

In the UK, *BTI 2014 LLC v Sequana SA* provides the most recent recognition of the fact that it is *no longer legally acceptable* that, for purposes of directors' fiduciary duty to act in the best interests of the corporation, for the directors only, and at all times, to treat 'the interests of a company as being the same as the interests of its members: that is to say its shareholders, in the case of a company with a share capital'.[165]

1.6.3.4 Reputational harm and directors' liability

The possibility of personal liability of directors when their acts and conduct have caused the corporation reputational harm was flagged in 2016 in a well-argued legal opinion by Noel Hutley SC and Sebastian Hartford-Davis in the context of disclosure (or the lack of disclosure) of climate change risks:[166]

> Further, the duty of care and diligence is capable of requiring company directors to consider and disclose the exposure to physical, transition and liability risks associated with climate change. It is likely to be only a matter of time before we see litigation against a director who has failed to perceive, disclose or take steps in relation to a foreseeable climate-related risk that can be demonstrated to have caused harm to a company (including, perhaps, reputational harm round).

Those authors were asked to update their position in context of 'greenwashing' (see discussion in Section 3.4.4) and did so in 2021, expressing their opinion as follows:[167]

> 7.1 The standard of care to be exercised by directors with respect to climate change has risen and continues to rise.
>
> 7.2 'Net zero' commitments by companies are becoming common and appear to be regarded by many directors as an appropriate or necessary step in the discharge of their duties. Consideration of the impact of these commitments and related developments would also appear to be regarded by many directors as an appropriate or necessary step in the discharge of their duties, regardless of whether or not the corporation to which they owe a duty has made such a commitment.

---

162 Ibid [77].

163 Ibid.

164 Ibid [78]. See also Langford, 'Dystopian accessorial liability' (2020)37 *Company and Securities Law Journal* 362.

165 [2022] 3 WLR 709, [19] (Lord Reed), explaining the traditional view. See further statements by Lord Reed at [20], [53].

166 Noel Hutley SC and Sebastian Hartford-Davis, 'Climate change and director's duties' (Memorandum of Opinion for the Centre for Policy Development, 7 October 2016) <https://cpd.org.au/wp-content/uploads/2016/10/Legal-Opinion-on-Climate-Change-and-Directors-Duties.pdf>.

167 Noel Hutley SC and Sebastian Hartford Davis, 'Climate change and directors' duties' (Further Supplementary Memorandum of Opinion for the Centre for Policy Development, 23 April 2021) 4 <https://cpd.org.au/wp-content/uploads/2021/04/Further-Supplementary-Opinion-2021-3.pdf>.

7.3   Companies making net zero commitments require 'reasonable grounds' to support the express and implied representations contained within such commitments at the time those commitments are made.

7.4   It is foreseeable that a company (and its directors) could be found to have engaged in misleading or deceptive conduct or other breaches of the law by not having had reasonable grounds to support the express and implied representations contained within its net zero commitment.

7.5   There are practical steps companies and directors can take to reduce the likelihood of liability arising from a net zero commitment and to increase the likelihood of available defences for their actions.[168]

Legal opinions that have broadly reached the same conclusions have been expressed in Hong Kong,[169] Singapore,[170] Canada[171] and India.[172] In another significant Memorandum of Opinion,[173] Hartford-Davis and Bush revisited the issue of 'nature-related risks'[174] and directors' duties', and again reached the conclusion that there are considerable risks for directors to be liable for a breach of their legal duties if disclosure of nature-related information is not done diligently and with due care, causing a corporation 'reputational damage. The potential of corporations to incur reputational damage by neglecting non-shareholder interests has also been recognised by the Global Reporting Initiative ('GRI').[175]

1.6.3.5 Recognising wider social responsibility duties

Returning to directors' duties, some commentators go one step further and argue for the recognition of a corporate social responsibility ('CSR') duty for directors, based on 'contemporary community expectations'.[176] They suggest that in framing the directors'

---

168 Point 7.5 seems to refer to the protection directors in Australia can get under the business judgment rule in s 180(2) of the *Corporations Act 2001* (Cth).

169 'Legal opinion on directors duties and disclosure obligations under Hong Kong law in the context of climate change risks and considerations', provided to the Commonwealth Climate and Law Initiative <https://ccli.ubc.ca/wp-content/uploads/2021/10/Hong-Kong-Directors-obligations-and-climate-change.pdf>.

170 Ernest Lim, *Directors' Liability and Climate Risk: White Paper on Singapore* (Commonwealth Climate and Law Initiative, April 2021).

171 Commonwealth Climate and Law Initiative, *Primer on Climate Change: Directors' Duties and Disclosure Obligations* (June 2021).

172 Shyam Divan, 'Legal opinion: Directors' obligations to consider climate change-related risk in India' (7 September 2021) <https://ccli.ubc.ca/wp-content/uploads/2021/09/CCLI_Legal_Opinion_India_Directors_Duties.pdf>.

173 Sebastian Hartford-Davis and Zoe Bush, 'Nature-related risks and directors' duties' (Joint Memorandum of Opinion between Commonwealth Climate and Law Initiative and Pollination [Instructing Solicitors], 24 October 2023).

174 Ibid 1, [2] where Hartford-Davis and Bush adopted the definition of 'nature-related risks' endorsed by the Taskforce on Nature-related Financial Disclosures ('TNFD'), namely: 'potential threats (effects of uncertainty) posed to an organisation that arise from its and wider society's dependencies and impacts on nature'. They were referring to TNFD, *Recommendations of the Taskforce on Nature-related Financial Disclosures* (Report, September 2023) 131.

175 Global Reporting Initiative, 'Towards stakeholder capitalism: How we can get there' (7 February 2022) <https://www.globalreporting.org/media/5qojzh2n/gri-perspective-towards-stakeholder-capitalism.pdf >.

176 See Du Plessis, 'Corporate social responsibility and "contemporary community expectations"' (2017) 35(1) *Company and Securities Law Journal* 30, 37–9. See also Tanusree Jain, Adrián Zicari

duty to act in the best interests of 'the corporation', the duty *should not* be interpreted as covering only 'the bests interests of the shareholders as a whole',[177] but should also cover other interests. This seems to be a logical conclusion based on the now well-established view that '[a] company's interests are not exclusively those of its shareholders'.[178]

Although this view would have been seen as controversial, or even radical, a few years ago, it is now getting traction. In 2019 the American Bar Association published an edited book, *The Lawyer's Corporate Social Responsibility Deskbook*.[179] The Editors' Note states:[180]

> Corporate social responsibility (CSR) was once a voluntary exercise taken up by companies for business reasons ranging from reduced energy costs, increased competitiveness in the market for talent, to improve corporate morale etc ... One could reasonably make the case that the increasing frequency with which in-house and outside counsel have been confronted with legal issues that in one way or another implicate CSR concerns is one of the most notable legal trends of the past decade. Such issues can arise in disparate contexts ranging from supply chain compliance requirements related to minerals sourcing or anti-trafficking, to investor inquiries regarding environmental, social, and governance performance, to board governance regarding sustainability issues. The issues typically span various legal practices areas such as securities law, corporate governance, compliance, commercial law, labor law, and trade law, amongst others; *indeed it is difficult to find an area of law or legal practice that is not in some way impacted by CSR considerations* [emphasis added].

This change of attitude is refreshing. It is also worth nothing that the Editors' Note to *The Lawyer's Corporate Social Responsibility Deskbook* does not shy away from acknowledging that CSR is emerging as a discrete legal field by referring to terms like 'CSR laws and regulations', 'CSR-related legal issues' and, most notably, 'CSR law'.[181] This provides further support that CSR cannot remain an area that directors turn a blind eye to. A CSR legal duty for directors should be recognised based on community expectations.[182]

The reality is that CSR law is now taking shape. Although these recent developments will not guarantee that directors of corporations will consider non-shareholder interests more diligently, ignoring those other interests when exercising their duty to act in

---

and Ruth V Aguilera, 'Corporate governance and corporate social responsibility: Revisiting their inter-relationship' in Talaulicar (ed), *Research Handbook on Corporate Governance* (2023) 113; and Paul Redmond, 'The ASX Corporate Governance Principles and Recommendations and the idea of corporate responsibility' (2023) 40(2) *Company and Securities Law Journal* 116.

177 Du Plessis, 'Directors' duty to act in the best interests of the corporation' (2019) 34(1) *Australian Journal of Corporate Law* 3. See also Julia Dreosti, Bimaya de Silva and Kate Walsh, 'A civil law solution to social licence to operate and directors' duties conundrum in Australia' (2021) 38(6) *Company and Securities Law Journal* 404, 418–20.

178 *Cassimatis v Australian Securities and Investments Commission* (2020) 275 FCR 533, [453], [470] (Rares J).

179 Alan S Gutterman et al, *The Lawyer's Corporate Social Responsibility Deskbook* (American Bar Association, 2019).

180 Ibid xi–xiii.

181 Ibid.

182 Du Plessis, 'Directors' duty to act in the best interests of the corporation' (2019) 34(1) *Australian Journal of Corporate Law* 3.

the best interests of the corporation may have serious legal implications for company directors. This provides another good reason for introducing specific law reform, as is suggested in Section 2.4.2.

1.6.3.6 Neglect of non-shareholder interests and poor corporate culture

There is probably no better illustration of the neglect of non-shareholder interests and an underlying problem of poor corporate culture[183] than what was revealed by the Interim (2018) and Final (2019) Hayne Reports. These reports uncovered serious wrongful, and even illegal, conduct by the majority of Australian corporations operating in the financial and banking sector. The root of the problem was identified as boards of directors being driven and motivated primarily by profit maximisation for shareholders:[184]

> [M]any of the case studies considered in the Commission showed that the financial services entity involved had chosen to give priority to the pursuit of profit over the interests of customers and above compliance with the law ... Some have sought to explain this emphasis on the pursuit of profit as reflecting the fact that a financial services entity is ultimately accountable to its shareholders ... [Different forms of accountability by boards towards shareholders] are, of course, important. But they do not mark the boundaries of the matters that the boards of financial services entities must consider in the course of performing their duties and exercising their powers.

Although the focus of the Hayne Royal Commission was on banks and other financial service providers, it is highly likely that the same problems exist in most for-profit public corporations in all other industries in Australia as well. It is, therefore, an issue that cannot be ignored. The community's expectations of financial institutions were also commented on judicially in *Australian Competition and Consumer Commission v Australia and New Zealand Banking Group Ltd*:[185]

> There is a legitimate community expectation that Australian financial institutions will develop and maintain a good corporate culture which ensures that their staff do not engage in illegal, unethical and unprofessional conduct and do not act in disregard of the interests of their customers. The Australian public is entitled to expect that Australia's major corporations act as exemplary corporate citizens wherever in the world they may operate.

Promoting good corporate culture in Australia was recently a focus point for the ASX Corporate Governance Council. This was largely as a result of the widespread negative media coverage of poor corporate culture in the financial sector following the Hayne

---

183 See generally Hanrahan, 'Corporate governance in these "exciting times"' (2017) 32(2) *Australian Journal of Corporate Law* 142, 153–6. For several examples of the bad corporate culture in Australia, refer to the Owen Report, *The Failure of HIH Insurance* (2003) vol 1.
184 Final Hayne Report (2019) 399.
185 (2016) 118 ACSR 124, 151, [123] (Wigney J).

Royal Commission. Although the 'social licence to operate' did not survive from the draft to appear in the final published fourth edition (2019) of the Australian corporate governance code, Principle 3 was expanded. In the third edition (2014), Principle 3 simply stated that listed entities should '[a]ct ethically and responsibly'. In the fourth edition the heading of Principle 3 was expanded slightly: 'Instil a culture of acting lawfully, ethically and responsibly'. The explanation of what that means was clarified slightly: 'A listed entity should instil and continually reinforce a culture across the organisation of acting lawfully, ethically and responsibly.' Under this Principle non-security stakeholders are also mentioned *subordinately* to security holder:[186]

> In formulating its values, a listed entity should consider what behaviours are needed from its officers and employees to build long term sustainable value *for its security holders*. This includes the need for the entity to preserve and protect its reputation and standing in the community and with key stakeholders, such as customers, employees, suppliers, creditors, law makers and regulators [emphasis added].

Under Principle 6 ('Respect the rights of security holders'), stakeholders are again only mentioned *in passing*:

> A listed entity's investor relations program *may also* run in tandem with a wider stakeholder engagement program involving interactions with politicians, bureaucrats, regulators, unions, employees, consumer groups, environmental groups, local community groups and other stakeholders [emphasis added].

This is unfortunate, as the current trend in Australia, and internationally, is to move away from a shareholder-focused approach and instead embrace an all-inclusive stakeholder approach.

1.6.3.7 The price of neglecting non-shareholder interests: The James Hardie case

In 2017 Hanrahan cited the James Hardie case in support of her claim that there has been a shift from a 'compliance culture' to a focus on 'the social purpose of corporations and the interests they should serve'. Hanrahan asks the questions: 'Should all corporations have a culture of "doing the right thing", and if so, by whom and by whose lights?'[187] She did not attempt to answer these questions as the cruel reality of 'not doing the right thing' based on the current shareholder primacy approach underlying the Australian corporate law model was shockingly illustrated by the James Hardie case. This was a series of legal actions brought by employees who had suffered tremendously from illnesses caused by asbestos mining and asbestos products manufactures by James Hardie.[188]

---

186 ASX Corporate Governance Council, *Corporate Governance Principles and Recommendations* (4th ed, 2019) 16.
187 Hanrahan, 'Corporate governance in these "exciting times"' (2017) 32(2) *Australian Journal of Corporate Law* 142, 156.
188 A case study of this is available at <www.cambridge.org/highereducation/isbn/9781009287388/resources>.

The directors of James Hardie argued that they had avoided considering the interests of suffering employees because *legally* their duty was to act 'in the best interests of the company' and this dictated that they could only act in the best interests of the 'shareholders as a whole'. Redmond explains what legal advice the James Hardie directors received and that they originally relied on:[189]

> There are clear indications that Hardie directors perceived themselves as constrained by the law on directors' duties in any disposition they might have to contribute to compensation for asbestos victims especially in view of their litigation strategy of quarantining liabilities in the former subsidiaries. Through the long restructuring process, Hardie directors were advised by external lawyers 'that directors could not provide ... "more than that for which [the parent company] was legally responsible, without honestly believing that ... what [they] were doing was of benefit to [its] shareholders."'[190] When the inadequacy of the foundation's funding became clear, Hardie justified its refusal to contribute on the grounds that 'there can be no legal or other legitimate basis on which shareholder's [sic] funds could be used to provide additional funds to the Foundation and the duties of the company's directors would preclude them from doing so.'[191] The chair of the James Hardie board later referred to the 'immense difficulty, ... [and] immense complexity' involved in adjusting conflicting expectations upon directors. Their understanding of available options reflected the legal advice the Hardie directors received on their duties from a first-tier law firm. It is reasonable to assume that such advice is given regularly in Australian boardrooms in similar contexts.

Although eventually there was some relief for the suffering employees because of considerable political and community pressure, it is shocking that a dated and probably an incorrect interpretation of the meaning of 'corporation' for the purposes of directors' duty 'to act in the best interests of the corporation' was the core reason why the James Hardie directors blatantly ignored the interests of suffering employees.

1.6.3.8 The price of inaction and the case for law reform in Australia

The James Hardie legal saga ran from roughly 2000 to 2011 (employees were exposed to asbestos from their work for James Hardie companies long before that), but since then *nothing* has changed *legally* as far as interpreting 'corporation' and directors' duty to act

---

189 Paul Redmond, 'Directors' duties and corporate social responsiveness' (2012) 35(1) *University of New South Wales Law Journal* 317, 318–19. On the analysis of the James Hardie decision in *Australian Securities and Investments Commission v McDonald (No 11)* (2009) 256 ALR 199, see Anil Hargovan, 'Australian Securities and Investments Commission v Macdonald [No 11]: Corporate governance lessons from James Hardie' (2009) 33(3) *Melbourne University Law Review* 984.

190 Redmond, 'Directors' duties and corporate social responsiveness' (2012) 35(1) *University of New South Wales Law Journal* 317, referring to David Jackson, *Report of the Special Commission of Inquiry into the Medical Research and Compensation Foundation* (September 2004) 196 [14.45(d)] (testimony of chair of James Hardie board).

191 Jackson, *Report of the Special Commission of Inquiry into the Medical Research and Compensation Foundation* (September 2004) 557 [30.22], citing James Hardie Industries NV, 'Possible asbestos funding shortfall suggests significant change in claims' (Media Release, 29 October 2003).

'in the best interests of *the corporation*': Directors today can still rely on High Court cases where it has been held that 'corporation' in context of this fiduciary duty means 'the shareholders as a whole'.[192]

In the context of the long-running James Hardie litigation, it is surprising that two reports in 2006 concluded that no law reform was required as far as the meaning of the 'best interests of the corporations is concerned'.[193] By then but even more so at the date of writing (2023) there are several reasons why law reform should proceed.

First, although both the Parliamentary Joint Committee on Corporations and Financial Services (June 2006)[194] and the Corporations and Markets Advisory Committee ('CAMAC') (December 2006)[195] rejected the introduction of a statutory provision similar to s 172 of the *Companies Act 2006* (UK),[196] the position taken in these reports was influenced by the dominant view in the UK at that stage,[197] namely that the 'enlightened shareholder value' approach provides answers to the neglect of non-shareholder interest.[198] As is clear from the British Academy's recent re-evaluation of the state of play regarding recognition of non-shareholder interests (see discussion in Section 1.6.2), the enlightened shareholder value approach, as embedded statutorily in s 172 of the *Companies Act 2006* (UK), has had little or no influence on steering directors toward an all-inclusive stakeholder approach.

Second, these reports pointed out that Australian corporate law 'allows directors sufficient flexibility to take relevant interests and broader community considerations into account',[199] and 'it is currently sufficiently open to allow companies to pursue a strategy of enlightened self interest'.[200] However, the practical reality is very different. As was seen above (Sections 1.2.2 and 1.6.3.6), the many case studies examined in the Interim (2018)

---

192 See references in Du Plessis, 'Directors' duty to act in the best interests of the corporation' (2019) 34(1) *Australian Journal of Corporate Law* 3, 13–14.
193 Parliamentary Joint Committee on Corporations and Financial Services, *Corporate Responsibility: Managing Risk and Creating Value* (Commonwealth of Australia, June 2006) xix, 6 <http://www.aph.gov.au/Parliamentary_Business/Committees/Joint/ Corporations_and_Financial_Services/ Completed_inquiries/2004-07/corporate_responsibility/report/index>; CAMAC, *The Social Responsibility of Corporations Report* (2006) 111–12. See generally Langford, 'Social licence to operate and directors' duties' (2019) 37(3) *Company and Securities Law Journal* 200, 208.
194 Parliamentary Joint Committee on Corporations and Financial Services, *Corporate Responsibility* (June 2006) 54, quoting cl 156 of the Company Law Reform Bill 2005 (UK), which became s 172 of the *Companies Act 2006* (UK), but rejecting the British approach: see 55 [4.46].
195 CAMAC, *The Social Responsibility of Corporations Report* (2006) 103–7, 111–12.
196 Parliamentary Joint Committee on Corporations and Financial Services, *Corporate Responsibility* (June 2006) 55–6.
197 Before the introduction of s 172 of the *Companies Act 2006* (UK) there were extensive discussions and debates in the UK about the shareholder primacy model of corporate law, and these impacted on views in Australia.
198 Parliamentary Joint Committee on Corporations and Financial Services, *Corporate Responsibility* (June 2006) xiii, 63 [4.76]–[4.77], 181 [1.55]. See Paul Redmond, 'Directors' duties and corporate social responsiveness' (2012) 35(1) *University of New South Wales Law Journal* 317, 329. The shareholder-primacy corporate law model, and alternatives to it, was discussed extensively in the UK during the period preceding the adoption of the enlightened shareholder value approach in the *Companies Act 2006* (UK), and that naturally did not escape attention in Australia: see RP Austin, 'Australian company law reform and the UK Companies Bill' in RP Austin (ed), *Company Directors and Corporate Social Responsibility, UK and Australian perspectives* (Ross Parsons Centre of Commercial, Corporate and Taxation Law, 2007) 3.
199 CAMAC, *The Social Responsibility of Corporations Report* (2006) 7.
200 Parliamentary Joint Committee on Corporations and Financial Services, *Corporate Responsibility* (June 2006) xiv.

and Final (2019) Hayne Reports illustrated that Australian companies neglect non-shareholder interests because of their relentless pursuit of profit maximisation.[201]

Third, recent judiciary recognition of other interests by Australian courts (see discussion in Section 1.6.3.3) strongly suggests that *statutory recognition* that directors should consider non-shareholder interests when they exercise their duty to act in the best interest of the corporation is required.

Fourth, recent developments towards a more stakeholder-orientated approach to corporate law and corporate governance in the US provide another reason why the legal meaning of 'the best interests of the corporation' should be revisited in Australia and that statutory amendments are required to embed this as part of Australian law.

Finally, a need for law reform[202] is supported by commentators who have conducted detailed and comprehensive analyses of the serious consequences of still perceiving 'the corporation' as 'the shareholders as a whole' for the purposes of directors' core duty 'to act in the best interest of the corporation'.[203]

Although the case for law reform in this section focused specifically on Australia, similar considerations will apply, by analogy, to all jurisdictions where the common law meaning of 'corporation', as part of directors' duty 'to act in the best interests of the corporation', is still based on older case law equating it with 'the best interests of the shareholders as a whole'.

1.7 Conclusion

There are various definitions of 'corporate governance'. We believe, however, that the most realistic approach to corporate governance is the so-called inclusive approach – viewing all stakeholders as part of the corporate governance debate. At the end of the day, corporate governance deals with the system of regulating and overseeing corporate conduct, balancing the interests of all internal stakeholders and other parties who may be affected by the corporation's conduct in order to ensure responsible behaviour by corporations and creating their long-term, sustainable growth. There is ample evidence that there are real economic benefits in following good practice in corporate governance – by doing so, boards of directors and managers will potentially be able to add significant shareholder value and investors will be prepared to pay a premium for investments in companies in which good corporate governance practices are followed.

---

201 Final Hayne Report (2019) 401–3.
202 See generally Redmond, 'Directors' duties and corporate social responsiveness' (2012) 35(1) *University of New South Wales Law Journal* 317, who argues that directors should be given explicit discretion to respond to negative social impacts and stakeholder expectations despite profit sacrifice. See also the collection of essays on directors' duties in (2012) 35(1) *University of New South Wales Law Journal* 248; and generally Julia Dreosti, Bimaya de Silva and Kate Walsh, 'A civil law solution to social licence to operate and directors' duties conundrum in Australia' (2021) 38(6) *Company and Securities Law Journal* 404, 433–4.
203 Edelman, 'The future of the Australian business corporation' (Conference Paper, 29 October 2019) 9. See also Du Plessis, 'Directors' duty to act in the best interests of the corporation' (2019) 34(1) *Australian Journal of Corporate Law* 3.

2 RECENT DEVELOPMENTS AND DEBATES

2.1 Introduction: A brave new corporate world

Since at least 2018 there has been a major shift within 'Business America' away from 'shareholder capitalism' towards 'stakeholder capitalism' – we discuss this development in Chapter 1 and Section 2.2. That shift already has had some global impact and will probably continue to have impact over the coming years, as will be seen in Section 2.3. Our approach is, however, realistic and in Section 2.4 we make the reader aware of the challenges for countries, particularly where shareholder primacy is deeply embedded in statutory law and case law, to move from shareholder primacy to an all-inclusive stakeholder model of corporate law and corporate governance. In this chapter we also extract some of the 'essential' principles of corporate governance (Section 2.5) and illustrate that there is a 'business case' for good corporate governance since, among other things, it adds value to corporations (Section 2.6). We conclude by discussing (in Section 2.7) broader trends and debates with a present and likely future impact on corporate governance. These include what can be described as the 'Fourth Industrial Revolution' (Section 2.7.2); the widening gap between the 'rich' and the 'poor', or, put differently, 'the price of inequality' (Section 2.7.3); the growing problem regarding profit-sharing or capital distribution in large public corporations (Section 2.7.4); and the call for a so-named 'Great Reset' (Section 2.7.5).

2.2 A move towards an all-inclusive, multistakeholder approach: Stakeholder capitalism

2.2.1 Some significant recent US developments

There have been some significant recent developments in the United States ('US') impinging on corporate governance since the publication in 2018 of the fourth edition of this book.

In 2018, Larry Fink, the CEO of BlackRock, one of the world's largest Investment Funds,[1] started to promote the idea that companies needed to take their 'social purpose' seriously and he laboured the point that companies must not only deliver financial performance but show that they make a positive contribution to society. He insisted

---

1   BlackRock, 'About BlackRock' <https://www.blackrock.com/sg/en/about-us>. See also Rebecca Henderson, *Reimagining Capitalism in a World on Fire* (PublicAffairs, 2020) 10, 49–84.

that the companies in which BlackRock invests illustrate that they have a long-term value-creation strategy in place. He also emphasised that '[c]ompanies must benefit all of their stakeholders, including shareholders, employees, customers, and the communities in which they operate'.[2] Fink expressed specific expectations of companies in which BlackRock invests, insisting that they should ask the following questions (presented here as bullet points for emphasis) about themselves as far as stakeholders were concerned:[3]

- What role do we play in the community?
- How are we managing our impact on the environment?
- Are we working to create a diverse workforce?
- Are we adapting to technological change?
- Are we providing the retraining and opportunities that our employees and our business will need to adjust to an increasingly automated world?
- Are we using behavioural finance and other tools to prepare workers for retirement, so that they invest in a way that that will help them achieve their goals?

Fink's 2019 Letter to CEOs was titled 'Purpose and Profit'. In this letter he focused on 'sustainable, long-term growth and profitability' for corporation and gave prominent mention of companies' responsibilities to look after the interests of employees, customers and communities as stakeholders – stakeholders are mentioned five times in this short piece.[4] His tone was distinctly different to his previous statements which were often concerned with investment banking – although whether or not BlackRock's investment strategies are meeting its founder's lofty aims is yet to become clear.

There has been some revolt against this new direction taken by BlackRock. The US Republican Party threatened to withdraw billions of dollars of investments in BlackRock and advertising campaigns were launched to encourage other investors to boycott investments in BlackRock, because of its new stakeholder-orientated approach to corporate governance and because of it taking climate change and environmental, social and governance reporting ('ESG') 'too seriously'.[5] In addition, in March 2023 the Republicans used their majority in the House of Representatives to pass a bill intended to overturn a ruling by the Department of Labor that allowed retirement funds to take into

2   Larry Fink, 'A sense of purpose' [2018 Letter to CEOs]' (2018) <https://www.blackrock.com/corporate/investor-relations/2018-larry-fink-ceo-letter>.
3   Ibid.
4   Larry Fink, 'Purpose and profit', [2019 Letter to CEOs] (2019) <https://www.blackrock.com/corporate/investor-relations/2019-larry-fink-ceo-letter>.
5   For media coverage of this, see Tsvetana Paraskova, 'Republicans withdraw $1 billion from BlackRock due to its ESG policies', *OilPrice.com* (10 October 2022) <https://oilprice.com/Latest-Energy-News/World-News/Republicans-Withdraw-1-Billion-From-BlackRock-Due-To-Its-ESG-Policies.html>; Ramsey Touchberry, 'BlackRock strikes back against Republicans who say investment firm has gone 'woke' for climate', *The Washington Times* (online, 7 October 2022) <https://www.washingtontimes.com/news/2022/oct/7/blackrock-strikes-back-against-republicans-who-say/>; and Eamonn Barrett, 'Republicans accused BlackRock of being too 'woke' on climate change. Activists say the firm isn't woke enough', *Fortune* (online, 14 September 2022) <https://fortune.com/2022/09/14/blackrock-republicans-letter-woke-capitalism-esg-investing/>.

consideration climate change and other non-financial factors when considering which companies they wanted to invest in. This resulted in President Biden using his veto to block this legislation.[6]

2.2.2 The US Business Roundtable's endorsement of stakeholder capitalism

Another noteworthy development, particularly significant in the US context, was the new strategic direction to corporate governance taken by the influential Business Roundtable ('BRT').[7] In 2019 the BRT announced it was moving away from a shareholder primacy approach to a stakeholder-orientated approach by redefining its position on 'the purpose of a corporation'.[8]

It was to be expected that shareholder interest groups would object strongly to this new strategic direction of the BRT, with the influential American Council of Institutional Investors ('CII')[9] 'respectfully' disagreeing with the BRT statement, which the CII stated 'suggests corporate obligations to a variety of stakeholders, placing shareholders last, and referencing shareholders simply as providers of capital rather than as owners'.[10]

The BRT revisited its 2019 statement in 2020, promoting it as its 'stakeholder capitalism' approach,[11] a strategy endorsed by Klaus Schwab in his 2021 book, *Stakeholder Capitalism: A Global Economy for Progress, People and Planet*.[12] It became clear from the debates that followed the BRT's 2019 statement 'that people viewed the BRT statement as heralding a major change'.[13] Stakeholder capitalism appears to be gaining momentum,[14] with the idea also promoted by the World Economic Forum.[15]

---

6   Charles Dane, 'What is going on with the backlash to ESG?' *Governance Institute of Australia*, (12 April 2023) <https://www.governanceinstitute.com.au/news-media/news/2023/apr/what-is-going-on-with-the-backlash-to-esg/>.
7   See *Business Roundtable* <https://www.businessroundtable.org/>.
8   Business Roundtable, 'Business Roundtable redefines the purpose of a corporation to promote "an economy that serves all Americans"' (19 August 2019) <https://www.businessroundtable.org/business-roundtable-redefines-the-purpose-of-a-corporation-to-promote-an-economy-that-serves-all-americans>.
9   See generally Dorothy S Lund and Elizabeth Pollman, 'The corporate governance machine' (2021) 121(8) *Columbia Law Review* 2563, 25921–3.
10   Council of Institutional Investors, 'Council of Institutional Investors responds to Business Roundtable statement on corporate purpose' (19 August 2019) <https://www.cii.org/aug19_brt_response>.
11   Geoff Colvin, 'Revisiting the Business Roundtable's "stakeholder capitalism," one year later' (19 August 2020) <https://fortune.com/2020/08/19/business-roundtable-statement-principles-stakeholder-capitalism-corporate-governance/>,.
12   Klaus Schwab, *Stakeholder Capitalism: A Global Economy for Progress, People and Planet* (Wiley, 2021).
13   Alex Edmans, 'Two years later, has the Business Roundtable statement transformed capitalism?' (7 September 7 2021) <https://www.promarket.org/2021/09/07/business-roundtable-shareholder-capitalism-promise/>. However, the shareholder primacy approach is still at the heart of American corporate law and significant change will only be brought about by fundamental legislative law reform. For a sceptical view of the aims of business initiatives in the US, see Lund and Pollman, 'The corporate governance Machine' (2021) 121(8) *Columbia Law Review* 2563, 2590–1.
14   Global Reporting Initiative, 'Towards stakeholder capitalism: How we can get there' (7 February 2022) <https://www.globalreporting.org/media/5qojzh2n/gri-perspective-towards-stakeholder-capitalism.pdf>.
15   Martin Lipton, *The New Paradigm: A Roadmap for an Implicit Corporate Governance Partnership between Corporations and Investors to Achieve Sustainable Long-Term Investment and Growth* (World

2.2.3 2020 and beyond: 'A Fundamental Reshaping of Finance' and 'The Power of Capitalism'?

In 2020 Larry Fink's Letter to CEOs was titled 'A Fundamental Reshaping of Finance', but a transparent stakeholder-orientated approach to doing business again featured prominently in the piece, linking it to the long term-profits and long-term sustainability of corporations. Fink, in fact, explained the business case for an all-inclusive and transparent stakeholder approach.[16]

In Fink's 2021 Letter[17] he emphasised the importance of stakeholders by stating that 'sustainability and deeper connections to stakeholders drives better returns'. In his 2022 Letter (titled 'The Power of Capitalism')[18] he made the following wise observations:

> It is clear that being connected to stakeholders – establishing trust with them and acting with purpose – enables a company to understand and respond to the changes happening in the world. Companies ignore stakeholders at their peril – companies that do not earn this trust will find it harder and harder to attract customers and talent, especially as young people increasingly expect companies to reflect their values ... I cannot recall a time where it has been more important for companies to respond to the needs of their stakeholders.

In his 2022 Letter Fink endorsed stakeholder capitalism to its fullest extent, even though he observed that 'the fair pursuit of profit is still what animates markets; and long-term profitability is the measure by which markets will ultimately determine [a] company's success':[19]

> Stakeholder capitalism is not about politics. It is not a social or ideological agenda. It is not 'woke.' It is capitalism, driven by mutually beneficial relationships between you and the employees, customers, suppliers, and communities your company relies on to prosper. This is the power of capitalism.
>
> In today's globally interconnected world, a company must create value for and be valued by its full range of stakeholders in order to deliver long-term value for its shareholders. It is through effective stakeholder capitalism that capital is efficiently allocated, companies achieve durable profitability, and value is created and sustained over the long-term.

Economic Forum, 2 September 2016) <https://www.wlrk.com/webdocs/wlrknew/AttorneyPubs/WLRK.25960.16.pdf>. See, however, Stephen M Bainbridge, *The Profit Motive: Defending Shareholder Value Maximization* (Cambridge University Press, 2023).

16   Larry Fink, 'A fundamental reshaping of finance [2020 Letter to CEOs]' (2020) <https://www.blackrock.com/corporate/investor-relations/2020-larry-fink-ceo-letter>. See also Henderson, *Reimagining Capitalism in a World on Fire* (2020) 160; and Australian Council of Superannuation Investors ('ACSI') and Financial Services Council ('FSC'), *2015 ESG Reporting Guide for Australian Companies* 14 <https://www.asx.com.au/documents/asx-compliance/acsi-fsc-esg-reporting-guide-final-2015.pdf>.

17   Larry Fink, 'Larry Fink's 2021 Letter to CEOs' (2021) <https://www.blackrock.com/au/individual/2021-larry-fink-ceo-letter>.

18   Larry Fink, 'The power of capitalism [2022 Letter to CEOs]' (2022) <https://www.blackrock.com/au/individual/2022-larry-fink-ceo-letter>.

19   Ibid.

This approach is far removed from the 'Friedman capitalism' discussed in Chapter 1, where profit maximisation is achieved for shareholders only, even at the expense of all other stakeholders this was the motto and driving force of capitalism until very recently. Fink, the BRT and others are no longer tainted by a socialist brush; if non-shareholder interests are promoted actively and unashamedly, this is not 'preaching pure and unadulterated socialism'.[20]

2.2.4 A refreshing approach

Whether it is called an all-inclusive stakeholder approach, a multistakeholder approach or stakeholder capitalism, the recognition of non-shareholders is to be welcomed and is in line with the approach adopted in this book since the publication of its first edition in 2005. Such an approach is also more important in the wake of the Fourth Industrial Revolution (see Section 2.7.2) and how that will shape the world in future.[21] Schwab summarises it well:[22]

> If we can muster our courage and act in the service of the common good, there is significant hope that we can continue an upward trajectory of human well-being and development. Past industrial revolutions have been a significant source of progress and enrichment, though it is up to us to solve for the negative externalities, such as environmental damage and growing inequality. Involving all relevant stakeholder groups will help us overcome the core challenges ahead – distributing the benefits of technological disruptions, containing the inevitable externalities and ensuring that emerging technologies empower, rather than determine, all of us as human beings.

2.3 Global impact of the new direction towards an all-inclusive stakeholder/stakeholder capitalism approach

2.3.1 Winds of change noted in Australia

In Australia, the new approach of the BRT has been acknowledged as a 'major policy change'.[23] However, the Australian Institute of Company Directors ('AICD') was careful in its view on this issue, only pointing out that 'directors' duties differ between the US and Australia and the two systems should not be conflated'. Similar to the 2006 reports of the Parliamentary Joint Committee on Corporations and Financial Services and the Corporations and Markets Advisory Committee (see Section 1.6.3.8), the AICD stated that the issue of what is meant by directors' duty 'to act in the best interests of the corporation is a live issue in Australia and that through its Forward Governance Agenda the Institute was examining how the best practice duty applies in practice.[24] It expressed that '[t]he

---

20 See quote of Milton Friedman from *The New York Times* cited in Section 1.5.1.3.
21 Klaus Schwab, *Shaping the Future of the Fourth Industrial Revolution: A Guide for Building a Better World* (World Economic Forum, 2018) 2, 16, 30, ch 4.
22 Ibid 239–40.
23 AICD, 'Where to now for shareholder primacy?' (25 September 2019) <https://aicd.companydirectors.com.au/membership/membership-update/where-to-now-for-shareholder-primacy>.
24 Ibid.

community needs *to trust* that directors take account of stakeholder, ethical and societal considerations as part of their duties [emphasis added]'.[25] Unfortunately, this *trust* has been seriously broken, in at least the banking, superannuation and financial services industry sector, if one looks at the Interim and Final Hayne Reports, published in 2018 and 2019 respectively. This was at the very time that the AICD asked the community to simply *trust* that directors will 'take account of stakeholder, ethical and societal considerations as part of their duties'.

Ross Grantham sums up the practical reality of how directors still prioritise the financial interests of shareholders:[26]

> Taken together, an overwhelming number of the companies surveyed adopted a shareholder primacy approach, where the 'interests of shareholders' was understood almost exclusively in terms of the financial returns to shareholders. In Australia, of the 100 companies examined listed the maximising of the financial returns to shareholders as their sole or primary objective.

The AICD suggests that there is still great uncertainty among Australian company directors regarding how to balance the interests of shareholders and other stakeholders, with 91 per cent indicating they want 'further guidance on duties and stakeholder engagement'.[27] However, research by Shelly Marshall and Ian Ramsay published in 2012 indicated that more than half of the directors surveyed understood that 'their primary obligation to act in the best interests of the company meant that they should balance the interests of all stakeholders'. No directors gave the response that they believed they were required to act only in the short-term interests of shareholders, and only a small percentage believed they were required to act in the long-term interest of shareholders only.[28] This uncertainty may only be addressed by clearer statutory guidance through legislative reforms (see Section 2.4.2). One can argue that it is exactly what Australian directors long for, drawing from the results of the AICD's 2019 survey based on its Forward Governance Agenda.

2.3.2 All-inclusiveness core to business success

All of the above means that predictions made several years ago are now part of the contemporary corporate governance field. The predictions or views include: 'in future the development of loyal, inclusive stakeholder relationships will become one of the most important determinants of commercial viability and business success';[29] 'recognition of stakeholder concern is not only good business, but politically expedient and morally and ethically just, even if in the strict legal sense [corporations] remain directly accountable

25 Ibid.
26 Ross Grantham, *The Law and Practice of Corporate Governance* (LexisNexis, 2020) 219.
27 AICD, *Forward Governance Agenda: Results of Member Consultation* (August 2019) 12 <https://www
    .aicd.com.au/content/dam/aicd/pdf/news-media/forward-governacne-agenda/Forward-Agenda-
    Finding-Report-Results-Next-Steps.pdf>.
28 Shelley Marshall and Ian Ramsay, 'Stakeholders and directors' duties: Law, theory and evidence'
    (2012) 35(1) *University of New South Wales Law Journal* 291, 304.
29 David Wheeler and Maria Sillanpää, *The Stakeholder Corporation* (Pitman, 1997) ix. See further
    James E Post, Lee E Preston and Sybille Sachs, *Redefining the Corporation: Stakeholder Management
    and Organizational Wealth* (Stanford Business Books, 2002) 1–3; and Mark J Roe, 'Preface' in Margaret
    M Blair and Mark J Roe (eds), *Employees and Corporate Governance* (Brookings Institute, 1999) v.

only to shareholders';[30] and 'the corporation as a legal entity grew out of its ability to protect not only the shareholders but also other stakeholders'.[31]

The importance of corporations considering the interests of stakeholders, outside areas where there is existing legal protection for them, has become an inevitable practical reality as is observed in the *G20/OECD Principles of Corporate Governance.*[32]

2.3.3 Solid foundation for a stakeholder-orientated model

As already indicated, the stakeholder-orientated approach to corporate governance has been promoted very strongly in this book since its first edition in 2005[33] and this was always reflected in the definition suggested for the term 'corporate governance' in later editions of the book.[34] Thus, these recent developments in the US are to be welcomed as they reflect progression in the corporate governance field that we have anticipated for several years.

2.4 Challenges in moving away from a shareholder primacy corporate law model

2.4.1 Shareholder capitalism still deeply embedded in the US

Staring with the US, the next natural step will be to ensure that the practical reality of stakeholder capitalism is embedded through legal principles. In other words, it needs to be ensured that *Dodge v Ford Motor Co* does not remain the dominant authority for directors seeking only to pursue profit maximisation for shareholders. This is a huge challenge that might only be realised through legislative change in the various states (which is highly unlikely), or at federal level (which is also unlikely currently),[35] as it is highly

---

30   SR Leighton and Donald H Thain, *Making Boards Work* (McGraw-Hill Ryerson, 1997) 23.
31   Morten Huse, *Boards, Governance and Value Creation: The Human Side of Corporate Governance* (Cambridge University Press, 2007) 29. Gilson argues that corporate governance models or theories that focus on single elements in the corporate governance mix, namely shareholder primacy or director primacy, are too simple to explain the real-world dynamics. He states that there is no one 'right' governance model and that governance models should be contextual and dynamic. See Ronald J Gilson, 'From corporate law to corporate governance' in Gordon and Wolf-Goerg (eds), *The Oxford Handbook of Corporate Law and Governance* (Oxford University Press, 2015) 36 <https://papers.ssrn .com/sol3/papers.cfm?abstract_id=2819128>.
32   Organisation for Economic Co-operation and Development ('OECD'), *G20/OECD Principles of Corporate Governance* (2015) 34 <https://www.oecd.org/publications/g20-oecd-principles-of- corporate-governance-2015-9789264236882-en.htm>. In September 2023, the 2015 Principles were replaced by the 2023 *G20/OECD Principles of Corporate Governance* <https://doi.org/10.1787/ed750b30- en>. The *G20/OECD Principles of Corporate Governance* are set out in the Appendix to the OECD *Recommendation on Principles of Corporate Governance* (OECD/LEGAL/0413) adopted by the OECD Council on 8 July 2015 and revised on 8 June 2023. See discussions in Sections 12.2 and 12.3.
33   Jean J du Plessis, James McConvill and Mirko Bagaric, *Principles of Contemporary Corporate Governance* (Cambridge University Press, 1st ed, 2005) 6–7, ch 2.
34   Jean J du Plessis, Anil Hargovan and Mirko Bagaric, *Principles of Contemporary Corporate Governance* (Cambridge University Press, 2nd ed, 2011) 10, ch 2; Jean Jacques du Plessis, Anil Hargovan and Mirko Bagaric, *Principles of Contemporary Corporate Governance* (Cambridge University Press, 3rd ed, 2015) 13, ch 2; and Jean J du Plessis, Anil Hargovan and Jason Harris, *Principles of Contemporary Corporate Governance* (Cambridge University Press, 4th ed, 2018) 13–14, ch 2.
35   See Lund and Pollman, 'The corporate governance machine' (2021) 121(8) *Columbia Law Review* 2563, 2580–1, 2609, 2629.

unlikely that the courts in a state like Delaware will be brave enough to set the tone and move away from the law as laid down in *Dodge v Ford Motor Co*, *Katz v Oak Industries* and other cases such as *Smith v Van Gorkom*.[36]

In the US-context, even if a radical restatement of directors' fiduciary duties moves away from a shareholder focus and profit maximisation for shareholders is endorsed by the Delaware Supreme Court, it is wishful thinking that courts in other states will follow suit. Lund and Pollman contend that a more 'substantial shock to the system' will be required at federal level,[37] but there seems to be little political or economic affinity for such a radical change in the US. Ultimately one cannot disagree with Lund and Pollman's conclusion that, at least in the foreseeable future, it is unlikely that 'stakeholderism' will 'dethrone shareholder primacy' in the US.[38] Moore and Petrin reach a similar conclusion by pointing out that it looks likely that shareholder primacy will remain the dominant Anglo-American governance model, notwithstanding growing dissatisfaction with it.[39] In this sense, the contentious claim by Henry Hansmann and Reinier Kraakman in their 2001 article, 'The End of History for Corporate Law',[40] that the shareholder primacy corporate model will continue to reign supreme due to path dependency, has not been disproved convincingly, at least not in the US, since 2001.[41]

2.4.2 Challenges and solutions: Directors' duties are owed to the company as a separate legal entity

Similar challenges will face law reforms in other jurisdictions if, legally, a shift away from a shareholder focus is to be implemented. In Australia, for instance, the common law meaning of 'the bests interests of the corporation' has been considered by the courts to mean the best interests of the 'shareholders as a whole';[42] changing this will have to be addressed at the highest level of law reform, namely, through legislation. That is the only way to resolve the confusion experienced by directors when they consider non-shareholder interests.[43] In South Africa there has been an attempt to deal with

---

36 See Section 1.5.1.1 discussing *Dodge v Ford Motor Co*, 170 NW 668, 684 (Mich 1919); *Katz v Oak Industries Inc*, 508 A 2d 873 (Del Ch, 1986); *Smith v Van Gorkom* 488 A 2d 858 (Del, 1985) were quoted.

37 Lund and Pollman, 'The corporate governance machine' (2021) 121(8) *Columbia Law Review* 2563, 2567–8, 2579, 2582, 2631, 2567–8.

38 Ibid 2633–4.

39 Marc Moore and Martin Petrin, *Corporate Governance: Law Regulation and Theory* (Macmillan International, 2017) 45–6.

40 Henry Hansmann and Reinier Kraakman, 'The end of history for corporate law' (2001) 89(2) *Georgetown Law Journal* 439.

41 For some of the many challenges to Hansmann and Kraakman's claim, see, inter alia, Douglas M Branson, 'The very uncertain prospect of "global" convergence in corporate governance' (2001) 34(2) *Cornell International Law Journal* 321; Thomas Clarke, 'The continuing diversity of corporate governance: Theories of convergence and variety' (2016) 16 *Ephemera Theory and Politics in Organization* 19, 23; Bob Tricker, *Corporate Governance: Principles, Policies, and Practices* (Oxford University Press, 4th ed, 2019) 503. See also Donald H Chew and Stuart L Gillan, 'Introduction' in Donald H Chew and Stuart L Gillan (eds), *Global Corporate Governance* (Columbia Business School, 2009) ix; and Huse, *Boards, Governance and Value Creation* (2007) 103–4.

42 See *Mills v Mills* (1938) 60 CLR 150; and *Ngurli Ltd v McCann* (1953) 90 CLR 425, 438. For a discussion of these and other cases, see Jean J du Plessis, 'Directors' duty to act in the best interests of the corporation: "Hard cases make bad law"' (2019) 34(1) *Australian Journal of Corporate Law* 3.

43 For a very good summary of the confusion caused by different models regarding directors' 'duty of care' and their 'duty of loyalty', see OECD, *Climate Change and Corporate Governance: Corporate*

the issue, not in legislation, but through the South African corporate governance code ('King IV'). A practically oriented solution has been found by emphasising the significance of the company as a separate legal entity and by adopting the following approach:[44]

> The position taken in King IV is that 'directors owe their duties to the company and the company alone as the company is a separate legal entity from the moment it is registered until it is deregistered ... The company is represented by several interests and these include the interests of shareholders, employees, consumers, the community and the environment. Thus requiring directors to act in good faith in the interests of "the company" cannot nowadays mean anything other than a blend of all these interests, but first and foremost they must act in the best interest of the company as a separate legal entity ... An interest that may be primary at one particular point in time in the company's existence may well become secondary at a later stage'.[45]

This approach is based on the 'entity theory of the corporation', probably best explained in its distilled form by Marc Moore and Martin Petrin in *Corporate Governance: Law Regulation and Theory*.[46] It is also an approach that clearly shines through in the recent UK case of *BTI 2014 LLC v Sequana SA*.[47] The Court reiterated the importance of the core company law concept that the company is a separate legal entity (see discussion in Section 1.6.3.2), but provided insightful perspectives on the importance of non-shareholder interests as part of the best interests of the corporation. The Court emphasised, correctly in our view, that just as directors do not owe fiduciary duties directly towards individual shareholders (as was held in *Percival v Wright* [1902] 2 Ch 421),[48] they also do not owe fiduciary duties directly towards creditors.[49] However, it is expected of directors to make 'commercial judgments' and, as part of these judgments, it will be expected of directors, depending on the particular circumstances, to consider the interests of 'creditors'.[50] However, making commercial judgments might, again depending on circumstances, also require of them to consider other interests of the corporation as separate legal entity.[51] Lady Arden explains this in a practical and very clear way:

Governance (2022) 37–8 <https://www.oecd.org/corporate/climate-change-and-corporate-governance-272d85c3-en.htm>.

44 *Report on Corporate Governance* ('King IV Report') (Institute of Directors in Southern Africa, 2016) 26.

45 Irene-marié Esser and Jean J du Plessis, 'The stakeholder debate and directors' fiduciary duties' (2007) 19(3) *South African Mercantile Law Journal* 346, 359–60. See also Monray Marsellus Botha, 'First do no harm! On oaths, social contracts and other promises: How corporations navigate the corporate social responsibility labyrinth' in Hermie Coetzee and Carika Fritz (eds), *De Serie Legenda, Developments in Commercial Law, Entrepreneurial Law* (LexisNexis, 2019) vol III, 14, 20, fn 59.

46 Moore and Petrin, *Corporate Governance* (2017) 26–9. For a more comprehensive and nuanced discussion of the 'real entity theory', see Michael J Phillips, 'Reappraising the real entity theory of the corporation' (1994) 21(4) *Florida State University Law Review* 1061.

47 [2022] 3 WLR 709.

48 Ibid [276] (Lady Arden).

49 Ibid [277], [405], [435] (Lady Arden); [11] (Lord Reed).

50 Ibid [238] (Lord Hodge).

51 Ibid [238] (Lord Hodge); [176] (Lord Briggs).

> Normally, the interests of shareholders and creditors row in the same direction.
> Lord Reed, addressing the situation where they diverge focuses on the interests
> of creditors in contrast to the interests of shareholders. I would respectfully say
> that the interests of shareholders and creditors do not occupy the whole field. A
> company is, as it were, polycentric ...[52]
>
> That leads to the question who should decide whether a particular interest
> in the company should be favoured over another, assuming they are both for
> the benefit of shareholders. In my judgment, the prioritisation of interests in a
> company is in general a matter for the directors' commercial judgment.[53]

That then leads her to the broader application of the principle, not specifically related to
shareholder and creditor interests:

> When there is no question of creditors' interests being materially and adversely
> prejudiced, it is for directors to prioritise the various interests and the courts
> leave such matters to the commercial judgment of the directors.[54]

A more accentuated and precise statutory formulation of the approach adopted by King IV
in core corporate law legislation in South Africa, but also in other parts of the world, will
go a long way to eliminate confusion for directors and reflect what the BRT, inter alia,
proposes: to be 'legitimate contemporary legal views and community expectations'.[55]

2.5 'Essential' principles of corporate governance

In recent years there have been several attempts to identify and explain the 'essential'
principles of corporate governance. Although there are several examples,[56] different
principles have been identified as 'essential' and, over time, views have changed. There
is nothing wrong or inconsistent with this evolutionary process. As we stated at the beginning of Chapter 1, corporate governance is a subject area that grows and expands, and
it adjusts according to new insights and new challenges. As Mervyn King puts it, 'good
governance is a journey and not a destination'[57] or, as Tricker puts it, '[a]t the moment,
there is no universally accepted theory of corporate governance'.[58]

A good illustration of the evolutionary nature of corporate governance as a subject
area is provided by the various South African King Reports. In the King II (2002) Report,[59]

---

52 Ibid [294].
53 Ibid [295].
54 Ibid [296].
55 This particular approach seems to be easily reconcilable with approaches by others (see Pamela
    Hanrahan, 'Corporate governance in these "exciting times"' (2017) 32(2) *Australian Journal of
    Corporate Law* 142, 148–9), although the significance of the company as a separate legal entity and the
    variety of interests represented in that entity is not accentuated enough. See also Tricker, *Corporate
    Governance* (2019) 500–2.
56 See, eg, OECD, *Principles of Corporate Governance* (April 2004); and ECGI, *The Combined Code on
    Corporate Governance* (UK Combined Code, 2008) <https://www.ecgi.global/code/combined-code-
    corporate-governance-revised-june-2008 >.
57 *King Report on Corporate Governance* ('King III Report') (Institute of Directors in Southern Africa,
    2009) 4.
58 Tricker, *Corporate Governance: Principles, Policies, and Practices* (2019) 488.
59 *King Report on Corporate Governance* ('King II Report') (Institute of Directors in Southern Africa, 2002).

seven 'essential' principles of corporate governance were identified: (1) discipline, (2) transparency, (3) independence, (4) accountability, (5) responsibility, (6) fairness and (7) social responsibility.

In the King III (2009) Report,[60] the emphasis shifted slightly: 'The philosophy of the Report revolves around leadership, sustainability and corporate citizenship'.

The South African King IV (2016) Report[61] continued to recognise the importance of ethical leadership, sustainability and corporate citizenship. Ethical and effective leadership, in particular, is cited in the Preface as an enduring foundational value. However, the report strongly focuses on governance in a broader context and lists as its underpinning philosophies the organisation as an integral part of society, stakeholder inclusivity, integrated thinking and integrated reporting. The report is drafted against the background of and informed by three interrelated 'paradigm shifts' in the corporate environment: the shift from financial capitalism to inclusive capitalism, from short-term capital market to long-term, sustainable capital markets and from siloed reporting to integrated reporting. The concepts of inclusiveness and integration lie at the heart of King IV.[62]

Another illustration of changing views on 'essential' principles of corporate governance is revealed by comparing the original (1st edition, 2003)[63] version of the ASX *Principles of Good Corporate Governance and Best Practice Recommendations* and the 2014 (3rd edition), the ASX *Corporate Governance Principles and Recommendations*. In 2003, 10 essential principles of good corporate governance were identified; these 10 were consolidated to eight essential principles in 2007 (2nd edition) and they are still the eight principles contained in the ASX *Corporate Governance Principles and Recommendations* (4th edition, 2019). However, refinements were made in every edition.

2.6 Is 'good corporate governance' important and does it add value?

2.6.1 Former scepticism

When corporate governance was raised in conversation and commentaries in the 1990s and early 2000s, there were often references to the need for corporations to implement and maintain 'good governance practices'. However, there has been a continuing debate as to whether a focus on governance practices comes at the expense of what is really important to the company and its stakeholders – creating long-term, sustainable growth for the corporation. Did giving attention to 'conformance', in terms of adhering to corporate governance rules and principles, come at the expense of 'performance'? Was implementing good corporate governance practices a necessary ingredient for corporate

---

60 King III Report (2009).
61 The report was published on 1 November 2016. It is effective in respect of financial years commencing on or after 1 April 2017 and replaces King III in its entirety. The report contains the first outcomes-based governance code in the world.
62 See generally Botha, 'First do no harm! On oaths, social contracts and other promises' in Coetzee and Fritz (eds), *De Serie Legenda, Developments in Commercial Law, Entrepreneurial Law* (LexisNexis, 2019) vol III, 14, 23, 34–5.
63 ASX, *Principles of Good Corporate Governance and Best Practice Recommendations* (1st ed, 2003).

success, or merely a distraction from the real business of the company? Naturally, given that there is still debate and uncertainty as to what 'corporate governance' means, there are varying perspectives on what constitutes good practice in corporate governance, and whether good corporate governance is indeed important to the company and actually adds value or 'makes a difference'.[64]

2.6.2 The 'business case' for good corporate governance

Nowadays, however, these questions seem almost rhetorical, as it is easy to find numerous reasons – and even empirical proof – that good corporate governance is important to companies and that it does add value and make a difference. As will be clear from the sources quoted in the next footnote, recognition of the need for good corporate governance is still gaining momentum. This is especially so in light of the broader and long-term focus on sustainable and responsible corporations.[65] There is also the acceptance that corporate social responsibility ('CSR') forms part of a corporation's existence,[66] just as much as recognising stakeholders other than shareholders, as explained in greater detail in Section 2.2. In short, there is an undisputable 'business case' for following good corporate governance practices, including corporations fulfilling their CSR duties[67] and looking after the interests of all stakeholders in accordance with the *G20/OECD Principles of Corporate Governance*.[68]

Lins, Servaes and Tamayo illustrate well how an approach of looking after social capital, taking CSR seriously and fostering a relationship of trust among all stakeholders add value and enhance firm performance, especially during a crisis like the Global Financial Crisis ('GFC').[69]

The considerable momentum that ESG reporting has gained recently (see Section 2.2.1) is another indicator that good corporate governance and transparency

---

64 See generally Jonathan Charkham, *Keeping Better Company* (Oxford University Press, 2nd ed, 2005) 23–4; Sir Geoffrey Owen, 'The role of the board' in Ken Rushton (ed), *The Business Case for Corporate Governance* (Cambridge University Press, 2008) 11.

65 See, eg, Report of the HIH Royal Commission ('Owen Report'), *The Failure of HIH Insurance – Volume I: A Corporate Collapse and Its Lessons* (Commonwealth of Australia, 2003) xxxiii, 104–5 [6.1.2], 133 [6.6]; Rushton (ed), *The Business Case for Corporate Governance* (2008); Chew and Gillan, in Chew and Gillan (eds), *Global Corporate Governance* (2009) IX; and René M Stulz, 'Globalization, corporate finance, and the cost of capital' in Chew and Gillan (eds), *Global Corporate Governance* (Columbia University Press, 2009) 108 *et seq;* Henry Bosch, 'The changing face of corporate governance' (2002) 25(2) *University of New South Wales Law Journal* 270, 271; Rick Sarre, 'Responding to corporate collapses: Is there a role for corporate social responsibility?' (2002) 7(1)*Deakin Law Review* 1; Sir Bryan Nicholson, 'The role of the regulator' in Ken Rushton (ed), *The Business Case for Corporate Governance* (2008) 100; and Scott Miller, 'Assessing the components of effective corporate governance' (2013) 7 *Strategic Management Review* 47.

66 Lund and Pollman, 'The corporate governance machine' (2021) 121(8) *Columbia Law Review* 2563, 2614.

67 See generally Tricker, *Corporate Governance* (2019) 512; Garin Pratiwi Solihati, 'Good corporate governance and corporate social responsibility disclosure on company value and return on asset as moderating variable' (2022) 4 *International Journal of Management Studies and Social Science Research* 287.

68 *G20/OECD Principles of Corporate Governance* (2015) 34. See also Steve Letza, Xiuping Sun and James Kirkbride, 'Shareholding versus stakeholding: A critical review of corporate governance' (2004) 12(3) *Corporate Governance* 242, 250–2, explaining the 'instrumental stakeholder theory'.

69 Karl V Lins, Henri Servaes and Ane Tamayo, 'Social capital, trust, firm performance: The value of corporate social responsibility during the financial crisis' (2017) 72(4) *The Journal of Finance* 1785.

do matter – investors will only invest in corporations adhering to good corporate governance practices and striving for the long-term and sustainable success of the corporation. Investors also want to see, through material and reliable reporting standards, that corporations cater for the interests of all stakeholders, not only shareholders, as discussed in greater detail in Section 3.4.

2.7 A few broader trends and debates with a potential impact on corporate governance

2.7.1 General

We turn now to a discussion of current trends and debates that have a potential impact on corporate governance.

2.7.2 The Fourth Industrial Revolution[70]

There is almost no aspect of our daily lives that has not been affected in some way or another by the mind-boggling advances of technology over the past 100 years. The internet is probably the most notable example, but as Klaus Schwab explains, the 'Fourth Industrial Revolution' is even more transformational:[71]

> Mindful of the various definitions and academic arguments used to describe the first three industrial revolutions, I believe that today we are at the beginning of a fourth industrial revolution. It began at the turn of this century and builds on the digital revolution. It is characterized by a much more ubiquitous and mobile internet, by smaller and more powerful sensors that have become cheaper, and by artificial intelligence and machine learning.

Clearly, corporations and corporate governance have been greatly impacted by this. Meetings hardly take place in a single physical location, but through communication tools like Zoom, Microsoft Teams and Webex, and by the time this book is published there will probably be many other web-based software programs released for social media and online meeting applications. Boards of directors have had to adjust to this and deal with the reality of disruptive technologies, ubiquitous computing and the interconnectivity of every part of their corporations. In fact, these technologies, especially with the presence of dominating companies like Google and Microsoft, have changed the way in which capitalism is perceived. They have also had a huge impact on directors' powers and duties. The reason for this is that in most jurisdictions, the power to manage the business of the corporation will be conferred on the board of directors.[72] This power is then normally accompanied by a duty directors have, under the common law and often

---

70   Klaus Schwab, *The Fourth Industrial Revolution* (Penguin UK, 2017).
71   Ibid 7.
72   This will normally be done in a company's articles of association or constitution. In Australia, for instance, s 198A(1) of the *Corporations Act 2001* (Cth) provides that '[t]he business of a company is to be managed by or under the direction of the directors'.

provisions in the corporations legislation, to exercise their powers and discharge their duties with reasonable 'care and diligence',[73] implying that they cannot simply ignore the significant issues associated with the 'Fourth Industrial Revolution'.

Shoshana Zuboff, in her fascinating and largely ground-breaking book, *The Age of Surveillance Capitalism*[74] explores the overwhelming developments in technology, the impact and how it changed everything, including how the global economy is conducted. She describes in colourful language the uncertain times in which we live:[75]

> The digital realm is overtaking and redefining everything familiar even before we have had a chance to ponder and decide. We celebrate the networked world for the many ways in which it enriches our capabilities and prospects, but it has birthed whole new territories of anxiety, danger, and violence as the sense of a predictable future slips away.

There is no doubt that the digital world will transform every aspect of corporate governance in the future. We will need to deal with many challenging questions including: How will digitally orientated organisations be controlled and governed? What will be the new corporate governance rules? How will the powers of boards be impacted? How will shareholders and other stakeholders exercise their rights and how will they be held responsible for their conduct? What imbalances will be created in corporations that are not dependent on the physical labour of employees, but on their intellectual labour? It is, therefore not surprising that as part of an extensive review of the 2015 *G20/OECD Principles of Corporate Governance*, the Organisation for Economic Co-operation and Development ('OECD')[76] had prominent focus on new digital technologies and their opportunities and risks (see Section 12.3.3.5).[77]

A similar focus on cyber-risk and cyber resilience is evident from a review of the Australian Securities and Investment's ('ASIC') approach in this space, with six reports since 2015 focused on cyber resilience.[78]

Conduct of corporations might nowadays go further than just neglecting certain stakeholders, but a greater, almost unimaginable impact on global society is still to come. We predict that issues related to the Fourth Industrial Revolution will become increasingly prominent from a corporate governance point of view. A glimpse of future impacts is

---

73 See, eg, s 180(1) of the *Corporations Act 2001* (Cth), which provides as follows:

(1) A director or other officer of a corporation must exercise their powers and discharge their duties with the degree of care and diligence that a reasonable person would exercise if they:
   (a) were a director or officer of a corporation in the corporation's circumstances; and
   (b) occupied the office held by, and had the same responsibilities within the corporation as, the director or officer.

74 Shoshana Zuboff, *The Age of Surveillance Capitalism* (Profile Books, 2019).

75 Ibid 3.

76 See OECD, 'Who we are' <https://www.oecd.org/about/>.

77 See OECD, *OECD Secretary-General's Second Report to G20 Finance Ministers and Central Bank Governors on the Review of the G20/OECD Principles of Corporate Governance, Indonesia, July 2022* (2022) 8 <www.oecd.org/corporate/oecd-secretary-general-report-G20-FMCBG-review-G20-OECD-principles-corporate-governance-2022.pdf>.

78 See, eg, 'Resources on cyber resilience', *ASIC* <https://asic.gov.au/regulatory-resources/corporate-governance/cyber-resilience/resources-on-cyber-resilience/>.

given by the headings of some parts in Schwab's *Shaping the Future of the Fourth Industrial Revolution*: these refer to extending digital technologies, reforming the physical world and altering the human being, and integrating environment.[79]

2.7.3 Widening gap between the rich and the poor: 'The price of inequality'[80]

Another new issue we introduce readers to briefly in this fifth edition is not the widening gap between the rich and the poor sectors of society – that gap has increasingly widened since the 1970s – but rather the blatant unfairness of this widening gap, necessitating mention of it in the context of corporate governance. It has considerable potential to impact on perceptions of economic systems and on how corporations are governed. It also impacts on several issues covered in this book, namely how corporations view, treat and respect corporate stakeholders; corporate social responsibility ('CSR'); the definition of the directors' duty to act in the best interests of a corporation; the role and purpose of businesses in society, and so on. Rebecca Henderson deals with this issue under 'inequality', referring to it as one of 'the three great problems of our time' – the other two she mentions are 'massive environmental degradation' and 'institutional collapse'.[81] The dire and depressing consequences of the growing gap between the rich and the poor in a developed country like the US is described in great detail by Anne Case and Angus Deaton in their book *Deaths of Despair and Future Capitalism*.[82]

In 2012, Joseph E Stiglitz, winner of the Nobel Prize for Economics in 2001,[83] former senior vice president and chief economist of the World Bank, and a former member and chairman of the (US President's) Council of Economic Advisers, published his book *The Price of Inequality*.[84] The book is very much focused on the US, with US case studies and US politics the main focus, but it is enlightening in that it demonstrates the considerable dangers lurking behind the growing gap between the rich and the poor. It reminds us of the severe reaction of 'the poor' in setting up a tent city in Wall Street in 2011 that became known as the 'Occupy Wall Street Movement',[85] but spread wider to other countries under the guise of the 'Occupy Movement'. The most important concern the protesters wanted to draw attention to was existing economic and social inequalities[86] – the fact that a very small percentage of the population holds a very large percentage of economic wealth ('one per cent of the population holds

---

79 Schwab, *Shaping the future of the Fourth Industrial Revolution* (2018) pts 2.1–2.4.
80 Joseph E Stiglitz, *The Price of Inequality* (Penguin Books, 2013).
81 Henderson, *Reimagining Capitalism in a World on Fire* (2020) 7.
82 Anne Case and Angus Deaton, *Deaths of Despair and Future Capitalism* (Princeton University Press, 2020).
83 See 'Joseph Stiglitz', *Wikipedia* <https://en.wikipedia.org/wiki/Joseph_Stiglitz>.
84 Stiglitz, *The Price of Inequality* (2012, 2013). Another noteworthy book that highlights the problems associated with social and economic inequalities is Schwab, *Stakeholder Capitalism* (2021).
85 Schwab, *Stakeholder Capitalism* (2021) 39.
86 David Ignatius, 'The path forward: the global economy – interview with IMF Managing Director, Kristalina Georgieva', *Washington Post Live* (3 June 2020) <https://www.imf.org/en/News/Articles/2020/06/03/tr060320-the-path-forward-the-global-economy>.

99 per cent wealth' was the slogan),[87] discussed by Stiglitz in his Chapter 1, 'America's 1 Percent Problem':[88]

> One of the darkest sides to the market economy that came to light was the large and growing inequality that has left the American social fabric, and the country's economic sustainability, fraying at the edges: the rich were getting richer, while the rest were facing hardships that seemed inconsonant with the American dream. The fact that there were rich and poor in America was well known; and even though this inequality was not caused solely by the subprime crisis and the downturn that followed – it had been building up over the past three decades – the crisis made matters worse, to the point where it could no longer be ignored. The middle class was being badly squeezed in ways we'll see later in this chapter; the suffering of the bottom was palpable, as weaknesses in America's safety net grew obvious and as public support programs, inadequate at best, were cut back further; but throughout all this, the top 1 percent managed to hang on to a huge piece of the national income – a fifth – although some of their investments took a hit.

The Occupy Wall Street tents have long been removed and the protesters silenced, but the underlying problem of the widening gap between the rich and the poor has not been addressed and did not disappear – the gap has widened since 2011. As Schwab points out, this disturbing trend has been observed for several decades since the 1970s.[89]

In 2020 the COVID-19 pandemic again illustrated, as was mentioned in Chapter 1, that employees would be left out in the cold at a time of crisis. The pandemic also accentuated the fact that 'our world and civil society is plagued by maddening inequality' and that '[t]hose with more money, better connections, or more impressive ZIP codes were affected by COVID at far lower rates'.[90] The very dark side of the current state of play is summarised well by Stiglitz, again in a global context.[91] Globally the picture is indeed dark.

---

87 That this is a particular problem in America was illustrated with figures from the period 1913–1998 provided by Thomas Pikkety and Emmanual Saez, 'Income inequality in the United States (2003) 118(1) *Quarterly Journal of Economics* 1, 8–12 – referred to by Stiglitz, *The Price of Inequality* (2012, 2013) xii, fn 9 (Preface to the paperback edition). See also Thomas Blanchet, Emanual Saez and Gabriel Zucman, *Real Time Inequality* (Working Paper 30229, National Bureau of Economic Research, July 2022) 5 <https://eml.berkeley.edu/~saez/BSZ2022.pdf> where they comment on the impact of COVID-19:

> [G]overnment programs enacted during the pandemic led to an unprecedented – but short-lived – improvement in living standards for the working class. After accounting for taxes and cash and quasi-cash transfers, disposable income for adults in the bottom 50 per cent was 20 per cent higher in 2021 than in 2019. However, disposable income fell in the beginning of 2022, as the expansion of the welfare state enacted during the pandemic – e.g., an expanded child tax credit and earned income tax credit – was rolled back. The only reason why disposable income for the bottom 50 per cent was higher in 2022 than in 2019 (by about 10 per cent in real terms) was the higher market income for this group, driven by wage gains.

See also Schwab, *Stakeholder Capitalism* (2021) 37–8.
88 Stiglitz, *The Price of Inequality* (2012, 2013) 1–35; see also 83–4, 334.
89 Schwab, *Stakeholder Capitalism* (2021) 38.
90 Ibid 2–3.
91 Stiglitz, *The Price of Inequality* (2012, 2013) 4.

Abhijit Banerjee and Esther Duflo, in the foreword to the *World Inequality Report 2022*, highlight the reality of the growing gap between the rich and the poor by citing statistics pointing to the inequalities in global wealth distribution.[92]

Social and financial inequalities will potentially be accelerated by the Fourth Industrial Revolution, and the danger for societies is extremism and violent unrest.[93] It is beyond the scope of this book to discuss the widening gap between the rich and the poor in detail, but the matter should not be ignored from a corporate governance point of view and in the context of all the principles of contemporary corporate governance we cover in this book.

2.7.4 Growing problem regarding profit-sharing or capital distribution in large public corporations

There are three areas of particular concern as far as profit-sharing or capital distribution by corporations is concerned, namely corporate profits distributed as excessive executive and director remuneration; disproportionate percentages of company profits distributed as dividend to shareholders; and astronomical amounts spent on share buy-backs (that is, companies buying back shares from their own shareholders). Each one of these areas is huge, complex and controversial, but for current purposes only a few general observations will be made about them.

As a general background it is interesting to look at the Gini Index,[94] which illustrates in which countries there are the biggest gaps between the 'haves' and 'have-nots'. It is a blunt measuring tool, but has a long history and seems generally to be a good indicator of wealth distribution in countries.[95]

There is ample evidence that executive remuneration has, proportionally to pay of ordinary employees, risen considerably faster over at least the last 20 years or so. This has occurred in Australia,[96] and in other jurisdictions as well.[97] One particularly interesting illustration of this is the research undertaken by Lawrence Mishel and Jessica Schieder, clearly explaining the disproportionality.[98]

This is a concern as it is part of the bigger problem of the widening gap between the rich and the poor, but because there is a legitimate expectation by employees to share

---

92   Abhijit Banerjee and Esther Duflo, 'Foreword' in Lucas Chancel et al (eds), *World Inequality Report 2022* (United Nations Development Programme, 2022) 3. See also Schwab, *The Fourth Industrial Revolution* (2017) 92–3; and Schwab, *Shaping the Future of the Fourth Industrial Revolution* (2018) 12–13.

93   Schwab, *The Fourth Industrial Revolution* (2017) 47, 80, 91–4; Schwab, *Shaping the Future of the Fourth Industrial Revolution* (2018) 30; Schwab, *Stakeholder Capitalism* (2021) 87–8.

94   See 'Gini coefficient', *Wikipedia* <https://en.wikipedia.org/wiki/Gini_coefficient>.

95   Frank A Farris, 'The Gini index and measures of inequality' (2010) 117 *The American Mathematical Monthly* 851.

96   John Shields, Michael O'Donnell and John O'Brien, 'The bucks stops here: Private sector executive remuneration in Australia' (Labor Council of NSW, 2014) 3.

97   Wojciech Prychodzen and Fernando Gómez-Bezares, 'CEO–employee pay gap, productivity and value creation' (2021) 14 *Journal of Risk Financial Management* 196; Susan J Stabile, 'One for A, two for B, and four hundred for C: The widening gap in pay between executives and rank and file employees' (2002–03) 36 *Michigan Journal of Law Reform* 115.

98   Lawrence Mishel and Jessica Schieder, 'CEO compensation surged in 2017', *Economic Policy Institute* <https://www.epi.org/publication/ceo-compensation-surged-in-2017/>.

fairly in the success of corporations.[99] In the ASX's *Corporate Governance Principles and Recommendations*, 'fairness' regarding remuneration only applies to directors, executives and senior executives: 'Principle 8: Remunerate fairly and responsibly'.[100] In fact, the word 'fair' is used sparingly outside the accounting standard expectation that the financial report 'give a true and fair view of the financial position and performance of the entity'.[101] The only other place 'fair' appears is under the suggestions for a code of conduct, reminding entities following the code to 'deal with customers and suppliers *fairly*' (emphasis added).[102] There is no principle specifically dealing with 'employees' and, as far as employee remuneration is concerned, it is reduced to a footnote reference, namely that '[t]he individual remuneration packages to be awarded to employees other than senior executives are generally matters left to management'.[103]

Although there has been a slight slowdown in CEO and executive remuneration increases in Australian companies, the *Aon and Governance Institute Board and Executive Remuneration Report of 2021*, covering the period when the impact of the COVID-19 pandemic was at its peak for ordinary employees, did not show any significant slow-down or claw-back of CEO and senior executive remuneration.[104]

The COVID-19 pandemic illustrated again that many corporations have little regard for employee interests and that there is little forward-planning in good years to look after employees in difficult years, even if the suffering of employees is not caused by a pandemic. Corporations remain focused on the short term and consider shareholder interest to be primary, which causes considerable anxiety for employees:[105]

> The realisation that short-termism and shareholder greed affected all stake-holders, in particular millions of employees who lost their jobs worldwide because of COVID-19, resulted in something that could be described as a revolution. Employees are 'up in arms' and it seems to be a dangerous trend if their pleas for greater employee democracy and codeterminations is ignored.

Du Plessis and Anastasi analysed another problem, the enormous amounts companies spend on dividends and sharebuy-back.[106] Earlier in 2019, the controversy surrounding stock buy-backs was also analysed by Jeff Desjardis.[107] The trend of a disproportionate percentage of company profits not being reinvested in the company, but used to pay dividends

---

99 Leo E Strine and Dorothy S Lund, 'How to restore strength and fairness to our economy', *The New York Times* (online, 10 April 2020) <https://www.nytimes.com/2020/04/10/business/dealbook/coronavirus-corporate-governance.html>.

100 ASX, *Corporate Governance Principles and Recommendations* (4th ed, 2019) <https://www.asx.com.au/documents/asx-compliance/cgc-principles-and-recommendations-fourth-edn.pdf> 29.

101 Ibid 19–20.

102 Ibid 17.

103 Ibid 29, fn 72.

104 Governance Institute of Australia, *Aon and Governance Institute Board and Executive Remuneration Report of 2021* (2021) 11.

105 Jean J du Plessis and Andrea Anastasi, '2020 vision: current reflections and stakeholder governance in a post-COVID-19 world' (2020) 37(7) *Company and Securities Law Journal* 495, 499.

106 The rest of this section is extracted from ibid 495, 499.

107 Jeff Desjardins, 'The controversy around stock buybacks explained: Stock buybacks surpassed $1 trillion last year', *Visual Capitalist* (online, 1 March 2019) <https://www.visualcapitalist.com/stock-buybacks-explained/>.

to shareholders was noticed several years ago. In a 2015 BBC interview hosted by Duncan Weldon, Andy Haldane, the then Chief Economist of the Bank of England, pointed out that in 1970 only 10 per cent of company profits were paid to shareholders as dividends. In 2015 the estimate was that 60–70 per cent of company profits were paid to shareholders as dividends.[108] As evidenced in the charts in Jeff Desjardis's analysis, matters got even worse after 2015 when proportions of company profits used for share buy-backs and dividend payments are combined.[109] This concerning trend has also received attention in more thorough scholarly financial analyses and reviews.[110] Share buy-backs do not only dispro-portionally divert company profits away from stakeholders, other than shareholders, but can be dangerous to the economy.[111] The problem is illustrated well by charts, relying on Deutsche Bank research, showing that corporate profits that were used on capital spending in the past are nowadays used to pay dividends and to fund share buy-backs.[112] Rebecca Henderson, with her open-minded and realistic stance on why 'Friedman Capitalism' as we know it needs re-engineering focuses on the problems created by the existing endemic 'trickle-up' profit distribution in public corporations in developed countries:[113]

> The vast majority of the fruits flowing from the productivity growth of the last twenty years have gone to the top 10 percent of the income distribution, partic-ularly in the United States and the United Kingdom. Real incomes at the bottom have stagnated. The populist fury that has emerged as a result is threatening the viability of our societies – and of our economies.

In 2020 (during the early days of COVID-19 and lockdowns) Strine and Lund observed the following disturbing trend:[114]

> After a 10-year economic expansion that led to record increases in earn-ings, plus huge corporate tax relief, American corporations should have had

---

108 Duncan Weldon, 'Shareholder power "holding back economic growth"', *BBC* (online, 24 July 2015) <https://www.bbc.com/news/business-33660426>.

109 Desjardins, 'The controversy around stock buybacks explained', *Visual Capitalist* (online, 1 March 2019). For more recent analyses, see Nessa Anwar, 'Share buybacks: The case for and against a company repurchasing its own stock', *CNBC* (online, 18 May 18 2020) <https://www.cnbc.com/2020/05/18/share-buybacks-case-for-and-against-a-company-buying-back-its-own-stock.html>; Cory Janssen (reviewed by Samantha Silberstein and fact checked by Suzanne Kvilhaug), 'Stock buybacks: A breakdown', *Investopedia* (19 May 2020) <https://www.investopedia.com/articles/02/041702.asp>; and Sara O'Brien, 'Stock buybacks: What are they and how do they impact investors?', *CNBC* (online, updated 14 May 2020) <https://www.cnbc.com/2020/03/20/stock-buybacks-what-are-they-and-how-do-they-impact-investors.html#:~:text=Here's%20the%20deal%3A%20First%2C%20when,Fide%20Wealth%20in%20New%20York>.

110 See William Lazonick, 'Profits without prosperity', *Harvard Business Review* (online, September 2014) <https://hbr.org/resources/pdfs/comm/fmglobal/profits_without_prosperity.pdf>; and Robert Homan, 'Think different', *Boston Review* (21 August 2018) <http://bostonreview.net/class-inequality/robert-homan-think-different>.

111 M Lazonick, ME Sakinç and Hopkins, 'Why stock buybacks are dangerous for the economy', *Harvard Business Review* (online, 7 January 2020) <https://hbr.org/2020/01/why-stock-buybacks-are-dangerous-for-the-economy>.

112 Gillian Tett, 'Does capitalism need saving itself', *Financial Times* (online, 6 September 2019) <http://digamo.free.fr/ftagenda919.pdf>.

113 Henderson, *Reimagining Capitalism in a World on Fire* (2020) 18–19.

114 Strine and Lund, 'How to restore strength and fairness to our economy', *The New York Times* (online, 10 April 2020) <https://www.nytimes.com/2020/04/10/business/dealbook/coronavirus-corporate-governance.html>.

substantial cash reserves to sustain them during a short period without revenue. But many did not, and instead were highly leveraged, lacked adequate
reserves and lived paycheck to paycheck, so to speak. What happened to that
cash? Much of it was returned to shareholders in dividends and stock buy-
backs. At the same time, American corporations weakened the traditional
gain-sharing between the workforce and stockholders that characterized the
post-World War II era. During that period, when corporate profits went up,
workers shared equitably in the gains. Not any more.

The problem of corporations being so focused on enriching shareholders and distrib-
uting profits primarily into the pockets of shareholders, rather than reinvesting into the
corporation itself or in key stakeholders, has been described by Haldane as corporations
'eating themselves'.[115] William Lazonick explains it as follows:[116]

> [The problem is that] [c]orporate profitability is not translating into economic
> prosperity in the United States. Instead of investing profits in innovation and
> productive capabilities, U.S. executives are spending them on gigantic stock
> repurchases (and paying shareholders generous dividends).

This, in fact, as Robert Homan explains, results in a 'trickle-up', not a 'trickle-down' of
profit distribution. The concentration of capital at the top 'results in even more money
being made for people who do not have to perform labor to watch it grow' and it 'is the
root mechanism by which corporations like Apple contribute to an increasingly unequal
society'.[117] The disturbing aspect of this 'trickle-up' phenomenon has been illustrated
convincingly in a very highly regarded and award-winning[118] work by Thomas Piketty,
Capital in the Twenty-First Century, the translated version of which was published in
2014.[119] Piketty illustrates the scale of unequal wealth distribution through historic analyses, reaching the following disturbing (although not surprising) conclusion, but also suggesting what could be done to deal with the problem:[120]

> When the rate of return on capital exceeds the rate of growth of output and
> income, as it did in the nineteenth century and seems quite likely to do again

---

115 Duncan Weldon, 'Shareholder power "holding back economic growth"', *BBC* (online, 24 July 2015)
<https://www.bbc.com/news/business-33660426>
116 Lazonick, 'Profits without prosperity', *Harvard Business Review* (September 2014).
117 Homan, 'Think different', *Boston Review* (21 August 2018).
118 Winner of the Financial Times and McKinsey Business Book of the Year Award; Winner of the
British Academy Medal and Finalist, National Book Critics Circle Award. See also Robert M
Solow, 'Thomas Piketty is right: Everything you need to know about "Capital in the Twenty-First
Century"', *The New Statesman* (online, 27 April 2014) <https://www.newstatesman.com/business/
economics/2014/04/thomas-piketty-right-everything-you-need-know-about-capital-twenty-first-
century>.
119 For a condensed explanation of core aspects he discusses in his book, see Thomas Piketty, 'Putting
distribution back at the center of economics: Reflections on *Capital in the Twenty-First Century*'
(2015) 29(1) *Journal of Economic Perspectives* 67. It is not surprising that some, especially as far as
his recommendations regarding progressive and punitive taxes are concerned, would challenge
his recommendations: see Curtis S Dubay and Salim Furth, 'Understanding Thomas Piketty
and his critics' *Backgrounder: No 2954* (12 September 2014) 1, 4–6; and Carlos Obregón, *Thomas Piketty
is Wrong* (CreateSpace Publishing Platform, 2015).
120 Thomas Piketty, *Capital in the Twenty-First Century*, tr Arthur Goldhammer (Belknap Press, 2014).

in the twenty-first, capitalism automatically generates arbitrary and unsustainable inequalities that radically undermine the meritocratic values on which democratic societies are based. There are nevertheless ways democracy can regain control over capitalism and ensure that the general interest takes precedence over private interests, while preserving economic openness and avoiding protectionist and nationalist reactions. The policy recommendations I propose later in the book tend in this direction. They are based on lessons derived from historical experience, of which what follows is essentially a narrative.

Visually, the problem is illustrated well by presenting figures used by Desjardins as a pie chart, based on data collected from a large number of American public corporations prior to 2019 (see Figure 2.1).

Our own research, undertaken by two research assistants (James Royce and Brody Wons) in 2020, illustrates an interesting pattern based on collecting data on ASX50 corporations and comparing what amounts were spent on executive remuneration, dividends and share buy-back in the financial year 2018–19: (Figure 2.2).

In the media, excessive executive remuneration normally makes headlines. When the public (and possibly shareholders) gets worked up about excessive executive remuneration, all sorts of mechanisms are proposed to deal with 'the problem': 'Say-on-Pay'; 'Two-strikes and a Spill; 'claw-back' of excessive executive remuneration under certain circumstance, and so on. But is that the real problem? If any conclusion could be drawn from the Figure 2.2, and more comprehensive data available internationally, the far bigger issue is amounts distributed on dividends and spent via share buy-backs.

Figure 2.1 Distribution of tax savings

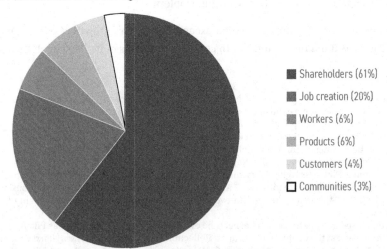

- Shareholders (61%)
- Job creation (20%)
- Workers (6%)
- Products (6%)
- Customers (4%)
- Communities (3%)

Source: Drawn from Jeff Desjardins, 'The controversy around stock buybacks explained: Stock buybacks surpassed $1 trillion last year', *Visual Capitalist* (online, 1 March 2019) <https://www.visualcapitalist.com/stock-buybacks-explained/>.

Figure 2.2 Total executive remuneration, dividends paid, and amounts spent on share buy-backs, ASX50 corporations, 2018–19

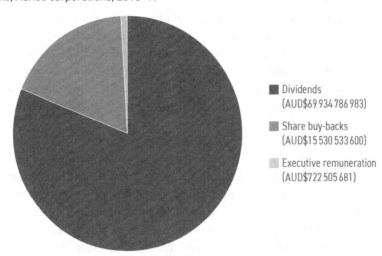

■ Dividends
(AUD$69 934 786 983)

■ Share buy-backs
(AUD$15 530 533 600)

■ Executive remuneration
(AUD$722 505 681)

Is it not perhaps time that the focus shifted to these bigger evils as far as excesses are concerned, which show blatantly unfair and unequal treatment of all non-shareholder interests?

A central theme in Rebecca Henderson's excellent book, *Reimagining Capitalism in a World on Fire,* is that the problem of 'inequality' (she does not only focus on financial inequality) cannot be effectively addressed without government interference and a concerted effort among all societal and business organisations, firms and entities.[121] However, how likely is that to happen? How seriously has it been addressed by politicians and government in any Western country and what impact did it have? If it had a high impact, a discussion of this would have been unnecessary for Henderson, as would devoting part of this book to one aspect of inequality, the growing gap between the rich and the poor. Is a broader, more grandiose plan required? This is probably where Klaus Schwab's very controversial 'Great Reset' proposal deserves a short mention.

2.7.5 The 'Great Reset'

In general terms, the 'Great Reset' proposal states that radical steps are required to deal with the inequalities in the world and this cannot be done in baby steps but, as with 'big bang theory', a great (economic and social) reset is required globally 'to save the world!'. The 'Great Reset' idea is linked to several conspiracy theories referencing the illuminati; world dominance by a few; a brave new world; the rise of a new world order; 'Klaus Schwab and his Davos buddies', and so on.[122]

---

121 Henderson, *Reimagining Capitalism* (2020) 163–3, 195, 201–4, 244, 253.
122 See, eg, Alex Jones, *The Great Reset and the War for the World* (Skyhorse Publishing, 2022); Vernon Coleman, *Endgame: The Hidden Agenda 21* (eBook, 2021); J Macha-el Thomas Hays, *Rise of the New World Order: The Culling of Man* (eBook, 2013); and Dean and Jill Henderson, *Illuminati: Agenda 21* (eBook, 2018).

There is, however, something real about the Great Reset given the interest in it by the World Economic Forum ('WEF'), an international non-governmental lobbying organisation based in Geneva, Switzerland, founded by Klaus Schwab in 1971.[123] It is an active organisation, with admirable sustainability goals[124] and is squarely based on a stakeholder approach to corporate governance since it was founded,[125] but also drives controversial agenda points. Greta Thunberg's powerful 2019 'Our House Is on Fire' speech that she gave at the 2019 WEF Forum is one example,[126] and the Great Reset initiative is another highly political, emotional and controversial one.[127] In 2021 an entire summit was dedicated to the initiative.[128]

There are many views, opinions and commentaries on the Great Reset. However, for the purposes of this book, we want to make the reader aware of this idea without any judgment on how realistic it will be to achieve a 'great global social and economic reset' or whether it stands on any theoretical sound foundations, or whether there are any hidden agendas. What is significant, however, is that it was probably Klaus Schwab, the driving force behind the Great Reset, who coined the term 'stakeholder capitalism',[129] which is now the flavour of the month in at least the US, as was seen in Section 2.2. From a more theoretical point of view, and linking the Great Reset to the COVID-19 pandemic, the book by Klaus Schwab and Thierry Malleret, *COVID-19: The Great Reset*,[130] provides interesting perspectives on some of the significant global issues we are faced with and that require attention. If not by way of a Great Reset, we touch on many of these issues in our book given their importance from a corporate governance point of view.

2.8 Conclusion

The recent development in the US whereby the interests of all corporate stakeholders are receiving greater recognition is indeed refreshing. Although not reflected in US law, in any state or at federal level, there is an apparent shift in approach to be detected in US business and, as the law often lags behind business, it is to be hoped that the current business realities will continue to transform and a stakeholder capitalism approach will gain more legal recognition over time. As pointed out, there has been immediate pushback from institutional investor organisations, and even political financial pressure from the Republicans who have sought to send a message that shareholder primacy and profit

---

123 See World Economic Forum <https://www.weforum.org/>.
124 See World Economic Forum, 'Leading by example: Our responsibility' (2023) <https://www.weforum.org/sustainability-world-economic-forum>.
125 See World Economic Forum, 'About – our mission' (2023) <https://www.weforum.org/about/world-economic-forum/>.
126 Greta Thunberg, 'Our house is on fire' (25 January 2019) <https://www.weforum.org/agenda/2019/01/our-house-is-on-fire-16-year-old-greta-thunberg-speaks-truth-to-power/>.
127 Ivan Wecke, 'Conspiracy theories aside, there is something fishy about the Great Reset', *Open Democracy* (16 August 2021) <https://www.opendemocracy.net/en/oureconomy/conspiracy-theories-aside-there-something-fishy-about-great-reset/>.
128 IISD, 'World Economic Forum Annual Meeting 2021' <https://sdg.iisd.org/events/world-economic-forum-annual-meeting-2021/>.
129 Schwab, *Stakeholder Capitalism* (2021) 86.
130 Klaus Schwab and Thierry Malleret, *COVID-19: The Great Reset* (Forum Publishing, World Economic Forum, 2020).

maximisation for shareholders should remain the main purpose of for-profit corporations in America. However, it is to be hoped that common sense and what is really in the best interests of corporations and society will prevail over time. Being such a dominant economic force, the US approach will have a ripple effect on the rest of the world, and hopefully it will be positive, leading to an all-inclusive stakeholder approach for all corporations. This theme of the importance of stakeholders and corporate social responsibility ('CSR') is the focus of Chapter 3.

3 GOVERNANCE OF STAKEHOLDERS AND CORPORATE SOCIAL RESPONSIBILITY

3.1 Introduction

As touched upon in Chapter 1, contemporary commentary on corporate governance can, in general terms, be divided into two main camps: those who consider corporate governance as being about building effective mechanisms and measures to satisfy the expectations of the variety of individuals, groups and entities (collectively, 'stakeholders') that inevitably interact with the corporation (stakeholder primacy), and those who focus on it in relation to the narrower expectations of shareholders (shareholder primacy).

This chapter focuses on the first of these objectives.[1] We commence the chapter by pointing out that an approach to accentuate the differences between a shareholder versus a stakeholder theory of the corporation is probably a contradiction and a false dichotomy (Section 3.2). In Section 3.3 we deal with the important aspect of corporate social responsibility ('CSR'). Closely related to CSR is disclosure of and reporting on non-financial matters, which we deal with in Section 3.4. As part of this discussion we cover, in Section 3.4.4, the controversial and highly topical issue of companies exaggerating their image as environmentally friendly corporations (greenwashing) to please investors and to attract more investments, which allows them to also smartening their image on other issues (greenscreening). We deal with the dangers associated with greenwashing and greenscreening in Section 3.4.5.

In Section 3.5 we deal with a relatively new, but currently prominent issue, namely 'the social licence to operate'. This issue has become prominent as part of the debate on the true role and purpose of corporations and also as a response to poor corporate culture, with the latter resulting in the questioning of corporate privileges and licence granted by society that allows companies to operate. The focus in Section 3.6 shifts to CSR and directors' duties. To what extent do the responsibilities that corporations have towards society reflect a community expectation that there is a legal duty on

---

1   For a broader discussion on competing corporate law theories and the public and private dimensions of corporate law, see Stephen Bottomley, *The Constitutional Corporation – Rethinking Corporate Governance* (Ashgate, 2007).

directors to heed the company's social responsibilities? In Section 3.7 we deal briefly with the meaning of 'stakeholders' and, again briefly, consider the position of clearly recognisable stakeholders such as shareholders, employees, creditors, customers, the community, the environment and government. In Section 3.8 we explain how all corporate stakeholders have vested interests in the sustainability of corporations. In Section 3.9 we draw conclusions in respect of the aspects of governance dealt with in this chapter.

3.2 A shareholder versus stakeholder focus: A contradiction and false dichotomy?

As pointed out in Chapter 1, a corporation is a separate legal entity and the directors owe their duties to the corporation as a separate legal entity – these are now firmly embedded principles of corporate law, at least in Australia and all common law juris-dictions. When these principles are accepted as trite law, and it is accepted that in the corporation as a separate legal entity various interests are represented and affected by the conduct of that separate corporate entity, then the shareholder *versus* stakeholder focus becomes a contradiction and false dichotomy. It is, therefore, quite misleading to argue as follows:[2]

> [I]f the directors of a company were held to be responsible to shareholders and the various stakeholders groups alike, then what would be the corporate objec-tive? How could the board function effectively if there were a multiplicity of different objectives, no one of which took priority over the others? … This could actually lead to quite a dangerous situation where directors and managers were not really accountable.

There should be no inherent tension between shareholders, on the one hand, and other stakeholders, on the other hand. When directors exercise their powers and discharge their duties with due care and diligence, in good faith and in the best interests of the corporation, the duty provides no legal prioritisation of which interest/s should come first for directors. The only consideration is the corporation as a separate legal entity. The directors do not serve more than one master, as has been argued in the past.[3] They only serve one master, and that master is the corporation as a separate legal entity. The practical reality that one of the interests, namely the interests of shareholders, is deeply imbedded in most Western corporate law models is beyond dispute. However, that does not detract from the fundamental principles associated with the doctrine of separateness of the company as legal entity that is so pertinently illustrated by the bedrock UK case of *Salomon v A Salomon & Co Ltd*.[4]

---

2   Christine Mallin, *Corporate Governance* (Oxford University Press, 2nd ed, 2007) 58.
3   Frank H Easterbrook and Daniel R Fischel, *The Economic Structure of Corporate Law* (Harvard University Press, 1991) 38: 'A manager told to serve two masters … has been freed of both and is answerable to neither.'
4   [1897] AC 22.

Steve Letza, Xiuping Sun and James Kirkbride explain the difference between the two corporate governance paradigms, 'shareholding' and 'stakeholding', illustrating how the false dichotomy evolved in the later 20th century.[5]

The *G20/OECD Principles of Corporate Governance*,[6] a non-binding statement of what the OECD believes to constitute best practice in corporate governance, is discussed in greater detail in Section 12.3 of this book. Since the 2004 edition of this statement, the OECD has recognised three key non-shareholder stakeholders: creditors, employees and government.[7]

3.3 Corporate social responsibility ('CSR')[8]

3.3.1 Background and inappropriate perceptions

Although profit maximisation for shareholders overshadowed all other corporate governance issues since the early 1970s, gradually the focus turned to 'the link between corporate social responsibility and financial performance' and on the 'business case' for corporate social responsibility ('CSR').[9] In the mid-2000s, this began to be referred to as the 'business approach' to 'stakeholders and CSR',[10] which in fact illustrates that a clear 'business case' has been made out for corporations' social responsibilities and an all-inclusive stakeholder approach.[11] More recently, at least since 2018, the business case for an all-inclusive stakeholder approach has been defended unreservedly as was illustrated in Sections 2.2.2 and 2.6.[12]

---

5   Steve Letza, Xiuping Sun and James Kirkbride, 'Shareholding versus stakeholding: A critical review of corporate governance' (2004) 12(3) *Corporate Governance* 242, 243.

6   In September 2023, the 2023 *G20/OECD Principles of Corporate Governance* <https://doi.org/10.1787/ed750b30-en> were introduced to replace the previous (2015) version. The *G20/OECD Principles of Corporate Governance* are set out in the Appendix to the Organisation for Economic Co-operation and Development ('OECD') *Recommendation on Principles of Corporate Governance* (OECD/LEGAL/0413) adopted by the OECD Council on 8 July 2015 and revised on 8 June 2023. See discussions in Sections 12.2 and 12.3.

7   OECD, *OECD Principles of Corporate Governance* (2004) 12 <https://www.oecd.org/corporate/ca/corporategovernanceprinciples/31557724.pdf>. For reinforcement of this approach, see pt IV of the *G20/OCED Principles of Corporate Governance* (2015) 34–6 <https://www.oecd.org/publications/g20-oecd-principles-of-corporate-governance-2015-9789264236882-en.htm> which discusses the role of stakeholders in corporate governance.

8   For a good explanation of the relationship between corporate governance and corporate social responsibility, see Andreas Rühmkorf, 'The promotion of corporate social responsibility in English private law' (PhD thesis, University of Sheffield, 2013) 58–62. See also several of the chapters in Michel Magnan and Giovanna Michelon (eds), *Handbook on Corporate Governance and Corporate Social Responsibility* (Edward Elgar, 2024).

9   Dorothy S Lund and Elizabeth Pollman, 'The corporate governance machine' (2021) 121(8) *Columbia Law Review* 2563, 2613.

10   Corporations and Markets Advisory Committee, *The Social Responsibility of Corporations Report* (2006) 56–7, 74, 78. See also Tanusree Jain, Adrián Zicari and Ruth V Aguilera, 'Corporate governance and corporate social responsibility: Revisiting their inter-relationship in Till Talaulicar (ed), *Research Handbook on Corporate Governance* (Edward Elgar, 2023) 113.

11   See generally Garin Pratiwi Solihati, 'Good corporate governance and corporate social responsibility disclosure on company value and return on asset as moderating variable' (2022) 4 *International Journal of Management Studies and Social Science Research* 287.

12   See in particular Larry Fink, 'A fundamental reshaping of finance [2020 Letter to CEOs]' (2020) <https://www.blackrock.com/corporate/investor-relations/2020-larry-fink-ceo-letter>; and Hilary Sale, 'The corporate purpose of social license' (2021) 94(4) *Southern California Law Review* 785 788–90.

Since at least the 1930s with the famous Berle and Dodd debates, the concept of CSR has been criticised as vague and as making it impossible for directors to exercise their duty to act 'in the bests interests of the corporation.[13] It should not be forgotten how some CEOs perceived their roles in the past, and it is not unthinkable that some CEOs still see their roles in the same light and would still express strong opinions on why there should be no duty to enforce CSR. In 2006 a former CEO of Macquarie Bank (Australia), John Green, spoke at a high-profile conference organised by the Supreme Court of New South Wales and the Law Society of New South Wales. His speech was transcribed verbatim and published in a monograph by the University of Sydney's Ross Parsons Centre of Commercial and Taxation Law. Green expressed his views strongly, as follows:[14]

> [T]his CSR stuff is not just fuzzy at the edges it is so mushy and fluffy that if you put your foot anywhere near it, it will suck you in and smother you like quicksand ...
>
> What is really lurking behind CSR is the insidious and false assumption that CSR really stands for 'Crooks, Spivs and Retards' – caricatures of rich white thieving bastards who yearn for nothing better than ripping off their customers with shoddy goods, screwing their employees with lousy pay and working conditions, all so they can spend the afternoons sinking back in their soft leather armchairs and puffing on fat cigars while they count their ill-gotten greenbacks. Maybe that was a fair generalization once, but it is not today [2006].

His comments were made during a time that the abuses, misuses of power, wrongful acts and even illegal conduct by banks[15] were probably rife, eventually leading to a Royal Commission into just those activities.[16]

3.3.2 Rising prominence of CSR

Although the term 'CSR' has had a rollercoaster existence since the 1930s, it has stayed the course and nowadays there is a pretty good understanding of it,[17] as will be seen

13   AA Berle, 'Corporate powers as powers in trust' (1931) 44(7) *Harvard Law Review* 1049; E Merrick Dodd, 'For whom are corporate managers trustees?' (1932) 45(7) *Harvard Law Review* 1145; AA Berle, 'For whom corporate managers are trustees: A note' (1932) 45(8) *Harvard Law Review* 1365; E Merrick Dodd, 'Book review: *Bureaucracy and Trusteeship in Large Corporation*' (1942) 9(3) *University of Chicago Law Review* 538, 546–7.

14   John M Green, 'Should the Corporations Act require directors to consider non-shareholder "stakeholders"' in RP Austin) (ed), *Company Directors and Corporate Social Responsibility: UK and Australian Perspectives* (Ross Parsons Centre of Commercial, Corporate and Taxation Law, 2007) 44, 45–6.

15   *Royal Commission into Misconduct in the Banking Industry, Superannuation and Financial Services Industry* (Final Report, February 2019) vol 1 ('Final Hayne Report') 127–8, 145, 182; *Royal Commission into Misconduct in the Banking Industry, Superannuation and Financial Services Industry* (Interim Report, September 2018) vol 1 ('Interim Hayne Report') 94, 175.

16   Interim Hayne Report (2018) 86–7. See also Julia Dreosti, Bimaya de Silva and Katie Walsh, 'A civil law solution to social licence to operate and directors' duties conundrum in Australia' (2021) 38(6) *Company and Securities Law Journal* 404, 432.

17   For analysis of CSR types, see Monray Marsellus Botha, 'First do no harm! On oaths, social contracts and other promises: How corporations navigate the corporate social responsibility labyrinth'

in Section 3.4.1. There is also progressively a more theoretical justification for of CSR, with the concept moving 'from the margins to the mainstream of corporate policy and practice'.[18] Redmond adopts a realistic approach regarding the meaning of CSR:[19]

> While definitions abound, corporate social responsibility ('CSR') is, in sophisticated modern conceptions, understood as 'the responsibility of enterprises for their impacts on society'.[20] The term CSR is sympathetically used to refer to a range of voluntary measures undertaken by companies to integrate social, environmental and business concerns in their operations and their interaction with stakeholders.

The continued relevance and importance of companies being 'good corporate citizens' and having corporate social *responsibilities* is highlighted by the sheer number of articles and books dedicated to corporate citizenship[21] as well as CSR, especially since 1990.[22]

---

in Hermie Coetzee and Carika Fritz (eds), *De Serie Legenda, Developments in Commercial Law, Entrepreneurial Law* (LexisNexis, Durban, 2019) vol III, 14, 28–34.

18   Thomas Clarke, *International Corporate Governance: A Comparative Approach* (Routledge, 2nd ed, 2017) 411, 428–35.

19   Paul Redmond, 'Directors' duties and corporate social responsiveness' (2012) 35(1) *University of New South Wales Law Journal* 317, 320. See also Paul Redmond, 'The ASX Corporate Governance Principles and Recommendations and the idea of corporate responsibility' (2023) 40(2) *Company and Securities Law Journal* 116; Ray Broomhill, 'Corporate social responsibility: Key issues and debates' (2007) 1 *Dunstan Papers* 1, 9–11; Ina Freeman and Amir Hasnaoui, 'The meaning of corporate social responsibility: The vision of four nations' (2011) 100(3) *Journal of Business Ethics* 419.

20   Redmond, 'Directors' duties and corporate social responsiveness' (2012) 35(1) *University of New South Wales Law Journal* 317, 320, referring to European Commission, *A Renewed EU Strategy 2011–14 for Corporate Social Responsibility* (Communication No 681, European Commission, 25 October 2011) 6.

21   For example, the following books, in their entirety, focus on corporate citizenship: Mervyn King, *The Corporate Citizen: Governance for All Entities* (Penguin, 2008) and Jesús Conill, Christoph Luetge and Tatjana Schönwälder-Kuntze (eds), *Corporate Citizenship, Contractarianism and Ethical Theory: On Philosophical Foundations of Business Ethics* (Ashgate, 2008). See also Ingo Pies and Peter Koslowski (eds), *Corporate Citizenship and New Governance: The Political Role of Corporations* (Springer, 2011); Karin Svedberg Helgesson and Ulrika Mörth (eds), *The Political Role of Corporate Citizens: An Interdisciplinary Approach* (Palgrave Macmillan, 2013); and Dr Christoph Luetge, Tatjana Schönwälder-Kuntze and Jesús Conill (eds), *Corporate Citizenship, Contractarianism and Ethical Theory: On Philosophical Foundations of Business Ethics* (Ashgate, 2013).

22   A few could be mentioned: Güler Aras and David Crowther (eds), *Global Perspectives on Corporate Governance and CSR* (Gower Publishing Ltd, 2009); Frankden Hond, Frank G Ade Bakker and Peter Neergaard, *Managing Corporate Social Responsibility in Action: Talking, Doing and Measuring* (Ashgate, 2007); Ana Maria Dávila Gómez and David Crowther (eds), *Ethics, Psyche and Social Responsibility* (Ashgate, 2007); Wim Vandekerckhove, *Whistleblowing and Organizational Social Responsibility: A Global Assessment* (Ashgate, 2006); David Crowther and Lez Rayman-Bacchus (eds), *Perspectives on Corporate Social Responsibility* (Ashgate, 2004); H Kent Baker and John R Nofsinger, 'Socially responsible finance and investing: An overview' in H Kent Baker and John R Nofsinger (eds), *Socially Responsible Finance and Investing* (Wiley, 2012) 1; Jill Solomon, *Corporate Governance and Accountability* (John Wiley & Sons, 2011); Lorenzo Sacconi et al (eds), *Corporate Social Responsibility and Corporate Governance: The Contribution of Economic Theory and Related Disciplines* (Palgrave Macmillan, 2010); and Kathryn Haynes, Alan Murray and Jesse Dillard, *Social Responsibility: A Research Handbook* (Taylor & Francis, 2012). Ironically, despite the wealth of literature on the topic of CSR, confusion and inconsistency as to what it means in practice remain. See David Chandler, *Corporate Social Responsibility: A Strategic Perspective* (Business Expert Press, 2015) xxiv.

What is clear is that over time there has been an inevitable move away from the view that the primary aim of corporations is simply 'to make a profit' or 'to make money'[23] for their 'shareholders' towards a more inclusive approach whereby corporations, especially large public corporations, 'have a responsibility for the public good'[24] and should strive 'to build a better society'.[25]

Based on these views, a new trend or imperative has developed, namely, for corporations, again especially large public corporations, to illustrate, in a practical way, that they behave in a *responsible* way.

3.4 Disclosure of and reporting on non-financial matters: A powerful corporate governance tool or a smokescreen?

3.4.1 Demonstrating good CSR practices

The developments outlined above resulted in a huge drive for 'responsible investment'[26] and ways for investors to determine whether they invest in corporations that are sensitive towards environmental and climate change issues, social issues, governance issues and the long-term sustainability of these corporations. Thus, reporting on non-financial issues (also referred to as 'sustainable or triple bottom line reporting') became fashionable.[27] The 'triple bottom line' refers to reporting not only on financial issues, but also on environment and social issues and was coined by Elkington in 1997.[28] This type of reporting is referred to as 'the three Ps', which stands for planet, people and profit. Regulation began to be introduced for disclosure of and reporting on non-financial matters and issues ('CSR disclosure'; also referred to in this chapter as 'non-financial reporting').[29] In addition, investors and stakeholders started to insist that corporations, especially large public ones, take seriously non-mandatory measures for CSR disclosure.

The widest and most common umbrella terminology used to reflect the expectation that corporation should engage in non-financial reporting – that is, reporting on

---

23 Paul Hawken, *The Ecology of Commerce* (Harper Business, rev ed, 2010) 1–2 makes this point very clear.

24 Rühmkorf, 'The promotion of corporate social responsibility in English private law' (2013) 18, fn 47, referring to M Blowfield and A Murray, *Corporate Responsibility: A Critical Introduction* (Oxford University Press, 2008) 13.

25 Alan C Hutchinson, *The Companies We Keep* (Irwin Law, 2005) 326.

26 Clarke, *International Corporate Governance* (2017) 445–50.

27 CAMAC, *The Social Responsibility of Corporations Report* (December 2006) 69–74, 115–16. See also Ross Grantham, *The Law and Practice of Corporate Governance* (LexisNexis, 2020) 392.

28 John Elkington, *Cannibals with Forks: The Triple Bottom Line of 21st Century Business* (Capstone, 1997) vii, 70. See also John Elkington, '25 years ago I coined the phrase "triple bottom line". Here's why it's time to rethink it' (2018) 25 *Harvard Business Review* 205; Katayun I Jaffari and Stephen A Pike (eds), *ESG in the Boardroom: A Guidebook for Directors* (American Bar Association, 2022) xli; Markus Milne and Rob Gray, 'W(h)ither ecology? The triple bottom line, the global reporting initiative, and corporate sustainability reporting' (2013) 118(1) *Journal of Business Ethics* 13.

29 Australian Government, Treasury, *Climate-related Financial Disclosure: Consultation Paper* (June 2023) <https://treasury.gov.au/sites/default/files/2023-06/c2023-402245.pdf> 6–9.

environmental, social and governance matters – is abbreviated as 'ESG' reporting. However, terminology in the space of non-financial reporting by corporations overlaps and different classifications occur. There is currently no strict theoretical distinction drawn between the various descriptions or labels for non-financial reporting. ESG might be the umbrella description, but where the focuses is on the 'S' ('social') part of ESG, the term 'CSR reporting' is commonly used.

As CSR disclosure gained traction, academics started to look for theories to justify it. For instance, Omran and Ramdhony[30] analysed the legitimacy theory, the stakeholder theory,[31] the social contract theory and the signalling theory as possible justifications for CSR disclosure. They make a convincing case that the stakeholder theory provides a good theoretical justification for CSR disclosure.[32] With respect to the legitimacy theory,[33] whereby corporations seek to justify their legitimacy by showing that they adhere to the social contract between organisations and the societies in which they operate, Omran and Ramdhony see this as a solid justification for expecting corporations to disclose and report on CSR matters. This is the corporation's 'social licence to operate' (discussed in Section 3.5)[34]. Omran and Ramdhony highlight that the social contract forms the basis by which businesses are legitimised, compelling businesses to continuously disclose beyond their legal obligations in order to maintain their legitimacy, thereby illustrating their credibility and trustworthiness to all stakeholders.

In the mid-2000s the prevailing view was still that non-financial reporting should not be based on mandatory legislation or government regulation, but should remain voluntary. However, at the same time the tide was turning 'in support of additional mandatory social and environmental reporting'.[35] We focus on this briefly in the next section.

3.4.2 Mandatory reporting

Although there are sound practical reasons for drawing a distinction between 'disclosure of' and 'reporting on' non-financial matters,[36] the discussion in this section will use the

---

30 Mohamed A Omran and Dineshwar Ramdhony, 'Theoretical perspectives on corporate social responsibility disclosure: A critical review' (2015) 5 *International Journal of Accounting and Financial Reporting* 38. See generally Clarke, *International Corporate Governance* (2017) 450–3.

31 For a review of the history and nature of the stakeholder theory, see also Emerson Wagner Mainardes, Helena Alves and Mario Raposo, 'Stakeholder theory: Issues to resolve' (2011) 49(2) *Management Decision* 226, 229 and Corina Gavrea and Roxana Stegerean, 'Comparative study on corporate governance' (2011) 20(2) *Annals of the University of Oradea, Economic Science Series* 674.

32 Omran and Ramdhony, 'Theoretical perspectives on corporate social responsibility disclosure' (2015) 5 *International Journal of Accounting and Financial Reporting* 38, 44.

33 Ibid 43–4.

34 Ibid 44–5.

35 CAMAC, *The Social Responsibility of Corporations Report* (December 2006) 138.

36 Giacomo Pigatto et al, 'A critical reflection on voluntary corporate non-financial and sustainability reporting and disclosure lessons learnt from two case studies on integrated reporting' (2022) 19(2) *Journal of Accounting and Organizational Change* 250, 251:

[T]he distinction between reporting and disclosure is relevant here and comes from linguistic and practical roots. To report means 'to give a formal or official account or statement of' something. Therefore, reporting has to do with corporations providing periodic accounts of their activities to interested stakeholders. Alternatively, to disclose means 'to make known or public' and 'expose to view'. Therefore, disclosure occurs when unknown or secret information is voluntarily made public by a corporation or involuntarily uncovered by other actors.

terms more generically to refer to ways in which information is made available publicly (for example, to investors). It is the impact of corporations on the environment and society that made it inevitable that reporting on ESG issues would be made mandatory. The most significant development in this regard took place in the European Union ('EU') in 2014.[37] On 22 October 2014 the European Parliament adopted Directive 2014/95/EU, which amended the important Directive 2013/34/EU (on disclosure of non-financial and diversity information by certain large undertakings and groups). The Explanatory Preamble to Directive 2014/95/EU states that since 2011 the European Commission aimed at harmonisation of the level of transparency regarding social and environmental information provided by undertakings in all sectors among EU Members. Since then there has been a particular focus in the EU on CSR and on developing a model for the EU that would foster accountability, transparency and responsible business behaviour and sustainable growth by promoting society's interests and achieving a sustainable and inclusive recovery of the EU's economies. The ultimate aim is explained well in [3] of the Explanatory Preamble to Directive 2014/95/EU:[38]

> The European Parliament acknowledged the importance of businesses divulging information on sustainability such as social and environmental factors, with a view to identifying sustainability risks and increasing investor and consumer trust. Indeed, disclosure of non-financial information is vital for managing change towards a sustainable global economy by combining long-term profitability with social justice and environmental protection.

3.4.3 Voluntary reporting initiatives

As already suggested, in the mid-2000s investors,[39] as well as several securities exchanges worldwide, started to expect reporting on ESG issues.[40] Since the late 1990s guidance on reporting on non-financial issues and matters has been provided by the Global Reporting Initiative ('GRI'), founded in Boston with current headquarters in Amsterdam.[41] In addition to this initiative, several other organisations, institutions, boards and councils developed frameworks and standards for CSR disclosure. The most notable are the Sustainability Accounting Standards Board ('SASB'), the International Accounting Standards Board ('IASB') and the International Financial Reporting Standards ('IFRS') Foundation.[42]

These initiatives, frameworks and standards are, to say the least, confusing because of the sheer number of different organisations, associations, foundations and initiatives

---

37 The following is partly based on Jean J du Plessis, 'Disclosure of non-financial information: A powerful corporate governance tool' (2016) 34(1) *Company and Securities Law Journal* 69.

38 Green Finance Platform, 'Non-Financial Reporting Directive (NFRD) – Directive 2014/95/EU and the proposal for a Corporate Sustainability Reporting Directive (CSRD)' <https://www.greenfinanceplatform.org/policies-and-regulations/non-financial-reporting-directive-nfrd-directive-201495eu-and-proposal#:~:text=The%20European%20Union%20(EU)%20Directive, of%20employees%2C%20respect%20for%20human>.

39 Jean J du Plessis and Andreas Rühmkorf, 'New trends regarding sustainability and integrated reporting for companies: What protection do directors have? (2015) 36(2) *Company Lawyer* 51.

40 For a succinct discussion of the ESG movement, see Lund and Pollman, 'The corporate governance machine' (2021) 121(8) *Columbia Law Review* 2563, 2612–15.

41 See Global Reporting Initiative ('GRI') <https://www.globalreporting.org/about-gri/contact-us/>.

42 See further the discussion in Section 7.3.

attempting to lead the way and trying to set the best possible standards, and to provide the best possible frameworks for reporting on non-financial issues.[43] The intentions are good, but the matrix of entities has created terrible confusion and uncertainty, not only for corporations who wish to report on non-financial matters, but also for investors and other stakeholders who are desperately looking for 'material' and 'reliable' information. The quest for all involved in the non-financial reporting space can be summarised as seeking information based on stakeholder inclusiveness, sustainable context, materiality and completeness.[44]

A small step toward harmonisation and standardisation has been taken recently. In 2021 and 2022 there were some serious efforts to find common ground on reporting standards for non-financial matters, eventually resulting in the formation of the IFRS Foundation in August 2022. The consolidation was explained as follows in a press release of 1 August 2022:[45]

> The IFRS Foundation has today announced the completion of the consolidation of the Value Reporting Foundation (VRF) into the IFRS Foundation. It follows the commitment made at COP26[46] to consolidate staff and resources of leading global sustainability disclosure initiatives to support the IFRS Foundation's new International Sustainability Standards Board's (ISSB) work to develop a comprehensive global baseline of sustainability disclosures for the capital markets.

More progress towards standardisation of frameworks and standards on reporting on non-financial matters has been made. On 25 July 2023, the International Organization of Securities Commissions ('IOSCO)' announced its endorsement of the sustainability-related Financial Disclosure Standards produced by the International Sustainability Standards Board ('ISSB').[47] The IFRS Foundation welcomed the new standards.[48]

It is to be hoped that a more specific and standardised framework will become the global standard, rather than the current differences and similarities being explained, as was done before by the GRI and SASB.[49] Exciting initiatives, involving common reporting standards and frameworks on non-financial disclosure, seem to be happening with initiatives like the GRI and the IFRS Foundation establishing a 'Sustainability Innovation Lab'.[50]

---

43 Ibid.
44 Clarke, *International Corporate Governance* (2017) 451.
45 IFRS, 'IFRS Foundation completes consolidation with Value Reporting Foundation' (1 August 2022) <https://www.ifrs.org/news-and-events/news/2022/08/ifrs-foundation-completes-consolidation-with-value-reporting-foundation/>.
46 'COP26' refers to the UN Climate Change Conference held on 31 October – 12 November 2021 in Glasgow: see <https://ukcop26.org/>.
47 See IOSCO, 'IOSCO endorses the ISSB's Sustainability-related Financial Disclosures Standards' (Media Release, 25 May 2025) <https://www.iosco.org/news/pdf/IOSCONEWS703.pdf> and IFRS, 'Cover note – Adoption Guide overview' <https://www.ifrs.org/supporting-implementation/supporting-materials-for-ifrs-sustainability-disclosure-standards/cover-note-adoption-guide-overview/>.
48 IFRS, 'IFRS Sustainability Disclosure Standards endorsed by international securities regulators' (25 July 2023) <https://www.ifrs.org/news-and-events/news/2023/07/issb-standards-endorsed-by-iosco/>.
49 See, eg, GRI and SASB, *A Practical Guide to Sustainability Reporting Using GRI and SASB Standards* (2021) <https://www.globalreporting.org/media/mlkjpn1i/gri-sasb-joint-publication-april-2021.pdf>.
50 IFRS, 'GRI establishes Sustainability Innovation Lab in coordination with the IFRS Foundation' (9 November 2023) <https://www.ifrs.org/news-and-events/news/2023/11/gri-establishes-sustainability-innovation-lab-in-coordination-with-the-ifrs-foundation/>.

3.4.4 Non-financial reporting, smokescreening, greenwashing and greenscreening

As discussed above, there has been considerable momentum in moving away from a voluntary arrangement ('nice to do') to a mandatory ('must do') regime for non-financial reporting. Investors are indeed insisting on reliable information on non-financial issues to enable them to make responsible investments in responsible companies that are focused on more than short-term financial profits. It is no wonder that there are now even stronger calls for more *formalised and mandatory reporting* on human, natural, and social capital.[51] The Integrated Reporting ('IR') Framework provides sensible guidelines for public companies reporting on not only financial capital but also the following five types of capital: human; intellectual; manufactured; natural; and social and relationship.[52]

Pigatto et al analyse developments in the field of voluntary corporate non-financial and sustainability reporting and disclosure ('VRD') critically, focusing on two case studies, and on integrated reporting ('IR') in particular, and come to some interesting conclusions.[53] First, corporations' motivation for VRD is not consistent; thus there is no consistency in how organisations voluntarily disclose information. Compliance with voluntary frameworks is done informally, and not always in a substantial way, which may not be meaningful to those relying on the disclosed information. Also, Pigatto et al found that 'at times, organisations serendipitously chance upon VRD practices such as IR instead of rationally recognising the potential ability of such practices to provide useful information for decision-making by investors'.[54] VRD practices may even be used by powerful groups in organisations 'to establish, maintain or restore power balances in their favour'.[55] Pigatto et al argue for 'reporting institutions to tone down any investor-centric rhetoric in favour of more substantial disclosures',[56] which in fact means that the authors appreciate that voluntary reporting and disclosure often is no more than 'window-dressing' or 'puffery' – a facade to impress investors.[57] The authors' (Pigatto et al) plea is for reporting organisations to approach the different frameworks for reporting (for example, IR, GRI, sustainability reporting) 'with a critical eye and read between the lines of these frameworks' to establish what they actually want to achieve'.[58] A clear trend of improved ESG reporting has also been noticed among the ASX200 corporations, but scepticism remains: '[A]re we getting the full story or just the good story'?[59]

---

51   Colin Mayer, *Prosperity* (Oxford University Press, 2018) 145–6.
52   IFRS Foundation, *International <IR> Framework* (January 2021) 18–19 <https://www .integratedreporting.org/wp-content/uploads/2021/01/InternationalIntegratedReportingFramework .pdf>.
53   Pigatto et al, 'A critical reflection on voluntary corporate non-financial and sustainability reporting and disclosure lessons learnt from two case studies on integrated reporting' (2022) 19(2) *Journal of Accounting and Organizational Change* 250.
54   Ibid 250.
55   Ibid.
56   Ibid 251.
57   See generally Grantham, *The Law and Practice of Corporate Governance* (2020) 481.
58   Pigatto et al, 'A critical reflection on voluntary corporate non-financial and sustainability reporting and disclosure lessons learnt from two case studies on integrated reporting' (2022) 19(2) *Journal of Accounting and Organizational Change* 250, 251.
59   PwC, 'ESG Reporting improves among the ASX200 – but are we getting the full story, or just the good story?' (2021) <https://www.pwc.com.au/media/2021/esg-reporting-among-asx200-improves.html>.

3.4.5 The dangers of greenwashing and greenscreening

The analysis of Pigatto et al also reveals the shortcomings of all voluntary forms of disclosure of and reporting on non-financial matters: corporations can smarten up their image (applying 'lipstick on a pig')[60] considerably, without being held liable under the rather complex legal rules applying to misleading and deceptive conduct. They disclose or report information against the backdrop of a studio green screen, allowing them to pick the background from millions of backgrounds available to let the corporation look very good – this is 'greenscreening'. In the context of climate change and environmental issues, making corporations look 'greener' than they really are when reporting on and disclosing environmental and climate change matters is known as 'greenwashing'.[61]

Greenwashing has been considered to comprise 'inaccurate climate-related statements and disclosures, including flawed climate scenario analysis and "net zero" commitments that are misleading or made without a reasonable basis'.[62] Apart from the possibility that directors and corporations involved in greenwashing can be held liable for misleading and deceptive conduct (probably only in extreme cases of misrepresenting facts regarding climate change and risk-mitigation), directors may also be liable if the greenwashing is discovered and causes the company serious reputational harm[63] – see the discussion in Section 1.6.3.4.

It is noteworthy that Australian Securities and Investments Commission ('ASIC'), the corporate watchdog in Australia, issued eight infringement notices for alleged greenwashing in 2022 and brought further enforcement action against a listed company in January 2023.[64]

Additional to ASIC, the Australian Prudential Regulation Authority identified interest in how entities are managing climate-related risk with a 2019 information paper focussed on climate change, and their Practice Guide 2021 incorporating climate

---

60   See *Gill v Ethicon Sarl (No 12)* [2023] FCA 902, [162].
61   The word 'greenwashing' combines the word 'green' (environmentally friendly) with 'whitewashing' ('to conceal or gloss over wrongdoing'): Katayun I Jaffari and Stephen A Pike (eds), *ESG in the Boardroom: A Guidebook for Directors* (American Bar Association, 2022) xxv. For some scholarly discourses on greenwashing see Riccardo Torelli, Federica Balluchi and Arianna Luzzini, 'Greenwashing and environmental communication: Effects of stakeholder's perceptions' (2020) 29(2) *Business Strategy and the Environment* 407; Sebastião Vieira de Freitas Netto et al, 'Concepts and forms of greenwashing: A systematic review' (2020) 32 *Environment Sciences Europe* 1; Lucia Gatti, Peter Seele and Lars Rademacher, 'Grey zone in – greenwash out. A review of greenwashing research and implications for the voluntary-mandatory transition of CSR' (2019) 4(1) *International Journal of Corporate Social Responsibility* 1; Christopher Marquis, Michael W Toffel and Yanhua Zhou 'Scrutiny, norms, and selective disclosure: A global study of greenwashing' (2016) 27(2) *Organization Science* 483; Magali A Delmas and Vanessa Cuerel Burbano, 'The drivers of greenwashing' (2011) 54(1) *California Management Review* 64; and William S Laufer, 'Social accountability and corporate greenwashing' (2003) 43(3) *Journal of Business Ethics* 253.
62   Noel Hutley SC and Sebastian Hartford Davis, 'Climate change and directors' duties' (Further Supplementary Memorandum of Opinion for the Centre for Policy Development, 23 April 2021) 3 <https://cpd.org.au/wp-content/uploads/2021/04/Further-Supplementary-Opinion-2021-3.pdf>.
63   Ibid 2, 3. See further ASIC, 'How to avoid greenwashing when offering or promoting sustainability-related products (Information Sheet No 271, June 2022) <https://asic.gov.au/regulatory-resources/financial-services/how-to-avoid-greenwashing-when-offering-or-promoting-sustainability-related-products/>.
64   ASIC, 'ASIC issues infringement notices to energy company for greenwashing' (Media Release, 5 January 2023) <https://asic.gov.au/about-asic/news-centre/find-a-media-release/2023-releases/23-001mr-asic-issues-infringement-notices-to-energy-company-for-greenwashing/>.

vulnerability assessments into stress-testing of the financial system. The Australian Accounting Standards Board ('AASB') and the Auditing and Assurance Standards Board ('AUASB') issued a joint bulletin on assessing climate-related risks in the context of financial statement materiality, highlighting that 'entities can no longer treat climate-related risks as merely a matter of corporate social responsibility and should consider them also in the context of their financial statements'.[65] They further suggested that climate change related assumptions have the potential to be a material accounting estimation variable, impacting on 'the useful lives of assets', 'fair valuation', impairments and provisions for bad and doubtful debts.[66] They also noted the impact in integrated reporting. More recently, the AASB and the AUASB published joint research identifying climate-related disclosures and associated assurance practices in ASX-listed entities, which identified that there was demand for ESG disclosure, but that most climate-related disclosure was outside of the financial statements and was therefore non-audited.[67] The Reserve Bank of Australia observed in its October 2019 Financial Stability Report that 'climate change is exposing financial institutions and the financial system more broadly to risks that will rise over time, if not addressed'.[68]

Similarly, ASIC has recently released an information sheet on greenwashing[69] in relation to financial products where the issuer incorporates sustainability-related considerations (such as ESG matters) into its investment strategies and decision-making.[70] ASIC defines greenwashing in relation to investments as 'the practice of misrepresenting the extent to which a financial product or investment strategy is environmentally friendly, sustainable or ethical'.[71] The *Corporations Act 2001* (Cth) and the *Australian Securities and Investments Commission Act 2001* (Cth) contain prohibitions against making statements or disseminating information which is false or misleading, and against engaging in dishonest, misleading or deceptive conduct in relation to a financial product or service. To avoid greenwashing, ASIC recommends considering whether the product is true to label (i.e. its labelled name reflects the reality of the product on offer), whether there is a use of vague terminology, whether the headline claims are potentially misleading, and a variety of questions in relation to metrics, targets, screening criteria and decision-making.[72]

---

65 AASB and AUASB, *Climate-related and Other Emerging Risks Disclosures: Assessing Financial Statement Materiality Using AASB/IASB Practice Statement 2* (April 2019) 3 <https://www.aasb.gov.au/admin/file/content102/c3/AASB_AUASBJointBulletin.pdf>.

66 Ibid 11.

67 Jean You and Roger Simnett, *Climate-related Disclosures and Assurance in the Annual Reports of ASX Listed Companies* (AASB and AAUASB, 2022) <https://aasb.gov.au/media/xu5leeby/aasb-auasb_rr_climaterelateddisclosures_12-22.pdf>.

68 Reserve Bank of Australia, *Financial Stability Review* (October 2019) <https://www.rba.gov.au/publications/fsr/2019/oct/>.

69 ASIC, 'How to avoid greenwashing when offering or promoting sustainability-related products' (Information Sheet No 271, June 2022) <https://asic.gov.au/regulatory-resources/financial-services/how-to-avoid-greenwashing-when-offering-or-promoting-sustainability-related-products/>.

70 The definition of 'sustainability-related product' is provided in a Note to the top of Information Sheet No 271: see ibid.

71 Ibid.

72 Ibid.

In the United States ('US'), Goldman Sachs Asset Management ('GSAM') agreed to pay the Securities and Exchange Commission ('SEC') a US\$4 million penalty for GSAM 'policies and procedures failures involving two mutual funds and one separately managed account strategy marketed as Environmental, Social, and Governance (ESG) investments'.[73] In the United Kingdom ('UK'), the Financial Conduct Authority ('FCA') is 'proposing a package of new measures including investment product sustainability labels and restrictions on how terms like "ESG", "green" or "sustainable" can be used'.[74]

The message is clear: as long as reporting on and disclosure of non-financial information is not mandatory, all stakeholders, including investors, need to be on the lookout for what images or figures are used to make corporations look as good as possible against the backdrop of a studio 'green screen' – caveat emptor (investor/stakeholder)! Based on, inter alia, the dangers of greenwashing, there has recently been calls for the entire ESG reporting approach to be revisited to ensure it has real impact. In this regard, a strong call for change was made by Henry Tricks in *The Economist* in 2022, proposing much 'tighter regulatory oversight of ESG'.[75]

3.5 The social licence[76] to operate

3.5.1 What is the 'social licence to operate'?

In Chapter 1 we dealt with some general developments in the area of corporate governance, including the meaning and definition of 'corporate governance'. It is clear that there has been a signal, not only in the US, but also in the UK and Australia, away from a purely shareholder-orientated model of corporate governance towards a more stakeholder or pluralistic orientation. That is the impression created when business and corporate perceptions are to be taken seriously. However, we concluded in that chapter that there is good authority that *legally* the Australian, UK and US corporate governance models are still based on the shareholder primacy model – albeit with scope to adopt an enlightened shareholder value approach.

It is beyond the scope of this book to discuss in detail the theoretical justifications for all corporate law and corporate governance models, such as the stakeholder (or pluralistic) theory, the fiction (or concession) theory, the realist (or natural entity) theory, the economic (or contractarian) theory, progressive (communitarian) perspectives and feminist perspectives, and aggregate theory.[77] It is, however, appropriate to say a few words about the social licence

---

73   US Securities and Exchange Commission, 'SEC charges Goldman Sachs Asset Management for failing to follow its policies and procedures involving ESG investments' (Press Release, 22 November 2022) <https://www.sec.gov/news/press-release/2022-209>.

74   FCA, 'FCA proposes new rules to tackle greenwashing' (Press Release, 25 October 2022); https://www.fca.org.uk/news/press-releases/fca-proposes-new-rules-tackle-greenwashing Public consultations closed on 25 January 2023. See FCA, *Sustainability Disclosure Requirements (SDR) and Investment Labels* (Consultation Paper, October 2022) <https://www.fca.org.uk/publication/consultation/cp22-20.pdf>.

75   Henry Tricks, 'In need of a clean-up' (Special Report (ESG Investing), *The Economist* (23 July 2022).

76   Note that the American spelling of the noun, 'licence', is 'license', explaining the different spelling in the titles of US articles and books.

77   For summaries of these models, see Jason Harris, *Company Law: Theories, Principles and Applications* (LexisNexis, 2nd ed, 2015) 16–33; Stephen Bottomley et at, *Contemporary Australian Corporate Law* (Cambridge University Press, 2nd ed, 2021) ch 2; and Michael J Phillips, 'Reappraising the real entity theory of the corporation' (1994) 21(4) *Florida State University Law Review* 1061, 1064–73.

to operate, an idea that has become trendy over recent years. It is related to the place and role of businesses and corporations in society and their impact on society. The social licence to operate is relevant not only for the purposes of directors' corporate social responsibilities (see Section 3.3)[78] and directors' legal duties,[79] but also for the purposes of corporations' responsibilities to stakeholders other than shareholders.

3.5.2 The meaning of 'the social licence to operate'[80]

Sally Wheeler relies on the definition of Gunningham, Kagan and Thornton,[81] who she describes as having done the most influential analysis of the social licence to operate theory.[82] They describe 'the social licence to operate' as:

> [The implied licence] which governs the extent to which a corporation is constrained to meet societal expectations and avoid activities that societies (or influential elements within it) deem unacceptable, whether or not those expectations are embodied in law ...[83] [T]he demands on and expectations for a business enterprise that emerge from neighbourhoods, environmental groups, community members and other elements of the surrounding civil society ...[84] The social license is based not on legal requirements but, rather, on the degree to which a corporation and its activities meet the expectations of local communities, the wider society, and various constituent groups.[85]

Other influential contemporary proponents of the idea of a social licence to operate include Thomas Donaldson and Thomas W Dunfee,[86] and Geert Demuijnck and Bjön Fasterling[87] (although they use slightly different terminology). Donaldson and Dunfee focus on the 'Ties that Bind in Business Ethics: Social Contracts and Why They Matter'.[88]

---

78 Sally Wheeler, 'Global production, CSR and human rights: The courts of public opinion and the social licence top operate' (2015) 19(6) *International Journal of Human Rights* 757, 765; Pamela Hanrahan, 'Corporate governance in these "exciting times"' (2017) 32(2) *Australian Journal of Corporate Law* 142, 144–50; Diana-Abasi Ibanga, 'Is there a social contract between the firm and community: Revisiting the philosophy of corporate social responsibility?' (2018) 7 *International Journal of Development and Sustainability* 355, 358–64.

79 Rosemary Teele Langford, 'Social licence to operate and director's duties: Is there a need for change?' (2019) 37(3) *Company and Securities Law Journal* 200.

80 Jean Jacques du Plessis would like to thank Ruby Morrissy and James Royce for the research they undertook for on 'Social Contract Theory and Its Application to Companies', a project funded by research funds provided by the Deakin Law School in 2021. Parts of this discussion were extracted from a summary provided by Morrissy and Royce.

81 Neil Gunningham, Robert A Kagan and Dorothy Thornton, 'Social license and environmental protection: Why businesses go beyond compliance' (2004) 29(2) *Law and Social Inquiry* 307.

82 Sally Wheeler, 'Global production, CSR and human rights' (2015) 19(6) *International Journal of Human Rights* 757, 765.

83 Gunningham, Kagan and Thornton, 'Social license and environmental protection' (2004) 29(2) *Law and Social Inquiry* 307, 307 (Abstract).

84 Ibid 308.

85 Ibid 313.

86 Thomas Donaldson and Thomas W Dunfee, 'Ties that bind in business ethics' (2002) 26(9) *Journal of Banking and Finance* 1853.

87 Geert Demuijnck and Bjön Fasterling, 'The social license to operate' (2016) *Journal of Business Ethics* 675.

88 For a summary of Donalsson and Dunfee's work, see Geert Demuijnck and Bjön Fasterling, 'The social license to operate' (2016) 136(4) *Journal of Business Ethics* 675, 677–8.

They developed the integrative social contract theory ('ISCT'). At the basis of this theory is the concept of 'trust'[89] and this derives from the fact that over time it became clear to 'all' that 'capital markets either become distorted or fail altogether owing to a fundamental lack of trust'.[90] Distortions or failures will occur if, for instance, promises are not kept; prosperity of societies in which business operates is not respected; violence and coercion are used to obtain economic advantages.[91]

Demuijnck and Fasterling focus specifically on the social licence to operate. The Abstract and Introduction of Demuijnck and Fasterling's article provides an overview of the fundamentals of the social licence to operate:

> An SLO ['social licence to operate') can be defined as a contractarian basis for the legitimacy of a company's specific activity or project. 'SLO', as a fashionable expression, has its origins in business practice. From a normative viewpoint, the concept is closely related to social contract theory, and, as such, it has a political dimension.[92]

3.5.3 Scant attention to the concept from the ASX Corporate Governance Council

The idea of a social licence to operate received some consideration during the drafting and consultation undertaken in the preparation of the fourth edition of what can be called the Australian corporate governance code (the ASX *Corporate Governance Principles and Recommendations*).[93] In the Review of the ASX Corporate Governance Council's Principles and Recommendations[94] the Corporate Governance Council identified the concept of 'social licence to operate' as something to be addressed but ultimately nothing come of this reference.[95] In the published fourth edition of the ASX *Corporate Governance Principles and Recommendations*, there is not a single mention of the 'social licence to operate'. This change of approach by the ASX Corporate Governance Council was seemingly in response to concerns by business that the term was vague and could lead to uncertainty, with threats that the ASX Guidelines would not be followed if the social licence to operate was included in the final fourth edition of the *Corporate Governance Principles and Recommendations*.[96]

---

89   Morrison, *The Social License* (2014) 33, 76 *et seq*; Sale, 'The corporate purpose of social license' (2021) 94(4) *Southern California Law Review* 785, 827–30.

90   Donaldson and Dunfee, 'Ties that bind in business ethics' (2002) 26(9) *Journal of Banking and Finance* 1853, 1857.

91   Ibid 1854–7. See also Thomas W Dunfee, 'Business ethics and extant social contracts' (1991) 1(1) *Business Ethics Quarterly* 24, 39–40.

92   Demuijnck and Fasterling, 'The social license to operate' (2016) 136(4) *Journal of Business Ethics* 675 (Abstract).

93   ASX, *Corporate Governance Principles and Recommendations* (ASX Corporate Governance Council, 4th ed, 2019) <https://www.asx.com.au/documents/asx-compliance/cgc-principles-and-recommendations-fourth-edn.pdf>. For a general discussion, see Dreosti, de Silva and Walsh, 'A civil law solution to social licence to operate and directors' duties conundrum in Australia' (2021) 38(6) *Company and Securities Law Journal* 404, 427–31.

94   ASX, *Review of the ASX Corporate Governance Council's Principles and Recommendations* (2 May 2018).

95   Ibid 4.

96   See, eg, Tony Boyd, 'David Murray's defiant plan for AMP', *Financial Review* (1 August 2018); Patrick Durkin, 'Board outrage over push to have a social licence', *Financial Review* (1 August 2018).

3.6 CSR and directors' duties

In Chapter 1 we discussed directors' duties generally, but it is worth summarising how these duties affect how directors exercise their powers and fulfil their duties as far as corporations' CSR is concerned.[97] We pointed out (see Sections 1.6.1 and 1.6.2.2–1.6.2.4) that in the UK, s 172 of the *Companies Act 2006* (UK) stipulates that directors, in fulfilling their duty to promote the success of the company, *must* ultimately do so 'for the benefit of its members as a whole'.[98] In fulfilling this duty, directors *may* consider the consequences of their decisions in the context of the long-term interests of the corporation.[99] In addition, they *may* have regard to other non-shareholder interests. The interests mentioned specifically are employees, suppliers, the community and the environment.[100] Directors may also consider the company's interest in its reputation, in particular the 'desirability of the company maintaining a reputation for high standards of business conduct'.[101] All of these are entrenched statutorily, but legally it is only the core duty to act 'for the benefit of its members as a whole' that is significant. All the other interests mentioned can collectively be described as directors' 'social' responsibility. CSR thus forms part of the adopted 'enlightened shareholder value' approach underpinning the UK corporate law model, although getting it embedded more sharply in the UK will be complex and a long drawn-out process.[102]

It was pointed out in Chapter 1 (see Sections 1.5.2.2, 1.6.2.3 and 1.6.3.8) that in Australia, the shareholder primacy model forms the basis of Australian corporate law on the common law interpretation of 'company' as meaning the 'shareholders as a whole'. However, there has been increasing recognition in recent times in Australia that directors owe their duty towards *the corporation*. As stated in Chapter 1, Australian courts have confirmed that it is illogical, and probably legally incorrect, to consider the interests of shareholders to be primary under all circumstances, irrespective of the factual context in which directors need to exercise their powers and fulfil their duties. The special circumstances associated with insolvency, and how creditors' interests then 'intrude' to become part of the corporation's interests and directors' duties,[103] has been accepted in Australia for at least the last 30 years.[104] In more recent times Australian courts have gradually started to judicially recognise non-shareholder interests as part of the interests of the corporation. In addition, a corporation's reputational

---

97 This aspect received quite extensive attention in 2006 in Corporations and Markets Advisory Committee, *The Social Responsibility of Corporations Report* (2006) 81–110.

98 *Companies Act 2006* (UK) s 172(1).

99 Ibid s 172(1)(a).

100 Ibid s 172(1)(b)–(d).

101 Ibid s 172(1)(e).

102 British Academy, *Policy and Practice for Purposeful Business: The Final Report of the Future of the Corporation Programme* (2021) 22 <https://www.thebritishacademy.ac.uk/publications/policy-and-practice-for-purposeful-business/>.

103 See *Bell Group Ltd (in liq) v Westpac Banking Corporation (No 9)* (2008) 39 WAR 1, [4439], [4440].

104 *Walker v Wimborne* (1976) 137 CLR 1; *Kinsela v Russell Kinsela Pty Ltd (in liq)* (1986) 4 NSWLR 722; Senate Standing Committee on Legal and Constitutional Affairs, *Company Directors' Duties: Report on the Social and Fiduciary Duties and Obligations of Company Directors* (Parliament of Australia, 1989) ch 5.

interests – that is, how it is perceived by the society, employees, creditors and stake-holders – have also been recognised judicially, most recently in the case of *Australian Securities and Investments Commission v Cassimatis* (court a quo as well as the Court of Appeal – see discussion in Section 1.6.3.3). Although there is not yet any case where the courts have recognised a CSR duty for directors based on community expecta-tions,[105] developments in Australia make CSR a relevant issue for directors, and prob-ably inevitable for them to take it seriously. If they do not, this is at their own peril, especially if ignoring their social responsibilities causes the corporation to suffer seri-ous reputational harm (as explained in Section 1.6.3.4). A Canadian court was willing, 50 years ago, to highlight that if a director were to 'observe decent respect for other interests lying beyond those of the company's shareholders in the strict sense'[106] – in particular, for example, the interests of the employees, but perhaps extending on an individual basis to wider stakeholders – it could be considered to be acting in good faith in the interests of the company.[107]

In the US, there is no general legal duty imposed on directors to take into con-sideration non-shareholder interests, or for directors to be brought to task legally for neglecting a corporations' social responsibilities. However, as was suggested in Sections 1.5.2, 1.6.3.5 and 2.2, non-shareholder interests can no longer be safely ignored by directors of American companies. Due to the expectations of powerful and influential business groups like the US Business Roundtable and major investors such as BlackRock, social considerations can potentially become more important for American corporations. Ignoring non-shareholder interests or not fulfilling their responsibilities to society can have a devastating impact on the potential to attract investment from investors who have a very strong focus on responsible investments. Thus, in the American context there is potential for CSR to be linked with directors' legal duties.

In the remaining sections of this chapter we will focus on what a 'stakeholder' is, even though we acknowledge that there is no fixed definition of the term. We then provide a discussion of some of the stakeholders that are generally recognised in corporate law and the corporate governance literature. As well as showing how stakeholders, other than shareholders, can impact corporate behaviour and corpo-rate conduct, we discuss how the James Hardie case illustrates the devastating conse-quences that can occur if a company ignores its responsibilities towards stakeholders such as employees.[108]

---

105 Jean J du Plessis 'Corporate social responsibility and "contemporary community expectations'''
 (2017) 35(1) *Company and Securities Law Journal* 30.
106 *Teck Corporation Ltd v Millar* (1972) 33 DLR (3d) 288, 314.
107 Bottomley et al, *Contemporary Australian Corporate Law* (2021) 337.
108 A case study on James Hardie's handling of its employees' asbestosis claims is available at <www
 .cambridge.org/highereducation/isbn/9781009287388/resources>. For an additional analysis of the
 James Hardie case in the context of the social licence to operate, see Lin Tozer and Fin Hamilton,
 '"Aethical" corporations: Is there a case to answer under a "social contract"', 9–18 <https://www
 .wgtn.ac.nz/sacl/about/events/past-events-temporary/past-conferences/csear2006/documents/
 tozer-hamilton.pdf>.

3.7 Stakeholders in the corporation[109]

3.7.1 What is a stakeholder?

The definition of 'stakeholder'[110] is not set in stone.[111] We intentionally made our own definition of stakeholder particularly wide. It includes examples of stakeholders that are discussed in this book as follows

> [A]ll internal parties (for example, shareholders and employees) and other parties (external stakeholders, governments and local communities) who can be affected by the corporation's conduct ...

However, it is useful to also be aware of other definitions or descriptions of the word 'stakeholder'. Indeed, there are almost as many definitions of what a 'stakeholder' is, and who can be characterised as a stakeholder, as there are individuals who have written about stakeholders in corporate governance.[112]

Christine Mallin provides the following definition of 'stakeholder', which informed our own definition:

> The term 'stakeholder' can encompass a wide range of interests: it refers to any individual or group on which the activities of the company have an impact.[113]

According to Mallin, apart from shareholders, corporate stakeholders include employees, suppliers, customers, government, providers of credit, interest groups and local communities.[114]

A definition of 'stakeholder' that recognises a mutual relationship between stakeholders and the corporation is provided by James E Post and colleagues in *Redefining the Corporation: Stakeholder Management and Organizational Wealth*:[115]

> The stakeholders in a corporation are the individuals and constituencies that contribute, either voluntarily or involuntarily, to its wealth-creating capacity and activities, and that are therefore its potential beneficiaries and/or risk bearers.[116]

109 For empirical evidence on the way in which Australian directors perceive their obligations to various stakeholders, see Shelley Marshall and Ian Ramsay, 'Stakeholders and directors' duties: Law, theory and evidence' (2012) 35(1) *University of New South Wales Law Journal* 291.

110 For a review of the history and nature of the stakeholder theory, see Emerson Wagner Mainardes, Helena Alves and Mario Raposo, 'Stakeholder theory: Issues to resolve' (2011) 49(2) *Management Decision* 226, 229 and Corina Gavrea and Roxana Stegerean, 'Comparative study on corporate governance' (2011) 20(2) *Annals of the University of Oradea, Economic Science Series* 674.

111 CAMAC, *The Social Responsibility of Corporations Report* (December 2006) [2.4] notes that the notion of 'stakeholders' has no precise or commonly agreed meaning. See further Bryan Horrigan, 'Fault lines in the intersection between corporate governance and social responsibility' (2002) 25(2) *University of New South Wales Law Journal* 515.

112 See generally Redmond, 'Directors' duties and corporate social responsiveness' (2012) 35(1) *University of New South Wales Law Journal* 317, 320.

113 Mallin, *Corporate Governance* (2019) 79.

114 Ibid 80.

115 James E Post, Lee E Preston and Sybille Sachs, *Redefining the Corporation: Stakeholder Management and Organizational Wealth* (Stanford Business Books, 2002).

116 Ibid 19. See also PM Vasudev, 'Corporate stakeholders in New Zealand – the present, and possibilities for the future' in PM Vasudev and Susan Watson (eds), *Corporate Governance after the Financial Crisis* (Edward Elgar, 2012) 120.

In 1990, Freeman and Evan, relying on the work done by Oliver Williamson in the 1970s and 1980s,[117] referred to the corporation as consisting of 'multiple bilateral contracts' between the enterprise and various stakeholders. A broad distinction could be made between 'internal' and 'external' stakeholders.[118] 'Internal' stakeholders typically include employees, managers and shareholders. 'External' stakeholders typically include customers, suppliers, competitors and special interest groups. Finally, governments and local communities set the legal and formal rules within which businesses must operate.[119]

Over time the identification of what the stakeholder *interests* are, particularly those that directors need to take into consideration when fulfilling their duty to act in the best interests of the corporation (see the discussion in Sections 1.6.3.3–1.6.3.4), became increasingly more important. In addition, as more pressure was put on corporations to report on non-financial issues (see the discussion in Section 3.4 above), the definition of 'stakeholder' became more influential as corporations need to ensure their reports reflect true stakeholder engagement. Mainly for these two reasons, the all-inclusive stakeholder approach became prominent in corporate governance codes, and 'stakeholders' were also defined more specifically for the purposes of reporting on non-financial issue and matters.

As far as corporate governance codes are concerned, it is useful to focus on the South African experience, as the all-inclusive stakeholder approach was already adopted in 1994 (King I) and refined in two further versions of the King Reports (King II and King III). The following description of 'stakeholders' was ultimately adopted in the 2016 (King IV) South African corporate governance code:[120]

> **Stakeholders:** Those groups or individuals that can reasonably be expected to be significantly affected by an organisation's business activities, outputs or outcomes, or whose actions can reasonably be expected to significantly affect the ability of the organization to create value over time.
>
> 'Internal stakeholders' are directly affiliated with the organization and include its governing body, management, employees and shareholders.
>
> 'External stakeholders' could include trade unions, civil society organizations, government, customers and consumers.
>
> Internal stakeholders are always material stakeholders, but external stakeholders may or may not be material.

As far as reporting is concerned, international reporting standards, frameworks and initiatives started to provide definitions of 'stakeholders'. The ISO Standards, which have been considered to be top-notch international standards since their introduction in 1946,[121]

---

117 R Edward Freeman and William M Evan, 'Corporate governance: A stakeholder interpretation' (1990) 19 *Journal of Behavioural Economics* 337.
118 Ibid 337, fn 1 (appearing as an endnote on 354).
119 Ibid 343, 347–9.
120 *Report on Corporate Governance for South Africa 2016* ('King IV Report') (Institute of Directors in Southern Africa, 2016) 17 ('Glossary of Terms').
121 The origin of the word 'ISO' is explained on the website of the International Organization for Standardization: 'Because 'International Organization for Standardization' would have different acronyms in different languages (IOS in English, OIN in French for Organisation internationale de

currently define 'stakeholder' in ISO 26000 in the widest possible terms, namely any 'individual or group that has an interest in any decision or activity of an organization'.[122] The Global Reporting Initiative ('GRI') is an 'independent, international organization that helps businesses and other organizations take responsibility for their impacts, by providing them with the global common language to communicate those impacts' through its GRI Standards.[123] 'The GRI Guidelines and ISO 26000 both aim at improving organizations' social responsibility and sustainability performance.'[124] The GRI sets reporting standards and provides a framework for multistakeholder reporting in the context of sustainable reporting, and defines 'stakeholders' as follows:[125]

> [E]ntities or individuals that can reasonably be expected to be significantly affected by the organization's activities, products, and services; and whose actions can reasonably be expected to affect the ability of the organization to successfully implement its strategies and achieve its objectives.

It was a former version of this wide GRI definition of 'stakeholders' that was quoted with approval in 2006 by the Corporations and Markets Advisory Committee's ('CAMAC')[126] report entitled *The Social Responsibility of Corporations*.[127] A useful summary of a definition of 'stakeholders' was provided in this report, pointing out that the term can include:

- shareholders, who, unlike other stakeholders have a direct equity interest in the corporation
- other persons with a financial interest in the company (financiers, suppliers and other creditors), or those in some other commercial legal relationship with the company (for instance business partners)
- persons who are involved in some manner in the company's wealth creation (employees and consumers)
- anyone otherwise directly affected by a company's conduct (for example, communities adjacent to a company's operation)
- pressure groups or non-government organisations ('NGOs'), usually characterised as public interests bodies that espouse social goals relevant to the activities of companies.

---

normalisation), our founders decided to give it the short form ISO. ISO is derived from the Greek 'isos', meaning equal. Whatever the country, whatever the language, we are always ISO': <https://www.iso.org/about-us.html>.

122 ISO 26000, cl 2.

123 GRI <https://www.globalreporting.org/about-gri/>.

124 GRI and ISO, *GRI G4 Guidelines and ISO 26000:2010: How to Use the GRI G4 Guidelines and ISO 26000 in Conjunction* (January 2014) 6.

125 Ibid 9.

126 CAMAC was established in 1989, but abolished as part of the 2014–15 Australian Budget under a government restructuring initiative: see Australian Government, Treasury, 'Corporations and Markets Advisory Committee (CAMAC)' <https://treasury.gov.au/policy-topics/business-and-industry/CAMAC>. It brought out some significant reports during its existence: see Australian Government, Treasury, 'Corporations and Markets Advisory Committee (CAMAC) – Publications' <https://treasury.gov.au/policy-topics/business-and-industry/CAMAC/publications>.

127 CAMAC, *The Social Responsibility of Corporations* (December 2006) 55–6.

It is important to note that different attitudes towards the place of stakeholders in corporate governance are evident in different jurisdictions, and that these are influenced by differences in tradition and culture. This will be demonstrated in Chapters 11 and 12. In Chapter 11 the focus is on corporate law models where a unitary or one-tier board system is the norm. In Chapter 12 some jurisdictions with the two-tier board structure as the default board structure are discussed. It will be seen that in the two-tier board structure in particular, employee interests are taken into account, with a specified number of supervisory boards seats filled by board members elected directly by employees, with no involvement of shareholders.

3.7.2 Discussion of stakeholders

This section provides a basic account of the role of some of the key stakeholders in the governance of a company. It should be kept in mind that discrete areas of legal regulation operating independently of company law and corporate governance principles also have a direct and significant impact on the relationship between particular stakeholders and the company. Due to space limitations these aspects are not discussed in this book.

3.7.2.1 Shareholders

As the stakeholder approach is often discussed as an alternative to the traditional shareholder-oriented approach to corporate governance (emphasising wealth maximisation), shareholders are regularly excluded from the definition of 'stakeholder'.

Mallin includes shareholders as part of her concept of 'stakeholder', but deals with shareholders separately from all the other constituents that are also stakeholders. She defines 'shareholder' as 'an individual, institution, firm, or other entity that owns shares in a company'.[128] As Mallin appreciates, however, the reality of shareholding is more complex than this definition suggests, once beneficial ownership and cross-holdings are considered.

Mallin treats shareholders differently from other stakeholders for two reasons: '[F]irst, shareholders invest their money to provide risk capital for the company and, secondly, in many legal jurisdictions, shareholders' rights are enshrined in law whereas those of the wider group of stakeholders are not.'[129]

3.7.2.2 Employees

It is remarkable that probably the most praised father of a free economic system, Adam Smith, not only made the idea of an 'invisible hand' prominent, but also identified the three factors of production, namely labour, capital, and land, expressed in the formula $(Y=K, L, N)$.[130] Smith opened his *An Inquiry into the Nature and Causes of the Wealth of Nations* with the following words:[131]

---

128 Mallin, *Corporate Governance* (2019) 79.
129 Ibid.
130 'Adam Smith theory of development in economics (main features)', *Economics Discussion* <https://www.economicsdiscussion.net/economics-2/adam-smith-theory-of-development-in-economics-main-features/4514>.
131 Adam Smith, *An Inquiry into the Nature and Causes of the Wealth of Nations, published in The World's Classics: Volume LIV* (Grant Richards, 1904) 1.

The annual labour of every nation is the fund which originally supplies it with all the necessaries and conveniences of life which it annually consumes, and which consist always either in the immediate produce of that labour, or in what is purchased with that produce from other nations.

According, therefore, as this produce, or what is produced with it, bares a greater or smaller proportion to the number of those who are to consume it, the nation will be better or worse supplied with all the necessaries and conveniences for which it has occasion.

But this proportion must in every nation be regulated by two different circumstances: first, by the skill, dexterity, and judgment with which its labour is generally applied; and, secondly, by the proportion between the number of those who are employed in useful labour, and that of those who are not so employed. Whatever be the soil, climate, or extent of territory of any particular nation, the abundance or scantiness of its annual supply must, in that particular situation, depend on those two circumstances.

Smith's *first book* dealt with these aspects, but it is also good to be reminded that Smith was very much aware of the interaction between labour and capital, thus dedicating his *second book* to 'the nature of capital stock, of the manner in which it is gradually accumulated, and of the different quantities of labour which it puts into motion, according to the different ways in which it is employed'.[132] He observed, with foresight in 1776, that '[n]ations tolerably well advanced as to skill, dexterity, and judgement, in the application of labour, have followed very different plans in the general conduct or direction (of labour)' and that 'those plans have not all been equally favourably to the greatness of its produce'.[133] This was the focus of his *third book*.

In his *fourth book* Smith focused on how labour and capital interacted, especially because of plans, 'introduced by the private interests and prejudices of particular orders of men, without any regard to or foresight of, their consequences upon the general welfare of society'.[134] Thus, in 1776, Smith had a clear concern about societal interests and how they could be impacted by the self-serving personal interests of the providers of capital.

His *fifth and last book* dealt with 'the revenue of the sovereign, or commonwealth', but again with a very specific focus on what parts of government expenses should be covered ('defrayed') by 'the general contribution of the whole society' and what parts should be covered by the private sector or, as he put it, which government expenses should come from 'some particular part only, or of some particular members (of society only)'.[135]

Smith's observations are remarkably prescient as it seems that gradually the significance of labour as a production factor became subordinated to that of capital as a production factor, and only because certain ideas grabbed the imagination of many. These include perceptions and principles like 'shareholders as owners of the corporation'; 'a business corporation is organized and carried on primarily for the profit

132 Ibid 2–3.
133 Ibid 3.
134 Ibid.
135 Ibid 4.

of the stockholders'; 'the social responsibility of business is to increase its profits'; 'directors, executives and managers are the agents of the shareholder'; and 'one can only serve one master [the shareholders]'. In modern lingua we would refer to 'human capital', and over time 'the evidence has become overwhelming that significant invest-ments in human capital are essential for economic growth'.[136] Bob Tricker, in 2023, had no hesitation in stating that '[e]mployees are the most significant resource in any corporate entity' and that 'all boards have a vital responsibility to the employ-ees in their organisation, whatever the form of that corporate body'.[137] It is, there-fore, not surprising that nowadays, for the purposes of disclosure of and reporting on non-financial matters (see Section 3.4), 'human capital' forms a key pillar of all the other forms of capitals upon which corporations rely to be financially successful and which they will apply to ensure the long-term and sustainable success of their corpo-rations (see again our definition of 'corporate governance' in Section 1.2).

It has required many years of laborious, painful and costly efforts to open the eyes of corporations to their social responsibilities and the merits of an all-inclusive stakeholder approach (as discussed in Sections 1.2.2 and 2.2) and for employees to really be seen as an indispensable and core production factor and as core stakeholders, at least on par with shareholders.

The place of employees *as stakeholders* is explained by Mallin as follows:[138]

> The employees of a company have an interest in the company as it provides their livelihood in the present day and at some future point, employees would often also be in receipt of a pension provided by the company's pension scheme. In terms of present-day employment, employees will be concerned with their pay and working conditions, and how the company's strategy will impact on these. Of course, the long-term growth and prosperity of the company is important for the longer term view of the employees, particularly as concerns pension benefits in the future ...

There are several rationales for promoting employee share ownership,[139] but the primary aim is to provide employees with another way of having 'an interest' in the corporation. The idea is that ongoing shareholder interests can lead to greater employee engagement and improved business outcomes. Stripped to its basics, the rationale behind employee share option plans ('ESOPs') and employee stock purchase plans ('ESPPs') is that if employees hold such an interest, they would work towards the goal of keeping share value as high as possible, as it will be in their best interests as holders of shares in their own company to do so.

---

136 Gary S Becker, 'The Adam Smith Address: Education, labor force quality, and economy' (1992) 27(1) *Business Economics* 7, 8. Investing in human capital is nowadays even more important than in the past, with education needed especially to cope with a diminishing role for low-cost, unskilled labour and for a demand for technologically skilled labour: see Klaus Schwab, *Shaping the Future of the Fourth Industrial Revolution: A Guide for Building a Better World* (World Economic Forum, 2018) 54.
137 Bob Tricker, *Corporate Governance in Practice* (CRC Press, 2023) 53.
138 Mallin, *Corporate Governance* (2019) 81.
139 Ingrid Landau, Ann O'Connell and Ian Ramsay, *Incentivising Employees* (Melbourne University Press, 2013) 11–13.

At first glance this seems a genuine and logical way for employees to strengthen their interests in the corporation, but a deeper analysis quickly reveals that it is no more than another way of entrenching a shareholder primacy model and justifying not recognising employees as significant stakeholders – unless they also own shares. For instance, shares owned by employees are held in trust, without any possibility of individual employee shareholders selling their shares on the open market at will. In addition, there is no employee shareholder scheme anywhere in the world, except for companies which are formed by employees and have shares issued to employees, where the employees can exercise any influence over company decisions through their voting rights as sharehold-ers.[140] The percentage of shares held by employees is normally so miniscule that it is not even worth mentioning voting rights attached to shares as an advantage for employee shareholders. In 2013 only about five per cent of employees in the US took part in ESOPs and only about 15 per cent in ESSPs. However, it should be mentioned that the participa-tion rate in ESOPs and ESSPs was primary for managers and salespeople[141] highly inter-ested in short-term gains and in 'grab and run' techniques. Examples like Avis, where the employees held the majority shares before 1994, and United Airlines, where employees agreed to an ESOP, acquiring 55 per cent of company stock in exchange for salary conces-sions, making it the largest 'employee-owned corporation in the word', ceased appearing after 2000.[142]

A far more long-lasting and meaningful way of recognising the employees as core stakeholders is to work towards a shared purpose between senior management and employees. Rebecca Henderson uses the CEO of Aetna as a case study in Chapter 4 of her book and points out the many advantages of keeping employees engaged and 'on board' as far the corporation's purpose and goals are concerned.[143] Henderson is, how-ever, realistic that a universal change to adopt such an approach is unlikely because of path dependency, or, as she puts it, influenced by worldviews that are 'over a hundred years old'.[144] The recent Qantas saga, where Qantas neglected the interests of employees and used outsourcing in an illegal way to save costs (around $100 million) by sacking employees, resulted in considerable reputational damage to Qantas. In *Qantas Airways Ltd v Transport Workers Union of Australia*[145] the Court ordered Qantas to pay millions of dollars of damage because of the illegal way that Qantas used outsourcing. It should be noted that the High Court did not hold that outsourcing as such is illegal, just the way it was used by Qantas during the COVID-19 pandemic.

Another emerging area of discourse that emphasises the importance of employee involvement in the overall governance framework of the corporation is the 'participatory management' philosophy. Commentators have referred to participatory management as the most important industrial relations phenomenon of the past three decades.[146]

---

140 Henry Hansmann, *The Ownership of Enterprises* (Belknap Press, 1996) 106–8.
141 Rebecca Henderson, *Reimagining Capitalism in a World on Fire* (PublicAffairs, 2020) 149.
142 Ibid.
143 Ibid 92–5.
144 Ibid 105–8.
145 (2023) 412 ALR 134.
146 Stephen M Bainbridge, 'Corporate decision-making and the moral rights of employees: Participatory management and natural law' (1998) 43(4) *Villanova Law Review* 741.

According to Stephen Bainbridge, there are two basic forms of participatory management: operational participation and strategic participation.[147]

3.7.2.3 Creditors

Creditors always rate a mention as one group of key stakeholders in the corporation. Apart from the rapidly increasing literature on corporate governance, over the years there has been extensive commentary on whether company directors can[148] and should owe a duty to act in the best interests of creditors while serving the company.[149]

In Australia, the majority judgment in the Appeal Court of the Supreme Court of Western Australia decision in *Westpac Banking Corporation v Bell Group Ltd (in liq) (No 3)*[150] reaffirms that the precise nature and scope of directors' duties to creditors upon corporate insolvency remains an unresolved judicial issue. In particular, following the majority judgment in this case, it is now unclear whether directors must go beyond consideration of creditors' interests and ensure that creditors are protected in conformity with the pari passu principle.[151] However, the seminal decision by the UK Supreme Court in *BTI 2014 LLC v Sequana SA*[152] has unanimously affirmed that the creditor duty is not a free-standing duty.

3.7.2.4 Customers

Mallin provides the following brief explanation of how a company's customers also fit the description of 'stakeholder' from a corporate governance perspective:

> Increasingly customers are also more aware of social, environmental, and ethical aspects of corporate behaviour and will try to ensure that the company supplying them is acting in a corporately socially responsible manner.[153]

---

147 Ibid 742.
148 Directors have no direct fiduciary duties to creditors: *Spies v The Queen* (2000) 201 CLR 603.
149 For a discussion of the vexed issue of directors' fiduciary duties to creditors following the High Court decision in *Spies*, see the scholarly debate, starting with James McConvill, 'Directors' duties towards creditors in Australia after *Spies v The Queen*' (2002) 20(1) *Company and Securities Law Journal* 4; in reply Anil Hargovan, 'Directors' duties to creditors in Australia after *Spies v The Queen* – is the development of an independent fiduciary duty dead or alive?' (2003) 21(6) *Company and Securities Law Journal* 390; James McConvill, 'Geneva finance and the "duty" of directors to creditors: Imperfect obligation and other imperfections' (2003) 11(1) *Insolvency Law Journal* 7; in reply Anil Hargovan, 'Geneva finance and the "duty" of directors to creditors: Imperfect obligation and critique' (2004) 12(3) *Insolvency Law Journal* 134. The debate appears to be resolved: Justice Owen in *Bell Group Ltd (in liq) v Westpac Banking Corporation (No 9)* (2008) 39 WAR 1, [4398] held that the question was 'determined authoritatively' by the High Court in *Spies*. For a comprehensive examination of this topic, see Andrew Keay, *Company Directors' Responsibilities to Creditors* (Routledge-Cavendish, 2006).
150 (2012) 44 WAR 1.
151 For exploration of this issue and the extent to which the judiciary can intervene to adjudicate directors' beliefs and business judgments in an insolvency context, see Anil Hargovan and Jason Harris, 'For whom the bell tolls: Directors' duties to creditors after *Bell*' (2013) 35(2) *Sydney Law Review* 433. The *Bell* case was settled by the parties on the eve of the High Court appeal hearings. For a comparative perspective with the law in the US, see Anil Hargovan and Tim Todd, 'Financial twilight re-appraisal: Ending the judicially created quagmire of fiduciary duties to creditors' (2016) 78(2) *University of Pittsburg Law Review* 135.
152 [2022] UKSC 25.
153 Mallin, *Corporate Governance* (2019) 82. See also Tricker, *Corporate Governance in Practice* (2023) 55.

The Australian Consumer Law ('ACL'), as set out in sch 2 of the *Competition and Consumer Act 2010* (Cth), confirms the importance of ensuring that the interests of customers are a central consideration of the corporation in its day-to-day activities. There is an extensive number of rules under in Chapter 2 of the ACL, 'Consumer Protection', including the general prohibition on misleading and deceptive conduct and unconscionable conduct, and further measures to protect and uphold the interests of consumers through rules on product recalls, defective goods and anti-competitive conduct.

These requirements (as well as a number of others) work together so that, in Australia, the role of customers in corporate governance is neatly aligned with Mallin's description above.

3.7.2.5 The community

A great deal has been written about whether society as a whole is also a specific stakeholder of the modern corporation, and the implications for directors' duties and corporate regulation more generally if society is, indeed, a stakeholder. Referring to 'society' as a whole as being a stakeholder presents some difficulties, as it makes it difficult to provide any meaningful conception of what obligation this imposes on the corporation. Mallin's approach of examining society at the micro-level of the 'local community' seems useful and workable.[154]

3.7.2.6 The environment

In the first edition of this book, it was noted that:

> just as contentious as the question of whether 'society' is a stakeholder of the corporation is whether 'the environment' can be considered to be a stakeholder. Perhaps this is because the implications of both, in terms of how a company must structure its affairs and do business, are enormous.

The call for environmental change has progressed rapidly since then, with a growing sense of urgency[155] that negates the need for the 'contentious' claim made earlier.[156] Following the launch of the *Kyoto Protocol* in 2005,[157] managing greenhouse gas emissions has become a routine part of doing business in key global trading markets, and shareholders and financial analysts increasingly assign value to companies that prepare for and capitalise upon business opportunities posed by climate change – whether from greenhouse gas regulations, direct physical impacts or changes in corporate reputation.[158]

---

154 Mallin, *Corporate Governance* (2019) 82.
155 See, eg, Intergovernmental Panel on Climate Change, *Climate Change 2007: The Physical Science Basis – Contribution of Working Group 1 to the Fourth Assessment Report of the Intergovernmental Panel on Climate Change* (Cambridge University Press, 2007).
156 See generally Janet Dine and Marios Koutsias, *The Nature of Corporate Governance: The Significance of National Cultural Identity* (Edward Elgar, 2013) 56–62.
157 The *Kyoto Protocol* was adopted at the Third Session of the Conference of the Parties to the UN *Framework Convention on Climate Change* in 1997 in Japan. Countries signatory to the Protocol undertook legally binding commitments to reduce greenhouse gas emissions in the commitment period 2008–12.
158 This account is drawn from Douglas Cogan, *Corporate Governance and Climate Change: Making the Connection* (March 2006) 1 – this report was commissioned from the Investor Responsibility Center.

In a report on climate change and corporate governance, the following observations were made:[159]

> For corporations, climate change is a financial problem that presents significant economic and competitive risks and opportunities. Corporate boards, executives and shareholders simply cannot afford to ignore it[160] ... Given the sweeping global nature of climate change, climate risk has become embedded, to a greater or lesser extent, in every business and investment portfolio.[161]

Mallin speaks not just of the 'environment' as being a stakeholder, but also of the various environmental lobby groups, both on the domestic and international level, that operate to ensure that companies meet environmental standards.[162] These standards can be either self-imposed or derived from obligations under environment protection and other legislation. Legislation on environmental protection has increased worldwide exponentially. There is no reason to believe that this will not continue for the foreseeable future. Climate change is driving the agenda. Governments and regulators cannot be passive in this space. In addition, climate change puts a lot of air under the wings of companies to show that they strive for long-term sustainability and being environmentally friendly. As discussed, this is done to attract investments. Disclosure of and reporting on non-financial matters is currently undertaken on a voluntary basis, but it will probably become mandatory in many countries in the near future.

There has been a growing trend in Australia whereby shareholder and superannuation fund members use judicial proceedings to seek more detailed information on investments made, on their behalf, by banks and superannuation funds where these may be affected by climate change. Beth Nosworthy outlines a series of cases in the 2010s against the Commonwealth Bank of Australia,[163] and against the Retail Employees

---

159 Ibid 11. The report is the first comprehensive examination of how 100 of the world's largest corporations are positioning themselves to compete in a carbon-constrained world. For an update on the main trends, issues and implications of climate change for corporate governance see OECD, *Climate Change and Corporate Governance* (2022) <https://doi.org/10.1787/272d85c3-en> ('OECD 2022 Report').

160 The OECD 2022 Report notes: 'Corporations [were] defendants in at least 18 climate-related court cases filed globally between May 2020 and May 2021.' See OECD, *Climate Change and Corporate Governance* (2022) <https://doi.org/10.1787/272d85c3-en>. For an interesting discourse on the corporate and securities law obligations on US companies in the context of climate change, see Perry Wallace, 'Climate change, fiduciary duty, and corporate disclosure: Are things heating up in the boardroom?' (2008) 26(1) *Virginia Environmental Law Journal* 293; Roshaan Wasim, 'Corporate (non) disclosure of climate change information' (2019) 119(5) *Columbia Law Review* 1311; and H Justin Pace and Lawrence J Trautman, 'Climate change and Caremark doctrine, imperfect together' (2023) 25(3) *University of Pennsylvania Journal of Business Law* 777.

161 The OECD 2022 Report notes: 'By mid-February 2021, shareholders had filed 66 resolutions specifically related to climate change for the year's US proxy season (in addition to 13 proposals about climate-related lobbying). Twenty-five of those climate-related proposals asked for the adoption of greenhouse gas emission reduction targets in line with the Paris Agreement.' See OECD, *Climate Change and Corporate Governance* (2022) <https://doi.org/10.1787/272d85c3-en>.

162 Mallin, *Corporate Governance* (2019) 82–3.

163 *Australasian Centre for Corporate Responsibility v Commonwealth Bank of Australia* (2015) 325 ALR 736; *Australasian Centre for Corporate Responsibility v Commonwealth Bank of Australia* (2016) 248 FCR 280; *Abrahams v Commonwealth Bank of Australia*, VID879/2017.

Superannuation Trust ('REST'),[164] where members used provisions of the *Corporations Act 2001* (Cth) to seek further information from companies as to their exposure to climate risk.[165] In most instances, the companies agreed to provide information after the suit was filed, and, in the matter of REST, the fund acknowledged that 'Climate change is a material, direct and current financial risk to the superannuation fund across many risk categories, including investment, market, reputational, strategic, governance and third-party risks'. REST committed to taking steps to 'ensure that investment managers take active steps to consider, measure and manage financial risks posed by climate change and other relevant ESG risks'.[166]

3.7.2.7 Government

As noted earlier, Mallin's account of the place of stakeholders in contemporary corporate governance identifies government as a key stakeholder.[167]

Interestingly, the Australian federal Minister for the Environment was found, at first instance in *Sharma v Minister for the Environment*,[168] to owe a duty of care in tort to future generations of Australian children. This action was brought by the applicants against the Commonwealth Government, and formulated that the Minister had a duty to exercise her statutory power, as provided by ss 130 and 133 of the *Environment Protection and Biodiversity Conservation Act 1999* (Cth), with reasonable care. The applicants sought to restrain an apprehended breach of that duty by the Minister in the approval of a specific coal mine expansion. Although Bromberg J found, at first instance, that a duty to the children existed, this was overturned by the Full Federal Court.[169] Regardless of this outcome, the role of government as a stakeholder in the governance of companies cannot be overlooked.

3.8 All stakeholders have vested interests in the sustainability of corporations

At the end of the day, it is not difficult to conclude that all stakeholders have vested interests in the sustainability of corporations[170] and that is linked to profit-making; as Larry Fink puts it: 'Profits are essential if a company is to effectively serve all of its stakeholders over time – not only shareholders, but also employees, customers, and communities.'[171] The *shareholders* want to maximise returns on their investment, not only by receiving good dividends, but also by making profits when they sell securities

164 *McVeigh v Retail Employees Superannuation Pty Ltd* [2019] FCA 14.
165 B Nosworthy, 'The Corporations Act and climate change – appetite for change?' (2020) 94(6) *Australian Law Journal* 411, 411–13.
166 REST, 'REST reaches settlement with Mark McVeigh' (Media Release, 2 November 2020) <https://rest .com.au/why-rest/about-rest/news/rest-reaches-settlement-with-mark-mcveigh>.
167 Mallin, *Corporate Governance* (2019) 83.
168 *Sharma v Minister for the Environment* (2021) 391 ALR 1.
169 *Minister for the Environment v Sharma* (2022) 291 FCR 311.
170 King, *The Corporate Citizen* (2006) 63.
171 Larry Fink, 'Purpose and profit, 2019 Letter to CEOs' (2019) <https://www.blackrock.com/corporate/ investor-relations/2019-larry-fink-ceo-letter>.

in a corporation. The *employees* are dependent on the company, not only to support themselves and their families, but in some cases as holders of employee benefits, including retirement benefits. The *creditors* have a strong interest in the sustainability of the company, as their expectation is that they are paid in accordance with the conditions agreed upon with the corporation, while other creditors are reliant on the corporation's continued existence and engagement with them for their own ongoing business needs. *Customers* want to continue trading with corporations that provide excellent goods and services, and they will deal with the company to enforce guarantees and warranties against suppliers. The *communities* in which corporations do business, manufacture their goods or deliver their services gain by corporations providing job opportunities and creating wealth that leads to the improvement of living conditions, as long as the corporations adhere to good practice in corporate governance and do business in an environmentally friendly manner. The *environment* is our 'pearl', and is highly dependent on sustainable and environmentally friendly corporations. The *government* has an interest in the sustainability of corporations, as not only do they provide job opportunities to citizens, but they are also responsible for the majority of governmental income through taxes, levies, licences etc, which income is eventually reinvested into a country's infrastructure, health, education etc to ensure prosperity for its citizens.

3.9 Conclusion

The inherent tension between the shareholder primacy theory and the stakeholder theory, famously identified in the public debate in the 1930s in the *Harvard Law Review* between Berle and Dodd, remains unsolved.[172] However, we have argued that these tensions might have been exaggerated in order to promote a shareholder primacy model, rather than a corporate law model based on the fact that the company is a separate legal entity and within that entity several interests (internal and external) are represented. However, value judgments will have to be made whether, at a particular moment of time, the bests interests of the corporation might require the interests of a particular group of stakeholders to be prioritised over other stakeholders. According to one commentator, 'in the current market-based economy, directors all over the world are questioning whether corporations should exist solely to maximize shareholder profit' and 'many corporate directors no longer abide by Milton Friedman's famous declaration that a corporation's only social responsibility is to provide a profit for its owners'.[173]

The debate on CSR is as alive now, in the 2020s, as it has been since the early 1930s, and much has been achieved to align these responsibilities with contemporary community expectations and directors' duties. We have pointed out that disclosure of and reporting

---

172 See, eg, I Esser and Jean J du Plessis, 'The stakeholder debate and directors' fiduciary duties' (2007) 19(3) *South African Mercantile Law Journal* 346, 347–51.
173 Alissa Mickels, 'Beyond corporate social responsibility: Reconciling the ideals of a for-benefit corporation with director fiduciary duties in the US and Europe' (2009) 32(1) *Hastings International and Comparative Law Review* 271, 272.

on non-financial issues became very important because of ESG and other non-financial reporting standards, initiatives and frameworks.

We conclude that there is a much better understanding of who could and should be identified a 'stakeholders' of the corporation. What is beyond dispute is that all stakeholders have a vested interest in the sustainability of corporations and that is why a focus on them, and the way in which corporations look after their interests, will remain a dominant issue in the areas of corporate law and governance in the future.

4 | BOARD FUNCTIONS AND STRUCTURES

4.1 Higher community expectations of directors

4.1.1 Historical low standards of care, skill and diligence expected of directors

Directors' statutory duties and liability are discussed in greater detail in Chapter 8. It is, however, important to first make a few observations regarding the higher modern community expectations of directors.

English precedents from the 1800s and before held that directors were not liable for a breach in their duty of care, skill and diligence if they merely acted negligently. One of the first indications that more than ordinary negligence was required is found in an English case decided in 1872, where it was held that directors are liable only for a breach of their duty of care, skill and diligence if they acted with *crassa negligentia* (gross negligence).[1] This rule was confirmed in a later case (1899) by Lord Lindley MR, one of the most famous English commercial Lords:

> The inquiry, therefore, is reduced to want of care and bona fides with a view to the interests of the nitrate company. The amount of care to be taken is difficult to define; but it is plain that directors are not liable for all the mistakes they may make, although if they had taken more care they might have avoided them: see *Overend, Gurney & Co v Gibb* (1872) LR 5 HL 480. Their negligence must be not the omission to take all possible care; it must be much more blameable than that: it must be in a business sense culpable or gross. I do not know how better to describe it.[2]

These sentiments were repeated in several later English cases,[3] and the fact that negligence alone was once not enough to hold directors liable for a breach of their common law duties or equitable duties was also referenced in the leading Australian case, *Daniels v Anderson*.[4] In *Daniels v Anderson* the majority (Clark and Sheller JJA) referred to the concept of 'negligence' as used in the context of equitable remedies, and concluded that 'The

---

1   *Overend & Gurney Co v Gibb* [1872] LR 5 HL 480, 487, 488, 489, 493, 496, 500.
2   *Lagunas Nitrate Co v Lagunas Syndicate* [1899] 2 Ch 392, 435.
3   *Re National Bank of Wales Ltd* [1899] 2 Ch 629, 672; *Re Brazilian Rubber Plantation and Estates Ltd* [1911] 1 Ch 425; *Re City Equitable Fire Insurance Co Ltd* [1925] Ch 407, 427.
4   (1995) 37 NSWLR 438, 493.

negligence spoken of was something grosser or more culpable determined by subjective rather than objective tests'.[5] The subjective test referred to by Clark and Sheller JJA was that a director was to exercise only *the care which can reasonably be expected of a person of his (or her) knowledge and experience.*

The combined effect of a higher requirement than ordinary negligence and the fact that subjective elements were used to judge whether a particular director was in breach of her or his duty of care, skill and diligence, ensured that well into the late 1900s it was rare to find cases in which directors were held liable for a breach of those duties.

In *Daniels v Anderson*[6] the Court referred to the low standards of care, skill and diligence expected of directors in the past and observed that 'However ridiculous and absurd the conduct of the directors, it was the company's misfortune that such unwise directors were chosen'.[7] There were several reasons given by the courts and commentators as to why in the past the courts were reluctant to expect high standards of directors. Or, to put it differently, why the courts were reluctant to scrutinise closely the business decisions taken by directors. Some of the reasons given were that:

- taking up a position as non-executive director on a part-time basis was simply 'an appropriate diversion for gentlemen but should not be coupled with onerous obligations'[8]
- 'directors are not specialists, like lawyers and doctors'[9]
- directors are expected to take risks and they are dealing with uncertainties, which would be compromised if too high standards of care were expected of them[10]
- courts are ill-equipped to second-guess directors' business decisions[11]
- the internal management of the company is one that companies can arrange as they wish, and courts should be reluctant to interfere with internal company matters.[12]

As will be seen below, the expectations of directors' care and diligence have changed considerably, as reflected in several court cases decided since the early 1990s.[13] The courts continue to be reluctant to interfere with internal company matters, but are more willing to view directors as specialist professionals with attendant obligations.

---

5 Ibid.
6 (1995) 37 NSWLR 438.
7 Ibid 494–5.
8 RBS Macfarlan, 'Directors' duties after the National Safety Council case: Directors' duty of care' (1992) 9(3) *Australian Bar Review* 269, 270. See also J Dodds, 'New developments in directors duties – the Victorian stance on financial competence' (1991) 17(1) *Monash University Law Review* 132, 134.
9 P Redmond, 'The reform of directors' duties' (1992) 15(1) *University of New South Wales Law Journal* 86, 98, quoting from *Barnes v Andrews*, 298 Fed 614, 618 (1924).
10 Jean J du Plessis, 'A comparative analysis of directors' duty of care, skill and diligence in South Africa and in Australia' (2010) (1) *Acta Juridica* 263, 274.
11 Ibid.
12 Ibid.
13 *Daniels v Anderson* (1995) 37 NSWLR 438; *Permanent Building Society (in liq) v Wheeler* (1994) 11 WAR 187; *Vrisakis v Australian Securities Commission* (1993) 9 WAR 395; *Australian*

4.1.2 Legal recognition of changed community expectations of directors

That the scene has changed considerably for directors in recent years was strikingly illustrated by the case of *Daniels v Anderson*.[14] Although the Court specifically recognised the potential tension in expecting objective professional standards of all directors in all types of companies, the Court did not hesitate to conclude that community expectations of the standards of performance of directors have increased in recent times, perhaps as the role of the director became a professional post. Thus, the Court held that it is the modern law of negligence that should be used to determine whether a director was in breach of his or her duty of care, skill and diligence.[15] In fact, the Court held that the modern law of negligence (also called the tort of negligence) has developed sufficiently to cope with expecting objective professional standards of all types of directors (for example, executive directors and non-executive directors) in all types of companies (from the one-person proprietary company to the multinational listed public company).

The general principles of the tort of negligence and the duty of care were relied on to emphasise three important things.[16] First, there were historic reasons why directors' duties of care, skill and diligence were viewed in a particular manner by the English courts of the late 1800s and early 1900s. Referring to the article by Jennifer Hill,[17] the Court made the following observation:

> The nature and extent of directors' liability for their acts and omissions developed as the body corporate evolved from the unincorporated joint stock company regulated by a deed of settlement and was influenced by the partnership theory of corporation whereunder shareholders were ultimately responsible for unwise appointment of directors.[18]

Second, in embracing the tort of negligence as the basis of liability for a breach of a director's duty of care, skill and diligence, the Court took into consideration that 'the law about the duty of directors' had developed considerably in the past century.[19]

Securities and Investments Commission v Adler (2002) 41 ACSR 72; Australian Securities and Investments Commission v Rich (2003) 44 ACSR 341; Australian Securities and Investments Commission v Maxwell (2006) 59 ACSR 373; Australian Securities and Investments Commission v Macdonald (No 11) (2009) 256 ALR 199; Australian Securities and Investments Commission v Healey (2011) 196 FCR 291; Cassimatis v Australian Securities and Investments Commission (2020) 275 FCR 533.

14 *Daniels v Anderson* (1995) 37 NSWLR 438.

15 Ibid 500–2.

16 Du Plessis, 'A comparative analysis of directors' duty of care, skill and diligence in South Africa and in Australia' (2010) (1) *Acta Juridica* 263, 273.

17 J Hill, 'The liability of passive directors: *Morley v Statewide Tobacco Services Ltd*' (1992) 14(4) *Sydney Law Review* 504.

18 *Daniels v Anderson* (1995) 37 NSWLR 438, 493.

19 Ibid 661, discussing in particular *Re City Equitable Fire Insurance Co Ltd* [1925] Ch 407. See also The Honourable Sir Douglas Menzies 'Company directors' (1959) 33(4) *Australian Law Journal* 156, 156–8, 163–4; Macfarlan, 'Directors' duties after the National Safety Council case' (1992) 272–3.

The Court then, in roughly seven pages,[20] painstakingly quoted from contemporary cases before reaching the conclusion that the tort of negligence and the modern concept of a duty of care now form an acceptable basis for liability of directors for breach of their duty of care.[21] Third, the Court mentioned that the law of negligence has also developed considerably in the past century, alongside the developments in directors' duties.[22]

Since *Daniels v Anderson*, it can safely be stated that the standard of care expected of Australian directors under the common law has reached new heights – *Daniels v Anderson* brought an abrupt end to the notion that directors' duty of care, skill and diligence should be judged subjectively and that their negligence 'must be in a business sense culpable or gross'.

As will be seen in Chapter 8, directors' liability in Australia is dominated by liability for a breach of their statutory duties under the *Corporations Act 2001* (Cth). Also, it will be seen that it is the primary corporate regulator (the Australian Securities and Investments Commission ['ASIC']) that takes a lead role in instituting actions against directors for a breach of their statutory duties.[23] However, as was illustrated above, the standards of skill, care and diligence expected of directors have risen considerably since the 1990s, and the statutory standards of care found under s 180(1) of the *Corporations Act 2001* (Cth) ('the Act') reflect these higher standards.[24]

---

20 *Daniels v Anderson* (1995) 37 NSWLR 438, 497–504.
21 Ibid 505.
22 Ibid 497.
23 An empirical study of court proceedings brought by ASIC and the Commonwealth Director of Public Prosecutions ('CDPP') for breach of directors' duties provisions of the *Corporations Act 2001* (Cth) from 2005 to 2014 reflects that ASIC and the CDPP initiated approximately half of all public and private proceedings involving breach of directors' duties. See Jasper Hedges et al, *An Empirical Analysis of Public Enforcement of Directors' Duties in Australia: Preliminary Findings* (Centre for Corporate Law and Securities Regulation, 2015) One of the co-authors of this study, Ian Ramsay, separately examined ASIC's power to litigate to enforce breaches of directors' duties, and found that, as an active litigant, ASIC is setting the standards for directors in the boardroom and that in some circumstances, ASIC-instigated litigation is desirable. See Ian Ramsay, 'Increased corporate governance powers of shareholders and regulators and the role of the corporate regulator in enforcing duties owed by corporate directors and managers' (2015) 26(1) *European Business Law Review* 49. Although corporations law in Australia is heavily influenced historically by English common law and statute, archival work of Rosemary Teele Langford and colleagues found evidence that the first statutory duty of care in Australia and perhaps the common law world was introduced in the *Companies Act 1896* (Vic): Rosemary Teele Langford, Ian Ramsay and Michelle Welsh, 'The origins of company directors' statutory duty of care' (2015) 37(4) *Sydney Law Review* 489. See also Jason Harris, Anil Hargovan and Janet Austin, Shareholder primacy revisited: Does the public interest have any role in statutory duties? (2008) 26(6) *Company and Securities Law Journal* 355.
24 *Australian Securities and Investments Commission v Maxwell* (2006) 59 ACSR 373; *Vines v Australian Securities and Investments Commission* (2007) 73 NSWLR 451; *Australian Securities and Investments Commission v Macdonald (No 11)* (2009) 256 ALR 199; *Australian Securities and Investments Commission v Healey* (2011) 196 FCR 291; *Australian Securities and Investments Commission v Flugge and Geary* (2016) 342 ALR 1; *Australian Securities and Investments Commission v Cassimatis (No 8)* (2016) 336 ALR 209; *Cassimatis v Australian Securities and Investments Commission* (2020) 275 FCR 533; *Australian Securities and Investments Commission v Mitchell (No 2)* (2020) 382 ALR 425; *Australian Securities and Investments Commission v Big Star Energy Ltd (No 3)* (2020) 389 ALR 17.

4.2 The organs of governance[25]

Although now 20 years old, the Report of the HIH Royal Commission ('Owen Report')[26] summarises clearly the concept of organs of a corporation in the context of corporate governance.[27] Justice Owen explained that a corporation is a legal entity separate and apart from its board of directors (one of the primary organs of a corporation) and shareholders (the other primary organ of a corporation), and that the corporation can only 'act through the intervention of the human condition'.[28]

Historically, the power to manage the business of all companies and corporations was conferred upon the board of directors. The fact that it was impossible for a board of directors to manage the day-to-day business of large public corporations was only openly acknowledged in the past three decades (see Section 4.3). Today, the board of directors is seen as the primary governance or supervisory organ.

The powers conferred upon shareholders are primarily conferred upon them by the Act. The powers to appoint directors and to remove directors are some of the most important powers of shareholders, but there are also several other decisions in a company that cannot be taken without the approval of the shareholders by way of a special resolution (75 per cent majority of the shareholders present at a shareholders' meeting in person or by proxy).[29]

The general public may understand shareholders as 'the owners' of the company. However, as discussed in Section 1.5.1.2, this is inaccurate, even under the presumption that shareholders provide the original capital ('share capital'), which may enable a company to commence commercial activities. As there is no minimum share capital requirement, or minimum issue price for shares, it is possible for proprietary companies to be incorporated with no significant share capital at all. In addition, there is a growing trend to recognise other forms of capital apart from financial capital, namely manufactured, intellectual, human, social and relationship, and natural capital.[30]

The current view, that directors are accountable to the body of shareholders, is partly based on the incorrect assumption that the shareholders 'own' the company, but also on the fact that it is the shareholders who appoint the directors and who normally have

---

25 This section presents and reflects on the prevailing approach in corporate decision-making processes: that is, the board of directors are appointed by, and accountable to, the body of shareholders. Andrew Keay, however, suggests that the board must be accountable to the company entity, either to an accountability council or to the general meeting of shareholders. See Andrew Keay, 'Board accountability and the entity maximization and sustainability approach' in Barnali Choudhury and Martin Petrin (eds), *Understanding the Company: Corporate Governance and Theory* (Cambridge University Press, 2017) 271.

26 Report of the HIH Royal Commission ('Owen Report'), *The Failure of HIH Insurance – Volume I: A Corporate Collapse and Its Lessons* (Commonwealth of Australia, 2003).

27 Ibid 103.

28 Ibid.

29 One of the most important powers that the shareholders have is to change the company's constitution (if any) by way of a special resolution: see *Corporations Act 2001* (Cth) s 136(2).

30 See International Integrated Reporting Council ('IIRC'), *International <IR> Framework* (IIRC, 2021) 2, 18–20 <https://www.integratedreporting.org/wp-content/uploads/2021/01/InternationalIntegratedReportingFramework.pdf>.

the power to remove the directors.[31] The dominance of shareholders is reflected in the shareholder primacy theory of corporate law, which was discussed in greater detail in Section 1.5.2; however, as was explained, that theory has long been under attack by the countervailing view that the board must be accountable to the company as a separate legal entity[32] and that there are stakeholder interests other than those of shareholders in the company as a separate legal entity.[33]

4.3 Board functions[34]

AWA Ltd v Daniels[35] is one of the few cases in which an attempt has been made to explain the division of functions between the board of directors and management; non-executive directors and the chief executive officer ('CEO') or managing director; and the chairman and the board of directors.[36] Rogers CJ explained that, apart from statutory ones, a board's functions are said to be normally fourfold, namely:

(1) to set goals for the corporation
(2) to appoint the corporation's chief executive
(3) to oversee the plans of managers for the acquisition and organisation of financial and human resources towards attainment of the corporation's goals
(4) to review, at reasonable intervals, the corporation's progress towards attaining its goals.[37]

Rogers CJ pointed out the practical limitations on the ability of the board of a large public corporation to manage the day-to-day business of the corporation:

> The Board of a large public corporation cannot manage the corporation's day to day business. That function must of necessity be left to the corporation's executives. If the directors of a large public corporation were to be immersed in the details of the day to day operations the directors would be incapable of taking more abstract, important decisions at board level ...[38]

---

31 *Corporations Act 2001* (Cth) s 203D gives the shareholders an inalienable right to remove directors of public companies by ordinary resolution, following the procedures prescribed in s 203D.
32 See Keay, 'Board accountability and the entity maximization and sustainability approach' in Choudhury and Petrin (eds), *Understanding the Company: Corporate Governance and Theory* (Cambridge University Press, 2017) 271.
33 See Jean J du Plessis, 'Corporate social responsibility and "contemporary community expectations"' (2017) 35(1) *Company and Securities Law Journal* 30, 33–5; Jean J du Plessis, 'Directors' duty to act in the best interests of the corporation: "Hard cases make bad law"' (2019) 34(1) *Australian Journal of Corporate Law* 3; and Tim Connor and Andrew O'Beid, 'Clarifying terms in the debate regarding "shareholder primacy"' (2020) 35(3) *Australian Journal of Corporate Law* 276.
34 For some interesting reflections on the gap between what directors in fact do and what the business literature professes that they *should* do, see Myles L Mace, 'Directors: Myth and reality' in Thomas Clarke (eds), *Theories of Corporate Governance: The Philosophical Foundations of Corporate Governance* (Routledge, 2004) 96 *et seq*, based on his book, Myles L Mace, *Directors: Myth and Reality* (Harvard University Press, 1971). For a more theoretical analysis, distinguishing between 'board tasks' and 'board functions', see Morten Huse, *Boards, Governance and Value Creation* (Cambridge University Press, 2007) 33, 38–40.
35 *AWA Ltd v Daniels* (1992) 7 ACSR 759.
36 Ibid 865–8.
37 Ibid.
38 Ibid 866.

This distinction is now also widely accepted in legislation. In the past the power 'to manage the business of the company' was invariably conferred upon the board of directors by way of the model set of articles of association ('Table A') that accompanied most of the Companies Acts that preceded the Act. The practical reality that in large public corporations the business of the corporation is not done by the board as such, but under the direction of the board, is currently reflected in s 198A(1) of the Act, which provides that 'The business of a company is to be managed by or under the direction of the directors'. In proprietary companies, the business of the company will be managed 'by' the board, but in large public corporations it will be managed 'under the direction' of the board.

The distinction between managing and directing the business of a corporation is well accepted in managerial circles. As early as 1997, Bob Garratt explained it as follows:

> But there is a vast difference between 'directing' and 'managing' an organisation. Managing is literally, given its Latin root, a hands-on activity thriving on crisis action. On the operations side of an organisation it is a crucial role. Directing is different. Directing is essentially an intellectual activity. It is about showing the way ahead, giving leadership. It is thoughtful and reflective and requires the acquisition by each director of a portfolio of completely different thinking skills.[39]

The Australian Securities Exchange's ('ASX') *Corporate Governance Principles and Recommendations* (2019) contains a useful summary of the responsibilities of the board. Readers are advised to have a look at it for a practical understanding of the board's role and functions.[40]

The language of a number of these responsibilities set out in the commentary in 2014 changed between the third and fourth editions of the Principles, which were updated at the same time that the Royal Commission into Misconduct in the Banking Industry, Superannuation and Financial Services Industry was taking place. The commentary now focuses on the board satisfying itself about, rather than simply approving, the risk management framework and remuneration policies – and explicitly encourages the board to challenge management and hold it to account. The Final Hayne Report identified a key concern that boards in the financial sector were not getting appropriate information, particularly about non-financial risks, were not seeking out information and were not engaging with management positions in relation to these risks.[41]

Ultimately the board's functions and responsibilities could be summarised as being to 'direct, govern, guide, monitor, oversee, supervise and comply'. Some literature on management and managerial strategy makes a distinction between two primary roles of the board, namely a 'performance role' and a 'conformance role'. Tricker classifies

39   Bob Garratt, *The Fish Rots from the Head* (HarperCollins Business, 1997) 4. See also Robert AG Monks and Nell Minow, *Corporate Governance* (Blackwell, 3rd ed, 2004) 195, 202–3; JB Reid, *Commonsense Corporate Governance* (Australian Institute of Company Directors], 2002) 22; Stephen M Bainbridge, *Corporation Law and Economics* (Foundation Press, 2002) 194–5.
40   ASX, *Corporate Governance Principles and Recommendations* (4th ed, 2019) 6 <www.asx.com.au/ documents/asx-compliance/cgc-principles-and-recommendations-fourth-edn.pdf>.
41   *Royal Commission into Misconduct in the Banking Industry, Superannuation and Financial Services Industry* (Final Report, February 2019) vol 1, 395 ('Final Hayne Report').

'contributing know-how, expertise and external information' and 'networking, repre-senting the company and adding status' as being part of directors' performance role. Under their conformance role he includes 'judging, questioning and supervising exec-utive management' and a 'watchdog, confidant and safety-valve role'.[42] Garratt sees accountability (for quality of thinking, high ethical standards and values, with the aim of obeying the law and treating stakeholders in a consistent way) and supervision of man-agement (conformance to key performance indicators, cash flow, budgets and projects) as part of the board's conformance task.[43] Among its performance tasks he lists policy formulation and foresight and strategic thinking.[44] The distinction between the board's 'performance' and 'conformance' tasks seems a realistic reflection of directors' roles and mirrors the primary functions of the board. Other theories referenced in the broader literature include agency theory, stewardship theory, resource dependency theory and stakeholder theory. There is also growing recognition that the role of the board is com-plex and cannot be adequately characterised by only two primary roles.

Directors need to have some practical guidelines to ensure that they fulfil their duties and responsibilities diligently. Mervyn King, in his book *The Corporate Citizen*, provides some excellent guidelines for directors taking decisions or making business judgments. He suggests that directors, when making decisions or business judgments, must ask 10 questions:

(1) Do I as a director of this board have any conflict in regard to the issue before the board?

(2) Do I have all the facts to enable me to make a decision on the issue before the board?

(3) Is the decision being made a rational business decision based on all the facts available at the time of the board meeting?

(4) Is the decision in the best interests of the company?

(5) Is the communication of the decision to the stakeholders of the company trans-parent, with substance over form, and does it contain all the negative and posi-tive features bound up in that decision?

(6) Will the company be seen as a good corporate citizen as a result of the decision?

(7) Am I acting as a good steward of the company's assets in making this decision?

(8) Have I exercised the concepts of intellectual honesty and intellectual naivety in acting on behalf of this incapacitated company?

(9) Have I understood the material in the board pack and the discussion at the board-room table?

(10) Will the board be embarrassed if its decision and the process employed in arriv-ing at its decision were to appear on the front page of the national newspaper?[45]

---

42 Robert I Tricker, *International Corporate Governance* (Prentice-Hall, 1994) 98–100. See also Bob Tricker, 'From Manager to director: Developing corporate governors' strategic thinking' in Bob Garratt (ed), *Developing Strategic Thought: Rediscovering the Art of Direction-giving* (McGraw-Hill, 1995) 1, 16–18; and Alice Klettner, *Theories of Corporate Governance and Its Regulation* (Routledge, 2016) 7, ch 3.

43 Garratt, *The Fish Rots from the Head* (Profile Books, 2003) 109 *et seq*, 131 *et seq*.

44 Ibid 57 *et seq*, 88 *et seq*.

45 Mervyn King, *The Corporate Citizen* (Penguin, 2006) 53–8.

Some may say it is unrealistic to expect that directors, making decisions 'on the run', ask all these questions. On the other hand, especially as far as Australian directors are concerned, there is very little doubt that if all the directors of James Hardie had asked all these 10 questions and could answer 'no' to questions 1 and 10 and 'yes' to questions 2–9, they would not have been held liable.[46] Also, the names of the directors of Centro Properties Group would not have been mentioned so prominently in the media during October 2009, when ASIC announced that it would institute action against the directors for a breach of their statutory duty of care and diligence,[47] if those directors had asked the 10 questions King suggests and could answer 'no' to questions 1 and 10 and 'yes' to questions 2–9. A similar observation can be made for the directors of Storm Financial Pty Ltd[48] and Vocation Ltd.[49]

4.4 Board structures

Generally speaking, there are two types of board structure, namely the unitary board and the two-tier board. It is, however, not easy to make an exact distinction between these two structures, as most developed countries have moved away from the traditional unitary board structure in the case of large public corporations. In most developed countries, board structures for large corporations have some characteristics that are reminiscent of the more traditional two-tier board. A good way to understand this point is to start with a basic distinction drawn by Tricker in *Corporate Governance: Principles, Policies and Practices*[50] between a 'managerial pyramid' and a 'governance circle'. His conceptualisation is illustrated by way of seven figures (Figures 4.1–4.6 are reproduced from *Corporate Governance: Principles, Policies and Practices* with Tricker's original numbering in square brackets).[51]

Figure 4.2 illustrates the typical board structure for proprietary companies and the board structure most public corporations have used historically. With the drive to have objective checks on management and to increase board independence, there has been a move towards the board structure depicted in Figure 4.3. There has also been a move to have a majority of non-executive directors and, in particular, a majority of independent non-executive directors (Figure 4.4).

---

46   See *Australian Securities and Investments Commission v Macdonald (No 11)* (2009) 256 ALR 199.
     See further Anil Hargovan, '*Australian Securities and Investments Commission v Macdonald [No 11]*: Corporate governance lessons from James Hardie' (2009) 33(3) *Melbourne University Law Review* 984.
47   See 'ASIC commences proceedings against current and former directors of Centro' (Media Release, 21 October 2009) <www.asic.gov.au/asic/asic.nsf/byheadline/09-202AD+ASIC+commences+proceedings+against+current+and+former+officers+of+Centro?openDocument>. See further *Australian Securities and Investments Commission v Healey* (2011) 196 FCR 291 (liability decision); and *Australian Securities and Investments Commission v Healey (No 2)* [2011] FCA 1003 (penalty decision).
48   *Australian Securities and Investments Commission v Cassimatis (No 8)* (2016) 336 ALR 209; *Cassimatis v Australian Securities and Investments Commission* (2020) 275 FCR 533.
49   *Australian Securities and Investments Commission v Vocation Ltd (in liq)* (2019) 371 ALR 155.
50   Bob Tricker, *Corporate Governance: Principles, Policies and Practices* (Oxford University Press, 4th ed, 2019) 46–52.
51   For some refinements and practical explanations of these Figures, see Bob Tricker, *Corporate Governance in Practice* (CRC Press, 2023) 22–5, 30–5.

Figure 4.1 [2.5] The board and management differentiated

Figure 4.2 [2.9] All-executive board

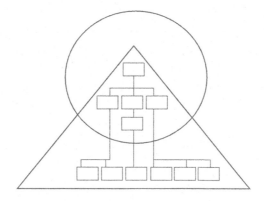

Figure 4.3 [2.10] Majority executive board

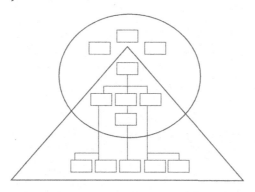

Figure 4.4 [2.11] Majority outside board

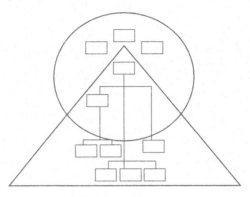

Figure 4.5 [2.13] Two-tier board

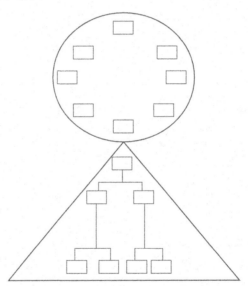

Figure 4.6 [3.12] The all non-executive director board

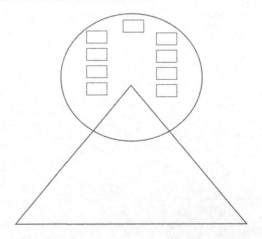

Figure 4.7 The statutory arrangement for South African close corporations

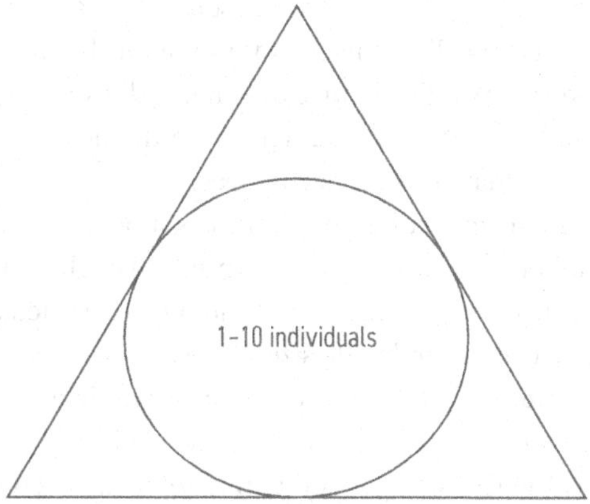

1–10 individuals

The German system is perhaps best described by Figure 4.5, with the governance circle representing the supervisory board and the managerial pyramid representing the management board.[52] The recent trends towards having independent non-executive directors will be explained in greater detail in Chapter 5, while the German two-tier board will be discussed briefly in Section 12.4. Figure 4.6 illustrates a board with no executive director. It is rare to find this in listed public companies, but Tricker points out that it is sometimes the board structure for not-for-profit entities such as charitable organisations, arts, health and sports organisations, and 'quangos' (quasi-autonomous non-government organisations).[53] Figure 4.7 depicts the South African close corporation, where the statutory presumed or default arrangement is based on the premise that there is a complete overlap between the governance circle and the managerial triangle in small businesses.[54]

Tricker's basic models could be used to further refine and explain board structures and an effective corporate governance model. There are several indications that traditional common law jurisdictions recognise the distinctive roles of 'the board' and 'management'. The primary function of 'the board' is to 'direct, govern, guide, monitor, oversee, supervise and comply', and 'management's' function is to 'manage the day-to-day business of the corporation'. This becomes clear if one looks at what is nowadays understood as coming under the 'functions of the board', as explained above. There is no longer a place in large corporations for the board to 'manage the business of the corporation', but there is a place for it to provide strategic direction to the corporation; the development and implementation of risk management policies are also key functions of the board.

In various reports, such as the Cadbury Report (UK), the King Reports (South Africa) (1994, 2002, 2009 and 2016), the Higgs Report (UK) and the Owen Report (Australia), the

---

52 See also Tricker, *Corporate Governance in Practice* (2023) 35, 48–9.
53 Ibid 50–1.
54 See further Jean J du Plessis, 'Reflections and perspectives on the South African close corporation as business vehicle for SMEs' (2009) 15(4) *New Zealand Business Law Quarterly* 250, 252–3, 257 for some of the reasons for having separate legislation applying to SMEs.

unitary board structure was preferred to the two-tier structure, but these are not really alternative structures to each other in the strict sense of that description; rather, they have some similarities and some differences. Additional problems with simply accepting the unitary board as the preferred structure are that it does not allow consideration of other possibilities and it does not stimulate debate on the best possible board structure or the relative merits of alternative board structures.

We do not propose that the unitary board structure is superior to the two-tier board structure or vice versa, but rather that a unitary board structure ought not simply be rejected in favour of a two-tier board structure or vice versa. Deciding on a particular board structure will depend on many variables (for example, the size of the company, the quality of persons sitting as non-executive directors, and the corporate culture within a particular corporation).[55]

As will be seen in Chapter 12, Japan and China, as well as Germany, use the two-tier board system; however, the German model is unique because co-determination[56] is so deeply embedded in its corporate governance model. It is to be expected that – depending on one's understanding and definition of a 'unitary board' or 'two-tier board' along with historical preference within the relevant incorporating jurisdiction – strong support for one or the other will continue to be expressed.[57]

4.5 Conclusion

We started this chapter by focusing on the organs of a company and then discussed the main functions of a board of directors. It is clear that there is an important distinction between managing the business of the company and directing, supervising and overseeing the management of the business of corporations in large public companies. The board is responsible for directing, supervising and overseeing the management of the business of corporations. Managing the business of large public corporations is normally left to management, but under control of the board.

As was pointed out in Chapters 1 and 2, there is now an expectation that corporations should also strive to build a better society and that they should be focused on responsible behaviour and long-term and sustainable growth. The idea that the primary aim of corporations is profit maximisation for shareholders and other investors can no longer be taken for granted. We have moved away from the single bottom-line (financial) approach. Boards of directors, as the ultimate control centres of corporations (the organ theory and the board primacy model), need to take serious notice of these trends and of their own ultimate responsibility for sustainability, and for reporting on and disclosing information regarding non-financial matters (see Section 3.4). It is, therefore, important to point out here (as well as in Chapter 8), the responsibilities of directors and the special position in which they are placed. This can hardly be illustrated better than

---

55 See Owen Report, *The Failure of HIH Insurance* (2003) vol 1, 105 [6.12].
56 As will be seen in Chapter 12, the supervisory board in Germany is based on co-determination between shareholders, providers of share capital and employees, representing human capital: up to half of the seats of supervisory boards are filled by employees and the other half are filled by shareholder representatives.
57 See Garratt, *The Fish Rots from the Head* (1997) 42–3, 210.

by quoting Justice Middleton in his judgment in *Australian Securities and Investments Commission v Healey*:

> A director is an essential component of corporate governance. Each director is placed at the apex of the structure of direction and management of a company. The higher the office that is held by a person, the greater the responsibility that falls upon him or her. The role of a director is significant as their actions may have a profound effect on the community, and not just shareholders, employees and creditors.[58]

There can be no doubt that in future all investors, especially large institutional investors, will be under tremendous pressure to invest only in corporations that adopt a long-term sustainable and responsible approach to conducting their businesses, now that reporting on and disclosing information regarding non-financial matters have become so prominent. Further, whether or not they adopt such an approach will be measurable. It is within these parameters that boards will have to fulfil their duties – no longer can the shareholder primacy model, in its pure and traditional form, be justified. The concept of 'profit maximisation' for shareholders will have to be toned down to a 'good return on investment in the long term'. We should strive for law reform that reflects the practical reality of a corporate environment that recognises the interests of multiple stakeholders.[59] In our view, all these developments will ensure that corporate governance as a subject area will remain of considerable importance in future.

---

58 (2011) 196 FCR 291, [14].
59 See Du Plessis, 'Corporate social responsibility and "contemporary community expectations"' (2017) 35(1) *Company and Securities Law Journal* 36, 45–6; and Du Plessis, 'Shareholder primacy and other stakeholder interests' (2016) 34(3) *Company and Securities Law Journal* 238, 242.

5 TYPES OF COMPANY DIRECTORS AND OFFICERS

5.1 Introduction

In the previous chapter we saw that modern community expectations are for all types of directors to fulfil their duties of care and diligence meticulously. No longer can directors hide behind ignorance or inaction; nor are the duties of non-executive directors seen as being of an intermittent nature. All directors have a positive duty to challenge, inquire and investigate when controversial or potentially risky matters are discussed at board level, as was illustrated by the 2009 case of *Australian Securities and Investments Commission v Macdonald (No 11)*,[1] discussed in Chapter 8.

5.2 Definition of 'director'

Identifying who is a director has practical significance for the law on directors' duties and sanctions for breach under the *Corporations Act 2001* (Cth) ('the Act'), in particular the civil penalty provisions (pecuniary penalty, compensation, disgorgement and disqualification orders) discussed in Chapter 8. The decision in *Murdaca v Australian Securities and Investments Commission*[2] reminds us that a person who is not, strictly speaking, a director may nevertheless be disqualified from managing a company if that person is involved in management in ways that are considered to constitute directing or controlling the affairs of that company, either alone or jointly with others. The expansive definition of 'director' also has significant ramifications for those people who occupy the position of director and cause the company to trade while insolvent.[3] Section 588G of the *Corporations Act 2001* (Cth) ('the Act'), discussed in greater detail in Chapter 8, imposes personal liability upon those who occupy the office of director or who discharge functions attaching to that office of the kind normally performed by a director.

---

1   (2009) 256 ALR 199; affirmed by the High Court of Australia in *Australian Securities and Investments Commission v Hellicar* (2012) 247 CLR 345.
2   (2009) 178 FCR 119.
3   See further Jason Harris and Anil Hargovan, 'Potential liability for directors during corporate restructuring: comparative perspectives' in Paul Omar and Jennifer Gant (eds), *Research Handbook on Corporate Restructuring* (Elgar, 2021) 584.

Importantly, s 201B contains rules about who can be a director of a corporation:

(1)   Only an individual who is at least 18 may be appointed as a director of a company.

(2)   A person who is disqualified from managing corporations under pt 2D.6 may only be appointed as director of a company if the appointment is made with permission granted by the Australian Securities and Investments Commission ('ASIC') under s 206GAB or leave granted by the Court under s 206G.

5.2.1 De jure and de facto directors covered

The corporations laws of most common law jurisdictions contain a definition of 'director'. Although there are some differences in these definitions, a common feature is that each aims to define the term quite widely in order to ensure that those who fulfil directorial functions do not escape the provisions of corporations legislation. Thus, the definition of 'director' will typically include a reference to the fact that a person could be considered a director irrespective of the fact that the person is not *called* a director,[4] but is known by a name such as 'governor', 'executive', or 'manager'. The definitions of director will also cover, as a general rule, not only those individuals who were validly appointed to the position of director (de jure directors), but also those acting as a director (de facto directors). Legislation often also includes 'shadow directors' under the definition: individuals who are neither appointed to the position nor act directly as directors, but who manipulate the board 'from behind the scenes'.

The labels accorded to directors as 'de facto' or 'shadow' directors are not intended to be prescriptive.[5] In expressing caution on becoming fixated with labels, Justice Gordon in 2008, in *Australian Securities and Investments Commission v Murdaca*,[6] warned:

> Such descriptions can, at times, be misleading. Names and labels aside, what is required is a critical assessment of the way in which a corporation is managed and then an assessment as to whether the conduct of the person concerned falls within one or more of the categories identified.

5.2.2 Shadow directors

Section 9AC(1)(b)(ii) of the Act encompasses 'shadow directors', but the proviso to this section was included in order to exclude from its parameters those persons in accordance with whose directions the directors usually act, where that advice is given by the outsider in that person's professional capacity (for example, as solicitor or accountant) or because of their business relationship with the directors or company (for example, as the company's banker).

---

4   See Bob Tricker, *Corporate Governance: Principles, Policies and Practices* (Oxford University Press, 4th ed, 2019) 103.

5   See *Grimaldi v Chameleon Mining NL (No 2)* (2012) 200 FCR 296 for discussion of legal principles in this area.

6   (2008) 105 ALD 461, [11].

The expanded definition of 'director' has caused concern among banks, financial institutions and business and professional advisers.[7] These institutions and persons clearly have a strong interest in the company's affairs, especially when companies are in financial difficulty and steps are being taken to send representatives to the board to investigate and make suggestions as to how to overcome these difficulties. The problem is succinctly stated by Vinelott J in *Re Tasbian (No 3)*:[8]

> The dividing line between the position of a watchdog or adviser imposed by an outsider investor and a de facto or shadow director is difficult to draw.

However, in *Buzzle Operations Pty Ltd (in liq) v Apple Computer Australia Pty Ltd*[9] the NSW Court of Appeal held that a secured creditor that imposes conditions on continuing to provide financial support for a debtor company is not a shadow director, even if the debtor's directors felt that they practically had no choice but to agree to the creditor's demands. In such a case the creditor is not acting as part of the governing structure of the debtor company, and hence is making demands or imposing conditions to protect its own independent commercial interest rather than making decisions for the debtor company.

The use of the plural, 'directors', in s 9AC(1)(b)(ii) of the Act suggests that the board, rather than a single director, must be accustomed to acting in accordance with the shadow director's directions or instructions before the subsection is satisfied. This was confirmed in the *Buzzle* case, where it was held that the influence must be exerted over a majority of the board.

That 'accustomed to act' is a tough threshold to satisfy is highlighted further in *Natcomp Technology Australia Pty Ltd v Graiche*,[10] in which Stein JA said that in order for directors to be 'accustomed to act' on the instructions or directions of an outsider for the purposes of the Act, it must be established that the outsider is involved in the principal aspects of the company's business. This threshold is, nonetheless, not insurmountable, as evidenced in *Ho v Akai Pty Ltd (in liq)*,[11] where it was found that the directors or officers of Akai Australia (a company in financial difficulty) were accustomed to acting in accordance with the instructions and wishes of Grande Holdings (a Singaporean company) – the latter being held to be a shadow director and therefore exposed to liability under the insolvent trading provisions in s 588G of the Act. Similarly, in *Damcevski v Demetriou*,[12] the Court held a father to be a shadow director of the company in which his daughter was the sole director because, at all relevant

7   See, eg, *Buzzle Operations Pty Ltd (in liq) v Apple Computer Australia Pty Ltd* (2011) 81 NSWLR 47, which contains a useful collection of the legal principles applicable to shadow directors. See also *Re Akron Roads Pty Ltd (in liq) (No 3)* (2016) 348 ALR 704.
8   *Re Tasbian (No 3)* [1992] BCC 358, 363.
9   (2011) 81 NSWLR 47, [229].
10 (2001) 19 ACLC 1117.
11 (2006) 247 FCR 205.
12 [2018] NSWSC 988, [283].

times, he acted as a director or alternatively that his daughter was accustomed to act in accordance with his instructions or wishes.[13]

It was held in the British case *Vivendi SA v Richards*[14] that shadow directors owe fiduciary duties to the company; this illustrates the huge potential for their liability towards the company.

5.2.3 Nominee directors

The term 'nominee director' is sometimes loosely used to refer to a director who has been nominated to the board by a majority shareholder or other stakeholder.[15] This practice is common in company groups in which the holding company appoints directors to the boards of its subsidiaries. Conflicts of interest may easily arise for these 'nominee directors', putting them in an unenviable position where they need to consider their duties towards the company upon whose board they serve or the shareholder (another company in the group context) that appointed them, and in groups of companies they will often be senior managers or executives of the holding company. The law is very clear. A director owes his or her duties to the company upon whose board he or she serves, not to the shareholder or stakeholder who nominated the person to be a director.[16] Thus, the director will be in breach of his or her statutory, common law and/or equitable duties if he or she does not act in good faith and in the best interests of the company upon whose board he or she serves, but instead in the best interests of the nominator or appointer. There is one exception, and that is provided for in s 187 of the Act. In terms of this section, a director of a corporation that is a wholly owned subsidiary of a body corporate is taken to act in good faith in the best interests of the subsidiary if the following three conditions apply:

(a) the constitution of the subsidiary expressly authorises the director to act in the best interests of the holding company

(b) the director acts in good faith in the best interests of the holding company

(c) the subsidiary is not insolvent at the time the director acts and does not become insolvent because of the director's act.

Apart from the obvious dilemma for the 'nominee director' as far as conflicts of interests are concerned, there are also other dangers involved for the nominator or appointer. First, the nominator or appointer could be considered to be a 'shadow director' (see discussion above), thus owing duties similar to other directors towards the company (the holding company in the group context).[17] Second, if the 'nominee directors' are controlled and manipulated by the nominator or appointer, the nominator or appointer could be held vicariously liable for the acts and conduct of the 'nominee directors'.[18]

---

13 Ibid [283].
14 [2013] EWHC 3006 (Ch).
15 See Tricker, *Corporate Governance* (2019) 105.
16 *Scottish Co-operative Wholesale Society Ltd v Meyer* [1959] AC 324, 367 (Lord Denning).
17 *Standard Chartered Bank of Australia v Antico* (1995) 38 NSWLR 290.
18 *Kuwait Asia Bank v National Mutual Life Nominees Ltd* [1991] AC 187.

5.3 Definition of 'officer'

5.3.1 Statutory definition

The provisions of the Act often extend beyond directors to any 'officer'. The aim is to ensure that other individuals in the company, not appointed as directors or acting as directors or shadow directors, are also covered by certain provisions of the Act and cannot escape liability if they are in breach of certain provisions. The High Court of Australia reviewed the statutory definition of 'officer' in *Australian Securities and Investments Commission v King*[19] (see Section 5.3.2).

Under s 9AD of the Act:

> An *officer* of a corporation is
> (a) a director or secretary of the corporation; or
> (b) a person:
>   (i)   who makes, or participates in making, decisions that affect the whole, or a substantial part, of the business of the corporation; or
>   (ii)   who has the capacity to affect significantly the corporation's financial standing; or
>   (iii) in accordance with whose instructions or wishes the directors of the corporation are accustomed to act (excluding advice given by the person in the proper performance of functions attaching to the person's professional capacity or their business relationship with the directors or the corporation); or
> (c) a receiver, or receiver and manager, of the property of the corporation; or
> (d) an administrator of the corporation; or
> (e) an administrator of a deed of company arrangement executed by the corporation; or
> (f) a restructuring practitioner for the corporation; or
> (g) a restructuring practitioner for a restructuring plan made by the corporation; or.
> (h) a liquidator of the corporation; or
> (i) a trustee or other person administering a compromise or arrangement made between the corporation and someone else.

5.3.2 Senior employees and senior executives as 'officers'

The aim with the broad statutory definition of 'officer' is also to ensure that there is no doubt that certain duties imposed by the Act apply to a group of people who will not necessarily fall under the definition of 'director'. It is a well-established principle that senior employees or senior officers of a corporation owe duties similar to those of directors towards the company. The clearest expression of this principle, recognised in most common law jurisdictions, is the case of *Canadian Aero Service Ltd v O'Malley*:[20]

> I do not think it matters whether O'Malley and Zarzycki were properly appointed as directors of Canaero or whether they did or did not act as directors. What is not

---

19   (2020) 270 CLR 1.
20   (1973) 40 DLR (3d) 371.

in doubt is that they acted respectively as president and executive vice-president of Canaero for about two years prior to their resignations. To paraphrase the findings of the trial Judge in this respect, they acted in these positions and their remuneration and responsibilities verified their status as senior officers of Canaero. They were 'top management' and not mere employees whose duty to their employer, unless enlarged by contract, consisted only in respect for trade secrets and for confidentiality of customer lists. Theirs was a larger, more exacting duty which, unless modified by statute or contract (and there is nothing of this sort here), was similar to that owed to a corporate employer by its directors.[21]

As with directors, an individual will be held to be an officer due to their conduct – making or participating in making key decisions for the company, having the capacity to affect the company's financial standing, or influencing the board in their decision-making – rather than being limited to those who hold or occupy a named office. This argument was rejected in *Australian Securities and Investments Commission v King*,[22] where the High Court held that 'the definition extends the scope of the term "officer" beyond its ordinary meaning of "officer holder".'[23]

5.3.3 Middle management as 'officers'

In the HIH Royal Commission Report, Justice Owen was struck by the role of middle management as a component of a company's governance systems. He observed that it is customary to focus upon the role of senior or executive-level management when the organs of governance are discussed. However, Justice Owen observed that 'middle management' had played a significant role in HIH and that they were involved in undesirable practices. He was frustrated by the disinclination of those individuals to accept responsibility in relation to such practices. Justice Owen suggested that the primary duties imposed upon directors and officers be made applicable to middle managers.[24]

As part of the CLERP 9 amendments to the Act in 2004 the term 'employee' was included in several of the provisions of the Act.[25] However, the legislature did not accept Justice Owen's suggestion. The question of reform in this area was referred to the Corporations and Markets Advisory Committee ('CAMAC') for consideration. In May 2005, CAMAC released a discussion paper titled *Corporate Duties Below Board Level*. In that paper, CAMAC put forward preliminary proposals to, inter alia: (1) extend the duties in s 180 (due care and diligence), and s 181 (good faith and proper purpose) to apply to 'any other person who takes part in, or is concerned, in the management of that corporation'; and (2) extend the prohibitions in ss 182 and 183 (regarding improper use of company position or information) to apply to 'any other person who performs functions, or otherwise acts, for or on behalf of that corporation'. CAMAC sought comments as to whether

---

21 Ibid 381 [22].
22 (2020) 270 CLR 1.
23 Ibid 15 [24]. See further Anil Hargovan, 'Who is a company officer? High Court analysis in ASIC v King and its implications' (2020) 72(4) *Governance Directions* 225.
24 Report of the HIH Royal Commission ('Owen Report'), *The Failure of HIH Insurance – Volume I: A Corporate Collapse and Its Lessons* (Commonwealth of Australia, 2003) 122 [6.4].
25 See the *Corporate Law Economic Reform Program (Audit Reform and Corporate Disclosure) Act 2004* (Cth) ('CLERP 9'), amending, inter alia, the following sections to include 'employees': ss 411, 418, 422, 436.

'management' should be defined and, if so, whether it should be defined along the lines of activities that 'involve policy and decision-making related to the business affairs of a corporation, to the extent that the consequences of the formation of those policies or making of those decisions may have some significant bearing on the financial standing of the corporation or the conduct of its affairs'.[26]

These proposals of CAMAC have not, so far, been taken up in the Act, but it should be noted that the duty not to use one's position to gain a personal advantage or to cause the company detriment (s 182) and the duty not to use information to gain a personal advantage or to cause the company detriment (s 183) apply to 'directors', 'officers' and 'employees'. In other words, all employees, including middle and senior management, fall under these provisions and will be liable if they are in breach of these provisions. For example, in *Central Innovation Pty Ltd v Garner (No 4)*,[27] the Court held that a former business development manager at a CAD software company had breached s 183 by improperly obtaining and misusing his former employer's information in subsequent employment with a competitor. Similarly, in *Spotlight Pty Ltd v Mehta*,[28] the Court granted an ex parte interim freezing order of the respondents' assets (which included former Spotlight distribution centre employees) for an alleged fraudulent scheme between the respondents to engage services for unauthorised payments and to sell company products and retain the profits. For the Spotlight employees, this would likely amount to an improper use of their positions for personal advantage, a breach of s 182(1).

5.4 Types of company officer

5.4.1 Executive and non-executive directors

It will be clear from the discussion above that the Act makes no distinction between 'executive' and 'non-executive'[29] directors. All 'directors' fall under the same definition and, *as a general rule*,[30] have the same duties. That this is the correct interpretation of the Act was confirmed in *Daniels v Anderson*.[31]

Although there is, as a general rule, no difference between the duties expected of 'executive' and 'non-executive' directors in the Act, the distinction between 'executive' and 'non-executive' directors is nowadays a very important one in practice.[32] This distinction has become progressively more important with the emphasis on the board's role

---

26   CAMAC, *Corporate Duties Below Board Level* (Report, April 2006).
27   *Central Innovation Pty Ltd v Garner (No 4)* [2020] FCA 1796.
28   *Spotlight Pty Ltd v Mehta* [2019] FCA 1422.
29   In the United States, the term 'outside director' is used rather than 'non-executive director'.
30   The words '*as a general rule*' are emphasised because there is a clear recognition in s 180(1) of the Act that although all directors or other officers of a corporation 'must exercise their powers and discharge their duties with the degree of care and diligence that a reasonable person would exercise', there are a number of factors that will be taken into consideration in determining whether there was a breach of a particular director's duty of care and diligence under this provision. These include the specific type of corporation (eg a small proprietary company or a large multinational, listed public company) in which the director fulfilled his or her duties, the specific position the person occupied and the specific responsibilities allocated to the person (eg an independent non-executive director or the chief financial officer or CEO, who are also board members).
31   (1995) 37 NSWLR 438.
32   *Australian Securities and Investments Commission v Rich* (2009) 75 ACSR 1, [7203].

to 'direct, govern, guide, monitor, oversee, supervise or comply', as explained in greater detail in Chapter 4. The more prominent role of 'independent non-executive directors' has further accentuated this practical distinction.[33]

Although there is no general distinction between the duties of executive and non-executive directors, for the purposes of determining a breach of a director's duty of care and diligence, the specific type of company involved and the responsibilities of the particular director will be taken into consideration by the courts. This is clear from the elements emphasised in s 180(1) of the Act.

> **180 Care and diligence – civil obligation only**
> Care and diligence – directors and other officers
> (1)   A director or other officer of a corporation must exercise their powers and discharge their duties with the degree of care and diligence that a reasonable person would exercise if they:
> > (i)   were a director or officer *of a corporation in the corporation's circumstances*; and
> > (ii) *occupied the office held by, and had the same responsibilities within the corporation as, the director or officer* [emphasis added].

5.4.2 Independent non-executive directors

It has been realised for several years that non-executive directors can play an important role on boards of larger corporations in particular, because they 'bring to bear a broader perspective, more background, a wider range of skills on a particular issue or indeed on the management of the company'.[34] Apart from any expertise they may bring to the company, non-executive directors often provide a beneficial objective/independent viewpoint and thus a crucial check on self-interest and abuse within corporate management.[35] Therefore, the idea of appointing *independent* non-executive directors to boards of listed companies has been promoted in the United Kingdom ('UK'), and in many other parts of the Commonwealth,[36] since the publication of the 1992 Cadbury Report (see Section 5.4.6).

---

33   See generally Murray Steele, 'The role of the non-executive director' in Ken Rushton (ed), *The Business Case for Corporate Governance* (Cambridge University Press, 2008) 50.
34   Evidence presented to the Senate Standing Committee on Legal and Constitutional Affairs, *Report on the Social and Fiduciary Duties and Obligations of Company Directors* (Parliament of Australia, 1989) 618. Most major Asian jurisdictions have implemented rules for appointing independent directors to their companies' boards since 2016: see Harald Baum, 'The rise of the independent director: A historical and comparative perspective' in Harald Baum, Luke R Nottage and Dan W Puchniak (eds), *Independent Directors in Asia: A Historical, Contextual and Comparative Approach* (Cambridge University Press, 2017) 21.
35   Suzanne Le Mire, 'Independent directors: Partnering expertise with independence' (2016) 16(1) *Journal of Corporate Law Studies* 1. As early as 1994 Tricker had suggested that the growing concern that inside directors tend to be self-serving explained the shift away from insider-controlled boards: see Bob Tricker, *International Corporate Governance: Text, Readings and Cases* (Prentice Hall, 1994) 15. See also Zahid Riaz, Sangeeta Ray and Pradeep Ray, 'The synergistic effect of state regulation and self-regulation on disclosure level of director and executive remuneration in Australia' (2015) 47(6) *Administration and Society* 623, 627.
36   See, eg, Pamela Hanrahan and Anil Hargovan, 'Legislating the concept of the independent company director: Recent Indian reforms seen through Australian eyes' (2020) 20(1) *Oxford University Commonwealth Law Journal* 86.

It was, however, the UK Higgs Report (2003) that recommended that at least half of the board (excluding the chair) should be 'independent non-executive directors',[37] and defined 'independence' in great detail.[38] These recommendations were accepted and incorporated[39] into the 2008 UK *Combined Code on Corporate Governance* (now called the *UK Corporate Governance Code* – see Chapter 11).

In Australia, it is now also expected that listed companies must explain why they do not have a majority of 'independent directors'.[40] It is also expected that the chair of the board be independent, and in particular he or she not be the same person as the CEO of the company.[41]

There are extensive guidelines in the Australian Securities Exchange ('ASX') *Corporate Governance Principles and Recommendations* for assessing whether a non-executive director is 'independent'.[42] The current edition (2019) of the *Principles and Recommendations* contains detailed provisions to guide companies in determining this question:[43]

> In each case, the materiality of the interest, position, or relationship needs to be assessed by the board to determine whether it might interfere, or might reasonably be seen to interfere, with the director's capacity to bring an independent judgement to bear on issues before the board and to act in the best interests of the entity as a whole, rather than in the interests of an individual security holder or any other party.

The shift towards expecting a majority of the directors of listed corporations to be 'independent non-executive directors' has gone hand in hand with a considerable expansion of the role envisaged for independent non-executive directors over recent years. Perceptions of what an 'independent director' is have also changed rapidly over recent times.[44]

In 2014, the Murray Review, an inquiry into the Australian financial system, recommended that there must be a majority of independent directors on the board of corporate trustees of public offer superannuation funds, including an independent chair.[45]

---

37 *Review of the Role and Effectiveness of Non-Executive Directors* ('Higgs Report') (January 2003) [9.5].
38 Ibid [9.11] and box following [9.13] at 37. See also Richard Smerdon, *A Practical Guide to Corporate Governance* (Sweet & Maxwell, 4th ed, 2010) 67 *et seq.*
39 Financial Reporting Council ('FRC'), *The UK Corporate Governance Code* (September 2012) 4. The new revised and updated Code applies to accounting periods beginning on or after 1 January 2019. FRC, *The UK Corporate Governance Code* (2018) <https://www.frc.org.uk/getattachment/88bd8c45-50ea-4841-95b0-d2f4f48069a2/2018-UK-Corporate-Governance-Code-FINAL.pdf>.
40 ASX, *Corporate Governance Principles and Recommendations* (4th ed, 2019) 15, Recommendation 2.4 <https://www.asx.com.au/documents/asx-compliance/cgc-principles-and-recommendations-fourth-edn.pdf>.
41 Ibid, Recommendation 2.5.
42 Ibid 13–15, Recommendation 2.3.
43 Ibid.
44 See generally Robert AG Monks and Nell Minow, *Corporate Governance* (Wiley, 5th ed, 2011) 227 *et seq.* For a comparative discussion, see Hanrahan and Hargovan, 'Legislating the concept of the independent company director: Recent Indian reforms seen through Australian eyes' (2020) 20(1) *Oxford University Commonwealth Law Journal* 86.
45 Australian Government, *Financial System Inquiry* (Final Report, November 2014) xxiii, Recommendation 13.

The Australian Government responded to this recommendation by proposing legislation that requires a minimum of one-third independent directors, including an independent chair, for superannuation trustee boards.[46] However, the Fraser Review,[47] commissioned by industry groups Industry Super Australia and the Australian Institute of Superannuation Trustees, concluded that setting a quota of independent directors would not necessarily deliver improved governance. The review found that the focus should be on appointing directors with skills, commitment and values, and recommended that a mandatory code of conduct be introduced instead.[48]

Several factors or barriers may stand in the way of non-executive directors fulfilling their role effectively:

- The appointment processes for non-executive directors are often inadequate on close personal relationships with board members, the CEO or the chairperson of the board.[49]
- Some are still too closely allied with management.
- They rely on information prepared by and received from management to fulfil their monitoring or supervisory functions.[50]
- There is no guarantee that they will challenge the CEO; they lack detailed knowledge of the company's business.
- They have limited time to spend on their directorships.[51]
- 'Independence' is a state of mind, rather than something to be determined by ticking a few boxes on a checklist.[52]
- There are various meanings attached to 'independence'.[53]
- The more 'involved and engaged' non-executive directors become, the less independent they become.[54]

---

46 Superannuation Legislation Amendment (Trustee Governance) Bill 2015 (Cth).
47 Bernie Fraser, *Board Governance of Not for Profit Superannuation Funds* (16 February 2017).
48 Sally Rose, 'Bernie Fraser Review finds no need for independents', *Investment Magazine* (16 February 2017) <https://investmentmagazine.com.au/2017/02/bernie-fraser-review-finds-no-need-for-independents/>.
49 See generally Tricker, *Corporate Governance* (2019) 103–4.
50 For some sceptical, but enlightening, views of the role of boards by young CEOs in Canada, see David Leighton and Donald H Thain, *Making Boards Work* (McGraw-Hill Ryerson, 1997) 6–7. See also Lawrence Mitchell, 'Structural holes, CEOs and the informational monopolies: The missing link in corporate governance' (2005) 70(4) *Brooklyn Law Review* 1313.
51 Bonnie Buchanan, Tom Arnold and Lance Nail, 'Beware the ides of March: The collapse of HIH Insurance' in Jonathan A Batten and Thomas A Fetherston (eds), *Social Responsibility: Corporate Governance Issues* (JAI, 2003) 199, 213; and John C Shaw, 'The Cadbury Report, two years later' in K J Hopt et al (eds), *Comparative Corporate Governance: The State of the Art and Emerging Research* (Clarendon Press, 1998) 21, 27–9.
52 See also Tricker, *Corporate Governance* (2019) 33–5, 506 where he focuses on the current role of boards and directors in terms of the scope of corporate governance and board culture and dynamics. Bernie Fraser echoed this sentiment when he argued that the values, skills and experience of board members should weigh more than the mere question of independence as such. See Fraser, *Board Governance of Not for Profit Superannuation Funds* (2017) 7.
53 See in particular Donald Clarke, 'Three concepts of the independent director' (2007) 32(1) *Delaware Journal of Corporate Law* 73.
54 Steele, 'The role of the non-executive director' in Rushton (ed), *The Business Case for Corporate Governance* (2008) 56–9.

Murray Steele summarises the challenges for non-executive directors very well:

> [A]s a result both of their responsibilities and of the rapidly changing environment in which companies operate, the NED [non-executive director] role today is complex and demanding. It requires skills, experience, integrity, and particular behaviours and personal attributes. NEDs have to deal with interesting dilemmas: they need both to challenge and support the executive directors; be both engaged and non-executive; and [be] both independent and involved.[55]

Research on the practical impact of having a majority of independent non-executives on boards is contradictory. On the one hand, Peter Fischer and Marc-Oliver Swan concluded that the approach in Australia – expecting (the 'comply or explain' or 'if not, why not' principle) a majority of independent non-executive directors – did not add to firm performance; to the contrary, they concluded:

> [I]t would appear that the ASX governance recommendation to declare significant shareholders as not independent and have 'independent' directors constitute the board majority has destroyed considerable shareholder wealth. This destruction is of no discernible benefit to other than executives and fellow board members. We estimate these losses conservatively at about AUS$69 billion over the period 2003–2011.[56]

This was confirmed by Peter Swan and David Forsberg.[57] In contrast, Kathy Fogel, Liping Ma and Randall Morck found that companies with 'powerful' independent directors have significantly higher firm valuations. They contend that powerful independent directors are better able to monitor CEOs, because they have better access to information and/or greater credibility in challenging errant top managers.[58] Despite such contrasting study results, having independent directors is still regarded as a core governance tool.[59]

There are also widely diverging views on what the actual effect of 'independence'[60] is on directors' perceptions of their role and functions. It has been argued that all directors should have an interest in the corporation through shareholdings;[61] that

---

55 Ibid 65.
56 Peter L Fischer and Marc-Oliver Swan, 'Does board independence improve firm performance? Outcome of a quasi-natural experiment' (2013) 1 <www.researchgate.net/publication/272241996_Does_Board_Independence_Improve_Firm_Performance_Outcome_of_a_Quasi-Natural_Experiment>. See also Peter L Swan and David Forsberg, 'Does board "independence" destroy corporate value?' (Conference Paper, Australasian Finance and Banking Conference 2013; Australasian Finance and Banking Conference 2014, 15 August 2014) 18.
57 Swan and Forsberg, 'Does board "independence" destroy corporate value?' (2014).
58 Kathy Fogel, Liping Ma and Randall Morck, 'Powerful independent directors' (2021) 50(4) *Financial Management* 935.
59 Baum, 'The rise of the independent director' in Baum, Nottage and Puchniak (eds), *Independent Directors in Asia* (2017) 33, 34.
60 Leighton and Thain, in *Making Boards Work* (1997) 64–5, give good reasons for their belief that 'director independence is a myth'.
61 See further Mirko Bagaric and James McConvill, 'Why all directors should be shareholders in the company: The case against "independence"' (2004) 16(2) *Bond Law Review* 40.

'the best boards consist of directors who are also substantial, as opposed to nominal, shareholders';[62] and that it 'has proven hollow at best' to expect 'outside directors with little or no equity stake in the company [to] effectively monitor and discipline the managers who selected them'.[63]

There is a definite place in the corporate governance picture for independent non-executive directors, as long as expectations of them are realistic and their role is seen as but one part of ensuring good corporate governance. In other words, the role of independent non-executive directors in the overall picture of good corporate governance should not be overemphasised.

5.4.3 The managing director, managing directors, the chief executive officer, executive directors and senior executives

In terms of s 201J[64] of the *Corporations Act 2001* (Cth), the directors of a company may appoint one *or more of themselves* to the office of managing director for such period, and on such terms (including remuneration), as the directors may think fit. Section 198C(1)[65] specifically allows the directors to confer on a managing director any of the powers that the directors may exercise, and s 198C(2) allows for revocation or variation of that conferral. In addition, s 203F(1) provides that a managing director who ceases to be a director (for example, a director who is removed as a director – which could be done under statutory provisions such as s 203D of the Act, or provisions in a company's constitution) ceases also to be a managing director, and s 203F(2) provides for the variation of the terms of his or her appointment, as distinct from his or her powers.

There is, however, no definition of 'managing director' in the Act. The term has been used, especially in the past, to indicate all those directors involved in managerial functions. Nowadays it is less common to use the term 'managing directors' or '*the* managing director' in public companies. Under the influence of the United States, it is now common to use the term 'executive directors'. It is common for public companies to appoint a chief executive officer ('CEO').[66] The CEO does not need to be appointed as director as well, but the person could also be appointed as a director. Under the ASX *Corporate Governance Principles and Recommendations* listed companies will have to explain (under the 'if not, why not' principle) if the CEO is also the chair of the board or if the chair of the board does not meet the independence definition.[67]

There is no reference to 'the managing director' or 'managing directors' in the *Principles and Recommendations*: the distinction made throughout is between 'directors', 'senior executives', 'executives' and 'employees'. The term 'senior executive' is defined differently for different types of corporations, but in essence it:

62 John L Colley Jr et al, *Corporate Governance* (McGraw-Hill, 2003) 78.
63 Michael C Jensen, as quoted by Mahmoud Ezzamel and Robert Watson, 'Executive remuneration and corporate performance' in Kevin Keasey and Mike Wright (eds), *Corporate Governance: Responsibility, Risks and Remuneration* (Wiley, 1997) 61, 70.
64 The provision is entitled in the Act '201J Appointment of managing directors *(replaceable rule – see section 135)*'.
65 The provision is entitled in the Act '198C Managing director *(replaceable rule – see section 135)*'.
66 JB Reid, *Commonsense Corporate Governance* (Australian Institute of Company Directors, 2002) 68.
67 ASX, *Corporate Governance Principles and Recommendations* (4th ed, 2019) 15, Recommendation 2.5.

- includes executive directors
- includes members or executive of the key management personnel of a corporation
- excludes non-executive directors.

The acronym 'CEO' is defined in the *Principles and Recommendations* as 'the chief executive officer ... (by whatever title called)',[68] which provides a clear indication that it will be the most senior executive and may well be the managing director of the company if the directors have appointed a person with that title.

5.4.4 Chairperson

It is striking that the Act, and many other equivalent statutes in Commonwealth countries, does not make any express reference to the roles or functions of the chair of the board, as observed by the Federal Court of Australia in *Australian Securities and Investments Commission v Mitchell (No 2)*.[69] To bridge that gap, reliance is placed upon the various replaceable rules in the Act (for example, s 248E), case law,[70] and the guidance offered in Recommendation 2.5 of the ASX *Corporate Governance Principles and Recommendations*.

Helpfully, Justice Beach in *Australian Securities and Investments Commission v Mitchell (No 2)*[71] offered insights into the power, authority and responsibility of the chair, indicating that the role goes far beyond procedural duties. He identified the role and functions of a chair as follows:[72]

- 'setting the agenda items for board meetings' (which can be done in consultation with the CEO)
- ensuring 'the board has before it sufficient information, whether presented in written or oral form, such as to be able to meaningfully consider, discuss and decide on the agenda items'
- managing 'the board to ensure that sufficient time is allowed for the discussion of complex or contentious matters'
- ensuring 'that the board members work effectively together and that their skill sets and personalities complement each other'
- ensuring there is 'workable and harmonious relations' between various parties (the executive and non-executive directors; the board and executive management; and the Chair and the CEO)

---

68   Ibid 35.
69   (2020) 382 ALR 425. See further Andrew Clarke, 'The lacuna in corporate law: The unwritten role of the chair' (2018) 33(2) *Australian Journal of Corporate Law* 125; and Anil Hargovan, 'Governance lessons from Tennis Australia: *ASIC v Mitchell (No 2)*' (2020) 72(8) *Governance Directions* 384. Mervyn King, in his book *The Corporate Citizen, Governance for All Entities* (Penguin, 2006) 39–45, devotes a chapter to the role of the chairperson. He lists some important key aspects that chairpersons should keep in mind when fulfilling their role. For another discussion of the practical importance of the chairperson, see Tricker, *Corporate Governance* (2019) 109–10, 373–78, 500.
70   See, eg, *Australian Securities and Investments Commission v Rich* (2003) 44 ACSR 1; *Australian Securities and Investments Commission v Mitchell (No 2)* (2020) 382 ALR 425.
71   (2020) 382 ALR 425.
72   Ibid [1410]–[1420].

- 'defining and ensuring that the board sets and implements the corporate culture of the organisation'
- 'defining and ensuring that the board sets and implements the appropriate corporate governance structure within the organisation'
- 'assisting to identify new directors, dealing with [their] induction ... and ensuring continuing education and development of each director'
- 'monitoring the performance of the board, board members and board committees'.

The above judicial insights affirm, from a governance perspective, that it will be foolish for a chair to view their role as being ceremonial only or to merely engage in a public relations exercise on behalf of the company.

Section 248E[73] of the Act allows the board to appoint one director to chair their meetings. This section further provides that 'the directors must elect a director present to chair a meeting, or part of it, if (i) a director has not already been elected to chair the meeting; or (ii) a previously elected chair is not available or declines to act for the meeting or part of the meeting'.

If a director is the chairperson of a meeting, he or she is still acting in his or her capacity as a director of the company. If, however, the chairperson is acting as a proxy (an agent for the member), the chairperson owes duties to the individual members who directed their proxies to him or her. Accordingly, in such circumstances a chairperson owes duties distinct from the duties owed by a director – they are not mutually exclusive – and both sets of duties must be complied with: see *Whitlam v Australian Securities and Investments Commission.*[74]

There are good reasons for the ASX *Corporate Governance Principles and Recommendations* expecting companies to explain if the chair of the board is also the CEO. First, the roles of management and the board are different and it is almost impossible for the same individual to properly fulfil the role of the most senior manager/executive of the company and the role of chairperson. Second, it is also considered to be too much of a concentration of power to combine the roles of CEO and chairperson.[75] However, it should be pointed out that whether or not the CEO is also the chairperson, it is unlikely that other executive directors serving on the board will challenge the CEO on managerial decisions taken by the CEO at board level. The reason for this is simply that such a challenge will probably result in them having to face the wrath of the CEO the next day, when they will again be the subordinates of the CEO who is their boss as far as line management is concerned. One can also imagine that executive directors will normally not like their internal differences to be displayed at board level, as that can easily get in the way of a harmonious and collegial running of the company by the senior executives. Having someone other than the CEO as chairperson of the board allows sensitive issues related to all executive matters to be discussed with the chairperson.

---

73 The provision is entitled in the Act '248E Chairing directors' meetings *(replaceable rule – see section 135)'*.
74 (2003) 57 NSWLR 559.
75 See generally Steele, 'The role of the chairman' in Rushton (ed), *The Business Case for Corporate Governance* (2008) 29.

5.4.5 Alternate director

Section 201K[76] of the Act empowers a director to appoint an alternate director to exercise some or all of the director's powers for a specific period. This power is useful when a director is unable to be present at meetings. The appointment of an alternate director must be in writing[77] and must be approved by the other directors.[78] This approval will presumably be by way of a resolution of the board. If so requested by the appointing director, the company must give the alternate director notice of directors' meetings.[79] When an alternate exercises the appointing director's powers, it is just as effective as if the powers were exercised by the appointing director.[80] Although the alternate director may be appointed to act as agent of the appointing director, the alternate is nevertheless a director in the eyes of the law, with all the rights, duties and responsibilities of a director.[81]

The appointing director may terminate the alternate's appointment at any time.[82] ASIC must be given notice of the appointment and termination of appointment of an alternate director.[83]

5.4.6 Secretary

The Cadbury Report (1992) explained in great detail the vital role the company secretary should play in ensuring that correct procedures and good corporate governance practices are followed.[84] This has been confirmed by the Hampel Report (1998).[85]

In Australia, a public company must have at least one secretary.[86] A proprietary company is no longer required to appoint a secretary, but if it does have one or more secretaries, at least one must ordinarily reside in Australia.[87] Section 188(2) of the Act serves as an encouragement for even proprietary companies to appoint a secretary, by providing that the directors of such a company will be liable if s 142, 145, 205B or 345 is contravened.

The power to appoint a company secretary rests with the board[88] and the appointee holds office on the terms and conditions (including remuneration) that the directors

76 The provision is entitled in the Act '201K Alternate directors *(replaceable rule – see section 135)*'.
77 *Corporations Act 2001* (Cth) s 201K(5).
78 Ibid s 201K(1).
79 Ibid s 201K(2).
80 Ibid s 201K(3).
81 Business Council of Australia, *Corporate Practices and Conduct* ('Bosch Report, 1993') (Information Australia, 1993) 18.
82 *Corporations Act 2001* (Cth) s 201K(4).
83 Ibid s 205B(2), (5).
84 Committee on the Financial Aspects of Corporate Governance, *The Financial Aspects of Corporate Governance* ('Cadbury Report') (Burgess Science Press, 1992) [4.25]–[4.27]. Joseph Lee points out that the need to ensure investor confidence resulted in the company secretary's role developing beyond mere administration to that of custodian of transparency and board independence. See Joseph Lee, 'From "housekeeping" to "gatekeeping": The enhanced role of the company secretary in the governance system' (1 October 2015) <http://dx.doi.org/10.2139/ssrn.2733180>. See generally Smerdon, *A Practical Guide to Corporate Governance* (2010) 93 et seq.
85 Committee on Corporate Governance ('Hampel Report'), *Final Report* (1998) [1.7] <www.econsense .de/_CSR_INFO_POOL/_CORP_GOVERNANCE/images/hampel_report.pdf>.
86 *Corporations Act 2001* (Cth) s 204A(2).
87 Ibid s 204A(1).
88 Ibid s 204D.

determine.[89] The secretary must be a natural person who is at least 18 years old, and no person disqualified from being a director may be a secretary without the approval of ASIC.[90] The secretary, or one of the secretaries, must be ordinarily a resident in Australia.[91] The company secretary may also be a director of the company. Unlike in the UK,[92] there is no requirement in Australia for the company secretary to have any relevant business experience or formal educational qualifications. It is not uncommon, however, for a company secretary to have a legal background and to also serve as the company's general counsel.[93]

5.5 Training and induction of directors

5.5.1 Training

After the collapse of the HIH Insurance company, Trevor Sykes, one of the leading commentators on corporate collapses and the impact they have on society, wrote:

> The whole [HIH] episode underlines the long-established lesson that whatever structures are devised to impose corporate honesty, they won't work unless you have the right people in them.[94]

This is almost stating the obvious as, in practical terms, the real difficulty is to find the right people and, once they have been found, to train them and then to monitor, over time, their performance: they need to be efficient, and to adhere to good corporate governance practices.

The importance of training directors was emphasised in the Cadbury Report. Training was considered to be 'highly desirable' because directors come from a range of backgrounds and their qualifications and experience vary considerably.[95] It was also emphasised that the training of directors is a very important way to ensure that directors adhere to good corporate governance practices.[96] The simple reality is that directors should be trained so that they understand and can discharge their

---

89 Ibid s 204F (replaceable rule).
90 Ibid s 204B(2).
91 Ibid s 204A(2).
92 *Companies Act 2006* (UK) s 273. This section applies to secretaries of public companies.
93 For liabilities issues arising from this dual capacity, see Anil Hargovan, 'Dual role of general counsel and company secretary: Walking the legal tightrope in *Shafron v ASIC*' (2012) 27(1) *Australian Journal of Corporate Law* 112. Ian Maurice contends that there is a move towards a separation of the roles in the top 100 companies listed on the London Stock Exchange. He acknowledges that combining the roles facilitates the presence of general counsel at board meetings and increases the focus on risk management at board level. However, the increasingly onerous responsibilities of general counsel and company secretaries and the complexity of both roles point towards diversion. See Ian Maurice, 'General counsel and company secretary: To combine or not to combine' (2011) 3 *Experts* 15. Joseph Lee discusses the question of combining the position of company secretary and general counsel. He points out that in the context of public interest disclosures there is an advantage for companies in appointing a legally qualified person to act as the company secretary. See Lee, 'From "housekeeping" to "gatekeeping"', 1 October 2015).
94 Trevor Sykes, 'Cocktail of greed, folly and incompetence', *Australian Financial Review* (14 January 2003).
95 Cadbury Report (1992) [4.19].
96 Ibid.

duties as directors.[97] Bob Garratt, however, exposed a serious problem with director training in the past: that is, that the training was based upon managerial training at a higher level, or a type of 'mini-MBA' training. He argues that 'managing' and 'directing' require completely different types of training.[98]

Kendall and Kendall emphasise the need for director training in at least the following areas:[99]

- statutory and regulatory obligations
- ethical obligations
- what constitutes good operational practice.

In his first edition (2009), Tricker provided a useful list of types of director training, including formal external training courses on aspects of the director's work; relevant higher degree courses in corporate governance, corporate strategy and other board-related topics; and one-to-one mentoring.[100] In the fourth edition (2019) of his book, Tricker added 'site visits to different company locations', which has become important because of the significance of supply chains for multinational corporations. He observes that the demands for proper director training have 'increased dramatically'[101] and that it is challenging for directors to remain up to date because of constant new expectations and changes in the law.[102]

5.5.2 Induction

It is worth mentioning that the UK Institute of Chartered Secretaries and Administrators ('ICSA') provides some useful practical guidance on what non-executive directors should consider before they join a board, as well as what first steps they should take once they have been appointed.[103] Once appointed, as part of the training process directors should be properly introduced to the company; this is especially important for independent non-executive directors, because the ways in which companies conduct their business may vary considerably or, to put it differently, 'corporate cultures' may differ hugely among corporations. The appointment of directors will normally be based upon their proven skills, experience, qualifications and past track record, but they may know nothing about the corporate culture or about the other directors and senior executives of the corporation. A good induction process for non-executive directors was considered to be of great importance by a large number of the non-executive directors surveyed two years after the Cadbury Report.[104]

---

97 Shaw, 'The Cadbury Report, two years later' in Hopt et al (eds), *Comparative Corporate Governance* (1998) 27.
98 Bob Garratt, *Thin on Top* (Nicholas Brealey Publishing, 2003) 214–15.
99 Nigel Kendall and Arthur Kendall, *Real-World Corporate Governance* (Pitman, 1998) 9.
100 Tricker, *Corporate Governance* (2009)
101 Tricker, *Corporate Governance* (2019) 434.
102 Ibid 434–5.
103 ICSA, *ICSA Guidance on Liability of Non-executive Directors: Care, Skill and Diligence* (Guidance Note 130117, January 2013).
104 Shaw, 'The Cadbury Report, Two years later' in Hopt et al (eds), *Comparative Corporate Governance* (1998) 30.

Particularly useful guidelines regarding a proper induction program formed part of the 2003 UK *Combined Code on Corporate Governance*. These guidelines were based on recommendations made by the Higgs Committee (2003).[105]

Interestingly, the 2018 *UK Corporate Governance Code* moved away from direct references to induction and training of board appointees, which had existed in the previous edition. The Code now merely states that the 'board and its committees should have a combination of skills, experience and knowledge'[106] with the provisions requiring 'formal and rigorous annual evaluation of the performance of the board, its committees, the chair and individual directors'.[107] The chair of the board is responsible for following up on the evaluations, and each director is individually tasked to 'take appropriate action when development needs have been identified'.[108]

5.6 Ethical behaviour of directors

Ethical behaviour by directors is one of the most important cornerstones of corporate governance, as it sets the tone for the ethical behaviour of the corporation and that, in turn, goes a long way to ensure that the corporation adheres to corporate governance practices.

Principle 3 of the 2019 ASX *Corporate Governance Principles and Recommendations* states that listed companies should instil a culture of acting lawfully, ethically and responsibly and that the entity's values are the guiding principles and norms that define what type of organisation it aspires to be.[109] The expectation that a corporation must have 'ethics, morals and values' became prominent with the recognition of the corporation as a person and of the 'social responsibilities of corporations'.[110] As was pointed out in Chapters 1 and 2, there is now an expectation that companies will carry out sustainability, and integrated and corporate social responsibility reporting to enable investors to, inter alia, see whether companies actually adhere to high ethical values. Ultimately it is the responsibility of the board of directors to promote ethical decision-making in the corporation.

The 2003 ASX *Principles of Good Corporate Governance and Best Practice Recommendations* was one of the first corporate governance documents to deal specifically with the

---

105 FRC, *The Combined Code on Corporate Governance* (July 2003) 75–6; *Review of the Role and Effectiveness of Non-Executive Directors* ('Higgs Report') (January 2003) 111–12. See also Smerdon, *A Practical Guide to Corporate Governance* (2010) 38–40.
106 FRC, *The UK Corporate Governance Code* (2018) 8, Principle K.
107 Ibid 9, Provision 21.
108 Ibid 9, Provision 22.
109 ASX, *Corporate Governance Principles and Recommendations* (4th ed, 2019) 16. Principle 10 of the *Not-for-profit Governance Principles* highlights the potential for culture to influence an organisation's ability to achieve its purpose and the pivotal role of the board and its directors in shaping the culture of the organisation: AICD, *Not-for-Profit Governance Principles* (2019) 96.
110 Kendall and Kendall, *Real-World Corporate Governance* (1998) 17, 139 *et seq*. See also Batten and Fetherston (eds), *Social Responsibility* (2003) 1, 5–6; Philip TN Koh, 'Responsibilities of corporate governance and control of corporate powers' in Philip TN Koh (ed), *3Rs of Corporate Governance* (Malaysian Institute of Corporate Governance, 2001) 1, 5–6; and Monks and Minow, *Corporate Governance* (2004) 17–18, 77 *et seq*.

ethical behaviour of directors. It recommended that corporations establish a code of ethical and legal conduct to guide the board and executives as to:[111]

(a) the practices necessary to maintain confidence in the company's integrity, and

(b) the responsibility and accountability of individuals for reporting and investigating reports of unethical practices.[112]

The expectation in the 2019 ASX *Corporate Governance Principles and Recommendations* is that these aspects are dealt with in the company's code of conduct.[113]

The importance of 'ethics, morals and values' was also commented on by Justice Owen in the HIH Royal Commission Report, under the heading 'The Royal Commission: A personal perspective':

> Right and wrong are moral concepts, and morality does not exist in a vacuum. I think all those who participate in the direction and management of public companies, as well as their professional advisers, need to identify and examine what they regard as the basic moral underpinning of their system of values. They must then apply those tenets in the decision-making process.[114]

The Appellate Court in *Australian Securities and Investments Commission v Ingleby*[115] was scathing about the conduct of a company officer involved in the company's 'oil for food' scandal in Iraq. The officer was held to be 'wilfully blind' to the company's corrupt practices, which were later investigated by a Royal Commission and found to be corporate bribes. The Court held:

> It is essential that those who accept the rewards of important offices also accept the responsibilities which go with them. Proper corporate and professional behaviour depends upon that acceptance, and must be supplemented by the knowledge that the courts will play their part in the maintenance of appropriate standards.[116]

'Ethics, morals and values' for corporations will become increasingly important considerations in the future. 'Ethical behaviour' adds value to the corporation:

> [A] highly ethical operation is likely to spend much less on protecting itself against fraud and will probably have to spend much less on industrial relations to maintain morale and common purpose.[117]

It is difficult to define 'business ethics': it is often closely linked to concepts such as 'business culture' and 'cultural values', as well as to perceptions about business

---

111 ASX, *Principles of Good Corporate Governance and Best Practice Recommendations* (2003) 25, Recommendation 3.1.

112 ASX, *Principles of Good Corporate Governance and Best Practice* (2007) 25.

113 ASX, *Principles of Good Corporate Governance and Best Practice Recommendations* (2003) 20; ASX, *Corporate Governance Principles and Recommendations* (4th ed, 2019) 16, Recommendation 3.2.

114 Owen Report, *The Failure of HIH Insurance* (2003) vol l, xiii.

115 (2013) 39 VR 554.

116 Ibid [95].

117 Kendall and Kendall, *Real-World Corporate Governance* (1998) 139. See also Stephen Cohen and Damien Grace, 'Ethics and the Sustainability of Business' in John D Adams et al, *Collapse Incorporated: Tales, Safeguards and Responsibilities of Corporate Australia* (CCH Australia, 2001) 99, 105–6.

in a particular country or community. Some would say that business 'is all about business', and that ethics has little place in the hard business world. Others would simply say that the ways in which people view ethics differ so much that we will never be able to find common ground on what is meant by 'ethical behaviour' – what is seen as a good and sound business deal or a clever business strategy by some would be considered 'unethical behaviour' by others. However, as Kendall and Kendall illustrate, there are certain general guidelines against which 'ethical behaviour' can be judged, and which will assist in detecting 'unethical behaviour'.[118]

The internationalisation and globalisation of business make it imperative that we strive to find common ground on what is meant by 'ethical behaviour' by corporations, and that we promote such behaviour as a core practice in good corporate governance.

5.7 Remuneration of directors and executives

5.7.1 A controversial and politically sensitive issue

The debate on excessive executive remuneration became particularly sensitive politically as a result of the GFCs, which commenced in 2007, but it is not a new topic. In 1995, the Greenbury Report in the UK was one of the first corporate governance reports to promote transparency and disclosure of executive remuneration. This was taken further in the 1998 UK Hampel Report, and Australia followed suit, reiterating the call for disclosure of executive remuneration in the Bosch and Hilmer corporate governance reports.[119] As a result, legislation was introduced to ensure disclosure in both jurisdictions.

As discussed in Chapter 2, it is not remuneration of directors and executives as such that causes resentment from the public and politicians, but 'excessive' remuneration.

The 2022 edition of the Australian Council of Superannuation Investors Report on CEO pay found that over the 10 years prior to the 2021 financial year, median fixed pay for CEOs in Australia's top companies had fallen by 0.6 per cent per annum, with the average declining by 0.8 per cent. Given the impact of the COVID-19 pandemic on the previous financial years this is perhaps unsurprising. However, as a result of the unwinding of temporary pay cuts in response to the pandemic as well as other contributing factors, CEO pay in the 2021 financial year surpassed several records in terms of fixed pay, bonuses and cash pay.[120]

5.7.2 Disclosure of remuneration and emoluments in Australia

Australia has one of the most extensive disclosure regimes in the world in relation to the remuneration of directors and key management personnel.[121] The *Corporate Law*

---

118 Kendall and Kendall, *Real-World Corporate Governance* (1998) 142.
119 For a detailed discussion of early corporate governance reports in Australia such as the Bosch and Hilmer reports, see Jean Jacques du Plessis, James McConvill and Mirko Bagaric, *Principles of Contemporary Corporate Governance* (Cambridge University Press, 2008) ch 5.
120 Australian Council of Superannuation Investors ('ACSI'), *CEO Pay in ASX 200 Companies* (Research Report, July 2022).
121 The regulatory framework for executive remuneration in Australia is explained in Kym Sheehan, 'The regulatory framework for executive remuneration in Australia' (2009) 31(2) *Sydney Law Review* 273. See also Zahid Riaz, Sangeeta Ray and Pradeep Ray, 'The synergistic effect of

Economic Reform Program (Audit Reform and Corporate Disclosure) Act 2004 (Cth) introduced s 300A into the *Corporations Act 2001* (Cth) – it requires enhanced disclosures, either in the directors' remuneration report or the financial report, both of which are audited. These disclosures include:

- the board's remuneration policy (s 300A(1)(a))
- the relationship between remuneration policy and company performance (s 300A(1)(ba))
- details of remuneration of key personnel (s 300A(1)(c))
- reasons for failing to subject to performance conditions any remuneration made via shares or options (s 300A(1)(d))
- the relative proportion of remuneration related to performance, value of options granted, and aggregate and percentage values of remuneration via options (s 300A(1)(e)).

Further major reforms to both disclosure of and accounting for share-based payments have occurred since 2004. In particular, Accounting Standard AASB 2 *Share-based Payment* requires calculation of the 'fair value' of options granted under remuneration packages and expensing of this value, along with disclosures around the method and assumptions involved in calculating the fair value. Alissa Irgang, however, provides evidence that 'disclosure' does not necessarily ensure that companies will not remunerate executives above averages in the industry. Companies may see above-average pay as making them more attractive for top and high-performing executives; this phenomenon has been described as an example of the 'Lake Wobegon effect'.[122] As will be seen in the next subsection, there have been several further developments regarding executive remuneration in Australia.

5.7.3 Some provisions of the ASX *Corporate Governance Principles and Recommendations* dealing with remuneration

It is to be expected that the ASX *Corporate Governance Principles and Recommendations*, like most voluntary corporate governance codes, would contain provisions on the remuneration of directors, executives and employees. The board of directors is ultimately responsible for 'satisfying itself that the entity's remuneration policies are aligned with the entity's purpose, values, strategic objectives and risk appetite',[123] and listed companies should have a 'formal, rigorous and transparent process for developing [their] remuneration policy and for fixing the remuneration packages of directors and senior executives'.[124] Apart from suggesting that the remuneration of executive and non-executive directors

---

state regulation and self-regulation on disclosure level of director and executive remuneration in Australia' (2015) 47(6) *Administration and Society* 623, 629 for an excellent exposition of the Australian context.

122 Alissa Irgang, 'Capping and corporate governance: An analysis of executive remuneration in Australia' (2013) 31(3) *Company and Securities Law Journal* 145, 149–51. See also 'Lake Wobegon' <http://en.wikipedia.org/wiki/Lake_Wobegon>. See further Zahid Riaz et al, 'Disclosure practices of foreign and domestic firms in Australia' (2015) 50(4) *Journal of World Business* 781, 789.

123 ASX, *Corporate Governance Principles and Recommendations* (4th ed, 2019) 6.

124 Ibid 29.

and senior executives should be agreed contractually, there are several provisions dealing specifically with the determination of remuneration and the disclosure of remuneration. The overall aim is to remunerate 'fairly and responsibly'.[125]

The ASX *Corporate Governance Principles and Recommendations* provides that all Australian listed companies must have a remuneration committee and that the remuneration committee must have at least three members, a majority of whom are independent directors; the chair should also be an independent director. The remuneration committee must disclose its charter and, for every reporting period, the number of times it met.[126] The overall aim of having a remuneration committee becomes clear when one looks at the ASX *Corporate Governance Principles and Recommendations*: it explains that the remuneration committee is usually tasked with reviewing and making recommendations to the board in relation to:

- the entity's remuneration framework for directors, including the process by which any pool of directors' fees approved by security holders is allocated to directors
- the remuneration packages to be awarded to senior executives
- equity-based remuneration plans for senior executives and other employees
- superannuation arrangements for directors, senior executives and other employees
- whether there is any gender or other inappropriate bias in remuneration for directors, senior executives or other employees.[127]

There is a strong suggestion that key performance indicators should be developed and that part of senior executives' remuneration should be linked to achieving them.[128] Recommendation 8.2 expects listed companies to disclose their policies and practices regarding the remuneration of non-executive directors and their policies and practices regarding the remuneration of executive directors and other senior executives. It is also expected that the roles and responsibilities of non-executive directors, executive directors and other senior executives are reflected in the level and composition of their remuneration.[129]

5.7.4 Further measures to counter excessive remuneration of directors and executives

In Australia, the Federal Government requested the Australian Prudential Regulation Authority ('APRA'), which regulates entities in the insurance, superannuation and authorised deposit-taking industries, to produce best practice guidelines for both the design and the disclosure of executive remuneration. On 30 November 2009, APRA released Prudential Practice Guide PPG 511 – *Remuneration*. This guide was most recently updated on 18 October 2021.[130]

---

125 Ibid 29, Principle 8.
126 Ibid 29.
127 Ibid.
128 Ibid 9.
129 Ibid 30.
130 APRA, *Prudential Practice Guide: CPG 511 Remuneration* (2021) <https://www.apra.gov.au/sites/default/files/2021-10/Final%20Prudential%20Practice%20Guide%20CPG%20511%20Remuneration.pdf>.

Briefly, the governance standards require the establishment of remuneration commit-tees and the design of remuneration policy that, in rewarding individual performance, is designed to encourage behaviour that supports the risk management framework of the regulated institution (para 43). Further, in designing remuneration arrangements, the board remuneration committee will need to consider, among other matters:

- the balance between fixed (salary) and variable (performance-based) components of remuneration. Performance-based components include all short-term and longer-term incentive remuneration, payable with or without deferral
- whether cash or equity-related payments are used and, in each case, the terms of the entitlements, including vesting and deferral arrangements (para 44).

In March 2009 the Federal Government initiated a Productivity Commission review into the regulation of director and executive remuneration in Australia. The Productivity Commission's final report[131] was released publicly in January 2010. Perhaps the most noteworthy[132] recommendation was the introduction of the 'two-strikes and spill' approach.[133] This approach entails that if 25 per cent or more of shareholders at two successive annual general meetings vote negatively on the board's pay report there should be an immediate vote on whether the entire board should face re-election. If that vote is carried by a majority of those voting at the meeting, all board positions would be up for election, one by one, at a special meeting (the spill meeting) held within three months. This approach became law on 1 July 2011 with the passing of the *Corporations Amendment (Improving Accountability on Director and Executive Remuneration) Act 2011* (Cth). These provisions are currently contained in ss 250U–250Y of the *Corporations Act 2001* (Cth).

The findings of misconduct in the banking sector by the Hayne Royal Commission (see Chapter 1) cast a long shadow at the 2018 round of annual general meetings. The adverse findings of poor governance and questionable ethical practices did not sit well with investors and Australian banks bore the brunt of investor dissatisfaction with dubi-ous performance and executive remuneration. National Australian Bank Ltd had a his-toric 88.43 per cent of shareholders vote against the remuneration report at the 2018 AGM. It is the biggest vote against a remuneration report recorded against an ASX300 company since voting was introduced in 2005.[134]

At the 2018 AGM of Westpac Ltd, shareholders voted 64.16 per cent against the remu-neration report. However, at the 2019 AGM, Westpac failed to avoid a second strike on its executive remuneration report, with 35 per cent of shareholders voting against the report. The second strike meant a motion was moved to spill the board, although a spill was avoided as Westpac managed to secure the backing of major investors (such as the Australian Council of Superannuation Investors), with 91 per cent of votes cast against

---

131 Productivity Commission, *Executive Remuneration in Australia* (2009).
132 See, eg, Allan Fels, 'Shareholders can turn up the heat on executive pay', *Sydney Morning Herald* (5 January 2010) 20.
133 See Productivity Commission, *Executive Remuneration in Australia* (2009) xxxii, 296–301.
134 James Frost, 'NAB attracts 88 per cent no vote against banker pay at AGM', *Australian Financial Review* (online, 19 December 2018) <https://www.afr.com/companies/financial-services/we-got-it-wrong-nab-chairman-ken-henry-tells-shareholders-at-agm-20181218-h198k8>.

sacking the entire board.[135] At the 2021 AGM, Westpac suffered a protest vote for the company's financial management and climate change policy, causing the chair to apologise.[136] Close to 30 per cent of the shareholders voted against the bank's pay plans.

The highest number of remunerations 'strikes' (26) across the ASX300 since the 'two-strikes rule' was introduced in 2011 occurred in 2021. Executive pay remained in close focus in 2022 against a backdrop of falling equity markets, economic and geopolitical uncertainties, and the ongoing impact of COVID-19.[137] It is, however, impossible to determine how many companies' remuneration practices for executives were adjusted or influenced by the fact that the rule exists.[138]

In December 2012, the government released an Exposure Draft of the Corporations Legislation Amendment (Remuneration Disclosures and Other Measures) Bill 2012. This legislation deals, inter alia, with some further recommendations made by CAMAC in its *Executive Remuneration Report* of April 2011.[139] The Exposure Draft proposed new requirements for the disclosure of clawbacks. The proposed reforms included requiring listed companies to disclose in the remuneration report whether any overpaid remuneration has been 'clawed back', and if not, an explanation, and requiring more transparent disclosure of termination payments or 'golden handshake' payments.[140] Since these proposals there have been several changes of government in Australia and it remains to be seen whether the current Labor Government (2023) will proceed with the proposed legislation, especially as the intended legislation was met with considerable resistance.[141] The fact that a considerable period of time has elapsed since the Exposure Draft was released (2012) is perhaps an indication that the current government is unlikely to proceed with the legislation. However, the market has already responded to it, with the ASX *Corporate Governance Principles and Recommendations* (2019) suggesting that the remuneration contract of executive directors or other senior executives specify the circumstances in which remuneration may be clawed back (for example, in the event of serious misconduct or if there was a material misstatement in the entity's financial statements).[142]

135 David Chau, 'Westpac cops second strike on pay but shareholders decline to spill "incompetent' board"', *ABC News* (12 December 2019) <https://www.abc.net.au/news/2019-12-12/westpac-chairman-agm-protest-vote/11792010>; see further Alex Co, 'Australia: Westpac: The issues, regulators and lessons to be learnt' (3 February 2020) <https://www.mondaq.com/australia/executive-remuneration/889534/westpac-the-issues-regulators-and-lessons-to-be-learnt>.
136 James Thomson, 'Westpac gets the protest vote it deserves', *Australian Financial Review* (online, 16 December 2021) <https://www.afr.com/chanticleer/westpac-gets-the-protest-vote-it-deserves-20211215-p59hwt>.
137 Morrow Sadali, 'AGM Season 2022 points to trends to watch in 2023' (21 December 2022) <https://morrowsodali.com/insights/agm-season-2022-points-to-trends-to-watch-in-2023>.
138 John Egan highlights an unintended consequence of the two-strike rule: that the board of a company, although supported by more than 85 per cent of shareholders, could be forced to stand for re-election if a significant minority of shareholders choose to vote against the remuneration report. He cites UGL Limited as an example where less than 12 per cent of shareholders pushed a negative vote of 30 per cent against its remuneration report. John Egan in Tony Featherstone, 'Two strikes round one', *Morningstar* (24 February 2017) <www.morningstar.com.au/funds/article/two-strikes/4311?q=printme>.
139 CAMAC, *Executive Remuneration Report* (April 2011).
140 See further AICD, *Company Director* (April 2013).
141 See ibid. See also Savo Kovacevic, 'Executive remuneration developments in Australia: Responses and reactions' (2012) 23(1) *Economic and Labour Relations Review* 99, 105–7.
142 ASX, *Corporate Governance Principles and Recommendations* (4th ed, 2019) 30.

There is, internationally, considerable pressure from shareholders, especially minority shareholders, to have a bigger say on directors' compensation. Under the banner 'Say on Pay', law reforms that would ensure that shareholders have some say on directors' pay were propagated internationally. In 2002 the UK adopted legislation that compels public companies to give shareholders a vote on the compensation of their top executives. This vote is not binding, but a significant vote by the shareholders against the compensation of their top executives sends a strong message to the directors. Since that time there has been a wave of such legislation enacted in countries around the world, including the US, Belgium, the Netherlands and Sweden; Switzerland, Germany and France appear to be moving rapidly in the same direction.[143] Research that examined the impact of 'Say on Pay' legislation on actual CEO and other executive compensation revealed significant changes in executive compensation policies and firm valuations following the passage of these laws.[144]

It is interesting to note that while such a non-binding vote was also adopted in Australia (previously s 250R of the *Corporations Act 2001* (Cth)),[145] Australia has now taken the lead in going one step further with the 'two-strikes and spill' approach. It is reasonably clear that this approach will capture the imagination of many shareholders in many other countries, and it is to be expected that shareholder lobby groups will put pressure on the legislatures of other countries to adopt comparable provisions with actual – not only non-binding – consequences for directors if the shareholders are not satisfied with directors' and executives' compensation.[146] In the UK there is already a move towards a binding 'Say on Pay' vote.[147]

The more litigious climate of the US may provide a different solution in that jurisdiction, where the Dodd-Frank Wall Street Reform introduced 'Say on Pay' provisions into the *Consumer Protection Act* in 2010. In July 2023, the directors of Tesla Inc returned US$725 million to the company to settle claims of gross overpayment brought by a pension fund,

---

143 Randall S Thomas and Christoph Van der Elst, 'The International Scope of Say on Pay' (Law Working Paper No 227, European Corporate Governance Institute, September 2013). See also Marinilka Barros Kimbro and Danielle Xu, 'Shareholders have a say on executive compensation: evidence from say-on-pay in the United States' (2016) 35(1) *Journal of Accounting and Public Policy* 19.

144 Ricardo Correa and Ugur Lel, 'Say on Pay Laws, Executive Compensation, CEO Pay Slice, and Firm Value around the World' (International Finance Discussion Paper No 1084, Governors of the Federal Reserve System, July 2013) <www.federalreserve.gov/pubs/ifdp/2013/1084/ifdp1084.pdf>.

145 For some background on the initial 'Say on Pay' provision in Australia see Larelle Chapple and Blake Christensen, 'The non-binding vote on executive pay: A review of the CLERP 9 reform' (2005) 18(3) *Australian Journal of Corporate Law* 263; and Thomas and Van der Elst, *The International Scope of Say on Pay* (2013) 18–20.

146 For a more comprehensive explanation of the approach in Australia, see Thomas and Van der Elst, *The International Scope of Say on Pay* (2013) 20–3. Recent research on the impact on corporate accountability of Australia's unique 'two strikes' rule found that it has been effective in reining in abnormally high CEO pay. It curbs excessive CEO pay, reduces the growth rate of pay and changes the pay mix. It also found that negative 'Say on Pay' votes are associated with negative market reaction, a lower share price, long-run underperformance and an increase in CEO turnover. However, directors do not appear to suffer reputational costs, as evidenced by the loss of outside directorships. Martin Bugeja et al, 'Life after a Shareholder Pay "Strike": Consequences for ASX-Listed Firms' (Working Paper No 130, Centre for International Finance and Regulation, 28 November 2016).

147 Thomas and Van der Elst, *The International Scope of Say on Pay* (2013) 17–18, 66.

the Police and Fire Retirement System of the City of Detroit.[148] The directors were accused of unfair and excessive remuneration from 2017 to 2020, having issued themselves approximately 11 million Tesla stock options. The equivalent value returned represents approximately 3.1 million Tesla stock options. In addition to returning the equivalent value, the directors also agreed not to receive compensation for 2021, 2022 and 2023.[149]

5.8 Board diversity[150]

5.8.1 Another controversial and politically sensitive issue

Board diversity has been a hot topic for several years. However, it is only in recent years that pertinent questions have been asked about what is meant by the term 'board diversity' and what would constitute ideal diversity. In the past the debate on board diversity has always been dominated by questions about the very low numbers of women on boards. This has been a fact in most countries with sophisticated corporate law and corporate governance systems. The issue of the percentage of women on boards still dominates the board diversity debate, but other forms of diversity, including age, cultural, nationality and race, have also become part of the debate.[151] The Governance Institute of Australia, in conjunction with Watermark Search International, published the Board Diversity Index 2022, which represents a comprehensive investigation of the diversity in the ASX300. This eighth iteration of reporting on diversity identified a stagnation of cultural diversity on Australian boards, and called for 'powerful advocacy and accelerated change [as] urgently required for cultural diversity'.[152]

'Stagnation' was reflected by data across several areas:

- Race: 90 per cent of directors come from Anglo-Celtic backgrounds, a figure which has not shifted from the 2021 Index. When combined, Anglo-Celtic and European backgrounds made up 93 per cent of board members in both the ASX100 and the ASX300.
- Age: directors aged over 70 years have increased from 16 per cent to 22 per cent.

148 This claim and settlement does not include the US$56 billion compensation package of Elon Musk, which is subject to a separate lawsuit which went to trial in 2022: Reuters, 'Tesla directors pay $735 million to settle lawsuit over excess compensation' (17 July 2023) <https://www.cnbc.com/2023/07/17/tesla-directors-settle-lawsuit-over-compensation-for-735-million.html>.
149 Ibid. See also Rebecca Bellan, 'Tesla directors pay $735m to settle claims they overpaid themselves', *TechCrunch* (18 July 2023) <https://techcrunch.com/2023/07/17/tesla-directors-pay-735m-to-settle-claims-they-overpaid-themselves/>.
150 This section is partly based on Jean J du Plessis, Ingo Saenger and Richard Foster, 'Board diversity or gender diversity? Perspectives from Europe, Australia and South Africa' (2012) 17(2) *Deakin Law Review* 207; and Jean du Plessis, James O'Sullivan and Ruth Rentschler, 'Multiple layers of gender diversity on corporate boards: To force or not to force diversity' (2014) 19(1) *Deakin Law Review* 1.
151 See Global Network of Director Institutes ('GNDI'), *Board Diversity: GNDI Perspectives* (February 2013) <www.gndi.org/papers>; FRC, *Developments in Corporate Governance 2013* (December 2012) 11–12. Michael Adams points out that diversity based on race and cultural heritage (expressed as 'ethnicity'), education, professional background and age are critical factors in a board's composition. See Michael Adams, 'Board diversity: More than a gender issue? (2015) 20(1) *Deakin Law Review* 123, 124.
152 Governance Institute of Australia and Watermark Search International, *2022 Board Diversity Index* (May 2022) <https://www.watermarksearch.com.au/2022-board-diversity-index>.

- Diversity of board holdings: 19 per cent of women directors hold 48 per cent of women-occupied seats on boards, slipping back from 29 per cent of women directors holding 51 per cent of women-occupied seats in the 2021 Index.
- Educational focus: 80 per cent of all directors held an undergraduate degree, which is no change from the 2021 Index, and 20 per cent of directors held an MBA. Women directors were more likely than men to hold a Phd, an MBA or other Masters qualification.

There were improvements in other areas. The number of boards with no women decreased from 30.2 per cent to 22.3 per cent. Tenure for women remains significantly shorter than for men, but is extending – for the first time, the 2022 Index reported women chairs and directors in the 15 years-plus tenure category. There was also a slight increase in independent director appointments across the ASX300, with approximately only 20.1 per cent of directors regarded as non-independent. Relatedly, there are significantly fewer non-independent women directors, which the Index suggests may be the result of the lack of women in c-suites who can be internally appointed, and consequently lack independence.

5.8.2 Gender diversity and quota legislation

There is ample evidence all over the world that in the past, women were under-represented on boards, and there is not a single country in the world without quota legislation where this is still not the case.[153] In countries such as Norway, Spain, Switzerland, France, Israel and the Netherlands,[154] where mandatory quotas for females on boards are set through legislation, the percentages have changed in recent times and there will surely be further improvements in the gender balance on boards. Organisation for Economic Co-operation and Development ('OECD') data confirms that there is not a single country in the world where women form more than 50 per cent of the boards of listed companies. Australian representation by women still lags behind: in 2022, Bloomberg reported that the percentage of directorships of companies listed on the S&P/ASX200 occupied by women in Australia had reached 35 per cent[155], far behind the 2021 numbers attained by the world leaders of Iceland (nearing parity at 47.1 per cent), France (45.3 per cent) and New Zealand (43.5 per cent).[156] In most countries, especially Western countries, where there are no mandatory quotas, there are serious attempts through voluntary

---

153 See Deloitte, *Women in the Boardroom: A Global Perspective* (November 2011); and Jennifer Whelan and Robert Wood, *Targets and Quotas for Women in Leadership: A Global Review of Policy, Practice, and Psychological Research* (Gender Equality Project, Centre for Ethical Leadership, Melbourne Business School, University of Melbourne, May 2012) 5, 6. See generally Boris Groysberg, *2011 Board of Directors Survey* (2011) 3–4.

154 Jo Armstrong and Sylvia Walby, *Gender Quotas in Management Boards* (Directorate-General for Internal Policies, European Parliament, 2012) 4. See Du Plessis, O'Sullivan and Rentschler, 'Multiple layers of gender diversity on corporate boards' (2014) 19(1) *Deakin Law Review* 1 for a short discussion of the legislation in these companies.

155 Andreea Papuc, 'Women now hold 35% of board seats at Australia's biggest companies', *Bloomberg* (27 June 2022) <https://www.bloomberg.com/news/articles/2022-06-27/women-reach-35-of-board-seats-at-australia-s-biggest-companies#xj4y7vzkg>.

156 OECD.Stat, 'Employment: Female share of seats on boards of the largest publicly listed companies' <https://stats.oecd.org/index.aspx?queryid=54753>. These figures are confirmed by research conducted by the AICD: AICD, 'Board diversity statistics' (30 November 2021) <https://www.aicd.com.au/about-aicd/governance-and-policy-leadership/board-diversity/Board-diversity-statistics.html>.

codes of good governance to increase female representation on company boards. It has been shown in Australia, in several European companies and in South Africa that the process of appointing more women as employees, executives and directors is taken seriously.[157] Also, there is considerable investor pressure on companies – especially listed companies – to appoint more women to their boards.[158] There is, indeed, solid research showing that if a country stops short of setting mandatory gender quotas, there should at least be very specific targets set by work units within companies, particularly at top executive levels, to achieve gender equality.[159]

Ensuring qualitative as well as quantitative gender equality at board level requires that the number of women and the remuneration of women on boards must be addressed. Women in the EU continue to earn less per hour than men, although this has dropped from 16.3 per cent in 2013 to 13 per cent in 2020.[160] The World Economic Forum suggested alarmingly: 'In 2022, the global gender gap has been closed by 68.1 per cent. At the current rate of progress, it will take 132 years to reach full parity.'[161]

The reasons for the under-representation of women on boards are somewhat perplexing.[162] In essence, there are those who argue that senior executive positions and board positions were (and still are) filled by men who are the gatekeepers, and who make it almost impossible for more women to be appointed to those positions. There is then a vicious circle: because women are not given the opportunity to fill the positions, the pool of competent and experienced women remains small, providing another excuse for not appointing more women to these positions. There are many who argue that this cycle should be broken, and some argue strongly that it can only be broken through mandatory gender quota legislation. Others argue that a 'one size fits all' approach is not desirable and that board diversity and gender diversity on boards will be achieved through voluntary codes of corporate governance.

5.8.3 Quota legislation

The first corporate board gender quota law in the world was introduced by Norway (not an EU member) through amendments to the *Norwegian Public Limited Liability Companies Act*.[163] In February 2012 it remained 'the only example of fully implemented

---

157 Du Plessis, Saenger and Foster, 'Board diversity or gender diversity?' (2012) 17(2) *Deakin Law Review* 207.
158 Yi Wang and Bob Clift, 'Is there a "business case" for board diversity?' (2009) 21(2) *Pacific Accounting Review* 88, 89; Nicole Sandford, 'Board diversity: Are we on the eve of real change?' (2011) 35(4) *Directors & Boards* 70.
159 Whelan and Wood, *Targets and Quotas for Women in Leadership* (2012) 5, 24–7.
160 Eurostat, 'Gender pay gap in unadjusted form' in European Women on Boards, *Gender Diversity on European Boards, Realizing Europe's Potential: Progress and Challenges* (April 2016) 47; European Commission, 'The gender pay gap situation in the EU' <https://commission.europa.eu/strategy-and-policy/policies-list-page/justice-and-fundamental-rights/gender-equality/equal-pay/gender-pay-gap-situation-eu_en>.
161 World Economic Forum, *Global Gender Gap Report 2022* (Insight Report, July 2022) <https://www3.weforum.org/docs/WEF_GGGR_2022.pdf>.
162 See Du Plessis, Saenger and Foster, 'Board diversity or gender diversity?' (2012) 17(2) *Deakin Law Review* 207, 240–2.
163 Aagoth Storvik and Mari Teigen, 'Women on board: The Norwegian experience' (June 2010) *Friedrich Ebert Stiftung* 3 <http://library.fes.de/pdf-files/id/ipa/07309.pdf>, cited in Armstrong and Walby, *Gender Quotas in Management Boards* (2012) 4, 6.

legislation (in the sense that the date for meeting the target has passed)'.[164] Norway's model was successful due to the strictness of the sanctions supporting it: the ultimate sanction for a company not achieving the mandatory gender quotas is the dissolution or deregistering of the company.[165]

Australia's 2020–21 Gender Equality Scorecard revealed that women make up half of the nation's workforce but earn only 77.2 per cent of men's average full-time income, a figure nearly identical to the 2015–16 value of 66.9 per cent.[166] Despite this, there is currently no indication from the Australian Government that it will consider gender quota legislation in the near future.[167]

5.8.4 Impact of women in the corporate world

What the actual effect of more women sitting on company boards will be from a business point of view is impossible to predict, but most studies show that gender-diverse corporate boards enhance corporate governance.[168] The fact that women will have a bigger say in the corporate world in future is beyond dispute even though the pace at which change is happening is still very slow.[169] The problem of under-representation of women on boards can be addressed through mandatory gender quota legislation,[170] through targets and through requirements for more women on boards in voluntary codes of corporate governance. Although the 'business case' for having more women on boards is probably still inconclusive, a number of studies have found significant correlations between the presence of women on corporate boards and strong corporate performance.[171] A meta-analysis of the relationship between women on boards and firm financial performance by Corinne Post and Kris Byron found that board diversity is 'neither wholly detrimental nor wholly beneficial to firm financial performance'. Their findings suggest that deriving optimal benefit from having more females on boards requires a better understanding of the particular firm and industry, and of the sociocultural context in which the board gender diversification occurs.[172]

---

164 Armstrong and Walby, *Gender Quotas in Management Boards* (2012) 4, 6.

165 Ibid 4; Deloitte, *Board Effectiveness Corporate Australia: Bridging the Gender Divide* (2010) 3, 21.

166 Workplace Gender Equality Agency, *Australia's Gender Equality Scorecard* (December 2022) 14–15.

167 Peta Spender contends that the time is ripe for Australia to legislate for mandatory gender quotas for corporate boards. See Peta Spender, 'Gender quotas on boards – is it time for Australia to lean in?' (2015) 20(1) *Deakin Law Review* 95.

168 See Mary Jane Lenard et al, 'Female business leaders and the incidence of fraud litigation' (2017) 43(1) *Managerial Finance* 59, 72; Meggin Thwing Eastman, Damion Rallis and Gaia Mazzucchelli, *The Tipping Point: Women on Boards and Financial Performance* (Women on Boards Report, December 2016) 6; and Linda Peach, 'We need women on boards for many reasons: Ethics isn't one', *The Conversation* (online, 20 February 2015) <http://theconversation.com/we-need-women-on-boards-for-many-reasons-ethics-isnt-one-37472>.

169 See Fei He, 'Gender quota on boards in Germany' (2016) 10 *Journal of International Scientific Publications* 77.

170 Kate Stary, 'Gender Diversity Quotas on Australian Boards: Is It in the Best Interests of the Company?' (Corporate Governance and Directors' Duties Paper 2, Law School, University of Melbourne, 2015).

171 See Thwing Eastman, Rallis and Mazzucchelli, *The Tipping Point* (December 2016).

172 See Corinne Post and Kris Byron, 'Women on boards and firm financial performance: A meta-analysis' (2015) 58(5) *Academy of Management Journal* 1546, 1563.

In 2020, the Bankwest Curtin Economics Centre together with the Australian Government's Workplace Gender Equality Agency found that:

- an increase of 10 percentage points or more in female representation on the boards of Australian ASX-listed companies leads to a 4.9 per cent increase in company market value
- an increase of 10 percentage points or more in the share of female key management personnel leads to a 6.6 per cent increase in the market value of Australian ASX-listed companies
- the appointment of a female CEO leads to a 5.0 per cent increase in the market value of Australian ASX-listed companies.[173]

Longitudinal studies will be required to see whether these increases remain across future years for the companies, or whether they are a short-term bump. Even for those focused solely on the market implications for companies of gender equality in the board room, this is a promising sign.

5.9 Conclusion

There is no doubt that there are much higher community expectations of company directors and company officers now than there were in the past. These higher expectations do not apply only to the exercise of directors' and other officers' general duties, but also to the ethics of their behaviour – company directors' and company officers' conduct is under constant scrutiny, not only by the media and the general public, but also by the regulators. As a corollary, there is constant pressure on politicians to ensure that the law is able to enforce these higher community expectations of company directors and company officers.

In this chapter we have seen that there are various types of company directors and officers, although the basic position is that the law will expect the same duties of all directors and that senior employees and senior executives owe duties to the company comparable to those of directors. The discussion in this chapter has also revealed that the practical distinction between, and expectations of, the various types of directors (for example, independent non-executive directors, executive directors, and senior or lead independent directors) are becoming increasingly important. Also, the roles, functions and expectations of CEOs and chairpersons have become more easily identifiable over time. This is the case not only because various corporate governance reports have begun to accentuate the various responsibilities associated with these positions, but also because the corporate regulator has started to focus on the higher responsibilities associated with, and higher standards expected of, persons occupying certain key positions in large public corporations.[174]

---

173 R Cassells and A Duncan, *Gender Equity Insights 2020: Delivering the Business Outcomes* (BCEC|WGEA Gender Equity Series, Issue No 5, March 2020).
174 See, eg, *Australian Securities and Investments Commission v Sino Australia Oil and Gas Ltd (in liq)* (2016) 115 ACSR 437; *Australian Securities and Investments Commission v Flugge and Geary* (2016) 342 ALR 1; *Australian Securities and Investments Commission v Vocation Ltd (in liq)* (2019) 371 ALR 155; *Australian Securities and Investments Commission v Mitchell (No 2)* (2020) 382 ALR 425; and *Australian Securities and Investments Commission v King* (2020) 270 CLR 1.

Several themes and issues of emerging importance have also been identified in this chapter. They include the training and induction of directors; the ethical behaviour of directors; the remuneration of directors and executives; and board diversity, in particular measures aimed at achieving gender balance. In the second edition of this book (2011) we identified some of these issues and predicted that they would become of increasing importance. That prediction was correct, and we would once again suggest that they will stay core areas of focus in the process of developing principles of contemporary corporate governance.

CORPORATE GOVERNANCE IN AUSTRALIA

REGULATION OF CORPORATE GOVERNANCE AND ROLE OF REGULATORS

6

6.1 Introduction

It will be clear from Chapter 4 that we consider regulation of corporate governance to be prominent in a good corporate governance model. This chapter builds upon that model by focusing on the regulation of corporate governance in particular. It deals specifically with the various mechanisms, legislative and non-legislative, which regulate the corporation and which set in place, collectively, a framework by which good governance can be achieved. Overall, this collective body of mechanisms forms part of what has recently been described as an emerging 'law of corporate governance'.

The regulation of corporate governance in Australia is achieved through binding and non-binding rules, international recommendations and industry-specific standards, the commentaries of scholars and practitioners, and the decisions of judges. The legislature acts to facilitate the achievement of good corporate governance directly by refining corporate law, and indirectly through the entire panoply of rules and regulations which have an impact on the corporation and its activities. There are other agencies that also assume a role in the regulation of corporate governance.

Section 6.2 explores the common and unifying aims and objectives of regulation, with reference in particular to the *G20/OECD Principles of Corporate Governance* (2015),[1] and similar statements made when corporate governance reforms were introduced in Australia: namely, the Australian Securities Exchange's ('ASX') *Corporate Governance Principles and Recommendations*.[2] Section 6.3 explains the mechanisms (or 'sources'), both traditional and more recent, which regulate corporate governance

---

1   Organisation for Economic Cooperation and Development ('OECD'), *G20/OECD Principles of Corporate Governance* (2015) <https://www.oecd.org/publications/g20-oecd-principles-of-corporate-governance-2015-9789264236882-en.htm>. A revised version was released in 2023: see Chapter 12.

2   ASX, *Corporate Governance Principles and Recommendations* (4th ed, 2019) <https://www.asx.com.au/documents/asx-compliance/cgc-principles-and-recommendations-fourth-edn.pdf>. The first edition was called *Principles of Good Corporate Governance and Best Practice Recommendations* and was published in March 2003. The second edition was published in 2007, and there were some important amendments made to this edition in 2010. The name was changed in 2007: since then the document has been called *Corporate Governance Principles and Recommendations*.

in Australia. These mechanisms are categorised as being examples of 'hard law', 'hybrids' or 'soft law'.[3]

Section 6.4 explains the role and powers of ASIC and presents research data on law enforcement patterns. Section 6.5 focuses on the ASX and the development and content of the ASX *Corporate Governance Principles and Recommendations*. Sections 6.6 and 6.7 offers a critical analysis of the Australian Securities and Investments Commission's ('ASIC') performance as a corporate regulator and Section 6.8 concludes with a broad philosophical question on corporate regulation and enforcement.

6.2 Objectives in regulating corporate governance

The impetus for corporate governance regulatory reform, both domestically and internationally (examples include the *Sarbanes-Oxley* and *Dodd-Frank Acts*[4] in the United States ['US'] and CLERP 9[5] in Australia), has been a series of corporate collapses and the perceived need to restore confidence in the market. As a result, financial objectives appear to be the driving factor for most contemporary corporate governance regulation. Most, if not all, contemporary corporate governance reports, guidelines, commentaries and legislative packages strongly emphasise the link between sound corporate governance practices and success within the corporation and throughout the economy. For example, the *G20/OECD Principles of Corporate Governance* states that:

> The Principles are developed with an understanding that corporate governance policies have an important role to play in achieving broader economic objectives with respect to investor confidence, capital formation and allocation. The quality of corporate governance affects the cost for corporations to access capital for growth and the confidence with which those that provide capital – directly or indirectly – can participate and share in their value-creation on fair and equitable terms. Together, the body of corporate governance rules and practices therefore provides a framework that helps to bridge the gap between household savings and investment in the real economy. As a consequence, good corporate governance will reassure shareholders and other stakeholders that their rights are protected and make it possible for corporations to decrease the cost of capital and to facilitate their access to the capital market.[6]

At the domestic level, in Australia, important sources of corporate governance reform – the CLERP 9 amendments to the *Corporations Act 2001* (Cth) ('the Act'), the ASX *Corporate*

---

3   For a discussion on the strengths and weakness of soft law, see Dimity Kingsford Smith, 'Governing the corporation: The role of "soft regulation"' (2012) 35 *UNSW Law Journal* 378; and Layan Charara, 'Introduction to Symposium on the Role of "Soft Law" in International Insolvency and Commercial Law' (2019) 40 *Michigan Journal of International Law* 411 <https://repository.law.umich.edu/mjil/vol40/iss3/2>.
4   See Chapter 11.
5   See Chapter 7.
6   *G20/OECD Principles of Corporate Governance* (2015) 10.

Governance Principles and Recommendations, and the Financial Services Council's Guidance Notes for the financial services industry[7] – all emphasise the financial objectives underlying contemporary regulation of corporate governance.

6.3 Sources of regulation in Australia

The key definitions of 'regulation'[8] highlight some of the main sources of regulation. We now apply this background discussion to the specific context of corporate governance in Australia, and provide an account of the mechanisms, both traditional and more recent, which regulate corporate governance in Australia.

John Farrar has engaged in the very useful task of categorising the various sources of corporate governance regulation in Australia into 'hard law', 'hybrids' and 'soft law'.[9] Although Farrar does not provide a working definition of any of these categories, it could be said that 'hard law' means 'traditional black-letter law'; 'soft law' includes voluntary sources of corporate governance standards that companies have the freedom to adopt or not; and 'hybrids' fall somewhere between the two, being neither mandatory nor purely voluntary. Below we identify the main sources of corporate governance regulation under the category headings provided by Farrar. We also detail our perspective on each of these sources and add to Farrar's analysis our own viewpoint on corporate governance regulation.

6.3.1 'Hard law'

6.3.1.1 Statutory regulation – corporate law

Australia's primary companies legislation, the *Corporations Act 2001* (Cth), contains a number of provisions that influence, both directly and indirectly, all aspects of a company's governance arrangements. The provisions range from directors' duties and liabilities[10] and shareholder rights and remedies[11] (which influence the relationship between directors, management and shareholders) to the financial reporting provisions under Chapter 2M[12] (which are intended to ensure that the financial aspects of a company's governance practices are characterised by transparency and accountability) and to the provisions under Chapter 2G governing company meetings (both directors' meetings and meetings of members). Many of these provisions are mandatory, with sanctions imposed for non-compliance.

---

7   See Financial Services Council ('FSC'), 'FSC Guidance Notes' <https://www.fsc.org.au/resources/fsc-standards-and-guidance-notes/guidance-notes>.

8   See Helen Bird et al, *ASIC Enforcement Patterns* (Public Law Research Paper No 71, University of Melbourne, 27 April 2004) <https://ssrn.com/abstract=530383>. For recent research on this topic, see Jasper Hedges et al, 'The policy and practice of enforcement of directors' duties by statutory agencies in Australia: An empirical analysis' (2017) 40(3) *Melbourne University Law Review* 905.

9   John H Farrar, 'Corporate governance and the judges' (2003) 15(1) *Bond Law Review* 65.

10   For a discussion, see Anil Hargovan, Michael Adams and Catherine Brown, *Australian Corporate Law* (LexisNexis, 8th ed, 2023) chs 15–18.

11   Ibid ch 19.

12   Ibid ch 21.

While there are many important corporate governance 'mandates' under the Act, this does not mean that all the corporate governance rules that stem from the Act are prescriptive in nature. Indeed, the opposite is the case. The Act provides companies with a great deal of say on the internal arrangements and management of their company. Most of the rules governing a company's internal arrangements and management may be contained in the company's constitution (if the company has one); this is specifically drafted by each company to meet its particular needs and may contain whatever rules the company desires (subject to a special majority of the company's shareholders approving the changes). Instead of a constitution, a company's internal management may be governed by a set of 'replaceable rules'. These are contained in s 141 of the Act – they are rules that the company may abide by or 'opt out of' by adopting alternative arrangements in its constitution. A company may use a combination of a constitution and replaceable rules.

Most companies, and all listed companies on the ASX, have a constitution. The main reason, in practice, for adopting a constitution is to displace one or more of the 'replaceable rules' under the Act that would otherwise apply to the company. This is implied in s 135(2) of the Act – replaceable rules are so named because they can be modified or displaced by adopting a constitution with alternative procedures.

The replaceable rules regime was introduced in 1998. The key objective of this move was to provide a simplified procedure for setting up and running a company. It is explained in the Explanatory Memorandum to the Company Law Reform Bill 1997:

> The concept of memorandum of association will be abolished (the memorandum of existing companies will be treated as part of their constitution). Also, the adoption of a constitution will be optional. The basic rules that are available to the internal management of companies (Table A of the Law) will be updated and moved into the main body of the Law as replaceable rules. Companies will be able to adopt a constitution displaying some or all of these rules. These reforms will reduce the cost of registering a company for the approximately 80,000 new companies that are registered each year.[13]

Under the ASX *Listing Rules*, publicly listed companies are required to have their own constitution. However, for smaller proprietary companies where there are only a few shareholders with no specific reason to adopt complex internal governance arrangements, the replaceable rules will cover all internal governance needs. The advantage is that the replaceable rules might be amended by the legislature to address shortcomings or to keep up with new developments, and these new replaceable rules will then apply to the company without its needing to amend the constitution by way of a special resolution.

6.3.1.2 Statutory regulation – other than corporate law

As explained in Chapter 4 the manner in which the internal arrangements and management of companies is achieved, and the relationship between the company and

---

13   Explanatory Memorandum, Company Law Reform Bill 1997, [10].

its various stakeholders, are also influenced by legal rules operating outside of company law. These rules derive from areas of law such as superannuation, industrial relations, tax, environmental law, and banking and finance law.

6.3.1.3 'Corporate governance and the judges' – the place of judge-made law

In Australia, 'company law' (including the rules of corporate governance) as a collective body of rules has traditionally been statute-based, unlike in the United Kingdom, where much of company law – including directors' duties and shareholder rights – has principally been governed by common law and equitable principles (although this has progressively changed as a result of modern company law reform). Within this statute-based regulatory framework, as the above statement suggests, judges have an important role in developing and applying the principles of the law as interpreters (particularly when provisions are vaguely expressed or overly complex).[14] Thus, while the common perception is that regulation of corporate governance comes in the form of black-letter rules – legislative or quasi-mandatory codes and principles – it is important to understand that judges continue to play a significant role.[15]

Probably the best account of this important role in Australia comes from Farrar. He states:

> If we turn to corporate governance consisting of statutory rules and case law rules and principles, [they have] traditionally been regarded as justiciable [that is, capable of being determined by a court acting judicially]. Indeed, it was left to the courts to fill in the substantial gaps left by the legislation in terms of directors' fiduciary and other duties, and shareholder remedies ... Court proceedings of any sort are expensive and occasion delay. ASIC prefers to avoid them if possible for these reasons and uses its administrative powers wherever possible and is seeking to impose its own penalties ... This needs to be considered, as does the question whether the courts have a role in respect of self-regulation.[16]

Farrar also discusses high-profile cases in Australia (for example, relating to the HIH and One.Tel collapses) to highlight the importance of the continuing role of the courts in corporate governance where self-regulation fails. He gives the following explanation:

> What these situations demonstrate is that self-regulation sometimes fails and there is no alternative to court involvement. Self-regulation lacks an effective

---

14 See, eg, the long-awaited development of the legal principle on the nature of a director's duty to consider creditor interests seen in *BTI 2014 LLC v Sequana SA* (2022) 3 WLR 709. There are, however, still unresolved issues surrounding the trigger for such a duty.

15 Paul L Davies, *Gower and Davies' Principles of Modern Company Law* (Sweet & Maxwell, 2008) 61. See also Angus Corbett and Stephen Bottomley, 'Regulating corporate governance' in Christine Parker et al (eds), *Regulating Law* (Oxford University Press, 2004) 60.

16 John Farrar, *Corporate Governance: Theories, Principles and Practice* (Oxford University Press, 2008).

system of sanctions, which can only be provided by the courts. In the case of HIH, retribution has been swift. There was not time and perhaps inclination for minority shareholders to seek redress. ASIC took prompt action.[17]

6.3.2 'Hybrids'

'Hybrid' mechanisms of corporate governance regulation have been described in the literature from a broader theoretical context as constituting a strategy of 'enforced self-regulation'. According to Ayres and Braithwaite in *Responsive Regulation*,[18] enforced self-regulation occurs where the law delegates to private-sector bodies (such as self-regulatory organisations, which loosely describes the ASX) the task of formulating substantive rules, to which certain legal sanctions are then attached.

6.3.2.1 ASX *Listing Rules*

The ASX provides a market for trading in securities. The ASX engages in market surveillance in relation to securities issued by entities that are accepted onto the official list of the ASX ('listed entities'). One way that the ASX does this is through setting the standards of behaviour for listed entities; these are contained in ASX *Listing Rules*.

Compliance with the *Listing Rules* is a requirement for admission to the official list. Non-compliance is a ground for removal from the official list. The corporate governance rules in the *Listing Rules* typically require a listed entity to disclose to the market and/or shareholders certain information, or to obtain shareholder approval for a particular transaction or arrangement. Some of the corporate governance–related *Listing Rules* include:

- LR 3.1 (dealing with continuous disclosure of information upon discovering the information's 'materiality')
- LR 10.1 (requiring shareholder approval for, among other things, certain related party transactions)
- LR 11.1 (requiring provision of details to the ASX if an entity proposes to make a significant change, either directly or indirectly, to the nature and scale of its activities).

6.3.2.2 ASX *Corporate Governance Principles and Recommendations*

Farrar includes the ASX *Corporate Governance Principles and Recommendations* under the category of 'soft law'.[19] The rationale for this is that they differ from the *Listing Rules* in that they are not strictly mandatory rules backed up by statutory force; rather, the ASX *Corporate Governance Principles and Recommendations* operate under a 'comply or explain' ('if not, why not') regime: ASX-listed companies must either comply with each of the recommendations or, if they do not comply, clearly explain why they do not comply. This must be done in their annual report.

---

17   Ibid 80.
18   Ian Ayres and John Braithwaite, *Responsive Regulation* (Oxford University Press, 1992).
19   Ibid 384 *et seq.*

6.3.2.3 Accounting standards

The importance of having in place within a company proper procedures and policies to ensure accurate and transparent financial reporting (which involves complying with standards of accounting and auditing practice) has been highlighted by the collapses of large companies such as Enron and WorldCom in the US and HIH in Australia.

Farrar distinguishes accounting standards from the *Corporations Act*, categorising accounting standards as 'hybrids' rather than 'hard law', for similar reasons as those given for his position on the ASX *Listing Rules*.

6.3.2.4 Auditing standards

Since the implementation of the CLERP 9 reforms in 2004, we can now similarly refer to auditing standards (standards of proper auditing practice which, if adhered to, assist auditors in satisfying their duty to use reasonable care and skill) as 'hard law'. Section 307A of the Act, introduced by CLERP 9, provides that if an individual auditor, audit firm or an audit company conducts:

(a)   an audit of the financial report for a financial year; or

(b)   an audit or review of the financial report for a half year;

the individual auditor or audit company must conduct the audit or review in accordance with the auditing standards.

6.3.3 'Soft law'[20]

The Australian Law Reform Commission has noted that soft law may also be referred to as 'quasi-legislation' or 'quasi-regulation'.[21] The *Australian Government Guide to Regulatory Impact Analysis*, for example, describes 'quasi-regulation' as:

[a]ny rule or requirement that is not established by a parliamentary process, but which can influence the behaviour of businesses, community organisations or individuals. Examples include industry codes of practice, guidance notes, industry-government agreements (co-regulation) and accreditation schemes.[22]

According to the *G20/OECD Principles of Corporate Governance*:

[C]orporate governance objectives are also formulated in voluntary codes and standards that do not have the status of law or regulation. While such codes play an important role in improving corporate governance arrangements, they might leave shareholders and other stakeholders with uncertainty concerning their status and implementation. When codes and principles are used as a

---

20   For a discussion of the impact of 'soft law', see Kent Greenfield, 'No law?' in Jean J du Plessis and Chee Keong Low (eds), *Corporate Governance Codes for the 21st Century: International Perspectives an Critical Analyses* (Springer Verlag, 2017) 57. For wider discussion, see Greg Weeks, 'The use and enforcement of soft law by Australian public authorities' (2014) 42(1) *Federal Law Review* 1.

21   Australian Law Reform Commission, *Interim Report B Financial Services Legislation* (Report 139, September 2022) [3.74] <https://www.alrc.gov.au/wp-content/uploads/2022/09/ALRC-FSL-Interim-Report-B-139.pdf>.

22   Department of the Prime Minister and Cabinet, *Australian Government Guide to Regulatory Impact Analysis* (2nd ed, 2020) 60.

national standard or as an explicit substitute for legal or regulatory provisions, market credibility requires that their status in terms of coverage, implementation, compliance and sanctions is clearly specified.[23]

'Soft law' therefore involves the purely voluntary[24] codes and guidelines articulating benchmarks for what is considered best practice in corporate governance, as well as scholarly[25] and trade writings (books, reports and articles) that have had some role in influencing how companies shape their internal arrangements and management to achieve best practice.

Examples of these codes/guidelines include the Financial Services Council's Guidance Notes for the financial services industry and Standards Australia's series of corporate governance standards (released since 2003), which contain benchmarks for a number of governance matters. The latter standards are similar to those in the ASX *Corporate Governance Principles and Recommendations* but are used mostly by public sector bodies, non-listed entities and non-profit organisations.

In terms of reports and other writings, a plethora of such material has been produced and published in Australia (mainly since the early 1990s) – as in other jurisdictions – creating a rich and valuable collection of corporate governance 'soft law'.

A fourth category of regulation that Farrar refers to is 'business ethics'. In this book, we deal with business ethics separately in Chapter 10.

6.3.4 The role of market forces

Another important source of influence, and perhaps control, over the internal arrangements and management of a company, but one that does not sit comfortably under any of the categories of regulation above,[26] is 'market forces'.

In their 1997 book, *Making Boards Work*, David SR Leighton and Donald H Thain referred to common examples of market forces acting as 'alternatives to self-motivated board improvement'. This lends support to our decision to include market forces as a form of regulation in this chapter. It is perhaps difficult for some to envisage how market forces, which are the natural forces of an intangible entity, could actually be said to be a form of regulation; however, the label 'alternatives to self-motivated board improvement' could be useful in easing 'market forces' into the dialogue on corporate governance regulation.[27]

---

23 *G20/OECD Principles of Corporate Governance* (2015) 30.
24 This means that no formal sanctions arise from non-compliance.
25 For an excellent analysis on the role of soft regulation in corporate governance, see Kingsford Smith, 'Governing the corporation' (2012) 35(1) *University of New South Wales Law Journal* 378.
26 In reference to 'hard law', 'hybrids' and 'soft law', it could perhaps be argued that market forces are 'hybrids', in that they cannot be described either as traditional black-letter law or as purely voluntary – market forces have an important influence on governance practices regardless of the wishes of the company and its management.
27 In their book, Leighton and Thain discuss five such 'alternatives' (some of which are often discussed as market forces, some of which are not): (1) takeovers (ineffective boards leave companies wide open for takeovers); (2) proxy contests (using voting powers to remove inefficient directors and appoint more effective directors); (3) 'power investing' (investment bankers who pool their money with pension funds and other institutional investors to take control of major corporations); (4) shareholder activism (self-explanatory); and (5) legal action (e.g. class action and oppression remedy). See David SR Leighton and Donald H Thain, *Making Boards Work* (McGraw-Hill Ryerson, 1997) 10–12.

The significant role of market forces in contributing towards good corporate governance and strong corporate performance has for some time been emphasised in economic literature on the corporation and corporate law.[28] In fact, many consider market forces an effective substitute for formal legal regulation.[29]

The *G20/OECD Principles of Corporate Governance* also recognises the role of market forces in the decisions of directors and managers in relation to the internal arrangements of companies. It explains that, in order to achieve the most efficient deployment of resources, policy-makers need to undertake analyses 'of the impact of key variables that affect the functioning of markets, [such as] incentive structures, the efficiency of self-regulatory systems and dealing with systemic conflicts of interest'.[30]

6.4 The role of the regulators: ASIC and the ASX

6.4.1 Introduction

This section highlights the roles of and relationship between the twin regulators, the Australian Securities and Investments Commission ('ASIC') and the Australian Securities Exchange ('ASX') in the Australian corporate governance regime. ASIC's functions complement those of other regulators such as Australian Prudential Regulation Authority's ('APRA') and the Australian Competition and Consumer Commission's ('ACCC') but a consideration of that working relationship falls outside the scope of this chapter. The exercise of ASIC's powers is reviewed and enforcement patterns are commented upon. This chapter sketches the role of the ASX in corporate governance and concludes with remarks addressing the broad philosophical debate on the role of the regulator in light of the carnage (the widespread corporate collapses or near collapses)[31] arising from the 2008 Global Financial Crisis ('GFC'), and the relatively recent pressure put on ASIC by the Royal Commission into Misconduct in the Banking Industry, Superannuation and Financial Services Industry ('Banking Royal Commission') to be more proactive and to perform to a higher standard.[32]

---

28 See Frank H Easterbrook and Daniel R Fischel, *The Economic Structure of Corporate Law* (Harvard University Press, 1991); consider, eg, Larry E Ribstein, 'Market vs regulatory responses to corporate fraud: A critique of the Sarbanes-Oxley Act of 2002' (2002) 28(1) *Journal of Corporation Law* 1.

29 The classic article on the role of market forces as an alternative regulatory mechanism to traditional legal regulation is LA Bebchuk, 'Federalism and the corporation: The desirable limits on state competition in corporate law' (1992) 105(7) *Harvard Law Review* 1435 (which examines the operation of the various markets that may affect the decisions of managers); another significant contribution is JC Coffee, 'Regulating the market for corporate control: A critical assessment of the tender offer's role in corporate governance' (1984) 84(5) *Columbia Law Review* 1145. Bebchuk's article ultimately contends that there are limits to the effectiveness of market forces and that, at least in the US, there remains a strong place for traditional legal rules in corporate law, if corporate law is truly to maximise shareholder value.

30 *G20/OECD Principles of Corporate Governance* (2015) 14.

31 Opes Prime Stockbroking Ltd, Tricom Equities Ltd, Chimaera Capital Ltd, Allco Finance Group Ltd, Babcock & Brown Ltd, Storm Financial Ltd, ABC Learning Ltd, Timbercorp Ltd, Great Southern Ltd, to name a few.

32 *Royal Commission into Misconduct in the Banking Industry, Superannuation and Financial Services Industry* (Final Report, February 2019) vol 1 ('Final Hayne Report').

6.4.2 The Australian Securities and Investments Commission ('ASIC')

ASIC was first called the National Companies and Securities Commission ('NCSC') and later the Australian Securities Commission ('ASC').[33] The Wallis Report (released in April 1997) recommended several regulatory changes, including the establishment of ASIC, which occurred on 1 July 1998.[34]

ASIC is Australia's corporate, markets and financial services regulator. It regulates companies, financial markets, financial services organisations and professionals who deal in and advise on investments, superannuation, insurance, deposit-taking and credit. ASIC's work covers consumers, investors and creditors of corporations and other businesses.

As the market regulator, ASIC assesses how effectively authorised financial markets are complying with their legal obligations to operate fair, orderly and transparently in markets.[35] As the financial services regulator, ASIC licenses and monitors financial service businesses to ensure that they operate efficiently, honestly and fairly.[36] As the corporate regulator, ASIC is responsible for ensuring that company directors and officers carry out their duties honestly, diligently and in the best interests of the company.[37] This chapter focuses on ASIC's role as corporate watchdog.[38]

6.4.3 Statutory powers under the *ASIC Act*[39]

ASIC is a federal government body, currently (in 2023) led by Chair Joseph Longo, with the assistance of commissioners. The chair and commissioners are accountable to the Minister for Financial Services, Superannuation and Corporate Law and the Parliament under the *Australian Securities and Investments Commission Act 2001* (Cth) ('the *ASIC Act*').

The objects of the *ASIC Act* are described in general terms in s 1 of the Act. Section 1(2) of the *ASIC Act* provides, in part, that in performing its functions and exercising its powers, ASIC must take whatever action it can take, and is necessary, in order to enforce and give effect to the laws of the Commonwealth that confer functions and powers upon it.

---

33 This chapter focuses on contemporary developments following the rebadging of ASC as ASIC. For a study of the many complexities (political, legal, social and institutional) that have influenced, motivated and constrained the development of the present system of Australian companies and securities regulation, see Bernard Mees and Ian Ramsay, 'Corporate regulators in Australia (1961–2000): From companies' registrars to ASIC' (2008) 22(3) *Australian Journal of Corporate Law* 212.

34 A Cameron, 'Not another regulator!!!' (1998 Suncorp-Metway Bob Nicol Memorial Lecture, Brisbane, 10 November 1998).

35 ASIC, 'Our role' <http://asic.gov.au/about-asic/what-we-do/our-role/>.

36 Ibid.

37 Ibid.

38 For an insight into the gatekeeping role expected of directors by the regulator, see Belinda Gibson and Diane Brown, 'ASIC's expectations of directors' (2012) 35(1) *University of New South Wales Law Journal* 254. For a perspective on ASIC's unique role as law-maker, see Stephen Bottomley, 'The notional legislator: The Australian Securities and Investments Commission's role as law-maker' (2011) 39(1) *Federal Law Review* 1.

39 For a fuller discussion, see Anil Hargovan, Michael Adams and Catherine Brown, *Australian Corporate Law* (LexisNexis, 7th ed, 2020) ch 2.

In order to ensure compliance with the law, ASIC is vested with special powers of investigation and information-gathering. These powers are set out in pt 3 of the *ASIC Act*. Where ASIC decides to undertake an investigation, it can require any person to render to it all necessary assistance in connection with the investigation.

ASIC is authorised under s 13 of the *ASIC Act* to initiate an investigation if it suspects, on reasonable grounds, that there is a contravention of the corporations legislation. Following an investigation or examination, ASIC may, if it is in the public interest to do so, commence proceedings under s 50 of the *ASIC Act* seeking civil remedies from the court. Section 50 has been under-utilised to date.[40]

6.4.4 The role of ASIC in corporate governance[41]

Jillian Segal (a former deputy chair of ASIC), in addressing the role of the regulator, captures the complex and multifaceted role that ASIC plays in Australia with the following observation: '[T]he regulator's role is a continuum of responses. It is bounded by enforcement at one end and education at the other, with policy guidance, industry support and disclosure guidelines in between.'[42]

ASIC has clearly recognised that it has a key and active role to play in corporate governance in Australia. Berna Collier (a former commissioner of ASIC) outlined the role of ASIC in corporate governance as follows:

> So what exactly is our role in corporate governance? What do we do on a daily basis to improve corporate governance in Australia? Essentially, ASIC's role in corporate governance is threefold:
>
> (1) monitors, enforces and administers compliance with the broad range of corporate governance provisions in the Corporations Act;
> (2) has a public education or advocacy role; and
> (3) contributes to law reform in relation to corporate governance.[43]

In more recent times, flowing from the legacy of the Banking Royal Commission, ASIC has focused on non-financial risks – in other words, risks such as operational risk, conduct risk (including risks from not treating customers fairly) and compliance risk (that is, risks from not following the rules).[44]

The first of these roles mentioned in the above quote, in particular enforcing compliance, was prominent in ASIC's dealings with the corporate collapses in Australia of HIH

---

40 ASIC, 'ASIC to pursue compensation for Westpoint investors' (Media Release, 8 November 2007). For the major reported instances of s 50 actions taken by ASIC, see Janet Austin, 'Does the Westpoint litigation signal a revival of the ASIC s 50 class action?' (2008) 22(1) *Australian Journal of Corporate Law* 8.

41 For some comparative perspectives and the role and functions of ASIC, see Jean J du Plessis and Niklas Cordes, 'Claiming damages from members of management boards in Germany: Time for a radical rethink and possible lessons from down under?' (2015) 36(11) *Company Lawyer* 335, 344–52.

42 Jillian Segal, 'Corporate governance: Substance over form' (2002) 25(1) *University of New South Wales Law Journal* 1, 5.

43 Berna Collier, 'The role of ASIC in corporate governance' (Speech, Corporate Governance Summit, 27 November 2002) 5.

44 See ASIC, 'ASIC releases report on director and officer oversight of non-financial risk' (Media Release, 2 October 2019).

Insurance Ltd, One.Tel Ltd, AWB Ltd, Sino Australia Oil and Gas Ltd, Storm Financial Pty Ltd[45] and more recent failures of corporate governance, such as in relation to GIO Ltd, James Hardie, Vocation Ltd and Tennis Australia.[46]

There is no doubt that in the aftermath of the massive corporate collapses referred to above, ASIC fulfilled its role with assiduousness, and it has remained highly active since then, with several actions instituted against directors, albeit with a mixed record of success (discussed below). It should be noted that ASIC's role as regulator, which also involves instituting action against directors to enforce the duties they owe to the company, is one of the most distinctive aspects of Australian corporate law and our corporate governance model.[47] In other jurisdictions the task of enforcing directors' duties is largely left to the shareholders, and it has been shown in several jurisdictions that even with statutory derivative actions available, legal actions against directors for a breach of their fiduciary duties and duty of care and diligence are few.[48] This is not so in Australia because of ASIC's active role in enforcing these duties on behalf of companies.[49]

ASIC's reputation for law enforcement has suffered somewhat a decade ago,[50] when it lost some high-profile civil cases: against the directors of One.Tel Ltd (Jodee Rich and Mark Silbermann)[51] and against Fortescue Metals Group Ltd's chairman and chief executive officer (Andrew Forrest).[52] Critical comments on ASIC's litigation strategy made by

45   For discussion of enforcement actions taken against officers of Water Wheel Holdings Ltd, GIO Insurance Ltd, HIH Insurance Ltd, One.Tel Ltd, AWA Ltd, James Hardie Ltd, Centro Ltd, AWB Ltd, Storm Financial, Sino Australia Ltd, Vocation Ltd and Tennis Australia, see Hargovan, Adams and Brown, *Australian Corporate Law* (2020) chs 15–18 (on directors' and officers' duties). See also Anil Hargovan, 'Failure to make adequate enquiries: Civil penalties for former chair of AWB Ltd' (2017) 69(5) *Governance Directions* 307; and Anil Hargovan, 'Foreign directors of Australian companies put on notice: No leniency for ignorance of duties' (2017) 69(1) *Governance Directions* 37.

46   See, eg, *Australian Securities and Investments Commission v Macdonald (No 11)* (2009) 256 ALR 199, discussed in Anil Hargovan, 'Corporate governance lessons from James Hardie' (2009) 33(3) *Melbourne University Law Review* 984; *Gillfillan v Australian Securities and Investments Commission* (2012) 92 ACSR 460; *ASIC v Vocation Ltd (in liq)* [2019] FCA 807; *ASIC v Vocation Ltd (in liq) (No 2)* [2019] FCA 1783, discussed in Anil Hargovan 'Stepping stone liability for non-executive chair in Vocation Ltd' (2019) 71(11) *Governance Directions* 659; and *Australian Securities and Investments Commission v Mitchell (No 2)* (2020) 382 ALR 425, discussed in Anil Hargovan 'Governance lessons from Tennis Australia: *ASIC v Mitchell (No 2)*' (2020) 72(8) *Governance Directions* 384.

47   See Michelle Welsh, 'Realising the public potential of corporate law: Twenty years of civil penalty enforcement in Australia' (2014) 42(1) *Federal Law Review* 217.

48   See Andrew Keay, 'The public enforcement of directors' duties: A normative inquiry' (2014) 43(3) *Common Law World Review* 89; Renee M Jones and Michelle Welsh, 'Towards a public enforcement model for directors' duty of oversight' (2012) 25(3) *Vanderbilt Journal of Transnational Law* 343.

49   See Chapter 8.

50   See Vicki Comino, *Company Law Watchdog – ASIC and Corporate Regulation* (Thomson Reuters Australia, 2015); Ben Woodhead, 'ASIC hits and misses', *Australian Financial Review* (3 May 2012); Adele Ferguson, Ben Butler and Ruth Williams, 'Scrutinising ASIC: Is it a watchdog or a dog with no teeth?', *Sydney Morning Herald* (23 November 2013).

51   *Australian Securities and Investments Commission v Rich* (2009) 75 ACSR 1: Justice Austin of the NSW Supreme Court held that ASIC failed to prove any facet of its pleaded case against either defendant.

52   *Forrest v Australian Securities and Investments Commission* (2012) 247 CLR 486. For stinging judicial criticism by the High Court of Australia of ASIC's poor pleading in its litigation strategy, see *Forrest v Australian Securities and Investments Commission* (2012) 247 CLR 486. See further Anil Hargovan, 'Sharp message to ASIC as Forrest wins High Court Appeal', *The Conversation* (online, 3 October 2012) <http://theconversation.com/sharp-message-to-asic-as-forrest-wins-high-court-appeal-9934>; John Humphrey and Stephen Corones, '*Forrest v ASIC*: "A perfect storm"' (2014) 88(1) *Australian Law Journal* 26, 37.

each of the sitting judges, independently and in different jurisdictions, painted a disturbing picture. A hostile media humiliated ASIC, questioning its ability to carry out complex litigation and its judgment.[53] Ian Ramsay commented on the need for a review of the manner in which ASIC conducts complex litigation.[54]

Similar comments and concerns were expressed by the judiciary in *Australian Securities and Investments Commission v Mitchell (No 2)*.[55] This case is interesting for many reasons, aside from the significant loss by the corporate regulator in this case in which 41 out of 44 allegations of breach of directors' duties were not upheld by the Court.[56] The case arose when ASIC alleged that key board members of Tennis Australia breached their duty of care and diligence (under s 180(1) of the *Corporations Act*) when negotiating with the Seven Network Holdings in securing domestic broadcast television rights.

Stringent judicial remarks on ASIC's role in this case, together with the regulator's narrow victory, indicates that this was a poor choice of case for ASIC to litigate. ASIC's misguided view of the commercial deal-making process revealed in the case, which lacked commercial nous, left the regulator vulnerable to the following judicial criticism:[57]

> ASIC's case assumed that a commercial negotiation was an adversarial contest intended to produce a winner and a loser, and in which the negotiating parties had to behave at all times as if they were protagonists. But the negotiations between Tennis Australia and Channel Seven (media) were between two parties who had had a fruitful relationship over decades. They were parties who were exploring whether a win-win deal could be negotiated between them ...

A substantial part of ASIC's construction of its evidence was held to have displayed 'confirmatory bias'.[58] The Court noted that many of the cover-up and conspiracy theories floated by ASIC lacked substance.[59] On the contrary, the Court was satisfied that the directors of Tennis Australia had the information necessary to make an informed choice, when approving the commercial deal, and therefore had not breached their duty of care and diligence.

Moreover, the failure by ASIC to lead expert evidence on the usual corporate practices within the organisation made it difficult to compare the conduct of Tennis Australia's chair and to measure it against any usual or normative corporate practices.

The ill-conceived nature of this case highlights the need for ASIC not to be too quick to pull the litigation trigger and to intrude into the boardroom without a plausible cause for legal action.

---

53 See, eg, Matthew Stevens, 'Laughter and jeers over ASIC failure', *The Australian* (31 December 2009); Jennifer Hewett, 'Three strikes prove regulator is out of touch', *The Australian* (24 December 2009).

54 Stuart Washington, 'Academics Question ASIC's Ability', *Brisbane Times* (25 December 2009). For the complexities involved in litigation concerning civil penalty proceedings, see the judgment of Justice Austin in *Australian Securities and Investments Commission v Rich* (2009) 75 ACSR 1. See further Tom Middleton, 'The privilege against self-incrimination, the penalty privilege and legal professional privilege under the laws governing ASIC, APRA, the ACCC and the ATO: Suggested reforms' (2008) 30(3) *Australian Bar Review* 282.

55 (2020) 283 ALR 425.

56 See further Anil Hargovan, 'Governance lessons from Tennis Australia: *ASIC v Mitchell (No 2)*' (2020) 72(8) *Governance Directions* 384.

57 *Australian Securities and Investments Commission v Mitchell (No 2)* (2020) 382 ALR 425, [1806].

58 Ibid [9].

59 Ibid [10].

6.4.5 ASIC enforcement patterns

Research on ASIC's enforcement patterns was undertaken in 2003[60] and in 2017.[61] The 2003 research revealed that ASIC was more likely to pursue court-based enforcement against individuals than against companies. This illustrated the point that actions by ASIC are aimed at deterrence: the Commission hopes that making individuals aware of the possibility of liability influences the behaviour of directors. It was also discovered that more actions are instituted against directors of private companies than against directors of public companies. This is perhaps understandable, as there are far more private companies than public companies and directors of public companies will often also be directors of subsidiary private companies of the public company: see the case study on the HIH Insurance Ltd collapse (*Australian Securities and Investments Commission v Adler*) in Chapter 8.

The 2003 research examined 1438 court-based ASIC enforcement actions, all occurring between January 1997 and December 1999. It found that these actions were predominantly penal enforcement actions rather than civil enforcement actions. ASIC would mainly use settlements – rather than court processes – as outcomes for civil enforcement. ASIC was 'more likely to pursue penal enforcement in relation to laws that were mandatory (rather than enabling) in nature' and laws 'oriented towards social (rather than economic) regulation', preferring to focus on 'laws with an ethical foundation' and address 'conduct that is widely condemned because it exploits and defrauds shareholders and creditors'.[62]

Significantly, the findings of an empirical analysis of sanctions imposed in proceedings brought by ASIC and the Commonwealth Director of Public Prosecutions for contraventions of the directors' duties provisions of the *Corporations Act 2001* (Cth) and its predecessor, the *Corporations Act 1989* (Cth), from 1 January 2005 to 31 December 2014, reaffirmed aspects of the findings of the 2003 research.

6.5 The Australian Securities Exchange Ltd ('ASX')

Securities exchanges have been part of Australia's corporate landscape since the 1840s. The ASX was formed in 1987 after an amalgamation of the separate state-based stock exchanges. It serves as an important mechanism for the non-legal regulation of publicly listed companies. The ASX *Listing Rules*, referred to earlier, provide a range of corporate governance and compliance mechanisms for listed companies.

The entire face of corporate governance in Australia changed rapidly with the collapses of HIH, Harris Scarfe, One.Tel Ltd, Pasminco Ltd, Centaur and Ansett Australia

---

60   Helen Bird et al, *ASIC Enforcement Patterns* (Research Paper No 71, Centre for Corporate Law and Securities Regulation, University of Melbourne, 27 April 2004). See also Helen Bird et al, 'Strategic regulation and ASIC enforcement patterrns: Results of an empirical study' (2005) 5(1) *Journal of Corporate Law Studies* 191. For an empirical study on the enforcement of directors' duties by private litigants in Australia, see Jenifer Varzaly, 'The enforcement of directors' duties in Australia: An empirical analysis' (2015) 16 *European Business Organization Law Review* 281.
61   See Jasper Hedges et al, 'The policy and practice of enforcement of directors' duties by statutory agencies in Australia: An empirical analysis' (2017) 40(3) *Melbourne University Law Review* 905.
62   Helen Bird et al, *ASIC Enforcement Patterns* (2004) xiii–xiv.

between 2000 and 2003. These collapses, together with corporate collapses in the US (such as Enron), were in part the catalyst for the establishment by the ASX of the Corporate Governance Council ('CGC') on 15 August 2002. The CGC is currently composed of representatives of the 20 most important players in the financial markets.[63] Its first task was to produce a set of consolidated and up-to-date standards of best governance practice. The CGC developed these guidelines with great speed, approving the *Principles of Good Corporate Governance and Best Practice Recommendations* in March 2003.

6.5.1 ASX *Corporate Governance Principles and Recommendations*

As mentioned in Chapter 1, the 2003 ASX *Principles of Good Corporate Governance and Best Practice Recommendations* were amended in 2007, 2010 (becoming known as the ASX *Corporate Governance Principles and Recommendations* with 2010 amendments) and 2014. A fourth edition was introduced in 2019.[64]

The current, fourth edition retains the eight core Principles (with slight amendments) as follows, with the same expectation that the reporting of an entity's compliance be on an 'if not, why not' basis:

- Principle 1: Lay solid foundations for management and oversight
- Principle 2: Structure the board to add value
- Principle 3: Act ethically and responsibly
- Principle 4: Safeguard integrity in corporate reporting
- Principle 5: Make timely and balanced disclosure
- Principle 6: Respect the rights of security holders
- Principle 7: Recognise and manage risk
- Principle 8: Remunerate fairly and responsibly.

There are, however, significant changes from the third edition – namely, there are 35 specific recommendations in the fourth edition (compared to 29 in the 2014 edition), with a strong focus on the link between culture, values and community expectations – themes reflective of the issues arising from the Banking Royal Commission (discussed below). There is emphasis on monitoring and taking responsibility for corporate culture, values, behaviour and for setting the tone from the top – these improvements align with the recommendations of the Banking Royal Commission.

To this end, Principle 3 was substantially modified to pick up on the governance concerns arising from the Banking Royal Commission and now includes the need for companies to 'instil a culture of acting lawfully, ethically and responsibly'. Significantly, the expression 'social licence to operate', which received prominence following the release of the Consultation Draft, was abandoned by the CGC and replaced with references to 'reputation' and 'standing in the community.' The latter references are seen by the ASX CGC as being similar to the expression 'social licence to operate.'

---

63 The Council consists of representatives of 20 business and investor groups
64 ASX, *Corporate Governance Principles and Recommendations* (4th ed, 2019).

New recommendations under Principle 3 include an expectation for a listed entity to articulate and disclose its values, whistleblower policy and anti-bribery and corruption policy. Recommendation 3.2 now also expects that the board or a committee of the board is informed of any material breaches of the code of conduct.

Efforts to increase gender diversity in board composition are given a boost with the recommendation that if the entity is part of the S&P/ASX300, the entity should have a measurable objective of 30 per cent of directors of each gender.

6.5.2 The roles of and relationship between the ASX and ASIC

Since 1998 there has been a memorandum of understanding between ASIC and the ASX regarding their respective supervisory roles that has been refined over the years. In 2011 some of the supervisory responsibilities of the ASX were transferred to ASIC, as the 'front-line' regulator of the securities exchange. The aim of this reform was to ensure that Australia has only one 'whole-of-market supervisor', and to thus eliminate any potential conflicts of interest arising from the ASX being both a regulator and a player on the securities market.[65] Before these reforms, the ASX was one of only a few major exchanges with such dual functions[66] and had been continually dogged by allegations of inherent conflicts of interest. For example, during the GFC, the ASX faced criticism when stockbroking firms such as Opes Prime collapsed. Concerns were raised that the ASX neglected managing conflicts of interest involving its supervision of firms, who also traded on its market and paid it fees.[67]

Fresh allegations of conflict of interest have arisen since the collapse of the ASX's upgrade to the CHESS settlement and clearing system. The situation is ripe for a conflict of interest as the ASX is the main player in share trading and, as owner of the CHESS technology, has a virtual monopoly over the settlement and clearing system. Accordingly, ASX is open to criticism that it failed to account for conflicts of interest when it designed the upgrade.[68]

Members of Parliament have recently raised questions as to whether the structure of the ASX is fit for purpose. Robert Austin, former judge of the NSW Supreme Court, expressed concern about the ASX structure:

> With the benefit of hindsight, it is clear that as part of the ASX demutualisation, settlement services should have been ring-fenced much more tightly with separate governance arrangements because the conflict of interest is manifest, as

65 Gill North, 'The corporate disclosure co-regulatory model: Dysfunctional and rules in limbo' (2009) 37(2) *Australian Business Law Review* 75, 80–1. On concerns arising around conflicts of interest under the old regulatory system, see Adele Ferguson, 'Query on ASX's supervisory power', *The Australian* (17 September 2007); Danny John, 'ASX cited for conflict of interest', *Sydney Morning Herald* (5 April 2008).

66 'Securities exchange had conflicting roles', *The Australian* (25 August 2009).

67 See James Eyers, 'ASX conflicts of interest points to utility model to settle equities', *Australian Financial Review* (online, 5 December 2022) <https://www.afr.com/companies/financial-services/asx-conflicts-of-interest-point-to-utility-model-to-settle-equities-20221129-p5c23n>. See further Tony Boyd, 'Call to end ASX conflicts', *Australian Financial Review* (online, 12 October 2022) <https://www.afr.com/chanticleer/call-to-end-asx-conflicts-20221012-p5bpb8>.

68 Eyers, 'ASX conflicts of interest points to utility model to settle equities' *Australian Financial Review* (5 December 2022).

subsequent events have shown ... I'm not sure the problem will be fixed by ASX structural governance changes unless they are mandated by legislation.[69]

It remains to be seen whether Parliament will intervene and legislate for regulatory change by granting increased powers of oversight to ASIC and the Reserve Bank of Australia over the clearing system, as reported in the press.[70]

6.6 Parliamentary critique of ASIC's performance

At the time of writing, ASIC is facing yet another Senate inquiry into its performance. On 27 October 2022, the Senate referred an inquiry into 'the capacity and capability of [ASIC] to undertake proportionate investigation and enforcement action arising from reports of alleged misconduct' to the Senate Economics References Committee for report by the last sitting day in June 2024.[71]

The reasons for a 2014 parliamentary inquiry into ASIC's performance centred around revelations about the misconduct of financial advisers and concerns about serious short-comings in corporate conduct and ASIC's response to them.[72] The recommendations of the resulting report aimed at encouraging the fulfilment of ASIC's responsibilities and obligations more effectively. The report authors made these trenchant remarks:

> However, many of the issues with ASIC's performance cannot be addressed by anyone other than ASIC. In the committee's opinion, ASIC has been in the spotlight far too frequently for the wrong reasons. It is acknowledged that not all of the criticisms levelled at ASIC are justified; ASIC is required to perform much of its work confidentially and in a way that ensures natural justice. It is also constrained by the legislation it administers and the resources given to it for this purpose. Nevertheless, the credibility of the regulator is important for encouraging a culture of compliance. That ASIC is consistently described as being slow to act or as a watchdog with no teeth is troubling. The committee knows, however, that ASIC has dedicated and talented employees that want to

---

69 Quoted in ibid.

70 Ibid. See further ASIC, 'ASIC RBA further regulatory response regarding the ASX CHESS Replacement Program' (Media Release, 15 December 2022) <https://asic.gov.au/about-asic/news-centre/find-a-media-release/2022-releases/22-357mr-asic-rba-further-regulatory-response-regarding-the-asx-chess-replacement-program/>. See also a speech by the ASIC Chair in which he addressed ASIC's limited intervention powers to ensure ASX compliance: Joseph Longo, 'Opening Statement' (Speech, Joint Committee on Corporations and Financial Services, 5 December 2022) <https://asic.gov.au/about-asic/news-centre/speeches/parliamentary-joint-committee-on-corporations-and-financial-services-opening-statement-5-december-2022/>.

71 The terms of inquiry, which include whether ASIC is meeting the expectations of government, business and the community with respect to regulatory action and enforcement, can be found here: <https://www.aph.gov.au/Parliamentary_Business/Committees/Senate/Economics/ASICinvestigation/Terms_of_Reference>.

72 On 20 June 2013, the Senate referred the performance of ASIC to the Economics References Committee for inquiry. Based on 578 public submissions, and five days of public hearings, a critical report on ASIC's performance was tabled in June 2014, making sweeping recommendations for improvements in ASIC's enforcement reputation and for law reform. See further Senate Economics and References Committee, Parliament of Australia, *Performance of the Australian Securities and Investments Commission* (Final Report, June 2014) <https://www.aph.gov.au/Parliamentary_Business/Committees/Senate/Economics/ASIC/Final_Report/index>.

rectify the agency's reputation. This inquiry has been a wake-up call for ASIC. The committee looks forward to seeing how ASIC changes as a result.[73]

As a partial response to such criticism, ASIC has made repeated calls for increases in its enforcement power. Following the appointment of a taskforce in October 2016 to review the enforcement regime of ASIC, the federal government significantly boosted the penalty regime under the *Corporations Act 2001* (Cth) through passage of the *Treasury Laws Amendment (Strengthening Corporate and Financial Sector Penalties) Act 2019* (Cth). Effective from March 2019, a new and tougher penalty regime was introduced into the *Corporations Act 2001* (Cth). The results of this initiative are yet to filter through court cases as many penalty judgments are still currently founded on causes of legal action that pre-dates commencement of the new penalty regime.

6.7 Royal Commission critique of ASIC's performance

The Interim Report on the Royal Commission into Misconduct in the Banking, Super-annuation and Financial Services Industry by Commissioner Haynes was released in September 2018,[74] followed by the Final Report on 1 February 2019.[75] Two dominant themes are striking in the Final Report on the law enforcement culture of the conduct regulator, ASIC.

The first relates to ASIC's enforcement strategy. The Commissioner criticised the choices made by ASIC when selecting an enforcement tool from its regulatory toolkit. For example, Commissioner Haynes noted that the use of infringement notices may be convenient and expeditious but it achieves 'neither punishment nor deterrence'.[76] Further, the Commissioner expressed concern about the widespread use of enforceable undertakings. It runs the risk that the promise made by the entity could be seen as 'no more than the cost of doing business or the cost of placating the regulator'.[77]

ASIC was also criticised by Commissioner Haynes for inadequate deterrence and weak regulatory enforcement action:[78]

> ASIC's starting point [as a response to misconduct] appears to have been: How can this be resolved by agreement. This cannot be the starting point for a con-duct regulator ...
>
> [ASIC and APRA] must always ask whether it can make a case that there has been a breach and, if it can, then ask why it would not be in the public interest to bring proceedings to penalise the breach.
>
> Laws are to be obeyed. Penalties are prescribed for failure to obey the law because society expects and requires obedience to the law.

---

73 Ibid xxii.
74 *Royal Commission into Misconduct in the Banking Industry, Superannuation and Financial Services Industry* (Interim Report, September 2018) vol 1 ('Interim Hayne Report'). See further A Hargovan, 'Hayne Royal Commission Interim Report: Unclogging the central artery' (2018) 70(11) *Governance Directions* 691.
75 Final Hayne Report (2019). See further A Hargovan, 'Banking royal commission final report: Cultural issues and implications' (2019) 71(3) *Governance Directions* 128.
76 Final Hayne Report (2019) vol 1, 436.
77 Final Hayne Report (2019) vol 1, 442.
78 Interim Hayne Report (2018) 277–8.

On the relationship between misconduct and the lack of effective deterrence (inadequate use of civil and criminal penalties by the regulator), Commissioner Haynes said:[79]

> Rewarding misconduct is wrong. Yet incentive, bonus and commission schemes throughout the financial services industry [in Australia] have measured sales and profit, but not compliance with the law and proper standards. Incentives have been offered, and rewards have been paid, regardless of whether the sale was made, or profit derived, in accordance with law ...
>
> ... [T]oo often, financial services entities that broke the law were not properly held to account. Misconduct will be deterred only if entities believe that misconduct will be detected, denounced and justly punished.
>
> Misconduct, especially misconduct that yields profit, is not deterred by requiring those who are found to have done wrong to do no more than pay compensation.

The second theme concerned Commissioner Hayne's concern over regulatory capture, where it appears that ASIC is susceptible to losing sight of its role as a conduct regulator. These concerns lie behind Recommendation 6.2 in the Final Report which states that ASIC should adopt an approach to enforcement that:

- takes, as its starting point, the question of whether a court should determine the consequences of a contravention
- recognises that infringement notices should principally be used in respect of administrative failings by entities, will rarely be appropriate for provisions that require an evaluative judgment and, beyond purely administrative failings, will rarely be an appropriate enforcement tool where the infringing party is a large corporation
- recognises the relevance and importance of general and specific deterrence in deciding whether to accept an enforceable undertaking, and the utility in obtaining admissions in enforceable undertakings
- separates, as much as possible, enforcement staff from non-enforcement related contact with regulated entities.

In October 2018, in response to the Interim Hayne Report, ASIC announced the adoption of the 'why not litigate' enforcement strategy.[80] This new enforcement strategy was explained further in ASIC's Corporate Plan (2020–24):[81]

> Over the next four years, we will conduct intensive surveillance and enforcement work to deter poor behaviour and misconduct and punish wrongdoers. In particular, we will continue to focus on cases of high-deterrence value and those involving egregious harm or misconduct.

---

79   Final Hayne Report (2019) vol 1 2–4.
80   ASIC, *ASIC Update on Implementation of Royal Commission Recommendations* (February 2019) <https://download.asic.gov.au/media/5011933/asic-update-on-implementation-of-royal-commission-recommendations.pdf>.
81   ASIC, *ASIC Corporate Plan 2020–24: Focus 2020–21* (August 2020) 25 <https://download.asic.gov.au/media/5828033/corporate-plan-2020-24-published-31-august-2020-2.pdf>.

> Our Office of Enforcement will continue to identify, prioritise and be accountable for the most important enforcement matters across ASIC. We continue to be guided by our 'Why not litigate?' discipline, which addresses the community expectation that unlawful conduct should be punished and publicly denounced through the courts.

However, ASIC's commitment to this path has been questioned by the media[82] and politicians following removal of all references to the 'why not litigate' strategy in ASIC's 2021–25 Corporate Plan.[83] In response to a parliamentary oversight inquiry question as to whether this strategy still continues to be in ASIC's frame, the current ASIC chair (Joseph Longo) replied:[84]

> The ... Royal Commission ... was a very significant contribution to the way we think about law enforcement and regulation in Australia. I think my starting point ... is that ASIC will always be an active, credible law enforcement agency. Now, the why-not-litigate mantra that came out of the royal commission was a very useful approach to ... the question of enforcement. But, to my mind, no particular mantra is ever going to really capture the subtlety or the complexity of what we're talking about ... We're never going to be able to investigate everything that's brought to our attention. We have to make choices, so our case-selection criteria ... all require judgement, and I think the concept that Commissioner Hayne came up with was a useful concept. But I think we all need to be reminded that what we're really talking about is active, credible, targeted law enforcement, and to my mind that's what we're about, and that's not going to change.

The ASIC chair, however, also offered the following rebuke when acknowledging the wide regulatory toolkit available to ASIC:[85]

> But the point Commissioner Hayne was making – that we look for agreement as our first option and a soft result – I don't think is an accurate view of how we approach enforcement.

6.8 Conclusion

The formalisation of corporate governance regulation, including hard law, and soft law such as the 'if not, why not?' regime underpinning the ASX *Corporate Governance Principles and Recommendations*, has been considered a necessary response to high-profile

---

82 See, eg, Ronald Mizen, 'ASIC dumps "why not litigate" policy as Frydenberg resets path', *Australian Financial Review* (online, 26 August 2021) <https://www.afr.com/politics/federal/asic-dumps-why-not-litigate-as-frydenberg-resets-path-20210825-p58lyx>.

83 ASIC, *ASIC Corporate Plan 2021–25: Focus 2020–21* (August 2021).

84 Parliamentary Joint Committee on Corporations and Financial Services, 'Oversight of the Australian Securities and Investments Commission, the Takeovers Panel and the Corporations Legislation No 1 of the 46th Parliament' (18 June 2021) <https://parlinfo.aph.gov.au/parlInfo/search/display/display.w3p;query=Id%3A%22committees%2Fcommjnt%2F1a409708-99b5-4311-bca8-c3784e95be18%2F0003%22>.

85 Ibid.

corporate collapses and poor stockmarket performance, which have been perceived as being attributable to less-than-desirable corporate governance practices. While corporate governance practices may have been a cause of the problems we have recently witnessed, this does not mean that formalising the regulation of corporate governance is the appropriate – or only – solution. Indeed, many commentators stress that a focus on conformance rather than performance will not resolve the recent problems.

Corporate governance continues to be high on the corporate law agenda in Australia. Challenging economic times, associated with the GFC and the COVID-19 pandemic, together with misconduct in the financial sector, have laid bare some of the shortcomings of the Australian regulators (ASIC and the ASX) in protecting investors.[86]

This raises a fundamental question that has had ongoing relevance: should the regulators in Australia be acting as an early warning system? In addressing the media on this question, former ASIC chair Tony D'Aloisio addressed the regulatory framework and, in turn, posed a number of challenging questions in a reply that is worth reproducing:[87]

> [A]s a community, is the regulatory framework one where the role of an ASIC is to actually prevent collapses of companies, or is it as it's been traditionally: that you really oversight the markets and you come in and you deal with issues as they unfold? ... what you're seeing is we're not having clear debate about that. I mean, traditionally a regulator such as ASIC has had roles of enforcement, compliance ... investigations ... it's never extended to the fact that ASIC is the guarantor of last resort, or that it actually has the resources to be able to go into every boardroom and every chief executive to make sure that things are being done properly. If that's where the community wants to go, then clearly there would be a need for quite substantial resources. Philosophically, in a free enterprise system I think the community also has to take into account the fact that failures in companies are part of the free enterprise system, as well as success ... you need to ... have a debate on whether ASIC should be preventative or ... should remain in its traditional role ...

The quote raises rich questions about policy settings and about whether the time is ripe for a review of the philosophical considerations underpinning the current regulatory system. It is reasonable to presume that, given a choice, the community would prefer the regulatory framework to be amended to facilitate ASIC's monitoring role becoming more prominent in future, as a way of detecting the signs of potential huge corporate collapses as soon as possible, rather than cleaning up after such collapses.

If this occurs, it will probably mean a much greater focus needs to be adopted by ASIC on monitoring companies, rather than strictly on regulating and enforcing. Fulfilling this role will likely be a far more demanding than the current role, which could be described as primarily picking up the leftovers on behalf of affected corporations and individuals after the 'corporate cowboys' and 'bold riders' have left the corporations

---

86 For example, millions of dollars were lost in the collapse of managed investment schemes such as Timbercorp Ltd and Great Southern Ltd, financial planners such as Storm Financial Ltd and Opes Prime Ltd, and other companies, such as Babcock & Brown Ltd and Allco Finance Group Ltd.

87 ABC, 'ASIC chairman defends role as corporate regulator', *Lateline* (Transcript, 22 May 2008).

they have ruined financially. Only time will tell whether ASIC will have the resources to be allowed to take up this challenge and live up to public expectations in this regard. As noted by the current ASIC chair (Joseph Longo), 'one of the challenges for a regulator is to strike the right balance to take decisive action against those who cause harm to consumers and investors but there is also a need to focus on deterrence, education, and prevention to reduce harms arising in the first place'.[88] The public, including commentators, politicians and investors, will be watching with interest to see if the corporate regulator gets the balance right.

---

88   Joseph Longo, 'Opening Statement' (Speech, ASIC Annual Forum 2022, 3 November 2022) <https:// asic.gov.au/about-asic/news-centre/speeches/asic-annual-forum-2022-chair-s-keynote/>.

ACCOUNTING GOVERNANCE

7

Helen Kang

7.1 Introduction

No matter which corporate code of conduct or corporate governance framework is used, the issue of 'transparency' is referred to, either directly or by implication. The application of 'transparency' to corporate reporting practices, covering both financial and non-financial conduct and performance, has come under increasing scrutiny from various stakeholder groups. The single most significant reform, to date, in this area in Australia came in response to the high-profile corporate collapses of the early 2000s. On 1 July 2004, the *Corporate Law Economic Reform Program (Audit Reform and Corporate Disclosure) Act 2004* (Cth) came into effect. This Act is commonly referred to as 'CLERP 9', as it was the ninth instalment under the government's Corporate Law Economic Reform Program ('CLERP').

As a result of CLERP 9, considerable parts of the *Corporations Act 2001* (Cth) ('*Corporations Act*' or 'the Act') are devoted to mandatory corporate governance mechanisms, especially in relation to the financial aspects of corporate governance, with substantial reforms in financial reporting and audit. For example, parts of the *Corporations Act* deal with executive remuneration and related disclosures and shareholder participation. Overall, CLERP 9 changed the way corporations are governed within and the role of the government and stock exchange regulators, such as the Australian Securities and Investments Commission ('ASIC') and the Australian Securities Exchange ('ASX') respectively.

CLERP 9 is broadly consistent with, and a complement to, the ASX *Corporate Governance Principles and Recommendations*, now in its fourth edition (2019). The aim was for the two documents together to promote good corporate governance practices within Australian listed companies and achieve effective regulation. The main difference between the two is that CLERP 9 is mandated to cover both listed and non-listed corporations, with formal non-compliance penalties, whereas the ASX *Corporate Governance Principles and Recommendations* operate under an 'if not, why not?' ('comply or explain') approach.[1]

These two documents potentially represent the most significant reforms affecting the corporate governance practices of companies in Australia since the first Companies Acts were introduced. Other important reforms in financial reporting

---

1   See Chapters 5, 6 and 11.

practices in Australia have been the adoption of International Financial Reporting Standards ('IFRS') and International Standards on Auditing ('ISA'), based on those issued by the International Accounting Standards Board ('IASB') and the International Auditing and Assurance Standards Board ('IAASB') respectively. Further, the creation of the International Sustainability Standards Board ('ISSB') in 2021, tasked with issuing sustainability-related disclosure standards, is likely to reform the way corporations report climate and other environmental, social and governance ('ESG') information in the future.

7.2 Key CLERP 9 reforms

7.2.1 Background

As discussed in various parts of this book, the international attention to corporate governance resulted from the collapse of two of the United States' ('US') largest companies, Enron and WorldCom, in 2001. In Australia, the collapse of HIH Insurance Ltd, Australia's largest-ever corporate failure, as well as the demise of Ansett Australia, followed soon after.

Regulators were quick to focus their attention on any role these companies' auditors may have played in the collapses: by exercising poor audit oversight, lacking transparency and accountability in their processes, or through the relevant audit firms being too close to their clients.

In the US, it was discovered that the global accounting firm Arthur Andersen & Co ('Andersen'), which subsequently collapsed under the weight of scandal, had signed off on Enron financial reports which overstated the company's earnings by US$586 million over five years, and had allegedly shredded a large volume of Enron's documents (although it was found later not to have been the case). It was argued that Andersen's negligence and, indeed, dishonest practices, were due to its dependence upon fees paid to the firm by Enron for non-audit services (such as consultancy and legal services). Unfortunately, these scandals were not isolated events limited to the early 2000s. There have been subsequent accounting irregularities and corporate scandals from all over the world, including in respect of the following companies: Satyam Computer Services (2009) in India, Tesco Supermarkets (2014) and Carillion plc (2018) in the United Kingdom, Dick Smith (2016) in Australia, Toshiba Corporation (2015) in Japan, and Wirecard (2020) in Germany.

It is not difficult to see why the problems that were believed to underlie these high-profile corporate collapses became the focus of corporate law reform, particularly in relation to corporate disclosures. The reform was seen as a possible way to restore market confidence by addressing the cause of those collapses and preventing further collapses. The following subsections address the four main categories of the CLERP 9 reforms.

7.2.2 Audit reform

The objectives of the auditor are to 'form an opinion on the financial report based on an evaluation of the conclusions drawn from the audit evidence obtained, and to express clearly that opinion through a written report' (ASA 700 para 6).[2] Key reforms under CLERP 9 covered auditor independence, auditor responsibilities and accountability, and regulatory requirements for audit. These reforms are discussed in detail in Sections 7.4–7.7.

7.2.3 Remuneration of directors and executives

CLERP 9 introduced enhanced disclosure requirements for listed companies in relation to the disclosure of director and executive remuneration, and the link between levels of executive pay and company performance. The major changes to s 300A of the *Corporations Act* required much greater disclosure by listed companies of director and executive remuneration in a specific 'remuneration report' to be included as a section in the directors' report. The report was to explain board policy in relation to remuneration and demonstrate to shareholders that levels of executive pay are based on company performance and how this is determined, and disclosure of the remuneration of each director and the five highest-paid managerial personnel in the company and in the group (if applicable).[3] Other CLERP 9 initiatives in relation to remuneration included:

- a requirement for listed companies to provide shareholders with a non-binding 'advisory' vote on the designated 'remuneration report' prepared by the directors (s 250R),[4] and
- a tightening of the termination payment rules, with shareholder approval generally being required for all termination payments that are greater than the relevant person's average remuneration for the last three years multiplied by the number of years the person has held an office in relation to the company (up to a maximum seven years) or the person's remuneration for the last 12 months (see s 200F).

7.2.4 Financial reporting

CLERP 9 introduced some significant financial reporting reforms requiring further information to be provided in the directors' report or the financial report as part of either the annual or half-yearly report of the company. The three key changes made under CLERP 9 were:

(1) that listed companies must include in the directors' report a declaration by the directors that they had received a chief executive officer ('CEO') and chief financial

---

2   Auditing and Assurance Standards Board, *Forming an Opinion and Reporting on a Financial Report* (Auditing Standard ASA 700, 2020) ('ASA 700').

3   See also Australian Accounting Standards Board ('AASB'), *Share-based Payment* (31 December 2017) for other required disclosures and accounting treatments.

4   Changes to the *Corporations Act* in 2011 required that a vote of more than 25 per cent against the remuneration report in two consecutive years gives rise to a board spill motion that could then lead to all directors being forced to stand for re-election at a special members' meeting: see *Corporations Act 2001* (Cth) pt 2G.2 div 9, and Chapter 5 for more detailed discussion.

officer ('CFO') joint declaration that the company's financial records have been properly maintained, that the financial statements and accompanying notes have been prepared in accordance with accounting standards, and that the financial statements and notes for the financial year provide a 'true and fair' view of the company's position (ss 295(4)(e), 295A)

(2) that the directors' report for a listed company must include a 'management discussion and analysis' ('MD&A'), which contains the information that investors would reasonably require to make an informed assessment of the company's operations and financial position, as well as business strategies and prospects for future financial years (s 299A)

(3) that if additional information is included in an entity's full year or half-year financial report to ensure a 'true and fair' view (of the financial performance and position of the company, satisfying the existing requirement under the Act (ss 297, 305)), then the directors' report must set out the reasons for the directors forming the view that the inclusion of this information was necessary and the location of this additional information in the financial report (s 298(1A)), and the auditor's report must include a statement as to whether the auditor believes the inclusion of this additional information was necessary to provide a 'true and fair' view (s 306(2)).

7.2.5 Continuous disclosure

The CLERP 9 reforms also made changes to the continuous disclosure regime which, under the *Corporations Act* and the ASX *Listing Rules*, requires that listed companies (and non-listed 'disclosing entities') immediately release to the market information that could have a material effect on the price or value of affected companies' securities. There were two changes:

(1) the introduction of personal liability for individuals who are deemed to be 'involved' in an entity's contravention of the continuous disclosure provisions (which essentially 'pick up' the continuous disclosure rules under the ASX *Listing Rules*). This personal liability provision is subject to a 'due diligence' defence[5]

(2) providing ASIC with the power to issue 'infringement notices' against an entity (but not against an individual 'involved' in a contravention) if ASIC considers that the entity has not met its continuous disclosure obligations. Complying with an infringement notice by paying the specified monetary penalty within the specified time period is not an admission of guilt, but it bars ASIC from commencing civil or criminal proceedings in relation to the alleged contravention.[6]

---

5   See *Corporations Act 2001* (Cth) s 674(2A) and *Australian Securities and Investments Commission v Sino Australia Oil and Gas Ltd (in liq)* (2016) 115 ACSR 437.
6   See *Corporations Act 2001* (Cth) pt 9.4AA, and ASIC's policy document, *Continuous Disclosure Obligations: Infringement Notices* (Regulatory Guide 73, 2012; reissued October 2017), which sets out ASIC's processes for administering the infringement notice regime, including how hearings are to be conducted and notices issued.

7.3 Accounting standards

7.3.1 Background

The Australian Financial Reporting Council ('FRC') is responsible for overseeing the effectiveness of the financial reporting framework in Australia[7] and has directed the 'AASB' to adopt IFRS as issued by the IASB, effective from 1 January 2005.

The statutory functions of the AASB under the *Australian Securities and Investments Commission Act 2001* (Cth) ('the *ASIC Act*') are to 'participate in and contribute to the development of a single set of accounting standards for worldwide use, and to advance and promote the main objects of pt 12 of the *ASIC Act*, which include 'reducing the cost of capital, enabling Australian entities to compete effectively overseas and maintaining investor confidence in the Australian economy'.[8]

According to the AASB's *Due Process Framework for Setting Standards*, the AASB sets 'standards that enable "publicly accountable" private sector entities to maintain IFRS compliance, and for others, use IFRS standards (where they exist), and transaction neutrality (modified as necessary), or develop Australian-specific standards and guidance'[9] under the broad strategic directions of the FRC.

7.3.2 The IFRS Foundation

The IFRS Foundation is a not-for-profit,[10] public interest organisation founded in 2001 to develop 'high-quality, global standards that result in corporate information that informs investment decisions'.[11] It comprises two standards-setting bodies: the IASB and the ISSB. As of January 2023, there are more than 140 jurisdictions around the world which require IFRS as their national accounting standards and, in addition, more than 20 jurisdictions permit the use of IFRS.[12] IFRS set out how a company prepares its financial statements, one of the most important components in accounting governance.

7.3.3 Sustainability reporting standards

One of the governance matters that has come under scrutiny at the IFRS Foundation is sustainability reporting. Investors around the world are calling for transparent information on climate and other ESG matters. This has also been the case in Australia where the AASB commenced a sustainability reporting project in February 2022 and earmarked the project as a high-priority standard-setting project for 2022–26.

On 3 November 2021, the IFRS Foundation Trustees announced the creation of a new standard-setting board, the ISSB, to help meet this demand. The intention is for the ISSB to establish a baseline of what sustainability-related disclosures should look

---

7   FRC, 'About the FRC' (2023) <https://frc.gov.au/about-frc>.
8   AASB, 'About the AASB' (2023) <https://aasb.gov.au/about-the-aasb/>.
9   AASB, *AASB Due Process Framework for Setting Standards* (September 2019) s 1.2.
10 See also Section 3.4.3.
11 IFRS, 'Who we are' (2023) <https://www.ifrs.org/about-us/who-we-are/>.
12 Refer to Deloitte, 'Use of IFRS by jurisdiction' (2023) <https://www.iasplus.com/en/resources/ifrs-topics/use-of-ifrs>.

like if they are to assist the decision-making processes of investors and other stake-holders.[13] In theory, sustainability-related disclosures should inform corporate stake-holders about companies' sustainability risks and opportunities, assisting them to make investment and other decisions.

In March 2022, the ISSB launched a consultation on its first two proposed sustainability standards: one on general sustainability-related disclosures and one on climate. The proposals have been developed in response to requests from G20 leaders, the International Organization of Securities Commissions ('IOSCO') and others for enhanced information from companies on sustainability-related risks and opportunities.

Two sustainability standards, IFRS S1 *General Requirements for Disclosure of Sustainability-related Financial Information* and IFRS S2 *Climate-related Disclosures*, were formally issued in June 2023, effective for reporting periods beginning on or after 1 January 2024. These two standards comprise overall disclosure requirements for an entity in respect of sustainability-related financial information, as well as any significant sustainability-related risks and opportunities by the entity. They also require entities to provide the market with a complete set of sustainability-related financial disclosures. After a comprehensive review of the standards, the IOSCO officially endorsed the two standards on 25 July 2023. The ISSB is working on an Adoption Guide for regulators that is due to be finalised in the first half of 2024. Going forward, these two sustainability standards should form a baseline for sustainability-related disclosures to meet the information needs of global investors in assessing corporate value and making investment decisions.[14]

The impact of sustainability reporting standards on accounting governance is likely to be enormous. According to Barker, Eccles and Serafeim (2020), if managers take sustainability issues into account, they will be able to make better strategy and capital allocation decisions. In turn, boards of directors will also view sustainability as a major governance issue to focus on, rather than considering it as a side issue. Having both the management and the board working together should lead to a better long-term corporate financial performance. As a consequence, investors will find companies with effective sustainability management and governance more attractive, and will demand the same consistency and clarity in a sustainability reporting as they expect for financial reporting. In other words, investors will demand transparent sustainability information, as well as financial information, prepared under respective standards by the management. They will also demand the opportunity to discuss both financial and sustainability performance, and how they are related to each other, with the management and the board.[15]

One component of accounting governance that will apply to both financial and sustainability reporting is the provision of external independent assurance of such reports provided by auditors. Section 7.4 considers current regulations on auditors and the role they play in accounting governance.

13 IFRS, 'About the International Sustainability Standards Board' (2023) <https://www.ifrs.org/groups/international-sustainability-standards-board/>.
14 Refer to this resource for more up-to-date details on the adoption and implementation of sustainability standards worldwide: IFRS, 'IFRS Sustainability Standards Navigator' (2023) <https://www.ifrs.org/issued-standards/ifrs-sustainability-standards-navigator/#sustainability-standards>.
15 R Barker, RG Eccles and G Serafeim, 'The future of ESG is ... accounting?' (*Harvard Business Review*, 3 December 2020) <https://hbr.org/2020/12/the-future-of-esg-is-accounting>.

7.4 Auditor independence

7.4.1 Background

As mentioned in Section 7.2.2, a key aim of the CLERP 9 reforms was to ensure greater auditor independence. Prior to those changes, the *Corporations Act* dealt with auditor independence in only a piecemeal fashion. The importance of auditor independence was underlined in the HIH Report,[16] where Justice Owen stated:

> Auditor independence is a critical element going to the credibility and reli-ability of an auditor's reports. Audited financial statements play a key role promoting the efficiency of capital markets and the independent auditor con-stitutes the principal external check on the integrity of financial statements. The Ramsay Report recognised the following four functions of an independent audit in relation to capital market efficiency:
>
> - adding value to financial statements
> - adding value to the capital markets by enhancing the credibility of financial statements
> - enhancing the effectiveness of the capital markets in allocating valuable resources by improving the decisions of users of financial statements
> - assisting to lower the cost of capital to those using audited financial state-ments by reducing information risk.

In addition to the above functions, an independent audit contributes to capital market efficiency by enhancing the consistency and comparability of reported financial infor-mation. It is therefore widely accepted that the auditor must be, and be seen to be, free of any interest that is incompatible with objectivity: for an audit to fulfil its func-tions, there must be public confidence in the auditor.[17] The responsibility of auditors to maintain independence in the carrying out of their function was stated by the US Supreme Court:

> The independent public accountant performing this special function owes alle-giance to the corporation's creditors and stockholders, as well as the investing public. This public watchdog function demands that the accountant maintain total independence from the client at all times and requires complete fidelity to the public trust.[18]

It seems striking that an 'independent' auditor could, in relation to another aspect of its business, be 'dependent' upon the fees paid by the company being audited. Human nature dictates that an auditor is likely to be less impartial in assessing a corporation's financial reporting if an unfavourable audit report may jeopardise substantial fees aris-ing from the provision of non-audit services. CLERP 9 attempted to address this issue

---

16 Report of the HIH Royal Commission ('Owen Report'), *The Failure of HIH Insurance – Volume I: A Corporate Collapse and Its Lessons* (Commonwealth of Australia, 2003).
17 Owen Report (2003) [7.2.1].
18 *United States v Arthur Young & Co*, 465 US 805, 817–18 (1984).

by introducing a range of reforms which aimed to improve both actual and perceived independence, which in turn would lead to greater confidence in the credibility and reliability of audited financial statements.

7.4.2 General requirement for auditor independence

Section 324CA of the *Corporations Act* establishes a general requirement for auditor independence which applies to auditors and audit companies.[19] An individual auditor or audit company is prohibited from engaging in 'audit activity'[20] if a 'conflict of interest situation' exists in relation to the audited body at that time. If the individual auditor or the audit company becomes aware that the conflict of interest situation exists, the individual auditor or the audit company is required to take all reasonable steps to ensure that the conflict of interest situation ceases to exist as soon as possible.

7.4.3 Conflict of interest

Section 324CD(1) of the *Corporations Act* provides that a 'conflict of interest situation' exists in relation to an audited body at a particular time, if circumstances exist at the time which:

- renders the auditor, or a professional member of the audit team, incapable of exercising objective and impartial judgment in relation to the conduct of an audit of the audited body (s 324CD(1)(a)), and
- would give a person, with full knowledge of the facts and circumstances, reasonable grounds for concern that the auditor, or a professional member of the audit team, is not capable of exercising objective and impartial judgment in relation to the conduct of an audit of the audited body (s 324CD(1)(b)).

In determining whether a conflict of interest situation exists, s 324CD(2) goes on to provide that regard is to be had to circumstances arising from any relationship (that either exists, has existed, or is likely to exist) between:

- the individual auditor, or
- the audit firm or any current or former member of the firm, or
- the audit company, any current or former director of the audit company or any person currently or formerly involved in the management of the audit company,

and any of the following persons and bodies:

- a company (including a person currently or formerly involved in the management of the company), or
- a disclosing entity (including a person currently or formerly involved in the management of the entity), or
- a registered scheme (including a person currently or formerly involved in the management of the responsible scheme or the entity).

---

19 A general independence requirement for members of audit firms and directors of audit companies, mirroring s 324CA, is contained in *Corporations Act 2001* (Cth) ss 324CB and 324CC respectively.
20 See the definition of 'engage in audit activity' in *Corporations Act 2001* (Cth) s 9.

If a 'conflict of interest situation' does exist, the individual auditor or audit company must notify ASIC in writing of the conflict of interest within seven days of the day they became aware of the conflict of interest (s 324CA(1A)). If the auditor or audit company does not then notify ASIC within 21 days of the notification (or such other period as ASIC determines) that the conflict has been removed, the audit appointment will terminate pursuant to s 327B(2A) if the audit is of a public company.

7.4.4 Specific independence requirements

Section 324 of the *Corporations Act* includes a limited number of specific restrictions on auditors to ensure independence. These are in the form of specific independence requirements applying to individual auditors (s 324CE), audit firms (s 324CF) and audit companies (s 324CG).

CLERP 9 introduced a cooling-off period concerning the involvement of auditors with firms they have audited. Under the Act, a person is prohibited from becoming an officer of an audited body for two years if the person:

- ceases to be a member of an audit firm or director of an audit company and was a professional member of the audit team engaged in an audit of the audited body (s 324CI), or
- ceases to be a professional employee of the auditor if the person was a 'lead auditor' or 'review auditor' for an audit of the audited body (s 324CJ).

Under the Act, a 'lead auditor' is the registered company auditor who is primarily responsible to the audit firm or audit company that is conducting the audit. A 'review auditor' is the registered company auditor (if any) who is primarily responsible to the individual auditor, the audit firm, or audit company for reviewing the conduct of the audit (s 324AF).

Additionally, CLERP 9 requires that a person who has been a member of an audit firm or director of an audit company cannot become an officer of an audited body if another person who is, or was, a member or director of the audit firm or company at a time when the auditor undertook an audit of the audited body is also an officer of the audited body (s 324CK).

7.4.5 Auditor rotation

The legislative framework for auditor rotation applies where an individual auditor, an audit firm or an authorised audit company has been appointed as auditor of a listed company or registered scheme. The provisions rely on the concept of an auditor having 'played a significant role', which is defined in s 9 of the Act. Where an individual plays a significant role in the audit of a listed company for five successive financial years, the individual cannot play a significant role in the audit of that company for at least another two successive financial years (s 324DA). Amendments in 2012 subsequently introduced a procedure that can allow the company to permit the auditor to serve another two successive financial years (s 324DAA).[21] This change was introduced following the Treasury's report, *Audit Quality in Australia: A Strategic Review* (March 2010), which found that audit

---

21   See the *Corporations Legislation Amendment (Audit Enhancement) Act 2012* (Cth) ss 324DAA–324DAD.

clients were losing valuable expertise because of the five-year rule. As some other jurisdictions allow for longer periods prior to mandatory rotation, the report recommended
a further two years be allowed in certain circumstances.

Section 324DA(2) goes on to provide that a person may not play a significant role as
auditor for more than five out of any seven successive financial years, although this too
is subject to the exception outlined above (s 324DA(3)). According to the Explanatory
Memorandum to the CLERP 9 Bill:

> This approach recognises that auditors may not necessarily audit a body in con-
> secutive years; however, the relationship between the auditor and the audited
> body can still give rise to a threat to independence.

7.4.6 Disclosure of non-audit services

The board of directors of a listed company must provide a statement in the company's
annual report identifying non-audit services that have been provided by the auditor,
audit firm or audit company, and a declaration that the provision of these services does
not compromise the auditor's independence (s 300(11B)). Where the company has an
audit committee, this statement must be made in accordance with advice provided by
that committee (s 300(11D)).

The *Corporations Legislation Amendment (Audit Enhancement) Act 2012* (Cth) has added
to the disclosure obligations of audit firms by introducing a new requirement: the annual
transparency report (pt 2M.4A). This requirement applies to auditors, audit firms and
audit companies that audit 10 or more listed companies or listed schemes or certain
APRA-regulated bodies in a given reporting year (s 332A). The content of the annual
transparency report is set out in sch 7A of the *Corporations Regulations 2001* (Cth).

7.5 Auditors' responsibilities

A good way to look beyond the often superficial nature of audit reports is to ask questions of
the auditors. CLERP 9 introduced s 250PA, which allows a shareholder of a listed company
to submit questions to the auditor about the contents of the audit report or the conduct of
the audit. Importantly, s 250PA(5) allows auditors to 'filter' questions according to their relevance to the audit report or conduct of the audit. While the filtering exercise is the task of
the auditor, the company can express its opinion to the auditor regarding the relevance of
individual questions. Section 250PA(7) requires the company to make the list of questions
provided by the auditor reasonably available to members attending the AGM. The list could
be provided through distribution of printed copies to shareholders or by other means.

Section 250RA of the Act requires auditors of a listed company to attend the company's AGM. Where the auditor is an individual auditor and is unable to attend the AGM,
the auditor can instead be represented by a member of the audit team who is 'suitably
qualified' and is in a position to answer questions regarding the audit (s 250RA(1)(b)).

Another change introduced by the CLERP 9 package of reforms involved expanding auditors' reporting obligations to ASIC to include a much wider range of suspected
or actual malfeasance. Section 311 requires individual auditors conducting an audit to
notify ASIC in writing within 28 days of becoming aware of any circumstances that:

- they have reasonable grounds to suspect amount to a contravention (either a significant contravention, or a contravention that the auditor believes 'has not been or will not be adequately dealt with by commenting on it in the auditor's report or bringing it to the attention of the directors') of the Act
- 'amount to an attempt, in relation to the audit, by any person to unduly influence, coerce, manipulate or mislead a person involved in the conduct of the audit', or
- 'amount to an attempt, by any person, to otherwise interfere with the proper conduct of the audit'.

7.6 Auditors' liability

7.6.1 Background

Like all parties, professional or otherwise, auditors may be legally liable where they do not properly discharge their legal duties.[22] This liability can arise in three main ways. First, the auditor is engaged by a company to perform an audit pursuant to a contract. The auditor can be liable for breach of contract if the audit function is not performed adequately. Parties to a contract are always free to agree to any express terms in the contract; however, in relation to audit services, the implied duties of an auditor include an undertaking by the auditor to use reasonable skill and care in the conduct of the audit.[23] As a result of the operation of the 'privity' doctrine, only the company may sue the auditor for breach of contractual promise. Other potentially affected parties, such as shareholders, are not a party to the contract and hence have no standing to sue under the contract.

Second, the law on negligence provides that the auditor will be liable to parties to whom they owe a duty of care if they do not complete the audit to the standard required of a professional auditor and the other party suffers loss as a result of the negligent audit. To this end, it is noteworthy that existing case law has held that not only do auditors owe a duty of care to the company, but in some cases the duty may extend to shareholders[24] and potentially also to other third parties, such as financiers of the company, where the financiers made the auditors aware of the fact that the information received from the auditors will be used to determine whether or not finance should be provided to the audited person or entity.

Finally, auditors can be held liable for breach of statutory duties. Where an auditor breaches duties imposed on the auditor by statute (such as s 311), the company may sue for damages for breach of this duty.[25] In these circumstances, only the company may sue, given that the statutory duties are enacted in order to protect the company.[26] There is a range of other statutory actions that might also be available to a company. The main one

---

22 For a detailed discussion regarding the legal liability of auditors, see RP Austin and IM Ramsay, *Ford Austin and Ramsay's Principles of Corporations Law* (LexisNexis, 16th ed, 2015) [11.530]–[11.580].
23 *Shire of Frankston and Hastings Corporation v Cohen* (1960) 102 CLR 607.
24 *Columbia Coffee & Tea Pty Ltd v Churchill* (1992) 29 NSWLR 141; *Strategic Minerals Corporation NL v Basham* (1996) 15 ACLC 1155; but cf *Esanda Finance Corporation Ltd v Peat Marwick Hungerfords* (1997) 188 CLR 241.
25 *AWA Ltd v Daniels (No 2)* (1992) 9 ACSR 983.
26 Ibid.

is the misleading and deceptive conduct cause of action pursuant to s 18 of the Australian Consumer Law (formerly s 52 of the *Trade Practices Act 1974* (Cth)).[27]

As a result of the operation of normal contract and, particularly, negligence principles, auditors might be burdened with a legal liability beyond their level of fault. A moment of inattention in checking company records can result in an auditor failing to observe a significant problem or defect in a company's finances. If the defect had been detected by the auditor it may have enabled the company to, say, stave off insolvency and thereby save many millions of dollars. In order to deal with this possibility, changes introduced as part of CLERP 9 reduced the potential liability of auditors.

Two key changes that were introduced by the CLERP 9 reforms were: (1) to enable audit firms to incorporate (so that liability is restricted to the auditors actually responsible); and (2) to introduce a system of 'proportionate liability' in relation to damages actions involving (but not limited to) auditors concerning economic loss or property damage stemming from misleading or deceptive conduct.

7.6.2 Registration of audit companies

Giving audit firms the option to incorporate was considered the best way to overcome this liability issue. Section 1299A requires companies to apply to ASIC for registration as an 'authorised audit company'. Section 1299B states that a company may only be registered as an authorised audit company if all of the following conditions are met:

- Each of the directors of the company is a registered company auditor and is not disqualified from managing a corporation under pt 2D.6.
- Each share in the company is held and beneficially owned by a person who is an individual or the legal representative of an individual.
- A majority of the votes that may be cast at a general meeting of the company attach to shares in the company that are held and beneficially owned by individuals who are registered company auditors.
- ASIC is satisfied that the company has adequate and appropriate professional indemnity insurance.
- The company is not an externally administered body corporate.

The CLERP 9 legislation also implemented a regime of 'proportionate' liability for all professional advisers, including auditors. The basic thrust of the provisions is that for claims not involving dishonesty or deliberate breaches, the liability of financial advisers would be commensurate with their degree of wrongdoing (ss 1041L–1041S).

7.7 Regulatory requirements for audit

7.7.1 Qualifications of auditors

The audit role can only be fulfilled properly if auditors have high-level skills and expertise. CLERP 9 comprises minimum competency requirements, and standards-based

---

27 *Competition and Consumer Act 2010* (Cth) sch 2 s 18. (The full text of the *Australian Consumer Law* (ACL) is set out in sch 2 of the *Competition and Consumer Act 2010* (Cth), formerly the *Trade Practices Act 1974* (Cth)).

practical experience requirements for all auditors in order to enhance public confidence in auditors. The specific amendments to the *Corporations Act* (ss 1280, 1280A) in this regard include:

- providing that the practical experience requirements for registration may be satisfied by completion of all the components of a competency standard in auditing
- revising the education requirements for registration to include completion of a specialist course in auditing
- making an auditor's continued registration subject to compliance with any conditions that may be imposed by ASIC in accordance with the regulations (with new corporations regulations introduced to deal with this)
- replacing the requirement for auditors to lodge a triennial statement with a new requirement to lodge an annual statement, and
- revising the types of matters that may be referred to the Companies Auditors and Liquidators Disciplinary Board ('CALDB', now known as 'CADB' after the disciplining of liquidators was removed in 2017) in light of the above.

7.7.2 Audit committees

An effective audit committee, which is a committee of the board of directors, can play a critical role in financial reporting by overseeing and monitoring the management and the auditor's participation in the financial reporting process. The committee can increase the credibility of the reporting process by monitoring the selection of financial accounting policies, and meeting regularly with internal and external auditors, and occasionally in the absence of management.

ASX Listing Rule 12.7[28] requires that an entity included in the S&P All Ordinaries Index at the beginning of its financial year have an audit committee during that year. If an entity is in the top 300 of that Index, the composition, operation and responsibilities of the audit committee must comply with the relevant recommendations found in the latest edition of the ASX *Corporate Governance Principles and Recommendations*.[29]

For an audit committee to be effective and not merely a cosmetic construct, research has shown that it should be composed entirely of independent or non-executive directors, at least some of whom have financial expertise; should have an audit committee charter; and should meet frequently. Recommendations 4.1(a)(1) and (2) of the 2019 ASX *Corporate Governance Principles and Recommendations* state that:

> The board of a listed entity should … have an audit committee which … has at least three members, all of whom are non-executive directors and a majority of whom are independent directors … and … is chaired by an independent director, who is not the chair of the board.

28 ASX, 'ASX Listing Rules – Chapter 12 Ongoing requirements' (1 December 2019) <https://www.asx .com.au/about/regulation/rules-guidance-notes-and-waivers/asx-listing-rules-guidance-notes-and-waivers.html>.

29 ASX, *Corporate Governance Principles and Recommendations* (4th ed, 2019) <https://www.asx.com.au/ documents/asx-compliance/cgc-principles-and-recommendations-fourth-edn.pdf>.

In terms of expertise, the Commentary to this Recommendation states that:

> The audit committee should be of sufficient size and independence, and its members between them should have the accounting and financial expertise and a sufficient understanding of the industry in which the entity operates, to be able to discharge the committee's mandate effectively.

Recommendation 4.1(a)(3) expects that the charter of the audit committee should be disclosed. The Commentary states that the charter should clearly set out the audit committee's role and, in order to achieve the role, the committee needs to have the right to obtain information, interview management and auditors, both internal and external, and seek advice from independent consultants or specialists if deemed necessary or appropriate.

Research has provided evidence of increased financial reporting and/or audit quality in association with effective audit committees: they reduced manipulation of accounting numbers,[30] and showed greater willingness to issue appropriately modified auditor's reports.[31] The following results were also found: a lower incidence of fraudulent financial reporting and financial restatements,[32] a lower incidence of auditor switching following an unfavourable auditor's report,[33] a lower incidence of auditor resignation[34] and a higher frequency of engagement of industry specialist auditors.[35]

7.7.3 Auditing standards

The FRC, being responsible for the effectiveness of the financial reporting framework in Australia, oversees both the AASB and the AUASB. The FRC monitors the development of international accounting and auditing standards by the AASB and the AUASB respectively, assists the development of a single set of global accounting and auditing standards, and promotes the adoption of these standards.[36]

The AUASB is an independent, non-corporate Commonwealth entity of the Australian Government, responsible for developing, issuing and maintain auditing and assurance standards. The AUASB standards are legally enforceable for audits or reviews of financial reports required under the *Corporations Act*. Similar to the vision and mission of the

---

30 A Klein, 'Audit committee, board of director characteristics, and earnings management' (2002) 33(3) *Journal of Accounting and Economics* 375; Q Yasser and A Mamun, 'Audit committee structure and earnings management in Asia Pacific' (2016) 2(1) *Economics and Business Review* 66.

31 JV Carcello and TL Neal, 'Audit committee composition and auditor reporting' (2000) 75(4) *Accounting Review* 453.

32 LJ Abbott, S Parker and GF Peters, 'Audit committee characteristics and restatements' (2004) 23(1) *Auditing: A Journal of Practice and Theory* 69; B Bratten, M Causholli and V Sulcaj, 'Overseeing the external audit function: Evidence from audit committees' reported activities' (2022) 41(1) *Auditing: A Journal of Practice and Theory* 1.

33 JV Carcello and TL Neal, 'Audit committee characteristics and auditor dismissal following "new" going concern reports' (2003) 78(1) *Accounting Review* 95.

34 HY Lee, V Mande and R Ortman, 'The effect of audit committee and board of director independence on auditor resignation' (2004) 23(2) *Auditing: A Journal of Practice and Theory* 131.

35 YM Chen, R Moroney and K Houghton, 'Audit committee composition and the use of an industry specialist audit firm' (2005) 45(2) *Accounting and Finance* 217; M Kao, M Shiue and C Tseng, 'Voluntary audit committees, auditor selection and audit quality: Evidence from Taiwan' (2021) 36(4) *Managerial Auditing Journal* 616.

36 FRC, 'About the FRC' (2023) <https://frc.gov.au/about-frc>.

AASB, the AUASB seeks to contribute to stakeholder confidence in the Australian economy, including its capital markets, and in external reporting. In addition, the board aims to contribute to the development of a single set of auditing and assurance standards and guidance for world-wide use.[37]

Section 307A of the *Corporations Act* requires audits of a financial report for a financial year and audits or reviews of a financial report for a half-year period to be conducted in accordance with auditing standards. Sections 308 (Auditor's report on annual financial report) and 309 (Auditor's report on half-year financial report) have been amended to require auditors to include in their reports any statements or disclosures required by the auditing standards: the provisions are ss 308(3A) and 309(5A).

In terms of sustainability reporting, which recently has gained much attention, the AUASB states that existing assurance standards are widely accepted and currently used for sustainability assurance engagements.[38] The issuance by the ISSB of the two sustainability standards in June 2023, along with the proposed International Standard on Sustainability Assurance 5000 and the General Requirements for Sustainability Assurance Engagements (ED-5000) in August 2023, however, is likely to bring further regulatory reforms in this area.

7.8 Conclusion

There have been some major changes in corporate governance regulations in Australia: from a disclosure-based approach, which preferred companies to disclose governance policies and practices implemented in accordance with their needs, to an interventionist approach. CLERP 9 reforms have contributed to the formalisation of best-practice governance benchmarks by introducing (or significantly enhancing) substantive corporate governance requirements under the *Corporations Act*.

There is still considerable debate as to whether many of the compliance-related requirements under CLERP 9 (particularly in relation to audit reform, financial reporting – including CEO/CFO declarations and the MD&A discussion in the directors' report – and executive remuneration) were necessary to improve the governance practices and performance of companies, and therefore to 'fireproof' companies from collapse, or whether they have merely imposed additional burdens on companies.

The 2008 Global Financial Crisis raised concerns about the efficacy of disclosure as the bedrock of corporate regulation. Companies, particularly publicly listed companies, are required to produce reams of often technical information that few find useful or intelligible. In a speech to the ASIC Annual Forum in June 2014,[39] ASIC Chair Greg Medcraft noted that future regulatory approaches may need to be better informed by developments in behavioural science and behavioural finance that provide valuable

37 AASB, 'About the AASB' (2023) <https://aasb.gov.au/about-the-aasb/>.
38 Auditing and Assurance Standards Board, 'AUASB Sustainability Assurance update' (20 April 2023) <https://auasb.gov.au/news/auasb-sustainability-assurance-update/>.
39 Greg Medcraft, 'Regulating for Real People, Markets and Globalization', (Speech, ASIC Annual Forum 2014, 24 March 2014) <https://asic.gov.au/about-asic/news-centre/speeches/asic-forum-2014-regulating-for-real-people-markets-and-globalisation/>.

insights into how investors gather and interpret information about their investments.[40] It seems that the debate concerning prescriptive regulation and mandatory disclosure has a long way to run.

For example, one of the more recent debates stems from the ever-increasing interest in how corporations can govern their sustainability-related activities and adapt their financial reporting to incorporate climate and other ESG information. While the initial steps have been taken by the ISSB to prescribe how sustainability-related information should be disclosed, there are still questions regarding how these disclosures can be utilised by investors and other stakeholders. In addition, the emergence of 'new' types of businesses relying on non-traditional assets and transactions, such as cryptocurrencies and data, is likely to further increase scrutiny: on how corporations disseminate both financial and non-financial information to stakeholders for decision-making processes, and on whether regulation can guide such reporting practices.

The ultimate objective of accounting governance is to ensure that financial statements better reflect the true financial position and performance of corporations. There is now a public expectation that corporations will engage in transparent reporting practices. While the reforms and regulations will not ensure that corporations do not collapse in future, they should, it is hoped, ensure that corporations (managers and the board of directors), auditors, and others involved in corporate reporting are held accountable in providing information needed for investors and other market participants to make informed economic decisions.

---

40 This was echoed in the Financial System Inquiry, *Final Report* (November 2014).

DIRECTORS' DUTIES AND ENFORCEMENT OF LIABILITY

8

8.1 Introduction

As a general rule, directors owe their duties to the company as a whole, not to individual shareholders.[1] Historically, directors' duties and liability were discussed under general law duties (duties at common law or in equity); subsequently,[2] they were added to under statutory duties. Under general law duties, most courts and commentators usually draw a distinction between equitable duties based on loyalty and good faith, with a particular focus on fiduciary duties, and the duty to act with due care and diligence (the duty of care). The duty of care may arise under principles of equity and at common law, in both contract and tort. Fiduciary duties in Australian law are proscriptive, not prescriptive.[3] That is, the duties prohibit the fiduciary from engaging in particular conduct rather than prescribing what the fiduciary must do in particular situations. The failure to act in a reasonable manner has traditionally fallen within the domain of the duty of care, whereas behaviour which falls foul of principles of loyalty is addressed more clearly in equity. The range of equitable duties that are owed by company directors are generally recognised as follows:

(1) the duty to act honestly and in the company's best interests
(2) the duty to act for a proper purpose
(3) the duty not to fetter their discretions
(4) the duty to avoid a conflict of interest
(5) the duty not to act so as to obtain a private profit.

Duties 4 and 5 are accepted as fiduciary duties. Duty 3 is not considered fiduciary in nature. As to duties 1 and 2, there is considerable debate as to whether these duties

---

1   *Percival v Wright* [1902] 2 Ch 421 is often cited as authority for this rule; however, the case involved the purchase of shares from shareholders by members of the board, when the company was subject to a private takeover which rendered the shares significantly more valuable. However, without doubt, significant case law has followed in the years since which reinforced this position. For examples of recognised exception, see *Brunninghausen v Glavanics* (1999) 46 NSWLR 538; *Crawley v Short* (2009) 262 ALR 654 (which deals with closely held family companies).
2   For discussion on the rationale and development of directors' statutory duties in Australia, see Jason Harris, Anil Hargovan and Janet Austin, 'Shareholder primacy revisited: Does the public interest have any role in statutory duties?' (2008) 26(6) *Company and Securities Law Journal* 355.
3   *Breen v Williams* (1996) 186 CLR 71.

are fiduciary or not. The majority of the WA Court of Appeal, in the long-running *Bell* case, held that the duties are fiduciary in nature,[4] but this decision has been strongly criticised.[5] Those arguing against duties 1 and 2 being fiduciary note that these duties seem to impose positive obligations on directors (to act honestly and to act properly) rather than to prohibit conduct.[6]

Unlike the duty of care, these duties are considered strict duties by the courts, which have held on numerous occasions that directors can be in breach of these duties irrespective of the fact that they acted without fault, in terms of either negligence or intent. It has also been held that, as a general rule, the fact that directors acted in what they believed to be the best interests of the company as a whole will not serve as a general defence for a breach of these duties. It also does not matter whether the company suffered any loss.[7] The remedies available will depend upon the nature of the breach. A breach of the duty of care will usually allow for a claim for damages by the company. A breach of the duty not to fetter discretion may give rise to a right to seek compensation or to specifically enforce a contract (depending on what the effect of the unlawful fetter is). Where directors act for an improper purpose, their conduct may be overturned and they may be liable to pay compensation for causing the company to engage in improper conduct. The most common example of this is the improper issue of shares by company directors, which may be challenged by existing members who can seek court orders to overturn the share issue.[8] Similarly, a failure to act in the best interests of the company may lead to the transaction being overturned in equity. This may also overlap with breaches of the duty of care and may give rise to damages payable to the company. The equitable remedy of an injunction may also be available for breaches of both fiduciary and non-fiduciary duties in equity.

The broadest remedies are available for breaches of fiduciary duties (duties 4 and 5, and possibly duties 1 and 2).[9] Remedies for breaches of fiduciary duties can include an account of profits (stripping away improper benefits from the defaulting fiduciary),[10] equitable compensation or a constructive trust over property held by a defaulting fiduciary or their associate.[11] Where a director has acted under a conflict of interest (for example,

4   *Westpac Banking Corporation v Bell Group Ltd (in liq) (No 3)* (2012) 44 WAR 1. For a discussion of the issues in this case see Anil Hargovan and Jason Harris, 'For whom the bell tolls: Directors' duties to creditors after *Bell*' (2013) 35(2) *Sydney Law Review* 433; Rosemary Langford, *Directors' Duties* (Federation Press, 2014); Dyson Heydon, Mark Leeming and Peter Turner, *Meagher Gummow and Lehane's Equity Doctrines and Remedies* (Lexis Nexis Butterworths, 5th ed, 2014) ch 2.

5   See, eg, TF Bathurst and Sienna Merope, 'It tolls for thee: Accessorial liability after *Bell v Westpac*' (2013) 87(12) *Australian Law Journal* 831; William Gummow, 'The equitable duties of company directors' (2013) 87(11) *Australian Law Journal* 753; Matthew Conaglen, 'Interaction between statutory and general law duties concerning company director conflicts' (2013) 31(7) *Company and Securities Law Journal* 403.

6   Stephen Bottomley et al, *Contemporary Australian Corporate Law* (Cambridge University Press, 2nd ed, 2021) 344–6.

7   *Regal (Hastings) Ltd v Gulliver* [1967] 2 AC 134.

8   See, eg, *Howard Smith Ltd v Ampol Petroleum Ltd* [1974] 1 NSWLR 68; *Whitehouse v Carlton Hotel Pty Ltd* (1987) 162 CLR 285.

9   For a useful discussion on the remedies available for breach of fiduciary duty, see *Western Areas Exploration Pty Ltd v Streeter (No 3)* (2009) 73 ACSR 494.

10 *Regal (Hastings) Ltd v Gulliver* [1967] 2 AC 134; *Furs Ltd v Tomkies* (1936) 54 CLR 583.

11 It remains unsettled, under Australian law, whether a breach of fiduciary obligation will enliven access to *Barnes v Addy* (1974) LR 9 Ch App 244 (which permits a beneficiary to seek a constructive

by entering into a transaction with the company) and the company wishes to reverse the transaction, the remedy of rescission may be available. However, the ability of the company to rescind the transaction is limited by a number of exceptions.[12]

In contrast with the judicial approach to directors' fiduciary duties, in the case of the directors' duty to act with due care and diligence the courts originally insisted that directors would only be in breach of this duty if they acted with gross negligence and only if the company suffered damages because the directors acted negligently.[13] In more recent times the courts have grappled with the overlapping nature of the duty as it arises in both equity and common law, and how these duties interact with the statutory duty recognised in s 180(1) of the *Corporations Act 2001* (Cth) ('*Corporations Act*' or 'the Act').[14] In addition, under the statutory duty of care, damages suffered by the company need not be proven; only a foreseeable risk of harm to the company needs to be proven.[15]

Historically, the directors' duty of care and diligence was considered to impose remarkably low standards on directors as the courts used gross negligence[16] as the yardstick for liability and judged a breach of these duties against subjective standards – '[a] director need not exhibit in the performance of his duties a greater degree of skill than may reasonably be expected from a person of his knowledge and experience'.[17] The idea was that the shareholders were ultimately responsible for the unwise appointments of directors that had led to the standards of care, skill and diligence being so low.[18] Then, directors were viewed as country gentlemen, and not expected to realise the significance of certain information in the financial accounts[19] or to even be aware of the company's affairs.[20]

---

trust over misappropriated trust property in the hands of a third party in certain circumstances): see, eg, *Consul Developments Pty Ltd v DPC Estates Pty Ltd* (1975) 132 CLR 373; *Farah Construction Pty Ltd v Say-Dee Pty Ltd* (2007) 203 CLR 89.

12   The exceptions are if the company affirmed the transaction with knowledge of its right to avoid it; innocent third parties would be prejudiced by the election to avoid the transaction; the company unduly delayed acting to exercise its right to avoid the transaction (a form of estoppel); or it became impossible for the parties' rights to be restored to the position obtaining before (*restitutio in integrum*) the transaction was entered into.

13   For historical development of the duty of care and diligence, see *Australian Securities and Investments Commission v Rich* (2009) 75 ACSR 1, [7193]; *Australian Securities and Investments Commission v Cassimatis (No 8)* (2016) 336 ALR 209. See further Rosemary Langford, Ian Ramsay and Michelle Welsh, 'The origins of company directors' statutory duty of care' (2015) 37(4) *Sydney Law Review* 489; Jason Harris, Anil Hargovan and Janet Austin, 'Shareholder primacy revisited: Does the public interest have any role in statutory duties? (2008) 26(6) *Company and Securities Law Journal* 355.

14   See, in particular, *Daniels v Anderson* (1995) 37 NSWLR 438, 652; *Australian Securities and Investments Commission v Rich* (2009) 75 ACSR 1, [7193]; *Vines v Australian Securities and Investments Commission* (2007) 73 NSWLR 451.

15   *Australian Securities and Investments Commission v Rich* (2009) 75 ACSR 1, [7193]; *Cassimatis v Australian Securities and Investments Commission* (2020) 275 FCR 533.

16   Lindley MR in *Lagunas Nitrate Co v Lagunas Syndicate* [1899] 2 Ch 392, 435.

17   *Re City Equitable Fire Insurance Co Ltd* [1925] Ch 407.

18   See, eg, *Turquand v Marshall* (1869) LR 4 Ch App 376.

19   See, eg, *Re Denham and Co* (1883) 25 Ch D 752.

20   In *Re Cardiff Savings Bank* [1892] 2 Ch 100 (*Marquis of Bute's case*), in dismissing a claim of negligence against the Marquis, who had become the president of the board of the bank at the age of six months and held that position for over 40 years (during which time he attended only one board meeting), the Court said that the Marquis was entitled to rely on the bank's managers to perform their duties properly and could not be liable for their neglect.

This laidback approach changed after the landmark 1995 decision in *Daniels v Anderson*,[21] which indicated that the Australian courts are in fact prepared to expect high standards of care and diligence of directors, including non-executive directors.[22]

Nowadays in Australia, the courts more often use the statutory duties of directors (rather than their duties at common law or in equity) to hold directors liable.[23] Under contemporary law, a discussion of directors' duties and liability can be adequately based on provisions in the *Corporations Act*, notwithstanding the fact that most of the primary statutory duties imposed upon directors 'have effect in addition to, and not in derogation of, any rule of law relating to the duty or liability of a person because of their office or employment in relation to a corporation'.[24] In other words, directors' statutory duties are most important, irrespective of the fact that the legislature did not intend to codify directors' duties at common law and in equity.

We have thus adopted the approach in this chapter of explaining directors' duties and liability primarily by way of the statutory provisions. Not only are these provisions comprehensive, but in more recent times they have formed the basis of most of the litigation in this area, due largely to the introduction in 1993 of the civil penalty provisions and the lower standard of proof (balance of probabilities) under those provisions.

The enforcement of directors' duties is of particular importance. Enforcement of the civil penalty provisions is discussed below with reference to two case studies: HIH Insurance (Section 8.3.2) and James Hardie (Section 8.3.3). This chapter first demonstrates (Section 8.2) that enforcement by the Australian Securities and Investments Commission ('ASIC') of civil penalty provisions has been its most common enforcement action in recent years. However, later, we address the enforcement of directors' duties by the corporation under the statutory derivative action (pt 2F.1A; Section 8.5) and the rights of minority shareholders to apply for various remedies in the case of unfairly prejudicial or unfairly discriminatory or oppressive conduct by the corporation or its directors (pt 2F.1; Section 8.6). Finally, we deal with injunctions under s 1324 of the *Corporations Act* (Section 8.7), which allow ASIC or 'a person whose interests have been affected' by a contravention of the Act to stop such conduct and to obtain damages for loss suffered because of such conduct.

---

21 *Daniels v Anderson* (1995) 37 NSWLR 438. See further Justice Geoffrey Nettle, 'The changing positions and duties of company directors' (2018) 41(3) *Melbourne University Law Review* 1402.
22 For discussion on the development of the modern law in this area, see Anil Hargovan, 'Corporate law's new love: Section 232(4) and the director's duty of care' (1994) 3(1) *Asia Pacific Law Review* 20; Sally Sievers, 'Farewell to the sleeping director – the modern judicial and legislative approach to directors' duties of care, skill and diligence – further developments' (1993) 21(2) *Australian Business Law Review* 111; and AS Sievers, 'Directors' duty of care: What is the new standard?' (1997) 15(7) *Company and Securities Law Journal* 392. See generally, as far as the United Kingdom is concerned, ICSA, *ICSA Guidance and Reports: Directors' Duty to Exercise Care, Skill and Diligence* (January 2013).
23 This was not always the case. Prior to the insolvent trading cases in the late 1980s and early 1990s (such as *Statewide Tobacco Services Ltd v Morley* (1990) 2 ACSR 405 and *Commonwealth Bank of Australia v Friedrich* (1991) 5 ACSR 115), which articulated higher standards of care, there was a dearth of reported cases on the directors' statutory duty of care and diligence. See further, Hargovan, 'Corporate law's new love' (1994) 3(1) *Asia Pacific Law Review* 20.
24 *Corporations Act 2001* (Cth) s 185(a).

8.2 Part 9.4B: Civil penalty provisions or pecuniary penalty provisions

8.2.1 Overview

As far as directors' duties and liabilities are concerned, the *Corporations Act* deals with the most important duties of directors, and breaches of them, under the 'civil penalty provisions'.[25] This means that if a breach of any of these provisions is proven, the court will make a declaration of contravention, which is then considered (under ss 1317F and 1317E(2) of the Act) to be conclusive evidence of the following matters:

(a) the court that made the declaration

(b) the civil penalty provision that was contravened

(c) the person who contravened the provision

(d) the conduct that constituted the contravention

(e) if the contravention is of a corporation/scheme civil penalty provision – the corporation or registered scheme to which the conduct related.

Once such an order of contravention is made, there are primarily four further orders that ASIC may seek: disqualification orders (for breaches of corporation/scheme civil penalty provisions), pecuniary penalty orders, relinquishment orders and/or compensation orders. In recent years it has been common for ASIC to pursue disqualification orders and penalty orders rather than compensation. The relevant corporation (or responsible entity of a registered scheme) may also apply for a compensation order,[26] and the corporation/scheme is also entitled to intervene in any proceedings for a disqualification order or pecuniary penalty (which may only be initiated by ASIC) and is entitled to be heard on all matters other than whether the declaration or order should be made.[27] It is important to emphasise that a declaration order must be made before a pecuniary penalty, relinquishment order or disqualification order can be sought by ASIC. A declaration of contravention is not, however, a necessary prerequisite to a compensation order being sought. We deal with disqualification orders, pecuniary penalty orders, relinquishment orders and compensation orders in some detail later in this chapter.

8.2.2 The civil penalty provisions

8.2.2.1 Section 180: Duty of care and diligence – civil obligation[28]

A director's duty of due care and diligence is captured in s 180(1) of the Act. This section provides that directors or other officers of a corporation must exercise their powers and

---

25 For a summary, see para 5.3 of pt 1.5 of the *Corporations Act*. It sets out some of the more important duties of directors and officers and the liability regime for breach.

26 Ibid s 1317H(2). See further *V-Flow Pty Ltd v Holyoake Industries (Vic) Pty Ltd* (2013) 93 ACSR 76.

27 See *Corporations Act 2001* (Cth) s 1317J(3). In relation to 'financial services civil penalty provisions', any person who suffers damage in relation to a contravention, or alleged contravention, of such a provision can also apply for a compensation order: s 1317J(3A).

28 For a fuller discussion, see Anil Hargovan, Michael Adams and Catherine Brown, *Australian Corporate Law* (LexisNexis, 8th ed, 2023) ch 17; Ian Ramsay and Ben Saunders, 'An analysis of the

discharge their duties with the degree of care and diligence that a reasonable person would exercise if they:

(1)   were a director or officer of a corporation in the corporation's circumstances, and

(2)   occupied the office held by, and had the same responsibilities within the corporation as, the director or officer.

The fact that this duty is judged against objective standards ('a reasonable person') means that the standards of this duty have been raised considerably; this is consistent with its common law counterpart, established in *Daniels v Anderson*.[29] No longer can directors escape a breach of this duty by relying on the fact that they lacked the knowledge or experience to take a certain decision. In other words, they would not be able to rely on the notion that in the performance of their duties they did not exhibit 'a greater degree of skill than may reasonably be expected from a person of [their] knowledge and experience'.[30] In order to ensure consistency in the application of this duty, several provisos have been included: first, the duty is to act as a reasonable *person* would act, not as a reasonable *director* would act. There is no applicable standard for what a reasonable director would do, because directors are not like lawyers or doctors, who apply industry-accepted professional standards. Every director and every company is different. Second, the duty of care and diligence is to be judged against the standards expected of directors or officers in corporations comparable to the corporation in which the accused director or officer held office. Third, the reasonable person benchmark is to be assessed by reference to the office and responsibilities that the director or other officer had within the corporation.[31] The duty posits a reasonable person in a similar position in a similar company and assesses what they would have done against what the director actually did or failed to do.

The expression 'same responsibilities' in s 180(1)(b) requires a consideration of all the work in fact undertaken by the relevant director or officer. So if a director or officer has dual roles – as, for example, a company secretary and in-house counsel – both roles are to be taken into account.

The courts adopt the following test to determine a breach of s 180(1):

> In determining whether a director has exercised reasonable care and diligence one must ask what an ordinary person, with the knowledge and experience of the defendant, might have been expected to have done in the circumstances if he or she was acting on their own behalf.[32]

---

enforcement of the statutory duty of care by ASIC' (2019) 36(6) *Company and Securities Law Journal* 497; and Bottomley et al, *Contemporary Australian Corporate Law* (2021) ch 11. See also Jean J du Plessis, 'A comparative analysis of directors' duty of care, skill and diligence in South Africa and in Australia' (2010) (1) *Acta Juridica* 263 and *Australian Securities and Investments Commission v Cassimatis (No 8)* (2016) 336 ALR 209.

29   *Daniels v Andrews* (1995) 37 NSWLR 438.

30   *Re City Equitable Fire Insurance Co Ltd* [1925] Ch 407. See further *Australian Securities and Investments Commission v Rich* (2009) 75 ACSR 1, [7207].

31   See further *Australian Securities and Investments Commission v Flugge and Geary* (2016) 342 ALR 1 for a detailed discussion of the role of expert evidence.

32   *Australian Securities and Investments Commission v Adler* (2002) 41 ACSR 72.

The precise degree or standard of care and diligence required is to be determined with reference to the particular circumstances of the company. These include:[33]

(a) the type of company
(b) the size and nature of the company's business
(c) the composition of the board
(d) the director's and officer's position and responsibilities within the company
(e) the particular function the director or officer is performing
(f) the experience or skills of the particular director or officer
(g) the circumstances of the specific case.

There is an expectation that all directors, regardless of their role and status as executive or non-executive, will have a degree of financial literacy.[34]

Business judgment rule

There is, however, some protection for directors against a breach of duty of care claim in a safe-haven provision called the 'business judgment' rule.[35] 'Business judgment' refers to any decision to take or not take action in respect of a matter relevant to the business operations of the corporation.[36] It is assumed that directors and other officers acted with the required degree of care and diligence if, in exercising business judgment, they met four standards (s 180(2)):

(1) They must have made the judgment in good faith for a proper purpose.
(2) They must not have had a material personal interest in the subject matter of the judgment.
(3) They must have informed themselves about the subject matter of the judgment to the extent they reasonably believed to be appropriate.
(4) They must have rationally believed that the judgment was in the best interests of the corporation.

The onus is on the defendant director to establish evidence to support each element of the business judgment rule defence.[37]

As far as the last requirement is concerned, it is provided that the director's or officer's belief that the judgment is in the best interests of the corporation is a rational one

---

33 *Australian Securities and Investments Commission v Rich* (2009) 75 ACSR 1, ch 23.
34 Established in *Commonwealth Bank of Australia v Friedrich* (1991) 5 ACSR 115, 126. For application, see *Australian Securities and Investments Commission v Healey* (2011) 196 FCR 291; and *Australian Securities and Investments Commission v Godfrey* (2017) 123 ACSR 478.
35 For discussion on the origins of the business judgment rule and its operation at common law, see Paul Redmond, 'Safe harbours or sleepy hollows: does Australia need a statutory business judgment rule?' in I Ramsay (ed), *Corporate Governance and the Duties of Company Directors* (Melbourne University Centre for Corporate Law and Securities Regulation, 1997) 185. For a practical illustration, see *Australian Securities and Investments Commission v Mariner Corporation Ltd* (2015) 241 FCR 502 where the Court held (obiter) that it would have successfully applied s 180(2) but it had already decided that s 180(1) was not contravened in this case.
36 *Corporations Act 2001* (Cth) s 180(3).
37 *Australian Securities and Investments Commission v Rich* (2009) 75 ACSR 1; *Australian Securities and Investments Commission v Mitchell (No 2)* (2020) 382 ALR 425, [1435].

unless the belief is one that no reasonable person in their position would hold. It should be noted that this provides considerable protection to directors, as the requirement is not the ordinary objective requirement that 'a reasonable person in their position will hold', but that 'no reasonable person in their position will hold'. This ensures that only in extreme circumstances, where a director or officer blindly believed something that 'no other person in their position' would believe, will a court withhold the protection of the business judgment rule based on the fact that it was not a rational belief that their business judgment was in the best interests of the corporation.

It is of considerable importance to note that the business judgment rule will only provide protection to directors when the courts must consider whether or not they acted with the required care and diligence. It does not operate in relation to duties under any other provision of the Act – for example, the duty to act in good faith (s 181); the duty not to use their position as director to gain personally or cause detriment to the corporation (s 182); the duty not to use information to gain personally or cause detriment to the corporation (s 183); and the duty to prevent insolvent trading (s 588G).

There have been suggestions that the business judgment rule be broadened to include other potential liabilities that may be incurred by directors, with both the Australian Institute of Company Directors and leading legal adviser, and former corporate law judge, the Hon Robert Austin (who decided the *Australian Securities and Investments Commission v Rich* case, among many others),[38] proposing potential models. It seems that the operation of the rule will continue to be a matter of keen public interest for the foreseeable future.[39]

Delegation and reliance

The ability to delegate responsibilities and rely on subordinates to carry out tasks is an essential part of effective management. The general law (*Australian Securities and Investments Commission v Adler*[40]) and ss 198D and 189 of the Act permit directors to delegate powers and to reasonably rely on others for information or advice.

In order to obtain the benefit of the reliance defence, the director's reliance on others must be reasonable, which is to be determined on the facts of each case. Justice Santow, in *Australian Securities and Investments Commission v Adler*,[41] collated the judicial authorities on this issue and offered the following general legal principles and factors in determining reasonableness:[42]

---

38 Robert Austin, 'Time to lift the grey cloud of litigation', *Australian Financial Review* (21 March 2014) 33. See further Jason Harris and Anil Hargovan, 'Revisiting the business judgment rule' (2014) 66(10) *Governance Directions* 634.

39 See Jean J du Plessis and Jim A Mathiopoulos, 'Defences and relief from liability for company directors widening protection to stimulate innovation' (2017) 31' *Australian Journal of Company Law* 1; Jason Harris and Anil Hargovan, 'Still a sleepy hollow? Directors' liability and the business judgment rule' (2016) 31(3) *Australian Journal of Corporate Law* 319. See also Jean J du Plessis, 'Open sea or safe harbour? American, Australian and South African business judgment rules compared' (2011) 32(12) *Company Lawyer* 377, 380–2.

40 *Australian Securities and Investments Commission v Adler* (2002) 41 ACSR 72.

41 Ibid.

42 For examples of cases where directors unsuccessfully relied on this defences, see *Australian Securities and Investments Commission v Vocation Ltd (in liq)* (2019) 371 ALR 155; *Australian*

(1)   The function that has been delegated is such that it is proper to leave it to the delegate.

(2)   The extent to which the director is put on inquiry or, given the facts of a case, should have been put on inquiry.

(3)   The relationship between the director and the delegate must be such that the director honestly holds the belief that the delegate is trustworthy, competent and someone upon whom reliance can be placed. Knowledge that the delegate is dishonest and incompetent will make reliance unreasonable.

(4)   The risk involved in the transaction and the nature of the transaction.

(5)   The extent of steps taken by the director: for example, inquiries made or other circumstances engendering trust.

(6)   Whether the position of the director is executive or non-executive (although, as noted by Santow J, the majority in *Daniels v Anderson* (1995) 37 NSWLR 438 moved away from this distinction).

The reliance defence is unavailable when management specifically brings a matter before the board for attention and the task for consideration is not an onerous one, as illustrated in *Australian Securities and Investments Commission v Macdonald (No 11)*, discussed in Section 8.3.

8.2.2.2 Section 181: Duty of good faith – civil obligation[43]

Under s 181, a director or other officer of a corporation is also expected to exercise their powers and discharge their duties:

(a)   in good faith in the best interests of the corporation, and

(b)   for a proper purpose.

This duty reflects a similar equitable duty of directors – that they must always act bona fide in the best interests of the corporation, and that they must act for proper purposes. Whether these duties in equity are a compound expression,[44] one duty with two separate limbs,[45] or some variation in between is unsettled[46] – but has no practical impact. The statutory provision expresses the duty as a singular duty, with two subsections, (a) and (b), as set out above – both must be satisfied or the duty is breached. In terms of acting for a 'proper purpose', the duty will be breached where an impermissible purpose for acting is 'causative in the sense that, but for its presence, "the power would

Securities and Investments Commission v Flugge (2016) 342 ALR 1; *Australian Securities and Investments Commission v Sino Australia Oil and Gas Ltd (in liq)* (2016) 115 ACSR 437; and *Australian Securities and Investments Commission v Macdonald (No 11)* (2009) 256 ALR 199. For examples of successful reliance, see *Australian Securities and Investments Commission v Mitchell (No 2)* (2020) 382 ALR 425; *Australian Securities and Investments Commission v Mariner Corporation Ltd* (2015) 241 FCR 502.

43   For a fuller discussion, see Hargovan, Adams and Brown, *Australian Corporate Law* (2023) ch 15; and Bottomley et al, *Contemporary Australian Corporate Law* (2021) ch 12. See further *Australian Securities and Investments Commission v Flugge and Geary* (2016) 342 ALR 1, [1965] *et seq*.

44   *Re Smith & Fawcett Ltd* [1942] Ch 304.

45   *Hogg v Cramphorn Ltd* [1967] Ch 254.

46   *Harlowe's Nominees Pty Ltd v Woodside (Lakes Entrance) Oil Co NL* (1968) 121 CLR 483.

not have been exercised'",[47] or where the substantial purpose for which the power was exercised was deemed improper.[48] Once the court has determined that primarily or substantially the power was misused, it will not help the directors to allege that they had not gained personally, that the company had benefited from the conduct or that they had acted honestly – the conduct of the directors under attack will then be set aside because of the breach of their strict fiduciary duty to exercise their powers for the purpose for which the power was conferred upon them.[49] The greater tension, currently, sits in an examination of which interests may be considered when determining how to act in 'the best interests of the company'. As discussed extensively in Chapters 1–3, although a narrow approach to this duty would suggest that acting in the best interests of the company can be equated with acting in the best interests of the members as a collective group,[50] other views, including permitting directors to have consideration of future members and the company as a commercial entity,[51] employees[52] and creditors (as the company nears insolvency),[53] are possible.[54]

8.2.2.3 Sections 182 and 183: Duty not to use position or information to gain personally or cause detriment to the corporation[55]

These two duties are discussed together because they deal with conflicts of interest, through the application to misuse of position and misuse of information. Directors occupy a unique position and have access to lots of information about the corporation's business, but they may not use their position or the information they obtain as directors to gain personally; or to gain an advantage for someone else; or to the detriment of the corporation. This duty will also cover situations in which directors use a corporate opportunity to make a secret profit or to allow someone else to gain from a corporate opportunity. It originates from the strict fiduciary duty on directors to act in the best interests of the corporation and to prevent a conflict between their duty to the corporation and their own self-interest, but is drafted with a slightly different emphasis in the *Corporations Act*.[56] Further, these provisions extend beyond directors and officers to also apply to the company's employees.[57]

---

47 *Whitehouse v Carlton Hotel Pty Ltd* (1987) 162 CLR 285, 294.
48 *Howard Smith Ltd v Ampol Petroleum Ltd* [1974] 1 NSWLR 68.
49 See Jean J du Plessis, 'Directors' duty to use their powers for proper or permissible purposes' (2004) 16(3) *South African Mercantile Law Journal* 308, 320.
50 *Parke v Daily News Ltd* [1962] Ch 927, *Ngurli Ltd v McCann* (1953) 90 CLR 425; *Ashburton Oil NL v Alpha Minerals NL* (1971) 123 CLR 614. See further Tim Connor and Andrew O'Beid, 'Clarifying terms in the debate regarding shareholder primacy' (2020) 35(3) *Australian Journal of Corporate Law* 276.
51 *Darvall v North Sydney Brick & Tile Co* (1989) 16 NSWLR 260.
52 *Teck Corporation Ltd v Millar* (1972) 33 DLR (3d) 288.
53 *Walker v Wimborne* (1976) 137 CLR 1; *BTI 2014 LLC v Sequana SA* [2022] 3 WLR 709.
54 See further Jean Jacques du Plessis, 'Directors' duty to act in the best interests of the corporation: "Hard cases make bad law"' (2019) 34(1) *Australian Journal of Corporate Law* 3.
55 For a fuller discussion, see Hargovan, Adams and Brown, *Australian Corporate Law* (2023) ch 16; and Bottomley et al, *Contemporary Australian Corporate Law* (2021) ch 13.
56 For further detail, see Bottomley et al, *Contemporary Australian Corporate Law* (2021) 374–5.
57 *Gunasegaram v Blue Visions Management Pty Ltd* (2018) 129 ACSR 265.

8.2.2.4 Chapter 2E: Duty relating to related-party transactions[58]

Chapter 2E of the *Corporations Act* stems from the recommendations made by the Companies and Securities Advisory Committee ('CSAC') in 1991 in its *Report on Reform of the Law Governing Corporate Financial Transactions*. The Committee's draft legislation was intended to introduce 'detailed procedures to monitor and control those matters which [are] otherwise vulnerable to abuse by corporate controllers', including loans to directors, inter-corporate loans, asset transfers and excessive remuneration.[59]

The underlying principle was that financial benefits given to persons who are in a position to significantly influence the decision to give the benefit should be subject to shareholder approval, unless they are on commercial terms. The legislation is based on the notion that 'uncommercial' transactions with related parties should be referred to disinterested shareholders before the transactions take place. These sentiments are currently echoed in s 207, which states the object of Chapter 2E as being 'to protect the interests of a public company's members as a whole, by requiring member approval for giving financial benefits to related parties that could endanger those interests'. Note that as a consequence of permitting proprietary companies to engage in crowd source funding, Chapter 2E has been amended to now also apply to such companies.

Chapter 2E prohibits a company from giving a financial benefit to a related party of the company unless:

(1) the giving of the financial benefit falls within one of several exceptions to the provision, or

(2) prior approval is obtained from shareholders to the giving of the financial benefit.[60]

For the purposes of Chapter 2E, each director of a public company is considered to be a related party of the public company. The core section for determining which parties are considered to be related parties is s 228 of the Act. It will be noted that not only the directors of the public company are considered to be related parties of the public company,[61] but also the directors of the entities that 'control'[62] the public company.[63] In addition, if the public is under control of an entity which is not a body corporate (for example, a partnership), all those forming these entities will also be considered to be related parties of the public company.[64] All the spouses, and all the parents and children of the individuals mentioned above, are also considered to be related parties to the public company.[65] Another noteworthy related party of the public company will be any entity controlled by any of the parties mentioned above and the meaning of control is also relevant here.[66]

---

58 For further detail, see Bottomley et al, *Contemporary Australian Corporate Law* (2021) 380–3.
59 CSAC, *Report on Reform of the Law Governing Corporate Financial Transactions* (1991) 11–12.
60 *Corporations Act 2001* (Cth) ss 208–229.
61 Ibid s 228(2)(a).
62 'Control' could be through shareholding or control over the board of directors: ibid ss 46, 47. 'Control' could also be through financial control: see ibid s 50AA.
63 Ibid s 228(2).
64 Ibid s 228(2)(c).
65 Ibid s 228(2)(d); s 228(3)(a), (b).
66 'Control' could be through shareholding or control over the board of directors: ibid ss 46, 47. 'Control' could also be through financial control: see ibid s 50AA.

'Financial benefit' is given a very wide meaning. In order to determine whether a transaction is a 'financial benefit', the economic and commercial substance of the transaction will be considered, and it is as a general rule irrelevant whether the related party delivered services or paid something (consideration given) to receive the financial benefit. 'Giving a financial benefit' includes things like making an informal agreement, oral agreement or agreement that has no binding force. It can be considered to be giving a financial benefit even if it does not involve paying money, but only confers a financial advantage on the related party. The following examples are financial benefits:

(1) giving or providing the related party finance or property
(2) buying an asset from or selling an asset to the related party
(3) leasing an asset from or to the related party
(4) supplying services to or receiving services from the related party
(5) issuing securities or granting an option to the related party
(6) taking up or releasing an obligation of the related party.[67]

Two of the main exceptions, where members' approval is not required when a financial benefit is given to a related party, are arm's-length transactions[68] and reasonable remuneration and reimbursement of expenses incurred by directors and other officers.[69]

The civil penalty provisions will be contravened if a financial benefit is given to a related party without prior approval of the general meeting or without it falling under one of the statutory exceptions.[70]

8.2.2.5 Parts 2M.2 and 2M.3: Duty relating to requirements for financial reports

Parts 2M.2 and 2M.3 contain detailed provisions regarding the keeping of financial records, financial reporting and directors' reports. As part of the CLERP 9 reforms, discussed in greater detail in Chapter 7, several of these provisions were refined, and new obligations were added to ensure that sound financial and other information is available to the public regarding the corporation's financial performance and financial practices. These provisions require directors to take all reasonable steps to comply with or to secure compliance with pts 2M.2 and 2M.3. These provisions were raised for consideration in the *Centro* decision (*Australian Securities and Investments Commission v Healey*),[71] where the directors of a large public company were found to have failed to take all reasonable steps to ensure that the company complied with its reporting obligations under pt 2M.3 and to keep adequate financial records under pt 2M.2. The directors were all experienced business professionals who acted with qualified professional advisers. The board established an audit committee, which reviewed the draft financial reports, but in approving the final accounts the board failed to

---

67 Ibid s 229.
68 Ibid s 210.
69 Ibid s 211.
70 Ibid s 1317E(1).
71 (2011) 196 FCR 291.

read all of the relevant information and hence could not be satisfied that the company was complying with its obligations.[72]

8.2.2.6 Part 5.7B: Duty to prevent insolvent trading[73]

Section 588G of the Act imposes a positive duty on directors to prevent insolvent trading by the corporation.[74] The statutory purpose of this section was considered by the NSW Court of Appeal in *Edwards v Australian Securities and Investments Commission*:

> [Its aim] is to discourage and provide a remedy for a particular type of commercial dishonesty or irresponsibility … [which] occurs when a company that is at or approaching insolvency obtains a loan, or obtains property or services on credit, and either there is a director who knows or suspects the insolvency or approaching insolvency, or a reasonable person in the director's position would know or suspect it. In that situation, any director … can be made personally liable … The section aims to encourage directors to carry out their duties properly if the company is at or approaching insolvency, and provides a sanction if they do not.[75]

Section 588G applies if:

(a) a person is a director of a company at the time when the company incurs a debt
(b) the company is insolvent at that time, or becomes insolvent by incurring that debt, or by incurring at that time debts including that debt, and
(c) at that time, there are reasonable grounds for suspecting that the company is insolvent, or would so become insolvent.[76]

It is important to note that the extended definition of director under s 9 of the Act discussed in Chapter 5, which includes de facto and shadow directors, applies to this provision,[77] but that the duty does not apply to officers.

Section 95A of the Act provides that a company is insolvent if, and only if, the company is unable to pay all the company's debts as and when they become due and payable. A temporary lack of liquidity does not mean there is insolvency.[78] The practical

---

72 See further Jean J du Plessis and Iain Meaney, 'Directors' liability for approving financial statements containing blatant incorrect items: Lessons from Australia for all directors in all jurisdictions' (2012) 33(9) *Company Lawyer* 273; and Philip Crutchfield and Catherine Button, 'Men over board: The burden of directors' duties in the wake of the Centro case' (2012) 30 (2)*Company and Securities Law Journal* 33.
73 For a fuller discussion, see Hargovan, Adams and Brown, *Australian Corporate Law* (2023) ch 18; and Bottomley et al, *Contemporary Australian Corporate Law* (2021) 321–7. See further Australian Securities and Investments Commission, *Duty to Prevent Insolvent Trading: Guide for Directors* (Regulatory Guide 217, September 2023), under review at the time of writing with an updated guide anticipated in 2024.
74 For a comparative analysis of insolvent trading law see Jason Harris, 'Director liability for insolvent trading: Is the cure worse than the disease?' (2009) 23(3) *Australian Journal of Corporate Law* 266.
75 (2009) 76 ACSR 369, [3] (Campbell JA).
76 For a list of relevant factors that may be used to determine whether or not there are reasonable grounds to suspect insolvency, see *ASIC v Plymin (No 1)* (2003) 46 ACSR 126.
77 See, eg, *Yeo, in the matter of Bradi Transport Pty Ltd (in liq) v Sklenovski* [2020] FCA 1540.
78 *Sandell v Porter* (1966) 115 CLR 666. The authorities on determining whether or not a company is insolvent are exhaustively analysed by Mandie J in *ASIC v Plymin (No 1)* (2003) 46 ACSR 126, [370]–[380] and *Quin v Vlahos* [2021] VSCA 205.

difficulties in assessing insolvent trading, and some of the indicia of insolvency, are recognised by Palmer J in the following passage in *Hall v Poolman*:

> The law recognises that there is sometimes no clear dividing line between solvency and insolvency from the perspective of the directors of a trading company which is in difficulties. There is a difference between temporary illiquidity and 'an endemic shortage of working capital whereby liquidity can only restored by a successful outcome of business ventures in which the existing working capital has been deployed' … The first is an embarrassment, the second is a disaster. It is easy enough to tell the difference in hindsight, when the company has either weathered the storm or foundered with all hands; sometimes it is not so easy when the company is still contending with the waves. Lack of liquidity is not conclusive of insolvency, neither is availability of assets conclusive of solvency.[79]

Section 588E assists in proving insolvency under s 588G by allowing for the following rebuttable presumptions to be made:

(1) continuing insolvency – if it can be proved that a company was insolvent at a particular time during the 12 months ending on the 'relation-back day' (as defined in s 9 of the Act: the date of filing the application for a compulsory winding up), it is presumed that the company remained insolvent thereafter

(2) absence of accounting records – if the company has contravened either s 286(1) or (2) by failing to keep or retain adequate financial records for seven years (except for a minor or technical breach), it is presumed that the company is insolvent during the period of contravention.

The Act does not contain a definition of 'debt'. What, then, is a debt for purposes of the insolvent trading provisions? Section 588G captures trading debts[80] (including contingent debts such as guarantees)[81] and a range of 'deemed debts' under s 588G(1A) linked to certain share capital transactions undertaken by the company. For example, when the directors make a decision to pay dividends, the debt so incurred will be considered to be incurred 'when the dividend is paid or, if the company has a constitution that provides for the declaration of dividends, when the dividend is declared'.

It is by failing to prevent the company from incurring the debt that the person contravenes this civil penalty provision: s 588G(2). There are certain further requirements for a contravention:

(1) the person was aware at that time that there were grounds for suspecting that the debt would render the company insolvent, or

(2) a reasonable person in a like position in a company in the company's circumstances would be so aware.

---

79 (2007) 65 ACSR 123, [266].

80 For consideration of the question 'when does a company incur a debt?', see the collection of authorities discussed in *Quin v Vlahos* (2021) 64 VR 319.

81 *Hawkins v Bank of China* (1992) 7 ACSR 349.

Directors need to be vigilant about this duty as it has the potential to make them liable for huge amounts.[82] A non-executive, honorary director of a company limited by guarantee, in *Commonwealth Bank of Australia v Friedrich*,[83] was found personally liable (under the predecessor provisions to s 588G) for a substantial corporate debt of $97 million (owed to the bank). Apart from civil liability, where insolvent trading is accompanied by a dishonest intent, there is a separate criminal offence that may result in a fine and/or imprisonment (up to five years).

In 2015, the Australian Productivity Commission recommended revisions to introduce a 'safe harbour' for directors in relation to s 588G. In 2017, a provision of similar purpose to s 180(2) (see Section 8.2.2.1) came into force,[84] providing a safe harbour for directors facing personal liability under s 588GA for debts incurred while developing 'courses of action that are reasonably likely to lead to a better outcome for the company'.[85] The safe harbour is limited to a reasonable period after the suspicion of insolvency,[86] and the burden of proof that the debts fall within the safe harbour lies on the director seeking its protection.[87]

A director is entitled to rely on any one or more of the following statutory defences listed in s 588H.

Reasonable expectation of solvency (s 588H(2))[88]

The courts require evidence greater than a mere hope or possibility that the company will be solvent. In explaining the concept of 'expectation', Austin J in *Tourprint International Pty Ltd v Bott*[89] held:

> Expectation ... means a higher degree of certainty than 'mere hope or possibility' or 'suspecting' ... The defence requires an actual expectation that the company was and would continue to be solvent, and that the grounds for so expecting are reasonable. A director cannot rely on complete ignorance of or neglect of duty ... and cannot hide behind ignorance of the company's affairs which is of their own making or, if not ... has been contributed to by their own failure to make further necessary inquiries.[90]

Palmer J, in *Hall v Poolman*,[91] offered guidance on the approach required to discharge the defence in s 588H(2):

---

82 Insolvent trading is made a civil penalty under *Corporations Act 2001* (Cth) ss 588G(2) and 1317E(1).
83 (1991) 5 ACSR 115.
84 *Treasury Laws Amendment (2017 Enterprise Incentives No 2) Act 2017* (Cth). See further Ian Ramsay and Stacey Steele, 'The "safe harbour" reform of directors' insolvent trading liability in Australia: Insolvency professionals views' (2020) 48(1) *Australian Business Law Review* 7.
85 *Corporations Act 2001* (Cth) s 588GA(1)(a).
86 Ibid s 588GA(1)(b).
87 Ibid s 588GA(3). For unsuccessful reliance, see *Re Balmz Pty Ltd (in liq)* [2020] VSC 652.
88 For case examples on the operation of this defence, see *Statewide Tobacco Services Ltd v Morley* (1990) 2 ACSR 405; *Metropolitan Fire Systems v Miller* (1997) 23 ACSR 699; *Tourprint International Pty Ltd v Bott* (1999) 32 ACSR 201; *Hall v Poolman* (2007) 65 ACSR 123; and *Re McLellan; Stake Man Pty Ltd v Carroll* (2009) 76 ACSR 67.
89 (1999) 32 ACSR 201. See also *Treloar Constructions Pty Ltd v McMillan* (2017) 120 ACSR 130.
90 Ibid [67].
91 *Hall v Poolman* (2007) 65 ACSR 123, [269].

There comes a point where the reasonable director must inform himself or herself as fully as possible of all relevant facts and then ask himself or herself and the other directors: 'How sure are we that this asset can be turned into cash to pay all our debts, present and to be incurred, within three months? Is that outcome certain, probable, more likely than not, possible, possible with a bit of luck, possible with a lot of luck, remote, or is there is no real way of knowing?' If the honest and reasonable answer is 'certain' or 'probable', the director can have a reasonable expectation of solvency. If the honest and reasonable answer is anywhere from 'possible' to 'no way of knowing', the director can have no reasonable expectation of solvency.

Reasonable reliance on others providing the information on the solvency of the company (s 588H(3))[92]

Directors will not be able to rely on s 588H(3) where they are put on inquiry as to whether the delegate was fulfilling their responsibilities and they do not make inquiries and receive reasonable assurances that the duties are being performed.[93] Distrust of the person relied upon for financial information will also negate the defence.[94]

Illness or some other good reason resulting in absence from management (s 588H(4))[95]

The law's intolerance of 'sleeping, or passive, directors or a director who is absent from management because of their total reliance on their spousal director due to their love and faith' is captured in the following passage by Chief Justice Spigelman in *Deputy Commissioner of Taxation v Clark*:[96]

[Sections 588G and 588H were] based on the assumption that a director would participate in the management of the company. This assumption strongly suggests that a total failure to participate, for whatever reason, should not be regarded as a 'good reason' for failing to participate at a particular time … it is a basal structural feature of corporations legislation in Australia that directors are expected to participate in the management of the corporation.

Reasonable steps to prevent the company from incurring any debts (s 588H(5))

This defence may be established if the director has acted swiftly in their decision to appoint a voluntary administrator to take over the management of the company: s 588H(6).

---

92   For case examples on the operation of this defence, see *Manpac Industries Pty Ltd v Ceccattini* (2002) 20 ACLC 1304; *Williams v Scholz* [2007] QSC 266; *Re McLellan; Stake Man Pty Ltd v Carroll* (2009) 76 ACSR 67; and *Re Forgione Family Group Pty Ltd (in liq) v Forgione* (2015) 239 FCR 285. See further Anil Hargovan, 'Relevance of directors' unsecured borrowings, guarantees and honesty in determining liability for insolvent trading' (2009) 17(1) *Insolvency Law Journal* 36.
93   *Australian Securities and Investments Commission v Plymin (No 1)* (2003) 46 ACSR 126; affirmed in *Elliott v Australian Securities and Investments Commission* (2004) 10 VR 369.
94   *Williams v Scholz* [2007] QSC 266; affirmed in *Williams v Scholz* [2008] QCA 94.
95   For case examples on the operation of this defence, see *Deputy Commissioner of Taxation v Clark* (2003) 57 NSWLR 113 and *Williams v Scholz* [2007] QSC 266.
96   (2003) 57 NSWLR 113, [114], [116].

If the director is unable to persuade the board to pass a written resolution to appoint a voluntary administrator, the director should either seek to wind up the company or resign to protect themselves from personal liability.[97]

8.2.2.7 Chapter 6CA: Duty relating to continuous disclosure

We deal with the introduction of the continuous disclosure provisions in Chapter 7 as part of the CLERP 9 reforms. It suffices here to point out that non-compliance with the continuous disclosure provisions is considered a contravention of a 'financial services civil penalty provision' to which a higher maximum penalty applies.[98]

8.2.2.8 Insider trading[99]

Part 7.10 div 3 contains the general prohibition on a person trading in financial products (defined in div 3: for instance, securities, derivatives and debentures) when that person is in possession of inside information. 'Inside information' is defined as information that is not generally available or information that, if it were generally available, a reasonable person would expect it to have a material effect on the price or value of a particular financial product.[100]

A person with inside information (the insider) may not apply for, acquire or dispose of any of the defined financial products, or enter into an agreement to apply for, acquire or dispose of such financial products, or procure another person to apply for, acquire or dispose of such financial products.[101] 'Procuring' is defined as inciting, inducing or encouraging an act or omission of another person by a person in possession of inside information.[102]

The insider must also not, directly or indirectly, communicate the inside information ('tipping'), or cause the information to be communicated, to another person if the insider knows, or ought reasonably to know, that the other person would or would be likely to apply for, acquire or dispose of the defined financial products, or enter into an agreement to apply for, acquire or dispose of such financial products, or procure another person to apply for, acquire or dispose of such financial products.[103]

Any contravention of the insider trading provisions is a contravention of a 'financial services civil penalty provision'.[104]

8.2.2.9 Relief from civil liability

Section 1317S gives the court discretion to relieve from liability, either wholly or partly, persons held liable to pay compensation if it appears that the person acted honestly and,

---

97 *Statewide Tobacco Services Ltd v Morley* (1990) 2 ACSR 405; affirmed *Morley v Statewide Tobacco Services Ltd* [1993] 1 VR 423.
98 Under s 1317E(1) the continuous disclosure provisions are treated as civil penalty provisions.
99 See Gregory Lyon and Jean J du Plessis, *The Law of Insider Trading in Australia* (Federation Press, 2005) for a comprehensive analysis of all legal aspects of insider trading.
100 *Corporations Act 2001* (Cth) s 1042A.
101 Ibid s 1043A(1).
102 Ibid s 1042A.
103 Ibid s 1043A(2).
104 Ibid s 1317E(1).

having regard to all the circumstances of the case, ought fairly to be excused. Section 1318 provides similar relief against breaches of civil penalty provisions. As was pointed out in *Daniels v Anderson*,[105] the purpose of these sections is 'to excuse company officers from liability in situations where it would be unjust and oppressive not to do so, recognising that such officers are businessmen and women who act in an environment involving risk in commercial decision-making'.[106] Acting honestly, which underpins both sections, means to act 'without moral turpitude'.[107] In *Hall v Poolman*,[108] Palmer J considered the following factors as relevant in assessing honesty:

> whether the person has acted without deceit or conscious impropriety, without intent to gain improper benefit or advantage for himself, herself or another, and without carelessness or imprudence to such a degree as to demonstrate that no genuine attempt at all has been made to carry out the duties and obligations of his or her office imposed by the Corporations Act or the general law.

There have not been many cases in which the directors have benefited from the operation of these discretionary provisions. Indeed, it is more commonly rejected, as it was in the matter of *Australian Securities and Investments Commission v Healey (No 2)*.[109] There, Justice Middleton reiterated that the consideration involves three stages of inquiry, determining the following: whether the applicant for relief has acted honestly; whether, having regard to all of the circumstances, the applicant ought fairly be excused; and whether they should be relieved of their liability wholly or in part, and to what extent.[110] His Honour accepted that the making of the order to impose liability was discretionary, and in doing so the court could consider a wide range of factors – and equally, those matters would be relevant to a decision whether to grant relief from such liability.[111] His Honour 'declined' to exercise the Court's discretion to relieve the defendants from liability in that case.[112] The decisions in *Hall v Poolman* and in *Re McLellan; Stake Man Pty Ltd v Carroll*[113] are notable exceptions to the trend of judicial reluctance in this regard. In the former case, a director was partially absolved from liability for debts incurred during insolvent trading (in breach of s 588G, discussed above). Significantly, the latter case is the first in which a director has been fully exonerated from personal liability through the exercise of judicial discretion.

The Court in *Hall v Poolman* was influenced by the commercial conduct of the director, who was found to have acted in a reasonable manner, for a limited time, when

---

105 *Daniels v Anderson* (1995) 37 NSWLR 438.
106 Ibid 525.
107 *Commonwealth Bank of Australia v Friedrich* (1991) 5 ACSR 115, 198; *Australian Securities and Investments Commission v Vines* (2005) 56 ACSR 528; affirmed in *Vines v Australian Securities and Investments Commission* (2007) 73 NSWLR 451, [568] (Ipp JA); [797], [800] (Santow JA).
108 (2007) 65 ACSR 123, [325].
109 (2011) 196 FCR 430.
110 Ibid [84].
111 Ibid [91].
112 Ibid [97].
113 *Hall v Poolman* (2009) 65 ACSR 123; *Stake Man Pty Ltd v Carroll* (2009) 76 ACSR 67. For commentary, see Anil Hargovan, 'Director's liability for insolvent trading, statutory forgiveness and law reform' (2010) 18(2) *Insolvency Law Journal* 96.

attempting to save the business while negotiating over a large debt with the Australian Taxation Office. In adopting an approach widely regarded by commentators as commercially realistic, Palmer J, in *Hall v Poolman*,[114] made the following observations:

> Experienced company directors ... would appreciate that, in some cases, it is not commercially sensible to summon the administrators or to abandon a substantial trading enterprise to the liquidators as soon as any liquidity shortage occurs. In some cases a reasonable time must be allowed to a director to assess whether the company's difficulty is temporary and remediable or endemic and fatal. The commercial reality is that creditors will usually allow some time for payment beyond normal trading terms, if there are worthwhile prospects of an improvement in the company's position.

Honesty, by itself, is insufficient to justify relief.[115] In *Williams v Scholz*,[116] the Queensland Court of Appeal declined to exercise judicial discretion under s 1318 and excuse the directors from liability for insolvent trading on the basis of their knowledge of deteriorating financial conditions, their suspicions of mismanagement and their failure to take remedial steps. Under these circumstances, despite the honest conduct of the directors, it was held that the function of s 1318 is not to subvert the operation of the insolvent trading laws.

It is an irrelevant consideration, for the exercise of judicial discretion for relief, that directors do not have directors' and officers' liability insurance to meet any judgment debt and have to rely on their own resources. In *Hall v Poolman*,[117] Palmer J considered this issue and held:

> The fact that a director has no insurance to meet a judgment debt arising from an insolvent trading claim cannot, without more, play a part in the consideration of discretionary defences under s.1317S and s.1318. Most creditors are not insured against the insolvency of their debtors. The Court should not, in the exercise of discretion under s.1317S or s.1318, hold accountable only a director whose insurer will absorb the pain of a judgment.

8.3 Case studies regarding civil penalty provisions

8.3.1 Overview

Australian Securities and Investments Commission v Adler,[118] a complex judgment arising from the fallout of the collapse of HIH Insurance Ltd (then Australia's second largest insurance company), remains one of the best cases to illustrate how the civil penalty provisions are used by ASIC in practice. This is because of both the lucid judgment of Santow J (leading to the development of the 'Santow Principles' on the exercise of the

114 (2007) 65 ACSR 123, [331].
115 *Kenna & Brown Pty Ltd v Kenna* (1999) 32 ACSR 430.
116 [2008] QCA 94.
117 (2007) 65 ACSR 123, [342].
118 *Australian Securities and Investments Commission v Adler* (2002) 41 ACSR 72.

civil penalty provisions) and the fact that the *Adler* case involved multiple breaches of statutory duties and civil penalty provisions. However, there were several other significant cases that ASIC brought against directors and officers that either clarified or demonstrated the operation of the statutory duties of directors. We now provide brief overviews of the key legal issues in *Australian Securities and Investments Commission v Adler*,[119] and in the James Hardie case (*ASIC v Macdonald (No 11)*),[120] another significant case for corporate governance due to the liability of the entire board for breach of the *Corporations Act*.

8.3.2 *ASIC v Adler* (2002) 41 ACSR 72

8.3.2.1 Summary of the facts

This case deals with four different sets of transactions in the lead-up to the collapse of HIH Insurance Ltd. The main defendants were Rodney Adler (director and shareholder in HIH, officer of the HIH subsidiary HIHC, and controller of Adler Corporation Pty Ltd ['Adler Corp']), Ray Williams (CEO, shareholder and founder of HIH, and a director of HIHC) and Dominic Fodera (director and CFO of HIH, and director of HIHC).

(1) *Transfer of funds*: The first transaction took place on 15 June 2000, when an amount of $10 million was transferred from one of HIH's subsidiaries, Casualty & General Insurance Company Limited ('HIHC'), to a company, Pacific Eagle Equity Pty Limited ('PEE'). The sole share in PEE was held by Adler Corporation, and PEE was incorporated on 15 June 2000 – the same day as the first transaction. This payment followed correspondence, commencing 9 June 2000, between Rodney Adler and Ray Williams and later steps involving various officers of HIH and HIHC. This transfer was executed by Dominic Fodera, the CFO of HIH and HIHC and also a director of both companies, after Adler requested such a transfer and the CEO of HIH, Williams, concurred with it and also directed the transfer.

(2) *Purchase of HIH shares*: The second set of transactions took place between 16 and 30 June 2000, when PEE began to purchase shares in HIH to the extent of $3 991 856.21. All these purchases were instigated by Rodney Adler. This was in circumstances in which, according to ASIC – but disputed – the stockmarket was led to believe by Adler that the purchases were made by Adler or family interests associated with Adler in order to shore up the HIH share price. On 7 July 2000, the Australian Equities Unit Trust ('AEUT') was established, by execution of a trust deed, with PEE as trustee. Units of different classes were issued to HIHC and Adler Corp. The $10 million investment by HIHC, including the HIH shares purchased with it, then became part of this trust ('AEUT').[121] The HIH shares were subsequently sold by AEUT at a loss of $2 121 261.11 on 26 September 2000 – barely three months after they had been purchased.

119 Ibid.
120 *Australian Securities and Investments Commission v Macdonald (No 11)* (2009) 256 ALR 199.
121 Jason Lang and Giselle McHugh, 'HIH Insurance – Related Party Transactions, Financial Assistance and Directors' Duties' (2002) (55) *Corporate Law Electronic Bulletin*.

(3) *Purchase of unlisted investments*: The third set of transactions relates to AEUT buying three unlisted investments (unlisted technology and internet companies) from Adler Corp. Adler was the sole director of Adler Corp, and he and his wife the only shareholders. AEUT bought dstore Limited ('dstore') on 25 August 2000 for $50 002, Planet Soccer International Limited ('Planet Soccer') on 25 August 2000 for $820 748 and Nomad Telecommunications Limited ('Nomad)' on 26 September 2000 for $2 539 000 – collectively called 'the unlisted investments'. These sales were all financed with the funds still available (after the purchase of the HIH shares) from the original $10 million payment by HIHC, which became AEUT's after the execution of the trust deed. AEUT suffered a loss on all three transactions totalling $3 859 750 (without interest taken into consideration).

(4) *Making of unsecured loans*: The fourth set of transactions deals with unsecured loans. Between 26 July 2000 and 30 November 2000, Adler caused three unsecured loans totalling $2 084 345 to be made by AEUT, without adequate documentation, to companies or funds associated with him and/or Adler Corp, to the latter's advantage and allegedly to the disadvantage of AEUT.

8.3.2.2 Contraventions of civil penalty provisions[122]

Related party transactions (Chapter 2E)

It was held that the payment of $10 million by HIHC to PEE on 15 June 2000 amounted to the 'giving of a financial benefit' to PEE, Adler Corp and Adler within the meaning of s 229 of the Act. Thus, HIH and HIHC had contravened s 208 of the Act. The transaction was not an 'arm's length' transaction under s 210. The subsequent entering into of the trust deed was also not held to fall within the 'arm's length' exception in s 210 because the trust deed lacked proper safeguards in circumstances in which Adler had a potential conflict of interest, and was significantly one-sided against HIHC.

It was also held that the transaction was carried out at Adler's request and with Williams's concurrence and direction. Both of them were 'involved' in the giving of a financial benefit within the meaning of s 79. Both contravened s 209(2) by being 'involved' in the contravention of s 208 by HIH and HIHC. Fodera was also in breach of s 209(2). He had sufficient knowledge of the essential elements of the contravention, and his attempts to subsequently distance himself from the transaction by referring matters to others did not alter this.

Financial assistance (Part 2J.3)

HIHC suffered material prejudice as a result of financially assisting PEE to acquire shares in HIH and, in so doing, contravened s 260A of the Act. The material prejudice arose from the fact that the rights that HIHC obtained from PEE were of a materially lesser value than the cash handed over. In other words, HIHC was 'impoverished' by this transaction.

---

122 Ibid: this section is based on Lang and McHugh JJ's excellent summary of the findings of Santow J and on the headnote to the Australian Corporations and Securities Reports: *Australian Securities and Investments Commission v Adler* (2002) 41 ACSR 72, 72–7.

The Court relied on *Charterhouse Investment Trust Ltd v Tempest Diesels Ltd* [1986] BCLC 1, looking 'at all interlocking elements in a commercial transaction as a whole'.

The material prejudice for HIHC resulted from the fact that there was no security or documentation and no control over the disposition of the funds. The AEUT trust deed was also one-sided and did not include safeguards to protect against Adler's potential conflict of interest. A loss on the HIH shares traded by PEE was inherently likely from the start, and did in fact occur.

It was held that Adler and Williams were sufficiently involved in the contravention of s 260A to have breached s 260D(2). They knew that HIHC was providing assistance for the purchase of HIH shares, but it was not necessary for them to have actual knowledge of material prejudice. Fodera's involvement was more remote and, on the facts, Santow J was not able to conclude that Fodera, while having knowledge that financial assistance was given, also had knowledge that it would materially prejudice HIHC. However, as the onus lay on the defendants to prove that giving the financial assistance was not materially prejudicial, this element of s 260A was essentially a defence, and proof of knowledge of material prejudice was therefore not necessary for s 260D(2). Accordingly, Fodera was also found to have breached s 260D(2).[123] In making these findings, Santow J stated that 'a combination of suspicious circumstances and the failure to make appropriate enquiry when confronted with the obvious, makes it possible to infer knowledge of the relevant essential matters'.[124]

Duty of care and diligence (s 180)

It was held that a reasonably careful and diligent director or officer in the position of Adler would not have caused the payment of $10 million by HIHC to PEE to be applied in part to purchasing HIH shares. Adler failed to follow authorised practices relating to investments made by HIH/HIHC and to ensure that safeguards were in place to protect HIH or HIHC. In fact, Adler's object was to support the HIH share price (doing so for his own substantial shareholding in HIH), rather than to enable HIH to obtain, through its interests in AEUT, the benefit of a quick profit on the resale of the HIH shares.

Williams was aware the $10 million was to be used in whole or in part to pay for shares in HIH, and permitted that amount to be paid in advance of any documentation and with no stipulation of any necessary safeguards to deal with Adler's potential conflicts of interest, which is a circumstance requiring special vigilance. While the primary responsibility will fall on the director proposing to enter into the transaction, this does not excuse other directors or officers who become aware of the transaction. It was only common sense that a reasonably careful and diligent director would have brought the issue of a $10 million payment being made to a director, to be used at his or her discretion, before the board or at least the HIH Investment Committee.[125]

The directors' attempt to rely on the protection of the business judgment rule (see s 180(2)) failed. In Adler's case, there was no 'business judgment'; moreover, Adler clearly

123 Lang and McHugh, 'HIH Insurance (2002) (55) *Corporate Law Electronic Bulletin*.
124 *Australian Securities and Investments Commission v Adler* (2002) 41 ACSR 72, 163.
125 Lang and McHugh, 'HIH Insurance (2002) (55) *Corporate Law Electronic Bulletin*.

had a material personal interest in the 'subject matter of the judgment'. Williams failed to establish that he had made the decision in good faith for a proper purpose, and that he had informed himself to the extent that he could reasonably believe that the decision was a proper business decision.

Duty of good faith (s 181)

Adler was the only director found to be in breach of s 181. This was because Adler, quite apart from failing to make proper disclosure, promoted his personal interest by making or pursuing a gain (of maintaining or supporting the HIH share price) when there was a substantial possibility of a conflict between his personal interests and those of the company in pursuing a profit. The interests of HIH and HIHC were put at risk by illegality under ss 208 and 260A, and by concealing from the market that HIHC, not Adler or his interests, was funding the purchase of HIH shares.[126]

Use of position to gain advantage for oneself or another or to cause detriment to the corporation (s 182)

Justice Santow concluded that both Adler and Williams were in breach of s 182. Adler's conduct evinced his improper purpose in supporting the share price in HIH. This included passing up an early opportunity for AEUT to make a profit on the sale of HIH shares, as well as maximising the ultimate loss for AEUT by selling his own interests in HIH ahead of AEUT's when the market was falling. Williams likewise breached s 182 in authorising the $10 million payment without proper safeguards and without the knowledge or approval of the HIH Investment Committee. More generally, Adler was also found to have breached his duties under ss 180–182 in relation to PEE's acquisition of the three unlisted technology and internet investments from Adler Corp. No reasonable director in Adler's position and possessing his knowledge would have committed PEE to acquire investments in Nomad, dstore and Planet Soccer at the prices Adler Corp paid for them. The known radical change in market conditions relating to technology stocks, the lack of any due diligence, and the misleading statements and omissions made by Adler in relation to the on-sale of these investments all supported this conclusion. Despite being clearly aware of the financial dire straits of these investments, Adler and Adler Corp extricated Adler Corp from its position, at no loss to Adler Corp, but to the disadvantage of PEE, HIH and HIHC.

Adler was in further breach of ss 180–182 in relation to the three unsecured loans from AEUT to entities associated with Adler. These loans were not adequately documented and not one of them was even within the scope of the vaguely sketched mandate for AEUT, as discussed by Adler and Williams, to pursue investment in 'venture capital' or 'share trading'.[127]

Improper use of information (s 183)

Adler was also found to have breached his obligations under s 183, in relation to both the acquisition of the three unlisted investments from Adler Corp and the loans to

---

126 Ibid.
127 Ibid.

Adler-associated entities. Adler had improperly used information obtained by him to gain an advantage for himself.[128] It must be noted, however, that this part of Santow J's judgment was overturned on appeal. The NSW Court of Appeal held that neither Adler's disregard of HIH's investment guidelines and procedures, nor his knowledge of Williams' susceptibility, amounted to an improper 'use' of information for the purposes of s 183.[129]

8.3.2.3 Court orders

Santow J ordered that Adler should be disqualified for a period of 20 years and that he and Adler Corp should pay pecuniary penalties of $450 000 each (totalling $900 000). Williams was disqualified for a period of 10 years and was ordered to pay pecuniary penalties of $250 000. Fodera was not disqualified, but was ordered to pay pecuniary penalties of $5000. In addition, Adler, Williams and Adler Corp were ordered to pay aggregate compensation of $7 958 112 to HIH Casualty and General Insurance Limited (subject to verification of the calculation of interest).[130]

Criminal proceedings were later brought against Adler and Williams in relation to their activities.

8.3.3 *ASIC v Macdonald (No 11)* (2009) 256 ALR 199 – James Hardie litigation[131]

8.3.3.1 Background and summary of the facts

This case sheds light on the practical application of the scope and content of directors' and officers' duties in a large, publicly listed company. The judgments illustrate the standard of care expected by management and the board when considering strategic company decisions and market-sensitive information. They offer guidance on the standards expected under s 180(1), with particular reference to non-executive directors, executive directors, CFOs, company secretaries and in-house counsel.

In Sections 1.6.3.7–1.6.3.8 and in Section 3.6 we refer to the James Hardie litigation as a case study in the context of the importance of stakeholders and how stakeholders and pressure groups are able to influence corporate behaviour and corporate governance practices. The irony is that the agreement by James Hardie to establish a fund to cover future medical claims led to further litigation, resulting in the reported cases *Australian Securities and Investments Commission v Macdonald (No 11)*[132] and *Australian Securities and Investments Commission v Macdonald (No 12)*.[133] Most of the defendants (with the exception of Macdonald, the CEO), and ASIC, appealed these decisions, which led to

128 Ibid.
129 See *Adler v ASIC* (2003) 46 ACSR 504.
130 Lang and McHugh, *Corporate Law Electronic Bulletin* (2002); Jillian Segal, 'Corporate governance: Substance over form' (2002) 25 *University of New South Wales Law Journal* 320, 328.
131 Part of this discussion is based on Anil Hargovan, 'Corporate governance lessons from James Hardie' (2009) 33(3) *Melbourne University Law Review* 984.
132 *Australian Securities and Investments Commission v Macdonald (No 11)* (2009) 256 ALR 199.
133 *Australian Securities and Investments Commission v Macdonald (No 12)* (2009) 259 ALR 116.

two Court of Appeal decisions[134] and two High Court decisions.[135] After the High Court appeals, the penalties were then determined afresh by the NSW Court of Appeal.[136]

James Hardie Industries Limited ('JHIL') faced significant liability for damages claims for asbestos-related conditions resulting from the manufacture and use of its products since 1920. JHIL was the holding company of the James Hardie group. In order to separate JHIL from this liability, the board decided to establish the Medical Research and Compensation Foundation ('MRCF') which would manage and pay out asbestos claims against JHIL.

At a board meeting of JHIL held on 15 February 2001, the board decided to constitute JHIL as trustee of the MRCF. At the same meeting, a draft announcement to the Australian Securities Exchange ('ASX') was approved. Although this event was disputed by the 10 defendants (directors and officers), the judge rejected the chorus of non-recollection. This draft announcement explained that MRCF would be 'fully funded' (to meet the outstanding liability). At the same meeting, the board also agreed to execute the deed of covenant and indemnity ('DOCI'), which dealt with liability between JHIL and MRCF. The seven non-executive directors attended this meeting (two by phone from the United States), as did the CEO (Peter Macdonald), the board secretary and general counsel (Peter Shafron) and the CFO (Phillip Morley).

The minutes of the board meeting contained an entry to the effect that the company had explained the impact of the resolution passed at the meeting to approve an ASX announcement and to execute the ASX announcement and send it to the ASX. The minutes of the meeting were signed by the chairman at the following board meeting, held on 4 April 2001. On 7 April 2001, the minutes of the meeting of 15 February 2001 were sent to the secretary of the company. The evidentiary value of the minutes, however, was negated by the company's non-compliance with the relevant statutory provisions governing minutes, which thereby precluded the Court from relying on the minutes to establish the events that transpired at the board meeting.

ASIC alleged that the draft ASX announcement was approved at the board meeting of 15 February 2001 and that it stated that the MRCF would commence operations with assets of $284 million. The draft ASX announcement also contained a number of statements to the effect that MRCF would have sufficient funds to meet all legitimate asbestos claims; that it was fully funded; and that it provided certainty for people with legitimate asbestos claims.

The final ASX announcement included, inter alia, the following statements:

> The Foundation has sufficient funds to meet all legitimate compensation claims ...
> Mr Peter Macdonald said that the establishment of a fully-funded Foundation provided certainty for both claimants and shareholders ... In establishing the

---

134 *Morley v Australian Securities and Investments Commission* (2010) 81 ACSR 285 (which dealt with appeals by ASIC and the individual defendants relating to the breaches of directors' and officers' duties); and *James Hardie Industries NV v Australian Securities and Investments Commission* (2010) 81 ACSR 1 (which dealt with the company's appeal relating to disclosure contraventions).

135 *Shafron v Australian Securities and Investments Commission* (2012) 247 CLR 465 (which dealt with the company secretary and general counsel's appeal); and *Australian Securities and Investments Commission v Hellicar* (2012) 247 CLR 345 (which dealt with ASIC's appeal from the NSW Court of Appeal and the non-executive directors' appeal from the same court).

136 *Gillfillan v Australian Securities and Investments Commission* (2012) 92 ACSR 460.

Foundation, James Hardie sought expert advice ... James Hardie is satisfied that the Foundation has sufficient funds to meet anticipated future claims ...

8.3.3.2 Legal issues

Based on the facts discussed above, ASIC alleged in Supreme Court hearings in September 2008 that JHIL, its officers and the board breached several civil penalty provisions of the previous *Corporations Law* and the current *Corporations Act 2001* (Cth), which attracted civil penalties.[137] In particular, ASIC argued the following points:

(1) The draft ASX announcement approved at the board meeting on 15 February 2001 was false or misleading. The approval by the non-executive directors,[138] the CEO (Macdonald), the company secretary and general counsel (Shafron), and CFO (Morley) was in breach of the duty of care in s 180(1).

(2) JHIL's failure to disclose information in relation to the DOCI to the ASX was in breach of s 1001A(2).[139]

(3) The failure by the CEO and company secretary and general counsel to advise the board that the DOCI information should be disclosed to the ASX was in breach of s 180(1).

(4) The CEO had breached s 180(1) by failing to advise that the final ASX announcement on 16 February 2001 should not be released or that it should be amended to cure the defect.

(5) Statements made by the CEO at a press conference concerning the adequacy of funding for asbestos claims were false or misleading and involved a breach of s 180(1).

(6) A 'continuous disclosure' announcement to the ASX on 23 February 2001 by the CEO, which contained false or misleading statements, was in breach of s 180(1); the approval of an announcement released to the ASX on 21 March 2001 by the same officer, which contained false or misleading statements, was also in breach of s 180(1) and the good faith provisions in s 181(1).[140]

(7) In the publication of the final ASX announcement, the press conference statements and the further ASX announcements, referred to in (6) above, JHIL contravened ss 995(2)[141] and 999.[142]

---

137 ASIC concluded that there was insufficient evidence to refer any matter to the Commonwealth Director of Public Prosecution for criminal prosecution of the company's officers: ASIC, 'James Hardie Group Civil Action' (Media Release, 5 September 2008).

138 Mr Brown, Ms Hellicar, Mr Wilcox, Mr O'Brien, Mr Terry, Messrs Gillfillan and Koffel.

139 *Corporations Act 2001* (Cth) s 1001A(2), carried over into the *Corporations Act* until its repeal in 2002, dealt with breach of continuous disclosure obligations.

140 Ibid s 181 requires directors and officers of a corporation to exercise their power and discharge their duties in good faith in the best interests of the corporation and for a proper purpose.

141 Ibid s 995(2), carried over into the Act until its repeal in 2002, was modelled on the *Trade Practices Act 1974* (Cth) s 52 (now *Competition and Consumer Act 2010* (Cth) sch 2 s 18). The full text of the *Australian Consumer Law* is set out in sch 2 of the *Competition and Consumer Act 2010* (Cth) and prohibits misleading or deceptive conduct in connection with securities. There is a similar provision to s 995 in *Corporations Act 2001* (Cth) s 1041H(1).

142 *Corporations Act 2001* (Cth) s 999, carried over into the Act until repealed in 2002, prohibited false or misleading statements in relation to securities.

(8) The representations made by the CEO with respect to JHI NV at roadshows in Edinburgh and London and in slides for these United Kingdom ('UK') presentations, lodged with the ASX, were false and misleading and in breach of ss 180(1) and 181. On the same facts, it was argued that JHI NV was in breach of s 1041E[143] and, in making ASX representations, breached s 1041H.[144]

(9) JHI NV failed to notify the ASX of JHIL information in accordance with Listing Rule 3.1 and thereby contravened disclosure obligations in s 674(2).[145]

8.3.3.3 Judicial decisions and the significance of the litigation[146]

The following discussion centres on the findings made against the directors and officers of JHIL. We focus on the significance of the case for different types of directors and officers.

Non-executive directors

The Court addressed the question of whether the law differentiated, in the standard of performance expected, between executive and non-executive directors. Justice Gzell referred to the divergent judicial views expressed by Rogers CJ in *AWA Ltd v Daniels*[147] and the Court of Appeal in *Daniels v Anderson*.[148] In the former case, Rogers CJ appeared to show a readiness to accept a lower standard of care for non-executive directors.[149] In the latter case Clarke and Sheller JJA held that the approach of Rogers CJ on this issue did not represent contemporary company law[150] and that all directors are required to take reasonable steps to guide and monitor the management of the company.[151] After reviewing the case law on this point,[152] Gzell J reiterated the analysis of Santow J in *Australian Securities and Investments Commission v Adler*[153] and held that a director should become familiar with the fundamentals of the company's business and is under a continuing obligation to keep informed about the company's activities.

Satisfied that the same standards of care are imposed on all directors, Gzell J focused on the test to determine breach of s 180(1) and relied on *Australian Securities and Investments Commission v Adler* to adopt the following test:

---

143 Ibid s 1041E prohibits false or misleading statements that induce persons to, *inter alia*, apply for or dispose of financial products.
144 Ibid s 1041H prohibits misleading or deceptive conduct in relation to a financial product.
145 Ibid s 674(2) deals with a listed disclosing entity's continuous disclosure obligations.
146 This subsection is based on Hargovan, 'Corporate governance lessons from James Hardie' (2009) 33(3) *Melbourne University Law Review* 984 and Anil Hargovan, 'Directors' and officers' statutory duty of care following *James Hardie*' (2009) 61(10) *Keeping Good Companies* 586, 590.
147 *AWA Ltd v Daniels* (1992) 7 ACSR 759.
148 *Daniels v Anderson* (1995) 37 NSWLR 438.
149 (1992) 7 ACSR 759, 867.
150 (1995) 37 NSWLR 438; 16 ACSR 607.
151 Ibid 664.
152 *Statewide Tobacco Services Ltd v Morley* (1990) 2 ACSR 405; *Group Four Industries Pty Ltd v Brosnan* (1992) 59 SASR 22; *Vrisakis v Australian Securities Commission* (1993) 9 WAR 395; *Permanent Building Society (in liq) v Wheeler* (1994) 11 WAR 187; *Australian Securities and Investments Commission v Adler* (2002) 41 ACSR 72; *Australian Securities and Investments Commission v Maxwell* (2006) 59 ACSR 373; *Vines v Australian Securities and Investments Commission* (2007) 73 NSWLR 451.
153 *Australian Securities and Investments Commission v Adler* (2002) 41 ACSR 72.

> In determining whether a director has exercised reasonable care and diligence one must ask what an ordinary person, with the knowledge and experience of the defendant, might have expected to have done in the circumstances if he or she was acting on their own behalf.[154]

Justice Gzell commented on the failure of the non-executive directors to discharge their monitoring role as part of the statutory duty of care and diligence:[155]

> [I]t was part of the function of the directors in monitoring the management of the company to settle the terms of the Draft ASX Announcement to ensure that it did not assert that the Foundation had sufficient funds to meet all legitimate compensation claims.

The Court held that the directors' conduct thereafter, in releasing the defective ASX announcement, fell short of the standards expected to discharge obligations under s 180(1) for the following reasons:

> The *formation of the foundation* and the [restructure of the relevant entities described earlier] from JHIL *were potentially explosive steps*. Market reaction to the announcement of them was critical. This was a matter within the purview of the board's responsibility: what should be stated publicly about the way in which Asbestos Claims would be handled by the James Hardie group for the future [emphasis added].[156]

Although two of the non-executive directors attended the relevant board meeting by telephone, and claimed that the draft ASX announcement was neither provided nor read to them, the Court held that both directors had breached s 180(1) by voting in favour of the resolution. Justice Gzell, unimpressed by the conduct of both directors in such circumstances, found liability on the following basis:[157]

> Neither [non-executive director] raised an objection that [he] did not have a copy of the Draft ASX Announcement at the … meeting. Nor did they ask that a copy be provided to them. Nor did they abstain from approving the … Announcement.

The entire board's reliance upon, and delegation to, management and experts was held to be inappropriate on the facts of this case for these key reasons:

> This was not a matter in which a director was entitled to rely upon those of his co-directors more concerned with communications strategy to consider the Draft ASX Announcement. *This was a key statement in relation to a highly significant restructure of the James Hardie group*. Management having brought the matter to the board, none of them was entitled to abdicate responsibility by delegating his or her duty to a fellow director [emphasis added].[158]

---

154 *Australian Securities and Investments Commission v Macdonald (No 11)* (2009) 256 ALR 199, [239].
155 Ibid [332].
156 Ibid [333].
157 Ibid [233].
158 Ibid [260].

The NSW Court of Appeal overturned Gzell J's decision based on a different view of the evidence. The Court of Appeal did not accept that the evidence demonstrated that the board had been asked to approve the ASX release. This was based on a number of factors, including ASIC's failure to call a key witness, which the Court held was in breach of ASIC's duty of fairness as a litigant. If the directors were not asked to approve the release, then they could not be in breach of their duties for releasing the misleading document. However, the Court also held that if its finding on the evidence was not correct the decision of the trial judge regarding breach of duties was upheld.

ASIC successfully appealed this decision to the High Court of Australia (*Australian Securities and Investments Commission v Hellicar*),[159] which held that the directors did approve the ASX release, and that ASIC's role as a litigant did not give rise to a duty of fairness that would undermine the cogency of evidence. This meant that the decision of the trial judge regarding the directors' breach of duty was reinstated. The High Court appeal did not consider directors' duties, but only matters relating to admissible evidence and the role of ASIC as a model litigant. The other High Court appeal was *Shafron v Australian Securities and Investments Commission*,[160] which did consider the duties of executives and is discussed below.

Chief executive officer

The Court found that Macdonald, as a director and CEO of JHIL with reporting duties directly to the board, had ultimate responsibility for planning the separation proposals and was the driving force behind it. Furthermore, he was appointed to make public statements on behalf of JHIL on these matters and, in keeping with his position, was responsible for dealing with the board on this issue.

As a result of these responsibilities, Gzell J concluded that the CEO bore a high duty of care. In voting in favour of the resolution to approve the draft ASX announcement, the Court applied an objective test and found liability under s 180(1) based on reasons similar to those considered applicable to the non-executive directors.

The Court also found that the negligent conduct of the CEO resulted in multiple breaches of the statutory duty of care and diligence under s 180(1). These included the failure of the CEO to:

- advise the board of the limited nature of the reviews on the cash-flow model undertaken by external consultants. The review was restricted to issues concerning logical soundness and technical correctness. According to Gzell J,[161] a reasonable person with the same responsibilities would have informed the board that the external consultant had been specifically instructed not to consider the key assumptions adopted by the cash-flow model – namely, the fixed investment earnings rates, litigation and management costs and future claim costs
- advise the board that the draft ASX announcement was expressed in too emphatic terms and, in relation to the adequacy of funding, was misleading and deceptive

---

159 *Australian Securities and Investments Commission v Hellicar* (2012) 247 CLR 345.
160 *Shafron v Australian Securities and Investments Commission* (2012) 247 CLR 465.
161 *Australian Securities and Investments Commission v Macdonald (No 11)* (2009) 256 ALR 199, [363].

- correct the misleading statements on the adequacy of funding when making representations during international roadshows in Edinburgh and London to promote the company, and
- advise the board of the company's continuous disclosure obligations to release price-sensitive information in a timely manner.

The Court, however, rejected ASIC's allegation that the CEO had breached s 180(1) through failure to inquire of each director as to whether they had formed an opinion on the adequacy of the quantum expressed to meet all present and future asbestos claims. The imposition of such a duty, according to Gzell J, was unwarranted because a director is not obliged to analyse the basis upon which fellow directors intend to vote before determining his or her own course.[162]

The CEO failed to offer oral evidence to substantiate all of the statutory criteria under the business judgment rule in s 180(2) (discussed in Section 8.2.2.1). This strategic decision proved to be fatal to his defence. It is not easy, as recognised by the Court, to rely on documentation alone to discern, for example, if the director had a rational belief that the business judgment was in the best interests of the company.

Macdonald was the only defendant who did not appeal the trial decision and was not involved in either the Court of Appeal or High Court decision.

General counsel

Shafron, the company secretary and in-house counsel, was held to be a company officer due to his expansive role in the affairs of JHIL and, significantly, attracted the stringent statutory duties applicable to officers under ss 180–183 of the Act, which include the duty of care and diligence.

Shafron's failure to advise the board of the limited nature of the reviews on the cash-flow model undertaken by external consultants also constituted a breach of s 180(1), for the same reasons discussed above with respect to the conduct of the CEO. Similarly, Shafron's failure to advise the CEO and the board of the company's continuous disclosure obligations, in relation to the failure to release price-sensitive information to the market in a timely manner, constituted a breach of s 180(1).

The Court rejected Shafron's argument that he had no duty to warn the board of the emphatic statements in the draft ASX announcement because a reasonable director would be capable of assessing the statement as false and misleading. On the contrary, according to the Court, there was a compelling duty to speak in such circumstances:[163]

> [General counsel] had a duty to protect JHIL from legal risk and if the directors were minded to approve the release of the Draft ASX Announcement in its false and misleading form, there was the danger that JHIL would be in breach ... [of the statute]. Against that harm it was [the] duty [of Mr Shafron] to warn the directors that [such an] announcement should not be released in its too emphatic form.

---

162 Ibid [351].
163 *Shafron v Australian Securities and Investments Commission* (2012) 247 CLR 465, [402].

The High Court upheld the contraventions by Shafron relating to his failure to advise the company regarding the need to disclose the entry into the deed of covenant and indemnity to the market, and his failure to advise the board regarding the limited assumptions upon which the actuarial modelling was based and how this might adversely affect the validity of the modelling. Importantly, Shafron's argument that he had separate roles and responsibilities as company secretary (which was an officer position) and as general counsel (which was not specifically designated an officer position) and that his duties should be divided accordingly was rejected by the High Court. The Court held that his role could not be easily and cleanly divided into two. Shafron worked as a lawyer for the company and his roles and responsibilities covered a number of areas. Shafron's duties arose from the work he did for the company, not simply from the titles of the roles he held. The Court stated:[164]

> All of the tasks Mr Shafron performed were undertaken in fulfilment of his responsibilities as general counsel and company secretary. More particularly, because of his qualifications and the position in which he was employed, his responsibilities as general counsel and company secretary extended to proffering advice about how duties of disclosure should be met. And when he procured advice of others and put that advice before the board for its use, his responsibilities could, and in this case did, extend to identifying the limits of the advice that the third party gave.

Another important determination by the High Court was that Shafron's role did involve participation in the decision-making process, despite the fact that Shafron rarely had final authority over decisions. Shafron had argued that his role as general counsel was similar to the position of an external lawyer, and that this should not render him an officer. The Court held:[165]

> The fact that Mr Shafron was an employee of the company, and not an external adviser, is important. What he did was not confined to proffering advice and information in response to particular requirements made by the company. And what he did went well beyond his proffering advice and information to the board of the company. He played a large and active part in formulating the proposal that he and others chose to put to the board as one that should be approved. It was the board that ultimately had to decide whether to adopt the proposal but what Mr Shafron did, as a senior executive employee of the company, was properly described as his participating in the decision to adopt the separation proposal that he had helped to devise.

Chief financial officer

Morley, the CFO of JHIL, was also held to be an officer due to his participation in far-reaching decisions of the board. The CFO was responsible for all of the finance, audit, tax and treasury aspects of the James Hardie Group of companies.

---

164 Ibid [16].
165 Ibid [30].

Engaging in a similar analysis on this issue with respect to the conduct of the CEO and general counsel described earlier, it was held that s 180(1) was breached by Morley for identical reasons concerning the failure to address the limitations of the cash-flow model and its key assumptions and to communicate this to the board.[166] As CFO, Morley was responsible for verifying the sufficiency of financial information. The Court held that a reasonable CFO would have known that the range of limited assumptions meant that the press release could not state with certainty that the MRCF was fully funded. This was upheld by the NSW Court of Appeal. After the Court of Appeal reduced his penalty, Morley did not pursue an appeal to the High Court.

8.3.3.4 Court orders

Justice Gzell (the trial judge) rejected the defendants' submissions relating to the exoneration provisions in ss 1317S and 1318.[167] His Honour held that the contraventions were both serious and flagrant, and that despite the lack of findings of intentional dishonesty, the conduct could not be exonerated by the Court. The CEO, Macdonald, was ordered to pay a pecuniary penalty of $350 000 and was disqualified from taking part in the management of corporations for 15 years. As Macdonald did not appeal, this penalty remains unchanged by the later court decisions.

Morley was disqualified by the trial judge for five years and ordered to pay a pecuniary penalty of $35 000. Morley appealed and the NSW Court of Appeal reduced his penalty to $20 000 and his period of disqualification to two years. Following this reduction in penalties Morley decided not to pursue his High Court appeal.

The trial judge imposed a pecuniary penalty on Shafron for $75 000 and disqualified him for a period of seven years. This penalty was upheld by the NSW Court of Appeal. Shafron's appeal to the High Court was unsuccessful but the High Court remitted the determination of penalties. The NSW Court of Appeal reaffirmed Shafron's original penalty and period of disqualification; Shafron continues to work, as a corporate lawyer, in the United States.

With respect to the non-executive directors, the trial judge imposed penalties of $30 000 and disqualification periods of five years each. As noted above, the Court of Appeal allowed the appeal of the non-executive directors based on a point of evidence regarding whether it had been proved that they were asked to approve the ASX release; thus there were no penalties imposed on them by the Court of Appeal as there was no breach proved. After the High Court allowed ASIC's appeal the Court of Appeal was asked to determine penalties. In *Gillfillan v Australian Securities and Investments Commission*, the Court reduced the period of disqualification for the Australian-based directors from five years to two years and three months, and the penalty from $30 000 to $25 000.[168] The overseas-based directors had their period of disqualification reduced to one year and 11 months and their penalty was reduced to $20 000.

166 *Australian Securities and Investments Commission v Macdonald (No 11)* (2009) 256 ALR 199, [454].
167 *Australian Securities and Investments Commission v Macdonald (No 12)* (2009) 259 ALR 116.
168 *Gillfillan v Australian Securities and Investments Commission* (2012) 92 ACSR 460.

8.4 Enforcement of directors' duties

ASIC, as the primary corporate regulator, has had some spectacular successes,[169] as well as failures,[170] in enforcing the civil penalty provisions underpinning breach of directors' duties under the *Corporations Act*. ASIC has also played an active role in enforcing civil penalty provisions against directors and officers.[171] However, as noted by one commentator, ASIC has shown a marked reluctance in recent years to use its power under s 50 of the *Australian Securities and Investment Commission Act 2001* (Cth) to bring civil action in the name of the company, or a class action for shareholders or investors for the recovery of damages for corporate misconduct.[172] The purpose of s 50 was captured by Justice Lockhart in *Somerville v Australian Securities and Investments Commission*:

> An evident function of s 50 is to permit the commission, acting in the public interest, to cause proceedings to be taken where persons or corporations have suffered loss or harm arising from fraud, negligence or misconduct, but do not have the resources to maintain expensive and complicated litigation ... In the case of a company, the commission may cause the proceedings to be begun and carried on the company's name whether it consents or not.[173]

This reluctance can be attributed, in part, to the rise and rise of class actions,[174] which are discussed further in Chapter 9. Following the Financial Services Royal Commission,[175] when ASIC was exhorted most clearly to adopt the approach of 'Why not litigate?' when reviewing corporate conduct, this approach was, for a short time, adopted by the regulator as an enforcement strategy.[176] Less than two years later, ASIC released its

---

169 For discussion on some of ASIC's successes, see Jean J du Plessis, 'Reverberations after the HIH and other recent Australian corporate collapses: The role of ASIC' (2003) 15(3) *Australian Journal of Corporate Law* 225, 240–3; Hargovan, 'Corporate governance lessons from James Hardie' (2009) 33(3) *Melbourne University Law Review* 984; Anil Hargovan, 'Dual role of general counsel and company secretary: Walking the legal tightrope in *Shafron v Australian Securities and Investments Commission*' (2012) 27(1) *Australian Journal of Corporate Law* 112; and Anil Hargovan, 'Caution against board groupthink – civil penalties in James Hardie' (2013) 65(1) *Keeping Good Companies* 36.

170 *Australian Securities and Investments Commission v Rich* (2009) 75 ACSR 1; *Forrest v Australian Securities and Investments Commission* (2012) 247 CLR 486. See John Humphrey and Stephen Corones, '*Forrest v ASIC*: "A perfect storm"' (2014) 88(1) *Australian Law Journal* 26.

171 For some of the wide literature on the growth of civil penalties and their use, see Jasper Hedges et al, 'The policy and practice of enforcement of directors' duties by statutory agencies in Australia: An empirical analysis' (2017) 40(3) *Melbourne University Law Review* 905; Andrew Keay and Michelle Welsh, 'Enforcing breaches of directors' duties by a public body and Antipodean experiences' (2015) 15(2) *Journal of Corporate Law Studies* 255; Michelle Welsh, 'Civil penalties and responsive regulation: The gap between theory and practice' (2009) 33(3) *Melbourne University Law Review* 908; and Vicky Comino, 'The enforcement record of ASIC since the introduction of the civil penalty regime' (2007) 20(2) *Australian Journal of Corporate Law* 183.

172 Janet Austin, 'Does the Westpoint litigation signal a revival of the ASIC s 50 class action?' (2008) 22(1) *Australian Journal of Corporate Law* 8.

173 *Somerville v Australian Securities and Investments Commission* (1995) 60 FCR 319, 324.

174 Michael Legg and James Metzger (eds), *The Australian Class Action – A 30 Year Perspective* (Federation Press, 2023).

175 *Royal Commission into Misconduct in the Banking Industry, Superannuation and Financial Services Industry* (Final Report, February 2019) 427.

176 See, eg, Sean Hughes, 'ASIC's approach to enforcement after the Royal Commission' (Speech, Annual Conference of the Banking and Financial Services Law Association, 30 August 2019) <https://asic.gov.au/about-asic/news-centre/speeches/asic-s-approach-to-enforcement-after-the-royal-commission/>.

2021–25 Corporate Plan, which prioritised the promotion of Australia's economy and targeting of regulatory and enforcement action 'to areas of greatest harm', and removed all reference to the 'why not litigate' approach.[177] Similarly, the Corporate Plan for 2022–26 indicated 'strong and targeted action to protect consumers and investors from harm',[178] rather than the broader approach suggested by the Royal Commission.

The aim of this chapter, however, is to provide an overview of the enforcement actions available to shareholders and some other parties. It deals briefly with the statutory derivative action (Part 2F.1A; Section 8.5); actions aimed at unfairly prejudicial, discriminatory or oppressive conduct by the corporation or its directors (Part 2F.1; Section 8.6); and injunctions under s 1324 of the *Corporations Act* (Section 8.7).[179] The chapter also canvasses the criminal liability of directors and selected types of criminal offences under the *Corporations Act* (Section 8.8).

8.5 The statutory derivative action: Part 2F.1A

8.5.1 The case for introducing a statutory derivative action

> These provisions [statutory derivative action] basically make it easier for shareholders and others to institute proceedings (including proceedings against directors) where the directors refuse to do so. These provisions obviously increase the exposure of directors, as there is now greater potential for actions to be brought against directors in the name of the company.[180]

The derivative action allows an individual to bring an action that belongs to another. (It should be remembered that directors owe their duty to the corporation and that the corporation is thus the proper plaintiff in the case of any breach of these duties). Furthermore, the benefit of this action, brought by the shareholder, will not directly advantage that member; rather, it will accrue to the corporation which has, for whatever reason, decided not to pursue the matter. Thus, it allows the shareholder to usurp the authority that the corporate entity has vested in the board of directors. Significantly, it also allows the minority shareholders of the corporation to act as some sort of corporate watchdog over the majority, and to set the company in motion to establish their rights in situations in which the majority shareholders oppose the company doing so.[181]

---

177 ASIC, *ASIC 2021–25 Corporate Plan* (26 August 2021) <https://download.asic.gov.au/media/qzcaljce/asic-corporate-plan-2021-25-focus-2021-22-published-26-august-2021.pdf>.

178 ASIC, *ASIC 2022–26 Corporate Plan* (22 August 2022) <https://download.asic.gov.au/media/v3vhdqiw/asic-corporate-plan-2022-26-focus-2022-23-published-22-august-2022.pdf>.

179 For a fuller discussion, see Hargovan, Adams and Brown, *Australian Corporate Law* (2023) ch 19; Bottomley et al, *Contemporary Australian Corporate Law* (2021) 288–91, ch 14.

180 Emilios Kyrou, 'Directors' duties, defences, indemnities, access to board papers and D&O insurance post CLERPA' (2000) 18(8) *Company and Securities Law Journal* 555, 561.

181 See *Metyor Inc v Queensland Electronic Switching Pty Ltd* [2003] 1 Qd R 186. For insight into the operation of the derivative action in Asia, see Félix E Mezzanotte, 'The unconvincing rise of the statutory derivative action in Hong Kong: Evidence from its first 10 years of enforcement' (2017) (1) *Journal of Corporate Law Studies* 469; Dan Puchniak, 'The derivative action in Asia' (2013) 9(1) *Berkeley Business Law Journal* 1. For insight into the UK experience, see Andrew Keay, 'Assessing and rethinking the statutory scheme for derivative actions under the *Companies Act 2006*' (2016) (1) *Journal of Corporate Law Studies* 39.

8.5.2 Eligible applicants

Section 236(1) of the Act, outlining who is entitled to apply to bring a statutory derivative action, provides as follows:

> (1) A person may bring proceedings on behalf of a company, or intervene in any proceedings to which the company is a party for the purpose of taking responsibility on behalf of the company for those proceedings, or for a particular step in those proceedings (for example, compromising or settling them), if:
>
>   (a) the person is:
>
>   (i) a member, former member, or person entitled to be registered as a member, of the company or of a related body corporate; or
>
>   (ii) an officer or former officer of the company; and
>
>   (b) the person is acting with leave granted under section 237.

Under the common law, only members may institute derivative proceedings on behalf of a company. As noted in the Explanatory Memorandum, 'former members are included under the statutory provision because they may have been compelled to leave the company in view of the dispute giving rise to the litigation on behalf of the company. Members and former members of a related body corporate are also included as they may be adversely affected by the failure of the company to take action and therefore may have a legitimate interest in applying to commence a derivative action.'[182] This will be particularly relevant in a corporate group scenario where subsidiary companies wish to take action against the directors of the holding company; for example, the NSW Supreme Court decision in *Goozee v Graphic World Group Holdings Pty Ltd*.[183] In this case, however, leave to institute a derivative action was refused, as the Court held that the applicant was not acting in good faith, and the derivative action would not be in the best interests of each immediate holding company. The conferral of standing on officers recognises that they are most likely to be the first to become aware of a right of action that is not being pursued by the company.[184]

ASIC is not included as an eligible applicant, as one of the purposes of the procedure is to relieve some of the regulatory burden from ASIC.[185]

8.5.3 Cause of action

The statutory derivative action may be used in respect of a cause of action that a company has against either:

- a director of the company for breach of duties owed to the company, or
- a third party for a breach of contract or in respect of a tortious act committed by that third party. (It will, however, be presumed that where proceedings involve a third party, granting leave is not in the best interests of the company unless the contrary is proved (proposed s 237(3)).[186]

---

182 Explanatory Memorandum to the Corporate Law Economic Reform Program Bill 1998 (Cth) [6.27].
183 *Goozee v Graphic World Group Holdings Ltd* (2002) 42 ACSR 534.
184 Explanatory Memorandum to the CLERP Bill 1998 [6.26]–[6.28].
185 Ibid [6.30].
186 Ibid [6.20].

The provisions allow a person to intervene in proceedings to which a company is a party, on behalf of the company, for the purpose of taking responsibility on behalf of the company for those proceedings, or for a particular step in those proceedings. This includes continuing, defending, discontinuing, compromising or settling the proceedings on behalf of the company.[187]

8.5.4 Leave of court required to institute the action

Appropriate checks and balances are provided in the legislation to prevent abuse of the proceedings, to ensure that company managements are not undermined by vexatious litigation and that company funds are not expended unnecessarily. This is done by requiring, in s 237, that a court should only grant leave to proceed with the action if:[188]

- there is inaction by the company
- the applicant is acting in good faith
- the action appears to be in the best interests of the company[189]
- there is a serious question to be tried, and
- the applicant gave written notice to the company of the intention to apply for leave, and of the reasons for applying, at least 14 days before making the application, or circumstances are such that it is appropriate to grant leave in any case.

Upon the applicant establishing each of these five elements of s 237(2) to the court's satisfaction, the court is required to grant the application for leave under s 237(1). There is no residual discretion.[190]

Empirical evidence suggests that it is a moot point whether the introduction of the statutory derivative action, as framed in pt 2F.1A,[191] has served as an effective watchdog by empowering shareholders to litigate on behalf of the company to redress wrongs done to the company that the company itself declines to pursue.[192]

8.6 Oppressive conduct of affairs: Part 2F.1

8.6.1 Types of conduct covered

Section 232 of the *Corporations Act* specifies the grounds for a court order under Part 2F.1.[193] It provides that a court can make any order under s 233 (see discussion below) if certain

---

187 Ibid [6.21].
188 For discussion of the legal principles surrounding the operation of s 237, see *Swansson v RA Pratt Properties Pty Ltd* (2002) 42 ACSR 313; *Chahwan v Euphoric Pty Ltd* (2008) 65 ACSR 661; *Oates v Consolidated Capital Services Ltd* (2009) 76 NSWLR 69; *Blakeney v Blakeney* (2016) 113 ACSR 398; *Bzezinski v Shaw* [2022] VSCA 173.
189 For relevant factors under this section, see *Blakeney v Blakeney* (2016) 113 ACSR 398 and *Huang v Wang* (2016) 114 ACSR 586.
190 *Chahwan v Euphoric Pty Ltd* (2008) 65 ACSR 661; *Huang v Wang* (2016) 114 ACSR 586.
191 For criticisms of law reform proposals leading up to the introduction of pt 2F.1A, see Anil Hargovan, 'Under judicial and legislative attack: The rule in *Foss v Harbottle*' (1996) 113(4) *South African Law Journal* 631.
192 See further I Ramsay and B Saunders, *Litigation by Shareholders and Directors: An Empirical Study of the Statutory Derivative Action* (Centre for Corporate Law and Securities Regulation, University of Melbourne, 2005).
193 For a summary of the legal principles on ss 232 (oppression remedy) and 233 (judicial relief), considered to be settled by the Full Court of the Federal Court, see *Mackay Sugar Ltd v Wilmar*

specified conduct by the corporation is either 'contrary to the interests of the members as a whole', or 'oppressive to, unfairly prejudicial to, or unfairly discriminatory against, a member or members whether in that capacity or in any other capacity'. Three specified forms of conduct are listed:

(1) the conduct of a company's affairs
(2) an actual or proposed act or omission by or on behalf of a company
(3) a resolution, or a proposed resolution, of members or a class of members of a company.

The oppression remedy is frequently relied upon, especially by members in proprietary companies whose commercial interests may be exploited and who may be unable to sell their shares to exit the company. The *Corporations Act* does not define 'oppression'. The courts have defined it widely to mean conduct that is 'burdensome, harsh and wrongful'.[194] In the leading decision on the operation of s 232, the High Court in *Wayde v New South Wales Rugby League Ltd*[195] held that there is no need to establish any irregularity or breach of legal rights to succeed. Thus, conduct that is legal may still be oppressive. Furthermore, mere prejudice or discrimination is insufficient to establish a breach of s 232, as the wording in that section requires the prejudice or discrimination to be unfair. Oppression may occur even though all members of a company are treated equally.[196] There is no requirement to prove that the company or its officers intended to cause harm to the members.[197] The broad nature of this provision, together with the wide nature of relief available (identified below), makes it an important remedy for minority shareholders.[198]

8.6.2 Who may apply for relief

Section 234 allows the following parties to bring an application under pt 2F.1:

(a) a member of the company, even if the application relates to an act or omission that is against:
   (i) the member in a capacity other than as a member; or
   (ii) another member in their capacity as a member; or
(b) a person who has been removed from the register of members because of a selective reduction; or
(c) a person who has ceased to be a member of the company if the application relates to the circumstances in which they ceased to be a member; or
(d) a person to whom a share in the company has been transmitted by will or by operation of law; or

---

Sugar Australia Ltd (2016) 338 ALR 374. For discussion of potential interpretations of the duty in the context of insolvency, see generally Nadia Hess, 'Oppression in two sections: A study of the judicial interpretation of oppression in sections 232 and 445D(1)(f) of the Corporations Act 2001 (Cth)' (2022) 45(4) *University of New South Wales Law Journal* 1556.

194 *Scottish Co-operative Wholesale Society Ltd v Meyer* [1959] AC 324.
195 *Wayde v New South Wales Rugby League Ltd* (1985) 180 CLR 459.
196 *John J Starr (Real Estate) Pty Ltd v Robert R Andrew (Australasia) Pty Ltd* (1991) 6 ACSR 63.
197 *Campbell v Backoffice Investments Pty Ltd* (2009) 238 CLR 304.
198 See further Ian Ramsay, 'An empirical study of the use of the oppression remedy' (1999) 27(1) *Australian Business Law Review* 23.

(e)   a person whom ASIC thinks appropriate having regard to investigations it
is conducting or has conducted into:

(i)   the company's affairs; or

(ii)   matters connected with the company's affairs.

The discretion of ASIC under s 234(e) is now wide enough to allow any person to have
standing if ASIC thinks it to be appropriate.

8.6.3 Nature of relief available

Section 233(1) confers upon a court a broad discretion to make 'any order under this section that it considers appropriate in relation to the company'. Apart from this very wide
discretion, s 233(1) lists 10 specific orders the court could consider, namely:

(a)   that the company be wound up;

(b)   that the company's existing constitution be modified or repealed;

(c)   that conduct of the company's affairs be regulated in future;

(d)   for the purchase of any shares by any member or person to whom a share
in the company has been transmitted by will or by operation of law;

(e)   for the purchase of shares with an appropriate reduction of the company's
share capital;

(f)   for the company to institute, prosecute, defend or discontinue specified
proceedings;

(g)   authorising a member, or a person to whom a share in the company has
been transmitted by will or by operation of law, to institute, prosecute,
defend or discontinue specified proceedings in the name and on behalf of
the company;

(h)   appointing a receiver or a receiver and manager of any or all of the company's property;

(i)   restraining a person from engaging in specified conduct or from doing a
specified act; and

(j)   requiring a person to do a specified act.

It is clear that the judicial discretion afforded under s 233 may be exercised to mould a
remedy appropriate to each particular case. Section 233(2) ensures that the general law
applying to winding up will apply if the court orders that the company be wound up.

Where a court's order effects a change to the company's constitution the company
cannot, without leave of the court, alter the constitution in a manner that is inconsistent with the order, unless the order states that the company does have the power
to make such a change (s 232(3)(a)) or the company obtains the leave of the court
(s 232(3)(b)).

8.7 Section 1324 injunctions

8.7.1 Introduction

The injunctive relief provided for under s 1324 has not been used as often as originally
expected. Section 1324(1) allows ASIC or a person 'whose interests have been, are or

would be affected by the conduct' to apply for an injunction or interim injunction (s 1324(4)) restraining a person who engages in conduct which, in essence, directly or indirectly involves a contravention of the *Corporations Act*. Under s 1324(2), the court may require a person who fails or refuses to do an act required by the Act to do such an act. We emphasise that s 1324 applies to the contravention of any provision in the entire Act. The courts have emphasised that 'an injunction under s 1324 is intended to be remedial in character',[199] and that the court may make any mandatory or prohibitive order the court considers desirable.

8.7.2 Section 1324(1)

In essence, s 1324(1) provides that where a person has engaged, is engaging or is proposing to engage in conduct that constituted, constitutes or would constitute a contravention of the Act, the court may, on the application of ASIC or of 'a person whose interests have been, are or would be affected by the conduct', grant an injunction, on such terms as the court thinks appropriate, restraining the first-mentioned person from engaging in the conduct and, if in the opinion of the court it is desirable to do so, requiring that person to do any act or thing.

Importantly, the phrase 'a person whose interests have been, are or would be affected', has been interpreted broadly to apply to creditors, employees, shareholders and other stakeholders[200] – even though, as discussed earlier, directors owe their duties first and foremost to the company. Accordingly, while the general duties of directors[201] under ch 2D of the Act are owed to the company, and only ASIC or the company[202] has standing to initiate action for breach[203] if a shareholder or a creditor, for example, suffers some loss or damage due to a breach or potential breach of a ch 2D duty, he or she may utilise s 1324 to have the particular conduct stopped, and/or to obtain damages.[204] Without s 1324, stakeholders affected by corporate misconduct, but without standing, would be dependent on ASIC to take action. This highlights the power of s 1324 as a remedial tool for stakeholders, and explains why commentators are frustrated by the fact that it has to date been under-utilised.[205]

8.7.3 The court's discretion

Section 1324 provides the court with a broad discretion to make orders on such terms as it thinks appropriate and to discharge and vary such at any time (s 1324(1), (2) and (5)). The court may also order the person to pay damages to any other person in lieu of or in addition to an order under s 1324(1) and (2): s 1324(10). Moreover, the court may order relief under s 1324(1) or (2) whether or not it appears that:

---

199 *Australian Securities and Investments Commission v ActiveSuper Pty Ltd (in liq)* (2015) 235 FCR 181, [74].
200 See *Airpeak Pty Ltd v Jetstream Aircraft* (1997) 73 FCR 161; *Allen v Atalay* (1993) 11 ACSR 753. Cf *Mesenberg v Cord Industrial Recruiters Pty Ltd* (1996) 39 NSWLR 128 for a restrictive interpretation.
201 For example, due care and diligence, good faith, proper purpose.
202 If seeking a compensation order – see s 1317(2).
203 Since the duties are civil penalty provisions.
204 Under s 1324(10), discussed below.
205 See Victoria Baumfield, 'Injunctions and damages under s 1324 of the Corporations Act: Will *McCracken v Phoenix Constructions* revive the narrow approach? (2014) 32(7) *Company and Securities Law Journal* 453.

- the person will continue to engage, or refuse/fail to engage, in that conduct
- the person has previously engaged, or refused/failed to engage, in that conduct, and
- there is an imminent danger of substantial damage to any person if that person engages, or refuses/fails to engage, in that conduct (s 1324(6) and (7)).

8.7.4 Remedies in particular

The main force of s 1324 is to provide restraining and mandatory injunctive relief. However, s 1324(9) widens the relief available to include the Mareva-type relief provided under s 1323 of the *Corporations Act*. Section 1323 gives power to the court to prohibit payment or transfer of money, securities, futures contracts or property.

Section 1324(10) provides that:

> Where the Court has power under this section to grant an injunction restraining a person from engaging in particular conduct, or requiring a person to do a particular act or thing, the Court may, either in addition to or in substitution for the grant of the injunction, order that person to pay damages to any other person.

The Queensland Court of Appeal, in *McCracken v Phoenix Constructions (Qld) Pty Ltd*,[206] held that a creditor cannot obtain an award of damages under s 1324(10) against a director for breach of the director's duties. It was held that an award of damages could only be given where an injunction could be sought, and the award of damages was therefore ancillary to the power to grant an injunction.

Moreover, the Court reasoned that a construction of s 1324(10) that allowed any person adversely affected by a contravention to claim damages cannot be reconciled with the specific civil remedy provisions in Part 9.4B of the Act. Thus, after *McCracken v Phoenix Constructions (Qld)Pty Ltd*, it is unlikely that courts will allow creditors to claim damages directly from directors under s 1324(10) based on a breach of directors' core duties under ss 180–182 of the Act.[207] By the same token, as the company is the proper plaintiff, it is unlikely that s 1324 will in future be seen as an exception to the statutory derivative action.[208]

8.8 Criminal liability of directors

8.8.1 The importance of the criminal sanction in corporations law

The sanctions explained above could be described as civil sanctions based on statutory provisions. We have chosen not to deal with non-statutory civil sanctions (for example,

---

206 *McCracken v Phoenix Constructions Pty Ltd* [2013] 2 Qd R 27.
207 See Jean J du Plessis, 'Company law developments in South Africa: Modernisation and some salient features of the Companies Act 71 of 2008' (2012) 27(1) *Australian Journal of Corporate Law* 46, 62–3. See also Nishad Kulkarni, 'In defence of McCracken: A response to "Why do courts cut back on statutory remedies provided by Parliament under corporate law?"' (2015) 89(3) *Australian Law Journal* 175.
208 See *Corporations Act 2001* (Cth) pt 2F.1A. See the discussion of the relationship between s 1324 and the derivative action by RP Austin and IM Ramsay, *Ford's Principles of Corporations Law* (LexisNexis, 15th ed, 2013) 695–7 [10.310].

action against directors or other personnel for common law negligence or breach of trust in equity) because of limited space and because of the prominence of the statutory sanctions. The criminal sanction is, however, very prominent in Australian corporate law and some mention should be made of potential offences directors and officers can commit under the *Corporations Act*. A comprehensive discussion of possible offences for corporations, directors and other officers falls outside the scope of this work.[209]

There are numerous criminal offences that directors and officers can commit. Many are contained in the Act; however, many other criminal offences for directors and officers arise in other areas of the law, in particular in the areas of workplace health and safety and environmental law, and, of course, under general criminal law (for example, theft, complicity and a range of deception offences).[210]

Subject to the provisions of the Act, the *Criminal Code Act 1995* (Cth) ('the Code') applies to all offences against the Act.[211] The Code clarifies the operation of general principles of criminal liability by setting in place the 'physical' element (what traditionally was the *actus reus* or physical act of the offence) and the 'fault' element of an offence (traditionally the *mens rea*). The Code provides that the physical elements of an offence are:

- conduct
- the circumstances in which conduct occurs, or
- a result of conduct.

Part 2.5 of the Code is particularly significant in that it explains how the principles of criminal responsibility in the Code apply to bodies corporate in relation to offences against Commonwealth laws (including the *Corporations Act*). To determine whether the company will be criminally liable for intentional offences of directors or other officers under the Act, pt 2.5 needs to be consulted (unless the relevant provision states that the principles of criminal responsibility under the Code do not apply). Part 2.5 provides that the physical element of an offence will be attributed to a body corporate where it is committed by an agent or officer of the body corporate acting within the actual or apparent scope of their employment or authority. This is, in essence, a codification of the traditional common law principle attributing criminal liability to the company when a criminal act is committed by the 'directing mind' of the company.[212] In relation to the fault element, div 12.3(1) provides that where 'intention, knowledge or recklessness' is a fault element of an offence, that element can be attributed to the company if the company 'expressly, tacitly or impliedly authorised or permitted the commission of the offence'.

---

209 For a useful summary of the offence provisions of several Acts, see Report of the HIH Royal Commission ('Owen Report'), *The Failure of HIH Insurance – Volume I: A Corporate Collapse and Its Lessons* (Commonwealth of Australia, 2003) Appendix G. For a comprehensive discussion of the criminal context for corporations, see Australian Law Reform Commission, *Corporate Criminal Responsibility* (Report No 136, 2020).

210 See, eg, James McConvill and Mirko Bagaric, 'Criminal responsibility based on complicity among corporate officers' (2004) 16(2) *Australian Journal of Corporate Law* 172.

211 *Corporations Act 2001* (Cth) s 1308A.

212 See *Tesco Supermarkets v Nattrass* [1972] AC 153.

Division 12.3(2) of the Code is crucial here, as it provides that 'authorisation or permission' may be established by a number of means, including:

...

(c) proving that a corporate culture existed within the body corporate that directed, encouraged, tolerated or led to non-compliance with the relevant provision; or

(d) proving that the body corporate failed to create and maintain a corporate culture that required compliance with the relevant provision.

'Corporate culture' is defined under pt 2.5 (div 12.3(6)) of the Code as 'an attitude, policy, rule, course of conduct or practice existing within the body corporate generally or in the part of the body corporate in which the relevant activities take place'. The effect of pt 2.5, therefore, is that the intention of a company will be equated with its 'corporate culture'. It is generally accepted that pt 2.5 of the Code, by embedding the concept of corporate culture, will have a significant impact on the approach to determining criminal liability of companies for the actions of their directors as well as their employees and agents.[213] Part 2.5 may, indeed, impose a direct duty on companies to implement a compliance system to avoid systematic contravention of federal legislation, including the Act.[214]

8.8.2 Selected criminal offences under the *Corporations Act*

8.8.2.1 General

Schedule 3 to the Act contains all the penalties (criminal as well as civil) and maximum periods of imprisonment for each of the criminal offences created by the Act. These offences can be committed by a wide variety of persons, but they are primarily offences that can be committed by the directors and officers and employees of the company.

Since we have concentrated on the civil penalty provisions as far as directors' duties are concerned, we will give only an overview of the offences directors can commit in relation to those provisions. Apart from s 180 (duty of care and diligence) and ss 674(2A) and 675(2A) (continuous disclosure), all the other civil penalty provisions are also made offences under the Act.

8.8.2.2 Specific offences for breaches of duties

Whereas ss 181–183 reflect directors' civil obligations, s 184 lays down the requirements for when directors will commit criminal offences in contravening their duties of good faith, use of position and use of information. Under s 184(1) a director or other officer of a corporation commits an offence if they are reckless, or are intentionally dishonest, and fail to exercise their powers and discharge their duties in good faith in the best interests of the corporation, or for a proper purpose.

---

213 See James McConvill and John Bingham, 'Comply or comply: The illusion of voluntary corporate governance' (2004) 22(3) *Company and Securities Law Journal* 208, 213–14.

214 See Christine Parker and Olivia Conolly, 'Is there a duty to implement a corporate compliance system in Australian law?' (2002) 30(4) *Australian Business Law Review* 273, 282–3.

A director who fails to perform his or her duties under these sections may be fined the greater of 4500 penalty units or three times the benefit derived and detriment avoided – if that can be determined – or imprisoned for up to 15 years, or both. A body corporate can be subject to the greater of 45000 penalty units, three times the benefit derived and detriment avoided – if that can be determined – or 10 per cent of its annual turnover ending at the end of the month in which the offence was committed, or began being committed.

8.9 Conclusion

This chapter confirms the view of Lord Hoffman that it is far from easy to succinctly extract the duties expected of directors.[215] For two reasons we have chosen to use the statutory duties, and in particular the civil penalty provisions in the *Corporations Act 2001* (Cth), as the starting point for explaining directors' duties and their potential liability. First, the *Corporations Act* covers directors' general law duties (duties at common law and in equity) comprehensively, and provides a neat extraction of most of these. Second, the litigation in recent years dealing with breaches of directors' duties has predominantly been based on breaches of the statutory duties, not on breaches of the duties at common law and in equity. The case studies provided demonstrate the complex litigation which can proceed from even the most egregious breaches of the duties set out.

Further, in this chapter we have shown that there are several ways of enforcing the provisions of the *Corporations Act* and have highlighted the public and private enforcement dichotomy in Australia. Although ASIC has a prominent role to play in the enforcement of the law against corporate misconduct, shareholders, directors and officers, and creditors[216] are also given standing to enforce directors' duties either on behalf of the company or on their own behalf. The statutory derivative actions (pt 2F.1A) and oppressive remedies actions (pt 2F.1) are the most important actions available to shareholders, with the latter often used in unlisted private companies or in closely held quasi-partnership companies. The s 1324 injunction and damages provide a powerful remedy to any person affected by conduct of the company in contravention of provisions of the Act, but its actual use is limited, disappointingly, and constrained by judicial interpretation. There are numerous criminal sanctions for contraventions of the Act, with research showing that criminal enforcement of directors' duties by the Commonwealth Director of Public Prosecution is significantly more prevalent than civil enforcement by ASIC.[217]

---

215 Lord Hoffman, 'Duties of company directors' (1999) 10(3-4) *European Business Law Review* 78.
216 Creditors, of course, have limited standing under the *Corporations Act 2001* (Cth).
217 Jasper Hedges et al, *An Empirical Analysis of Public Enforcement of Directors' Duties in Australia: Preliminary Findings* (CIFR Paper No 105/2016, 4 March 2016) <https://ssrn.com/abstract=2766132>.

SHAREHOLDER ACTIVISM AND BUSINESS ETHICS

SHAREHOLDER ACTIVISM

9

9.1 Introduction

Australia has a long tradition of shareholder activism. What has changed in recent years is the nature of the shareholders who are taking activist positions.[1]

It is more common nowadays to speak of activist hedge funds, activist sovereign wealth funds (such as Australia's Future Fund) and activist fund managers (such as Allan Gray), in addition to individual shareholders and interest groups such as the Australasian Centre for Corporate Responsibility.

Institutional investors have always exercised some measure of influence over the management of large public corporations,[2] but recent developments in shareholder activism mean these manoeuvres are increasingly in the public spotlight.[3] Australia's corporate landscape has featured a range of high-profile boardroom battles involving activist investors, including fund managers advocating the break-up of interlocked listed companies Brickworks and Washington H Soul Pattinson, the Future Fund putting pressure on Telstra, and a consortium of institutional investors advocating change at AGL. In recent times Australia has seen a rise in United States ('US')–style activism tactics, with public criticism of existing board members and overall denouncement of management strategy being played out through both traditional and social media.

Australia is by no means alone in experiencing rising shareholder activism. A range of large and high-profile international hedge funds,[4] pension funds[5] and other collective

---

1   For a review of shareholder activism activities see Activist Insight and Arnold Bloch Leibler, *Shareholder Activisim in Australia* (2016) <https://www.abl.com.au/shareholder-activism-1/>.
2   For a discussion of the past reticent attitude of institutional investors towards taking activist stances see Geoff Stapledon, 'Disincentives to activism by institutional investors in listed Australian companies' (1996) 18(2) *Sydney Law Review* 152. Compare the position today: see Jennifer Hill and Tim Bowley, 'Australia: Fast-growing awareness and activism' (2022) 2(4) *USALI East-West Studies* <https://usali.org/asia-pacific-symposium-essays/australia-fast-growing-awareness-and-activism>; and Bernard Mees and Sherene Smith, 'Corporate governance reform in Australia: A new institutional approach' (2019) 30(1) *British Journal of Management* 75.
3   For a cross-disciplinary review of the literature on shareholder activism see Maria Goranova and Lori Ryan, 'Shareholder activism: A multidisciplinary review' (2014) 40(5) *Journal of Management* 1230.
4   The Children's Investment Fund Management LLP (based in the United Kingdom) and Carl Icahn Capital Management LP (based in the US) are two of the most high-profile activist hedge funds. See further Marcel Kahan and Edward Rock, 'Hedge funds in corporate governance and corporate control' (2007) 3(2) *Corporate Governance Law Review* 134; John Coffee and Darius Palia, 'The wolf at the door: The impact of hedge fund activism on corporate governance' (2016) 41(3) *Journal of Corporation Law* 545.
5   The California Public Employees' Retirement System ('CalPERS') has been an activist pension fund for several decades.

investment vehicles have built a business out of taking small positions in public companies in order to advocate change that will, in their view, improve returns. The US has had the most high-profile and sustained tradition of shareholder activism,[6] but numerous examples can also be found in England and, in more recent times, in countries with block-holder corporate governance systems, such as Japan, South Korea, Italy, France and Germany.[7] In 2023, major institutional investors in Europe, the United Kingdom ('UK') and Australia co-filed a shareholder resolution for discussion at Glencore plc's 2024 annual general meeting ('AGM'); the company is the world's largest coal trader. The resolution seeks more transparency in how Glencore's thermal coal production output meets the Paris objective of limiting the global temperature increase to 1.5°C.[8] The international group of institutional investors, collectively representing $US2.2 trillion of assets under management, include Legal and General Investment Management ('LGIM'); Swiss-based Ethos Foundation, advocating on behalf of large Swiss pension funds; Vision Super, an Australian industry super fund; and HSBC Asset Management.

Certain developments in corporate law and corporate governance have contributed to rising shareholder activism in Australia. First, Australian institutional investors have embraced participation in shareholder class actions. Large-scale shareholder class actions began in Australia with the GIO (a large public insurance company) class action in the late 1990s that resulted in a settlement of close to A$100 million. This was followed by a plethora of shareholder class actions against major Australian public companies, including Telstra (Australia's largest telco), Aristocrat (the world's largest gaming machine manufacturer), Multiplex (a large construction company), Downer EDI (a large construction and manufacturing company) and NAB (one of Australia's big four banks). Shareholder class actions will be discussed in Section 9.7.2. Second, changes to the rules relating to director elections at AGMs – allowing for a spill motion where more than 25 per cent of the voting shareholders vote against the company's remuneration report in two consecutive years[9] – have led to high-profile activist positions being taken by large investment funds such as Perpetual. The two-strikes rule has also emboldened proxy advisers such as Ownership Matters, CGI Glass Lewis, ISS Proxy and ACSI, who use their reports and recommendations for institutional investors to drive governance changes at large listed companies, sometimes recommending voting against remuneration reports in order to push for change on other matters.

6   See further Jay Eisenhofer and Michael Barry, *Shareholder Activism Handbook* (Aspen Publishers, 2005); and Stuart Gillan and Laura Starks, 'The evolution of shareholder activism in the United States' (2007) 19(1) *Journal of Applied Corporate Finance* 55.

7   A search of the respected journal *Corporate Governance: An International Review* reveals numerous studies on the effects of shareholder activism in dozens of both developed and developing countries.

8   ACCR, 'Global investors unite on first ever shareholder resolution targeting Glencore's coal production' (Media Release, 5 January 2023) <https://www.accr.org.au/news/global-investors-unite-on-first-ever-shareholder-resolution-targeting-glencore%E2%80%99s-coal-production/>.

9   See *Corporations Act 2001* (Cth) s 250U and the Productivity Commission, *Executive Remuneration in Australia* (Report No 49, Final Enquiry Report, December 2009).

This chapter explores the nature and scope of shareholder activism in Australia (including reference to international developments) and its implications for corporate governance.

9.2 What is shareholder activism?

'Shareholder activism' refers to attempts by one or more shareholders to influence the management of a particular company.[10] The goals of shareholder activism are to effect some form of management and/or strategic change in the company. This may involve pressuring existing managers to resign or pressuring the company to accept new candidates for the board. It is common for shareholder activists to pursue representation on the board, or at least to pursue having certain directors removed from the board as a consequence of alleged underperformance.

Activism may also involve persuading companies to change their operational plans; for example, refraining from pursuing a particular transaction or adopting a certain corporate strategy. Activist shareholders may also pursue personal agendas such as pressuring the company to adopt particular environmental policies or approaches to human rights and/or labour practices.[11]

Shareholder activism may be seen as one part of a broader debate concerning shareholder engagement and shareholder empowerment.[12] There have long been concerns raised about the low level of shareholder participation in shareholders' (or members', as the *Corporations Act 2001* (Cth) calls them) meetings and the high level of disengagement of shareholders from their companies.[13] In Australia, this has led to a wide-ranging review of the AGM and shareholder engagement undertaken by the Corporations and Markets Advisory Committee ('CAMAC') since 2011,[14] but with CAMAC's abolition the project (it has been transferred to Treasury) the review seems to have stalled.

The AGM as it currently stands is one of the most useful tools for shareholder activists, as they can use question time to ask challenging questions of the board and the CEO. Particularly in relation to large publicly listed companies, this can be an effective way of gaining publicity for the activist's agenda. This is the approach favoured by

---

10   See further ECGI ['European Corporate Governance Institute'], 'Activism' <https://www.ecgi.global/categories/activism>. For a detailed consideration of this issue, see Tim Bowley, *Activist Shareholders in Corporate Governance* (Hart Publishing, 2023).

11   See eg Lloyd Freeburn and Ian Ramsay, 'An analysis of ESG shareholder resolutions in Australia' (2021) 44(3) *The University of New South Wales Law Journal* 1142; Kirsten Anderson and Ian Ramsay, 'From the picket line to the board room: Union shareholder activism in Australia' (2006) 24(5) *Company and Securities Law Journal* 279; Shelley Bielefeld, 'Directors' duties to the company and minority shareholder environmental activism' (2004) 23(1) *Company and Securities Law Journal* 28; Susan Shearing, 'Raising the boardroom temperature? Climate change and shareholder activism in Australia' (2012) 29(6) *Environmental and Planning Law Journal* 479.

12   For a comparative study of shareholder empowerment and shareholder activism see Jennifer Hill, 'The rising tension between shareholder and director power in the common law world' (2010) 18 *Corporate Governance: An International Review* 344.

13   See generally Stephen Bottomley, *The Responsible Shareholder* (Edward Elgar Publishing, 2021).

14   See CAMAC, *The AGM and Shareholder Engagement* (Discussion Paper, December 2012).

individual shareholder activists, and by representatives of retail investors such as the Australian Shareholders' Association. Larger institutional shareholder activists may rely more on meetings with company management and on proxy advisory firms as a more forceful method of furthering their agenda, although high-profile proxy fights involving Westfield, UniSuper, Soul Pattison and Perpetual suggest that that may be changing, and that institutional investors are not hesitant to out themselves on a public platform to drive their change agenda.

9.3 What attracts shareholder activism?

Shareholder activists usually act against companies that they see as underperforming or as underutilising their assets, with the aim of benefiting investors. Another incentive to act has been underperformance at the board level, such as an apparent failure by a board to take responsibility for poor performance or misconduct by executives below board level – the proxy contest in Bellamy Australia[15] was a good recent example of this.

Another common target for shareholder activists is allegations of mishandled conflicts of interest and related-party dealings. Lastly, but most commonly, remuneration packages of senior executives and board members will often give rise to activism. The widespread industry benchmarking of executive remuneration makes it easy for activist investors to target companies whose remuneration programs are inconsistent with peer companies or are otherwise not believed to be justified based on the performance of management. Proxy advisory firms typically provide detailed reports on remuneration practices and how industry benchmarks stack up against individual company practices.

9.4 Does shareholder activism add value?

There is a large number of case studies that have examined the performance of companies following the intervention of activist investors, but the evidence is inconclusive, with numerous studies showing improved returns and other studies showing little or no improvement.[16] Shareholder activism does seem to affect management behaviour, with firms targeted by shareholder activism more likely than other firms to change their CEO.[17] It is also widely believed that shareholder activism provides value to the activist investor.[18] Indeed there is a growing number of hedge funds and individual institutional funds whose primary investment strategy is to take an activist stance against what they perceive to be underperforming companies.

---

15 Carrie LaFrenz, 'Proxy firms tell Bellamy's shareholders to vote against Jan Cameron', *Australian Financial Review* (16 February 2017).
16 Goranova and Ryan, 'Shareholder activism' (2014) 40(5) *Journal of Management* 1230.
17 Ibid. For a review of both financial and non-financial outcomes of investor activism in the US see Gillan and Starks, 'The evolution of shareholder activism in the United States' (2007) 19(1) *Journal of Applied Corporate Finance* 55.
18 See Ronald Gilson and Jeffrey Gordon, 'The agency costs of agency capitalism: Activist investors and the revaluation of governance rights' (2013) 113(4) *Columbia Law Review* 863.

9.5 Characteristics of shareholder activism

Shareholder activists use a range of private and public strategies to influence company management. It is difficult to gauge the level of private influence that activist shareholders have over particular companies, as such conduct occurs behind closed doors. Public companies, and other disclosing entities, in Australia are required to comply with continuous disclosure laws,[19] which limit the ability of management to give market-sensitive information to individual shareholders without also disclosing the same information to the market. However, this does not mean that company management cannot engage in private discussions with investors and their advisers, provided they do not disclose confidential and market-sensitive information.

The most common tactic of shareholder activists is to publicise their interactions with the target company, particularly by disclosing correspondence where the activists lay out the problems with the company and their demands for corporate governance change. High-profile activists may then further push their message by engaging in media activity to highlight their arguments for change. Well-known activist investors such as American Carl Icahn are regularly interviewed in the press. It is also becoming common for activist investors to use online media tools to further their arguments, using social media and blog sites to spread their message as widely as possible.

Activist institutional shareholders who want to pressure company management are likely to want a substantial stake in the company to use as a leverage point. In large public companies it may be expensive for an activist investor to purchase enough shares to build up a substantial stake in the company. Purchasing large parcels of shares in a publicly listed company will usually generate market rumours and suspicions of potential takeover activity that will drive the price of the shares up. Activist institutional investors are increasingly using derivatives[20] to assist with their portfolio purchases. It is possible to use equity swaps, which may be entered into with a number of investment counterparties (usually investment banks), to obtain millions of dollars' worth of shares within a relatively short period, without showing up on the company's register of members. This has been used in activist campaigns against Bellamy's and Echo Entertainment.

Under Australian law a substantial shareholder is required to disclose movements in their shareholdings of more than one per cent.[21] A substantial shareholder is one with a relevant interest of five per cent or more of the voting shares in a company.[22] However, the holder of an equity swap that is not physically settled will not fall within these provisions even though it may be relatively easy for the holder to request that the counterparty unwind the swap and settle by selling the shares to the holder. The practice of using derivatives to mask actual positions of control and influence in public

---

19 *Corporations Act 2001* (Cth) ch 6CA.
20 Derivatives are financial instruments which involve an obligation to pay money or to deliver a product sometime in the future, but where the value of the contract is referenced to something else, typically a commodity price or an interest rate, or an index rate. Futures, options, currency and interest rate swaps are the most common forms of derivatives: see further *Corporations Act 2001* (Cth) s 761D; Alastair Hudson, *Law of Financial Derivatives* (Sweet & Maxwell, 5th ed, 2012).
21 *Corporations Act 2001* (Cth) s 671B.
22 Ibid s 9.

companies has been the subject of extensive scholarly debate, particularly in the US, where Professor Henry Hu and Professor Bernard Black have undertaken a deep vein of scholarship on the issue.[23]

Another common technique used by activist fund managers is to 'move in packs'.[24] While not necessarily coordinating their activities so as to render themselves formally associated, it is common for multiple hedge funds to work simultaneously to put increased pressure on target management. They may be joined in such efforts by other institutional investors and private equity investors. Given the often dramatic effect of shareholder activism on the short-term share price of a public company, it is common for multiple activist funds to 'pile into a stock'[25] while it is under the spotlight of a public governance campaign.

Activist institutional investors may use their substantial holdings to requisition members' meetings, to distribute material to investors, to propose resolutions to members and ultimately to seek the replacement of incumbent directors or to vote against the remuneration report. Individual activist investors are usually not able to achieve the passage of resolutions at members' meetings due to their relatively small holdings in the company.

9.6 Internal activism

9.6.1 Overview

Shareholder activism may involve a number of actions taken within the company, usually actions that may only be taken by members. These will be regulated by the company's constitution and any subsidiary by-laws or board/committee charters as well as by the *Corporations Act 2001* (Cth) ('*Corporations Act*' or 'the Act') and by the listing rules of the licensed financial market if the company has its securities listed for public trading.

9.6.2 Obtaining information

The first element of shareholder activism is to obtain relevant information about what the company is doing or proposing to do or not do. Shareholders have a range of information rights, including access to periodic reports (pt 2M of the Act), and to notices of members' meetings.[26] However, much of this information will already be available because most target companies in shareholder activism cases are disclosing entities, so they are required to keep the financial market informed of material information on an immediate and ongoing basis.

---

23 See, eg, Henry Hu and Bernard Black, 'Hedge funds, insiders, and the decoupling of economic and voting ownership: Empty voting and hidden (morphable) ownership' (2007) 13(2) *Journal of Corporate Finance* 343; and Henry Hu and Bernard Black, 'The new vote buying: Empty voting and hidden (morphable) ownership' (2006) 79(4) *Southern California Law Review* 811.

24 See Carmen Lu, 'Unpacking wolf packs': Comment' (2016) 125(3) *Yale Law Journal* 560; Leo E Strine Jr, 'Who bleeds when the wolves bite? A flesh-and-blood perspective on hedge fund activism and our strange corporate governance *system'* (2017) 126(6) *Yale Law Journal* 1870.

25 This refers to multiple fund managers purchasing securities in the company in the expectation that they can benefit from the rising price of the securities or can benefit from price volatility in the securities (usually combined with hedging arrangements such as using derivatives to protect themselves from too much volatility, and thus risk).

26 *Corporations Act 2001* (Cth) s 249J.

Shareholders may request access to information that is not generally available, such as the company's register of members, and copies of such registers, provided that the use of the information is permissible under the *Corporations Act*.[27] Members may also seek access to books that are required to be kept by the company.[28] This provision was utilised in *Abrahams v Commonwealth Bank of Australia*[29] to seek access to documents relating to the bank's involvement in gas and fossil fuel projects in order to assess their compliance with the bank's Environmental and Social Framework and Environmental and Social Policy.

9.6.3 Convening members

Members with at least five per cent of the votes in a members' meeting may convene a members' meeting under s 249D of the Act. This will involve them paying for the meeting themselves, but they will also control the conduct of the meeting (within the terms of the constitution). A more common occurrence is for members with at least five per cent of the votes to require the company to convene a members' meeting (also s 249D). In these instances the company will control the conduct of the meeting, but the members can force the company to convene a meeting only if the purpose of the meeting is within the power of the meeting to determine, such as the removal and appointment of directors. If a meeting requisition is made for an improper purpose it may be ignored by the directors.[30]

9.6.4 Distributing information to members

Members with at least five per cent of the votes may require the company to put resolutions to the next members' meeting (s 249N) and may require the company to distribute information to members for the next meeting (s 249P).[31] There are limitations on how long the information may be and it must not be defamatory. Members may also obtain a copy of the share register in order to contact members about an upcoming meeting, although this would be at their own expense (ss 173 and 177).

9.6.5 Voting at members' meetings

One of the basic components of an ordinary share in an Australian company is the right to vote on a resolution at a members' meeting (s 250E – a replaceable rule). For activist shareholders this may be used to vote for changes in the composition of the board of directors, but even large shareholders are unlikely to have enough votes to successfully undertake this without the support of numerous other large shareholders, and usually one or more widely used proxy advisers.

27 Ibid ss 173, 177.
28 This ability is not restricted to members only: *Corporations Act 2001* (Cth) s 1300.
29 *Abrahams v Commonwealth Bank of Australia* [2021] NSD864/2021 (NSW District Registry of the Federal Court of Australia, Cheeseman J, 4 November 2021).
30 *NRMA Ltd v Parker* (1986) 6 NSWLR 517.
31 *Australasian Centre for Corporate Responsibility v Commonwealth Bank of Australia* (2016) 248 FCR 280. See further Jason Harris, 'Barbarians at the gate?' (2016) 34(3) *Company and Securities Law Journal* 151.

Proxy advisers are firms that assist institutional investors with voting on resolutions that are put to members' meetings, typically AGMs. Where an individual owns shares in a small number of companies it may not be too onerous to participate in voting either in person or by proxy. But an institutional fund manager may own shares in dozens or even hundreds of companies, most of which will have their AGMs around the same time each year. This makes it difficult for the institutional shareholder to properly evaluate each proposal for each company, leading them to rely on proxy advisers, who can give them (for a fee) an informed view about how to vote. In Australia there are a number of proxy advisers, from large-scale international operations such as ISS Proxy and CGI Glass Lewis, to local firms such as the Australian Council of Superannuation Investors and Ownership Matters. Proxy advisers have come under a great deal of scrutiny and criticism, particularly from the boards of major corporations, because of their power and influence over the institutional shareholders who control the majority of shares in most publicly listed companies.

There have been calls for regulation of proxy advisers,[32] but the Senate in Australia has resisted that trend by rejecting the *Treasury Laws Amendment (Greater Transparency of Proxy Advice) Regulations 2021* (Cth) introduced by the Morrison government without much public discussion or parliamentary scrutiny.[33] The government's reforms aimed to introduce stricter obligations by extending coverage of the Australian financial services licensing regime to a wider range of proxy adviser activities, and also by addressing independence concerns (namely, by mandating proxy advisers to be independent of their institutional clients).[34]

It is significant that a review of proxy engagement practices undertaken in 2018 by the corporate regulator, Australian Securities and Investments Commission ('ASIC'), did not find any pressing need for further regulation.[35] The political nature of proxy adviser regulation is underscored by recent events in the US where the legislators in Indiana and Montana introduced Bills to ban the states' pension funds from following shareholder advisers' voting recommendations that consider environmental, social and governance ('ESG') criteria.[36]

---

32   For a summary see Egan Associates, 'The influence of proxy advisors' <https://eganassociates .com.au/influence-of-proxy-advisers/>. See further Lars Klohn and Philip Schwarz, 'The regulation of proxy advisors' (2013) 8(1) *Capital Markets Law Journal* 90; and Holger Fleischer, 'Proxy advisors in Europe: Reform proposals and regulatory strategies' (2012) 9(1) *European Company Law* 12.

33   For contents of the vetoed Regulations, see Australian Government, Federal Register of Legislation, *Treasury Laws Amendment (Greater Transparency of Proxy Advice) Regulations 2021* (Cth) <https://www .legislation.gov.au/Details/F2021L01801>.

34   For the Morrison government's announcement, see Jane Hume, 'Reforms to bring greater transparency and accountability to proxy advice' (Media Release, Treasury, 17 December 2021) <https://ministers.treasury.gov.au/ministers/jane-hume-2020/media-releases/reforms-bring-greater-transparency-and-accountability-proxy>.

35   ASIC, *ASIC Review of Proxy Adviser Engagement Practices* (Report 578, June 2018) <https://asic.gov.au/ regulatory-resources/find-a-document/reports/rep-578-asic-review-of-proxy-adviser-engagement-practices/>.

36   See Patrick Temple-West, '*Republicans target proxy advisers ISS and Glass Lewis in ESG backlash*' *Financial Times*, (online, 18 January 2023) <https://www.ft.com/content/44323744-b145-4c49-a821-b1546b722aff>.

There are two areas where reform of proxy engagement practices in Australia has occurred: first, fund managers are required to disclose their use of proxy advisory services, and second, companies are required to formulate voting policies which are given to proxy advisers and disclosed to fund members.[37]

9.7 Court action

9.7.1 Individual actions

There is a variety of individual court actions that can assist with a shareholder activist agenda.[38] The obvious disadvantages of individual court actions are that the activist must meet the cost of the action, which can be high, and court actions often involve months, if not years, of work. For activist institutional investors (as opposed to hedge funds or private equity funds) there is also the reputational risk involved in litigation: it may jeopardise relationships with current or future clients. Many, perhaps most, institutional investors (such as insurance companies and pension funds) do not want to be seen to be picking fights with major corporates and potential future clients. However, for well-funded activists who are not concerned about the reputational risk, the goal may not be a final court order but rather the company management accepting their agenda. Sometimes the threat of expensive litigation can bring the parties together to negotiate a resolution of the dispute.

An activist's complaint that the company has issued shares improperly gives rise to an equitable right to seek a court order rescinding the share issue.[39]

Activist shareholders may also take advantage of a range of statutory rights of action, assuming that it could be argued that the conduct by the company or by the directors or executives is in breach of the *Corporations Act*. These include:

- actions for conduct that is oppressive or unfairly prejudicial or unfairly discriminatory (s 232)
- applying for a statutory injunction (s 1324).

Each of these statutory rights was explained in Chapter 8.

Where the conduct that the activist is targeting is a breach of a right held by the company, the activist shareholder may apply for a statutory derivative action under pt 2F.1A to enforce the company's rights. This may involve suing the directors or officers on behalf of the company or seeking to enforce a right that the company has against a third party. However, a statutory derivative action is unlikely to be frequently used because it is expensive – and the applicant bears the cost – and there is no guarantee that the court will order the company to indemnify them even if they win. Furthermore, a shareholder activist with a long-running dispute against the company may face difficulties satisfying

---

37   See Financial Services Council, *Standard 13 Voting Policy, Voting Record and Disclosure* (2004; updated in 2013 and 2019), which applies to all Financial Services Council members (this includes most of the largest fund managers in Australia).

38   For more detail in the context of climate litigation, see generally Beth Nosworthy, 'The Corporations Act and climate change – appetite for change?' (2020) 94(6) *Australian Law Journal* 411.

39   *Residues Treatment & Trading Co Ltd v Southern Resources Ltd (No 4)* (1988) 14 ACLR 569.

the good faith requirement under s 237(2)(b) when applying for leave to commence the proceedings. Statutory derivative actions were discussed in detail in Chapter 8.

If the conduct of the company is in breach of the company's constitution, the activist shareholder may seek to enforce the contractual nature of the constitution (s 140). This too is unlikely to be a major avenue for court action because the activist agenda will usually involve more than mere compliance with the company's constitution.

It is also possible that an activist investor may take action for alleged disclosure contraventions by the company, particularly where underperformance or undisclosed fraud is at issue. The *Corporations Act* contains a prohibition on misleading or deceptive conduct in relation to financial products (shares and debentures), as well as a positive obligation to disclose material information (for disclosing entities).[40] However, there have been very few cases of individual enforcement action for disclosure breaches against publicly listed companies. In recent times it is more likely that an activist investor would participate in a shareholder class action.

9.7.2 Class actions

It is possible for shareholder activists to become involved in a shareholder class action against a target company. Shareholder class actions are large-scale forms of litigation, often involving thousands of investors, which means they are always highly publicised. The publicity and large amounts of damages claimed can mean that they will drive institutional change inside the target company. However, activist investors are likely to pursue other means to push their agenda given the length of time – usually several years – that class actions take. Nonetheless, they are clearly one of many techniques that can be used to force corporate governance change.

A class action is a form of group litigation, the aim of which is to stop multiple parallel proceedings, which would waste court time and resources. Group proceedings have long been part of court procedure, but class actions allow a lead plaintiff to represent the class members, who thereby maintain anonymity and assume little risk in participating in the action.

Class actions have been in operation in Australia since 1992[41] and, except for the US,[42] Australia is regarded as the country with the highest risk in facing class action litigation.

According to a report by Insightia, Australia was third behind the US and the South Korea as the country with the greatest amount of activist activity during the first quarter

---

40   *Corporations Act 2001* (Cth) ss 674 (continuous disclosure) and 1041H (misleading or deceptive conduct). For the definitions of 'disclosing entity', 'listed disclosing entity' and 'unlisted disclosing entity', see *Corporations Act 2001* (Cth) ss 111AC, 111AL(1) and 111AL(2). See further Jason Harris and Suzanne Webbey, 'Personal liability for corporate disclosure problems' (2011) 29(8) *Company and Securities Law Journal* 463.

41   For an edited collection of essays marking the 30th anniversary of the introduction of class actions law in Australia, see Michael Legg and James Metzger (eds), *The Australian Class Action – A 30 Year Perspective* (The Federation Press, 2023); see also Damien Grave and Helen Mould (eds), *25 Years of Class Actions in Australia: 1992–2017* (Ross Parsons Centre of Commercial, Corporate and Taxation Law, 2017.

42   Jones Day, *Class Actions Worldview: Part I – United States and the European Union* (White Paper, August 2023) <https://www.jonesday.com/en/insights/2023/08/class-actions-worldview-part-i-us-and-the-eu>.

of 2022, with 18 Australia-based companies subject to activist attention (up from 14 companies in both the first quarters of 2021 and 2020).[43]

The right of shareholders to inspect company registers and obtain copies thereof has become prominent in the past decade, in part because of the increase in shareholder class actions, which some have branded Australia's 'new growth industry'.[44] Class actions, aided by litigation funding, are a regular feature of Australian law. In the 27-year period between their introduction in 1992 and 30 June 2019, there were 634 class actions, representing an annual average of 23.[45] The most common type during that period were shareholder class actions, of which there were 122.[46] Eighty-two (or 67 per cent) of the 122 shareholder class actions were brought against only the relevant companies, as opposed to their directors.[47] In 2020–21, there was a peak of 64 class-actions filed, the most in any year since 2012,[48] which coincided with a peak in consumer action claims (25 for that year alone).[49]

There appears to be very little appetite on the part of ASIC to use class actions to secure monetary relief for shareholders.[50] Research shows that in the class actions generated by the private sector, A\$888 605 232 has been paid out to 94 984 shareholders, which equates to individual compensation of A\$9355.[51]

More class actions are likely in relation to companies that may have delayed reporting material changes in financial circumstances arising from the global pandemic. The growth in class actions is aided by the support received from litigation funders. Based on access to justice considerations, the High of Australia has removed barriers to litigation funding, with the latter no longer seen as contrary to public policy.[52] It is now commonplace to observe third party funding in class actions.[53]

---

43 Insightia, *Shareholder Activism in Q1 2022* (April 2022) <https://www.insightia.com/q12022/. See further MinterEllison, 'Global report finds that shareholder activist activity globally is showing signs of bouncing back from the pandemic' (12 April 2022) <https://www.minterellison.com/articles/key-takeaways-from-insightia-report-shareholder-activism-in-q1-2022>.

44 Jennifer Hewett, 'The rise and rise of class actions', *The Australian Financial Review* (14 October 2019). Maurice Blackburn, a law firm specialising in class actions, claimed in January 2023 to have obtained more than A\$3.7 billion in settlements for its clients. See Maurice Blackburn, 'Past class actions' <https://www.mauriceblackburn.com.au/class-actions/past-class-actions/>.

45 Vince Morabito, *Shareholder Class Actions in Australia – Myth v Facts* (11 November 2019) <https://ssrn.com/abstract=3484660>.

46 Ibid.

47 Ibid.

48 King & Wood Mallesons, *The Review: Class Actions in Australia 2021/2022* (15 September 2022) 6 <https://www.kwm.com/au/en/insights/latest-thinking/the-review-class-actions-in-australia-2021-2022.html>.

49 Ibid 7.

50 Morabito, *Shareholder Class Actions in Australia* (11 November 2019).

51 Ibid.

52 Prior to significant judicial developments in Australia, litigation funding had traditionally been confined to financial assistance to liquidators, with the courts recognising an exception to the torts of maintenance and champerty (which arise for benefiting and encouraging litigation). Although these torts have been abolished in many jurisdictions, concerns remained about whether litigation funding was an abuse of process. Such concerns were erased in the significant case of *Campbell's Cash and Carry Pty Ltd v Fostif Pty Ltd* (2006) 229 CLR 386 in which the High Court held that litigation funding was not an abuse of process.

53 Australian Law Reform Commission, *Integrity, Fairness and Efficiency – An Inquiry into Class Action Proceedings and Third-Party Litigation Funders* (Report 134, December 2018). In 2020, the

Common causes of class action in Australia involve a claim of misleading or deceptive conduct in respect of statements and/or a failure to disclose or correct certain information; and breach of a listed company's continuous disclosure obligations.[54]

Many of the biggest companies listed on the ASX have been subjected to class actions in Australia, including Multiplex (a large construction company),[55] Aristocrat Leisure (one of the world's largest poker machine manufacturers),[56] Commonwealth Bank of Australia, National Australia Bank,[57] QBE Insurance,[58] Leighton (now CIMIC, an international construction company) and Centro (now Federation Centres, a large shopping centre owner).[59] Australia's largest class action may be waiting in the wings, given the significant breach of data suffered by former and current Optus customers in 2022, with a potential class-action pool of almost 10 million customers exposed in that data breach.[60]

It is relevant to note that all of these examples of successful class action cases represented out-of-court settlements. Equally relevant, in the class actions based on allegations of breach of continuous disclosure law, prior to recent statutory amendments (discussed below), the causes of legal action did not require proof of intent to mislead or defraud shareholders.

Morrison government enacted the *Corporations Amendment (Litigation Funding) Regulations 2020* (Cth) to regulate litigation funding. However, the current Albanese Labor government introduced regulations in 2022 to wind back these reforms. The *Corporations Amendment (Litigation Funding) Regulations 2022* (Cth), which took effect from 10 December 2022, once again exempts litigation funders from ASIC's managed investment scheme regime and its Australian Financial Services Licence requirements, and the product disclosure and anti-hawking provisions of the *Corporations Act.*

54   Morabito, *Shareholder Class Actions in Australia* (11 November 2019). See further Michael Duffy and Ellie Chapple, 'The rise of the securities nondisclosure class action in New Zealand and views from Australian and global practice' (2022) 41(4) *Civil Justice Quarterly* 408.

55   The Multiplex class action (2006–10) settled before trial for A$110 million, with shareholders alleging that the company failed to adequately disclose the full extent of substantial cost increases and delays in the construction of Wembley Stadium. See further Maurice Blackburn, 'Past class actions' <https://www.mauriceblackburn.com.au/class-actions/past-class-actions/>.

56   The Aristocrat class action alleged that the company's reported profits for 2001 and the first half of 2002 were overstated and in breach of accounting standards. Furthermore, the shareholders alleged the company, in breach of its continuous disclosure obligations, failed to inform the market that it was unlikely to achieve its 2002 profit forecast. In August 2008, the Federal Court of Australia approved the A$144.5 million settlement, the largest class action settlement in Australian legal history at that time. See further Maurice Blackburn, 'Past class actions' <https://www.mauriceblackburn.com.au/class-actions/past-class-actions/>.

57   The National Australia Bank ('NAB') class action (2010–12) was settled for A$115 million, with shareholders alleging that NAB failed to disclose provisions for losses in respect of the bank's exposure to over $1 billion of collateralised debt obligations.

58   The QBE Insurance Group Ltd class action lawsuit arose from the belated profit downgrade made in 2013 – this saw a significant drop in the value of its shares and wiped A$4 billion off the company's market value. Under the terms of the class action settlement in 2018, QBE was ordered by the Court to pay A$132.5 million. See further Maurice Blackburn, 'Past class actions' <https://www.mauriceblackburn.com.au/class-actions/past-class-actions/>.

59   The Centro class action (2008–12) was settled midway through the trial for A$200 million, with investors alleging that the Centro companies failed to adequately disclose the full extent of their maturing debt obligations. See further Maurice Blackburn, 'Past class actions', <https://www.mauriceblackburn.com.au/class-actions/past-class-actions/>.

60   Mirella Atherton and Eliezer Sanchez-Lasaballett, 'A class action against Optus could easily be Australia's biggest: Here's what is involved', *The Conversation* (5 October 2022).

Significantly, in the first class action case to run to full judgment in Australia, the *Myer* case (2019), the plaintiffs were unsuccessful.[61] This development, together with the recent reforms which have narrowed the scope of continuous disclosure laws,[62] suggests that there may be risks for future class action disclosure cases going to full trial. A fault element is now required to prove breach of continuous disclosure law.

Under the recently passed *Treasury Laws Amendment (2021 Measures No 1) Act 2021* (Cth), it must be established that a listed entity acted with 'knowledge, recklessness or negligence' in order to sound a breach of the continuous disclosure civil penalty provisions of s 674A(2) of the *Corporations Act*. It remains to be seen whether or not this legislative reform, together with the pronouncements in the *Myer* case on the difficult issue of causation, will slow the pace of developments in shareholder class actions.

Although shareholder class actions have been criticised for being expensive and complex and opening the door to frivolous claims, they are growing in number and have been embraced by institutional investors. These class actions have been recognised as having a valuable role in complementing public enforcement by ASIC.

9.8 Case studies

Carl Icahn

Carl Icahn is perhaps the most famous activist investor in the world.[63] He built a fearsome reputation as a corporate raider in the 1980s: his actions included the hostile takeover and eventual breakup of TWA ('Trans World Airlines'). In recent years Icahn has become a shareholder activist and advocate for corporate governance reform rather than merely a corporate raider. He has advocated corporate governance and business operations reforms in large public companies such as Yahoo (advocating the resignation of CEO Jerry Yang and the merger with Microsoft), Dell Computer (opposing the privatisation proposed by CEO Michael Dell) and eBay (advocating its divesture of PayPal).[64] Most recently, in 2022, his activism was less successful, specifically

---

61 *TPT Patrol Pty Ltd as trustee for Amies Superannuation Fund v Myer Holdings Ltd* (2019) 293 FCR 29. On the legal significance of the *Myer* case for class actions, see Michael Duffy, 'Causation in Australian securities class actions: Searching for an efficient but balanced approach' (2019) 93(10) *Australian Law Journal* 833; and Frank Castiglia, 'Practical guidance from the Myer case for directors and executives' (2019) 71(11) *Governance Directions Journal* 620. For similar result, see *Bonham as Trustee for the Aucham Super Fund v Iluka Resources Ltd* (2022) 404 ALR 15. Cf *Crowley v Worley Ltd* (2022) 293 FCR 438 where the Court remitted the case to the single judge for determination. This may give rise to the first order for damages in a shareholders' class action in Australia.

62 See further Michael Duffy, 'Modifications to continuous disclosure requirements and the role of corporate knowledge, intent, recklessness and negligence in breaches: A discussion' (2021) 38(2) *Company and Securities Law Journal* 138.

63 See 'Anything you can do, Icahn do better', *The Economist* (15 February 2014) 55. Carl Icahn has operated a number of enterprises over the years, including a securities firm (Icahn & Co), a hedge fund (Icahn Capital LP) and a diversified holding company with interests across a range of business lines (Icahn Enterprises LP). See further Matteo Tonello, 'The activism of Carl Icahn and Bill Ackman' (29 May 2014) <https://corpgov.law.harvard.edu/2014/05/29/the-activism-of-carl-icahn-and-bill-ackman/>.

64 For an empirical study of the Icahn effect on public companies see Vinod Venkiteshwaran, Subramanian Iyer and Ramesh Rao, 'Is Carl Icahn good for long-term shareholders? A case study in shareholder activism' (2010) 22(4) *Journal of Applied Corporate Finance* 45.

his ESG-focused proxy campaigns targeting McDonalds and Kroger. Icahn, along with his daughter Michelle Icahn Nevin, sought to hold the board of McDonalds to account in relation to promises around the treatment of pigs in their supply chains – this campaign was not successful, with less than two per cent of votes cast in favour of his board nominees.[65] A similar campaign targeting food retailer Kroger, but in respect of employee welfare in that instance, was withdrawn following the outcome of the McDonald's shareholder vote.[66]

In 2013–14 Icahn made a high-profile and sustained attack on Apple, arguing that Apple is the most overcapitalised company in history.[67] Apple, at the time, had over US$150 billion in cash reserves, which provoked widespread public criticism from the investment community. Activist hedge fund Greenlight Capital called for Apple to issue preference shares as a way of returning some of the excess capital to investors; this led Apple to announce a buy-back and dividend program that would involve more than US$100 billion over several years. Icahn then became involved by buying up over US$4 billion worth of Apple shares, and advocated loudly that Apple should both increase and accelerate its buy-back program. This action included a meeting with the Apple CEO and a pending proxy fight at an Apple shareholders' meeting. Apple responded to this by increasing its public buy-back program and by paying a large dividend in 2013. Icahn dropped his proxy proposal.

One major feature of Icahn's shareholder activism is the highly public nature of his battles with company management. Icahn has set up an X feed and his comments about companies often have an effect on the company's share price. As corporate governance expert Robert Monks said, Icahn has made 'it clear to the greediest people in the world that you can make a lot of money out of activism'.[68]

AGL

According to the Clean Energy Regulator, an independent statutory authority,[69] in 2020–21 931 corporations in Australia reported a total of 315 million tonnes of scope 1 greenhouse gas emissions. Australia's 10 highest emitting corporations, which amounted for almost half of these reported emissions, were predominantly electricity generators, and topping the list, reporting 40.2 million tonnes alone, was AGL Energy Limited ('AGL'). AGL is an Australian listed public company, operating Australia's largest electricity generation portfolio, which accounts for approximately 20 per cent of the total generation capacity within Australia's National Electricity Market.[70]

---

65 Glass Lewis, 'M&A roundup: ESG activism case studies' (11 January 2023) <https://www.glasslewis.com/ma-roundup-esg-activism-case-studies/>.

66 See Carl Icahn, 'Statement to shareholders of McDonalds and Kroger' (6 June 2022) <https://carlicahn.com/statement-to-shareholders-of-mcdonalds-and-kroger/>.

67 Carl Icahn, 'Open letter to Apple shareholders' (January 24, 2014) <https://carlicahn.com/apple_shareholder_letter/>.

68 'Anything you can do, Icahn do better', *The Economist* (15 February 2014) 55.

69 Established by the *Clean Energy Regulator Act 2011* (Cth).

70 See generally 'Who we are', *AGL* <https://www.agl.com.au/about-agl/who-we-are>.

In 2021, AGL unsuccessfully sued Greenpeace for parodying its logo, as part of a campaign to shift the company from coal to renewables, in which Greenpeace edited AGL's logo to declare it 'Australia's Greatest Liability'.[71] Justice Burley found that the 'ridicule potent in the message was likely to be immediately perceived. ... Many would see these uses of the modified AGL logo as darkly humorous, because the combined effect is ridiculous. AGL is exposed to ridicule by the use of its corporate imagery including by use of the modified AGL logo to convey a message that AGL would not wish to send.'[72] There was clear parody, and consequently access to s 41A of the *Copyright Act 1968* (Cth) affirmative defence of fair dealing for the purpose of parody or satire.[73]

In the same year, a demerger was announced: AGL would split its company into two new businesses, one to be called Accel Energy, which would take the coal-heavy generation portfolio; and the retail business, distributed energy, and gas-fired, hydro and solar power station projects to be retained by AGL.[74] Shareholders were to vote on the proposed demerger at an extraordinary general meeting in June 2022.

The Australasian Centre for Corporate Responsibility ('ACCR') put a shareholder resolution to the 2021 AGM, which requested that the board disclose, in relation to the demerger, short-, medium- and long-term targets for reductions in relation to emissions – aligned with arts 2.1(a) and 4.1 of the *Paris Agreement* details on how the demerged companies' capital expenditure would align with the targets, and details of how the demerged companies' remuneration policies would incentivise progress in that space.[75] This resolution was supported by 54 per cent of the shareholders.[76]

Mid-year, AGL posted a A$2 billion loss for the 2020–21 financial year. Mike Cannon-Brookes, a billionaire tech entrepreneur known initially for his role as co-founder and co-CEO of Atlassian, with a consortium including Canada's Brookfield Asset Management, approached AGL with a A$5 billion takeover bid.[77] The board of AGL rejected the unsolicited proposal, on the basis that it undervalued the company.

The demerger vote approached, and required a special resolution (that is, 75 per cent of votes case in favour) to proceed. The ACCR published a briefing, identifying that it would be voting against the demerger.[78] Cannon-Brookes, who by then held over 11 per cent of AGL, via

71 *AGL Energy Ltd v Greenpeace Australia Pacific Ltd* (2021) 395 ALR 275.
72 Ibid [63].
73 Some other uses of the AGL logo, generally without the accompanying tagline of 'Australia's Greatest Liability''' or 'presented by Greenpeace' were not able to meet the defence: ibid [65]–[66].
74 AGL, 'AGL announces intention to create two leading energy businesses' (Media Release, 30 March 2021) <https://www.agl.com.au/about-agl/media-centre/asx-and-media-releases/2021/march/agl-announces-intention-to-create-two-leading-energy-businesses>.
75 ACCR, 'Investor briefing: Shareholder resolution to AGL Energy Ltd on Paris-aligned goals and targets' (23 August 2021) <https://www.accr.org.au/research/accr-investor-briefing-on-agl-energy-aug-2021/>.
76 ACCR,' AGL Energy demerger: What should a climate aware investor consider?' (18 May 2022) <https://www.accr.org.au/research/agl-energy-demerger/>.
77 Mark Ludlow and Elouise Fowler, 'Cannon-Brookes plans to kill coal by 2030, invest $20b in renewables', *Australian Financial Review* (21 February 2022).
78 ACCR, 'AGL Energy Demerger' (18 May 2022) <https://www.accr.org.au/research/agl-energy-demerger/>.

his private investment vehicle Grok Ventures, also publicly opposed the demerger.[79] Climate-focused investor Snowcap and Greenpeace also weighed in against the demerger.[80]

One month before the AGM, AGL abandoned the demerger plans, with the board chair, the chief executive officer and one director resigning in the process, and another to leave a few months later.[81] The remaining board was immediately under pressure to act in relation to its portfolio, with Cannon-Brookes and other large shareholders voicing a preference for an accelerated timeline for AGL to exit from coal-powered energy generation.[82]

At the AGM in November 2022, shareholders endorsed four candidates for the board proposed by Grok Ventures and Cannon-Brookes, despite three of these candidates being opposed by the current members of the board. Further, the shareholders reappointed an existing non-executive director also endorsed by Grok Ventures,[83] expanding the total number of directors from five to nine. The existing chair, Patricial McKenzie, was reinstalled with 96 per cent approval, and AGL's climate transition plan – which included closure of all coal-fired power stations by 2035[84] and significant renewable investments – was backed by 70 per cent of the AGM shareholders. AGL's remuneration report was subject to a 'first strike', as discussed in Section 9.1.[85]

There is clearly a relationship between the impact of activism and the swift upheaval at AGL – from its business plans to the make-up of its board, AGL felt the heated pressure to make changes. David Ritter, the CEO of Greenpeace, declared it 'a triumph of the clean energy revolution over the vested interests of the fossil fuel order'.[86] Clear parallels can be drawn with the board campaign run in relation to Exxon Mobile Corp in 2021,[87] where Engine No 1 succeeded in installing three nominees to the board, on a much slimmer holding of 0.02 per cent.[88] Exxon director Ursula Burns was reported as describing the

---

79   Editorial Board, 'Australia's AGL Energy case shows the growing power of green capital', *Financial Times* (3 June 2022); Mark Ludlow, '"Godawful mess": AGL's "own goal" leaves it vulnerable for takeover', *Australian Financial Review* (30 May 2022).

80   Glass Lewis, 'M & A round up' (11 January 2023) <https://www.glasslewis.com/ma-roundup-esg-activism-case-studies/>.

81   Ludlow, '"Godawful mess"', *Australian Financial Review* (30 May 2022).

82   Angela Macdonald-Smith, 'Investors demand Paris alignment as AGL dumps split', *Australian Financial Review* (30 May 2022).

83   David Stringer, 'Billionaire Cannon-Brookes backed to overhaul AGL's board', *Bloomberg* (15 November 2022); David Simmons, 'Cannon-Brookes' Grok Ventures secures four key seats on AGL board', *Business News Australia* (15 November 2022).

84   AGL had already announced in September 2022 that it would close the Loy Yang A power plant in 2035 – 10 years earlier than previously planned: Bruce Mountain, 'The end of coal-fired power is in sight, even with private interests holding out', *The Conversation* (10 October 2022).

85   Mark Ludlow and Elouise Fowler, 'AGL Board must work as one, warns McKenzie', *Australian Financial Review* (15 November 2022).

86   David Ritter, 'Change of pace by AGL a giant tick for clean energy', *Independent Australia* (20 November 2022).

87   For more information, see Anna Christie, 'Battle for the board: Climate rebellion at Exxon marks a new era of shareholder activism', *Oxford Business Law Blog* (Blog Post, 12 July 2021) <https://www.law.ox.ac.uk/business-law-blog/blog/2021/07/battle-board-climate-rebellion-exxon-marks-new-era-shareholder>.

88   Jennifer Hiller and Svea Herbst-Bayliss, 'Exxon loses board seats to activist hedge fund in landmark climate vote', *Reuters* (27 March 2021); Samantha Subramanian, 'Engine No 1: The little hedge fund that shook Big Oil', *Quartz* (28 May 2021, updated 3 June 2021).

climate as a 'tidal wave of investor concerns on ESG issues'.[89] This climate is not limited to Australia and the US, and where investors around the world draw the line in coming years remains a focal point for corporations and the market.

9.9 Conclusion

Shareholder activism has been a hot topic of debate for the past decade, and continues to draw focus. A number of high-profile businesspeople have fashioned themselves as shareholder activists after discovering that control and influence over a company, even a large public company, can be achieved without the need for a full takeover. While activism has its critics, who highlight that profit motives, rather than a desire for corporate governance change, underpin the majority of activist agendas, there is no doubt that shareholder activism works and is here to stay.[90]

---

89 Jennifer Hiller and Svea Herbst-Bayliss, 'Engine No 1 extends gains with a third seat on Exxon board', *Reuters* (3 June 2021).

90 See further OECD, *The Role of Institutional Investors in Promoting Good Corporate Governance* (2011) <www.oecd.org/corporate/ca/corporategovernanceprinciples/theroleofinstitutionalinvestorsinpromotinggoodcorporategovernance.htm>.

10 BUSINESS ETHICS AND CORPORATE GOVERNANCE

Identifying who was responsible for the wrongdoing does not fully explain why things went wrong. That is a difficult task, but some explanations are possible. There are two standout reasons that help explain why wrongdoing occurred and also the extent of the wrongdoing.

The first is the prioritisation of profit over all other considerations, including the wellbeing of Crown Melbourne's customers and staff. ...

It is also too simple to explain what happened by reference only to profit maximisation. There is a second, and more insidious, cause at play. It is that Crown Melbourne took a risk based approach to legal and moral obligations. That approach focused more on the chance of getting caught (and preparing defensively for that event) than on the need for compliance with the law and adherence to ethical standards and community expectations.

This approach is what Mr Oliver Wendell Holmes, the great American jurist, referred to as the 'bad man's' view of legal rules: the rules are the price discounted by sanctions – or to reduce it even further, by the probability of the enforcement of sanctions. That is, laws are not norms of conduct but tariffs on conduct.

Royal Commission into the Casino Operator and Licence
(Report, October 2021) vol 1, ch 18 [43]–[47]

10.1 Introduction

One only has to scan media reporting to find plentiful examples of corporations being criticised for unethical conduct. It would take little more time to find businesses or business leaders who have suffered significant reputational damage, enforcement actions or damages claims. Since the 1970s, a considerable academic and practical literature has developed that considers and explores the field of business ethics, drawing on theory, practice and empirical data. Subjects that consider business ethics have become standard within university business courses,[1] and legal ethics are a compulsory component of most law

---

1   Henkvan Luijk, 'Business ethics: cases, codes and institutions' in Wim Dubbink, Lucvan Liedekerke and Henkvan Luijk (eds), *European Business Ethics Casebook: The Morality of Corporate Decision Making* (Springer, 2011) 3.

degrees. There can be no doubt that the conduct of corporations attracts considerable public interest. For a corporation, the consequences of perceived unethical activity can be profound: they include significant penalties for breaches that amount to regulatory infringements.[2] It can also lead to calls for enhanced regulation and broader scrutiny of corporate activity.[3] In this context the management of a corporation's ethical climate and conduct is increasingly seen as critical to its success, and a matter with which the senior management and the board should be deeply concerned. No book on corporate governance would, therefore, be complete without canvassing this topic.

Despite this considerable focus, it is not easy to navigate the complexities of the way organisations can, do and should manage business ethics. To traverse this area successfully it is critical to understand how ethical problems arise. The strategies for their management can then be tailored to respond to these pressure points. It is also vital that those governing corporations be intimately connected to the ethics of their organisation, and engage actively in developing a good 'corporate culture'. Without scrutiny, thoughtful responses and commitment from those leading the organisation, the risk of poor outcomes is considerable. Steven Brenner points out that 'all organizations have ethics programs' even if, as he asserts, 'most do not know they do'.[4] In fact, whatever they are, 'processes of governance and regulation imply particular sets of ethical values and norms'.[5] This chapter considers how the external regulatory settings, and processes of governance within corporations, can affect ethical conduct.

Before going any further, a note of caution. The discipline of ethics and the applied area of business ethics are complex, contested and important. While this chapter, and the others in this volume, consider and explain the ethical dimensions of corporate governance, by necessity they can only introduce some key concepts and ways of thinking about business ethics. They cannot provide the fullness of a deep consideration of the philosophical roots of ethical theory,[6] nor a comprehensive picture of business ethics theory and practice. Our aim is to be introductory.

It is also pertinent to note that business ethics is related to concepts of corporate social responsibility ('CSR'), and corporate responsibility, as discussed in Chapters 1, 2 and 3. Rosamund Thomas explains that:

2   Michael Janda, 'Westpac's record $1.3 billion AUSTRAC money laundering fine explained', *ABC News*, (24 September 2020); David J Lynch, 'VW admits guilt and pays $4.3bn emissions scandal penalty', *Financial Times* (12 January 2017); European Commission, 'Antitrust: Commission fines Google €2.42 billion for abusing dominance as search engine by giving illegal advantage to own comparison shopping service' (Fact Sheet, 27 June 2017) <https://ec.europa.eu/commission/presscorner/api/files/document/print/es/memo_17_1785/MEMO_17_1785_EN.pdf>.

3   James Frost, 'Westpac shredded again at penalty hearing', *Australian Financial Review* (21 October 2020); Justin O'Brien, 'Normal science and paradigmatic shifts: Political and regulatory strategies to develop investor protection in the aftermath of crisis' (2012) 52(1) *Accounting and Finance* 217, 224.

4   Steven N Brenner, 'Ethics programs and their dimensions' (1992) 11(5-6) *Journal of Business Ethics* 391, 391.

5   Glenn Morgan, 'Governance and regulation: An institutionalist approach to ethics and organizations' in Martin Parker (ed), *Ethics and Organizations* (Sage, 1998) 197, 229.

6   For an accessible account of ethical theory see Noel Preston, *Understanding Ethics* (Federation Press, 4th ed, 2014).

> Corporate Social Responsibility (CSR) differs from Business Ethics insofar as it concentrates principally on the social, environmental, and human rights concerns of business companies, more than their moral leadership. However, in practice, CSR and Business Ethics are frequently entwined in the company's Mission Statement or Code of Ethics.[7]

As this quote shows there is a practical link between CSR and business ethics. CSR and corporate responsibility relate to the way the corporation exercises its power, in particular its effects on external constituencies. Business ethics is relevant to this but operates across all corporate activities, including CSR, and will have a significant role to play in the internal functioning and decision-making within the corporation. It is the platform that underlies all corporate activity.

With those matters in mind, this chapter opens with a brief discussion in Section 10.2 of the nature of business ethics, its significance for corporations and the ethical dimensions of a corporation's stakeholder relationships. Section 10.3 is focused on the causes of ethical problems: bad apples, bad cases and bad barrels. In order to examine these it presents the theory related to each before drawing on three case studies: the HIH failure, the LIBOR case and the destruction of Juukan Gorge. The extent to which we attempt to encourage ethical conduct is discussed in Section 10.4. In particular, that section examines corporate accountability, individual accountability and organisation-level approaches that seek to shape the ethical conduct of corporations. Section 10.5 is devoted to some concluding remarks.

10.2 The case for business ethics

In order to understand the significance and complexities of business ethics, this section explores the concept of business ethics and its relationship to the way corporations operate – mediating between the interests of, and obligations to, various stakeholder groups.

10.2.1 The significance of the modern corporation

It is difficult to overestimate the reach and significance of the modern corporation in our daily lives, and in the progress of our economies. The products and services provided by corporations touch us in myriad ways every moment of our lives. Corporations almost invariably employ us, we use corporate vehicles to preserve and enhance our personal wealth, we rely on corporations for housing, transport, healthcare, entertainment and nutrition. We are avid consumers of the goods and services created by corporations across the globe. The pervasive nature of the corporation, and its ability to influence our lives at the personal and societal level, makes it a powerful actor in enhancing or undermining social and individual welfare.[8] As such, we are all

---

7   Rosamund M Thomas, *Business Ethics and Corporate Social Responsibility* (Ethics International Press, 2015) 83.
8   Christine Parker, *Open Corporation: Effective Self-Regulation and Democracy* (Cambridge University Press, 2002) 2.

vulnerable to negative impacts when corporations act unethically, and therefore, it might be expected that we take an interest in the extent to which corporations 'do the right thing'.

While the corporation is predominantly a source of progress and prosperity, there are certainly numerous instances where corporations have been conducted in ways that harmed others. Famous examples include the Ford Pinto case, the Enron scandal, the Rana Plaza factory collapse and the Deepwater Horizon oil spill.

Each of these examples provides concrete evidence about why we want corporations to act ethically. The impact of the corporate activity was profound, rippling out from each corporation to affect many beyond. Following these events, individual and corporate decision-making was scrutinised and in some cases significant penalties were visited on the corporations and some individuals.[9] In each case the conduct flowed from a decision or, more likely, a number of decisions or non-decisions. In these cases, the person or persons concerned either failed to see the ethical issue or made the wrong call. In some cases the ethical problems were deep-seated within structures, policies and processes, making ethical decision-making more difficult, or making the ethical dimensions of particular issues harder to spot. In this chapter, in Section 10.3, three case studies of unethical conduct will be examined.

10.2.2 What are business ethics?

Defining business ethics has been likened to 'nailing jello to a wall'.[10] Nonetheless, it is possible to capture at least a working definition using the general concept of ethics. The study of ethics can be focused on a singular question: what does it mean to be 'right, fair, just or good'?[11] According to Christine Parker and Adrian Evans:

> Ethics is concerned with deciding what is the good or right thing to do – the right or wrong action; and with the moral evaluation of our own and others' character and actions – what does it mean to be a good person? In deciding what to do and how to be, ethics requires that we look for coherent reasons for our actions and character – reasons that explain why it is right or wrong ...[12]

Logically then, business ethics provides a focus on the right thing to do in the context of business endeavour.

Part of the definitional difficulty associated with defining business ethics can be attributed to the fact that it has 'macro' and 'micro' aspects. As Noel Preston explains:

> At the micro level we may be concerned to identify virtues which make a good business person, for example, diligence and service; this level also includes the ethics of intra-organisational relationships, matters of employee

---

9   See, eg, Mike Spector and Mike Colias, 'VW cops $3.7bn fine for emissions rigging', *The Australian* (13 March 2017).

10 Phillip V Lewis, 'Defining "business ethics": Like nailing jello to a wall' (1985) 4(5) *Journal of Business Ethics* 377, 382.

11 Noel Preston, *Understanding Ethics* (Federation Press, 4th ed, 2014) 16.

12 Vivien Holmes and Francesca Bartlett, *Parker and Evans's Inside Lawyers' Ethics* (Cambridge University Press, 4th ed, 2023) 13.

well-being for instance, or respectful treatment of customers. The macro level refers to the moral duties of a company with respect to the rest of society. It implies leadership in business characterised by the virtue of civic responsibility.[13]

It is possible, however, to craft a definition that is capable of accommodating both of these perspectives, although it will necessarily be somewhat abstract. Phillip Lewis, after reviewing contemporary definitions in textbooks and articles, settled on the following: '"business ethics" is moral rules, standards, codes, or principles which provide guidelines for right and truthful behavior in specific situations'.[14] Such a definition can encompass both the micro and the macro aspects.

Drawing on this discussion, and turning to corporate governance, the question then becomes what is the right, good, fair and just approach for those leading corporations to take? At the macro level, as we can see from the discussion above, there is no doubt that the value choices made by those who lead corporations can have significant impact. At the micro level the rules, standards, codes, norms or principles that guide activity within a particular corporation can also affect those within and those outside the corporation in profound ways. Ultimately corporate boards are responsible for both of these aspects of the corporation's ethics. As Philip Styles and Bernard Taylor point out:

> Boards ... set the ethical tone with regard to their monitoring and accountability roles. What is expected of management, both by way of performance and behaviour, is ultimately the responsibility of directors. The board is thus recognized as crucial in the process of developing an ethical framework, implicit or explicit, for the formulation of strategy and policy, monitoring management and ensuring accountability.[15]

Turning first to the macro level, in the 1960s and 1970s the concerns about corporate activity prompted a public debate about how we should think about the ethics of corporate enterprise in the wider sense. This debate was not new. Professors Berle and Dodd canvassed similar issues several decades earlier.[16] However, the debate provides a useful starting point to understanding the ethics of corporations. The debate was championed on one side by Milton Friedman, the US economist, whose essay 'A Friedman doctrine – The Social Responsibility of Business Is to Increase Its Profits'[17] is still cited as representing a conservative view of the ethics of corporations.[18]

---

13   Noel Preston, *Understanding Ethics* (Federation Press, 2014) 171.

14   Lewis, 'Defining "business ethics"' (1985) 4(5) *Journal of Business Ethics* 377, 382.

15   Philip Styles and Bernard Taylor, *Boards at Work* (Oxford University Press, 2002) 39 (citations omitted).

16   Adolf A Berle Jr, 'Corporate powers as powers in trust' (1931) 44(7) *Harvard Law Review* 1049; E Merrick Dodd, 'For whom are the corporate managers trustees?' (1932) 45(7) *Harvard Law Review* 1145. See also John CC Macintosh, 'The issues, effects and consequences of the Berle–Dodd debate, 1931–1932' (1999) 24(2) *Accounting, Organizations and Society* 139.

17   Milton Friedman, 'A Friedman doctrine – The social responsibility of business is to increase its profits', *The New York Times* (13 September 1970).

18   James Arnt Aune, 'How to read Milton Friedman: Corporate social responsibility and today's capitalisms' in S May, G Cheney and J Roper (eds), *The Debate over Corporate Social Responsibility*

In that essay Friedman sought to clarify, and debunk, those who 'declaim that business is not concerned "merely" with profit but also with promoting desirable "social" ends'.[19] His argument is that the corporation itself could not have responsibilities, as it is purely an artificial construct, and therefore the more accurate articulation of the position is that individuals, such as corporate executives, have social responsibilities in their professional roles. He then asserted that the responsibility of these individuals must be to achieve the aims of the owners of the business, and that this is, most commonly, to generate profits. He argued that any allegiance by corporate executives to 'social goals', where they derogate from their primary profit-making function, would not only undermine the executives' devotion to the interests of the shareholders, but also mean that an executive 'self-selected or appointed directly or indirectly by stockholders ... is to be simultaneously legislator, executive and jurist'.[20] For Friedman, there are two legitimate checks on conduct. First, corporate executives should conform to the 'basic rules of society, both those embodied in the law and those embodied in ethical custom'. The 'invisible hand' of the market provides the second limit. In his view any external interventions or expectations beyond these are counterproductive.[21]

As identified earlier in Chapters 1–3, the contrary argument sees corporations as having a social role that goes beyond their economic impact.[22] This argument is formulated in various ways. Some suggest that as corporations are given significant benefits, such as separate perpetual legal existence and limited liability, they should then be expected to 'pay' for those advantages by prioritising social good, or at least considering the social impact of their activities.[23] Another strand of the argument is focused on ensuring that corporations are 'managed so that individuals are treated as "ends" instead of as "means"'.[24] A further point made is that market mechanisms cannot necessarily appropriately compensate for the costs visited on others by corporate activity,[25] and that both government intervention and internal ethical governance arrangements are required to reduce the costs imposed by corporations on external constituencies.

Nor is this debate consigned to history. When the James Hardie group of companies moved its parent company offshore, leaving behind a trust intended to address current

(Oxford University Press, 2007) 207, 207–8; Thomas Mulligan, 'A critique of Milton Friedman's essay "The Social Responsibility of Business Is to Increase Its Profits"' (1986) 5(4) *Journal of Business Ethics* 265, 265.

19 Friedman, 'A Friedman doctrine', *The New York Times* (13 September 1970).
20 Ibid.
21 Ibid; Helen Anderson, 'The theory of the corporation and its tortious liability to creditors' (2004) 16(1) *Australian Journal of Corporate Law* 1, 3; Kent Greenfield, *The Failure of Corporate Law* (University of Chicago Press, 2008) 31 (summing up the argument that any legal intervention in corporate governance should be minimal due to its private law nature).
22 David Millon, 'Communitarians, contractarians, and the crisis in corporate law' (1993) 50(4) *Washington and Lee Law Review* 1373, 1379.
23 Peter Nobel, 'Social responsibility of corporations' (1999) 84(5) *Cornell Law Review* 1255, 1257.
24 Timothy L Fort, 'The corporation as mediating institution: An efficacious synthesis of stakeholder theory and corporate constituency statutes' (1997) 73(1) *Notre Dame Law Review* 173, 196.
25 Millon, 'Communitarians, contractarians, and the crisis in corporate law' (1993) 50(4) *Washington and Lee Law Review* 1373, 1383.

and future liabilities arising from the manufacture and sales of asbestos by a number of its subsidiaries which was discovered to be significantly underfunded, questions were asked about the directors' responsibility for these corporate liabilities, and they were subject to significant litigation in the years which followed.[26] Donations by Australian corporations in the wake of the Boxing Day tsunami in 2004 drew similar critique,[27] as did the open letter signed by CEOs and leaders of major Australian corporations advocating for the legalisation of same sex marriage in the lead-up to the Australian Marriage Equality postal survey held in Australia in 2017.[28]

The distinction that appears to be drawn by critics is between: (a) conduct that directly advances the interests of stakeholders, which would be considered controversial; and (b) conduct that advances the interests of shareholders and that may also incidentally benefit other stakeholders – which is clearly acceptable. Le Mire suggests '[t]his could include conduct that enhances the corporate brand, increases employee, shareholder and consumer motivation and loyalty and avoids negative publicity, or regulatory sanctions. These rationales, on their face, provide significant latitude and support for those governing corporations to develop and support ethical conduct'.[29] As Peter Henley explains, '[t]he current law is capable of supporting a broad range of philanthropic and "socially responsible" activities and "sustainable" business practices'.[30] In 2006, a Commonwealth Parliamentary Joint Committee on Corporations and Financial Services reached a similar conclusion. It took the view that 'the Corporations Act permits directors to have regard for the interests of stakeholders other than shareholders'.[31]

We have dealt with various corporate law theories and the importance of an all-inclusive approach in detail in Chapters 1 and 2, but the importance of stakeholders needs to be borne in mind, as emphasised by the *G20/OECD Principles of Corporate Governance*:

> Corporations should recognise that the contributions of stakeholders constitute a valuable resource for building competitive and profitable companies. It is, therefore, in the long-term interest of corporations to foster wealth-creating co-operation among stakeholders.[32]

---

26 See Chapter 1 and the case study in Chapter 8.
27 Peter Henley, 'Were corporate tsunami donations made legally? Directors and corporate social responsibilities' (2005) 30(4) *Alternative Law Journal* 154, 158.
28 Rachel Baxendale and Dennis Shanahan, 'Sparks fly as chiefs tell Turnbull "marriage equality good for business"', *The Australian* (16 March 2017).
29 Suzanne Le Mire, 'CEOs and same sex marriage: Echoes of a longstanding debate' (5 May 2017) <https://blogs.adelaide.edu.au/law/2017/04/05/ceos-and-same-sex-marriage-echoes-of-a-longstanding-debate/>.
30 Henley, 'Were corporate tsunami donations made legally?' (2005) 30(4) *Alternative Law Journal* 154.
31 Parliamentary Joint Committee on Corporations and Financial Services, *Corporate Responsibility: Managing Risk and Creating Value* (2006) xiv.
32 Organisation for Economic Cooperation and Development ('OECD'), *G20/OECD Principles of Corporate Governance* (2015) 34 <https://www.oecd.org/publications/g20-oecd-principles-of-corporate-governance-2015-9789264236882-en.htm>. In September 2023, the 2015 Principles were replaced by the 2023 *G20/OECD Principles of Corporate Governance* <https://doi.org/10.1787/

More difficult questions arise where an ethical dilemma seems to lead to a decision that does not seem to advance, or even undermines, shareholder interests, perhaps in order to prioritise another stakeholder group. It is then going be up to corporate management to disclose and justify their decision or actions in a way that is satisfactory to the shareholders, assuming the shareholder primacy model still underpins our corporate law model,[33] and the board. The board would also have a role in monitoring management actions of this kind and ensuring that they are in the best interests of the company. And shareholders have mechanisms (which may or may not be effective) that enable them to discipline the directors if they fail.

While the debate outlined above seems to assume that ethical decision-making is a clean deliberative process, leading to ethical failure or success, in reality ethical failures are complex and not always deliberate. They can arise when the relevant actors fail to see and understand the ethical dimensions of particular decisions, policy settings or practices. Such failures can also flow when there is recognition of an ethical aspect to a particular part of business but a failure to act, or an action that is problematic. Failures can be predicated by decisions taken decades before, or the previous day. The dilemmas can be derived from external forces or entirely generated within the corporation. They can flow from one event or from a series of events over days, months, even years. In order to understand this complexity, the next step is to understand better how ethical problems emerge.

10.3 The causes of ethical problems

In their meta-analysis, Jennifer Kish-Gephart, David Harrison and Linda Klebe Treviño argue that the causes of unethical conduct in workplaces can be grouped into three categories.[34] First are 'bad apples' – individuals who engage in unethical behaviour. 'Bad cases' are the second group. These occur where the activity is such that it is difficult to identify the ethical dimensions, or the effect of the decision is seen as remote, unlikely or minor. Finally, 'bad barrels' are those organisational settings that encourage or allow unethical conduct. While these three categories provide a useful way to think about problematic conduct, of course, as the three case studies presented in this chapter indicate, there is potential for the categories to overlap and reinforce each other in complex ways. There may well be elements of each category present in any one event. Nonetheless, they provide a useful starting point for thinking about ethical risks and opportunities within the corporate governance sphere. Each category is considered more fully below.

---

ed750b30-en>. The *G20/OECD Principles of Corporate Governance* are set out in the Appendix to the OECD *Recommendation on Principles of Corporate Governance* (OECD/LEGAL/0413) adopted by the OECD Council on 8 July 2015 and revised on 8 June 2023. The Principles were endorsed by the G20 after the substantial writing of this chapter, which makes a number of references to the 2015 Principles. See discussions in Sections 12.2 and 12.3.

33 See Jean J du Plessis, 'Shareholder primacy and other stakeholder interests' (2016) 34(3) *Company and Securities Law Review* 238, 241.

34 Jennifer J Kish-Gephart, David A Harrison and Linda Klebe Treviño, 'Bad apples, bad cases, and bad barrels: Meta-analytic evidence about sources of unethical decisions at work' (2010) 95 *Journal of Applied Psychology* 1, 2.

10.3.1 Bad apples

It is common to see 'bad apples' as key contributors to ethical problems. This descriptor seeks to explain ethical problems by reference to particular individuals or individual characteristics. It is a familiar approach. The Australian Securities Exchange's ('ASX') *Corporate Governance Principles and Recommendations* assert that '[i]nvestors and the broader community expect a listed entity to act lawfully, ethically and responsibly',[35] and, particularly, that the board has responsibility for approving a statement of values, and that senior executives continually reference and reinforce those values (setting the 'tone from the top). Following a corporate scandal or collapse the significance of various individuals often becomes a focus of discussion. For example, the role and actions of Ray Williams and Rodney Adler in the collapse of the HIH insurance group were heavily criticised in the press and in the Royal Commission, and ultimately led to significant jail terms for the two men along with one other. In the wake of the Enron collapse, Fastow (the CFO), Skilling (the CEO), and Lay (the chairman), were prosecuted, and Fastow and Skilling were jailed.[36] In the LIBOR case (presented below), some of the sentencing remarks seem to fit with the 'bad apple' status attributed to Jay Merchant. The judge found that '[t]he evidence of the way in which manipulation of the rate began in earnest after you arrived in New York was compelling' and '[i]t was under your leadership on the desk that the requests to the LIBOR submitters really took off'.[37]

The basis of the 'bad apple' explanation lies in the understanding that each corporation acts through the agency of the individuals within it. It recognises that 'in order to conduct business or do anything at all, corporations must always have accomplices, since without people to run them, corporations are mere legal constructs – ideas, not things'.[38] When ethical problems emerge, it is often possible to trace those back to people within the organisation whose actions – or failures to act – are seen as having contributed to the problem. It is also consistent with the view that ethical or unethical conduct is a matter of personal, rather than collective, responsibility. In contrast, attributing ethical problems to bad cases and bad barrels shifts the focus to the corporation and its activities as a factor in the genesis and management of ethical issues. Having said that, there is clearly a role for those involved in the governance of a corporation in identifying and managing individuals who may be predisposed to ethically problematic conduct. And bad apples, particularly where they are in positions of influence and power, can have a significant impact on the way organisations see and manage ethical activity, hence potentially contributing to bad cases and barrels.

35   ASX, *Corporate Governance Principles and Recommendations* (4th ed, 2019) 16 <https://www.asx.com .au/documents/asx-compliance/cgc-principles-and-recommendations-fourth-edn.pdf>.

36   Lay died after his conviction and prior to serving a sentence: Kristen Hays and Anna Driver, 'Former Enron CEO Skilling's sentence cut to 14 years', *Reuters* (21 June 2013) <www.reuters.com/article/us-enron-skilling-idUSBRE95K12520130621>.

37   *R v Peter Johnson, Jonathan Mathew, Jay Vijay Merchant and Alex Pabon*, Sentencing remarks of HJ Anthony Leonard QC, Southwark Crown Court (8 July 2016).

38   Sean F Griffith, 'Afterword and comment: Towards an ethical duty to market investors' (2003) 35 *Connecticut Law Review* 1223, 1252.

A case study of the HIH collapse

We have discussed the HIH case from a legal point of view and as far as the liability of directors were concerned (see Section 8.3.2). The case is, however, also significant as far as ethical lessons are concerned. HIH had its origins in an insurance agency started by Ray Williams and Michael Payne in 1968: MW Payne Liability Agencies Pty Ltd.[39] Its descendant, CE Heath Underwriting Agencies, was listed on the ASX in 1992.[40] Once listed, the company engaged in a rapid expansion, with a series of mergers and acquisitions both within Australia and overseas.[41] By 2001, the year of its collapse, the corporation, then known as HIH, was a major player in the Australian insurance market. It held thousands of 'professional liability, public indemnity, home warranty and travel insurance policies'.[42]

The HIH collapse has the dubious honour of being Australia's largest corporate failure.[43] Ultimately, the corporation was revealed to have debts of at least $5.3 billion.[44] The subsequent Royal Commission identified the cause of the HIH failure as insufficient attention having been paid to the financial health of the corporation. In particular, there were inadequate systems and processes in place for the proper review of business practices and outcomes.[45] As a result, ongoing poor risk management led to insufficient premiums being charged and inadequate provision being made for claims. Fundamental problems with the bread-and-butter business of HIH were compounded by decisions to buy into several failing businesses, without due diligence. These transactions were entered into without a full appreciation of their complexities, and the ultimate effect that they might have on the viability of HIH. For example, the Allianz joint venture, entered into in September 2000, had the effect of requiring HIH to hand over its most profitable lines of business to Allianz. The agreement required payment into a trust of a lump sum of $500 million, to be followed by contributing the insurance premiums for these business lines to the trust until an actuarial analysis justified their quarterly distribution. By this time, HIH was so chronically short of funds that the purchase price from Allianz of $200 million had to be paid into the trust to satisfy the lump sum obligation. Then the delay associated with the actuarial report and distribution caused the cash flow crisis that hastened the end. The Royal Commission found that the 'trust provisions and their potential adverse effect on cash flow were either completely overlooked or not properly appreciated'.[46] In addition, a number of overseas ventures were spectacularly unsuccessful, draining the group of much-needed funds.

---

39 Report of the HIH Royal Commission ('Owen Report'), *The Failure of HIH Insurance – Volume I: A Corporate Collapse and Its Lessons* (Commonwealth of Australia, 2003) 3.1.
40 Ibid 54.
41 Farid Varess, '"The buck will stop at the board"? An examination of directors' (and other) duties in light of the HIH collapse' (2002) 16(1) *Commercial Law Quarterly* 12, 13.
42 Owen Report, *The Failure of HIH Insurance* (2003) vol 1, xiv.
43 Jean J du Plessis, 'Reverberations after the HIH and other recent Australian corporate collapses: The role of ASIC' (2003) 15(3) *Australian Journal of Corporate Law* 1, 1; Phillip Lipton, 'The demise of HIH: Corporate governance lessons' (2003) 55(5) *Keeping Good Companies* 273.
44 Tina Mak, Hemant Deo and Kathie Cooper, 'Australia's major corporate collapse: Health International Holdings (HIH) Insurance "May the force be with you"' (2005) 2 *Journal of American Academy of Business* 104.
45 Owen Report, *The Failure of HIH Insurance* (2003) vol 1, xvii.
46 Ibid xxvi.

A number of commentators have noted that HIH's failure can be traced to the corporation's rapid transition from a small private company to Australia's second-largest insurer.[47] Despite the tumult of the transition from private to public company, and the many suitors and substantial shareholders who at one stage or another had a finger in the HIH pie, one man, its CEO, Ray Williams, dominated HIH. This dominance had two aspects that were particularly problematic. First, he treated HIH's assets as his own.[48] Second, he surrounded himself with people he trusted, but who were deferential to his views.[49] This meant that HIH had a senior management team with insufficient experience and expertise:

> No one rivalled him in terms of authority or influence. Even as his business judgment faltered in the second half of the 1990s he remained unchallenged. No one else in senior management was equipped to grasp what was happening and to bring about a change of direction for the group.[50]

This deference meant that the proposals of Williams and the affairs of HIH were not subject to the 'countervailing effect of close review, debate and questioning'.[51] Even the board was not immune to Williams' preference for loyalty over rigour, with long-time associates being shoehorned into non-executive board roles. The board and its committees operated as rubber stamps of management decisions.

It was the practice of the HIH audit committee to meet before or after the main board meeting. The proximity to the board meeting, as well as a standing invitation to all members of the board to attend the audit committee meetings, meant that the committee operated as 'little more than an extension of the board'.[52] This had a number of consequences in terms of its effectiveness. It was potentially constrained in the time available to it to examine the necessarily complex issues arising from HIH's position. This issue was mentioned by a director, Head, in a detailed letter of complaint[53] to the company chairman, Geoffrey Cohen. Head's view was that the board was not being given sufficient information to enable it to make an informed contribution to the governance of the company. In the same month Justin Gardener, another HIH director,[54] had

47   Kamel Mellahi, 'The dynamics of boards of directors in failing organizations' (2005) 38(3) *Long Range Planning* 261; Owen Report, *The Failure of HIH Insurance* (2003) vol 1, xxvi–ii; note also that this criticism was made by Blake Dawson Waldron in a due diligence report in 1995, some six years before the collapse.
48   Williams' philanthropy was well known. HIH shareholders unknowingly bankrolled much of this: see Owen Report, *The Failure of HIH Insurance* (2003) vol 3, 310; Andrew Main, *Other People's Money: The Complete Story of the Extraordinary Collapse of HIH* (Harper Collins, 2005) 227. When questioned at the Royal Commission on the payment by HIH of more than $38 000 for airfares for Mrs Williams in the year prior to the collapse, Williams was unrepentant.
49   The executive directors were all close associates of Williams. Fodera had been headhunted from Arthur Andersen to take up a position as chief financial officer. Sturesteps and Cassidy had been working alongside Williams since 1969 and 1972 respectively. Wein had been retained after the Swiss insurer Winterthur sold its majority shareholding in HIH.
50   Owen Report, *The Failure of HIH Insurance* (2003) vol 1, xxvii.
51   Ibid xxvii.
52   Ibid vol 3, 279.
53   The text of the Head's letter is reproduced in ibid vol 3, 267–8. It cites a number of concerns about management not using the board effectively.
54   Despite the claims of HIH, analysis reveals that in fact Gardener's independence was compromised by his past association with the corporate auditor: Owen Report, *The Failure of HIH Insurance* (2003) vol 3, 261.

also approached the CEO, Ray Williams, with a list of matters for discussion.[55] The list revealed that Gardener was troubled by the lack of involvement of the board in the strategic direction of the company. Despite an apparent dismissal of these concerns,[56] Williams called a meeting of non-executive directors on 1 June 1999, when the other concerned director was away. Gardener explained his disquiet and Williams asked the directors present whether they were satisfied with HIH's governance arrangements:

> Ray asked, um, asked the um, er ... the board members whether they felt the board was operating satisfactorily – in response to my comment – and they all said, yes, they thought it was. I was somewhat nonplussed. I-I-I thought probably, er, Ray doesn't like, er, criticism. Er, and, um, he wanted to just make sure that, um, there was only one person that was being, being critical of him.[57]

Williams later asserted that Gardener had indicated that he was satisfied with the information provided in advance of the next board meeting.[58] No further action was taken in response to these concerns.[59]

One further incident provides an example of the way Williams discouraged free dialogue. Following an audit committee meeting where the auditors had signalled that HIH was facing serious difficulties, Alan Davies, then the HIH auditor, asked Head and Gardener to lunch. At the lunch a number of concerns that the auditors had were discussed. Williams appeared upset when he discovered that the meeting had occurred without his sanction or presence.[60] The end result for Davies was that Williams asked Arthur Andersen to remove him from the audit. Arthur Andersen duly complied.[61] It seems that the CEO felt it was inappropriate for the audit committee members to fulfil what would normally be seen as the standard role of an audit committee: that is, to meet with the auditor without management being present. This series of events had the potential to chill the free communication between the auditors and the non-executive directors.

10.3.1.1 Managing bad apples

The HIH case indicates the way an individual can influence the culture of a corporation. Kamel Mellahi argues that the board was passive and accepting of management dominance in the period before 1998. After 1998 'the CEO and management took deliberate steps to prevent the board from observing the warning signals'.[62] The formal complaints

---

55   Ibid 267: 'Gardener prepared an analysis of matters for discussion with Williams. The analysis covered the desired mindset of the board; matters to be reviewed with management including HIH's vision, purpose and strategy; oversight of management performance; and accountability' (citations omitted).
56   Gardener later described the meeting: 'Ray was very polite and said, "Well, thank you. But you don't have to worry about these things. You know, that's really the concern of management." And he, you know, metaphorically patted me on the head and sort of sent me on my way': 'Odds on to fail' (Australian Broadcasting Corporation, *Four Corners*, 2 July 2001).
57   Ibid.
58   Owen Report, *The Failure of HIH Insurance* (2003) vol 3, 269.
59   Ibid.
60   Main, *Other People's Money* (2005) 231; Owen Report, *The Failure of HIH Insurance* (2003) vol 3, 91.
61   Main, *Other People's Money* (2005) 231–3.
62   Mellahi, 'The dynamics of boards of directors in failing organizations' (2005) 38(3) *Long Range Planning* 261, 271.

of Head and Gardener provided the CEO with an opportunity to 'employ a number of political techniques to overcome board opposition, such as distortion, reduction of communication with the board, and threats of punishment'.[63] By these means it was made clear to all the board members that their role was to follow management's lead.

The analysis of Kish-Gephart, Harrison and Treviño identifies four factors that are correlated with the unethical conduct of individuals.[64] First, there are those who are obedient to the ethical directives of others or who are motivated only to avoid punishment. Second, there are those who are motivated by self-interest. The third group do not appreciate the link between their actions and outcomes. Finally, there are those who are moral relativists: that is, they are not convinced that there are moral absolutes but rather believe that ethical principles change according to the circumstances. In each case these traits are likely to contribute to ethical problems. From a corporate governance perspective, recruitment policy could be a useful way to reduce the likelihood that bad apples, and hence ethical problems, become part of the corporation. The ability of bad apples to influence others can be particularly problematic, and profoundly so where the bad apple is in a position of influence. The data suggest that there is a case for acting decisively where a bad apple emerges. This is important from the perspective of removing the bad apple and because the appearance of tolerating a bad apple can create a bad barrel.

10.3.2 Bad cases

Bad cases are those where the nature of the issue is such that it inhibits ethical action. Writing in 1991, Thomas Jones posited that the characteristics of the issue can affect its moral intensity and hence influence whether or not individuals respond ethically.[65] He identified six elements that could make ethical decisions less likely. First, he argued that the *magnitude of the consequences* is significant.[66] In contemplating an action or inaction, individuals will consider the extent to which their act affects others. The greater the number of persons negatively affected, and the more acute the harm done to those persons, the more likely it is that the individual will act ethically. The second factor is *social consensus*.[67] Where there is broad agreement that a particular action is wrong it is harder to rationalise taking that course. This would suggest that unethical activity that is also illegal is more likely to be avoided. Third, Jones considers the *probability of the effect* important.[68] So an act that is more likely than not to cause harm will be given greater ethical weight than one where the probability of the harm occurring is small. The *temporal immediacy* of the effect is the fourth factor identified by James as influencing the ethical choices of individuals.[69] Where an act would take years to cause harm it is less

---

63   Ibid 275.
64   Kish-Gephart, Harrison and Treviño, 'Bad apples, bad cases, and bad barrels' (2010) 95 *Journal of Applied Psychology* 1, 18.
65   Thomas M Jones, 'Ethical decision making by individuals in organizations: An issue-contingent model' (1991) 16(2) *Academy of Management* 366.
66   Ibid 374–5.
67   Ibid 375.
68   Ibid 375–6.
69   Ibid 376.

likely to be taken seriously. This might be a factor with harm from asbestos exposure, which can take up to 40 years to emerge, or tobacco consumption, which again tends not to emerge for many years. Fifth, *proximity* highlights the 'feeling of nearness (social, cultural, psychological, or physical) that the moral agent has for victims (beneficiaries) of the evil (beneficial) act in question' as a factor that increases moral intensity.[70] The final factor is *concentration of effect*.[71] An act that causes slight harm to many people will have less importance in the mind of an actor than one that causes profound harm to fewer people.

A case study of the LIBOR scandal

In the LIBOR scandal, the incentives to act unethically were considerable. LIBOR is the trimmed averaged interest rate used as the basis for a benchmark interest rate that is referenced in financial transactions worth more than $300 trillion.[72] The benchmark is determined by reference to a self-report from 18 banks that make up a panel.[73] Each panel member responds to the question: 'At what rate could you borrow funds, were you to do so by asking for and then accepting inter-bank offers in a reasonable market size just prior to 11am?'[74] The response is an estimate, with no requirements for any evidence or actual transaction to support it.[75] The responses are then trimmed, with the top 25 per cent and bottom 25 per cent being discarded and the remaining responses averaged.[76] At the time of the manipulations the bank submissions were made publicly available contemporaneously.[77]

This system can be seen as a bad case. First, the banks were both setting the benchmark and trading using the benchmark. This created an incentive to manipulate the rate to benefit the banks' trading arms. In relation to the manipulation by Barclays Bank, Professor Bainbridge notes:

> Because of the large amounts of financial contracts referencing LIBOR and the leverage inherent in the use of options and other derivatives, even very small changes in the LIBOR rate could earn a bank's trading desk significant profits. Evidence was emerging that Barclays derivatives traders pushed the bank employees who reported its LIBOR quote to provide high or low estimates depending on which would produce higher profits.[78]

70 Ibid 376–7.
71 Ibid 377–8.
72 UK Treasury, *Wheatley Review of LIBOR* (Final Report, 2012) 7.
73 The current panel composition and policy on the panel composition are available at <www.theice .com/iba/libor>. At the time of the impugned conduct the panel was made up of 16 banks.
74 ICE/ ICE Benchmark Administration, 'Libor: Frequently asked questions', *ICE* <www.theice.com/ publicdocs/IBA_LIBOR_FAQ.pdf>.
75 Stephen M Bainbridge, 'Reforming LIBOR: Wheatley versus the alternatives' (2013) 9(3) *New York University Journal of Law and Business* 789, 796.
76 ICE/ ICE Benchmark Administration, 'LIBOR: Frequently asked questions', *ICE* <www.theice.com/ publicdocs/IBA_LIBOR_FAQ.pdf>.
77 Bainbridge, 'Reforming LIBOR' (2013) 9(3) *New York University Journal of Law and Business* 789, 797.
78 Ibid 800–1 (citations omitted).

In the sentencing remarks for four Barclays' employees who took part in the activity, the judge noted that while there was no substantial bonus resting on the outcome of the manipulation, it was motivated by the fact that 'retaining your job or being promoted to the next level at the bank did depend on making a profit on your book, something which was under daily scrutiny at the bank'.[79]

The second incentive arose in the wake of the 2008 Global Financial Crisis when it became critically important to some banks not to reveal their precarious financial position, which was reflected in their inability to secure funds at low rates. This created an incentive to register a higher rate than that which was genuinely available to the bank. It has been suggested that sub-mitters were directed to present an inflated response by senior managers and also that the Bank of England gave an 'implicit nod' to this approach.[80] This indicates that there was little evident social consensus that the conduct was unethical.

This example provides almost a perfect storm of incentives, pressures and practices that encouraged unethical conduct: the apparent low risk of detection, the ease of implementation, the 'everyone's doing it' factor as banks joined forces to enable the manipulation, the fact that the harm caused was distant and not immediately obvious to the perpetrators, the sense of sanction from both those higher in the organisation and those outside it and the strong incentives to act dishonestly. As such it represents a 'bad case'.

10.3.2.1 Managing bad cases

From a corporate governance perspective the LIBOR case suggests that the board should be alert to the potential for certain activities to lead to unethical conduct. One way to address this is by strengthening the narrative associated with the potential harm. Kish-Gephart, Harrison and Treviño argue that 'unethical behavior may be reduced if employees learn to associate potential unethical behavior with severe, well-defined harm (magnitude of consequences) to a familiar or recognizable victim similar to the actor (proximity)'.[81] In addition, the way incentives work could have a downward or upward spiral effect by encouraging either ethical or unethical conduct where there is a bad case. Policy settings, such as incentives and codes of conduct, as well as actions of the leadership team and narratives that encourage ethical conduct, are all likely to play a significant role in shaping the consensus around acceptable and unacceptable conduct.

10.3.3 Bad barrels

The theory of the bad barrel is based on the idea that an organisation can significantly affect the ethical conduct of the individuals within it, in either positive or negative ways. A number of aspects of the organisation have been implicated in this process: the presence of organisational chaos, the lack of appropriate 'tone' at the top, the lack of a code of

79   *R v Peter Johnson, Jonathan Mathew, Jay Vijay Merchant and Alex Pabon,* Sentencing remarks of HHJ Anthony Leonard QC, Southwark Crown Court (8 July 2016).
80   Bainbridge, 'Reforming LIBOR' (2013) 9(3) *New York University Journal of Law and Business* 789, 801 (citations omitted).
81   Kish-Gephart, Harrison and Treviño, 'Bad apples, bad cases, and bad barrels' (2010) 95 *Journal of Applied Psychology* 1, 20.

conduct, or more compellingly, the lack of a code of conduct that matters, the presence of an ethic of self-interest, a gulf between policy and practice, a 'siloed' approach, a lack of accountability, and incentives to act unethically. More subtly, Fiona Haines argues that:

> Organizations, or more specifically organizational culture, may influence indi-
> vidual action in an unobtrusive and indirect manner by manipulating premises
> and providing normative frameworks, rather than [by] any authoritarian con-
> trol from above.[82]

It is possible that the way processes are organised could make it more difficult to identify and respond to ethical problems or that a focus on one corporate aim could drown out others. In the latter case, for example, a focus on efficiency might downgrade customer service below appropriate levels. As noted by Marianne Jennings and Lawrence Trautman, '[p]sychologically, humans respond to the pressures and pain in the present, not the future and non-quantifiable costs that accompany poor risk decisions'.[83]

A case study of the destruction of Juukan Gorge

The PKKP People are deeply hurt and traumatised by the desecration of a site which is profoundly significant to us and future generations. The Juukan Gorge disaster is a tragedy not only for the PKKP People. It is also a tragedy for the heritage of all Australians and indeed humanity as a whole.

> Puutu Kunti Kurrama People and Pinikura People, Submission to the Joint Standing
> Committee on Northern Australia, *Inquiry Into the Destruction of 46 000-year-old
> Caves at the Juukan Gorge in the Pilbara Region of Western Australia*[84]

On 24 May 2020, Rio Tinto detonated explosives to extend its Brockman 4 iron ore mine – action which 'destroyed two rock shelters of great cultural, ethnographic and archaeological significance, along with evidence of continuous occupation and cultural knowledge stretching back 46 000 years'.[85] The Juukan 1 and 2 rock shelters contained thousands of artefacts recording human occupation, long known to the Puutu Kunti Kurrama People and Pinikura People ('PKKP peoples')[86] but also recorded by publications dating to 2009[87] and archaeological excavations in 2014. The rock shelters held 'a "museum of information", harbouring thousands of

82 Fiona Haines, *Corporate Regulation: Beyond Punish or Persuade* (Clarendon Press, 1997) 93.
83 Marianne Jennings and Lawrence J Trautman, 'Ethical culture and legal liability: The GM switch crisis and lessons in governance' (2016) 22(2) *Boston University Journal of Science and Technology Law* 187, 207.
84 PKKP Aboriginal Corporation, Submission No 129 to the Joint Standing Committee on Northern Australia, *Inquiry Into the Destruction of 46 000-year-old Caves at the Juukan Gorge in the Pilbara Region of Western Australia*, 1 <https://www.aph.gov.au/Parliamentary_Business/Committees/Joint/Former_Committees/Northern_Australia_46P/CavesatJuukanGorge/Submissions>.
85 Joint Standing Committee on Northern Australia, *A Way Forward: Final report into the destruction of Indigenous heritage sites at Juukan Gorge* (18 October 2021) 1.
86 This discussion adopts the acronym PKKP, which is used by the Puutu Kunti Kurrama People and Pinikura People. In their words, 'the PKKP are two distinct Aboriginal socio-territorial groups': Joint Standing Committee on Northern Australia, *A Way Forward* (18 October 2021) 3.
87 Michael Slack, Melanie Fillios, Richard Fullagar, 'Aboriginal settlement during the LGM at Brockman, Pilbara Region, Western Australia' (2009) 44(1) *Archaeology in Oceania* 32.

artefacts, including grinding stones, rock seats, a blade quarry and flaked stone materials, and human hair from a hair belt that has been genetically identified to match PKK descendants'.[88] The gorge itself is identified as a 'significant spiritual place, ... of continuing spirituality and therefore sacredness', and the region was of both 'tangible and intangible cultural importance'.[89]

In the aftermath, the Joint Standing Committee on Northern Australia led an inquiry into the destruction of Juukan Gorge, which engaged with 177 submissions and 23 public hearings. The factual discussion below draws from the evidence provided to that Committee, and its final report, titled *A Way Forward*.[90]

Rio Tinto and the PKKP peoples had engaged in consultation over approximately 18 years, and there had been eight years of archaeological work directly involving Juukan Gorge. Indeed, Rio Tinto facilitated a salvage dig on the site in 2014, led by archaeologist Dr Michael Slack, which uncovered that the archaeological records in the site did not disappear during the last ice age, which was particularly unique.[91] This dig followed reporting from Dr Heather Builth, the PKKP peoples' heritage manager, in July and September 2013, in relation to which the Rio Tinto Board Review acknowledged that there was 'insufficient flexibility in our operating procedures in terms of responding to material new information about the cultural heritage significance of the Juukan Gorge area reflected in the reports'.[92]

Although Rio Tinto had appropriate licences and approvals in relation to its activities in the area, having received ministerial consent to mine the site in 2013, there was disagreement as to whether or not Juukan Gorge was included within a particular set of consents sought as a precaution against future collateral damage from adjacent mining activity.[93] Rio Tinto acknowledged that the 'Juukan 1 and Juukan 2 rock shelters were not within the indicative or conceptual pit outline at that point in time but were very close to the edge of the pit outline, such that they could not be expected to have avoided impacts to the rockshelters from mining activities, including blasting'.[94] Rio Tinto was required to take all practicable measures to avoid sites of special significance under its Regional Framework Deed and could take into account views and concerns presented to it. The Joint Standing Committee on Northern Australia ultimately found that Rio Tinto failed to present the PKKP peoples with different pit options in 2013, which breached its own Communities and Social Performance standards, and its commitment to international standards.[95] The report described this as 'a critical juncture where the destruction of the rockshelters at Juukan Gorge might have prevented if the opportunity for communication had been taken up'.[96]

88   PKKP Aboriginal Corporation, Submission No 129 to the Joint Standing Committee on Northern Australia, *Inquiry Into the Destruction of 46 000-year-old Caves at the Juukan Gorge in the Pilbara Region of Western Australia*, 14.
89   Ibid 14–15.
90   Joint Standing Committee on Northern Australia, *A Way Forward* (18 October 2021).
91   Calla Wahlquist, 'Rio Tinto blasts 46 000-year-old Aboriginal site to expand iron ore mine', *The Guardian* (26 May 2020).
92   Rio Tinto, *Board Review of Cultural Heritage Management* (23 August 2020) 15.
93   Joint Standing Committee on Northern Australia, *A Way Forward* (18 October 2021) 9–13.
94   Rio Tinto, Supplementary Submission No 25.1 to the Joint Standing Committee on Northern Australia, *Inquiry Into the Destruction of 46 000-year-old Caves at the Juukan Gorge in the Pilbara Region of Western Australia*, 27 <https://www.aph.gov.au/Parliamentary_Business/Committees/Joint/Former_Committees/Northern_Australia_46P/CavesatJuukanGorge/Submissions>.
95   Joint Standing Committee on Northern Australia, *A Way Forward*, 19–20.
96   Ibid 18.

Further, the PKKP peoples claimed that Rio Tinto had told them they would mitigate the effect of the blasting on Juukan 1 and 2, 'taking out the explosives from the holes over the top of the Juukan rock shelters'.[97] Explosives were loaded across a number of days in May, including on three extra sites where the appropriate approvals had not been granted, and so Rio Tinto employees consequently had to unload those explosives.[98] The PKKP people contended that, despite removing these other charges, Rio Tinto did not remove the charges most likely to damage Juukan 1 and 2 rock shelters,[99] which were subsequently destroyed when the blasting proceeded.

The Joint Standing Committee report, *A Way Forward*, records evidence from a number of submissions of the impact of internal structural and cultural changes in Rio Tinto from 2016 onwards as 'key contributing factors to the communications breakdown that preceded the destruction of the caves'.[100] Witnesses described a shift from a strategy of 'attempting to understand affected community concerns and respond to them' to '"managing communities", presumably to achieve their compliance with Rio Tinto's imperatives'.[101] Rio Tinto's own Board Review identified changes in personnel as a contributing factor, with the loss of institutional knowledge, including the location and significance of the rock shelters.[102]

For now, Rio Tinto maintains a specific web page recording the disaster, which is called 'Juukan Gorge – A breach of our values'.[103] There, in careful language, the company acknowledges that 'in allowing the destruction of the Juukan Gorge rock shelters', Rio Tinto 'fell far short of our values as a company and breached the trust placed in us by the Traditional Owners of the lands on which we operate'.[104] The page states that, in the years which followed its destruction of Juukan Gorge, Rio Tinto signed a remedy agreement with the Puutu Kunti Kurrama and Pinikura Aboriginal Corporation, and established the Juukan Gorge Legacy Foundation which the company will financially support. Attempts to remediate and re-excavate Juukan Gorge 2 commenced in July 2022, at the request of the PKKP peoples and 'under Traditional Owner oversight'. Rio Tinto indicates that it has undertaken a 'substantive independent review of our cultural heritage performance'... to redefine best practice for cultural heritage management.[105] It acknowledges deficiencies in its partnership management, along with a 'work culture that was too focused on business performance and not enough on building and maintaining relationships with Traditional Owners'.[106]

97 PKKP Aboriginal Corporation, Submission No 129 to the Joint Standing Committee on Northern Australia, *Inquiry Into the Destruction of 46 000-year-old Caves at the Juukan Gorge in the Pilbara Region of Western Australia*, 53.

98 PKKP Aboriginal Corporation, Supplementary Submission No 129.2 to the Joint Standing Committee on Northern Australia, *Inquiry Into the Destruction of 46 000-year-old Caves at the Juukan Gorge in the Pilbara Region of Western Australia*, 2.

99 PKKP Aboriginal Corporation, Submission No 129 to the Joint Standing Committee on Northern Australia, *Inquiry Into the Destruction of 46 000-year-old Caves at the Juukan Gorge in the Pilbara Region of Western Australia*, 55.

100 Joint Standing Committee on Northern Australia, *A Way Forward* (18 October 2021) 15.

101 Ibid.

102 Rio Tinto, *Board Review of Cultural Heritage Management* (23 August 2020) 16.

103 'Juukan Gorge – A breach of our values', *Rio Tinto* <https://www.riotinto.com/en/news/inquiry-into-juukan-gorge>.

104 Much further down on the page, beneath a video screened at their AGM, the website states more directly, 'we destroyed rock shelters of exceptional significance at Juukan Gorge'.

105 Ibid.

106 Ibid.

Almost a year later, at the Rio Tinto AGM, 61 per cent of votes cast rejected Rio Tinto's executive remuneration package.[107] This included the exit package for the outgoing chief executive, Jean-Sébastien Jacques, who resigned in September 2020 along with two other senior executives (the head of iron ore, Chris Salisbury, and the head of corporate affairs, Simone Niven) in the wake of the destruction. All three remained entitled to long-term bonuses, albeit reduced following a review in response to public outcry.[108]

10.3.3.1 Managing bad barrels

Learnings from a cultural tragedy such as the destruction of Juukan Gorge must be carefully and considerately undertaken. The harm caused by these events cannot be overstated – from our perspective, learning from this experience involves engagement with corporations' cultural norms to prevent future violations, rather than reducing this destruction to an educational discussion point.

To our minds, this case reveals a number of aspects of the bad barrel theory. While there is no general sense that individuals were corrupt or dishonest, not one of the many employees who handled this matter identified or responded effectively and promptly to it. The undertakings of Rio Tinto during this matter were undoubtedly legal, but the legislative framework had been the subject of five reviews up to and including 2011, which identified significant reforms were required, relevantly around protection of cultural heritage sites and improved consultation with traditional owners.[109] Despite the similarity of the recommendations from each review, nothing pertinent to the identified points for reform was enacted. The Joint Parliamentary Committee particularly noted that the key Western Australian Act, the *Aboriginal Heritage Act 1972* (WA), was enacted before native title rights were formally recognised by the High Court of Australia.[110] Rio Tinto was variously described as 'shelter[ing] under the legality of its actions' under the Act, or, more brutally, using the Act 'according to a strict interpretation of the law ... to destroy specified Aboriginal heritage objects and places'.[111] The Australian Archaeological Association identified the fundamental flaw: that a permit to destroy could be granted, and that subsequent significant archaeological or other finds did not justify any re-evaluation process. 'In such cases, any decision to mitigate the destruction of significant sites is entirely at the discretion of, and dependent on, the goodwill of the developer.'[112]

107 Neil Hume, 'Rio Tinto suffers huge revolt over pay', *Financial Times* (7 May 2021); BBC News, 'Juukan Gorge: Rio Tinto investors in pay revolt over sacred cave blast', *BBC News* (7 May 2021).
108 Ben Butler, Lorena Allam and Calla Wahlquist, 'Rio Tinto CEO and senior executives resign from company after Juukan Gorge debacle', *The Guardian* (11 September 2020).
109 Joint Standing Committee on Northern Australia, *A Way Forward* (18 October 2021) 67.
110 Ibid 72.
111 Ibid 75, citing Dr Sue-Anne Wallace, Submission No 17, and Mr Bruce Harvey, Submission No 19, to the Joint Standing Committee on Northern Australia, *Inquiry Into the Destruction of 46 000-year-old Caves at the Juukan Gorge in the Pilbara Region of Western Australia* <https://www.aph.gov.au/Parliamentary_Business/Committees/Joint/Former_Committees/Northern_Australia_46P/CavesatJuukanGorge/Submissions>.
112 Australian Archaeological Association, Submission No 37 to the Joint Standing Committee on Northern Australia, *Inquiry Into the Destruction of 46 000-year-old Caves at the Juukan Gorge in the Pilbara Region of Western Australia*, 2–4 <https://www.aph.gov.au/Parliamentary_Business/Committees/Joint/Former_Committees/Northern_Australia_46P/CavesatJuukanGorge/Submissions>.

Rio Tinto's internal review acknowledged the particular failures around managing its relationship with the PKKP peoples, the lack of integration between the company's heritage management team and its front-line operational teams, and a work culture 'too focused on business performance'. Employees knew that not only did they fall short of the company's own standards and guidance in relation to heritage protection, but they failed to escalate issues to senior management, the CEO and the Board.[113] Particularly, the archaeological reporting undertaken in both 2013 and 2014 was not escalated any higher than the mine general manager level.

There was clearly a range of factors that contributed to Rio Tinto's conduct in this case. In the context of an outdated legislative framework, with known weak protections for culturally significant sites, the reputational harm suffered by Rio Tinto for resting on its legal laurels cannot be overstated. Its internal standards and guidance 'talked the talk', but their practical application was constrained by poor communication channels to senior management. An emphasis on business performance – the value to be gained from the iron ore – was allowed to overshadow the cultural and spiritual value of the sites,. Frankly, their loss can never be remediated.

10.4 Mechanisms that regulate business ethics

As the preceding section illustrates, there is a range of ways in which unethical conduct can emerge. As noted above, the root causes of ethical problems can be attributed to individuals (bad apples), particular transactions (bad cases) or the corporation itself (bad barrels). There are also various ways that unethical conduct can be addressed and discouraged. The law has long been accustomed to regulating individuals using a variety of mechanisms, including education, incentives, personal liability and criminal law. However, given that unethical conduct is not just a consequence of individual conduct, simply regulating individuals is insufficient. Corporations are an important part of the picture. The following discussion is focused on ways corporations can be regulated so as to discourage unethical conduct.

10.4.1 Legal consequences

Friedman argued that 'the basic rules of the society, both those embodied in law and those embodied in ethical custom' provide an appropriate check on corporate activity.[114] In fact, according to his analysis these 'basic' rules and the markets are the only legitimate mechanisms for controlling corporate activity. The view that the corporation should abide by the general law is widely, although not universally, accepted. Interestingly, there is a line of argument in the United States ('US'), underpinned by sacrosanct following of the shareholder primacy theory, that directors and management only have a duty to comply with the law where the consequent penalty to the shareholders exceeds the benefit.[115]

113 Rio Tinto, *Board Review of Cultural Heritage Management* (23 August 2020) 17.
114 Friedman, 'A Friedman doctrine', *The New York Times* (13 September 1970).
115 Frank H Easterbrook and Daniel R Fischel, 'The proper role of a target's management in responding to a tender offer' (1981) 94(6) *Harvard Law Review* 1161, 1192–4. See also Kent Greenfield, *The Failure of Corporate Law* (University of Chicago Press, 2008) 73–4.

This position would not hold in Australia, where directors and officers can breach their duty of care if the corporation under their direction fails to comply with the law.[116] Directors or 'high managerial' agents could also potentially breach the *Criminal Code Act 1995* (Cth) if they 'intentionally, knowingly or recklessly carried out the relevant conduct, or expressly, tacitly or impliedly authorised or permitted' an offence under the *Criminal Code*,[117] or the corporation's culture 'directed, encouraged, tolerated or led to non-compliance with the relevant provision'.[118] The Code defines corporate culture as:

> an attitude, policy, rule, course of conduct or practice existing within the body corporate generally or in the part of the body corporate in which the relevant activities take place.[119]

In addition, persons, including professional advisers, can be subject to accessorial liability under s 79 of the *Corporations Act* where they 'aided, abetted, counselled or procured', induced or were 'knowingly involved in' a contravention of the *Corporations Act*.[120] This regulation, therefore, attempts to address the possibility of bad apples, bad cases and bad barrels.

It will not always be the case that unethical conduct is also illegal. However, ethical breaches that also breach the law may have particularly profound implications. Where unethical conduct is also illegal there is a possibility that the corporation might be subjected to some form of legal consequence. For example, the corporation may be subjected to criminal or civil penalties, there could be harm to the company's reputation, and employees and officers may be subjected to sanctions.[121]

The legal risk associated with illegal conduct has focused attention on legal compliance as a key governance function. The *G20/OECD Principles of Corporate Governance* state that a key function of the board is:

> ensuring the integrity of the corporation's accounting and financial reporting systems, including the independent audit, and that appropriate systems of control are in place, in particular, systems for risk management, financial and operational control, and *compliance with the law and relevant standards* [emphasis added].[122]

The ASX *Corporate Governance Principles and Recommendations* remain less forthright, even in the update between the third and fourth editions, advising only that '[a] listed entity should instil and continually reinforce a culture across the organization of acting lawfully, ethically and responsibly'. The commentary to Recommendation 3.1 explicitly discusses tone from the top, community expectations and the relationship between a

---

116 See, eg, *Corporations Act 2001* (Cth) s 180.
117 *Criminal Code Act 1995* (Cth) s 12.3(2)(a), (b).
118 Ibid s 12.3(2)(c).
119 Ibid s 12.3(6).
120 See, eg, *Australian Securities and Investments Commission v Somerville* (2009) 77 NSWLR 110.
121 For further discussion of the existing possibilities, see Senate Economic References Committee, *"Lifting the Fear and Suppressing the Greed": Penalties for White-collar Crime and Corporate and Financial Misconduct in Australia* (2017) ch 2.
122 OECD, *G20/OECD Principles of Corporate Governance* (2015) 49.

corporation's values and long-term sustainable value.[123] Interestingly, the Principles footnote a reference to the Australian Prudential Regulation Authority's Prudential Inquiry into the Commonwealth Bank of Australia, identifying that

> [c]onduct risk is 'the risk of inappropriate, unethical or unlawful behaviour on the part of an organisation's management or employees.' At its simplest, conduct risk management goes beyond what is strictly allowed under law and regulation ('can we do it?') to consider whether an action is appropriate or ethical ('should we do it').[124]

10.4.2 Market mechanisms

In theory the market should provide a powerful check on the unethical conduct of companies where investors are wary of regulatory fallout or of the potential for shares to diminish in value as a consequence of the misconduct. That is, investors should react negatively to shares that have an underlying unreported revenue problem, like that evident in the HIH scenario, or as Enron used special purpose vehicles deceptively to shore up their share price. Those investors should sell their shares, causing the share price to drop and thereby making the company an attractive prospect for takeovers and bringing the reign of management to an end. Should it operate effectively, the market for corporate control and the market for management could provide significant checks. This could therefore place pressure on both the corporation as a whole, and the individuals within it, to do the 'right thing', thus addressing both bad apple and bad barrel possibilities.

As Kent Greenfield explains:

> Perhaps the most important market protection for shareholders is the large and relatively efficient capital market, which rapidly incorporates information about a company into the prices for that firm's securities. If corporate management pursues actions that harm investors, the price of the firm's securities will fall in the capital market. The efficient market also allows investors to sell their interest in firms whenever they hear that managers are failing to maximize profits. The liquidity of the security means that existing shareholders can dispose of their security before they suffer significant harm because of the managers' actions. Potential shareholders are protected as well, since (unless there is fraud) the price of a firm's security will more or less reflect the management's diligence in maximizing returns to shareholders. If management is inefficient, the share price will likely be less than what it would be under efficient management. This will make a takeover of the company cheaper and more likely. Because takeovers usually result in a change in management, a manager who wants to keep her job will work to maintain a high share price.[125]

123 ASX, *Corporate Governance Principles and Recommendations* (4th ed, 2019) 16.
124 Australian Prudential Regulation Authority, *Prudential Inquiry into the Commonwealth Bank of Australia* (Final Report, 1 May 2018), 7.
125 Greenfield, *The Failure of Corporate Law* (2008) 49.

There are, however, considerable hurdles that can prevent these mechanisms from operating in the way described above. First, the information that could signal to investors that the corporation is compromised may not be publicly available, or sufficiently accessible. Even where the disclosure system is working, where fraud is involved, considerable efforts may be made to conceal the fraudulent activity from scrutiny. Disclosure is also a noisy system, so while critical information may well be disclosed, there is no guarantee that it will be noticed and acted on in any systematic way. Second, the kind of conduct that might prompt investor action is only a portion of the possible unethical conduct in which corporations could engage. Some unethical conduct may appear to be, at least in the short term, in the interests of shareholders. Accordingly, conduct that promotes or appears to promote shareholder wealth in unethical or illegal ways, such as the LIBOR activity, may not be subject to disclosure, but also may not, even if revealed, prompt shareholder exit.

10.4.3 Disclosure

Disclosure, as a regulatory technique, had its birth alongside incorporation legislation itself, featuring in the 'first general incorporation act', the *Joint Stock Companies Act 1844* (UK).[126] It gained further momentum in the reforms introduced in the US in the wake of the Depression.[127] Then, as now, its aims were to:

> improve the functioning of the securities markets by providing to investors the information they needed to evaluate the merits of a potential investment. Moreover, although this goal was distinctly secondary, it was also recognized that disclosure would help to deter fraud and self dealing.[128]

Over time, a third aim became evident as disclosure requirements were widened beyond matters related to the proper functioning of the securities market. That is, disclosure was used for 'influencing a wide range of corporate primary behavior that has only the most tenuous connection with the securities market'.[129] In Australia, it remains a key strategy for discouraging unethical conduct, exposing corporate activity to scrutiny and addressing the information asymmetry of investors and creditors. The use of disclosure to shape ethical outcomes is also an approach that is taken transnationally. The *G20/OECD Principles of Corporate Governance* state:

> In addition to their commercial objectives, companies are encouraged to disclose policies and performance relating to business ethics, the environment and, where material to the company, social issues, human rights and other public policy commitments. Such information may be important for certain investors and other users of information to better evaluate the relationship between companies and the communities in which they operate and the steps that companies have taken to implement their objectives.[130]

---

126 Paul Redmond, *Company and Securities Law: Commentary and Materials* (Lawbook, 8th ed, 2023) 56, 861.
127 *Securities Act* of 1933 and the *Securities Exchange Act* of 1934.
128 Russell B Stevenson, *Corporations and Information: Secrecy, Access and Disclosure* (Johns Hopkins University Press, 1980) 80.
129 Ibid 82.
130 OECD, *G20/OECD Principles of Corporate Governance* (2015) 38–9.

This suggests that social and ethical disclosure extending beyond financial matters could be relevant to investor choices. This could then encourage companies to act ethically in order to attract investor funds.

All corporations are subject to disclosure requirements, with listed companies subject to the most extensive obligations. These requirements are rationalised as the corollary of limited liability. As stated by RP Austin and IM Ramsay, '[p]roper financial record keeping and public disclosure of financial information are normally justified as the price to be paid for the privilege of limited liability'.[131] The effectiveness of the disclosure regime is often questioned. For creditors to absorb financial disclosure requires commitment and investment of time. This is only likely to occur in the case of large creditors, who arguably could bargain for the access to the information in any event or protect themselves through security arrangements.[132] Disclosure is more likely to be of moment for investors, but even then the density of the information provided and the marginal commitment of many investors constitute considerable hurdles.

Nevertheless, the commitment to disclosure has been evident in Australia since the 1970s[133] and it was substantially reinforced in the period following the excesses of the 1980s by the *Corporate Law Reform Act 1994* (Cth). Under the *Corporations Act*, all companies must provide basic information to the corporate regulator, including the details of their officeholders and their registered office.[134] Large proprietary companies and public companies must provide a financial report,[135] a directors' report[136] and an auditor report[137] each financial year. Specific disclosure requirements are triggered should a corporation embark on fundraising or in connection with a takeover. Additionally, the continuous disclosure regime applies to listed companies ('disclosing entities'[138]). Under this framework listed companies are required (by s 674 and the *Listing Rules*) to disclose to the ASX immediately any information of which they are, or become, aware that a reasonable person might expect to have a material effect on the price or value of the entity's securities.[139] Carve-outs contained in Listing Rule 3.1A indicate that disclosure is not required where it would be a breach of law to disclose the information or the information is related to an incomplete proposal or matters of supposition, is insufficiently definite, generated for internal management or is a trade secret, provided also that it is confidential and a reasonable person would not expect it to be disclosed.[140]

The consequences of a failure to disclose can be profound. Disclosure regulation generally relies on compelling a proper process for disclosure. That is, provided the

---

131 RP Austin and IM Ramsay, *Ford, Austin and Ramsay's Principles of Corporations Law* (LexisNexis, 16th ed, 2015) 774; see also Redmond, *Company and Securities Law* (2023) 56.
132 Austin and Ramsay, *Ford, Austin and Ramsay's Principles of Corporations Law* (2015) 775.
133 Ibid.
134 *Corporations Act 2001* (Cth) ss 201L, 142, 146.
135 Ibid s 292.
136 Ibid s 299.
137 Ibid ss 301, 307A, 308.
138 A listed disclosing entity is one that is listed and has issued 'enhanced disclosure securities'. This includes securities that are permitted to be traded on a prescribed financial market: *Corporations Act 2001* (Cth) ss 111AD, 111AE, 111AL, 111AM.
139 ASX, *Listing Rules* r 3.1.
140 ASX, *Listing Rules* r 3.1A.

discloser can establish that they adhered to a proper process in determining the information to be disclosed, they will have satisfied their obligations, even if the information turns out to be inaccurate.[141] Generally, persons involved in a contravention of the disclosure regime will contravene a civil penalty provision, and also commit a criminal offence.[142] For directors and officers, a failure to comply with any of the disclosure requirements could also be a breach of their duty of care and diligence under s 180 and the equivalent common law duty.[143] Again, this seems to cover the bad apple and bad barrel options.

10.4.4 Gatekeepers

A number of scholars have considered the role that professional experts, or 'gatekeepers', play in preventing unethical conduct by corporations. Gatekeeper theory suggests that professionals, such as lawyers, securities analysts, auditors, credit ratings agencies, and investment bankers,[144] who sign off or provide necessary consent to corporate activity, thereby vouch for the legitimacy of their client's activity. According to this theory, should the gatekeeper detect fraudulent or unethical conduct, they are incentivised to intervene to prevent such conduct, or to refuse to act, in order to protect their reputation. No single client is worth risking a hard-won reputation lost by colluding or consenting to unethical or illegal conduct.

John Coffee Jr defines a corporate gatekeeper as:

> an agent who acts as a reputational intermediary to assure investors as to the quality of the 'signal' sent by the corporate issuer. The reputational intermediary does so by lending or 'pledging' its reputational capital to the corporation, thus enabling investors or the market to rely on the corporation's own disclosures or assurances where they otherwise might not.[145]

According to this definition, the gatekeeper has an incentive to identify and prevent wrongdoing because its later revelation has the potential to harm their reputation. Reinier Kraakman first proposed that 'gatekeepers' could provide a check on corporate activity in the 1980s. He saw gatekeepers as supplementing the regulation that discourages corporations and their managements from misconduct. The central aspect of this concept is a duty imposed 'on private "gatekeepers" to prevent misconduct by withholding support'.[146]

While gatekeeper activity holds some promise as a way of monitoring and responding to corporate misconduct, it is by no means a comprehensive solution. The focus on reputation and its protection as the key motivator for effective gatekeeper action has been challenged as insufficient, and increased gatekeeper liability has been proposed as a means

---

141 Leif Gamertsfelder, *Corporate Information and the Law* (Lexis Nexis, 2nd ed, 2015) 116.
142 *Corporations Act 2001* (Cth) ss 674(2), 1317E(1), 1311(1).
143 See, eg, *Australian Securities and Investments Commission v Healey* (2011) 196 FCR 291.
144 John C Coffee Jr, *Gatekeepers: The Professions and Corporate Governance* (Oxford University Press, 2006) 1.
145 Ibid 2.
146 Reinier H Kraakman, 'Gatekeepers: The anatomy of a third-party enforcement strategy' (1986) 2(1) *Journal of Law, Economics, and Organization* 53, 54.

of providing further incentives for gatekeeper action.[147] The other aspect of the definition is that it identifies the gatekeeper's remit as related to the 'corporation's own disclosures or assurances'. Coffee also states that the gatekeeper provides 'certification or verification services' to investors.[148] The focus is, therefore, on a narrow band of activity where the gatekeeper's reputation is on the line or where a transaction requires gatekeeper consent or cooperation – that is, where there is public verification of corporate activity by a gatekeeper. This means that the reputation of the gatekeeper is only called into question in certain types of transactions. If the theory were to apply to matters beyond these transactions, the gatekeeper would have to be sensitive to reputational damage in these contexts. That is, the gatekeeper would have to be incentivised to decline to act or to offer resistance where corporate activity was unethical beyond the financial arena.

Moreover, the continued existence of corporate fraud suggests that gatekeeper failure is a problem. In his masterly analysis of the excesses of Australian corporations in the 1980s, Trevor Sykes colourfully describes the way the 'professions prostituted themselves – with the odd notable exception – to the bold riders'.[149] As Roger Crampton highlights, 'compliant lawyers as well as greedy executives, lazy directors and malleable accountants are necessary for large corporate frauds to come to life and persist long enough to cause major harm'.[150] Coffee attributes these failures to four factors: first, agency problems within gatekeeper firms that make acquiescence with the client make sense to individuals or teams; second, market failures that mean gatekeepers are not operating in sufficiently competitive markets; third, a decline in the value of gatekeeper reputation; and, finally, reduced litigation.[151] Reflecting on the failure of gatekeepers before the Enron failure, Sean Griffith noted that the 'responsibility of lawyers for the current crisis may arise from tensions in their dual role as gatekeepers and transaction engineers'. Their roles as 'authors' of corporate transactions may weaken their structural independence, as they are asked to sit in judgment on their own work.[152]

Despite the potential for gatekeeper failure, and the fact that gatekeepers will not be relevant in all areas of corporate endeavour, the role of the gatekeeper is an important one in the context of ethical conduct. Gatekeepers such as lawyers and accountants are committed to professional codes of ethics.[153] They are in a privileged position in that they can have information about problem transactions in advance, at a point when the course of action can be changed. In the boardroom, the prevalence of independent board members may mean that gatekeepers are particularly important as board advisers.[154] In addition, gatekeepers can provide a regulatory option that does not rely on state regulators, thus extending the regulatory reach in a context where resources are tight and remit is broad.

---

147 See, eg, Frank Partnoy, 'Strict liability for gatekeepers: A reply to Professor Coffee' (2004) 84(2) *Boston University Law Review* 365; and John C Coffee Jr, 'Gatekeeper failure and reform: The challenge of fashioning relevant reforms' (2004) 84(2) *Boston University Law Review* 301.
148 Coffee, *Gatekeepers* (2006) 2.
149 Trevor Sykes, *The Bold Riders behind Australia's Corporate Collapses* (Allen & Unwin, 2nd ed, 1996) 575.
150 Roger C Crampton, 'Enron and the corporate lawyer: A primer on legal and ethical issues' (2002) 58(1) *Business Lawyer* 143, 144.
151 Coffee, *Gatekeepers* (2006) 6.
152 Griffith, 'Afterword and comment' (2003) 35 *Connecticut Law Review* 1223, 1225.
153 See, eg, Law Society of South Australia, *Australian Solicitors Conduct Rules* (2014).
154 Coffee, *Gatekeepers* (2006) 7–8.

10.4.5 Whistleblowers

Whistleblowing is influentially defined as the 'disclosure by organization members (former and current) of illegal, immoral and illegitimate practices under the control of their employers to persons or organizations that may be able to effect action'.[155] The support and protection of whistleblowers has garnered significant regulatory attention in recent decades. This was founded in the post-war focus on the power and rights of the individual,[156] but is now anchored in the potential for whistleblowers to extend the regulatory ability of the state to respond to negative conduct. According to Ashley Savage and Richard Hyde, '[m]odern governance relies on decentred regulatory networks, and these networks involve whistleblowers'.[157]

In the corporate sphere, the *G20/OECD Principles of Corporate Governance* endorse the significance of whistleblowing. It recommends that the responsibility for encouraging whistleblowing should rest with the board:

> In fulfilling its control oversight responsibilities it is important for the board to encourage the reporting of unethical/unlawful behaviour without fear of retribution. The existence of a company code of ethics should aid this process, which should be underpinned by legal protection for the individuals concerned. A contact point for employees who wish to report concerns about unethical or illegal behaviour that might also compromise the integrity of financial statements should be offered by the audit committee or by an ethics committee or equivalent body.[158]

The key elements of the whistleblowing process are that there is a disclosure by an insider with special knowledge of wrongdoing to a party capable of intervention. The kind of wrongdoing that is contemplated is drawn broadly, to include conduct beyond, but encompassing, illegal conduct. AJ Brown has suggested defining whistleblowers to include those with a 'special relationship such as to mean that their disclosure comes "from within"'.[159] In addition to current employees and officers, this would include former employees and contractors. From a regulatory perspective, these parties have the potential to address the informational disadvantage of the regulator by providing inside knowledge, while the regulator can provide the heft necessary to respond to the wrongdoing.

Both the public and private sector approaches to whistleblowing in Australia were subject to reviews in the past decade, namely the Moss Review in 2016[160] and

---

155 J Near and Marcia P Miceli, 'Organizational dissidence: The case of whistle-Blowing' (1985) 4(1) *Journal of Business Ethics* 4.

156 Robert Vaughn, *The Successes and Failures of Whistleblowing Laws* (Edward Elgar, 2012); see also Ashley Savage and Richard Hyde, 'The response to whistleblowing by regulators: A practical perspective' (2015) 35(3) *Legal Studies* 408, 409–10.

157 Savage and Hyde, 'The response to whistleblowing by regulators' (2015) 35(3) *Legal Studies* 408.

158 OECD, *G20/OECD Principles of Corporate Governance* (2015) 49.

159 AJ Brown, 'Restoring sunshine to the Sunshine State: Priorities for whistleblowing law reform in Queensland' (2009) 18(3) *Griffith Law Review* 666, 684.

160 Philip Moss AM, 'Review of the *Public Interest Disclosure Act 2013* (Cth)' (20 October 2016) <https://www.ag.gov.au/about-us/publications/review-public-interest-disclosure-act-2013>.

the Parliamentary Joint Committee on Corporations and Financial Services review in 2016–17.[161] In Australia, from 1 January 2020, public companies, large proprietary companies and corporate trustees of registrable superannuation entities are required by the *Corporations Act* to have a whistleblower policy.[162] That policy must be available to officers and employees of the company. ASIC's Regulatory Guide 270 provides a practice guide on implementing and maintaining a policy that complies with these new legal obligations.[163] The ASX *Corporate Governance Principles and Recommendations*, which were in place before this provision was enacted in the *Corporations Act*, also recommend that listed companies have and disclose a whistleblower policy, and ensure that the board (or a committee of the board) is informed of any material incident reported under the policy.[164] The commentary and recommendations further encourage the policy to '[e]xplain how the confidentiality of the whistleblower's identity is safeguarded and the whistleblower is protected from retaliation or victimisation'.[165] Companies are increasingly appreciating the risk management potential associated with formalising channels for, and protection of, whistleblowers.[166]

The *Corporations Act* offers some protection for whistleblowers in pt 9.4AAA, which was expanded in 2019 to provide greater protection to whistleblowers. These provisions protect current and former officers, employees, contractors, associates[167] and their spouses, dependants and other relatives.[168] Reports can be made anonymously, but disclosure must be made to either a director, officer, senior manager, auditor or actuary of the company (or a related company), or a person authorised by the company to receive whistleblower disclosures – or to ASIC, APRA or a lawyer.[169]

The subject of the disclosure is also significant. Protection is extended to the whistleblower who has reasonable grounds to suspect that information concerns 'misconduct', or 'an improper state of affairs or circumstances', in relation to a regulated entity, which includes but is not limited to conduct in breach of the *Corporations Act* and the *Australian Securities and Investments Commission Act 2001* (Cth), among others, or which represents a danger to the public or the financial system.[170] If the disclosure relates to a substantial and imminent danger to the health and safety of people, or to the environment, 90 days have passed, and the discloser does not have reasonable grounds to believe that action is being or has been taken, then, after the provision of written notice to the

---

161 Parliamentary Joint Committee on Corporations and Financial Services, *Whistleblower Protections* (Report, 13 September 2017) <https://www.aph.gov.au/Parliamentary_Business/Committees/Joint/Corporations_and_Financial_Services/WhistleblowerProtections/Report>.

162 *Corporations Act 2001* (Cth) s 1317AI.

163 ASIC, *Whistleblower Policies* (Regulatory Guide 270, November 2019) <https://asic.gov.au/regulatory-resources/find-a-document/regulatory-guides/rg-270-whistleblower-policies/>.

164 ASX, *Corporate Governance Principles and Recommendations* (4th ed, 2019) 17.

165 Ibid.

166 Janine Pascoe and Michelle Welsh, 'Whistleblowing, ethics and corporate culture: Theory and practice in Australia' (2011) 40(2) *Common Law World Review* 144, 147; Sulette Lombard, Vivienne Brand and Janet Austin, *Corporate Whistleblowing Regulation* (Springer, 2020).

167 In the instance of a superannuation entity, this also extends to trustees, custodians and investment managers.

168 *Corporations Act 2001* (Cth) s 1317AAA.

169 Ibid s 1317AAC.

170 This is much broader than the previous provision to the 2019 amendments.

original recipient of the disclosure, a 'public interest disclosure' can be made to a member of state or federal Parliament, or a journalist.[171]

These provisions represent a substantially broader framework than previously existed in Australia, which had been subject to criticism.[172] The public sector remained, in 2022, subject to the criticisms that had previously been levelled at the private sector, with the Media Entertainment and Arts Alliance identifying improved whistleblower protection as a key demand for more than 20 years by that point.[173] In the same year, public sector whistleblowing cases involving Bernard Collaery, Richard Boyle and David McBride demonstrated the scant protection available, even under circumstances of disclosure involving clear public interest with significant ramifications for Australian society – as the recommendations of the Moss Review had not been actioned, after six years. An amending bill to the *Public Interest Disclosure Act 2013* (Cth) has been announced,[174] which proposes to implement 21 of the 33 recommendations of the Moss Review.[175]

10.5 Organisation-level approaches

In addition to the mechanisms for discouraging unethical conduct by corporations discussed above, elements within corporations will have profound effects on the way those interacting with, or working within, corporations see, understand and respond to ethical problems.

10.5.1 Leadership

Edgar H Schein sees leadership as critical to any organisation's culture.[176] He argues that there are 'six primary embedding mechanisms' that a leader can use to influence an organisation's culture: attention, reaction to crises, allocation of resources, role modelling, rewards and status, and criteria for selection and dismissal.[177] Bob Garratt also focuses on leadership, with a particular emphasis on the role of the board. He notes:

> It is the board's job to ensure sufficient numbers of members [of the organisation] are pointing in the same direction, committed to a common purpose, with similar values and behaviours, so that the organization can function effectively and efficiently.[178]

171 *Corporations Act 2001* (Cth) s 1317AAD.
172 Simon Wolfe et al, *Whistleblower Protection Laws in G20 Countries: Priorities for Action* (Melbourne University, Griffith University, Blueprint for Free Speech, Transparency International Australia, 2014).
173 Media Entertainment and Arts Alliance, 'Whistleblower protection' (29 April 2022) <https://pressfreedom.org.au/whistleblower-protection-8eeb6edea6a2#_edn1>.
174 Public Interest Disclosure Amendment (Review) Bill 2022 (Cth).
175 Mark Dreyfus, 'Public interest disclosure reform' (Media Release, Attorney-General's Department, 30 November 2022) <https://ministers.ag.gov.au/media-centre/public-interest-disclosure-reform-30-11-2022>.
176 Edgar H Schein, *Organizational Culture and Leadership* (Jossey-Bass, 4th ed, 2010) 219.
177 Ibid; see also Ronald R Sims and Johannes Brinkmann, 'Enron ethics (or: culture matters more than codes)' (2003) 45(3) *Journal of Business Ethics* 243.
178 Bob Garratt, *The Fish Rots from the Head: The Crisis in Our Boardrooms: Developing the Crucial Skills of the Competent Director* (Profile, 2003) xxix.

Ronald R Sims and Johannes Brinkmann argue that 'issues that capture the attention of the leader (ie what is criticised, praised or asked about) will also capture the attention of the greater organization and will become the focus of the employees'. In the Juukan Gorge case, management's focus on business performance and policy compliance did not prioritise building and maintaining relationships with the PKKP peoples.[179] In Enron the focus was on the bottom line.[180]

Similarly, the reaction of leadership to a crisis can be a powerful indicator of ethical values.[181] In the HIH case, the reaction of Williams to the challenge posed by the discussions between the auditor and some directors and the relaying of concerns by directors indicated a level of intolerance for constructive dissent. Relatedly, the modelling of ethical conduct by leadership can be significant to those observing it. The seeming acquiescence by leadership to the LIBOR manipulation, including by the Bank of England, provided a powerful example to more junior employees: 'Employees often emulate leaders' behavior and look to the leaders for cues to appropriate behavior'.[182] So at Enron, when the CEO 'bragged about Enron's sophisticated controls but undermined them at every turn',[183] it encouraged others to do the same.

The allocation of resources, rewards and punishments and the criteria for selection and dismissal are also critical: 'Reward systems can ... become unfair and, therefore, increase the likelihood of unethical conduct by tending to politicise the compensation and promotion system.'[184] For example, the significance of LIBOR manipulation for promotion indicated to employees that rule-breaking was accepted. At Enron, the 'rank and yank' performance review system placed employees in the bottom 15 per cent under extreme pressure to perform, while also rewarding those who broke the rules to get ahead.[185]

10.5.2 Corporate culture

Corporate culture is attracting considerable attention. Speaking in 2016, Greg Medcraft, the then chairman of ASIC, defined corporate culture as 'a set of shared values and assumptions within an organisation'. It reflects the underlying 'mindset of an organisation', the 'unwritten rules'.[186] For ASIC, the significance of culture is that:

> poor culture can be a driver of poor conduct – and we regulate conduct. Bad conduct can flourish, proliferate and may even be rewarded in a poor culture.

179 Rio Tinto, *Board Review of Cultural Heritage Management* (23 August 2020) 15; Joint Standing Committee on Northern Australia, *A Way Forward* (18 October 2021) 15.
180 Sims and Brinkmann, 'Enron ethics (or: culture matters more than codes)' (2003) 45(3) *Journal of Business Ethics* 243, 247.
181 Ibid.
182 Ibid.
183 Bethany McLean and Peter Elkind, *The Smartest Guys in the Room: The Amazing Rise and Scandalous Fall of Enron* (Portfolio, 2004) 114.
184 Lynne Dallas, 'Enron and ethical corporate Climates' in Nancy Rapoport, Jeffrey Van Neil and Bala Dharan (eds), *Enron and other Corporate Fiascos: The Corporate Scandal Reader* (Foundation Press, 2nd ed, 2009) 151, 158.
185 Duane Windsor, 'Business ethics at the Crooked E' in Rapoport, Neil and Dharan (eds), *Enron and other Corporate Fiascos: The Corporate Scandal Reader* (2009) 123, 139.
186 Greg Medcraft, 'The importance of corporate culture in improving governance and compliance' (Speech, Challenger Legal and Corporate Affairs team offsite, Sydney, 28 July 2016).

A good culture, on the other hand, can help uncover and inhibit bad conduct and reward and encourage good conduct.[187]

This emphasis from the Australian regulator is not unusual. Corporate culture has become the 'focus of attention in the business media and is a topic of discussion in corporate board rooms'.[188] This focus is also backed by empirical study. So, for example, Muel Kaptein found that 'the ethical culture of work groups has a negative relationship with the frequency of observed unethical behavior within work groups'.[189] In his study he further found:

> Six of the eight dimensions of ethical culture that were tested had a negative relationship with observed unethical behavior. These dimensions are: ethical role modeling of management, ethical role modeling of supervisors, capability to behave ethically, commitment to behave ethically, openness to discuss ethical issues, and reinforcement of ethical behavior.[190]

For some scholars concerned with ethical conduct in particular, the weight is given to the 'ethical climate ... [as] one component of the organizational culture'.[191] In this literature a distinction is drawn between ethical culture and ethical climate. For example, Muel Kaptein explains that 'ethical climate is substantive in that it pertains to the content of ethical and unethical behavior, whereas ethical culture is procedural in that it pertains to the conditions for ethical and unethical behavior'.[192] Lynne Dallas describes 'climate' as 'the ethical meaning attached by employees to organizational policies, practices and procedures'.[193] It is certainly plausible that culture, including as it does norms of conduct, written and unwritten rules and expectations, will be correlated with the attitudes that make up the ethical climate within a corporation. That is, a culture that creates the conditions for ethical conduct is likely to have values and perceptions consistent with that and vice versa.

Reflecting on the bad apples, cases and barrels discussion above, it is plausible that culture could have a positive or negative impact on all three. Haines, in her work exploring worker deaths, draws a contrast between two types of culture. She finds that '[a]t the core of each culture was the understanding of how to achieve "success" as an organization'.[194] She describes the 'virtuous' culture and 'blinkered' culture in a safety context by explaining how a virtuous culture was able to combine safety concerns with business priorities whereas the blinkered culture saw them as oppositional.[195] As Dallas

---

187 Ibid.
188 Jerome Want, *Corporate Culture: Illuminating the Black Hole* (St Martin's Press, 2006) 3.
189 Muel Kaptein, 'Understanding unethical behavior by unraveling ethical culture' (2011) 64(6) *Human Relations* 843, 858.
190 Ibid 843.
191 Bahram Soltani, 'The anatomy of corporate fraud: A comparative analysis of high profile American and European corporate scandals' (2014) 120(2) *Journal of Business Ethics* 251, 254.
192 Kaptein, 'Understanding unethical behavior by unraveling ethical culture' (2011) 64(6) *Human Relations* 843, 846.
193 Dallas, 'Enron and ethical corporate climates' in Rapoport, Neil and Dharan (eds), *Enron and other Corporate Fiascos: The Corporate Scandal Reader* (2009) 151, 157–8.
194 Fiona Haines, *Corporate Regulation: Beyond Punish or Persuade* (Clarendon Press, 1997) 99.
195 Ibid 97–9.

explains, 'the corporation itself creates a social environment that can increase or decrease the likelihood of ethical decision-making'.[196]

Apart from the 'bad apples' analogy we make above, we would also like to refer the reader back to what we said in Section 1.6.3.6 about how widespread 'poor corporate culture' seems to be in Australia. We mentioned that there are probably no better illustrations of the neglect of non-shareholder interests and an underlying problem of poor corporate culture,[197] also widespread in Australian companies,[198] than what was revealed by the Interim (2018) and Final (2019) Hayne Reports. These reports uncovered serious wrongful, and even illegal, conduct by the majority of Australian corporations operating in the financial and banking sector. Examples of such conduct included customers being overcharged or deceived about the payment of fees (which became know as the 'fee for no service' scandal).[199] The root of the problem was identified as boards of directors being driven and motivated primarily by profit maximisation for shareholders.[200] This could be attributed to a flawed culture within entities. Poor organisational culture was seen as a blameworthy factor which contributed to the poor management of regulatory, compliance and conduct risks. According to Commissioner Hayne, if the mistakes of the past misconduct in the financial sector are to be avoided in the future, 'entities have no choice but to grapple with culture, governance and remuneration. All three are related.'[201]

10.5.3 Codes of conduct

In 2017, the CEO of QBE, a large Australian insurance company, reportedly took a $550 000 pay cut for breaching the company's executive code of conduct by failing to advise the board of a personal relationship with a company employee immediately.[202] Corporate codes of conduct, such as the one that proved so costly for the QBE chief executive, have become common elements of the ethical infrastructure of large corporations. Moreover, beyond the individual corporation, there are a variety of supra-corporate and sector codes that seek to shape corporate conduct in positive ways.[203] The *G20/OECD*

---

196 Dallas, 'Enron and ethical corporate climates' in Rapoport, Neil and Dharan (eds), *Enron and other Corporate Fiascos: The Corporate Scandal Reader* (2009) 151, 155.

197 See generally Hanrahan, 'Corporate governance in these "exciting times"' (2017) 32(2) *Australian Journal of Corporate Law 142*, 153–6.

198 For several examples of the bad corporate culture in the Owen Report, see Commonwealth of Australia, Department of the Parliamentary Library, 'Report of the Royal Commission into HIH Insurance' (Research Note No 32, 13 May 2003) <https://parlinfo.aph.gov.au/parlInfo/search/display/display.w3p;query=Id:%22library/prspub/XZ896%22#:~:text=The%20Royal%20Commission%20noted%20that,circumstances%20in%20the%20insurance%20industry>.

199 For identification of many other examples of wrongful, and even illegal, conduct by entities in the financial sector, see Anil Hargovan 'Hayne Royal Commission Interim Report: Unclogging the central artery' (2018) 70(11) *Governance Directions* 691; Anil Hargovan 'Banking Royal Commission final report: Cultural issues and implications (2019) 71 *Governance Directions* 128.

200 Final (2019) Hayne Report at 399.

201 Ibid 334.

202 Christine Lacey, 'QBE CEO John Neal takes $550 000 pay cut over "personal decisions"', *The Australian* (27 February 2017).

203 See, eg, the Ethical Trading Initiative, 'The ETI Base Code' <www.ethicaltrade.org/resources/eti-base-code>; UN Global Compact, 'The Ten Principles of the UN Global Compact' <https://unglobalcompact.org/what-is-gc/mission/principles>.

Principles of Corporate Governance recommend that '[c]ompanies are also well advised to establish and ensure the effectiveness of internal controls, ethics, and compliance programmes or measures to comply with applicable laws, regulations, and standards'.[204] Corporate codes of conduct have also been given regulatory impetus through a variety of regulatory instruments in a number of jurisdictions.[205] Nonetheless, there remain significant questions about their effectiveness. The example of Enron is often cited as indicating that the presence of a lengthy and detailed code of conduct does not necessarily mean that ethical conduct is observed.[206] More persuasively, a meta-analysis of empirical studies fails to shore up the case for the effectiveness of these codes.[207]

Joshua Newberg defines corporate codes of conduct as follows:

> The typical CCOE [corporate code of ethics] of a large public company is a hybrid that combines some general statements of the firm's commitment to broadly expressed normative formulations of principled business conduct – such as acting with 'integrity', or adherence to 'the highest ethical standards' – with a number of specific pronouncements or rules addressing discrete areas of unlawful and/or unethical conduct.[208]

Codes have both an internal and external aspect. As Josef Wieland explains, '[w]hen firms design an explicit code of ethics, they are attempting to transform moral ambiguity in their environment into organizational self-commitment by rules and values'.[209] They can provide a framework for existing employees, and can be used to explain corporate expectations to new employees.[210] As such, they can be used to manage bad apple conduct, as well as having a more general application. They can reduce the risk of organisational chaos and enhance the likelihood that a large organisation will work consistently even where it is geographically separated. They can also signal to outsiders the organisation's commitment to ethical conduct.

The challenge for the code of conduct approach is that simply writing a code is insufficient. Michael Deck notes that 'of the 90% of companies that have codes, only 28% do any training'.[211] Following his empirical study, Kaptein advised that corporations should 'adopt at least eight components in the following sequence: a code; training and communication; accountability policies; monitoring and auditing; investigation

---

204 OECD, *G20/OECD Principles of Corporate Governance* (2015) 50.
205 See, eg, *Sarbanes-Oxley Act of 2002* (US) s 406; ASX, *Corporate Governance Principles and Recommendations* (4th ed, 2019) Recommendations 3.1–3.2; United States Sentencing Commission, *Guidelines Manual 2023*, 'Chapter 8 – Sentencing of organizations'.
206 Joshua A Newberg, 'Corporate codes of ethics, mandatory disclosure, and the market for ethical conduct' (2005) 29(2) *Vermont Law Review* 253, 265.
207 Patrick M Erwin, 'Corporate codes of conduct: The effects of code content and quality on ethical performance' (2011) 99(4) *Journal of Business Ethics* 535, 536.
208 Newberg, 'Corporate codes of ethics, mandatory disclosure, and the market for ethical conduct' (2005) 29(2) *Vermont Law Review* 253, 258 (citations omitted).
209 Josef Wieland, 'The ethics of governance' (2001) 11(1) *Business Ethics Quarterly* 73, 81 (citations omitted).
210 Lutz Preuss, 'Codes of conduct in organisational context: From cascade to lattice-work of codes' (2010) 94(4) *Journal of Business Ethics* 471, 473.
211 Michael C Deck, 'Corporate codes and ethics programs' in Laura P Hartman (ed), *Perspectives in Business Ethics* (McGraw-Hill Irwin, 3rd ed, 2005) 250.

and corrective policies; an ethics office(r); ethics report line; and incentive policies'.[212] Dallas highlights the:

> mission statement and code of ethics, the criteria for business decisions, the words and actions of leaders, the handling of conflicts of interest, the reward system, the guidance provided to employees concerning dealing with ethical issues, and the monitoring system.[213]

As this indicates, the code is only part of the picture. Codes of conduct are required by the general corporate governance codes of many countries, normally applying to listed companies and based on the 'comply or explain' principle. This 'soft law' approach has come under scrutiny in recent times,[214] but whether a more robust 'hard law' approach to the ethical conduct of corporations will be adopted is difficult to predict, as it is so difficult to define 'business ethics' (see Section 10.2.2). And legislation for 'corporate culture' is controversial too (see Section 10.5.2).

10.5.4 Structures

There is a connection between the way a corporation is structured and its culture. In the Juukan Gorge and the HIH cases, structures appear to have significantly affected the way the corporations responded to their challenges. In relation to Rio Tinto, for example, its internal audit following the destruction of Juukan Gorge identified that important information was not escalated to management. The evidence provided to the Joint Parliamentary Committee provided examples of personnel change affecting institutional knowledge, and structural impediments to information-sharing. In HIH the structure of the audit committee and its relationship with the board, CEO and the external auditor inhibited its effectiveness.

At the board level, 'the first and primary obligation of a board should be to ensure that its structure and operation are of the highest standards for integrity'.[215] The importance of board structure is recognised in corporate governance codes. So, for example, the ASX *Corporate Governance Principles and Recommendations* recommend that all corporations have audit, nomination and compensation committees. They also outline the preferred membership of these committees and their areas of responsibility.

The issue of fragmentation of responsibility and information is more complex, but clearly has a structural aspect to it. The *G20/OECD Principles of Corporate Governance* entrust the board with 'ensuring the integrity of the essential reporting and monitoring systems' and states that this 'will require the board to set and enforce clear lines of responsibility and accountability throughout the organisation'.[216]

212 Muel Kaptein, 'The effectiveness of ethics programs: The role of scope, composition, and sequence' (2015) 132(2) *Journal of Business Ethics* 415, 429.
213 Dallas, 'Enron and ethical corporate climates' in Rapoport, Neil and Dharan (eds), *Enron and Other Corporate Fiascos: The Corporate Scandal Reader* (2009) 151, 139.
214 See Jean J du Plessis and Chee Keong Low (eds), *Corporate Governance Codes for the 21st Century: International Perspectives and Critical Analyses* (Springer Verlag, 2017).
215 Dawn-Marie Driscoll, 'Ethics and corporate governance: Lessons learned from a financial services model' (2001) 11(1) *Business Ethics Quarterly* 145.
216 OECD, *G20/OECD Principles of Corporate Governance* (2015) 49.

10.5.5 Complaints handling

As was noted in the whistleblowing discussion above (Section 10.4.5), there is an increased interest in the potential for whistleblowers to contribute to the risk management of corporations by alerting senior management and the board to problems and concerns. The way an organisation responds to complaints and concerns is a powerful indicator of its ethical culture. For example, the response of HIH to the concerns raised by directors indicated to others the likely reception of any complaints. Such conduct can only inhibit the free flow of information to those who have the power to address risks. The importance of having proper complaints management is str in several key regulatory instruments.

The *G20/OECD Principles of Corporate Governance*, for example, highlight the need to provide avenues for complaints from employees and those external to the company to be made. They recommend that regulation be created to encourage boards to take this in hand:

> It is ... to the advantage of the company and its shareholders to establish pro-
> cedures and safe-harbours for complaints by employees, either personally or
> through their representative bodies, and others outside the company, concern-
> ing illegal and unethical behaviour. The board should be encouraged by laws
> and or principles to protect these individuals and representative bodies and
> to give them confidential direct access to someone independent on the board,
> often a member of an audit or an ethics committee.[217]

The ASX *Corporate Governance Principles and Recommendations* offer a gentle nudge in this direction within the commentary around the whistleblower policy, recommending that the policy should: clearly identify the types of concern to be reported under the policy – and to whom; explain how the identity of the whistleblower will be kept confidential, and how they will be protected from retaliation or victimisation; outline the processes to investigate reports made; provide training for both employees on reporting, and managers on receiving reports; and review the policy periodically.[218]

10.6 Conclusion

This chapter has explored the nature and significance of business ethics within the context of corporate governance. While difficult to define, business ethics can be seen at a macro level, taking account of the role of corporations in society, as well as at a micro level, in the way corporations operate as individuals. In order to unpack this further this chapter has used bad apples, bad cases and bad barrels as devices to explore the way ethical problems can arise, and analysed these with reference to three case studies: the HIH collapse, the LIBOR scandal and the destruction of Juukan Gorge. These case studies reveal the complex interactions that preceded the relevant events. In each case it is possible to attribute the outcomes to a mix of structures, policies, shared understandings and practices that together make up the ethics of the organisation.

---

217 Ibid 35.
218 ASX, *Corporate Governance Principles and Recommendations* (4th ed, 2019) 17.

In order to 'reduce unethical behavior, management first needs to understand and unravel the existing ethical culture'.[219] This will involve scrutiny of the way external regulation affects the corporation, as well as understanding internal processes, policies, narratives and practices that inhibit or encourage ethical action. External influences including general law, market activity, disclosure, gatekeeper activity and whistleblower regulation are all considered to be mechanisms that may change the way corporations respond to ethical matters. Internally, those leading corporations have a profound effect on the way those within the corporation see and respond to ethical dilemmas. The culture of the organisation, incorporating structures, policies and practices, will also be highly influential.

There can be no doubt that the interaction of business ethics with corporate governance poses many challenges. However, it also presents great opportunities. According to Tony Watson:

> Moralities are social constructions – guidelines for human action which people acting socially have devised to handle the problems of their existence in a contingent world. What we might try to do, therefore, as the inhabitants of organizations ... is to come fully to terms with the extent of our interdependencies and set out to create a good world.[220]

While this points out the agency of those working within organisations, it is also evident that a similar challenge is posed to policymakers, regulators, gatekeepers and community members.

---

219 Kaptein, 'Understanding unethical behavior by unraveling ethical culture' (2011) 64(6) *Human Relations* 843, 863.
220 Tony Watson, 'Ethical codes and moral communities: The Gunlaw Temptation, the Simon Solution and the David Dilemma' in Martin Parker (ed), *Ethics and Organizations* (Sage, 1998) 238, 267.

CORPORATE GOVERNANCE IN INTERNATIONAL AND GLOBAL CONTEXTS

11

CORPORATE GOVERNANCE IN THE UNITED STATES, THE UNITED KINGDOM, NEW ZEALAND, CANADA, SOUTH AFRICA, INDIA AND SINGAPORE

11.1 Introduction

In this chapter we give a brief overview of corporate governance in the United States ('US'), the United Kingdom ('UK'), New Zealand, Canada, South Africa, India and Singapore – some of the major Anglo-American corporate governance jurisdictions that are based on the unitary (one-tier) board model. In Chapter 12 we deal with corporate governance developments in the European Union ('EU'), the *G20/OECD Principles of Corporate Governance*, and corporate governance in Germany, Japan and China. The Principles include traditional Anglo-American corporate governance principles but go wider – as well as principles applying to a traditional unitary board structure, they include principles applying to a typical two-tier board structure.

11.2 United States

Lécia Vicente

11.2.1 Overview

The 2000s was a decade that saw a prolific number of corporate scandals worldwide, such as Enron, WorldCom, Tyco, Conseco, Adelphia, Skandia, Parmalat, Swissair, Mitsubishi Motors, Merrill Lynch, Waste Management, Sunbeam, and Seibu Railway. Such scandals were not unprecedented. When the Penn Central Company collapsed in the 1970s, the US witnessed what the Securities and Exchange Commission ('SEC') defined as 'the single largest bankruptcy in our nation's history'.[1]

---

1   Securities and Exchange Commission, *The Financial Collapse of the Penn Central Company: Staff Report of the Securities and Exchange Commission to the Special Subcommittee on*

The surprise and market disruption caused by the collapse of public companies worldwide changed corporate law history and ignited the development of corporate governance as a legal and regulatory discipline. This section examines the current corporate governance debates in the US, which will help the reader understand corporate governance models and legislative choices and how they may influence other parts of the world, including developing countries and emerging economies.

In the last two decades, corporate governance has evolved significantly. In the US, arguments in favour of corporate governance are sharper due to cyclical financial crises like the 2008 Global Financial Crisis ('GFC'), the COVID-19 pandemic and the 2021–23 global energy crisis.[2] Although corporate governance developed at the same time as the acceptance of shareholder primacy, the second decade of 2000s showed a clear trend towards stakeholders' interests and supporting environmental, social and governance ('ESG') reporting.[3]

Historically, corporate governance has been constantly reframed to respond to political and socioeconomic challenges, such as government shortcomings, corruption, corporate scandals, global financial crises, income inequality, racial inequities, gender discrimination and climate change.[4] Thus, the ongoing trend towards protecting stakeholders' interests may indicate corporations anticipate a paradigm shift.[5]

This section takes stock of corporate governance policies in the US, examines the current status of the corporate governance debate in that jurisdiction, reflects on future trends, and proposes new reflections and research avenues. Section 11.2.2 discusses the regulatory environment and the historical background of corporate governance in the US. Section 11.2.3 analyses the governing legislation and regulators, focusing on the legislative scope and aims. Section 11.2.4 covers the soft law in place, such as corporate governance codes, and enforcement. Section 11.2.5 contextualises corporate governance in the broader debate about sustainability. Section 11.2.6 outlines future areas of significance. Section 11.2.7 concludes by providing an overall perspective of corporate governance in the US.

11.2.2 Regulatory environment

11.2.2.1 The evolution of corporate governance in six periods

Historically, the evolution of corporate governance can be framed as six phases: the 1970s, following a widespread economic crisis and corruption scandals; the 1980s, a

Investigations (1972) <https://fraser.stlouisfed.org/files/docs/historical/house/1972house_fincolpenncentral.pdf>.

2   Nathan Rosenberg and Claudio R Frischtak, 'Technological innovations and long waves' (1984) 8(1) Cambridge Journal of Economics 7; Iyanatul Islam and S Verick, 'The Great Recession of 2008–09: Causes, consequences and policy responses' in Iyanatul Islam and S Verick (eds), From the Great Recession to Labour Market Recovery: Issues, Evidence and Policy Options (Palgrave Macmillan, 2011) 19; Stefano Ramelli and Alexander F Wagner, 'Feverish stock price reactions to COVID-19' (2020) 9(3) Review of Corporate Finance Studies 622.

3   Alex Edmans, Grow the Pie: How Great Companies Deliver both Purpose and Profit (Cambridge University Press, 2020); Gregory Louis, 'Unlocking progressive corporate governance: The black and brown HDFC key' (2021) 10(1) American University Business Law Review 79; Grant M Hayden and Matthew T Bodie, Reconstructing the Corporation: From Shareholder Primacy to Shared Governance (Cambridge University Press, 2021); Lucian A Bebchuk, Kobi Kastiel and Roberto Tallarita, 'Does enlightened shareholder value add value?' (2022) 77(3) Business Lawyer 731.

4   Mariana Pargendler, 'The corporate governance obsession' (2016) 42(2) Journal of Corporation Law 359.

5   Antoinette Handley, Business and Social Crisis in Africa (Cambridge University Press, 2020).

recovery period during which the market for corporate control emerged in the US; the 1990s, when the US corporate governance model spread throughout the world; the 2000s, which saw the collapse of Enron, WorldCom and other companies; the 2008 GFC; and post-2020, when the world was assaulted by the COVID-19 pandemic, corporate governance measures internalised racial reckoning following the summer of 2020, and climate change mitigation became the target of SEC regulations. It is important to understand the driving forces in each period.[6]

An excursion through economic crises: From the 1929 Great Depression to the 1970s

In 1932, Adolf Berle and Gardiner Means published *The Modern Corporation and Private Property*.[7] They called our attention to agency problems deriving from separation of ownership and control in publicly-held corporations in the US. However, their proposed solution for managers' disregard of shareholders' interests was not based on finding an internal equilibrium between interests of different corporate constituencies. Rather, they suggested the adoption of regulatory mechanisms to tame the managerial impetus, in line with the prominent role the federal government assumed with the New Deal.[8]

'Managerial capitalism' emerged between 1930 and 1970.[9] In what can be defined as true 'Berle-Means' firms, managers had extensive managerial power, and managerial hierarchies would often replicate themselves.[10]

It was not until the emergence of the theory of the firm in the 1970s that the firm's internal corporate governance became the focus of the business and economic literature. In the late 1970s and mid-1980s, Oliver Williamson applied transaction costs theory to firm behaviour.[11] In the late 1970s and early 1980s, Michael Jensen and William Meckling, Bengt Holmström, and Eugene Fama, individually and in co-authorship with Michael Jensen, created principal-agent models that led to the development of the agency costs theory of the firm.[12] In the late 1980s and 1990s, Sanford Grossman,

6 Henry Hansmann and Reinier Kraakman, 'The end of history for corporate law' (2001) 89(2) *Georgetown Law Journal* 439; Dorothy S Lund and Elizabeth Pollman, 'The corporate governance machine' (2021) 121(8) *Columbia Law Review* 2563; Pargendler, 'The corporate governance obsession' (2016) 42(2) *Journal of Corporation Law* 359.

7 Adolf A Berle and Gardiner C Means, *The Modern Corporation and Private Property* (Routledge, 2017) (first published in 1932 by Transaction Publishers).

8 Mark H Leff, *The Limits of Symbolic Reform: The New Deal and Taxation, 1933–1939* (Cambridge University Press, 1984).

9 Martin Gelter, 'The pension system and the rise of shareholder primacy' (2013) 43(3) *Seton Hall Law Review* 909, 910.

10 Ibid. See also Myles L Mace, *The Growth and Development of Executives* (Division of Research, Graduate School of Business Administration, Harvard University, 1950); Myles L Mace, *Directors: Myth and Reality* (Division of Research, Graduate School of Business Administration, Harvard University Press, 1971); and Detlev F Vagts, 'Directors: Myth and reality' (1976) 31 *Business Lawyer* 1227, 1232.

11 Oliver Williamson, *Markets and Hierarchies: Analysis and Antitrust Implications, A Study in the Economics of Internal Organization* (The Free Press, 1975); Oliver Williamson, *The Economic Institutions of Capitalism Firms, Markets, Relational Contracts* (The Free Press, 1985).

12 Michael C Jensen and William H Meckling, 'Theory of the firm: Managerial behavior, agency costs and ownership structure' (1976) 3(4) *Journal of Financial Economics* 305; Bengt Holmström, 'Moral hazard and observability' (1979) 10(1) *Bell Journal of Economics* 74; Eugene F Fama, 'Agency problems and the theory of the firm' (1980) 88(2) *Journal of Political Economy* 288;

Oliver Hart, and John More created models that shaped the property rights theory of the firm, also referred to as 'modern property rights theory' or the 'GHM model'.[13] Earlier, in the late 1930s, Ronald Coase had written his ground-breaking article, 'The Nature of Firm', in which he presented a model that conducted micro-analysis of the market to explain market participants' choices that led to the emergence of the firm.[14] Nevertheless, Coase's ideas were only subject to careful scrutiny nearly five decades later.

'Corporate governance' as a subject only became mainstream in the 1970s. Economic and political turmoil caused by the oil and energy crisis, the devastating collapse of the Penn Central Railroad, and the Watergate scandal brought corporate governance to the limelight.[15] In 1977, *Taming the Giant Corporation* by Ralph Nader, Mark J Green and Joel Seligman became one of the earliest academic accounts of corporate governance, denouncing the pervasiveness of corporate irresponsibility and enticing civil society and governments to make corporations accountable.[16]

Nader, Green and Seligman's book came a few years after Milton Friedman wrote a popular op-ed in the *New York Times*.[17] Friedman maintained that only people can have responsibilities, not businesses. He perceived managers as agents of the owners of the business. According to Friedman, managers' sole responsibility would be to the business owners and running a business to be profitable. Friedman's ideas influenced the next decade of the debate on corporate governance.

Economic recovery and the emergence of the market for corporate control

In the 1980s, there was increasing interest in corporate governance, coinciding with the US economic recovery. The emergence of hostile takeovers, the market for corporate control, and equity-based executive compensation signalled the recovery. Managerial capitalism gave way to investor capitalism where the market created incentives for managers to prioritise shareholders' interests and share value. Simultaneously, the rise of independent directors in the US was notable.[18]

Eugene F Fama and Michael C Jensen, 'Separation of ownership and control' (1983) 26(2) *Journal of Law and Economics* 301.

13 Sanford J Grossman and Oliver D Hart, 'The costs and benefits of ownership: A theory of vertical and lateral integration' (1986) 94(4) *Journal of Political Economy* 691; Oliver Hart and John Moore, 'Property rights and the nature of the firm' (1990) 98(6) *Journal of Political Economy* 1119; Jongwook Kim and Joseph T Mahoney, 'Property rights theory, transaction costs theory, and agency theory: An organizational economics approach to strategic management' (2005) 26(4) *Managerial and Decision Economics* 223, 224.

14 Ronald H Coase, 'The nature of the firm' (1937) 4(16) *Economica* 38.

15 Roger F Murray, 'The Penn Central debacle: Lessons for financial analysis' (1970) 26(2) *Journal of Finance* 327.

16 Ralph Nader, Mark J Green and Joel Seligman, *Taming the Giant Corporation: How the Largest Corporations Control Our Lives* (WW Norton & Company, 1977).

17 Milton Friedman, 'A Friedman doctrine – The social responsibility of business is to increase its profits', *The New York Times* (13 September 1970). For a slightly more detailed discussion and to consider the Friedman Doctrine in context, see Section 1.5.1.3.

18 Jeffrey N Gordon, 'The rise of independent directors in the United States, 1950–2005: Of shareholder value and stock market prices' (2007) 59(6) *Stanford Law Review* 1465.

The discussion about corporate governance intensified in 1982 with the drafting of the *Principles of Corporate Governance and Structure: Restatement and Recommendations* (the 'Principles') by the American Law Institute ('ALI'). The project was designed as a restatement of the law.

Unlike statutory laws, which are binding, restatements are not binding. US corporate law is essentially state (non-federal) law, and the application of these broad principles drafted by the ALI varies between states. The *Proposed Final Draft of the Principles of Corporate Governance* was approved in 1992. The final version of the Principles was published in 1994.[19]

The globalisation of the US corporate governance model

During this period of the rise of corporate governance, there were three noteworthy international events: the fall of the Berlin Wall in 1989, the end of the Cold War, and globalisation. Corporate governance itself became global as there was a shared goal to revitalise economies in the West. Rafael La Porta, Florencio Lopez-de-Silanes, Andrei Schleifer, and Robert W Vishny ('LLSV') created a line of research referred to as 'legal origin theory' ('LOT').[20] They used an empirical, statistical method to elaborate differences between legal families. They concluded that common law countries, such as the UK and the US, economically outperformed civil law countries because common law countries housed more efficient legal institutions. Despite criticism, their investigation was used as a foil for the development of corporate governance in the US and its export to other countries.

The new wave of corporate scandals in the 2000s

The shift from managerial to shareholder capitalism that had been gradually developing significantly influenced the corporation's internal dynamic. Political circumstances and economic constructions determined the change of the investment landscape.

The continuous rise of institutional investors and their activism is remarkable.[21] We have been witnessing a phenomenon of 'deretailisation', which alludes to retail investors' loss of power vis-à-vis institutional investors' increasing activism.[22] Shareholder activism influences how constituencies interact inside the corporation.

Economic models that substantiate transaction costs theory and agency costs theory of the firm were applied to the corporation. Corporate governance democratised the

19   Melvin A Eisenberg, 'An overview of the Principles of Corporate Governance' (1993) 48(4)
      The Business Lawyer 1271.
20   Rafael La Porta et al, 'Law and finance' (1998) 106(6) *Journal of Political Economy* 113; Rafael La Porta,
      Florencio Lopez-de-Silanes and Andrei Schleifer, 'The economic consequences of legal origins'
      (2008) 46(2) *Journal of Economic Literature* 285.
21   Sarah C Haan, 'Is American Shareholder Activism a Social Movement?' International Journal for
      Financial Services' (2022) *Revues Internationale des Services Financiers* 21.
22   See Neil Bhutta et al, 'Changes in US family finances from 2016 to 2019: Evidence from
      the Survey of Consumer Finances' (2020) 106(5) *Federal Reserve Bulletin* 18 <https://www
      .federalreserve.gov/econres/scfindex.htm>.

corporation by empowering shareholders' activism against agency problems and potential management abuses.[23] Shareholder wealth maximisation and shareholder primacy were widely taught in business schools due to the incentives managers received to align their interests with shareholders' interests.

In 2001, Henry Hansmann and Reinier Kraakman published their article 'The End of History for Corporate Law'.[24] Some commentators like Mark Roe maintained that political forces created a clear effect of path-dependence in corporate law.[25] Hansmann and Kraakman opined that the law of business corporations had already achieved an extraordinary degree of worldwide convergence toward shareholder primacy at the end of the 19th century. The Enron, WorldCom and other scandals took the world aback at the turn of the 20th century. Incentives, such as executive compensation for managers to align their interests with shareholders interests, led managers to pursue short-term share value-maximisation.

The 2008 GFC, the 2020 COVID-19 pandemic, social justice and political polarisation

The 2008 GFC had a tremendous impact on financial markets and made clear that corporate governance was unstable. It forced the reassessment of the paradigm based on shareholder wealth maximisation.[26] It is noteworthy that at this time the discussion about the separation of the roles of CEO and chairman of the board was front and centre.[27]

In 2020, the COVID-19 pandemic disrupted the world and increased the existing political polarisation over measures to curb the spread of the pandemic.[28] Furthermore, the broadcast of racially motivated acts of violence ignited a phenomenon of racial awakening led by the Black Lives Matter ('BLM') movement. Many corporations pledged to make diversity and inclusion efforts and create better workplace environments for their employees.[29]

23   It is important to note that, despite efforts to democratise the corporation, shareholders were blind to the risks of subprime mortgages that led to the 2008 GFC. Shareholders were powerless in curbing the wealth gap between CEOs and workers, and in getting companies to focus on their carbon footprints.

24   Hansmann and Kraakman, 'The end of history for corporate law' (2001) 89 *Georgetown Law Journal* 439.

25   Mark J Roe, *Strong Managers, Weak Owners: The Political Roots of American Corporate Finance* (Princeton University Press, 1994); Franklin A Gevurtz, 'The globalization of corporate law: The end of history or a never-ending story?' (2011) 86(3) *Washington Law Review* 475.

26   Sher Verick and Iyanatul Islam, *The Great Recession of 2008–2009: Causes, Consequences and Policy Responses* (Employment Working Paper No 61, International Labour Organization, 2012).

27   B Ram Baliga, R Charles Moyer and Ramesh S Rao, 'CEO duality and firm performance: What's the fuss?' (1996) 17(1) *Strategic Management Journal* 41.

28   Matt C Howard, 'Are face masks a partisan issue during the COVID-19 pandemic? Differentiating political ideology and political party affiliation' (2021) 57(1) *International Journal of Psychology* 153; John Kerr, Costas Panagopoulos and Sander van der Linden, 'Political polarization on COVID-19 pandemic response in the United States' (2021) 179 *Personality and Individual Differences* 110892; Joe Nogera and Bethany McLean, *The Big Fail: What the Pandemic Revealed about Who America Protects and Who It Leaves Behind* (Portfolio Penguin, 2023).

29   Blair Johnson, 'How the Black Lives Matter movement enhanced corporate governance in 2020' (2021) 8(1) *Emory Corporate Governance and Accountability Review* 99; Veronica Root Martinez and Gina-Gail S Fletcher, 'Equality metrics' (2021) 130 *Yale Law Journal Forum* 869. See also Alisha

The SEC proposed rules to increase board diversity, a measure that was accompanied by proposals by NASDAQ.[30] Additionally, concerns about climate change reignited the debate about corporations' role in promoting ESG matters and sustainability.[31]

11.2.3 Legislation and regulators

Besides Berle and Means' *The Modern Corporation and Private Property* (1932)[32] and Jensen and Meckling's *Theory of Firm* (1976),[33] important statutory and case law shaped the history of the public corporation and corporate governance. Federal securities law (1933, 1934),[34] the *Williams Act* (1968),[35] *Edgar v MITE Corporation* (1982),[36] *CTS v Dynamics* (1987),[37] the SEC 1992 Release,[38] the *Private Securities Litigation Reform Act* ('PSLRA') (1995),[39] the *Sarbanes Oxley Act* ('SOX') (2002),[40] the *Dodd-Frank Wall Street Reform and Consumer Protection Act* ('Dodd-Frank') (2010),[41] and the *Jumpstart Our Business Startups (JOBS) Act* (2012)[42] are but a few examples. At the state level, corporate law has been fundamentally shaped by case law.[43]

Ebrahimji, 'Nike is saying "Don't Do It" in a message about racism in America', *CNN* (30 May 2020) <https://edition.cnn.com/2020/05/30/business/nike-dont-do-it-message-trnd/index.html>; Fernando Duarte, 'Black Lives Matter: Do companies really support the cause?', *BBC World Service* (12 June 2020) <https://www.bbc.com/worklife/article/20200612-black-lives-matter-do-companies-really-support-the-cause>; Tom Braithwaite, 'How companies decided that black lives matter', *Financial Times* (online, 4 June 2020) <https://www.ft.com/content/6bd46c48-ee90-42b8-af70-78d949025c1d>.

30 Lisa M Fairfax, 'Board diversity revisited: New rationale, same old story?' (2011) 89 *North Carolina Law Review* 855; Lécia Vicente, Lucia Ruggeri and Kozue Kashiwazaki, 'Beyond lipstick and high heels: Three tell-tale narratives of female leadership in the United States, Italy and Japan' (2021) 32(1) *Hastings Women's Law Journal* 3; Jesse M Fried, 'Will Nasdaq's diversity rules harm investors?' (2021) 12 *Harvard Business Law Review Online* 1; June Carbone, 'Board diversity: People or pathways?' (2022) 85(1) *Law and Contemporary Problems* 167. See also US Securities and Exchange Commission, 'Statement on Nasdaq's Diversity Proposals – A Positive First Step for Investors (6 August 2021) <https://www.sec.gov/news/public-statement/statement-nasdaq-diversity-080621>.

31 Elizabeth Demers and Marcel Metzner, 'TCFD climate risk disclosures: Early evidence on the "gold standard"' (2021) (unpublished manuscript on file with the authors); Quinn Curtis, Jill E Fisch and Adriana Z Robertson, 'Do ESG mutual funds deliver on their promises' (2021) 120(3) *Michigan Law Review* 393; Elizabeth Pollman, *The Making and Meaning of ESG* (Research Paper No 22–23, University of Pennsylvania Institute for Law and Economics, 31 October 2022) <https://ssrn.com/abstract=4219857>.

32 Berle and Means, *The Modern Corporation and Private Property* (2017).

33 Jensen and Meckling, 'Theory of the firm' (1976) 3(4) *Journal of Financial Economics* 305.

34 *Securities Act of 1933*, 48 Stat 74, 15 USC 77a–77mm; *Securities Exchange Act of 1934*, 48 Stat 881, 15 USC 78a–78kk.

35 *Williams Act of 1968*, Pub L No 90–439, 82 Stat 454 (1968).

36 *Edgar v MITE Corporation*, 457 US 624 (1982).

37 *CTS Corporation v Dynamics Corporation of America*, 481 US 69 (1987).

38 'Regulation of Communications Among Shareholders', Release No 34-31326, 52 SEC Docket 2028, Release No IC-19031 (1992).

39 *Private Securities Litigation Reform Act of 1995*, Pub L No 104–67, 109 Stat 737 (1995).

40 *Sarbanes-Oxley Act of 2002*, Pub L No 107–204 (2002).

41 *Dodd-Frank Wall Street Reform and Consumer Protection Act*, Pub L No 111–203 (2010).

42 *Jumpstart Our Business Startups Act*, Pub L No 112–106 (2012).

43 There are important cases at the state level, such *as Rosenfeld v Fairchild Engine and Airplane Corporation*, 309 NY 168, 128 NE 2d 291 (1955); *Cheff v Mathes*, 41 Del Ch 494, 199 A 2d 548 (1964); *Smith v Van Gorkom*, 488 A 2d 858 (Del, 1985); *Unocal Corporation v Mesa Petroleum Co*, 493 A 2d 946 (Del 1985); *Moran v Household International, Inc*, 490 A 2d 1059 (Del Ch 1985); *Revlon, Inc v MacAndrews & Forbes Holdings, Inc*, 506 A 2d 173 (Del 1985); *Paramount Communications, Inc v Time Inc*, 571 A 2d 1140 (Del 1989); *Unitrin, Inc v American General Corporation*, 651 A 2d 1361 (Del 1995); *Lyondell Chemical Co v Ryan*, 970 A 2d 235 (Del 2009); and *Corwin v KKR Financial Holdings LLC*, 125 A 3d 304 (Del 2015).

Although corporate law is essentially state law, the role of securities law in the development of corporate governance should be stressed.[44] In 1933, Congress enacted the *Securities Act of 1933*, which requires companies issuing stock to disclose certain information, namely regarding the business and capital structure, and file periodic reports depending on the amount of the company's assets. The *Securities Exchange Act of 1934* established the SEC.

The *Securities Act of 1933* and the *Securities Exchange Act of 1934* revitalised the financial market by regulating security exchange and over-the-counter markets, preventing fraud, ensuring transparency, and protecting the public interest and investors. Achieving these goals was of utmost importance considering the excesses of the 1920s that led to the stock market crash of 1929 and the Great Depression.

The SEC is pivotal for achieving the political goals established by Congress. Pursuant to the 1933 Act, the SEC may engage in rule-making and be required to determine whether an action is necessary or appropriate in the public interest. The SEC will consider whether an action will promote not only investors' protection but also efficiency, competition, and capital formation.

The SEC's extensive powers to regulate the financial markets, investigate contraventions of the law, and impose civil and criminal sanctions to enforce the law have grown through the years. This phenomenon increases after each market disruption or crash, such as after World War II in 1945, in the late 1970s, in the early 2000s with the enactment of SOX, and after the GFC with the enactment of Dodd-Frank.[45]

Congress enacted SOX in 2002 to protect investors by improving accuracy and reliability of corporate disclosures made pursuant to securities law. The aim was to strengthen regulation of the auditing of US public companies, which became a priority after the public downfall of accounting firms like Arthur Andersen. To that end, SOX created a quasi-public institution: the Public Company Accounting Oversight Board ('PCAOB').[46]

Dodd-Frank, enacted in 2010, was crucial to developing corporate governance rules for publicly-held companies and financial institutions. Its impetus was to avoid the moral hazard, the 'too big to fail' financial institutions, conflicts of interest and lack of transparency, and market participants' bounded rationality[47] that contributed to the systemic risk that led to the 2008 GFC.[48]

---

44 Marc I Steinberg, Franklin A Gevurtz and Eric Chafee, *Global Issues in Securities Law* (West Academic Publishing, 2013).

45 Roberta Romano, 'The Sarbanes-Oxley Act and the making of quack corporate governance' (2005) 114(7) *Yale Law Journal* 1521; John C Coffee Jr, 'The political economy of Dodd-Frank: Why financial reform tends to be frustrated and systemic risk perpetuated' (2012) 97 *Cornell Law Review* 1019; Peter Conti-Brown and Michael Ohlrogge, 'Financial crises and legislation' (2022) 4(3) *Journal of Financial Crises* 1.

46 John C Coates IV, 'The goals and promise of the Sarbanes-Oxley Act' (2007) 21(1) *Journal of Economic Perspectives* 91; Coffee, 'The political economy of Dodd-Frank: Why financial reform tends to be frustrated and systemic risk perpetuated' (2012) 97(5) *Cornell Law Review* 1019, 1036–7.

47 Herbert A Simon, *Administrative Behavior: A Study of Decision-Making Processes in Administrative Organization* (The Macmillan Company, 1947).

48 Members of the Corporate Governance Committee, ABA Business Law Section, 'Dodd-Frank governance rules three years later' (2013) 69(1) *Business Lawyer* 133. One of the biggest risks facing corporations is climate risk. In 2010, the SEC managed to elaborate on a guidance on climate risk disclosure that was essentially abandoned, which has raised scepticism around the SEC's efforts in the aftermath of the GFC.

Market instability puts pressure on corporations as they anticipate political or economic crises and take measures for their survival.[49] The SEC's regulatory role has been vital, although its expanded powers have not been enough to prevent severe economic crises and market disruptions.[50]

11.2.4 Codes of practice

In the context of corporate scandals and broader political and economic crises, the Council of the American Law Institute ('ALI') authorised the Corporate Project in 1978.[51] The *Principles of Corporate Governance and Structure: Restatement and Recommendations* ('the Principles') emerged from that project to improve corporate law and governance.

The Principles were developed from the 1980s through the 1990s. They were published in 1994. In the 1980s, the draft was heavily criticised by many, including the Business Roundtable in 1983, for imposing non-consensual regulatory constraints on corporate boards.[52] Thirty-six years later, in 2019, the Business Roundtable issued a joint statement of 181 CEOs of major corporations committed to 'lead their companies for the benefit of all stakeholders – customers, employees, suppliers, communities and shareholders'.[53] This statement points to a trend towards protecting stakeholders' rights and contradicts the shareholder-centric approach that the Principles apply.[54]

The Principles are an essential tool to understand directors' and officers' roles, namely their duties and responsibilities vis-à-vis the corporation and shareholders. They combine the restatement of black-letter provisions with recommendations and commentators' notes. Given their nature as a restatement and a product of formal codification, the Principles are not binding. They restate the law by assembling principles and rules that have been laid out and developed by jurisprudence. Additionally, they make recommendations should there not be applicable or well-fitting case law or statutory law.

The Principles are divided in seven parts. A few issues, particularly those related to the corporation's purpose, directors' fiduciary duties and the business judgment rule, have been subject to longstanding scrutiny in the corporate law and governance literature. In pt II, § 2.01, the Principles define fundamental purpose to be 'the conduct of business activities with a view to enhancing corporate profit and shareholder gain'. However, managers' pursuit of profit and shareholder wealth maximisation may give way to legal requirements and ethical and humanitarian considerations.

---

49   Handley, *Business and Social Crisis in Africa* (2020); Jagdish Sheth, 'Business of business is more than business: Managing during the Covid crisis' (2020) 88 *Industrial Marketing Management* 261.
50   Vincent Barnett, *Kondratiev and the Dynamics of Economic Development: Long Cycles and Industrial Growth in Historical Context* (Palgrave Macmillan, 1998).
51   Joel Seligman, 'A sheep in wolf's clothing: The American Law Institute Principles of Corporate Governance Project' (1987) 55(2) *George Washington Law Review* 325.
52   Business Roundtable, *Principles of Corporate Governance* (Harvard Law School Forum on Corporate Governance, 8 September 2016) <https://corpgov.law.harvard.edu/2016/09/08/principles-of-corporate-governance/>.
53   Business Roundtable, 'Business Roundtable redefines the purpose of a corporation to promote "an economy that serves all Americans"' (19 Aug 2019) <https://www.businessroundtable.org/business-roundtable-redefines-the-purpose-of-a-corporation-to-promote-an-economy-that-serves-all-americans>.
54   For additional discussion of some recent developments in the US, see Section 2.2.1.

Part IV articulates directors' and officers' fiduciary duties, namely the duty of care and respective standards that are applied to the management of the corporation's ongoing operations and decision-making process. When they face liability, directors are protected by the business judgment rule set forth in § 4.01, which maintains that they are not liable for a mistake if their business judgment was in good faith. As posited in a report about the emergence of new legal forms for business in the US, this rule 'provides tremendous discretion for directors to balance shareholder and other stakeholder interests in all but the most extreme circumstances'.[55]

The Principles have shaped corporate governance in the US and been used as a reference for corporate governance debates in other jurisdictions. However, the approach used in the Principles is still controversial, particularly at a time when there is a renewed debate about corporate purpose and sustainability.

11.2.5 Sustainability

In 1987, the Brundtland Report defined sustainability as 'meeting the needs of the present without compromising the ability of future generations to meet their own needs'.[56] Although meritorious, that definition does not specify the role of corporations in implementing sustainability goals.

Corporations are inherently political.[57] Historically, corporate governance has constituted a means to allocate to the corporation what one might define as governmental functions: to protect the environment, and promote economic and social equality.[58] For authors who side with the idea of progressive corporate law, the corporation's public responsibility as an extension of the governmental arm results from the public nature of the corporation since its inception when it was created by charters issued by the government in the 19th century.[59] Thus, for such authors corporations ought to take a significant stand towards sustainability. It is noteworthy that the International Sustainability Standards Board ('ISSB') was created in November 2021 to help corporations meet international investors' concerns about sustainability and demands for reliable ESG reporting.

Delaware courts have upheld shareholder primacy and board of directors' decisions favouring the corporation's and shareholders' interests.[60] Former Delaware Supreme Court Chief Justice Leo E Strine argued that corporations are indifferent to 'societally

---

55 Lécia Vicente, 'The social enterprise: A new form of enterprise' (2022)70(1) *American Journal of Comparative Law* i155.

56 United Nations, World Commission on Environment and Development, *Report of the World Commission on Environment and Development: Our Common Future* (1987).

57 Handley, *Business and Social Crisis in Africa* (2020).

58 Pargendler, 'The corporate governance obsession' (2016) 42(2) *Journal of Corporation Law* 359.

59 Gregory Louis, 'Unlocking progressive corporate governance: The Black and Brown HDFC key' (2021)10(1) *American University Business Law Review* 79. See also Margaret M Blair, 'Locking in capital: What corporate law achieved for business organizers in the nineteenth century' (2003) 51(2) *UCLA Law Review* 387; Timothy Guinnane et al, 'Putting the corporation in its place' (2007) 8(3) *Enterprise and Society* 687, 714–23.

60 Empirically, further work needs to be done in this area to understand whether Delaware Courts tend to uphold managers' decisions that favour the corporation's and shareholders' interests or whether they uphold management decisions that favour managers' own interests, especially those of reputable managers, in the name of shareholder primacy.

destructive externalities';[61] they are designed to deliver short-term profits and take risks. He maintained that '[t]he public interest, in the end, depends on protection by the public's elected representatives in the form of law'.[62]

However, the rise of ESG investing over the last years in the US, which has been ignited by palpable concerns about climate change and social justice, seems to contradict the perception that corporations are or should understandably be only profit-driven. While the *Principles of Corporate Governance* postulate shareholder wealth maximisation, the ESG debate is based on the understanding that, although value is paramount, ESG issues matter.[63]

The ESG debate is not clear-cut because the definition of the term and impact of the concept have become a source of discord – ESG investing has been characterised as noisy, unreliable, 'greenwashing' and a marketing stunt.[64] Furthermore, ESG rating providers disagree on companies' ESG performance ratings which influences investing and the market's perception of companies, and makes it difficult to link executive compensation to ESG performance.[65]

Despite lack of consensus on the merit of ESG data, in reality, ESG considerations may influence how courts review board decisions, particularly regarding board members' discharge of their fiduciary duties.[66] Additionally, ESG considerations may impact internal dynamics of the corporation, relationships between different corporate constituencies, and the scope of those constituencies' rights, such as certain stakeholders' right to vote on ESG-related issues.

The ESG movement's purpose is to create incentives to change the corporation's design and integrate corporate objectives that change how the corporation makes a profit. Does corporate governance adequately equip the corporation to internalise environmental and social harm, to consider long-term rather than short-term goals, if necessary, to diversify its board, and use the political process to further its sustainability objectives?

This discussion is longstanding in the US, and it has been highlighted in a report about legal forms for social enterprise.[67] As stated therein, 'from *Dodge v Ford* in 1919[68] to Milton

---

61 Leo E Strine Jr, 'Our continuing struggle with the idea that for-profit corporations seek profit' (2012) 47 *Wake Forest Law Review*, 135, 136.

62 Leo E Strine, Jr, 'Our continuing struggle with the idea that for-profit corporations seek profit' (2012) 47 *Wake Forest Law Review* 135, 155. For an opposite view, see Alan Palmiter, *Capitalism, Heal Thyself* (2021) <https://papers.ssrn.com/sol3/papers.cfm?abstract_id=3940395>.

63 Stuart L Gillan, Andrew Koch and Laura T Starks, 'Firms and social responsibility: A review of ESG and CRS research in corporate finance' (2021) 66 *Journal of Corporate Finance* 101889; Quinn Curtis, Jill Fisch and Adriana Z Robertson, 'Do ESG funds deliver on their promises?' (2021) 120(3) *Michigan Law Review* 393.

64 Andy Kessler, 'The many reasons ESG is a loser', *The Wall Street Journal* (online, 10 July 2022) <https://www.wsj.com/articles/esg-loser-funds-costs-basis-points-blackrock-500-environment-green-sec-11657461127?mod=article_inline>; Sabrina Chevannes, 'Is sustainability just a PR stunt?' *Entrepreneur* (2 June 2022) <https://www.entrepreneur.com/business-news/is-sustainability-just-a-pr-stunt/426306>; Thomson Reuters Institute, *ESG: Navigating Past the Noise* (White Paper, 2023) <https://www.thomsonreuters.com/en-us/posts/esg/esg-navigating-past-the-noise/>.

65 Florian Berg, Julian F Kölbel and Roberto Rigobon, 'Aggregate confusion: The divergence of ESG ratings' (2022) 26(6) *Review of Finance* 1315. For an opposing view, see Quinn Curtis, Jill Fisch and Adriana Z Robertson, 'Do ESG funds deliver on their promises?' (2021)120(3) *Michigan Law Review* 393.

66 E Christopher Johnson Jr, John H Stout and Ashley C Walter, 'Profound change: The evolution of ESG' (2020) 75(4) *Business Lawyer* 2567, 2593. See also *Shlensky v Wrigley*, 95 Ill App 2d 173, 237 NE 2d 776 (Ill App Ct, 1968).

67 Vicente, 'The social enterprise' (2022) 70(1) *American Journal of Comparative Law* i155, i170.

68 *Dodge v Ford Motor Co*, 204 Mich 459, 170 NW 668 (Mich, 1919).

Friedman's 1970 *New York Times* op-ed,[69] the ALI's *Principles of Corporate Governance* in the 1980s through the 1990s[70] and the Business Roundtable Statement in 2019,[71] the corporation's purpose has been profusely debated'.[72] Currently, there are two different but reconcilable views. Some understand that the corporation is more integrative than we perceive, and its profit may arise from integrating the interests of all the corporation touches.[73] Others maintain that the corporation should realise its profit without integrative concerns.[74] Both views agree that the corporation's sole purpose is profit-making.

11.2.6 Future directions

Corporate governance will likely take new directions. A range of new developments will be subject to new regulation and market approaches devised by boards of directors, namely:

- significant monetary liquidity
- the role of policy and regulation vis-à-vis the market's self-regulatory capability to avoid or reduce market distortions and climate change's negative financial impact[75]
- the influence of technology and communication tools on financial markets
- the rise of artificial intelligence ('AI') and what can be called the Fourth Industrial Revolution[76]
- human capital management[77]
- cybersecurity risk governance[78]
- the increasing importance of institutional investors' demands and activism[79]
- new proxy-voting guidelines for these investors
- board of directors' compliance and oversight effectiveness
- sustainability disclosures imposed by the SEC, and
- a greater attachment of corporations to causes regarding equity, diversity, and political involvement.[80]

---

69 Friedman, 'A Friedman doctrine', *The New York Times* (13 September 1970).
70 The American Law Institute, *Principles of the Law, Corporate Governance: Analysis and Recommendations* (1994).
71 Business Roundtable, 'Business Roundtable redefines the purpose of a corporation to promote "an economy that serves all Americans"' (19 Aug 2019).
72 Vicente, 'The social enterprise' (2022)70 *The American Journal of Comparative Law* i155, i170.
73 Alan Palmiter, *Sustainable Corporations* (Aspen Publishing, 2022).
74 Strine, 'Our continuing struggle with the idea that for-profit corporations seek profit' (2012) 47(1) *Wake Forest Law Review* 135.
75 John Armour, Luca Enriques and Thom Wetzer, 'Mandatory corporate climate disclosures: Now, but how?' (2021) (3) *Columbia Business Law Review* 1085.
76 See discussion in Section 2.7.2.
77 George S Georgiev, 'The human capital management movement in US corporate law' (2021) 95(3) *Tulane Law Review* 639.
78 Kristen Eichensehr and Cathy Hwang, 'National Security Creep in Corporate Transactions (2023) 123(2) *Columbia Law Review* 549.
79 Matt Philips, 'Exxon's board defeat signals the rise of social-good activists', *The New York Times* (online, 9 June 2021) <https://www.nytimes.com/2021/06/09/business/exxon-mobil-engine-no1-activist.html>. See also Tom CW Lin, 'Incorporating social activism' (2018) 98(6) *Boston University Law Review* 1535.
80 Aaron A Dhir, *Challenging Boardroom Homogeneity: Corporate Law, Governance, And Diversity* (Cambridge University Press, 2015).

These changes require institutions, such as the SEC, the Commodity Futures Trading Commission and the Federal Reserve, to engage in a thorough evaluation of the financial market and assess the effects of varying policies implemented over the last two decades.[81]

11.2.7 Conclusion

Corporate governance in the US has come a long way since the time of the Great Depression in 1929 and the years that followed it. The power shift from corporate executives to financiers or institutional shareholders is remarkable. Institutional shareholders have taken on the function that the government never was able to assume. Depending on the market's characteristics, corporations may assume major political roles. Contemporaneously, the corporation's political role is less insular and more interconnected, for it follows global trends. Among those trends are activist investors open to changing the society through their financial investments. This trend has ignited empirical research on financial markets' behaviour.[82]

Additionally, enhanced scrutiny of board of directors by shareholders and regulators is indicative of several aspects. Corporate governance substitutes the lack of government in essential areas of social welfare; it helps corporations adjust to the signs of our time by embracing corporate social responsibility and ESG terminology that may expand the scope of compliance scrutiny and fiduciary duties.[83] Corporate governance influences the composition of the boardroom to circumvent the detachment of the board of directors from the make-up of the American society. The materiality of climate change, political polarisation, economic inequality and social injustice affects corporations' bottom line. Corporate governance rules are malleable as legislatures have been successful in creating new requirements. However, companies' performance standard continues to be significantly influenced by shareholder primacy that requires boards of directors prioritise shareholder wealth maximisation.

It is unclear whether there will be future statutory action that leads to a serious paradigm shift toward other stakeholders.[84] The manifest move of corporate power from the C-suite to institutional investors raises the question as to which factors contribute to profitability.

11.3 United Kingdom

Suren Gomtsian

11.3.1 Overview

The UK has been an early mover (but not the first)[85] in promoting high standards of corporate governance of firms. Most of the initial reforms in the country's corporate

81 Jens Frankenreiter et al, 'Cleaning corporate governance' (2021) 170(1) *University of Pennsylvania Law Review* 1.

82 Zaghum Umar et al, 'A tale of company fundamentals vs sentiment driven pricing: The case of GameStop' (2021) 30 *Journal of Behavioral and Experimental Finance* 100501.

83 Stephen Bainbridge, 'Don't compound the Caremark mistake by extending it to ESG oversight' (2022) 77 *Business Lawyer* 651.

84 Lund and Pollman, 'The corporate governance machine' (2021) 121(8) *Columbia Law Review* 2563.

85 The term 'corporate governance' was used routinely in the US as early as the 1970s. See Brian R Cheffins, 'The rise of corporate governance in the UK: When and why' (2015) 68(1) *Current Legal*

governance regime, which date back to early 1990s, were not path-breaking and endorsed ideas and recommendations already proposed in scholarly work or elsewhere. But the UK's innovative approach of using 'comply or explain' codes of best practice to promote good governance standards has become a standard model for corporate governance reforms in many countries and for the governance principles promoted by multilateral organisations.[86] The ambition to maintain the country's status as a corporate governance norm exporter, as well as the need to keep pace with the changing corporate landscape, have served as a strong encouragement for the promoters of UK corporate governance standards to innovate and regularly update the corporate governance regime.

Corporate governance in listed companies in the UK is based on two pillars: governance practices of the board of directors and stewardship by investors. The board of directors has a central role in overseeing the company's business and operating matters. Effectively functioning boards monitor corporate executives better and reduce managerial agency problems.[87] Accordingly, boards, as the 'most prominent actor in corporate governance',[88] have been the main target of corporate governance reforms in the UK, especially during the early 1990s and 2000s.

The second pillar – stewardship by shareholders and investors in general – aims to improve the effective and independent board oversight of a company's business by encouraging shareholders to create a strong and well-functioning board. Actively engaged shareholders achieve this by participating in the formation of the board of directors, monitoring the board's activities, and regularly communicating and engaging with the board. Additionally, where boards are not willing or incapable to accommodate shareholders' interests, shareholders can initiate shareholder-sponsored proposals or, as a measure of last resort, remove directors.

The effectiveness of these two pillars is supported by information disclosure and transparency rules. Boards rely on corporate disclosures to perform their oversight function in relation to executive officers; shareholders, in turn, use this information for monitoring the board in its capacity as an intermediary between shareholders and management. The following subsections offer more detail on statutory rules and soft law recommendations applicable to the two main corporate governance actors: corporate boards and shareholders. Like in most other jurisdictions, COVID-19 focused the attention in the UK on corporate governance, but the collapse of Carillion plc in 2018[89]

Problems 387, 390–1. Refer to Section 1.5 for a more comprehensive discussion of the origins of the corporate governance debate and changing views on it.

86 Brian R Cheffins, 'Corporate governance reform: Britain as an exporter' (2000) 8(1) *Hume Papers on Public Policy* 10, 12–14; Klaus J Hopt, 'Comparative corporate governance: The state of the art and international regulation' (2011) 59(1) *American Journal of Comparative Law* 1, 12, 69; Donald Nordberg and Terry McNulty, 'Creating better boards through codification: Possibilities and limitations in UK corporate governance, 1992–2010' (2013) 55(3) *Business History* 348, 349; Iain MacNeil and Irenemarié Esser, 'The emergence of "comply or explain" as a global model for corporate governance codes' (2022) 33(1) *European Business Law Review* 1, 25–8.

87 Kathleen M Eisenhardt, 'Agency theory: An assessment and review' (1989) 14(1) *Academy of Management Review* 57, 65.

88 Hopt, 'Comparative corporate governance' (2011) 59(1) *American Journal of Comparative Law* 1, 19.

89 See Section 1.6.2.4.

accentuated that there were still some work to be done in the space of corporate governance in the UK, irrespective of the introduction of the 'enlightened shareholder value
approach' (see below) through s 172 of the *Companies Act 2006* (UK).[90] As was discussed
in greater detail in Chapter 1, the British Academy also embarked on a comprehensive
project on the future of the corporation and the purpose of the corporation in 2017,
with a final report published in 2021.[91] At the date of finalising this chapter (August
2023) the practical impact of the British Academy's future of the corporation project is
still unclear.

11.3.2 Regulatory environment

Historically, corporate governance in the UK relied almost exceptionally on certain statutory responsibilities placed on company directors and auditors, according to which
directors and auditors were expected to fulfil their obligations honestly and with due
care.[92] Major paradigm shift took place in early 1990s in response to shortcomings in
managerial accountability laid bare by economic recession and, perhaps more importantly, a wave of high-profile scandals involving UK quoted companies.[93] These corporate scandals, in particular the BCCI and Maxwell scandals,[94] served as a catalyst for
strengthening corporate governance, primarily through soft law measures, as a means
for protecting the interests of shareholders and other corporate constituencies.[95]

Against this background, the Committee on the Financial Aspects of Corporate
Governance, better known as the 'Cadbury Committee', was set up with a narrow task to
review the aspects of corporate governance related to financial reporting and accountability.[96] In its final report, which was released in December 1992 and has become known
as the 'Cadbury Report', the Committee went further by putting forward proposals for the
promotion of good corporate governance as a whole.[97] The centrepiece of the Cadbury
Report was a code of best practice of corporate governance standards compliance which –
based on the 'comply or explain' principle – soon became a condition for admission and
continued listing on the London Stock Exchange.[98] The Cadbury Report was a landmark
document that had a profound impact on the rise and evolution of corporate governance
in the UK and in some other countries.[99] Several rounds of updates and revisions of the

---

90 See further Section 1.6.1.
91 See Section 1.6.2.
92 David Allvey, 'Corporate governance in the United Kingdom' in Eberhard Scheffler (ed), *Corporate Governance* (Springer, 1995) 58.
93 Cheffins, 'The rise of corporate governance in the UK' (2015) 68(1) *Current Legal Problems* 387, 409–11.
94 Committee on the Financial Aspects of Corporate Governance, *The Financial Aspects of Corporate Governance* ('Cadbury Report') (Burgess Science Press, 1992) Preface, [5.27], [4.60].
95 Corporate governance reforms have generally been reactions to corporate scandals and crises: Hopt, 'Comparative corporate governance' (2011) 59(1) *American Journal of Comparative Law* 1, 16, 17.
96 Laura F Spira and Judy Slinn, *The Cadbury Committee: A History* (Oxford University Press, 2013) 1, 45.
97 Cadbury Report (1992) [1.2].
98 Stock Exchange, *The Listing Rules* (London Stock Exchange, 1993) [12.43(j)]. This requirement, due to EU legislation transferring the listing decision from stock exchanges to special national listing authorities, was later incorporated in the Financial Conduct Authority's *Listing Rules*.
99 Spira and Slinn, *The Cadbury Committee* (2013) 4; Cheffins, 'The rise of corporate governance in the UK' (2015) 68 *Current Legal Problems* 387, 405.

Cadbury Report's best practice guidelines followed later, thereby setting the foundations of soft law corporate governance in the UK. The latest major revision took place in 2018, leading to the adoption of the *UK Corporate Governance Code* ('CGC 2018').[100]

The early initiatives directed at the promotion of high standards of corporate governance focused almost exclusively on the role and practices of the board of directors. Indeed, the Cadbury Report's code of best practice contained guidelines directed only at the board, non-executive and executive directors, and reporting.[101] A well-structured and composed board of directors with sound and transparent processes of operation was the sole bedrock of good corporate governance.[102] But the 2008 GFC illustrated how poor shareholder oversight of corporate boards can lead to excessive risk-taking and corporate failures, thereby exposing the limits of the one-sided focus on changing boards to improve corporate governance. As a result, the Financial Reporting Council ('FRC'), an independent government agency, building on the earlier work done by the Institutional Shareholders' Committee, published the first Stewardship Code for institutional investors in 2010.[103] This code and its subsequent revisions in 2012[104] and 2019[105] formed the second pillar of corporate governance in the UK.

At present, the corporate governance system in the UK comprises laws and regulations, soft law codes of best practice, and market guidance. The primary pieces of laws and regulations are the *Companies Act 2006*;[106] and the Financial Conduct Authority's ('FCA') rules governing the listing regime the *Listing Rules*, which set the requirements for admission to listing and the obligations of listed companies;[107] the *Prospectus Regulation Rules*, which govern the prospectus requirements for public offers;[108] and *Disclosure Guidance and Transparency Rules*, which define periodic disclosure requirements on UK financial markets.[109] The two main soft law codes of best practice are the CGC 2018 and the *UK Stewardship Code 2020* ('the SC 2020'), both designed by the FRC. Last, market guidance tools include various documents published by trade associations of market participants, such as the Investment Association's guidelines for listed companies.[110]

11.3.3 Legislation and regulators

Traditionally, corporate governance has been influenced by the mandatory and default rules of UK company law. These rules shape and influence the governance roles of both the board of directors and shareholders.

---

100 FRC, *UK Corporate Governance Code* (July 2018) ('the CGC 2018').
101 Cadbury Report (1992) 58–60.
102 Nordberg and McNulty, 'Creating better boards through codification' (2013) 55(3) *Business History* 348, 350–1.
103 FRC, *UK Stewardship Code* (July 2010).
104 FRC, *UK Stewardship Code* (September 2012).
105 FRC, *UK Stewardship Code 2020* (October 2019), hereinafter 'SC (2020)'.
106 *Companies Act 2006* (UK) c 46.
107 FCA, *FCA Handbook – Listing Rules ('LR')*, LR (July 2022).
108 FCA, *FCA Handbook – The Prospectus Regulation Rules Sourcebook* (July 2022).
109 FCA, *FCA Handbook – Disclosure Guidance and Transparency Rules Sourcebook* (July 2022).
110 The Investment Association, 'Guidelines for investee companies' (29 June 2023) <https://www.theia.org/industry-policy/guidelines/guidelines-listed-companies>.

11.3.3.1 Governance rules relating to the board

Statutory rules set the duties of directors and define how boards are formed. Directors must guide their actions by the duty to promote the success of the company on whose board they serve.[111] In the decision-making process, they must also exercise reasonable care, skill and diligence.[112] UK company law includes very few provisions on the structure, formation and composition of the board. Most of these matters are left to the discretion of the founders and shareholders of a company under the best practice standards and the specific company needs. But the statute provides shareholders with an unwaivable right to remove any director by a simple majority vote.[113]

11.3.3.2 Governance rules relating to shareholders

Statutory rules also form the basis of shareholder stewardship. In addition to the influence on the formation of the board through the right to remove a director, statutory rules give shareholders voting rights on fundamental matters related to the company's business,[114] on conflicted transactions[115] and on executive compensation ('say-on-pay' votes).[116] Shareholders also have a right to initiate shareholder proposals.[117] Importantly, the enabling rules on the division of powers between shareholders and boards allow companies to create their own optimal governance structure.[118] Nevertheless, as a matter of practice, many listed companies adopt a standard governance structure where shareholders retain limited decision-making powers that rarely go beyond their minimum statutory voting rights. One of the major exceptions to this practice is the annual shareholder vote on the (re-)election of directors, which is added to the internal governance documents of listed companies.[119]

11.3.3.3 Regulatory bodies

Two different regulatory bodies deal with corporate governance in the UK. The FCA, a regulatory body operating independently of the UK government, is responsible for promulgating rules, such as the *Listing Rules*, the *Disclosure Guidance and Transparency Rules* and the *Prospectus Regulation Rules*, and their enforcement. The FCA has wide enforcement powers in relation to these rules and can apply formal sanctions against the wrongdoers, including civil and criminal sanctions, disciplinary bans or the issue of a public censure.[120] More recently, the FCA has been involved in updating sustainability

---

111 *Companies Act 2006* (UK) s 172(1).
112 Ibid s 174(1).
113 Ibid s 168(1).
114 For example, a shareholder vote is required for amending the company's articles of association (*Companies Act 2006* (UK) s 21(1)) and approving mergers and divisions (ibid ss 907(1), 922(1)).
115 *Companies Act 2006* (UK) s 190(1).
116 Ibid ss 439(1), 439A(1).
117 Ibid s 338A(1).
118 Paul Davies, *Introduction to Company Law* (Oxford University Press, 2nd ed, 2010) 12.
119 CGC (2018) Provision 18.
120 John Armour, 'Enforcement strategies in UK corporate governance: A roadmap and empirical assessment' in John Armour and Jennifer Payne (eds), *Rationality in Company Law: Essays in Honour of DD Prentice* (Hart Publishing, 2009) 83.

disclosure requirements and the labeling of investment funds to enable the use of ESG factors in investment decision-making.[121]

The FRC, which is expected to be replaced by the new Audit, Reporting and Governance Authority ('ARGA') in 2024, is the regulator for corporate reporting, auditing, and corporate governance. The FRC is responsible for setting the UK corporate governance and stewardship codes. Given the soft law nature of these best practice codes, the FRC does not have powers to enforce their provisions. Instead, the enforcement of both codes is market driven based on information disclosed by companies and institutional investors.[122]

11.3.4 Codes of practice

11.3.4.1 Best practices of governance relating to the board

The early focus of best practice codes in the UK, as noted earlier, was on changing boards of directors as a means to improve corporate governance.[123] The Cadbury Report put strong emphasis on the structure and processes of the board of directors, including its independence and the separation of leadership roles.[124]

The subsequent review of corporate governance in the UK in 2003 in the aftermath of the Enron scandal, known as the 'Higgs Report', focused more on strengthening the role of independent non-executive directors in board decision-making.[125] As such, the Higgs Report offered formal criteria, the presence of which could impair director independence.[126] The final decision of whether a director is independent remains with the board; the formal definition of independence aims to assist the board in this process.[127] Furthermore, the Higgs Report recommended that independent directors, including the chair who should be independent on appointment, form the majority of the board.[128] As a means to strengthen the independence of directors, the Higgs Report also recommended limiting the terms of office of independent directors.[129] This report thus contributed to the growing role of independent directors in UK listed companies.

The 2008 GFC accelerated the planned review of corporate governance in the UK and resulted in the adoption of the *UK Corporate Governance Code* of 2010. The new Code incorporated many provisions from past codes of best practice and added an emphasis on the behaviour of directors.[130] A related aspect is the attempt to make boards and board committees more professional by appointing independent directors with relevant

---

121 FCA, *Sustainability Disclosure Requirements (SDR) and Investment Labels* (Discussion Paper DP21/4, November 2021).
122 Andrew Keay, 'Comply or explain in corporate governance codes: In need of greater regulatory oversight?' (2014) 34(2) *Legal Studies* 279, 280.
123 In general, corporate governance codes in many countries contain provisions that are primarily addressed to the board and its committees: Hopt, 'Comparative corporate governance' (2011) 59(1) *American Journal of Comparative Law* 1, 13.
124 Cadbury Report (1992) 58–60.
125 Nordberg and McNulty, 'Creating better boards through codification' (2013) 55 *Business History* 348, 364.
126 *Review of the Role and Effectiveness of Non-Executive Directors* ('Higgs Report') (January 2003). These circumstances are currently listed in Provision 10 of the CGC 2018.
127 Hopt, 'Comparative corporate governance' (2011) 59(1) *American Journal of Comparative Law* 1, 36.
128 Higgs Report (2003) 35 [9.5]. Currently, CGC (2018) Provisions 9 and 11.
129 Higgs Report (2003) 37. Currently, CGC (2018) Provision 10.
130 Nordberg and McNulty, 'Creating better boards through codification' (2013) 55(3) *Business History* 348, 364.

knowledge and professional backgrounds. In particular, the Code set an expectation on independent directors to offer 'appropriate balance of skills, experience, independence and knowledge of the company to enable them to discharge their respective duties and responsibilities effectively'.[131]

Finally, the CGC 2018, the latest revision of corporate governance in the UK, highlights the importance of sustainability and corporate culture in a company's long-term success. Companies 'need to build and maintain successful relationship with a wide range of stakeholders', according to the Code.[132] This is possible where a company's culture promotes integrity and openness, values diversity and is responsive to the views of different stakeholders, including shareholders.[133]

The result of the different iterations of the best practice corporate governance codes is the creation of corporate boards that include independent non-executive directors,[134] form different committees,[135] divide leadership roles within the board by separating the positions of chair and chief executive,[136] reduce the duration of office,[137] and become more professional in terms of time commitment[138] and skills, experience, and knowledge.[139]

11.3.4.2 Compliance with best practice governance codes

UK codes of best practice acknowledge that there is no standard governance structure that suits all companies. In recognition of this flexible approach, the Cadbury Code relied on the voluntary 'comply or explain' principle, which requires companies to comply with the Code's recommendations or explain any non-compliance, rather than on the binding force of laws.[140] Since the introduction of different types of best practice norms, principles and provisions, in 1995, the corporate governance codes have relied on a tiered model of implementation by partially moving to a stricter 'apply and explain' principle which requires companies to apply the code and explain its application.[141] The 'apply and explain' principle applies to the main principles of the CGC 2018; the Code's more detailed explanatory provisions, which form the second level of best practice guidelines, continue to be subject to the more flexible 'comply or explain' standard.[142] This subtle difference in the wording places a stronger emphasis on the expectation that

131 FRC, *UK Corporate Governance Code* (2010) Principle B.1.

132 CGC (2018) 1, Principle A.

133 Ibid Principle B.

134 Ibid Principle G.

135 Ibid Provisions 17, 24 and 32.

136 Ibid Principle G, Provision 9.

137 Ibid Principle K (generally for the board and individual members), Provisions 10 (for independent non-executive directors) and 19 (for the chair).

138 Ibid Principle H, Provision 15.

139 Ibid Principle K.

140 Marc T Moore, 'The end of "comply or explain" in UK corporate governance?' (2009) 60(1) *Northern Ireland Legal Quarterly* 85, 87; Nordberg and McNulty, 'Creating better boards through codification' (2013) 55(3) *Business History* 348, 362–3.

141 'The end of "comply or explain" in UK corporate governance?' (2009) 60(1) *Northern Ireland Law Quarterly* 85, 89; MacNeil and Esser, 'The emergence of "comply or explain" as a global model for corporate governance codes' (2022) 33(1) *European Business Law Review* 1, 17.

142 CGC (2018) 1–2.

companies need to follow the core recommendations of the Code. Giving reasons for non-compliance, unlike in the case of supporting provisions, is not considered to bean acceptable form of compliance with the Code's principles.

This tiered model is supported by the FRC's *Listing Rules* which require premium listed companies to disclose: (1) how they have applied the CGC 2018 principles;[143] and (2) whether they have complied with the provisions or, if not, give reasons for non-compliance.[144] While the failure to follow these rules is a formal breach of the *Listing Rules*, in practice the FCA does not take action against companies for non-compliance with the CGC 2018.[145] Neither do the FCA rules set the minimum required standard of explanations in the context of the 'apply and explain' and 'comply or explain' principles.[146] The Code's flexible approach to compliance relies, instead, on shareholder engagement to monitor and assess the credibility of (non-)compliance statements disclosed by companies.[147] This highlights the importance of informal private enforcement by institutional investors in promoting the broad application of best practice recommendations by listed companies.[148] Better engagement by institutional investors, the dominant shareholders in many listed UK companies, is the focus of the UK stewardship codes which complement corporate governance codes and are an integral part of the UK corporate governance regime.

11.3.4.3 Best practices of governance relating to investors

The SC 2020 is a soft law tool comprising a set of 'apply and explain' principles for institutional investors, which comprise asset owners (such as pension funds and insurance companies) and asset managers (firms providing investment management services).[149] The Code has introduced four major innovations to the concept of investor stewardship that distinguish it from the earlier versions. First, 'in addition to operating performance and corporate governance matters, the updated concept of stewardship covers other topics, including material ESG factors relevant for individual firms and broader market'.[150] Second, the new Code takes a broader perspective on the tools available to active stewards and embraces more explicitly the need to integrate stewardship preferences into investment decision-making along with investor stewardship through voting and private engagement.[151] Third, the Code marks a major change in the concept of stewardship by expanding the traditional and exclusive focus of stewardship codes on equity to

---

143 FCA, *Listing Rules* (2022) LR 9.8.6(5).

144 Ibid LR 9.8.6(6).

145 Armour, 'Enforcement strategies in UK corporate governance' in Armour and Payne (eds), *Rationality in Company Law* (2009) 103.

146 MacNeil and Esser, 'The emergence of "comply or explain" as a global model for corporate governance codes' (2022) 33(1) *European Business Law Review* 1, 11.

147 The Cadbury Report recognised the central role of shareholders and institutional investors in ensuring that companies comply with best practice codes. As acknowledged by the report's authors, '[t]he widespread adoption of our recommendations will turn in large measure on the support which all shareholders give to them': Cadbury Report (1992) [6.16].

148 Armour, 'Enforcement strategies in UK corporate governance' in Armour and Payne (eds), *Rationality in Company Law* (2009) 103, 104.

149 SC (2020) 4. See also Suren Gomtsian, 'Debtholder stewardship' (2023) 86(2) *Modern Law Review* 395.

150 SC (2020) 4 (on ESG stewardship).

151 Ibid (stewardship as the responsible allocation of capital).

a broader range of assets, including corporate debt.[152] Last but not least, the Code has moved away from asking signatories to report on their policies (what they say they are going to do) towards reporting on concrete activities and outcomes of stewardship.[153] These developments, given the UK's role as a 'stewardship norm exporter',[154] are likely to be adopted in other countries that closely follow stewardship developments in the UK.

11.3.5 Sustainability

11.3.5.1 Corporate purpose and stakeholder interests

The importance of wider interested groups in corporate governance has been recognised at the legislative level through the 'enlightened shareholder value' approach set out in the *Companies Act 2006* ('the Act').[155] Section 172 of the Act imposes a statutory duty on directors to promote the success of the company for the benefit of its shareholders, while having regard to the interests of a wider group of other stakeholders.[156] This approach has been widely accepted as ineffective in promoting the interests of stakeholders other than shareholders, for two reasons. First, under s 172, directors, at best, can promote the interests of non-shareholder stakeholders as far as this creates benefits for shareholders.[157] Second, even if s 172 establishes a right, it does not come with a clear remedy that can be used as an accountability mechanism for board decision-making.[158]

While there have been no meaningful legislative attempts to upgrade the interests of non-shareholder stakeholders in corporate governance, the UK government has sought to strengthen the consideration of the interests of stakeholders by directors through reporting requirements. This emphasis on the process of decision-making has led to the adoption of non-financial reporting obligations in the annual strategic report where companies must explain how they consider stakeholder interests in board decisions.[159] Public companies and large private companies must also report information on environmental and employee matters.[160]

The growing recognition of wider interested groups in corporate law has influenced the soft law corporate governance framework.[161] Both the CGC 2018 and the SC 2020 mark a shift away from the de facto shareholder-oriented model of corporate governance – where the main purpose is to protect shareholders from managers by strengthening the accountability, transparency and oversight of managerial decision-making – towards

---

152 Ibid 4, 7 (exercising stewardship no matter how capital is invested).
153 Ibid 6.
154 Dionysia Katelouzou and Mathias Siems, 'The global diffusion of stewardship codes' in Dionysia Katelouzou and Dan W Puchniak (eds), *Global Shareholder Stewardship* (Cambridge University Press, 2022) 645.
155 *Companies Act 2006* (UK) s 172(1).
156 Ibid.
157 Andrew Keay, 'Section 172(1) of the Companies Act 2006: An interpretation and assessment' (2007) 28(4) *Company Lawyer* 106, 108.
158 Georgina Tsagas, 'Section 172 of the Companies Act 2006: Desperate times call for soft law measures' in Nina Boeger and Charlotte Villiers (eds), *Shaping the Corporate Landscape: Towards Corporate Reform and Enterprise Diversity* (Hart Publishing, 2018) 138.
159 *Companies Act 2006* (UK) ss 414A(1), 414C(1).
160 Ibid s 414C(4).
161 MacNeil and Esser, 'The emergence of "comply or explain" as a global model for corporate governance codes' (2022) 33(1) *European Business Law Review* 1, 16.

more sustainable corporate behaviour. In particular, companies are expected to use one or the combination of three options to achieve improved engagement with the workforce: appoint a director from the workforce, create a formal workforce advisory panel, or designate one of the non-executive directors to communicate the interests of employees.[162]

11.3.5.2 Diversity in corporate life

In addition to the growing accommodation of stakeholder interests in corporate governance, another major theme of the recent decade has been the diversity – predominantly in relation to gender – of corporate boards and at the senior management level. In line with the general soft law nature of corporate governance initiatives in the UK, diversity has been encouraged through voluntary targets that are subject to periodic reviews and increase in ambition and coverage. The first target of achieving 25 per cent for women on the boards of the FTSE100 companies by the end of 2015 was set in 2011.[163] The most recent review shows substantial improvements in large listed companies on diversity, but – not surprisingly for a voluntary regime – there are also some laggards that are far below the set targets.[164] The latest target is set at minimum of 40 per cent women representation both for boards and executive leadership teams of the FTSE350 companies by the end of 2025.[165]

11.3.5.3 Sustainability and investor stewardship

The rise of sustainability is also visible in the stewardship pillar of corporate governance. The purpose of encouraging investor engagement has gradually changed from the initial focus on increasing value for shareholders to promoting long-term value and sustainability.[166] This evolution is reflected in the aims of the three different versions of the UK stewardship codes. If the 2010 and 2012 editions of the stewardship codes aimed to enhance the quality of shareholder engagement to improve long-term returns for shareholders,[167] the aim of the SC 2020 is to create 'long-term value for clients and beneficiaries [of asset managers and asset owners] leading to sustainable benefits for the economy, the environment and society'.[168] This updated aim puts the emphasis on sustainability and the link between the interests of various stakeholders, including shareholders, in the long-term perspective.

11.3.6 Future directions

The sustainability revolution in corporate governance in the UK is expected to continue. The CGC 2018 was released when the corporate landscape was a different place.

---

162 CGC (2018) Provision 5.
163 Department for Business, Innovation, and Skills, *Women on Boards: Independent Review* (2011) 18–19.
164 BEIS, *Hampton-Alexander Review on FTSE Women Leaders: Improving Gender Balance – 5 Year Summary Report* (2021) Appendices C and D.
165 BEIS, *FTSE Women Leaders Review: Achieving Gender Balance* (2022) 10.
166 Andrew Johnston, Rachelle Belinga and Blanche Segrestin, 'Governing institutional investor engagement: From activism to stewardship or custodianship?' (2022) 22(1) *Journal of Corporate Law Studies* 1.
167 Ibid 5–6.
168 SC (2020) 4.

The Code contains more references to responsible corporate behaviour than its predecessors; it sees the value of good corporate governance in contributing to a company's long-term sustainable success and achieving better outcomes for its shareholders and wider stakeholders. The increasing societal attention to environmental, including climate change, and social challenges means that the next version of the corporate governance code, which is expected to be released in the not too distant future, will place additional emphasis on sustainability. The FRC previously announced plans to change the corporate governance code by reinforcing the emphasis on sustainability and ESG reporting.[169]

The planned review comes against the backdrop of growing calls to reform the Code substantially or even abolish it completely. Strong corporate governance standards do not necessarily guarantee better performance, as evidenced by the underperformance of many UK companies compared to their peers in other countries. In a provocative call, Professors Brian Cheffins and Bobby Reddy propose abolishing the CGC 2018.[170] The irrelevance of the Code's many provisions, which state the obvious or duplicate what is mandated elsewhere, and the inadequacy of the shareholder-oriented 'comply or explain' principle for promoting wider stakeholder interests, are among the key justifications for this call.[171]

Similarly, the SC 2020 came under heavy criticism in 2018 by the committee set up to review the FRC and its work.[172] In a damning report branding the FRC a 'ramshackle house',[173] the review questioned the practical effectiveness of the Code and recommended fundamentally revising or abolishing it altogether.[174] In response, the FRC published a revised code at the end of 2019.[175] This means that the SC 2020 will remain in the spotlight in the coming years and the questions of its role in improving investor oversight and overall value in corporate governance are likely to come up again when the time comes for the Code's periodic review.

11.3.7 Conclusion

Corporate governance came to prominence in the UK earlier than in many other countries. The UK has sought to maintain its leading status as a country with a strong corporate governance framework since then. This has led to periodic reviews and updates of the existing corporate governance rules and best practice recommendations. In that latest turn, the corporate governance initiatives put stronger emphasis on sustainability in general and on the need to strengthen the voice of wider interested groups in

169 FRC, *Restoring Trust in Audit and Corporate Governance* (Position Paper, 2022) 4. See also Suren Gomtsian 'Stakeholder engagement: It's time to ditch public vs private', *Board Agenda* (13 December 2022) <https://boardagenda.com/2022/12/13/stakeholder-engagement-its-time-to-ditch-public-vs-private/>.

170 Brian R Cheffins and Bobby V Reddy, *Thirty Years and Done – Time to Abolish the UK Corporate Governance Code* (Working Paper No 654/2022, European Corporate Governance Institute Law, July 2022) 2.

171 Ibid 26–37, 44–50.

172 BEIS, *Independent Review of the Financial Reporting Council* (2018).

173 Ibid 5.

174 Ibid 46.

175 SC (2020).

decision-making, on improving corporate culture, and on the need to have companies with purpose. Evolving societal preferences are a major factor behind this turn. The planned reform of the FRC is another factor that is likely to lead to substantial changes, especially on sustainability matters, in the existing corporate governance framework.

Lastly, we are yet to see the influence of Brexit on the UK corporate governance regime. Brexit has had a big impact on UK companies by forcing them to operate under uncertain business conditions during a relatively long period of time and to adapt to new business realities. But the likely impact of Brexit on corporate governance is less clear. Although UK regulators may have more freedom of action and may become more responsive to the needs of companies after Brexit, Brexit has also scaled down expertise available for promoting regulatory reforms.

All these factors combined make for interesting times ahead for the observers of corporate governance in the UK.

11.4 New Zealand[176]

Matthew Berkahn

11.4.1 Overview

New Zealand is, by a considerable margin, the smallest economy surveyed in this work. It ranks just inside the world's 50 largest economies by GDP,[177] although is much higher in overall prosperity.[178] Even more than in other comparable jurisdictions, small enterprises predominate: the majority (over 95 per cent) of New Zealand companies are small or medium-sized enterprises ('SMEs'),[179] generally defined as those with 50 or fewer full-time equivalent employees. Most have far fewer – a 2019 study found that 70 per cent of New Zealand businesses had no employees at all.[180] This has led some commentators to conclude that 'corporate governance issues are of little or no importance' to most New Zealand companies because of the lack of the agency problem caused by the separation of ownership and control,[181] and because governance codes and guidelines are not taken seriously unless companies are legally compelled to observe them.[182] For that reason, the statutory directors' duties (arguably) codified in the *Companies Act 1993* (NZ) ('CA 1993') are the most significant aspect of the regulatory environment for most companies.

Other guidelines exist: the Financial Markets Authority ('FMA'), New Zealand's financial markets regulator with wide oversight and enforcement powers, has produced a set of guidelines on corporate governance. The New Zealand Stock Exchange ('NZX'),

---

176 This section draws on the equivalent section in the previous edition by Susan Watson.
177 See The World Bank (2022) <https://data.worldbank.org/indicator/NY.GDP.MKTP.CD>.
178 See the Legatum Prosperity Index 2021 <https://www.prosperity.com/globe/new-zealand>.
179 Mark A Fox, Gordon R Walker and Alma Pekmezovic, 'Corporate governance research on New Zealand listed companies' (2012) 29(1) *Arizona Journal of International and Comparative Law* 1, 3.
180 Tanya Jurado and Martina Battisti, 'The evolution of SME policy: The case of New Zealand' (2019) 6(1) *Regional Studies, Regional Science* 32, 38.
181 Fox, Walker and Pekmezovic, 'Corporate governance research on New Zealand listed companies' (2012) 2991) *Arizona Journal of International and Comparative Law* 1, 3.
182 Ibid 5. See also Susan Watson and Lynne Taylor (eds), *Corporate Law in New Zealand* (Thomson Reuters, 2018) 347.

New Zealand's only licensed market operator, has a set of listing rules by which all listed issuers are contractually bound. The New Zealand Corporate Governance Forum ('NZCGF'), formed by a group of influential institutional investors with the aim of improving corporate governance in listed companies, has produced guidelines that expand on the FMA Guidelines. And the Institute of Directors ('IOD'), the leading industry body for directors of listed companies, has a code to which members must adhere. These are all discussed below.

This section also discusses New Zealand's efforts to encourage corporate governance practices that are consistent with sustainable business, and future directions including the growing importance of Māori organisations and their governance.

11.4.2 Regulatory environment

New Zealand's first statement on corporate governance was produced in 2004 by the Securities Commission, then the main regulator of New Zealand's financial markets.[183] New Zealand has, however, since jumped enthusiastically onto the corporate governance bandwagon. The IOD has noted that, after an initial period of fragmentation and inconsistency between the various codes, making corporate governance reporting challenging for listed companies, 'a new level of consistency' has now been achieved.[184]

As in other jurisdictions, the 2008 GFC highlighted flaws in New Zealand's corporate governance practices. Although the direct impact on New Zealand was minimal (largely because its Australian-owned banks were not affected), a knock-on effect was the failure of finance companies, with the Securities Commission, fairly or unfairly, widely considered to be under-resourced and ineffective as a regulator and enforcer. A 2009 report on the Commission's effectiveness[185] influenced reform, leading to the enactment of the *Financial Markets Conduct Act 2013* (NZ) ('FMCA') and the establishment of the FMA to replace the Commission.

The COVID-19 pandemic, and resulting economic uncertainty, is – according to a 2020 article – 'rewriting the rules of corporate governance'.[186] New Zealand's response included temporary relief for company directors. A 'safe harbour' provision was enacted, allowing directors to carry on business and incur obligations between April and September 2020 without risk of breaching certain directors' duties.[187] The provision applied to directors who, in good faith, believed that the company had or was likely to have significant COVID-related liquidity problems and that it was more likely than not that the company would

183 Securities Commission, *Corporate Governance in New Zealand: Principles and Guidelines* (16 February 2004).

184 Felicity Caird, 'Governance Leadership Centre [Update]', *Boardroom, Magazine of the Institute of Directors* (October–November 2017) 30 <https://www.iod.org.nz/assets/Resources-insights/IoD-publications/Institute-of-Directors-Boardroom-November-2017-v2.pdf>. The article refers to a comparative table of corporate governance codes, the most recent version of which appears at Chapman Tripp, *Corporate Governance: Codes Compared* (March 2022) <https://chapmantripp.com/media/lvbfrkrt/corporate-governance-codes-compared-2022.pdf>.

185 Michel Prada and Neil Walter, *Report on the Effectiveness of New Zealand's Securities Commission* (September 2009).

186 Lynn S Paine, 'COVID-19 is rewriting the rules of corporate governance', *Harvard Business Review Digital Articles* (6 October 2020) <https://hbr.org/2020/10/covid-19-is-rewriting-the-rules-of-corporate-governance>.

187 Those set out in ss 135 and 136 of the CA 1993: see below.

be able to pay its due debts on and after September 2021.[188] A 'business debt hibernation' scheme was also enacted, enabling businesses to place existing debts into hibernation for up to seven months if they faced COVID-related liquidity problems.[189]

11.4.3 Legislation and regulators

Corporate governance in New Zealand has a statutory base, supplemented by other 'soft' or 'hard soft' requirements.[190]

The relevant statute is the CA 1993, the first objective of which is set out in its long title:

> ... to reaffirm the value of the company as a means of achieving economic and social benefits through the aggregation of capital for productive purposes, the spreading of economic risk, and the taking of business risks ...

Section 131 of the Act imposes a subjective duty of good faith on directors (see also Section 11.4.3). There are separate duties of care and to use powers for a proper purpose (ss 137 and 133), processes around conflicts of interest (ss 139–144) and on directors' share dealing (ss 148 and 149). There are also positive obligations on directors not to trade recklessly and not to allow the company to incur obligations that it will not be able to perform (ss 135 and 136). Although explicitly not owed to creditors, those duties primarily protect their interests.[191] There is also a duty to comply with the Act and the company's constitution (s 134).

Opinion is divided on whether these duties codify the common law duties. At the very least, the pre-existing case law remains relevant in understanding the origins of the rules and in helping to interpret them.[192] Heath J's statement in *Benton v Priore*, that ss 131–138 of the Act 'should be seen as a restatement of basic duties [developed by the common law] in an endeavour to promote accessibility to the law', rather than a codification as such, seems to represent the predominant view.[193]

The FMA initially adopted the Commission's 2004 guidelines, updating them in 2014 and 2018.[194] In the latest guidelines the FMA acknowledges that the NZX Code (see below) is the primary guide to governance practices for listed companies. The FMA has therefore refocused its guidelines on non-listed entities, many of which have a significant impact on New Zealand's financial markets.[195]

---

188 CA 1993 s 138B, in force 30 April 2020 to 31 May 2022.

189 CA 1993 s 395A, in force 30 April 2020 to 31 May 2022.

190 See Watson and Taylor (eds), *Corporate Law in New Zealand* (2018) 346–7; and Fox, Walker and Pekmezovic, 'Corporate governance research on New Zealand listed companies' (2012) 29(1) *Arizona Journal of International and Comparative Law* 1, 5.

191 CA 1993 s 169(3) provides that these duties are owed to the company and not to shareholders. In the leading case, *Nicholson v Permakraft (NZ) Ltd* [1985] 1 NZLR 242 (NZCA), it was held that, in situations of doubtful solvency, the directors' duties to the company require consideration of creditors' interests.

192 Susan Watson, 'Corporate law and governance' (2015) (2) *New Zealand Law Review* 239.

193 *Benton v Priore* [2003] 1 NZLR 564 (NZHC), [46], followed in *Sojourner v Robb* [2006] 3 NZLR 808 (NZHC), [100]. See also the comments of Heath J in *EBR Holdings Ltd v Van Duyn (No 2)* [2017] NZHC 1698, [128]–[135].

194 The latest version is: Financial Markets Authority ('FMA'), *Corporate Governance in New Zealand: Principles and Guidelines* (February 2018) <https://www.fma.govt.nz/library/guidance-library/corporate-governance-in-new-zealand-principles-and-guidelines/> ('FMA Guidelines').

195 Ibid 5.

The NZX is currently New Zealand's only licensed market operator. Under the FMCA, the NZX must have a set of contractually binding listing rules with which all listed issuers must comply.[196] The NZX has a corporate governance code ('NZX Code') that applies to entities that have equity securities quoted on the NZX.[197] The NZX Code has recently been revised to align it more closely with the FMA Guidelines.[198] The NZX *Listing Rules* and Code require entities to disclose in their annual reports the extent to which their governance practices follow the principles set out in the NZX Code and what, if any, alternative practices have been adopted.[199]

11.4.4 Codes of practice

11.4.4.1 The FMA Guidelines

The FMA Guidelines are intended to apply to non-listed companies and other entities that nonetheless have impact on New Zealand's financial markets or are accountable to the public. The FMA also states that the Guidelines can be useful to all entities and notes their relevance to companies wanting to raise capital and/or list on the NZX in the future, financial services providers, unlisted issuers, state-owned enterprises and other public-sector entities, Māori and iwi-owned entities and not-for-profit organisations, among others. The FMA acknowledges, however, that not all guidelines will apply to all entities; for example, public-sector entities do not have shareholders and have their own specific board-appointment processes.[200] The FMA states that it will 'take appropriate action, where [it] find[s] examples of poor governance'.[201]

The FMA has not adopted a UK-style 'comply or explain' principle. The Guidelines' focus is 'on principles, rather than checklists or rules':

> [W]e suggest boards explain to investors and stakeholders how they have applied each principle. The 'comply or explain' approach is appropriate for listed companies. The 'explain' approach of this handbook is intended to cater for reporting by the wide range of entities that may use [it].[202]

Principle 1 addresses ethical standards.[203] Listed issuers are required to have a code of ethics, and the FMA suggests that more '[w]idespread adoption and implementation' of such codes will help 'promote public confidence in governance structures and behaviour'. Ethics committees and regular independent verification of the implementation and

---

196 FMCA ss 327–329.
197 NZX Ltd, 'NZX Listing Rules' (17 June 2022) Appendix 1: NZX Corporate Governance Code <https://www.nzx.com/regulation/nzx-rules-guidance/nzx-listing-rules>.
198 Ibid 6.
199 NZX Ltd, 'NZX Listing Rules' (17 June 2022), r 3.8.1 and Appendix 1 3–5.
200 FMA Guidelines 4–5.
201 Ibid 5. Note that the FMA's functions extend beyond enforcement of the law and include promoting 'confident and informed participation ... in the financial markets, including ... issuing warnings, reports, or guidelines, or making comments, about any matter relating to those markets' and 'to monitor, and conduct inquiries and investigations into any matter relating to, financial markets': *Financial Markets Authority Act 2011* (NZ) s 9.
202 FMA Guidelines 5–6.
203 Ibid 8–9.

effectiveness of ethics codes are suggested. The FMA Guidelines recommend a written code of ethics that is 'a meaningful statement of the entity's core values'. It should include expectations for ethical decision-making in respect of matters including:

- conflicts of interest, including limitations on director participation in discussion of, and voting on, matters in which a director is interested
- proper use of an entity's property and information, including not taking advantage of it for personal gain, except as permitted by law
- giving and receiving gifts, koha (a Māori custom of giving gifts or donations, often by visitors to hosts), facilitation payments and bribes
- expectations when responding to and supporting whistleblowing.

The board is charged with putting a system in place to implement and review the code of ethics. Codes should be communicated to employees and should include processes for recording and evaluating compliance. Training should be provided.

Principle 2 addresses board composition and performance.[204] Board size should be 'appropriate to meet the needs of the entity', with each director having skills, knowledge and experience relevant to the needs of the entity and complementary to other directors. 'This includes diversity of gender, ethnicity, cultural background, age and skills' as well as a willingness to make the necessary time commitment. Directors should be selected and appointed through rigorous formal processes designed to achieve those ends. Regular performance reviews are encouraged.

Directors must endeavour to have an independent perspective when making judgments. The entity's interests are to be put ahead of other interests. Boards are encouraged to establish criteria for defining independent directors, but it is recognised that board effectiveness is not always enhanced by formal independence without independence of mind and the appropriate skills, knowledge, experience and time to contribute. It is also recognised that achieving high levels of formal independence may be difficult in New Zealand, with its relatively small pool of qualified and experienced directors.

As well as an independent perspective, the FMA considers that 'the underlying issues related to director independence can be addressed by':[205]

- a non-executive director being formally classified as independent only where he or she does not represent a substantial stakeholder, and where the board is satisfied that the director has no other direct or indirect interest or relationship that could reasonably influence decision-making
- the chair being independent
- boards meeting all disclosure obligations concerning directors and their interests
- boards of entities that intend to raise capital from the public, or that otherwise have a significant role in New Zealand's financial markets, being encouraged to have, or work towards, a majority of non-executive directors and a minimum one-third independent directors.

204 Ibid 10–13.
205 Ibid 11–12.

Boards are encouraged to consider issues around director tenure and to have a board charter setting out its role and responsibilities. Appropriate induction training for new appointees and ongoing training for directors should be provided. The role of the chair is critical; in particular, the relationship between the board and the CEO. It is desirable that the chair be an independent director and not a previous CEO. Only in special circumstances should the roles of chair and CEO be combined – for example, where an individual has skills, knowledge and experience not otherwise available and the circumstances are fully explained to stakeholders. The chair should be formally responsible for fostering a constructive governance culture and ensuring appropriate principles are applied. Larger boards are encouraged to consider nomination committees and non-executive directors are encouraged to make themselves familiar with the entity's activities.

Principle 3 addresses board committees.[206] Boards should use committees where they enhance effectiveness, while also retaining the ultimate decision-making authority of the board. They may not be appropriate or practical for every entity, but in larger or more complex businesses they can enhance effectiveness.

Audit committees are encouraged for larger entities, to recommend the appointment of external auditors, oversee the entity–auditor relationship and promote integrity and transparency in financial reporting. They should comprise non-executive directors, a majority of whom are independent, including at least one who is a qualified accountant or has some recognised financial expertise. The chair of the audit committee should be independent and not the board chair.[207]

Remuneration committees are encouraged for entities with larger boards. Risk committees, nomination committees and workplace health and safety committees are also suggested.

Principle 4 addresses reporting and disclosure, highlighting its importance for accountability between an entity and its stakeholders, and as an incentive for good governance.[208] Boards should have a rigorous process for ensuring the quality and integrity of financial statements. They 'should (in addition to all information required by law) include sufficient, meaningful information to enable investors and stakeholders to be well informed'.[209] The commentary suggests that entities other than public-sector entities, issuers and providers of financial services could adopt similar reporting standards. Non-financial reporting – 'considering the interests of ... stakeholders and material exposure to environmental, social and governance (ESG) factors'[210] – is also encouraged.

Entities should, where appropriate, make their codes of ethics and other governance documents readily available to investors and stakeholders online.

Principle 5 provides that remuneration should be transparent, fair and reasonable.[211] While acknowledging that '[a]dequate remuneration is necessary to attract, retain and motivate high quality directors and executives',[212] it is suggested that it be

206 Ibid 14–15.
207 Ibid 14.
208 Ibid 16–18.
209 Ibid 16.
210 Ibid.
211 Ibid 19–20.
212 Ibid 20.

reflected in performance. To allow shareholders to assess its quality, the commentary recommends that '[r]emuneration policies should be disclosed ... [as well as] total remuneration and a full breakdown of any other benefits and incentives paid to directors'.[213] A 'clear distinction between the remuneration packages of executive directors and non-executive directors'[214] should also be drawn, with performance incentives for executive directors recommended in the form of shares or options to reflect a longer-term view.

Principle 6 addresses risk management.[215] The commentary acknowledges that appropriate risk-taking is essential for business and that 'boards should be aware of and properly assess the nature and magnitude of risks faced by the entity',[216] including ESG matters. Rigorous processes for risk management and internal controls should be implemented. A risk management committee may be appropriate, 'depending on the size and circumstances of the entity'.[217] Annual reporting and review are recommended.

Principle 7 provides that boards 'should ensure the quality and independence of the external audit process'.[218] Good governance requires structures that promote auditors' independence from the entity and its management, protect auditors' professional objectivity, and facilitate access to information and personnel. When selecting auditors, boards should query whether auditors have been quality-reviewed by the FMA, and whether any issues identified have been addressed. While rotation of auditors is desirable (and required by professional and ethical standards), it needs to be balanced against the costs of a new engagement. It is noted that limiting non-audit work from a firm will help maintain independence and objectivity. Boards should explain in the annual report what non-audit work was undertaken and 'why this did not compromise auditor objectivity and independence'.[219] Boards should also report on audit fees paid, and differentiate them from fees for individually identified non-audit work.

Audit committees (see above) are crucial in the auditor appointment process and for dealing with complaints or disputes between auditors and entities. They should be open to the views of employees or others who raise concerns about auditor independence and objectivity.

The final principle, Principle 8, deals with shareholder relations and stakeholder interests.[220] Boards are encouraged to 'foster constructive relationships ... that encourage them to engage with the entity'. The guidelines appear to prioritise the interests of shareholders, describing them as 'the ultimate owners of companies' but that is qualified by the requirement to '[t]ake account of stakeholder interests' and an acknowledgement that the legal requirement to act 'in the best interests of the company'[221] will often involve advancing the interests of other stakeholders, such as employees and customers.

---

213 Ibid.
214 Ibid.
215 Ibid 21–2.
216 Ibid 22.
217 Ibid.
218 Ibid 23–5.
219 Ibid 23.
220 Ibid 26–8.
221 CA 1993 s 131.

Entities are encouraged to:[222]

- have clear policies for shareholder relations and regularly review practices
- maintain up-to-date online or other access to a comprehensive description of its business and structure, commentary on goals, strategies and performance, and key governance documents
- support shareholder participation in meetings by holding them in locations, and at times, that are convenient to shareholders and by providing clear and meaningful information about the business to be conducted thereat
- have clear policies on relationships with significant stakeholders, bearing in mind distinctions between public-sector and private entities. Compliance with these policies should be regularly assessed to ensure that such relations comply with the code of ethics and the law and align with accepted social, environmental, and ethical norms.

11.4.4.2 The NZX Code

The NZX last updated its corporate governance code in 2018 following a review that began in 2015.[223] The updated NZX Code aligns with the FMA Guidelines, discussed above. The specific reference in Principle 8 to stakeholder interests is omitted, although stakeholders are referred to, both there and in the other Principles. The new NZX Code has, since the previous substantive update in 2003, increased its focus on ESG and board diversity reporting, workplace health and safety risk management, and director and CEO remuneration reporting requirements.

Along with the improved alignment, the NZX Code gives issuers flexibility to tailor their governance practices to the needs of the entity. In line with the ASX *Corporate Governance Principles and Recommendations*,[224] the NZX Code adopts a three-tiered approach:

- the top tier sets out eight principles closely based on the FMA Guidelines
- the second tier contains recommendations that apply on a 'comply or explain' basis: the requirement for an explanation is new
- the third tier contains commentary and additional optional guidance on suggested good practice.

In addition to the NZX Code, the mandatory corporate governance provisions set out in the NZX *Listing Rules* continue to apply.[225]

The NZX Code suggests that: 'An issuer should provide non-financial disclosure at least annually, including considering environmental, economic and social sustainability factors and practices. It should explain how operational or non-financial targets are measured.'[226] The NZX recommends that issuers explain how they intend to manage ESG

---

222 FMA Guidelines, 26.

223 NZX Code 6.

224 ASX, *Corporate Governance Principles and Recommendations* (4th ed, 2019) <https://www.asx.com.au/documents/asx-compliance/cgc-principles-and-recommendations-fourth-edn.pdf>.

225 See NZX Code 4.

226 Ibid, Recommendation 4.3. A guidance note is available for listed issuers that are considering the disclosure of ESG factors under the NZX Code: NZX Ltd, 'Guidance Note: NZX ESG Guidance' (10 December 2020) <https://www.nzx.com/regulation/nzx-rules-guidance/corporate-governance-code>.

factors, that they report against a recognised international framework such as the Global Reporting Initiative, and that they describe how the business is performing against its strategic objectives.[227]

11.4.4.3 NZCGF Guidelines ('Forum Guidelines')

The Forum Guidelines[228] build on the FMA Guidelines, with a focus on shareholders: how information is presented to them and how their interests are considered and protected. Reporting should help shareholders understand a company's strategic objectives and report on ESG considerations specific to the company.[229] Additional ethical standards relate to a review of whistleblowing arrangements, a policy on the company's political engagement, and a policy on employee and director trading in company securities. They also recommend disclosure of policy and practices on related party transactions.[230] A diversity policy with measurable objectives is recommended, as is its disclosure, including reports on progress. Directors are considered independent if they have not been employed in the past three years and have not been a director of a related company.[231] The Forum Guidelines recommend a majority and the chair of committees be independent, and that boards should foster a culture where financial, strategic and ESG risks are considered.[232]

11.4.4.4 Institute of Directors' Code of Practice for Directors ('IOD Code')

The IOD Code[233] is not intended to be exhaustive and is designed to be read in conjunction with applicable law and other relevant codes such as the NZX Code.[234] It recommends monitoring and control of performance through reporting that provides shareholders with an assessment of the company's performance and position in a form that shareholders can readily understand.[235] As well as encouraging the adoption of a code of conduct by the company, directors should lead a culture of high ethical standards.[236] Boards should be balanced, with a mix of skills, knowledge and experience.[237] Listed companies should have a majority of non-executive directors and at least two independent directors. The CEO should generally not also be the chair.[238] Auditors should maintain communication with audit committees, meeting with them at least once a year, with auditors able to attend and speak at company meetings. Audit committees should be made up of independent directors, with the chair of the board ideally not the chair of the audit committee.[239]

---

227 NZX Code 21.
228 New Zealand Corporate Governance Forum, 'Guidelines' (July 2015) <www.nzcgf.org.nz/assets/Uploads/guidelines/nzcgf-guidelines-july-2015.pdf>.
229 Ibid 7.
230 Ibid 3.
231 Ibid 5.
232 Ibid 6, 9.
233 Institute of Directors (Inc), 'Code of Practice for Directors' (2022) <https://www.iod.org.nz/about-us/policies-and-documents/#>.
234 Ibid [1.3].
235 Ibid [3.16].
236 Ibid [3.1].
237 Ibid [3.6].
238 Ibid [3.7], [3.14].
239 Ibid [3.11], [3.12].

Remuneration should be fair, transparent and set to attract, motivate and retain the best people possible. Incentives should be aligned with strategy and performance, reviewed annually and disclosed in the annual report. Remuneration should be approved by shareholders, and it is recommended that remuneration policy is aligned with the objectives of the company. Remuneration committees should be comprised of independent directors.[240] Risk management plans, including systems of internal control within the company, should be implemented and maintained.[241]

Though not stated in its Code, the IOD also supports boards reporting on ESG matters and workplace health and safety performance.[242]

11.4.5 Sustainability

References to ESG matters appear in all of the codes of practice noted above, reflecting a growing awareness and concern about sustainability issues. New Zealand has a number of industry-led organisations in this space, including:

- the Sustainable Business Council, whose 'purpose is to mobilise New Zealand's most ambitious businesses to build a thriving and sustainable future for all',[243] and
- the Sustainable Business Network, which aims to 'collaborate to co-create solutions to some of the biggest problems in New Zealand in the areas of climate, waste and nature' and 'build sustainability capability in businesses by providing training, advice and resources'.[244]

A recent statutory amendment, originating as a member's Bill selected from the ballot, seeks to make sustainability an explicit consideration for company directors. The new provision:

> makes clear that a director, in acting as the mind and will of the company, can take actions which take into account wider matters other than the financial bottom-line. This accords with modern corporate governance theory that recognises that corporations are connected with communities, wider society, and the environment and need to measure their performance not only in financial terms, but also against wider measures including social, and environmental matters.[245]

Section 131 of the CA 1993, providing for the directors' duty to act in good faith and in the best interests of the company, was amended by the insertion of a new sub-s (5):

> To avoid doubt, in considering the best interests of a company or holding company for the purposes of this section, a director may consider matters other than the maximisation of profit (for example, environmental, social, and governance matters).

---

240 Ibid [3.8], [3.13].
241 Ibid [3.5].
242 See 'Corporate governance codes compared' (March 2022) <https://chapmantripp.com/media/lvbfrkrt/corporate-governance-codes-compared-2022.pdf>.
243 Sustainable Business Council, 'About the Sustainable Business Council' <https://sbc.org.nz/about-us/>.
244 Sustainable Business Network, 'Who we are' <https://sustainable.org.nz/about-sbn/who-we-are/>.
245 Companies (Directors Duties) Amendment Bill (NZ), Explanatory Note.

A member of public-policy think tank The New Zealand Initiative,[246] in condemning the amendment, somewhat optimistically concludes:

> The reality is that the current model of shareholder primacy does not need 'fixing.' Under it, directors are already able to take a broad view of what is in a company's best interests. Satisfying customers. Treating staff fairly. Repaying creditors. Meeting environmental obligations. Acting ethically. These are all interests the modern company – and its directors – must take into account. If they do not do so, they will quickly find their critical stake-holders jumping ship – including their customers, employees and even shareholders.[247]

In contrast, others have noted the growing pressure for law reform in this area, and that

> at a time when more and more is expected of directors, it is critical that direc-tors have more clarity in relation to which stakeholders they can or should legitimately have regard to, to what extent, and whether they can or should give priority to others over the stated preferences of shareholders.[248]

11.4.6 Future directions

Another area of growing significance is Māori business and governance. The loss of tribal land in the 19th century left iwi (tribes) with few resources to exploit. In recent times, however, assets have been returned to iwi ownership through *Treaty of Waitangi* settlements,[249] enabling investment in business. The revitalisation of Māori culture has led to greater acceptance of tikanga (Māori customary practices and principles), includ-ing in a business context.

According to Te Puni Kōkiri (the Ministry of Māori Development), 'good governance principles and practices are universal ... [but there are] particular characteristics of Māori organisations which bring extra dimensions to the practice of governance'.[250] Those noted include:

> the use of Te Reo [the Māori language], mihi [a greeting or introduction at the beginning of a gathering], karakia [prayers or incantations, for example, to open and close meetings], koha [gifts or donations, for example, by visitors to hosts], hospitality for manuhiri [guests], manaakitanga [respect, generosity

---

246 A successor to the New Zealand Business Roundtable, one of the main proponents of New Zealand's free-market-oriented economic reforms of the 1980s and 1990s.

247 Roger Partridge, 'Directors' Duties Bill is well-meaning but harmful' (4 May 2022) <https://www.nzinitiative.org.nz/reports-and-media/opinion/new-opinion-224/>.

248 Trish Keeper, 'The mainstreaming of climate change and the impact on directors' duties' (2020/2021) (13/14) *Journal of the Australasian Law Academics Association* 62, 74.

249 See Te Tai, 'What are Treaty settlements and why are they needed?' <https://teara.govt.nz/en/te-tai/about-treaty-settlements>.

250 Te Puni Kōkiri, 'What is governance?' (10 August 2022) <https://www.tpk.govt.nz/en/nga-putea-me-nga-ratonga/governance/effective-governance/what-is-governance>. See also Jade Newton, 'Reconciling traditional forms of Māori governance with models of Western corporate governance' (2019) 6 *Public Interest Law Journal of New Zealand* 15.

and care for others], whanaungatanga [connection between people; kinship], consensus decision-making and regular consultation hui [meetings] ... It can be important to have people with expertise in tikanga and kawa [Māori protocol and etiquette] on the board.[251]

11.4.7 Conclusion

A hallmark of New Zealand's corporate governance regime is flexibility, appropriate given the predominance of SMEs. The influential FMA Guidelines focus on general principles rather than rules and even the NZX Code gives listed issuers a degree of freedom to tailor their governance practices to their individual needs. The FMA, the main market monitor and regulator, has expressed a commitment 'to taking strong action and holding individuals and entities accountable when they break the law and fail to meet the standards that are expected of them', in contrast to the perceived ineffectiveness of its predecessor, while also advocating a flexible approach that 'ensure[s] the most appropriate and fit-for-purpose regulatory response to achieve the desired outcome'.[252]

While perhaps still not reflecting mainstream business practice in New Zealand, issues such as the place of non-shareholder stakeholders in board decision-making, sustainability and Māori approaches to governance are gaining a foothold.

11.5 Canada

Poonam Puri

11.5.1 Overview

Canadian corporate governance standards have both been shaped by Canada's ties with the UK and the US, and evolved in response to the unique Canadian context. They comprise formal requirements set out in corporate and securities legislation as well as industry norms and best practices promoted by private organisations. The result is a set of standards that are contextual, varying by the type of corporation and business activity. This is complicated, to an extent, by the division of powers between the federal and provincial/territorial governments, whereby there are multiple federal and provincial/territorial corporate statutes and multiple provincial/territorial securities regulations.

This section provides an introduction to the corporate governance framework in Canada. It begins with a description of distinctive features of the Canadian business context. It then explores the governing legislative and regulatory framework of Canadian corporations, taking an introductory view of corporate and securities legislation and the division of powers in Canada. It then discusses the corporate governance guidelines set out by securities regulations, stock exchange rules and other sources, and the enforcement mechanisms available to shareholders, stakeholders and regulators. The final

---

251 Te Puni Kōkiri, 'What is governance?' (10 August 2022) <https://www.tpk.govt.nz/en/nga-putea-me-nga-ratonga/governance/effective-governance/what-is-governance>.
252 FMA, 'Enforcement Policy' <https://www.fma.govt.nz/about-us/regulatory-approach/enforcement/enforcement-policy/>.

subsections discuss the role of sustainability and ESG in good corporate governance, as well as Canada's progress on climate change and diversity disclosure, and provide a forward-looking analysis of the challenge of adopting a stakeholder-centric governance framework.

11.5.2 Regulatory environment

Historically, Canada's corporate governance framework has been shaped by a variety of foreign legal traditions, including British common law and the American corporate and securities law regimes. Early Canadian corporate governance was rooted in the traditional English concept of majority rule, with the majority shareholders having broad discretion over the business of the corporation, even when it was at the expense of the minority shareholders.[253] Over time, the balance shifted to stronger protections for minority rights, which is reflected in Canadian case law, corporate statutes and securities regulations.[254]

Canada's corporate governance framework developed in the context of Canada's unique business landscape, which differs in significant ways from the UK, US and other common law jurisdictions. Two notable characteristics that have had a significant influence on how corporate laws, regulations and governance have evolved in Canada are: (1) the size and composition of Canadian capital markets; and (2) the high proportion of concentrated ownership structures.

11.5.2.1 Canadian capital markets

While its capital markets are small on a global scale, Canada has a large number of public companies in proportion to other countries. There is a large number of very small and micro-cap companies and a small number of very large companies. There is also significant variation between jurisdictions, with different provinces attracting companies from certain industries or with a certain level of market capitalisation.[255] For example, Alberta hosts many oil and gas companies, British Columbia hosts many micro-cap and venture companies, and Ontario hosts many financial services companies. A large proportion of Canadian companies are also cross-listed on an international exchange, meaning that they are subject to the securities rules of both Canada and the other jurisdiction(s). The Canadian corporate governance regime has had to develop to respond to the challenges of accommodating this unique range of public companies and local markets.

---

253 Philip Anisman, 'Majority-minority relations in Canadian corporation law: An overview' (1988) 13 *Canada-United States Law Journal* 85, 86.
254 Ibid. Starting in the late 1960s, a series of influential reports commissioned by the Ontario and federal governments served to modernise the corporate governance regime. In particular, the Kimber Report, published in 1966, ultimately served to entrench a shareholder-centric perspective of corporate governance in Canada, recognising that public confidence in the public markets is dependent on investors' ability to make informed choices and exercise shareholder rights. It resulted in the adoption of stronger investor protections under Ontario's securities legislation.
255 Poonam Puri, *Local and Regional Interests in the Debate on Optimal Securities Regulatory Structure* (Commissioned Reports, Studies and Public Policy Documents, Paper 118, Ottawa, 2003).

Jurisdictional differences partly account for the fact that Canada remains one of the only industrialised nations without a national securities regulator. Despite a number of attempts to create a national or common regulator, there have been significant concerns that a national entity would not appropriately respond to distinct jurisdictional needs.

Canadian regulators have also had to carefully balance investor protection with regulatory burden reduction. On the one hand, investors face greater risk when investing in smaller companies; therefore, robust disclosure and shareholder action rights are necessary to account for increased price volatility and illiquidity risk. On the other hand, stringent regulations may be unaffordable for smaller companies, and may ultimately force them to go private or push them out of Canada. In order to strike the right balance, the Canadian corporate governance framework has been designed flexibly, rather than as a one-size-fits-all regime. There are different corporate governance standards for public versus private companies, as well as for established companies versus venture issuers.

11.5.2.2 Concentrated ownership

Canada's corporate governance regime has also been influenced by how Canadian companies are owned and controlled. There are two main types of corporate ownership: (1) dispersed or widely held; and (2) concentrated or closely held. The first type means that the company is held by a large number of shareholders who do not individually have control over the company. The second type means that the company has a controlling shareholder or shareholders and can impact company decision-making.

Since the 20th century, the Canadian corporate sector has been marked by family-controlled concentrated ownership structures.[256] Today, a large proportion of Canadian companies remain family-controlled,[257] either through equity ownership or voting interests. As a result, the Canadian corporate governance regime has developed to include provisions aimed at limiting agency costs and protecting minority shareholder rights. For example, shareholders with greater than one per cent ownership in a company can submit proposals to be heard and voted on at annual meetings,[258] and in the event of a fundamental corporate change, shareholders who dissent have the right to require the company to buy back their shares at a fair market value.[259] Where shareholders believe that the company has acted in a way that is oppressive or unfairly prejudicial relative to their reasonable expectations, they have a right to seek a statutory oppression remedy.[260]

11.5.3 Legislation and regulators

The Canadian corporate governance framework derives from two primary sources: (1) federal and provincial/territorial corporate statutes; and (2) provincial/territorial

---

256 Randall Morck et al, *The Rise and Fall of the Widely Held Firm – A History of Corporate Ownership in Canada* (National Bureau of Economic Research, Working Paper No 10635, 2004).

257 In 2019, family-owned businesses comprised 63.1 per cent of all private companies in Canada. See The Conference Board of Canada, *The Economic Impact of Family- Owned Enterprises in Canada* (September 2019) <https://familyenterprise.ca/wp-content/uploads/2020/01/CBOC-2019-Family-Owned-Enterprises-Impact-Report.pdf>.

258 See, eg, *Canada Business Corporations Act,* RSC 1985 ('CBCA') s 137.

259 See, eg, ibid s 190.

260 See, eg, ibid s 241.

securities legislation, rules and policies. Public companies are also subject to the rules of the stock exchange(s) that their securities are listed on.

11.5.3.1 Corporate statutes

The division of federal and provincial powers in Canada is outlined by the *Constitution Act 1867*.[261] As both the federal and provincial governments have jurisdiction to incorporate companies,[262] Canada has both a federal corporate statute and 13 provincial/territorial corporate statutes. Each statute contains provisions on how to incorporate, sets out the duties and responsibilities of directors and officers, and establishes the rights and remedies available to shareholders and other stakeholders. In some cases, the requirements apply exclusively to public companies, although private companies may choose to implement them as best practices.[263]

Despite what might appear to be a ripe condition for fragmentation, and unlike in some other jurisdictions, Canadian federal and provincial/territorial incorporation statutes are quite similar, with provincial/territorial statutes largely mirroring provisions in the federal statute. The 'race to the bottom' phenomenon has mostly escaped Canadian corporate law, as provincial/territorial and federal statutes do not attempt to entice corporations to their own particular jurisdictions with statutory incentives and innovations.

Canada Business Corporations Act

The *Canada Business Corporations Act* ('CBCA'), which came into force in 1975, governs all Canadian companies that are incorporated federally. It sets out a basic corporate governance framework, including how to incorporate a company, the rights and responsibilities of directors and officers, shareholder rights and remedies, as well as financial accountability and disclosure. The CBCA does not prescribe detailed rules of how companies should be run, leaving the business affairs of the company to its management and directors.

In 2001, major amendments were passed to modernise the CBCA and increase the global competitiveness of Canadian businesses. Directors' duties and liabilities were amended, bringing the CBCA closer in line to the statutory regimes of US jurisdictions like Delaware, where directors are afforded greater flexibility in running the company.[264]

---

261 *Constitution Act 1867*, (Imp), 30 & 31 Vict, c 3.

262 Ibid, ss 91, 92(11). Provincial jurisdiction is expressly set out with respect to 'Incorporation of Companies with Provincial Objects'. Though no such express provision exists for the federal government, the courts have interpreted that the federal government has jurisdiction to incorporate through its general power to make laws for peace, order and good government. See *Citizens' and the Queen Insurance Cos v Parsons, Western Ins Co v Johnston* (1880) 4 SCR 215.

263 For example, public companies are typically required to appoint an external auditor, while private companies are exempted from this requirement. This recognises that for small, private companies, the benefits of an external audit may not outweigh the costs.

264 See KG Ottenbreit and JE Walker, "Learning from the Delaware experience: of the Canada Business Corporations Act and the Delaware General Corporation Law' (1998) 29(3) *Canadian Business Law Journal* 364, 369; and Ruth O Kuras, 'Corporate social responsibility: A Canada–US comparative analysis" (2002) 28(3) *Manitoba Law Journal* 303, 313.

These amendments included:

- broadened rules for indemnification of directors and officers for liabilities[265]
- expansion of director responsibilities from simply managing the business and affairs of a corporation to managing, or supervising the management of, the business and affairs of a corporation,[266] and
- creation of a general 'due diligence' defence, whereby directors are not held liable if they exercise the same degree of care, diligence and skill that a reasonably prudent person would exercise in comparable circumstances.[267]

These amendments were balanced by expanding shareholder rights, including by providing shareholders with enhanced opportunities to participate in companies' decision-making. These changes included:

- provisions permitting shareholders to communicate, participate in meetings and vote via electronic means[268]
- relaxed mechanisms for individual shareholders to submit proposals,[269] and
- clarification of expanded rules regarding unanimous shareholder agreements.[270]

The 2019 amendments to the CBCA demonstrate a growing role for the federal government in setting corporate governance standards. These amendments codified key elements relating to directors' and officers' duties as set out by the Supreme Court of Canada ('SCC') in *BCE Inc v 1976 Debentureholders*.[271] Under the CBCA, directors and officers are subject to a fiduciary duty to act honestly and in good faith with respect to the best interests of the corporation. The amendments provide that in satisfying this duty, directors and officers may, but are not required to, consider the interests of other stakeholders, including (but presumably not limited to) the following: shareholders, employees, retirees and pensioners, creditors, consumers and governments; the environment; and the best interests of the corporation.[272] Other amendments, which are not yet in force, include:

- requirements for prescribed companies regarding diversity, the well-being of employees, retirees and pensioners, and the clawback of director and officer compensation, and
- requirements for public companies to disclose their remuneration practices to shareholders and to hold an annual, non-binding shareholder 'say-on-pay' vote.[273]

The 2019 CBCA amendments were consistent with similar amendments that had been made to US corporate statutes, particularly with respect to their increased focus on stakeholder interests.[274] They reflect a larger shift in the corporate world from shareholder

---

265 CBCA s 124.
266 CBCA s 102(1).
267 CBCA s 123.
268 CBCA ss 132, 141.
269 CBCA s 137.
270 CBCA s 146.
271 *BCE Inc v 1976 Debentureholders* [2008] 3 SCR 560.
272 CBCA s 122(1.1).
273 CBCA, Amendments Not in Force (as at August 2023).
274 See, eg, *New York Business Corporation Law* s 717(3)(b).

primacy theory, which holds that the corporation's role is solely to maximise share-holder value,[275] to stakeholder theory, which holds that corporations should also take into account the interests of various stakeholders. The Canadian courts and federal government have recognised that companies have a responsibility not only to their shareholders, but also to the communities in which they operate.

The provincial/territorial statutes

Each province and territory has its own corporate statute. Companies can choose to incorporate under the CBCA or under the statute of their home jurisdiction. The provincial/territorial statutes have generally developed based on the CBCA model; however, the 2001 amendments to the CBCA resulted in greater divergence between the federal and provincial/territorial statutes. Provinces including British Columbia[276] and Ontario have since introduced their own amendments, which mirror some of the changes to the CBCA.

11.5.3.2 Securities regulation

Though securities regulation is not explicitly mentioned in the *Constitution Act 1867*, it has been interpreted as falling under provincial jurisdiction over 'Property and Civil Rights in the Province'.[277] As a result, Canada does not have a national securities regulator, nor a federal securities law statute. Each province and territory has its own securities regulatory authority and its own set of securities laws and regulations.

The Canadian securities regulations system is administered by 13 provincial/territorial securities regulatory authorities that are independent and are broadly tasked with administering the provincial/territorial securities Acts and other relevant legislation. The regulatory purposes of most of the securities Acts are to protect investors from unfair, improper or fraudulent practices and to promote efficient capital markets and confidence in those markets. After the 2008 GFC, the purpose of Ontario's *Securities Act*, RSO 1990 ('OSA') was revised to include the mitigation of systemic risk; and again, more recently to include fostering capital formation.[278] Practically, the primary responsibilities of the regulators include making rules, monitoring compliance with securities laws and investigating breaches of them, and enforcing those laws. Other day-to-day regulatory responsibilities are delegated to the recently amalgamated, pan-Canadian self-regulatory organisation ('SRO'),[279] and the stock exchanges.

Together, the 13 securities regulators have formed an organisation called the Canadian Securities Administrators ('CSA'), which works to harmonise the provincial/territorial securities regimes. The CSA issues national instruments ('NIs') and multilateral instruments (along with companion policies that provide further guidance), which are then incorporated into provincial/territorial laws by the regulators that have rule-making authority, or into policy in the other jurisdictions. However, the harmonisation is not absolute, as regulators have discretion to opt out or amend provisions of the NIs, and to enact other local rules.

---

275 AA Berle, 'Corporate powers as power in trust' (1931) 44(7) *Harvard Law Review* 1049, 1049–50.
276 *Business Corporations Act*, SBC 2002, c 57.
277 *Constitution Act 1867*, 30 & 31 Vict, c 3, s 92(13).
278 *Securities Act*, RSO 1990, c S.5, s 1.1(b.1), (c) [OSA].
279 The new SRO consolidated the functions of the two formerly existing SROs, the Investment Industry Regulatory Organization of Canada ('IIROC') and the Mutual Fund Dealers Association ('MFDA').

11.5.3.3 Stock exchange rules

Public companies that are listed on a stock exchange must also comply with the rules of that stock exchange. For example, companies listed on the Toronto Stock Exchange ('TSX') are subject to the rules in the *TSX Company Manual* ('TSX Rules').

Historically, the TSX Rules were the primary source of corporate governance disclosure requirements in Canada. In 2005, to provide greater transparency on corporate governance practices for public companies, the CSA published NI 58-101 – *Corporate Governance Practices* ('NI 58-101') and NP 58-201 – *Corporate Governance Guidelines* ('NP 58-201'), which now largely overlap with requirements under the TSX Rules. One additional requirement imposed by the TSX Rules is that companies must seek shareholder approval for certain transactions.[280]

11.5.4 Codes of practice

11.5.4.1 Corporate governance guidelines

Canada's corporate statutes do not contain formal corporate governance codes. Instead, companies must comply with the principles-based requirements and best practices that are set out in securities regulations and stock exchange rules.

Corporate governance guidelines are set out in NP 58-201 and NI 58-101. NP 58-201 sets out a number of corporate governance guidelines for public companies (other than investment funds), including with respect to board composition and mandate, code of business conduct and ethics, and nomination and compensation of directors. This instrument is not intended to be prescriptive, but rather, serves to provide guidance on best practices. However, NI 58-101 requires that companies either comply with the guidance in NP 58-201 or explain why they did not comply in their public disclosure. In creating this 'comply or explain' approach, the Canadian securities regulators have expressly encouraged public companies to implement the guidelines flexibly, in a way that suits their individual circumstances.[281] Private companies are not subject to these guidelines at all, but many choose to implement some of them as best practices. Venture issuers are subject to fewer disclosure obligations under NI 58-101.

Public companies may also be subject to additional corporate governance requirements when they engage in certain related-party transactions. For instance, in the event of a related-party transaction, some public companies may have to comply with procedural and reporting requirements under Multilateral Instrument 61-101 – *Protection of Minority Security Holders in Special Transactions*. This instrument ensures that minority shareholder rights are adequately protected against potential self-dealing.

11.5.4.2 Other sources

In addition to the primary sources of corporate governance requirements discussed above, Canadian corporate governance has been strongly shaped by Canadian

---

280 See, eg, *TSX Company Manual* s 611(c).
281 See Ontario Securities Commission, 'Request for Comment, Notice of Proposed Multilateral Policy 58-201 *Effective Corporate Governance* and Proposed Multilateral Instrument 58-101 *Disclosure of Corporate Governance Practices*, Forms 58-101F1 and 58-101F2' (16 January 2004).

institutional investors, proxy advisory groups, the media and professional director associations. For instance, the Canadian Coalition for Good Corporate Governance is a national institutional investor organisation that promotes good governance at public companies. Glass Lewis and Institutional Shareholder Services are proxy advisory firms which provide proxy voting guidelines for the shareholders of public companies. While these organisations have established themselves as influential proponents of corporate governance best practices, it is important to note that these practices are not necessarily required or even recommended by the relevant securities regulations.

11.5.4.3 Enforcement

The Canadian corporate governance enforcement regime is responsive to the various sources of Canadian corporate governance laws and regulations. Canadian corporate laws are typically enforced by private parties through the courts, while the securities regulations are enforced by the securities regulatory authorities and SROs. Stock exchanges are also able to enforce their rules by delisting companies in cases of non-compliance.

Private enforcement

The separation of ownership and control in corporations means that shareholders must place their trust in officers and directors to make sound business decisions that will protect their financial interests. Where management and/or directors do not appropriately carry out their duties or place their personal interests above those of the company, corporate law provides shareholder remedies to hold them accountable. There are two primary remedies under Canadian corporate law:

(1) *Oppression remedy* – this powerful remedy permits a complainant to apply for a range of orders from the court where that complainant feels that the company, its directors or officers has acted 'in a manner that is oppressive, unfairly prejudicial to, or which unfairly disregards, that complainant's individual interests'.[282] The court can make any order it sees fit, including compensating the aggrieved party, appointing or removing directors, dissolving the company etc.[283]

(2) *Derivative action* – this is the right to bring an action on behalf of the company, with permission of the court, for breach by directors and officers of the duties they owe to the corporation.[284] It is the only remedy available to shareholders for breach of directors' fiduciary duty since that duty is owed only to the company.[285]

Public enforcement

There are three types of public enforcement mechanisms available in Canada:

(1) *Criminal prosecution* – in Canada, criminal law is under the jurisdiction of the federal government. There are a number of securities-related offences under the *Criminal Code*, including insider trading, tipping and fraud.[286]

---

282 See, eg, CBCA s 241.
283 See, eg, CBCA s 241(3).
284 See, eg, CBCA s 239.
285 See, eg, CBCA s 122(1)(a).
286 *Criminal Code*, RSC 1985, c C-46, s 382.1(1), 382.1(2), 380(2).

(2) *Quasi-criminal prosecution* – while only the federal government can enact laws which carry criminal sanctions, securities regulatory authorities can lay quasi-criminal charges against companies and individuals for violations of certain securities laws. These charges carry serious consequences, including jail terms and fines, and are tried by the staff of the securities regulatory authorities in provincial/territorial courts.

(3) *Administrative proceedings* – securities regulatory authorities can also impose various sanctions for violations of securities law or conduct contrary to the public interest, including monetary penalties, disgorgement and trading bans.[287] Administrative sanctions are the most common type of public enforcement as they have a lower burden of proof.

11.5.5 Sustainability

Canada, like many other jurisdictions, has shifted over time from shareholder primacy to a stakeholder-centric approach. The SCC has established that while the fiduciary duty of directors is owed exclusively to the corporation, the board of directors may also consider the interests of various stakeholders including employees, consumers and the environment.[288] The SCC has also endorsed the business judgment rule, meaning that courts will not second-guess directors' judgment as long as their decision was reasonable under the circumstances.[289] From a policy perspective, this represents a 'nudge' in the direction of increased corporate social responsibility, while recognising that progress must be grounded in business reality.

On a global stage, environmental, social and governance ('ESG') considerations have become increasingly important. There has been an increase in ESG-driven investing worldwide, including in Canada, where 81 per cent of investors report integrating ESG principles into their investment decisions.[290] While Canada has so far adopted a disclosure-based approach to ESG matters related to climate change and diversity, many stakeholders are in favour of tougher standards to yield more substantive results.

11.5.5.1 Climate change

Under the current regime, Canadian public companies are only required to make disclosures with respect to climate-related information if that information is material.[291] Disclosures under the existing system have received a number of criticisms, including that the information provided is not complete, consistent and comparable across companies; and that companies engage in selective reporting against their preferred standard or framework. There has been growing pressure to improve the climate change

---

287 See, eg, OSA s 127.
288 *BCE Inc v 1976 Debentureholders* [2008] 3 SCR 560, [39].
289 Ibid 40.
290 RBC Global Asset Management, *ESG in a Pandemic World: Responsible Investment Survey 2021* (13 October 2021) <https://www.rbcgam.com/en/ca/about-us/responsible-investment/our-latest-independent-research>.
291 See CSA Staff Notice 51-333 *Environmental Reporting Guidance* (27 October 2010) and CSA Staff Notice 51-358 *Reporting of Climate Change-related Risks* (1 August 2019).

disclosure framework to ensure that the information provided is consistent and comparable and can be used by investors to make meaningful decisions.

In October 2021, the CSA published for comment the proposed NI 51-107 –*Disclosure of Climate-related Matters* ('NI 51-107') and its companion policy 51-107CP – *Disclosure of Climate-related Matters*.[292] This instrument will introduce disclosure requirements regarding climate-related matters for most public companies to help improve the consistency and comparability of Canadian companies' climate change disclosure. These requirements are largely based on the recommendations of the Taskforce on Climate-Related Financial Disclosures ('TCFD'), published in its report entitled *Recommendations of the Task Force on Climate-related Financial Disclosures* in June 2017. The requirements track the four core elements of the TCFD recommendations:

(1) *governance* – description of the board and management's oversight of climate-related risks and opportunities

(2) *strategy* – description of material climate-related risks and opportunities the company has identified over the short, medium and long term, and their impact on the company's businesses, strategy, and financial planning

(3) *risk management* – description of the company's processes for identifying, assessing and managing climate-related risks and how they are integrated within the company's overall risk management

(4) *metrics and targets* – disclosure of the metrics and targets used to assess climate-related risks and opportunities, where this information is material.

NI 51-107 was expected to come into effect in December 2022, bringing the Canadian climate-change disclosure regime in line with the new global standard.

However, the Canadian Government has already taken additional action to address climate change. In 2020, the Canadian Government introduced the Large Employer Emergency Financing Facility ('LEEFF') to help provide financing to businesses impacted by the COVID-19 pandemic.[293] To qualify for support under LEEFF, companies must publish annual climate-related disclosure reports that are consistent with the TCFD's recommendations. Tying climate change disclosure to financial incentives in this way reflects the reality that the existing non-mandatory disclosure model may not go far enough to affect meaningful corporate change.

11.5.5.2 Diversity

Canadian diversity disclosure requirements have expanded significantly since their initial introduction seven years ago, from a focus on gender diversity alone to include members of other minority groups. However, it is unclear whether the changes go far enough, and whether the 'comply or explain' model is sufficient to drive meaningful change. Based on increased pressure from the private sector, including proxy advisory

---

292 See CSA Notice 51-107 *Consultation Climate-related Disclosure Update* and CSA Notice and Request for Comment Proposed National Instrument 51-107 *Disclosure of Climate-related Matters* (18 October 2021).

293 Prime Minister of Canada, 'Prime Minister announces additional support for businesses to help save Canadian jobs' (Media Release, 11 May 2020) <https://pm.gc.ca/en/news/news-releases/2020/05/11/prime-minister-announces-additional-support-businesses-help-save>.

firms, it appears that the corporate governance framework may need to go further to keep up with the times.

Diversity disclosure requirements were first introduced in 2014 as part of amendments to NI 58-101. The amendments require (non-venture) public companies to make annual disclosure on the following:[294]

- director term limits and other mechanisms of renewal of the board
- policies regarding the representation of women on the board
- the board's or nominating committee's consideration of the representation of women in the director identification and selection process
- the company's consideration of the representation of women in executive officer positions when making executive officer appointments
- targets regarding the representation of women on the board and in executive officer positions
- the number of women on the board and in executive officer positions.

NI 58-101 did not require that companies set specific targets or quotas for women in executive positions or on boards. Rather, the CSA adopted the 'comply or explain' approach, whereby a company would have to either confirm that it had a policy regarding the disclosure requirements and provide disclosure regarding the policy, or otherwise explain why it did not have such a policy in place.

The CSA conducts an annual review of the impact of these diversity disclosure requirements. The data indicates that while some progress has been made over the past seven years, it has been slow. Between 2014 and 2021, the proportion of women on boards doubled to 22 per cent, but only 6 per cent of board chairs were women in 2021.[295] While 32 per cent of public companies adopted targets for the representation of women on their board in 2021 (as compared to 7 per cent in 2014), only 6 per cent adopted targets for the representation of women in executive officer positions (as compared to 2 per cent in 2014).[296]

In January 2020, new CBCA amendments came into force which require the directors of public companies (including venture issuers) to report to shareholders and Corporations Canada annually prescribed information regarding diversity among both the directors and members of senior management of the company.[297] Similarly to the framework under NI 58–101, the new requirements take a 'comply or explain' approach. However, this framework is broader, as it requires disclosure with respect not only to women, but also members of visible minorities, persons with disabilities and Aboriginal peoples.

In 2021, the final report of the Ontario Capital Markets Modernization Taskforce was published. The taskforce was established to review the status of Ontario's capital

---

294 Multilateral CSA Notice of Amendments to National Instrument 58-101, *Disclosure of Corporate Governance Practices* (15 October 2014).
295 CSA Multilateral Staff Notice 58-313, *Review of Disclosure Regarding Women on Boards and in Executive Officer Positions* – Year 7 Report (4 November 2021) 4.
296 Ibid 5.
297 CBCA s 172.1(1).

markets. It made a number of recommendations that go beyond the current 'comply or explain' model under NI 58–101 as well as the scope of the CBCA provisions, including:[298]

(1) requiring public companies to set targets for representation on their board of directors and executive management of individuals who identify as women, Black, Indigenous and people of colour, persons with disabilities or LGBTQ+

(2) requiring public companies to adopt written policies for their director nomination process that addresses the identification of candidates who identify as women, Black, Indigenous and people of colour, persons with disabilities or LGBTQ+

(3) requiring public companies to set 12-year tenure limits for their directors

(4) ensuring that diversity is similarly represented at the board and executive levels of the Ontario Securities Commission.

These recommendations demonstrate that while progress has been made, there is still much room for improvement with respect to meaningful representation of Canada's diversity in its boards and C-suites.

In addition to governments and regulators, other industry groups, including the Canadian Coalition for Good Corporate Governance, Glass Lewis and Institutional Shareholder Services have issued their own recommended best practices related to diversity. For example, Glass Lewis now recommends, for TSX-listed companies, voting against the chair of the nominating committee of a board with less than two gender diverse directors, or the whole nominating committee of a board with no gender-diverse directors.[299] As the conversation on diversity continues, Canada is likely to see the disclosure requirements continue to expand.

11.5.6 Future directions

As Canada and the rest of the world face significant challenges, including climate change, the COVID-19 pandemic, international conflict and a global recession, companies must be prepared to respond to the rapidly changing state of affairs. These crises have initiated important conversations, including on social inequities, both within and outside Canada's borders, on the future of work, the vulnerability of global supply chains and the importance of sustainable energy. These conversations present an opportunity for companies to re-evaluate their relationships with their stakeholders and what it means to be a good corporate citizen in 2022.

Arguably the most significant future direction for the evolution of corporate governance in Canada is related to the general shift from shareholder primacy to stakeholder primacy. Although the CBCA enumerates the various stakeholder interests that may be considered by directors in determining the best interests of the corporation, there are no existing guidelines on how boards should go about taking these interests into account in their decision-making.

---

298 *Ontario Capital Markets Modernization: Final Report* (January 2021) <https://files.ontario.ca/books/mof-capital-markets-modernization-taskforce-final-report-en-2021-01-22-v2.pdf>.
299 Glass Lewis, *2022 Policy Guidelines – Canada* (2021) 7, 30.

Peter Dey and Sarah Kaplan have recently published a report entitled *360° Governance: Where Are the Directors in a World in Crisis?*, which sets out 13 good governance guidelines for the 21st century.[300] The report includes guidelines to help directors establish an analytical framework to be able to better consider and balance the interests of stakeholders, including by establishing a corporate purpose that addresses all of the company's stakeholders, identifying who the company's stakeholders are, fostering a relationship with Indigenous peoples, reporting on stakeholder impact and tracking progress over time, and establishing a process to fairly consider stakeholder interests. While these guidelines are not mandatory under the law, companies that start thinking about implementing a stakeholder framework now will be better prepared for the emerging trends and practices that will continue to gain traction in the years to come.

11.5.7 Conclusion

As directors and officers approach the domestic and international challenges faced by Canadian corporations, the contextual nature of corporate governance in Canada and the lack of a comprehensive codified regime, along with the continued shift to stakeholder-centric corporate governance, provide both a degree of flexibility and uncertainty. Directors and officers are afforded great deference in applying their business judgement and shaping best practices and industry norms to tackle contemporary challenges, but they must be mindful of stakeholder expectations.

11.6 South Africa

Irene-marié Esser

11.6.1 Overview

Corporate governance in South Africa has been the primary focus of various reports since 1994, known as the King Reports (see below). The most recent King Report – King IV (2016) or 'King IV' – defines, for the first time, 'corporate governance' with reference to 'the exercise of ethical and effective leadership by a governing body towards the achievement of governance outcomes' like ethical culture, good performance, effective control and legitimacy.[301]

This section will provide a brief overview and discussion of King IV, focusing on its application, scope, aims and the governance outcomes, principles and practices. It will also refer to relevant provisions of the *Companies Act 2008* (South Africa) ('SACA 2008'). It will conclude by considering developments relating to environmental, social and governance ('ESG') issues in the South African context as well as expected areas of significance.

---

300 Peter Dey and Sarah Kaplan, *360° Governance: Where Are the Directors in a World in Crisis?* (Michael Lee-Chin Family Institute for Corporate Citizenship, University of Toronto, February 2021) <https://www.rotman.utoronto.ca/FacultyAndResearch/ResearchCentres/LeeChinInstitute/Sustainability-Research-Resources/360-Governance-Report>.

301 See *Report on Corporate Governance for South Africa 2016* (Institute of Directors in Southern Africa, 2016) 11 (definition of 'corporate governance'). The report is available at <https://www.iodsa.co.za/page/king-iv>. In these footnotes it is referred to as 'King IV' or 'King IV (2016)'.

11.6.2 Regulatory environment

In South Africa corporate governance became particularly prominent with the publication of the King Reports, referred to generally as King I (1994),[302] King II (2002),[303] King III (2009)[304] and King IV (2016).[305]

South Africa has a hybrid corporate governance system, meaning that directors' duties and principles of good governance are regulated by legislation, but also governed by several common law principles and rules. In addition, important corporate governance recommendations are also contained in codes of best practice, currently contained in King IV. Of specific significance is the fact that corporate social responsibility ('CSR') is dealt with in King IV as well as in the SACA 2008. Social and ethics committees, required for certain South African companies, are of particular importance as will be seen below.

The Johannesburg Stock Exchange Ltd (JSE) *Listings Requirements* add more additional requirements, providing that JSE-listed entities must implement certain specific corporate governance practices and disclose compliance therewith in their annual reports.[306] In addition to requiring listed companies to comply with King III (applicable at that stage), the JSE launched a Socially Responsible Investment Index ('SRI Index') in May 2004.[307] In this Index the JSE used criteria to measure the 'triple-bottom line' performance of the FTSE/JSE All Share Index.[308] The SRI Index was replaced at the end of 2015. The JSE has adopted the FTSE Russell ESG Ratings process to create the following two indices, launched on 12 October 2015: the FTSE/JSE Responsible Investment Index and the FTSE/JSE Responsible Investment Top 30 Index.

11.6.3 Legislation and regulators

Many of the recommendations of King III and King IV are now embedded in the SACA 2008.[309] It is not the purpose of this subsection to deal with the SACA 2008 in detail, but rather to discuss the position of stakeholders and the extent that directors have to consider their interests under the SACA 2008. The current provisions applying to stakeholders

302 *The King Report on Corporate Governance* (29 November 1994) ('King I').

303 *King Report on Corporate Governance for South Africa – 2002* (Institute of Directors in Southern Africa, 2002) ('King II').

304 *The King Code of Governance for South Africa 2009* and the *King Report of Governance in South Africa 2009* ('King III'). Both documents are together referred to as the King Report (2009). The King Report (2002), replacing King I, was applicable to South African enterprises until the end of February 2010, after which the King Report (2009) became effective. See <www.iodsa.co.za>.

305 The content of King IV was developed by building on the strengths of King III. The drafting of King IV was led by Ansie Ramalho and various team members. The consultation process was widely consultative.

306 See Listings Requirements 3.84 and 8.63(a) dealing with corporate governance requirements. It is stated that: 'The effect of incorporating certain practices from the King Code in the Listings Requirements is to make their implementation mandatory, this is notwithstanding the fact that application of the corporate governance practices in the King Code is generally voluntary.'

307 For the SRI Index see JSE, 'FTSE/JSE Responsible Investment Index' <https://www.jse.co.za/services/indices/ftsejse-responsible-investment-index>.

308 See JSE, 'Sustainability Segment' <http://www.jse.co.za/sri/index.htm>.

309 See A Loubser, 'The King Reports on corporate governance' in I-M Esser and M K Havenga (eds), *Corporate Governance Annual Review 2012* (LexisNexis, 2012) 20ff. This is based on King III but will be similar regarding King IV as the contents of King III and King IV are much aligned. The differences are more in application and scope.

under the SACA 2008 are important because there were no comparable provisions in the former *Companies Act 1973* (South Africa).[310]

A unique aspect of the South African legislation is that s 72 of the SACA 2008 introduces a compulsory social and ethics committee for all state-owned and listed companies, as well as other companies with a 'public interest score'[311] of more than 500.[312] The number of employees and the turnover are some of the factors that determine if a company is obliged to have such a committee. It is worth noting that it is the shareholders of the company, and not the board, that must appoint this committee.[313] A minimum of three directors or prescribed officers[314] must serve on a company's social and ethics committee. One of them must not, at least for the previous three financial years, have been involved in the day-to-day management of the company's business.[315] The social and ethics committee has the following functions:[316]

> To monitor the company's activities, having regard to any relevant legislation, other legal requirements or prevailing codes of best practice, in matters concerning social and economic development, including the company's position regarding the goals and purposes as envisaged in, for example, the *OECD Principles* and the *Global Compact Principles*, as well as record of sponsorships, consumer relationships and labour and employment.

The committee should report annually to the shareholders at the company's annual general meeting on the matters within its mandate.[317]

CSR issues enjoy more prominence in the SACA 2008 than in any previous company legislation in South Africa. Section 7(d) confirms that one of the purposes of the SACA 2008 is to reaffirm the concept of the company as a means of achieving economic

---

310 Act 61 of 1973.

311 The 'public interest score' is calculated at the end of a financial year, and is the sum of a number of things, including the average number of employees, the turnover of the company, and the nature and extent of the company's activities during that financial year. It is used to determine whether a company must comply with enhanced accountability requirements based on its social and economic impact. See *Companies Regulations, 2011* reg 26(2).

312 See SACA 2008 s 72(4) and *Companies Regulations, 2011* regs 43 and 26(2). See HJ Kloppers, 'Driving corporate social responsibility (CSR) through the *Companies Act*: An overview of the role of the social and ethics committee' (2013) 16(1) *Potchefstroom Electronic Law Journal* 165 for an overview of the social and ethics committee. See the Draft Companies Amendment Bill 2021 published in October 2021 where it is proposed that these committees produce a report annually, which would be subject to shareholder approval through an ordinary resolution.

313 This seems to be the case as there is a clear distinction between 'the board' and the 'company' in regs 43(2) and 43(3). In the Companies Amendment Bill 2021 this is also clear from s 72(10) (as amended) that the social and ethics committee of public and state-owned companies must be appointed at the annual general meeting. See also PA Delport (ed), *Henochsberg on the Companies Act 71 of 2008* (May 2022 edition) ('Henochsberg') 284.

314 Regulation 43(4). A prescribed officer is a person who, within a company, performs any function that has been designated by the Minister in terms of SACA s 66(10). It is clear in the *Companies Regulations, 2011* R38 that a prescribed officer is not necessarily a director, but rather anyone who 'exercises general executive control over and management of the whole, or a significant portion, of the business and activities of the company'.

315 See reg 43(4). See Natasha Bouwman, 'Are We Moving to a Two-Tier Board Structure?' (April 2010) *Without Prejudice* 14.

316 See reg 43(5) for the functions of this committee.

317 See reg 43(5).

and social benefit,[318] while s 72(4) provides for the establishment of the social and ethics committee mentioned above. Several sections in the SACA 2008 also afford protection to stakeholders,[319] but others refer to the primary role of shareholders.[320] Stakeholder protection is addressed in s 76(3)(b).

Subsections 76(3)(a) and (b) of the SACA 2008 provide as follows:

> A director of a company, when acting in that capacity, must exercise the powers and perform the functions of a director (a) in good faith and for a proper purpose; (b) *in the best interests of the company* ... (emphasis added)

This particular section does not clarify what is meant by 'the company' in the emphasised part. Does it mean the interests of 'the shareholders as a whole' (a shareholder primacy approach);[321] or the interests of various stakeholders on a case-by-case basis; or primarily the best interests of the shareholders (members), having regard to other stakeholders (an enlightened shareholder value approach)?[322] There is authority in South Africa that the all-inclusive stakeholder approach requires of directors to consider the interests of various stakeholders on a case-by-case basis, but in the end the decision must be in the best interests of the company, even if it could be to the detriment of the shareholders.[323]

An inclusive approach is advocated, through soft law, in King IV,[324] which entails that directors owe their duties to the company as a separate legal entity. In that separate legal entity several interests are represented, including the interests of shareholders, employees, consumers, the community and the environment. Considered on a case-by-case

---

318 Section 5(1) of the SACA 2008 states that the Act must be interpreted in such a way as gives best effect to the purposes listed in s 7.

319 See Irene-marié Esser and Piet Delport, 'The protection of stakeholders: The South African social and ethics committee and the United Kingdom's enlightened shareholder value approach,' Part 1 (2017) 50(1) *De Jure* 97 and Part 2 (2017) 50(2) *De Jure* 221.

320 See s 81(1)(d)(i)(bb) of the SACA 2008. It is also stated in Henochsberg at 54(1) that s 81(1)(d)(i)(bb) provides for the winding-up of a solvent company in deadlock if its business cannot be conducted to the advantage of shareholders generally. Clearly, this section focuses on profit maximisation of shareholders, as opposed to benefit to all stakeholders.

321 See discussion in Chapter 1.

322 See discussion in Chapter 1.

323 See *Swart v Beagles Run Investments 25 (Pty) Ltd* (2011) (5) SA 422 (GNP) on how the court balances the interests of shareholders and creditors in the context of business rescue proceedings. See also *Khammissa v Master of the High Court, Gauteng* [2020] JOL 48082 (GJ), 2021 (1) SA 421 (GJ) [24] where the Court said that 'the current company-law regime ... seeks to take account of a range of stakeholders', which is actually not what it does. The *Khammissa* judgment was confirmed on appeal on other grounds: *De Wet v Khammissa* [2021] JOL 50577 (SCA). See Henochsberg at 54(1) on this. See further the recent case in the UK of *BTI 2014 LLC v Sequana SA* (2022) 3 WLR 709 where the Court held that that the fiduciary duty owed by a company's directors, to act in good faith in the interests of the company, would sometimes include the interests of the creditors as a whole but the object of the duty is still the company; there is no standalone duty to creditors. See also Jean du Plessis, "'Shareholder capitalism' or an all-inclusive stakeholder model: What is the preferred corporate governance model for South Africa' in Howard Chitimira and Tapiwa Warikandwa (eds), *Financial Inclusion Regulatory Practices in SADC: Addressing Prospects and Challenges in the 21st Century* (Routledge, 2023) 60.

324 See King IV (2016) 26, fn 4.

basis, directors must exercise their powers and perform their functions as directors in good faith and for a proper purpose, keeping in mind that an interest of the company 'that may be primary at one particular point of time in the company's existence, may well become secondary at a later stage'.[325]

11.6.4 Codes of practice[326]

In the first draft of King IV reference was made to three paradigm shifts in corporate thinking that are specifically relevant:[327] (1) a shift from financial capitalism to inclusive capitalism;[328] (2) a move from silo reporting to integrated reporting; and (3) a shift from short-term capital markets to long-term sustainable markets, where value has to be created in a sustainable manner.

King IV focuses on mindful compliance, adding value across a broad front and an all-inclusive stakeholder approach. King IV strives to achieve these objectives by way of *governance outcomes, principles and practices*.[329]

King IV consists of seven Parts, with the actual *King IV Code on Corporate Governance* ('King IV Code') contained in Part 5. The Code operates in terms of principles, practices and governance outcomes.[330] The *principles* will state what organisations should strive toward. The *practices* must support the *principles* and this will lead to *governance outcomes*. *Governance outcomes* are thus the benefits that organisations could realise if the underlying *principles* are achieved. With King IV the focus is on the principles which embody the aspirations towards the journey of good governance. Practices may be scaled in accordance with proportionality considerations (size of turnover, resources and extent and complexity of activities are some factors to be taken into account regarding proportionality).[331]

King IV is, similar to its predecessors, a set of voluntary principles and practices.[332] Some of these practices have been legislated[333] and are in line with international 'hybrid systems of good governance' where corporate governance principles are legislated but also dealt with through soft law in codes of best practices.[334] The main objective of

---

325 This approach is taken from Irene-marié Esser and Jean J du Plessis, 'The stakeholder debate and directors' fiduciary duties' (2007) 19(3) *South African Mercantile Law Journal* 346. Reference is also made to Irene-marié Esser and Piet Delport, 'Shareholder protection philosophy in terms of the Companies Act 71 of 2008' (2016) 79(1) *Journal of Contemporary Roman Dutch Law* 1.

326 This subsection is based on Irene-marié Esser and Piet Delport, 'The South African King IV Report on corporate governance: Is the crown shiny enough?' (2018) 39(11) *Company Lawyer* 378. © 2018 Sweet and Maxwell. Reproduced with permission of Thomson Reuters (Professional) UK Limited through PLSClear.

327 See the Foreword of King IV (2016). See also Esser and Delport, 'The South African King IV Report on corporate governance' (2018) 39(11) *Company Lawyer* 378.

328 As set out in the International Integrated Reporting Council's 'Integrated Reporting <IR> Framework' as financial, manufactured, human, intellectual, natural and social and relationship capital.

329 King IV (2016) pt 2 [3]. For a detailed discussion of King IV see Esser and Delport, 'The South African King IV Report on corporate governance' (2018) 39(11) *Company Lawyer* 378.

330 King IV (2016) pt 4 for the application and disclosure of King IV.

331 King IV (2016) 36.

332 King IV (2016) 35.

333 For example, the social and ethics committee provided for in s 72 of the SACA 2008.

334 See I Esser, 'Corporate governance: Soft law regulation and disclosure – the cases of the United Kingdom and South Africa' in Jean J du Plessis and Chee Keong Low (eds), *Corporate Governance Codes for the 21st Century: International Perspectives and Critical Analyses* (Springer, 2017).

King IV was to make that regime applicable to as many organisations as possible and to make the practices adaptable according to organisation type. In view of this approach, King IV is based on an 'apply and explain' approach of disclosure, moving away from the more general approach of 'comply or explain'. The application of the principle is assumed as 'all principles are phrased as aspirations and ideals that organisations should strive to achieve to give effect to the governance outcomes'.[335] The 'explanation' that is required provides a high-level disclosure of the practices that have been implemented and the progress that has been made in the journey towards giving effect to each principle.[336] The expectation is that the 'explanation' should be provided in the form of a narrative account.[337] The detail provided in the narrative account should be guided by 'materiality' and should enable stakeholders to make informed assessments of the quality of the corporate governance of the specific organisation.

It is within the discretion of the governing body of entities that adopted the approach of the King IV Code to decide where disclosure of adhering to the principles should be made. This can be in the integrated report, social and ethics committee's report, online report or in a printed report. Disclosure can also be contained in more than one of these reports. Disclosure should at least be updated on an annual basis.

The King IV Code (Part 5 of King IV) consists of 17 Principles, with numerous practices recommended to attain the relevant governance outcomes of ethical culture, good performance, effective control and legitimacy. The King IV Code, as with most corporate governance codes, is based on 'soft law' and 'enforcement' depends on many factors. It can, indirectly, be enforced in law if it can be determined that the director has complied with the duties of care, skill and maybe also diligence.[338] In this respect the King IV Code is not law; however, direct application of the King IV Code is found in the regulations to the SACA 2008.[339] Under reg 54 every prospectus must include a narrative statement setting out the extent to which, and manner in which, the company has applied the principles of the King IV Code (by implication, as King III was applicable at that stage) and the reasons for any instance of not applying the recommended principles in the King IV Code.[340] If the company is listed on a South African exchange, the listing requirements of the exchange may prescribe that the company must apply King IV. The onus to 'enforce' King IV would then also lie with the investors and other stakeholders in the company or organisation who should, through potential disinvestment or failure to invest, be the incentive for the company or organisation to comply with King IV. This 'enforcement'

---

335 Esser and Delport, 'The protection of stakeholders', Part 1 (2017) 50(1) *De Jure* 97, 98.
336 King IV (2016) pt 3 [5.1]. King III operated on the 'apply or explain' approach. For the UK's approach on 'comply or explain' see Ridhar Arcot, Valentina Bruno and Antoine Faure-Grimaud, 'Corporate governance in the UK: Is the comply or explain approach working?' (2010) 30(2) *International Review of Law and Economics* 193; AR Keay, 'Comply or explain: In need of greater regulatory oversight?' (2014) 34(2) *Legal Studies* 279; and MT Moore, 'The end of "comply or explain" in UK corporate governance?' (2009) 60(1) *Northern Ireland Legal Quarterly* 85.
337 King IV (2016) 37. There is no need to disclose whether each practice has been implemented. The detail provided in the narrative should be guided by materiality.
338 See, eg, *Minister of Water Affairs and Forestry v Stilfontein Gold Mining Company Ltd* 2006 (5) SA 333 (W).
339 R351 in Government Gazette 34239 of 26 April 2011.
340 Non-compliance can result in civil and criminal statutory and common law sanctions. See ss 95 and 104 of the SACA 2008 and Henochsberg 371, 391.

works in two ways – on the one hand, it will be mere non-investment or potential disinvestment to convince the company or organisation to comply with King IV, while on the other hand the benefits of complying with King IV will be such that it would be beneficial for the investors to invest in the company or to do business with organisation. The benefit can be financial or 'social', in the sense that the investor or the person doing business with the organisation will be seen to be a responsible 'citizen'.

11.6.5 Sustainability

11.6.5.1 CSR, ESG and sustainability: Meaning and context

MacNeil and Esser argue that 'ESG investing evolved over time from the earlier concept of CSR. The process of evolution moved the focus from the external impact of corporate activities (CSR) to the risk and return implications for financial investors of failing to address ESG issues in their portfolio selection and corporate engagement.'[341] ESG focuses on the role of capital and investors in driving change and pays much less attention to the role of board decision-making and directors' fiduciary duties.[342] The latter is, however, reflected to an extent in directors' duties, recommendations of King IV and provisions like the requirement to have a social and ethics committee in certain instances.[343]

The consideration of ESG issues by directors during decision-making, and also by investors when making investment choices, has attracted a lot of attention in recent times. Various measures are proposed for ensuring a sustainable economy, such as detailed reporting and disclosure of non-financial matters; the expansion of directors' duties; linking executive remuneration to sustainable goals and criteria and the promotion of stewardship codes; encouraging investors to pursue ESG criteria in their investment choices; and disclosure of investor engagement policies.[344]

11.6.5.2 Regulation in the South African context

Regulation has also been a key driver in the context of ESG in South Africa. In this context one should refer to the *Pension Funds Act 1956* (reg 28), the *Public Investment Corporation Amendment Act 2019*, King IV, the *Code for Responsible Investing in South Africa* ('CRISA')[345] and the JSE *Listing Requirements*. Global reporting and disclosure standards are also relevant.[346]

---

341 Iain MacNeil and Irene-marié Esser, 'From a financial to an entity model of ESG' (2022) 23(1) *European Business Organization Law Review* 9, 9.

342 MacNeil and Esser, 'From a financial to an entity model of ESG' (2022) 23 *European Business Organization Law Review* 9.

343 For a detailed discussion of ESG developments in South Africa see ICLG, 'Environmental, social and governance law South Africa 2023' (26 January 2023) <https://iclg.com/practice-areas/environmental-social-and-governance-law/south-africa>.

344 MacNeil and Esser, 'From a financial to an entity model of ESG' (2022) 23(1) *European Business Organization Law Review* 9. On an investor-led approach see Wolf-Georg Ringe, 'Investor-led sustainability in corporate governance' (2022) 7(2) *Annals of Corporate Governance* 93.

345 CRISA 2, Section A: 'ESG factors are clearly linked to a company's purpose and long-term performance and should be considered not only in the context of engagement and voting, but also in investment decisions relating to valuation and the buying or selling of financial assets.'

346 Examples include the Global Reporting Initiative <https://www.globalreporting.org/>, the Financial Stability Board's Task Force on Climate Related Disclosure <https://www.fsb-tcfd.org/> and the Sustainability Accounting Standards Board <https://www.ifrs.org/groups/international-sustainability-standards-board/>, developed by IFRS in November 2021. See also Value Reporting

Legislation and regulatory guidance in South Africa are aiming to encourage institutional investors to integrate ESG issues into their investment decisions. Regulation 28 of the *Pension Funds Act 1956*[347] stipulates how retirement funds should invest their assets to ensure that their long-term obligations to members are met. It guides trustees on how to adopt responsible investment strategies that will provide benefits suitable for its members' retirements, and also determines asset limits. It explicitly states that prudent investing should take into account 'any factor which may materially affect the sustainable long-term performance of a fund's assets, including factors of an environmental, social and governance (ESG) character'.[348] Insurers, including life insurers, non-life and reinsurers, should also prepare their investment policies in line with Prudential Standard GOI 3, issued by the Prudential Authority.[349] It states that insurers have to take any factor into account that may materially affect the sustainable long-term performance of the assets, including ESG factors. The Public Investment Corporation (the largest asset management entity in Africa) must, as far as possible, seek to invest to promote sustainable development.[350]

CRISA is also relevant in this regard. The Code applies to institutional investors as asset owners (for example, pension funds and insurance companies) and their service providers (for example, asset managers, fund managers and consultants). It is a voluntary code that encourages investors to adopt its principles and practices where applicable. It operates on an 'apply and explain' basis.[351]

Both King IV and the United Nations–backed *Principles for Responsible Investment* require institutional investors to seriously consider ESG factors in investment decisions. Principle 17 of King IV is linked to CRISA, as both deal with the responsibilities of institutional investors. Both should ensure that 'responsible investment is practised by the organisation to promote the good governance and the creation of value by the companies in which it invests'.[352] As mentioned before, King IV also promotes a stakeholder inclusive approach, which will ultimately promote sustainability.

There is no explicit requirement on companies or organisations to report on ESG matters, but the JSE requires listed companies to annually report, on a 'apply and explain'

Foundation <https://www.valuereportingfoundation.org/. The latter has now consolidated into the IFRS Framework <https://www.ifrs.org/>. The IFRS standards are developed by two standard-setting boards: the International Accounting Standards Board ('IASB') and International Sustainability Standards Board ('ISSB').

347 *Pension Funds Act,1956* reg 28, FSCA Guidance Notice No 1 of 2019 (issued in terms of the *Pension Funds Act 1956*).

348 Ibid. See also Deloitte, 'The relationship between CRISA and regulation 28 of *Public Funds Act* and integrated reporting' (2014) <https://www2.deloitte.com/content/dam/Deloitte/za/Documents/governance-risk-compliance/ZA_TheRelationshipBetweenCRISAAndRegulation28OfPensionFundsAct04042014.pdf>.

349 See 'Prudential Standard GOI 3 – risk management an internal controls for insurers' (26 April 2017) <https://www.fsca.co.za/Regulated%20Entities/SAM%20DOCUMENTS/Prudential%20Standard%20GOI%203%20-%20Risk%20Management%20and%20Internal%20Controls%20for%20Insurers.pdf>.

350 *Public Investment Corporation Amendment Act, 2019.*

351 On the emergence of the 'comply or explain' approach, see MacNeil and Esser, 'The emergence of "comply or explain" as a global model for corporate governance codes' (2022) 33 *European Business Law Review* 1.

352 Delport, 'The South African King IV Report on corporate governance' (2018) 39(11) *Company Lawyer* 378.

basis, to what extent they have complied with King IV. This is often in an integrated report and informed by international guidance and standards. Integrated thinking was introduced in King III but has since evolved through the International Integrated Reporting Council's work.[353] King IV is now aligned with these international practices.

During March 2021 the EU regulation on sustainability-related disclosures came into effect[354] and it is expected to have an influence on the regulatory regime in South Africa and the potential of mandatory disclosures.

11.6.6 Future directions

Considering recent reform and other regulatory developments in South Africa, but also globally, it seems that diversity, remuneration, sustainability and ESG will continue to feature high on the corporate governance agenda. The South African Companies Act Amendment Bill 2021 included provisions on, *inter alia*, remuneration, the pay gap between the highest paid and the lowest paid employees and, as mentioned before, the social and ethics committee. In December 2021, the JSE published a draft Sustainability and Climate Change Disclosure Guidance which encourages transparency and good governance and guides listed companies on ESG disclosure best practice.[355] The South African National Treasury also recently published a draft technical paper on sustainable finance.[356] The draft paper 'encouraged voluntary sustainable finance initiatives and further stakeholder engagement to strengthen sustainable finance in South Africa'. An update to CRISA was also undertaken during 2020, but 'CRISA 2' is not in force yet.[357] The draft paper outlines principles and practice recommendations which focus on ESG and broader sustainable development issues and suggests shifting the application regime from 'apply or explain' to an 'apply and explain', focusing on outcomes.[358]

11.6.7 Conclusion

The JSE *Listings Requirements* impose a duty on all listed companies 'to report on social, health, environmental and ethical performance, the efficiency of risk management and

---

353 See Integrated Reporting, 'Integrated reporting framework' <http://integratedreporting.org/resource/international-ir-framework/>. The International Integrated Reporting Council ('IIRC') is a global coalition of regulators, investors, companies, standard-setters, the accounting profession and NGOs. See King IV (2016) pt 5.2 on integrated reporting.

354 See European Commission, 'Sustainability related disclosure in the financial services sector' (2023) <https://finance.ec.europa.eu/sustainable-finance/disclosures/sustainability-related-disclosure-financial-services-sector_en>.

355 See JSE, 'JSE's Sustainability and Climate Disclosure Guidance' (2023) <https://www.jse.co.za/our-business/sustainability/jses-sustainability-and-climate-change-disclosure-guidance>. It is intended to mainly assist JSE-listed companies, but it 'will also be of value to institutional investors and the different entities that they invest in (including non-listed companies and debt issuers), as well as a range of stakeholder groups interested in sustainability/ESG disclosure and performance'.

356 See National Treasury, Republic of South Africa, *Financing a Sustainable Economy* (Technical Paper 2020, Draft) <http://www.treasury.gov.za/publications/other/Sustainability%20technical%20paper%202020.pdf>. This was updated in October 2021.

357 See *CRISA Code for Responsible Investment in South Africa: 2020 Revision Consultation Draft* (November 2020).

358 See also Lexology, 'Shareholder rights and activism: South Africa' (20 August 2023) <https://thelawreviews.co.uk/title/the-shareholder-rights-and-activism-review/south-africa>.

internal control, and to disclose the degree of compliance with King IV'.[359] South Africa has an extensive and detailed corporate governance framework. King IV provides ample guidance on corporate governance issues and how company directors should act. Many of these recommendations, especially on CSR and directors' duties, were also embedded in the SACA 2008.

However, this does not mean that nothing will go wrong. The alleged accounting irregularities at Steinhoff[360] which came to light at the end of 2017, as well as the work done by the Zondo Commission of Inquiry into allegations of state capture,[361] are examples of instances where corporate governance has gone wrong, and it has renewed public interest in the matter in South Africa. Companies that are only paying lip service to recommendations or following a tick-box approach will have to account for it and will probably bear the consequences in the longer term.

When considering the role of stakeholders, the main issue is how the law can ensure that directors act in a sustainable manner and focus on long-term interests, rather than on short-term goals and profit maximisation for shareholders. The COVID-19 pandemic focused attention on stakeholder interests in South Africa, especially the interests of employees, who suffered tremendously because of lockdowns and companies not having provided for enough reserve funds to look after their employees during such a difficult time. The crisis caused by the pandemic revealed which companies have truly embodied the 'stakeholder model' and which ones have only paid lip service to it. Since March 2020, we have seen companies engaging in various activities and initiatives to try to deal with the devastating impact of COVID-19. However, not all have done so and it is an open question whether the majority of South African companies passed the test of being good 'corporate citizens', which is core to corporate governance in South Africa. Why did it require a pandemic to make companies focus on the real impact of share buy-backs, generous dividend payments to shareholders and excessive executives remuneration? Should all of these not be part of governing enterprises in a corporate governance model based on transparency, an all-inclusive stakeholder approach and striving for long-term sustainability?

It is not to be disputed that South Africa has an effective corporate governance framework based on and refined by the four King Reports. However, ultimately the question remains whether South African society and South African companies reflect the values, ethics and good governance principles[362] embedded in the legislation, codes of best practice and case law.[363]

---

359 Esser and Delport, 'The protection of stakeholders', Part 1 (2017) 50(1) *De Jure* 97, 109. See Listings Requirement 3.84 dealing with corporate governance requirements.
360 Tiisetso Motsoeneng and Emma Rumney, 'PwC investigation finds $7.4 billion accounting fraud at Steinhoff, company says', *Reuters* (16 March 2019) <https://www.reuters.com/article/us-steinhoff-intln-accounts-idUSKCN1QW2C2>. There is ample coverage on the Steinhoff scandal. For a very good discussion see Rob Rose, *Steinheist: Markus Jooste, Steinhoff and SA's Biggest Corporate Fraud* (Tafelberg, 2018).
361 *Commission of Inquiry into State Capture* (Web Page) <https://www.statecapture.org.za/>.
362 See the Fragile States Index of the Fund for Peace <https://fragilestatesindex.org/global-data/>, where South Africa is ranked 89/179 (179 being the best). Social, political and economic indicators are used to determine if a state is at an 'alert' phase or sustainable. See also the Corruption Perceptions Index 2013 <http://www.transparency.org/cpi2013/results>. South Africa has been ranked 72/177 (with 1 being best) with a 42% rating (with 0 as highly corrupt and 100 as very clean).
363 See, eg, *Minister of Water Affairs and Forestry v Stilfontein Gold Mining Company Ltd* 2006 (5) SA 333 (W).

11.7 India

Akshaya Kamalnath

11.7.1 Overview

This section outlines India's corporate governance journey from the pre-independence era to the present day. It is a journey of an erstwhile colony going from being a norm-importer to a country that, at least in some instances, has designed its own home-grown rules to address local corporate governance issues.

11.7.2 Regulatory environment

India's corporate governance regulation has shifted from voluntary guidelines to more mandatory rules. This subsection will trace the development of India's corporate governance regulation in context.

Since the seeds of the Anglo-American corporate law model were sown in India way back during its time as a British colony, adopting the Anglo-American model in India was less problematic than for many other emerging economies. Still, it was not without complications. Below is a brief historical overview of the development of the regulatory environment in this area.[364]

11.7.2.1 Pre-independence

Prior to independence (1947), India followed the Managing Agency System whereby managing agencies managed companies under agency contracts. These contracts were heavily in favour of the agencies and it was almost impossible for shareholders to remove them. Thus, shareholder activism was almost absent in this phase and abuse of power by the managing agencies was rampant.[365] After independence, the Indian government tried to maintain an equal mix of the role of the state and the private sector in the development of its economy.[366] It passed the *Companies Act 1956*, which put an end to the managing agency system by bringing the management of the company under the purview of the board of directors.[367] The 1956 Act was amended multiple times to accommodate policy changes relating to company administration, and was repealed by Act No 18 of 2013 (*Companies Act 2013*). The introduction of the New Economy Policy ('NEP') in 1991 by the Central (Federal) Government was the catalyst for the 2013 Act.

11.7.2.2 The 1990s

Prior to the 2013 Act and the NEP, industrial sectors were classified[368] as public or private, and the majority were not open for private investment. The NEP attempted to declassify a large number of the industrial sectors (mainly manufacturing sectors) and open them up

---

364 For a detailed discussion on this see Akshaya Kamalnath, 'Corporate governance reforms in India – accommodating local culture along with the drive for global convergence' (30 December 2013) <https://papers.ssrn.com/sol3/papers.cfm?abstract_id=2382595>.

365 Ibid 4.

366 *Industrial Policy Resolution 1948* <http://www.scribd.com/doc/38373070/Industrial-PolicyResolution-1948>.

367 *Companies Act 1956* ss 2(6), 292.

368 Industries were classified under the *Industries (Development and Regulation) Act 1952*.

for private and foreign direct investment. This is popularly known as the 'end of License Raj'. With this change in economic philosophy,[369] investment from the private sector escalated over time, which re-energised the demand for capital market and related institutional reforms. Business associations and conglomerates lobbied for the introduction of international standards in investor protection and management decision-making.

The government established a capital market regulator, the Securities and Exchange Board of India ('SEBI'). SEBI was entrusted with several responsibilities, including 'to protect the interests of investors in securities and to promote the development of, and to regulate, the securities market'.[370]

To develop the capital market and promote transparency, predictability and openness in the market, SEBI proposed several institutional reforms and adopted a series of guidelines, rules and regulations. The primary objectives of the reforms were to protect the market from initial distortions, and to allow further diversity in the economy. Companies, mainly private equity companies, emerged as the preferred business vehicle for major commercial and business activities in the post-reform period (that is, after 1990).

Corporate governance, as a concept, first came to India as an industry initiative. The Confederation of Indian Industries ('CII'), a leading business association, led a major initiative to introduce a code of corporate governance. In 1998 a committee was set up, under the leadership of Rahul Bajaj, a noted industrialist, to develop a voluntary code of corporate governance. The code, which drew heavily on the Anglo-American model of corporate governance, was titled *Desirable Corporate Governance: A Code*.[371] Many industrial houses and companies welcomed this move.[372]

Following the CII initiative, SEBI constituted a committee, under Kumar Mangalam Birla, to develop a standard of good corporate governance for public listed companies ('PLCs'). The committee made several recommendations, including regarding the composition and functions of audit committees and remuneration committees, the composition of the board of directors[373] and the appointment of independent directors, and the board's role in risk management. The committee observed that the board has responsibilities with respect to stakeholder well-being.[374]

11.7.2.3 The 2000s

SEBI adopted the recommendation and inserted a clause (cl 49) on corporate governance compliance for PLCs in the Listing Agreement in February 2000.[375] Clause 49 requires

---

369 For a discussion of the circumstances that gave rise to the change in economic philosophy, see Kamalnath, 'Corporate governance reforms in India' (2014) <https://papers.ssrn.com/sol3/papers.cfm?abstract_id=2382595>.

370 See *Securities and Exchange Board of India Act 1992*, Preamble.

371 *Desirable Corporate Governance: A Code (CII Code)* (Confederation of Indian Industries, April 1998) 1.

372 For critical appraisal see Umakanth Varottil, 'A cautionary tale of the transplant effect on Indian corporate governance' (2009) 21(1) *National Law School of India Review* 1.

373 In common with the Anglo-American model, India has a single-tier board system.

374 *Report of the Committee Appointed by the SEBI on Corporate Governance (Kumarmanglam Birla Committee)* (SEBI, 2000) 1 <www.sebi.gov.in/commreport/corpgov.html> (popularly known as the 'Kumarmagalam Birla Committee Report').

375 A Listing Agreement is entered into between a registered stock exchange (in India) and each PLC. The minimum standard of content of a Listing Agreement is prescribed by SEBI under the *Security Contract Regulation Act 1956*.

a PLC to include a dedicated section on corporate governance in its annual report. Key features of cl 49 included the need for disclosure of the following matters: ownership structure, the composition of the board, the ratio of executive to non-executive directors, the qualifications of directors, the number of board meetings, the composition and functions of the audit committee, and the CEO/CFO's certification of the company's financial result. The primary objectives of cl 49 are to protect the interest of investors and to strive for the equitable treatment of all stakeholders.

Under cl 49, PLCs are required to submit a quarterly compliance report to the stock exchange within 15 days of their quarterly financial reporting. The report is to be submitted by either the compliance officer or the CEO of the company after obtaining the approval of the board. Stock exchanges can obtain information from companies under eight subclasses: Board of Directors; Audit Committee; Shareholders/Investor Grievance Committee; Remuneration of Directors; Board Procedures; Management; Shareholders; and Report on Corporate Governance. Stock exchanges are required to set up independent groups to monitor compliance with the corporate governance provisions of Listing Agreements, and are required to submit a consolidated compliance report to SEBI within 30 days of each quarter end.

International corporate collapses, such as Enron and WorldCom in the US, prompted SEBI to set up a committee in 2003, under the chairmanship of Narayana Murthy, to review existing corporate governance practices and suggest measures to improve compliance. The Murthy Committee produced a report in 2003 which focused on strengthening the role and structure of the board, the role of independent directors and board subcommittees, and companies' disclosure practices.[376] The recommendations in this report were further revised following public consultation[377] and in October 2004 SEBI announced the revision of cl 49, which was effective from the end of the 2004–05 financial year.

The amended cl 49 requires companies to provide specific corporate disclosures relating to independent directors, whistleblower policy, performance evaluation of non-executive directors, mandatory training of non-executive directors, related party transactions, accounting treatment, reasons for deviations from accounting standards, risk management procedures, proceeds of various kinds of share issues, remuneration of directors and management discussions. There are also disclosure requirements in respect of general business conditions and outlook, and details of committee members and new directors.[378] The amended cl 49 further stipulates that non-executive members should comprise at least half of the board of directors.

---

376 *Report of SEBI Committee on Corporate Governance (Narayana Murthy Committee)* (Business, Security and Exchange Board of India, 8 February 2003) 43 <www.sebi.gov.in/commreport/corpgov.pdf>.

377 *Consultative Paper on Review of Corporate Governance Norms in India* (30 January 2013) <https://www.sebi.gov.in/sebi_data/attachdocs/1357290354602.pdf>.

378 Madan Bhasin and Adliya Manama, 'Corporate governance disclosure practices in India: An empirical study' (2008) 5 <https://www.researchgate.net/publication/228435019_Corporate_Governance_Disclosure_Practices_In_India_An_Empirical_Study>; Rajesh Chakrabarti, William Megginson and Pradeep K Yadav, 'Corporate governance in India' (2008) 20(1) *Journal of Applied Corporate Finance* 59, 64.

SEBI implemented cl 49 of its Listing Agreement in a phased manner. On 31 March 2001, it was made applicable to all the companies in the BSE200 and S&P CNX indices[379] and all newly listed companies. The application of the clause extended to companies with a paid-up capital of Rs 100 million, or with a net worth of Rs 250 million at any time in last five years (dated from 31 March 2002). On 31 March 2003, the clause was extended to other listed companies with a paid-up capital of over Rs 30 million.[380] By 1 January 2006, cl 49 applied to all PLCs. Further amendments were made to cl 49 in 2014, clarifying its contents on related party transactions and on board composition and powers, to align it with the new *Companies Act 2013*. A company's failure to comply with cl 49 can result in delisting, and in financial penalties.

Another landmark event that forms a defining moment in Indian corporate governance is the collapse in January 2009 of Satyam Computer Services Ltd, one of the largest IT companies in India. The failure of corporate governance in Satyam centred on three issues: (1) accounting fraud – fabricated accounts had been presented by the company for years; (2) related-party transactions – promoters of Satyam computers were personally interested; and (3) the failure of the independent directors to effectively monitor the company.

The Satyam scam shook the Indian corporate world and prompted CII,[381] the National Association of Software and Service Companies ('NASSCOM')[382] and the Institute of Company Secretaries of India ('ICSI')[383] to set up expert committees to recommend corporate governance reforms in response to the Satyam experience. The collective recommendation of the committees was to enlarge the role of independent directors; to incorporate/constitute various mandatory subcommittees of boards which would be chaired by the independent directors; to ensure that the chairman of the board would be an independent director; to evolve mechanisms to assess the performance of individual directors and the board subcommittees; and to reform the appointment procedure for internal and external auditors.[384] The committees emphasised that every related-party transaction should be critically examined by the board and subject to any measures necessary to protect the independence of the directors.[385] The recommendations also advocated that corporate governance orientation should shift towards stakeholders.[386]

---

379 Ibid 64.

380 *Report of SEBI Committee on Corporate Governance (Narayana Murthy Committee)* (2003) 4.

381 CII appointed Sri Naresh Chandra as the head of the Task Force Committee, and the report was submitted on November 2009: *Report of the CII Task Force on Corporate Governance Chaired by (Sri Naresh Chandra)* (Business, Confederation of Indian Industries, November 2009) 1 <www.mca.gov .in/Ministry/latestnews/Draft_Report_NareshChandra_CII.pdf>.

382 NASSCOM appointed an expert committee under the chairmanship of NR Narayana Murthy: *NASSCOM Corporate Governance Report* (27 April 2010) ('NASSCOM Report') <http://survey.nasscom .in/sites/default/files/upload/66719/Corporate_Governance_Report.pdf>.

383 *ICSI Recommendations to Strengthen Corporate Governance Framework* (Institute of Company Secretaries of India, 2009) <www.mca.gov.in/Ministry/latestnews/ICSI_Recommendations_ Book_8dec2009.pdf>.

384 See generally ibid and NASSCOM Report.

385 Ibid.

386 Ibid. See also Umakanth Varottil, 'Nasscom on corporate governance', *IndiaCorpLaw Blog* (12 May 2010) <https://indiacorplaw.in/2010/05/nasscom-on-corporate-governance.html>.

In late 2009, the Ministry of Corporate Affairs issued the *Corporate Governance Voluntary Guidelines 2009* ('*Voluntary Guidelines*'), based on the recommendations of the committees. The *Voluntary Guidelines* recognised that corporate governance 'may go well beyond the law and that there are inherent limitations in enforcing many aspects of corporate governance through legislative and regulatory means'.[387] The *Voluntary Guidelines* were for all private and public companies. Companies were to adopt the *Voluntary Guidelines* in their day-to-day operations. In cases of partial adoption, companies had to disclose the reasons for non-adoption to their shareholders. The *Voluntary Guidelines* did not replace any existing regulations; they were in addition to the existing framework.

Important matters covered by the *Voluntary Guidelines* included the appointment of independent directors, the remuneration of directors, the responsibilities of the board, the audit committee of the board, the auditors, the secretarial audit and the institutionalisation of whistleblower mechanisms.

Since then, India has adopted more mandatory corporate governance rules – these will be discussed in the next subsection.

11.7.3 Legislation and regulators

The Indian statutory framework has been influenced by international corporate governance best practices. The corporate governance mechanism for companies in India is generally found in the following enactments, guidelines and standards:

(1) The *Companies Act 2013*: this is the primary legislation concerned with the regulation of corporations in India. It contains provisions relating to board constitution, board meetings, board processes, independent directors, general meetings, audit committees, related party transactions, and disclosure requirements in financial statements.

(2) *Securities and Exchange Board of India ('SEBI') Guidelines:* SEBI is a regulatory authority with jurisdiction over listed companies. It issues regulations, rules and guidelines to companies to ensure the protection of investors.

(3) *Accounting Standards issued by the Institute of Chartered Accountants of India ('ICAI'):* ICAI is an autonomous body which issues accounting standards that operate as guidelines for disclosure of financial information. Section 129 of the *Companies Act 2013, inter alia,* provides that financial statements shall give a true and fair view of the state of affairs of the company or companies, and comply with the accounting standards notified in s 133 of the *Companies Act*.

(4) *Secretarial standards issued by the Institute of Company Secretaries of India ('ICSI'):* ICSI is an autonomous body which issues secretarial standards in terms of the provisions of the *Companies Act*. So far, the ICSI has issued secretarial standards on 'Meetings of the Board of Directors' (SS-1) and on 'General Meetings' (SS-2). These standards came into force on 1 July 2015. Section 118(10) of the *Companies Act 2013* provides that *every company* (other than a one-person company) shall observe secretarial standards specified by the ICSI with respect to general and board meetings.

---

387 *Corporate Governance Voluntary Guidelines 2009* (Ministry of Corporate Affairs, 2009) 1, 9 <www.mca .gov.in/Ministry/latestnews/CG_Voluntary_Guidelines_2009_24dec2009.pdf>.

11.7.3.1 The *Companies Act 2013*

The Companies Bill 2008 was reintroduced in Parliament as the Companies Bill 2009. The Ministry of Corporate Affairs ('MCA') received numerous suggestions for amendments from the various stakeholders. The Lok Sabha referred the Bill to the Parliamentary Standing Committee on Finance. The Standing Committee held several consultations with various stakeholders and suggested a number of amendments. The MCA decided to withdraw the Companies Bill 2009 and introduce a fresh Bill after incorporating the recommendation of the Standing Committee. At the end of 2011, the MCA reintroduced the Companies Bill 2011.

The Companies Bill 2011 was passed by the Indian Parliament (both Lok Sabha [Lower House] and Rajya Sabha [Upper House]) in 2013, thereby repealing the *Companies Act 1956*. The *Companies Act 2013* ('the Act') has extensive provisions on corporate governance[388] relating to directors and boards, auditors and auditing standards. Board composition and functions are also dealt with under the Act.

Board of directors

A maximum number of members for any board is 15 directors.[389] PLCs are required to have independent directors making up at least one-third of the board.[390] The Act defines who is an independent director,[391] and the appointment procedure of the independent director is specified in sch IV.[392] An independent director cannot be appointed for more than five consecutive years.[393] The Act addresses gender diversity and provides for the mandatory appointment of women directors for classes of companies.[394] Directors are required to make disclosures in the event of changes of their interest in respect of the company.[395] All related party transactions are to be scrutinised by the board.[396] The composition and responsibilities of board subcommittees – audit committee,[397] nomination committee,[398] remuneration committee,[399] stakeholder relations committee[400] and the CSR committee[401] – are addressed.

---

388 Most of the issues mentioned in the *Voluntary Guidelines for Corporate Governance 2009* were legislated under the *Companies Act 2013*.
389 *Companies Act 2013* s 149(1)(b).
390 Ibid s 149(4).
391 Ibid s 149(6). For critical discussion on definitional issues, see Pamela Hanarah and Anil Hargovan, 'Legislating the concept of the independent company director: Recent Indian reforms seen through Australian eyes' (2020) 20(1) *Oxford University Commonwealth Law Journal* 86.
392 *Companies Act 2013*.
393 Ibid s 149(10).
394 Ibid s 142(2) proviso.
395 Ibid s 184.
396 Ibid s 188.
397 Ibid s 177.
398 Ibid s 178.
399 Ibid.
400 Ibid s 178(6).
401 Ibid s 135: 'Every company having net worth of rupees five hundred crore or more, or turnover of rupees one thousand crore or more or a net profit of five crore or more during any financial year shall constitute a Corporate Social Responsibility Committee of the Board consisting of three or more directors, out of which at least one director shall be an independent director.' India also introduced mandatory CSR spending requirements for certain classes of companies through the *Companies Act 2013* (see Section 11.7.5).

The duties of directors are enumerated:

> [They] shall act in good faith in order to promote the objects of the company for the benefit of its members as a whole, and in the best interests of the company, its employees, the shareholders, the community, and for the protection of the environment.[402]

The board of directors also has a duty to comply with mandatory corporate social responsibility requirements, constituting an obligation to spend a certain percentage of the company's profits in the preceding three years on designated activities. This will be discussed in greater detail in Section 11.7.5.

Audit and accounting standards

Significant changes were introduced by the 2013 Act relating to audit and accounting standards. The listed companies belonging to a class or classes notified by the MCA may not reappoint any individual as an auditor for more than one term of five consecutive years, and as an audit firm for more than two terms of five consecutive years.[403] The Act lays down the rules on eligibility, qualification and disqualification of auditors. An audit firm shall not be engaged unless it is a limited liability partnership ('LLP') and provided that the partner of an LLP is not a former employee the company. Also, the auditor personally, or their relative or partner, shall not hold any securities or interest in the company or its subsidiary or its holding or associate company, or a subsidiary of such holding company.[404] The auditor, in their report, needs to mention the state of the company's internal financial control system and how effectively such control is operating.[405] The auditor also needs to certify if any director has failed to discharge their financial responsibilities (which disqualifies them from continuing as a director).[406] The Act was substantially amended by the Companies (Amendment) Bill 2016,[407] in accordance with the recommendations of the *Report of the Companies Law Committee*.[408] The amended Act strengthens compliance and procedure with respect to several activities, including financial reporting. For example, a financial statement of a company must include the consolidated financial statement of its subsidiary and associate companies. Every listed company having a subsidiary must publish the separate audited account in respect of its subsidiary/ies on its website. The policy on evaluation of director performance must also be published on the website of the company.

Parallel corporate governance requirements under cl 49

Mandatory and voluntary corporate governance practices in India developed in parallel, under cl 49 and other ancillary clauses of SEBI's Listing Agreement[409] and provisions of

---

402 *Companies Act 2013* s 166(2); *Corporate Governance Standards* (31 December 2009) s 303A.11.
403 *Companies Act 2013* s 139(2).
404 Ibid.
405 Ibid s 143(3)(i).
406 Ibid s 143(3)(g). Auditors need to certify if any company has not filed financial statements or annual returns or has failed to repay the deposits and interest or debentures accepted by the company during the tenure of the director in question.
407 Companies (Amendment) Bill 2016.
408 Government of India, Ministry of Company Affairs, *Report of the Companies Law Committee* (February 2016) 1 <www.mca.gov.in/Ministry/pdf/Report_Companies_Law_Committee_01022016.pdf>.
409 SEBI is empowered to administer the Listing Agreement under s 21 (Condition for Listing) of the *Security Contract Regulation Act 1956*.

the *Companies Act 1956* (now the *Companies Act 2013*). While the Listing Agreement is administered by SEBI, the *Companies Act* is administered by the MCA. Regulators in India did not adopt 'comply or explain principles', unlike other jurisdictions. Companies need to comply with mandatory and statutory provisions under the Listing Agreement and the *Companies Act* respectively. However, the voluntary provisions of the Listing Agreement are left to companies to report on a case-by-case basis.

11.7.3.2 Reforms introduced by SEBI

Following the *Consultative Paper on Review of Corporate Governance Norms in India* published by SEBI in 2013, significant reforms were made in the area of corporate disclosure by PLCs.[410] The approach taken in the paper was informed by the local problems faced by shareholders and Indian companies. Instead of amending cl 49 through notification, SEBI introduced *SEBI (Listing Obligations and Disclosure Requirements) Regulations 2015*,[411] which has emerged as a comprehensive corporate governance code for PLCs. The 2015 Regulation is also aligned with the corporate governance requirements under the *Companies Act 2013*.

The corporate governance compliance requirement under Regulation 2015 has enhanced timely disclosures relating to company promoters and shareholder holdings, boards and their functions, risk management and the protection of stakeholders. The board has also been entrusted with the responsibility of overseeing the governance practices of the subsidiaries. The audit committee of the holding company needs to assess the financial condition and the risk management status of the subsidiaries. The 2015 Regulation has made a board risk management subcommittee mandatory.

In 2018, the *SEBI (Listing Obligations and Disclosure Requirements) Regulations* were further amended to require top-listed companies to appoint at least one woman director who is also an independent director.[412] This was in response to some firms simply appointing a family member of existing directors to comply with the gender quota introduced by the *Companies Act 2013*.[413]

SEBI has also been actively monitoring international trends and tries to ensure that India remains an attractive market for investors and for entrepreneurs. For instance, SEBI introduced regulations to allow a restricted model of dual class shares[414] for 'new technology firms' where the founder is 'instrumental to the success of the firm'.[415] However, this has not had much uptake in the country.

---

410 SEBI, *Consultative Paper on Review of Corporate Governance Norms in India* (7 January 2013) 1 <www.sebi.gov.in/cms/sebi_data/attachdocs/1357290354602.pdf>.

411 'The regulations start by providing broad principles for periodic disclosures by listed entities and also have incorporated the principles of Corporate Governance. These principles underline specific requirements prescribed under different chapters of the Regulations': *SEBI (Listing Obligations and Disclosure Requirements Regulations) 2015*.

412 *SEBI (Listing Obligations and Disclosure Requirements Regulations) 2018*.

413 For a detailed discussion on this issue, see Akshaya Kamalnath and Annick Masselot, 'Corporate board gender diversity in the shadow of the controlling shareholder – an Indian perspective' (2019) 19(2) *Oxford University Commonwealth Law Journal* 179.

414 A share structure consisting of a set of shares with superior voting rights usually held by the company insiders, and another set of shares with regular or restricted voting rights.

415 SEBI, *Framework for Issuance of Differential Voting Rights (DVR) Shares* (2019).

11.7.4 Codes of practice

Unlike countries like the UK and Australia, India's corporate governance requirements have all become rule-based. Although the voluntary guidelines mentioned above still exist, companies are naturally more focused on the mandatory requirements.

11.7.5 Sustainability

11.7.5.1 Mandatory CSR

It is worth noting a novel provision of the *Companies Act 2013* dealing with CSR. The Act requires companies of a certain size to spend (on specific activities) at least two per cent of the average net profits made during the three immediately preceding financial years.[416] This requirement is applicable to companies which have:

- a net worth of at least INR 5 billion during any financial year
- a turnover of at least INR 10 billion during any financial year, or
- a net profit of at least INR 50 million during any financial year.

The spending must be in accordance with the CSR policy set out by a subcommittee of the board, and also with the list of prescribed CSR activities. The pre-scribed activities include eradication of poverty, promotion of education, promotion of gender equality and environmental sustainability.[417] This provision operates on a 'comply or explain' basis, meaning that if the company fails to spend the required amount on CSR activities per the legislation, the board must provide reasons for not doing so.[418]

While this requirement seems innovative, India's experience during the COVID-19 pandemic showed the limits of such a firm requirement. In response to the pandemic, the government imposed a nation-wide lockdown requiring all non-essential services, including businesses, to close their physical operations, allowing only remote work to continue. Since there was no government subsidy to pay employee salaries like in Australia, many big businesses promised not to cut staff salaries. Corporations also responded to the crisis by making charitable donations and engaging in other innovative measures. However, the *Companies Act 2013* only allows spending on designated categories to be classified as CSR, and the MCA issued a circular saying that companies' payment of salaries and wages of employees and workers could be considered CSR under the law. This shows the limitations of government mandates regarding CSR.[419]

---

416 *Companies Act 2013* s 135(5).
417 For a detailed discussion of the CSR provision in India and its impact on practice, see Sandeep Gopalan and Akshaya Kamalnath, 'Mandatory corporate social responsibility as a vehicle for reducing inequality: An Indian solution for Piketty and the millennials' (2015) 10(1) *Northwestern Journal of Law and Social Policy* 34.
418 *Companies Act 2013* s 135.
419 For a detailed examination of the CSR provision provision in light of the pandemic, see Akshaya Kamalnath, 'A post pandemic analysis of CSR in India' (2021) 16(2) *Journal of Comparative Law* 714.

11.7.5.2 Sustainability reporting

In addition to the CSR provision, in 2011 SEBI introduced a sustainability reporting framework ('Business Responsibility Reporting' or 'BRR') applicable to the top 500 listed companies. This was replaced in 2021 by a requirement to publishing a 'Business Responsibility and Sustainability Report' ('BRSR'), which will have mandatory effect for the top 1000 listed companies from the 2022–23 financial year.[420] The BRSR attempts to address the concern that companies will engage in mandatory CSR spending while disregarding sustainability issues.[421]

In line with the global trend, India introduced a stewardship code in 2019 for certain types of institutional investors.[422] As discussed earlier, the *Companies Act 2013* also addresses issues of gender diversity on company boards.

Despite these developments, greenwashing, or the phenomenon of companies marketing their work and philanthropic efforts as environmentally and socially conscious to conceal some other problematic conduct, is still a concern in India, like it is in other jurisdictions.[423] The market regulator is attempting to address this in different contexts.[424]

11.7.6 Future directions

Recent developments in India have shown that corporate governance developments may be locally sourced, or inspired by an international trend. In the latter case, history has shown that modifications in the rules were necessary to fit local needs. It is likely that the recently introduced stewardship code will have to be modified to suit local needs. Still, from recent developments, it can be said that Indian corporate governance has been taking a more sustainability-friendly path and that will continue.

11.7.7 Conclusion

Following the spectacular collapse of Satyam Computers and the 2008 GFC, Indian business and regulators have been active in focusing on making governance principles and rules compatible with international standards, taking account of the local variances. There have also been some homegrown innovations like the CSR spending provision of the *Companies Act 2013* and it will be interesting to see if India, at least in some areas of corporate governance (for example, CSR spending), goes from being a norm-taker to a norm-maker.

420 SEBI, 'Business responsibility and sustainability reporting by listed entities' (10 May 2021) <https://www.sebi.gov.in/legal/circulars/may-2021/business-responsibility-and-sustainability-reporting-by-listed-entities_50096.html).

421 While the content of this is similar to the global sustainability reporting frameworks (eg GRI standards), the format is different. To solve this, the GRI, in conjunction with Indian authorities, has developed a linkage guide that allows companies to link the BRSR to GRI standards: *Linking the GRI Standards and the SEBI BRSR Framework* (2022) <https://www.globalreporting.org/media/ioqnxtmx/sebi_brsb_gri_linkage_doc.pdf>

422 SEBI, *Stewardship Code for all Mutual Funds and all Categories of AIFs, in Relation to their Investment in Listed Equities* (2019).

423 Stephen Kim Park, 'Social responsibility regulation and its challenges to corporate compliance' (2019) 14(1) *Brooklyn Journal of Corporate, Financial and Commercial Law* 39, 51.

424 See, eg, SEBI, *Consultation Paper on ESG Disclosures, Ratings, and Investments* (20 February 2023) <https://www.sebi.gov.in/reports-and-statistics/reports/feb-2023/consultation-paper-on-esg-disclosures-ratings-and-investing_68193.html>.

11.8 Singapore

Luh Lan

11.8.1 Overview[425,426]

Since becoming a sovereign nation in 1965, Singapore has rapidly developed from a colonial backwater of the British empire to an international commercial and financial hub. Such unprecedented economic transformation appears to have been underpinned by Singapore's regulators' continuous commitment to keeping pace with the highest global standards of corporate governance. This has provided 'a climate conducive to the orderly development of the capital markets', 'to meet the increasing expectations of investors'[427] and to attract foreign investment.

Today, Singapore is regarded as having attained the highest international standards of corporate governance. This is illustrated by how it has been placed in the top two of the World Bank's Ease of Business Index for 16 consecutive years from 2004 to 2020,[428] and how it has consistently being placed in the top three positions in Asia by the Asian Corporate Governance Association's ('ACGA') CG Watch market rankings.[429] However, throughout the last five decades, Singapore's regulators have had to confront myriad challenges in achieving these accolades.

First, Singapore's corporate landscape has traditionally been dominated by highly concentrated shareholding structures. Over 90 per cent of Singapore listed companies have 'block shareholders who exercise controlling power'.[430] Second, Singapore's corporate landscape with regards to the companies listed on the Singapore Exchange ('SGX') is traditionally dominated by government-linked companies ('GLCs') – companies that are fully or partially state-owned (see discussion in Section 11.8.4). Third, since its founding, Singapore has confronted a spate of corporate governance scandals[431] and economic crises.[432] Fourth, the SGX, like most international securities/stock exchanges, must maintain a

---

425 This section is based on the author's article 'Corporate governance in Singapore – the road thus far' to be published in the forthcoming issue of *Journal of Business Law*. For a more comprehensive discussion of the Singapore corporate law and corporate governance landscape, see Lan Luh Luh, *Essentials of Corporate Law and Governance in Singapore* (Sweet & Maxwell, 2nd ed, 2023).

426 The author would like to thank her research assistant, Chan Yong Sheng Abraham, for his help in preparing this manuscript.

427 Corporate Governance Committee, *Report of the Corporate Governance Committee* (21 March 2001) [6] <https://www.mas.gov.sg/-/media/MAS/Regulations-and-Financial-Stability/Regulatory-and-Supervisory-Framework/Corporate-Governance-of-Listed-Companies/corfinalrpt.pdf>.

428 Available from The World Bank, 'Business Ready (B-READY) – Doing Business legacy' <https://www.worldbank.org/en/programs/business-enabling-environment/doing-business-legacy>.

429 ACGA, 'CG Watch' <https://www.acga-asia.org/cgwatch-detail.php?id=425>. Singapore tied at second place with Hong Kong in the ACGA's 2018 ranking but fell by to the third spot in the 2020 ranking. Australia remains at the top spot in both 2018 and 2020 in this pan-Asian study: ACGA, *CG Watch 2020: Future Promise* (2020) <https://www.acga-asia.org/cgwatch-detail.php?id=425>.

430 Tan Cheng Han, Dan W Puchniak and Umakanth Varottil, 'State-owned enterprises in Singapore: Historical insights into a potential model for reform' (2015) *Columbia Journal of Asian Law* 28(2) 61, 67.

431 Tabby Kinder and Hudson Lockett, 'Singapore Bourse tightens audit rules after string of scandals' (*Financial Times*, 12 January 2021).

432 Such as the 1997 Asian Financial Crisis and the 2008 Global Financial Recession ('2008 GFC'). Singapore was hit particularly hard by the 2008 GFC, which was caused by the US sub-prime mortgage crisis. It was the first country in East Asia to succumb to recession and caused Singapore's

'complex balance' between high corporate governance standards while ensuring these are not too onerous for foreign investors and multinational companies based in Singapore. It therefore has to be flexible in the implementation of the country's corporate governance regime.[433] Lastly, in the early 21st century, Singapore is increasingly facing the challenge of adopting the growing global trend of incorporating stakeholder interests, corporate social responsibility ('CSR') and sustainability goals into an Anglo-American influenced corporate governance framework which traditionally promotes shareholder value (the shareholder primacy model – see more detailed discussions in Sections 1.5.1.2, 1.5.2.2 and 1.6) as the pre-eminent purpose of a corporation. All these are factors which help to explain the Singapore corporate governance landscape as it is today.

11.8.1.1 History of corporate law and corporate governance in Singapore

Much of Singapore's law was heavily influenced by English law before its independence from Britain in 1959.[434] This continued in the area of corporate law by the adoption of the *Companies Act 1967* (Singapore), primarily based on the *Companies Act 1948* (UK).[435] At the turn of the 21st century, key international developments in the corporate governance scene – such as the publication of the Cadbury Report in the UK in 1992 and the issue of the first edition of the OECD *Principles of Corporate Governance* in 1999[436] – preluded Singapore's eventual gradual adoption of soft law measures to regulate corporate governance. Furthermore, poor corporate governance in various Asian jurisdictions was 'widely viewed as one of structural weaknesses' responsible for the outbreak of the Asian Financial Crisis in 1997.[437] This led many Asian jurisdictions, including Singapore, to undertake corporate governance reform in order to meet internationally-recognised standards of corporate governance while restoring investor confidence.

11.8.2 Regulatory environment

11.8.2.1 Monetary Authority of Singapore ('MAS')

The MAS is the primary institution regulating corporate governance in Singapore. It serves as Singapore's central bank as well as a consolidated regulator that regulates securities, banking and insurance. The mission of the MAS is 'to promote sustained and non-inflationary economic growth, and a sound and progressive financial services sector'.[438]

worst ever recession. For a comparison of the impact of these two crises on the Singapore economy, see Lan Luh Luh and Hans Tjio, 'Regulatory framework: The winning/losing architecture' in Seetharam Kallidaikurichi (ed), *A Tale of Two City – A Multidisciplinary Analysis* (Routledge, 2012).

433 Chanyaporn Chanjaroen and Ishika Mookerjee, 'Singapore corporate scandals spur push for regulatory transparency' in *Bloomberg* (9 March 2021) <https://www.bloomberg.com/news/articles/2021-03-08/singapore-corporate-scandals-spur-push-for-regulatory-transparency#xj4y7vzkg>.

434 Singapore gained full internal self-governance from the British on 3 June 1959, although it became an independent sovereign nation much later on 9 August 1965.

435 Walter Woon, 'Reforming company law in Singapore' (2011) 23 *Singapore Academy of Law Journal* 795.

436 See Sections 1.3 and 12.3.1.

437 Sang-Woo Nam and Il Chong Nam, *Corporate Governance in Asia: Recent Evidence from Indonesia, Republic of Korea, Malaysia and Thailand* (Asian Development Bank Institute, 2004) 1 <https://www.adb.org/sites/default/files/publication/159384/adbi-corp-gov-asia.pdf>.

438 Monetary Authority of Singapore, *Objectives and Principles of Financial Supervision in Singapore* (April 2004, revised in 2015) 1 <https://www.mas.gov.sg/~/media/MAS/News%20and%20Publications/

In December 1999, the MAS convened the Corporate Governance Committee ('CGC'), comprising industry representatives from various groups (including the corporate sector, legal profession and regulators), to review the approach, development and promotion of best practices in corporate governance in Singapore.[439] This led to the eventual adoption of the *Code of Corporate Governance* ('CCG') on 21 March 2001, making Singapore the second Asian nation to adopt a formal code.[440] Since the launch of the CCG, Singapore's regulators have recognised the need to evolve the Code 'to maintain its relevance and applicability with the changing corporate landscape'[441] and the Code has undergone three revisions in 2005, 2012 and 2018.

In addition to the CCG, which applies to all companies listed on the SGX, the MAS also issues guidelines on corporate governance that financial institutions, including all designated financial holding companies, banks, direct insurers, reinsurers and captive insurers which are incorporated in Singapore, must observe in relation to their corporate governance. The latest version was issued on 9 November 2021.[442]

11.8.2.2 The Singapore Exchange ('SGX')

Unlike the MAS, which is a statutory body, the SGX is an incorporated company listed on itself.[443] As Singapore's only approved exchange, the SGX, through its wholly-owned subsidiary, SGX RegCo,[444] plays a crucial role in regulating the corporate governance of SGX-listed companies. SGX RegCo's regulatory strategy involves monitoring the compliance of SGX-listed companies with the SGX's *Listing Rules* ('SGX LR') – the latter contain the CCG. The SGX LR are essentially a contract between SGX and its various listed companies. As such, breaches do not incur criminal liability under a court of law. Nonetheless, SGX RegCo's disciplinary committee is entitled to issue fines, public reprimands or impose suspension and even de-listing on listed companies that fail to comply with the SGX LR. The actions taken by SGX RegCo and SGX often result in major corporate governance changes in listed companies. For example, in 2017, SGX publicly reprimanded Singapore Post Limited, for, among other things, failing to 'have a robust and effective system of internal controls, addressing financial, operational and compliance risks'.[445]

Monographs%20and%20Information%20Papers/Objectives%20and%20Principles%20of%20
Financial%20Supervision%20in%20Singapore.pdf>.
439 Corporate Governance Committee, *Consultation Paper* (November 2000) 1.
440 Malaysia adopted its code in 2000.
441 Corporate Governance Committee, *Consultation Paper* (November 2000) 4, 8.
442 MAS, *Guidelines on Corporate Governance for Designated Financial Holding Companies, Banks, Direct insurers, Reinsurers and Captive Insurers Which are incorporated in Singapore* (9 November 2021) <https://www.mas.gov.sg/-/media/MAS-Media-Library/regulation/guidelines/ID/guidelines-on-corporate-governance/Guidelines-on-Corporate-Governance-9-November-2021.pdf>.
443 The SGX was formed in 1999 to effectuate the demutualisation and merger of the two exchanges: Stock Exchange of Singapore and Singapore International Monetary Exchange under the *Exchanges (Demutualisation and Merger) Act 1999*.
444 The SGX RegCo was established in 2017 to ensure the separation of the regulatory functions from the business functions of SGX. The majority of the SGX RegCo board, including the chairman, comprise directors independent from the SGX Group. Additionally, the entire board is independent of any corporations listed on SGX-ST and member firms of the SGX Group.
445 This eventually led to a total board change. See SGX, 'SGX reprimands Singapore Post Limited' (4 May 2017) <https://www.sgx.com/regulation/public-disciplinary-actions/sgx-reprimands-singapore-post-limited>.

11.8.2.3 The Accounting and Corporate Regulatory Authority ('ACRA')

ACRA is the regulator of business registration, financial reporting, public accountants and corporate service providers.[446] Although ACRA is not involved in the implementation and oversight of the CCG, it administers and enforces (with the assistance of the Attorney General's Office for criminal prosecution), *inter alia*, the *Companies Act 1967*. The Act contains sections relating to directors' duties, breach of which can attract disqualification and criminal sanctions, including a fine of up to S$5000 (approximately US$3500) and/or a jail term not exceeding 12 months.[447]

11.8.2.4 The Corporate Governance Advisory Committee ('CGAC')

The original CCG and the three editions that followed were proposed by ad hoc Corporate Governance Committees/Councils ('CGCs') established at different points in time by the MAS. It was not until 2019 that MAS established the CGAC as a permanent, industry-led body to advocate good corporate governance practices among listed companies in Singapore.

The CGAC has a few functions. First, it identifies current and potential risks to the quality of corporate governance in Singapore and monitors international trends. Second, it revises the Practice Guidance, and recommends updates to the CCG. Third, it provides opinions on corporate governance practices. Finally, it consults stakeholders, including listed entities, on proposed changes to the CCG or Practice Guidance and acts as a resource to regulators (SGX RegCo, MAS and ACRA), including advising regulators on corporate governance issues referred to it by regulators.[448] Unlike the MAS and SGX, CGAC's role is advisory in nature and does not carry any regulatory or enforcement powers.

11.8.3 Codes of practice

11.8.3.1 The *Code of Corporate Governance* ('CCG')

The CCG serves as the primary source of best practices regulating corporate governance practices in Singapore. It aims to promote 'high levels of corporate governance in Singapore by putting forth Principles of good corporate governance and Provisions with which companies are expected to comply'.[449] After considering the various approaches to regulating corporate governance around the world, the CGC in 2001 recommended that Singapore adopt a balanced approach in promoting good corporate governance, one influenced by Canada and UK's regulatory regimes.

This approach eschews a total adoption of the prescriptive approach as 'what is good corporate governance is likely to vary across companies and over time', such that a

---

446 ACRA was formed as a statutory board under the *Accounting and Corporate Regulatory Authority Act 2004* on 1 April 2004, following the merger of the Registry of Companies and Businesses, and the Public Accountants' Board.
447 See, eg, s 157(3) of the *Companies Act 1967*. See generally Singapore Police Force, 'Resident director sentenced to $3000 fine and disqualified from being a director for three years' (Media Release, 30 July 2021) <https://www.police.gov.sg/Media-Room/News/20210730_resident_dir_sentenced_to_$3000_fine_n_disqualified_from_being_a_cmpy_dir_for_3_years>.
448 Corporate Governance Advisory Committee, 'About the CGAC' <https://www.cgac.sg/about-cgac>.
449 Corporate Governance Committee, *Corporate Governance Committee Consultation Paper* (November 2000) 1.

prescriptive corporate governance code that assumes a 'one size fits all' approach is inappropriate in the Singapore context.[450] The CCG was also, to a certain extent, influenced by the non-prescriptive approach to corporate governance which is exemplified by the approach in the US. Ultimately, Singapore's balanced approach incorporates a US-style 'disclosure-based philosophy to regulation',[451] while providing fairly specific, albeit voluntary corporate governance practices that companies should adopt.[452]

In the latest revision of the CCG, Singapore shifted away from a voluntary approach to a partially mandatory approach with respect to corporate governance practices. During its review, the CGC recommended the adoption of an even 'more concise and less prescriptive Code to encourage thoughtful application and a move away from a box-ticking mindset'.[453] The 2018 version of the CCG has now been streamlined to focus on key tenets of corporate governance by: (a) shifting important requirements or baseline market practices to the SGX LR; (b) removing overly-prescriptive or duplicative requirements, already in the SGX LR, from the CCG; and (c) introducing a voluntary Practice Guidance to provide clearer 'guidance on the application of the Principles and Provisions with which companies are expected to apply'.

The CCG is now structured as follows:

- Introduction – broadly outlines the CCG's objectives, structure and its 'comply or explain' framework.[454]
- Principles – set out 'broadly accepted characteristics of good corporate governance'.[455]
- Provisions – describe the tenets of good corporate governance; they are designed to support compliance with the Principles.[456]

Compliance with the SGX-LR and the Principles is mandatory while the 'comply or explain' regime continues to apply to the Provisions. Adherence to the Practice Guidance is entirely voluntary.

11.8.3.2 Key aspects of corporate governance regulation

The CCG broadly seeks to regulate the following five key areas of corporate governance regulation in Singapore:

(1) role and composition of the Board (Principles 1–5)
(2) remuneration matters (Principles 6–8)
(3) matters of accountability and audit (Principles 9–10)
(4) shareholder rights and engagement (Principles 11–12)
(5) managing stakeholder relationships (Principle 13).

---

450 Corporate Governance Committee, *Report of the Committee and the Code of Corporate Governance* (21 March 2001) [10].
451 Ibid.
452 Ibid [13].
453 Corporate Governance Council, *Final Recommendations of the Corporate Governance Council Submitted to MAS* (2018) Annex A [2]; Allen and Gledhill, *Knowledge Highlights: MAS Issues Code of Corporate Governance* (13 August 2018).
454 CCG (2018).
455 Ibid [7].
456 Ibid [8].

In what follows, we highlight the important changes that have taken place in these key areas over recent years.

The board

General considerations

Singapore's regulation of the board is underpinned by the CCG's affirmation of 'the centrality of the Board to good corporate governance' in two regards. First, the Code establishes the 'appropriate culture, values and ethical standards of conduct at all levels of the company; and second, it encourages the formation of a well-constituted board to lead in better decision-making and 'enhanced business performance'.[457] In particular, the SCCG seeks to regulate three aspects of the board: its role (Principle 1) which includes the assessment of its performance (Principle 5); composition (Principles 2 and 3); and board membership (Principle 4).

It is required that there should be three main board committees: the audit committee,[458] the nomination committee[459] and the remuneration committee.[460] It is now mandatory for all directors, including executive directors, to submit themselves for re-nomination and reappointment at least once every three years.[461] A director who has no prior experience as a director of a listed company on the SGX must also undergo training in the roles and responsibilities of a director as prescribed.[462]

Over the last 20 years, the requirements in the SCCG on the board have evolved most in the following areas:

(1) the progressive strengthening of the requirement for an *independent element on the board*'[463]

(2) the broadening of the board's composition to include an appropriate level of *diversity of thought and background* to enable it to make decisions in the best interests of the company (emphasis added).[464]

Requirement of independence

It is now mandatory for independent directors to make up at least one-third of listed boards.[465] If the chairman is not independent, the CCG recommends that independent directors make up a majority (from at least half) of the board.[466] Other times, non-executive directors are to make up a majority of the board.[467] In addition, independent directors who have served for an aggregate period of more than nine years (whether before or after listing) can continue to be considered independent only until the conclusion of the next annual general meeting of the company.[468]

---

457 Ibid [3].
458 Ibid Principle 10.
459 Ibid Provision 4.1.
460 Ibid Provision 6.1.
461 *SGX Listing Rules (Mainboard)* r 720(5); *SGX Listing Rules (Catalist)* r 720(4).
462 *SGX Listing Rules (Mainboard)* r 210(5)(a); *SGX Listing Rules (Catalist)* r 406(3)(a).
463 CCG (2018) Principle 2; *Practice Guidance* (11 January 2023) Practice Guidance 2.
464 CCG (2018) Principle 2; *Practice Guidance* (11 January 2023) Practice Guidance 2.
465 See *SGX Listing Rules (Mainboard)* r 210(5)(c); *SGX Listing Rules (Catalist)* r 406(3)(c).
466 CCG (2018) Provision 2.2.
467 Ibid Provision 2.3.
468 *SGX Listing Rules (Mainboard)* r 210(5)(d)(iv); *SGX Listing Rules (Catalist)* r 406(3)(d)(iv).

Board diversity

The CCG requires that the Board must have a 'diversity of thought and background in its composition to enable it to make decisions in the best interests of the company'.[469] In addition, the listed companies are now required, for the first time, to disclose their board diversity policy and progress made in achieving the board diversity policy (including any objectives set by the companies) in their annual reports.[470]

However, Singapore's framework for promoting board diversity remains controversial in the following regards. First and foremost, there is inconclusive evidence (empirical or otherwise) that board diversity promotes good corporate governance. While various Singaporean organisations, including the Council for Board Diversity,[471] have touted that 'diverse boards are catalysts to robust governance',[472] such claims have yet to be supported by local empirical studies or evidence. Second, the CCG's 'comply or explain' framework is arguably inadequate in promoting board diversity. To begin with, unlike countries like Belgium and Norway with mandatory gender quota, the CCG does not mandate any specific targets/quotas for the minimum number of board directors to be from diverse gender or minority backgrounds. In addition, the CCG's 'comply or explain' framework can be justified in allowing for 'flexibility of implementation'.[473] It permits companies who may not have the resources to implement the diversity rules to explain their inability to comply. In the alternative, it allows companies to achieve 'diversity of thought and background' without employing traditional metrics of demographic diversity (such as age or gender).[474] This may explain the slow increase in women's representation on the top 100 SGX primary-listed boards, from 15.2 per cent as at end December 2018[475] to 19.7 per cent as at 1 January 2022.[476]

Remuneration matters

Disclosure of remuneration matters has always been a sensitive topic in Asian countries, especially Singapore.[477]

---

469 CCG (2018) Principle 2.
470 Ibid Provision 2.4. With effect from 1 January 2022, *SGX Listing Rules (Mainboard)* r 710A(1)/*SGX Listing Rules (Catalist)* r 710A(1) requires issuers to maintain a board diversity policy.
471 The Council for Board Diversity was set up in 2019 by the Singapore Ministry for Social and Family Development with the main aim of increasing women representation on boards of SGX listed companies. It has the President of Singapore, Madam Halimah Yacob, as its patron. See Counci for Board Diversity, 'Our journey' <https://www.councilforboarddiversity.sg/about/our-journey/>.
472 Council for Board Diversity, 'Our belief' <https://www.councilforboarddiversity.sg/about/our-belief/>.
473 Ernest Lim, *Sustainability and Corporate Mechanisms in Asia* (Cambridge University Press, 2020) 68.
474 Ibid 125–9. In particular, Lim is of the view that the Code's comply-or-explain regime fails to review the quality of diversity disclosures let alone make clear the 'criteria that it will adopt to determine the adequacy' of disclosures. This undermines the promotion of board diversity insofar as companies may, for instance, provide self-serving justifications for failing to employ a diverse board while omitting to disclose 'concrete measures that the board has taken or will take to promote board gender diversity'.
475 Diversity Action Committee, *Report on Women's Representation on Boards of SGX-listed Companies as at End December 2018* (January 2019).
476 Council for Board Diversity, *Report on Women's Representation on Boards as at End December 2021* (March 2022).
477 See Corporate Governance Committee, *Report of the Committee and Code of Corporate Governance* (21 March 2001) [34], defending non-disclosure of remuneration, *inter alia*, on 'personal privacy of directors of publicly listed companies, and that it 'might create inflationary pressure to ratchet directors' remuneration upwards'.

Listed companies are now required to be 'transparent on [their] remuneration policies, level and mix of remuneration, the procedure for setting remuneration, and the relationships between remuneration, performance and value creation'.[478] As far as the disclosure of the exact remuneration packages received by the concerned parties, the CCG still allows the listed company to disclose (on a 'comply or explain' basis) only the names, amounts and breakdown of remuneration of each individual director and the CEO. The disclosure on the remuneration packages for the top five key management personnel is in bands no wider than S$250 000 and in aggregate the total remuneration paid to the key management personnel.[479] Even for the remuneration packages for substantial shareholders or employees who are immediate family members of the relevant people,[480] disclosure is on a named basis in bands no wider than S$100 000 and only if the remuneration exceeds S$100 000.[481] It appears that the CCG still falls short of remuneration standards imposed by other leading Asian economies, such as Malaysia and Hong Kong.[482] Moving forward, remuneration transparency is certainly an area that Singapore companies can improve upon.

Matters of accountability and audit

Since the 2012 revision of the CCG, the board is tasked with the responsibility of risk governance.[483] The board is now required to comment on the adequacy and effectiveness of the company's internal controls and risk management systems, and to disclose in the company's annual report the weaknesses of the systems, if any, and steps taken to address the weaknesses, with the concurrence of the audit committee.[484]

Shareholder rights and engagement

The CCG started with two short principles on communications with shareholders in 2001.[485] In 2012, following global developments in shareholder stewardship by institutional investors and asset managers, the CCG was revised to put more emphasis on shareholder rights and engagement. In particular, companies were encouraged to 'put all resolutions to vote by poll and make an announcement of the detailed results showing the number of votes cast for and against each resolution and the respective percentages'.[486] This was in contrast to the usual practice then of voting by show of hands. Also for the first time, companies were urged to keep a dividend policy and disclose it to the shareholders.[487] Now, if the directors decide not to declare or recommend

---

478 CCG (2018) Principle 8.
479 Ibid Provision 8.1.
480 CEO, director or substantial shareholders.
481 CCG (2018) Provision 8.2. This was missing from the earlier editions of the Code.
482 These countries legislate and mandate the disclosure of remuneration of individual directors on listed companies. See Mak Yuen Teen, 'Poor remuneration disclosure is no laughing matter', *Governance for Stakeholders* (31 December 2021) <https://governanceforstakeholders.com/2021/12/31/poor-remuneration-disclosure-is-no-laughing-matter/>.
483 CCG (2012) Principles 10 and 11; CCG (2018) Principle 9.
484 *SGX Listing Rules (Mainboard)* rr 610(5) and 719(1)/*SGX Listing Rules (Catalist)* rr 407(4)(b) and 719(1).
485 CCG (2001) Principles 14 and 15; CCG (2005) Principles 14 and 15.
486 CCG (2012) Guideline 16.5.
487 Ibid Guideline 15.5.

a dividend, it is mandatory for the directors to announce this together with the rea-
son(s) for such decision.[488]

Managing stakeholder relationships and sustainability disclosures

With the global movement towards the board adopting more of a stakeholder approach
in its decision-making rather than the traditional shareholder-centric approach,[489] the
CCG in 2018 adopted a new Principle 13 and accompanying Provisions for companies
to consider and balance the needs and interests of material stakeholders. As the CGC
noted,[490] this is in line with the *G20/OECD Principles of Corporate Governance* (2015)[491] as
well as the corporate governance codes in other jurisdictions, including Australia, South
Africa and Malaysia, which have incorporated provisions for boards to consider stakeholders other than shareholders.

The CCG does not contain any principle or provisions on sustainability. However, the
SGX separately launched the sustainability reporting listing rules and reporting guide
in June 2016.[492] The guidelines apply to listed companies on a 'comply or explain' basis
from the financial year ending on, or after, 31 December 2017, with reports to be published from 2018.[493] After this there is a phased approach to mandatory climate reporting
depending on the industry based on the recommendations of the Task Force on Climate-
related Financial Disclosures – it takes effect from the financial year ending on, or after,
31 December 2022, with reports to be published from 2023.[494]

11.8.4 Corporate governance of Singapore government-linked companies ('GLCs')

Government-linked companies ('GLCs') play a huge role in the Singapore economy.
The Singapore government serves as the ultimately controlling shareholder of these
GLCs, through its holding company, Temasek Holdings Pte Ltd ('Temasek'), whose sole
shareholder is the Ministry of Finance. As at 31 March 2019, Temasek has at least 25
listings on the SGX, comprising 15 companies and 10 trusts with a combined market cap
of more than S$260 billion,[495] which is about 32 per cent of the total market capitalisa-
tion of SGX.[496] There are certain key features of Singapore's regulatory regime designed

---

488 *SGX Listing Rules (Mainboard)* r 704(24)/*SGX Listing Rules (Catalist)* r 704(23); CCG (2018) Provision 11.6.

489 For the legal justifications for the board to adopt a stakeholder-approach in decision-making, see
   Luh Luh Lan and Heracleous Loizos, 'Rethinking agency theory: The view from law' (2010) 35(2)
   Academy of Management Review 294.

490 Monetary Authority of Singapore, *Recommendations of the Corporate Governance Council*, P002–2018
   (Consultation Paper, January 2018) [7.1]–[7.3].

491 See Section 12.1 in Chapter 12 on the latest (2023) version of these Principles.

492 Institute of Singapore Chartered Accountants, *Sustainability Reporting Implementation Roadmap*
   (September 2017) <https://isca.org.sg/media/2238512/isca-sustainability-report-implementation-
   roadmap.pdf>.

493 *SGX Listing Rules (Mainboard)* rr 711A and 711B; Practice Note 7.6/*SGX Listing Rules (Catalist)*
   rr 11A and 711B and Practice Note 7Fs.

494 SGX, 'Sustainability reporting' <https://www.sgx.com/regulation/sustainability-reporting>.

495 SGX My Gateway, 'Highlights of Temasek's SGX-listed investment' (24 September 2019) <https://
   sginvestors.io/sgx-mygateway/2019/09/highlights-of-temasek-sgx-listed-investments>.

496 The total market capitalisation of SGX as at August 2020 was about S$815.46 billion: SGX,
   'Market statistics' (August 2020) <https://www.sgx.com/research-education/historical-data/
   market-statistics>.

to address some of the common corporate governance issues faced by state-owned enterprises, including undue political influence and/or the pursuit of political objectives over long-term shareholder value. We do not have space to discuss this in detail, but the reader is advised to study the sources referred to in the footnote.[497]

11.8.5 Future directions and conclusion

In the 21 years since the first version of the CCG was launched, Singapore's corporate governance framework has evolved to ensure that it remains effective and relevant, with supporting business growth and innovation as its chief objectives. Although there have been gaps along the way, the corporate governance benchmarks have been constantly raised over the years. As pointed out by the CGC in its 2018 Consultation Paper,[498] a balance has to be struck 'between the need to keep the [CCG] progressive and on par with international developments, while tailoring it to Singapore's context and the profile of the listed companies in Singapore'.[499] The idea of building and fostering a supportive corporate governance eco-system rather than merely suggesting amendments to the CCG was thus a key concern of the CGC when it recommended the 2018 revisions.[500] The result was a leaner and more concise CCG focusing on good corporate governance tenets, with the important requirements or baseline market practices integrated to form part of the mandatory SGX LR. Although the CCG still operates on a 'comply or explain' basis, the key principles of good corporate governance are now mandatory and must be embraced and practised by all listed companies in Singapore. Moving forward, the broad principles of corporate governance are unlikely to change in the CCG. What we can expect to see in the future would be a more refined and thoughtful series of suggestions of the applications of the principles through the issuance of the Provisions and Practice Guidance, especially in the areas of diversity[501]

---

497 Dan W Puchniak and Luh Luh Lan, 'Independent directors in Singapore: Puzzling compliance requiring explanation' (2017) 65(2) *American Journal of Comparative Law* 265; Tan Cheng Han, Dan W Puchniak and Umakanth Varottil, 'State-owned enterprises in Singapore: Historical insights into a potential model for reform' (2015) 28(2) *Columbia Journal of Asian Law* 61; Christopher Chen, 'Solving the puzzle of corporate governance of state-owned enterprises: The path of the Temasek model in Singapore and lessons for China' (2016) 36(2) *Northwestern Journal of International Law and Business* 303; Isabel Sim, Steen Thomson, Gerard Yeong, *The State as Shareholder: The Case of Singapore: Research Report* (Centre for Governance, Institutions & Organisations, 2014). See also the yearly reports on the Governance and Transparency Index ('GTI') published by the NUS Business School Centre for Governance and Sustainability (formerly known as Centre for Governance, Institutions and Organisations): 'Centre for Governance and Sustainability – corporate governance', *NUS Business School* (Web Page) <https://bschool.nus.edu.sg/cgs/research/corporate-governance/>.

498 Corporate Governance Council, *Recommendations of the Corporate Governance Committee 2018* (Consultation Paper, 16 January 2018).

499 Ibid [2.5].

500 Ibid.

501 On 25 March 2022, the CGAC through MAS issued an updated set of Practice Guidance on how company should not only publish a board diversity policy that minimally addresses gender, skills and experience. The Nominating Committee also has the responsibility to monitor the progress towards meeting the policy targets and keep the board updated. See Allen & Gledhill, 'MAS revised Practical Guidance in Code of Corporate Governance to provide updated guidance on board diversity policy' (28 April 2022) <https://www.allenandgledhill.com/sg/publication/articles/21622/mas-revises-practice-guidance-in-code-of-corporate-governance-to-provide-updated-guidance-on-board-diversity-policy>.

and remuneration disclosure[502] by the various regulatory authorities. Hopefully, all these improvements will be sufficient to help Singapore companies weather the next global economic storm, when it arrives.

---

502 In October 2022, SGX RegCo released a public consultation paper proposing to amend the *Listing Rules* to impose a hard nine-year limit on the tenure of independent directors, removing the current two-tier voting rule. The SGX RegCo has also proposed mandatory disclosures of the actual amounts of the remuneration of each listed company director and CEO. See SGX, *Consultation Paper on Board Renewal and Remuneration* (27 October 2022) <https://www.sgx.com/regulation/public-consultations/20221027-consultation-paper-board-renewal-and-remuneration>.

12 CORPORATE GOVERNANCE IN THE EUROPEAN UNION, THE *G20/OECD PRINCIPLES OF CORPORATE GOVERNANCE,* AND CORPORATE GOVERNANCE IN GERMANY, JAPAN AND CHINA

12.1 Introduction

In Chapter 11 we discussed corporate governance in the United States ('US'), the United Kingdom ('UK'), New Zealand, Canada, South Africa, India and Singapore. These are some of the major traditional Anglo-American corporate governance jurisdictions. There are among them some fundamental differences in approach.

In this chapter the focus is on corporate governance developments in countries where the two-tier board system is used. Section 12.2 examines the situation in the European Union ('EU'). EU member states have different corporate law systems. This makes corporate governance harmonisation quite difficult, but also leads to very interesting and dynamic discussions within the EU.

Section 12.3 discusses the *G20/OECD Principles of Corporate Governance* (2023) ('the Principles'). As the main international benchmark for good corporate governance, the Principles have a global reach and influence the corporate governance frameworks in EU jurisdictions. The Principles reflect the experiences and ambitions of a wide variety of jurisdictions with varying legal systems and at different stages of development. They apply to both one-tier and two-tier board structures.

In Section 12.4 we turn to Germany, which has a two-tier board structure, with employee representatives forming part of the supervisory board. Elements of the German corporate governance model influenced the original Japanese corporate governance model (Section 12.5), but Anglo-American influence emerged after World War II. Section 12.6 discusses the approach taken by China. This jurisdiction has a unique corporate governance model because Chinese corporations were traditionally state-owned and many major corporations are still either state-owned or state-controlled. Nevertheless, elements of both the German model and the Anglo-American model, especially as far as independent, non-executive directors for listed companies are concerned, have influenced the Chinese corporate governance model.

12.2 European Union

Rosalien van 't Foort-Diepeveen, Jeroen Veldman and Tineke Lambooy

12.2.1 Overview

The domain of corporate governance is undergoing a massive transformation in the EU. The introduction of the European Green Deal in 2019[1] was probably the most significant recent EU development in the context of contemporary corporate governance. Not only does it present significant targets in the areas of corporate social responsibility ('CSR') and sustainability, but because of its effect on, for instance, supply chains, its impact will be felt globally.

The European Green Deal ('the Green Deal') seeks to engage with concerns about the current impacts of economic activity and the likely economic impacts of a belated and/or disorderly transition scenario on societies and organisations. It aims to reallocate EU$1 trillion before 2030[2] and makes significant amendments to the institutional setting for corporate governance in the EU.

Introduced in 2019, the Green Deal's purpose is to allow for a timely and orderly transition to a low-carbon economy by making the EU climate-neutral by 2050.[3] The stated aim of the Green Deal is as follows:[4]

> [To provide] a new growth strategy that aims to transform the EU into a fair and prosperous society, with a modern, resource-efficient and competitive economy where there are no net emissions of greenhouse gases in 2050 and where economic growth is decoupled from resource use. It also aims to protect, conserve and enhance the EU's natural capital, and protect the health and

---

1 European Commission, *Communication from the Commission to the European Parliament, the European Council, the Council, the European Economic and Social Committee and the Committee of the Regions: The European Green Deal* ('*The European Green Deal*') (COM/2019/640 final).

2 See Beate Sjåfjell and Jeroen Veldman, 'SMART reflections on policy coherence, legal developments in the Netherlands and the case for EU harmonisation' (2019) (4) *Erasmus Law Review* 111.

3 *The European Green Deal* (COM/2019/640 final) 4.

4 Ibid 2.

well-being of citizens from environment-related risks and impacts. At the same time, this transition must be just and inclusive.

Accordingly, the aims of the Green Deal include, among other things:[5]

(1) reducing greenhouse gas emissions at a faster rate for 2030 to ensure that the EU is climate-neutral by 2050[6]

(2) providing clean renewable energy at an affordable price

(3) helping industries to innovate to use circular products and becoming more sustainable

(4) constructing and renovating buildings to reduce greenhouse gas emissions

(5) ensuring sustainable transportation

(6) producing food in a more sustainable way

(7) preserving and restoring natural resources, ecosystems and biodiversity

(8) preventing pollution.

To achieve these goals, the European Commission has presented a series of legislative initiatives. Some of these initiatives have already entered into force, such as the *Sustainable Finance Disclosure Regulation* ('SFDR') and the *Regulation on Sustainable Investment*, while a number of other proposals are still under review.

12.2.2 Legislative context

With the Green Deal guiding reforms, over the past decade the EU has enacted several Acts pertaining to corporate governance and corporate law that have focused on sustainability and climate change. Most of this legislation is in the form of directives, which aim to harmonise the national laws of the member states by giving instructions on how the directive should be transposed into national law, while leaving it to member states to choose the form and method of implementation.[7]

12.2.3 Codes of practice

In the EU context one cannot refer to a single approach towards codes of conduct or corporate governance codes as there are diverging corporate law models and different board models, such as the one-tier board system and the two-tier board system. In this book, the German model (see Section 12.4) and the UK model (see Section 11.3) are discussed. Apart from formal differences, there are different ways of approaching issues that form part of codes of practices. For instance, although the UK is no longer

---

5   Ibid 4–15.

6   The climate neutrality target and the reduction of greenhouse gas emissions by 55 per cent in 2030 are included in the European Climate Law: *Regulation (EU) 2021/1119 of the European Parliament and of the Council of 30 June 2021 Establishing the Framework for Achieving Climate Neutrality and Amending Regulations (EC) No 401/2009 and (EU) 2018/1999* ('European Climate Law') arts 2, 4. See also European Commission, *Communication from the Commission to the European Parliament, the Council, the European Economic and Social Committee and the Committee of the Regions: Stepping up Europe's 2030 Climate Ambition – Investing in a Climate-neutral future for the Benefit of Our People* (COM/2020/562 final).

7   *Treaty on the Functioning of the European Union* art 288.

a member of the EU after Brexit, the impact of the UK on EU corporate governance remains strong. The 'comply and explain' principle that originated in the UK is still one that EU member states must adopt because of Directive 2014/95 (see Section 12.2.4.4). In the EU, general guidance in respect of corporate governance codes has been derived from the 2015 *G20/OECD Principles of Corporate Governance*. In September 2023, the 2015 Principles were replaced by the 2023 *G20/OECD Principles of Corporate Governance* (see Section 12.3).[8] In this section (12.2) we will primarily focus on developments regarding sustainability and speculate on some future EU developments.

12.2.4 Sustainability, the Green Deal and EU directives

12.2.4.1 Background and context

Within the larger setting of the Green Deal, the EU framework for sustainable finance and corporate sustainability details how the private sector, and the operation of corporate governance in particular, can be redeveloped to enable a sustainable transition. To achieve this goal, the Green Deal presents a series of comprehensive and interlinked reform proposals across the areas of company law, reporting, and issues related to finance in four major areas:

(1) a classification system, or 'taxonomy', of sustainable activities
(2) a disclosure framework for sustainability-related information for both financial market participants and non-financial companies
(3) proposed requirements for corporate sustainability due diligence
(4) standards and tools to develop sustainable investment solutions which further support the framework.

12.2.4.2 *Taxonomy Regulation*

The *Regulation on Sustainable Investment* (also known as, and hereafter referred to as, the '*Taxonomy Regulation*')[9] provides for a classification system that determines the criteria that allow participants and issuers on the financial market to identify, evaluate and report on which of their economic activities, or the economic activities they invest in, can be deemed 'environmentally sustainable'. It defines 'environmentally sustainable' activities as economic activities that contribute substantially to at least one of the EU's environmental objectives,[10]

---

8   Organisation for Economic Co-operation and Development ('OECD'), *G20/OECD Principles of Corporate Governance 2023* <https://doi.org/10.1787/ed750b30-en>. The Principles are set out in the Appendix to the OECD *Recommendation on Principles of Corporate Governance* (OECD/LEGAL/0413) adopted by the OECD Council on 8 July 2015 and revised on 8 June 2023. The Principles were endorsed by the G20 in September 2023, after the substantial writing of Sections 12.2 and 12.3. For access to the official text of the Recommendation, as well as other related information, please consult the Compendium of OECD Legal Instruments <https://legalinstruments.oecd.org>.

9   *Regulation (EU) 2020/852 of the European Parliament and of the Council of 18 June 2020 on the Establishment of a Framework to Facilitate Sustainable Investment, and Amending Regulation* (EU) 2019/2088.

10 The EU has the following environmental objectives: climate change mitigation; climate change adaptation; sustainable use and protection of water and marine resources; transition to a circular economy; pollution prevention and control; and protection and restoration of biodiversity and ecosystems. See *Taxonomy Regulation* arts 10–16. See also Holly Pettingale, Stéphane de Maupeou

that, at the same time, do 'not significantly harm' any of these objectives and meet minimum social safeguards.[11]

12.2.4.3 Sustainable finance

The *Sustainable Finance Disclosure Regulation* ('SFDR'),[12] applicable from 10 March 2021, requires financial service providers and owners of financial products to publicly assess and disclose the integration of sustainability matters into their investment considerations.

The goal of the SFDR is to make the sustainability profile of investment funds more comparable and easier to understand for investors by providing categories and metrics for assessing the sustainability impacts of the investment process for each investment fund that falls within the scope of the *Taxonomy Regulation*.

The *Proposal for a Regulation on the Green Bond Standard* ('GBS')[13] provides a voluntary standard available to all private and sovereign issuers to enable investors to assess whether and to what extent investments are sustainable, thereby reducing the risk of greenwashing. The aim of the GBS is to provide a framework for the development of green bonds in accordance with the classifications of the *Taxonomy Regulation*. It introduces a registration and supervision system for companies that operate as external reviewers of bond compliance – this is registered with and supervised by the European Securities Markets Authority.[14]

12.2.4.4 *Corporate Sustainability Reporting Directive* ('CSRD')

The *Corporate Sustainability Reporting Directive* ('CSRD'),[15] which entered into force on 5 January 2023, followed the *Directive on Non-financial Information* ('NFRD'),[16] which was adopted in 2014.[17] The NFRD requires large public-interest entities (mainly companies listed on a stock exchange, such as insurance companies) with on average 500 employees to include a non-financial statement in their management report. This non-financial statement includes information and discloses risks in respect of business activities in the

and Peter Reilly, 'EU taxonomy and the future of reporting', *Harvard Law School Forum on Corporate Governance* (19 December 2023) <https://corpgov.law.harvard.edu/2022/04/04/eu-taxonomy-and-the-future-of-reporting/>.

11   *Regulation (EU) 2020/852 of the European Parliament and of the Council of 18 June 2020 on the Establishment of a Framework to Facilitate Sustainable Investment, and Amending Regulation (EU) 2019/2088* art 3.

12   *Regulation (EU) 2019/2088 of the European Parliament and of the Council of 27 November 2019 on Sustainability-related Disclosures in the Financial Services Sector* (OJ L 317, 9.12.2019). It was amended by the *Taxonomy Regulation*.

13   *Proposal for a Regulation of the European Parliament and of the Council on European Green Bonds* (COM/2021/391 final 2021/0191 (COD).

14   Ibid 1.

15   *Directive (EU) 2022/2464 of the European Parliament and of the Council of 14 December 2022 Amending Regulation (EU) No 537/2014, Directive 2004/109/EC, Directive 2006/43/EC and Directive 2013/34/EU, as Regards Corporate Sustainability Reporting.*

16   *Directive 2014/95/EU of the European Parliament and of the Council of 22 October 2014 Amending Directive 2013/34/EU as Regards Disclosure of Non-financial and Diversity Information by Certain Large Undertakings and Groups* (Text with EEA relevance).

17   The CSRD needs to be transposed into the member states' national laws by 6 July 2024.

value chain with regard to environmental, employee and social matters, human rights, anti-corruption and bribery.[18]

The CSRD aims to amend the NFRD by implementing new criteria. It stipulates that companies must report in line with the SFDR and the *Taxonomy Regulation*[19] and that they have to provide both retrospective and forward-looking information. This information includes targets and progress relating to intangibles, including environmental protection, social responsibility, treatment of employees, respect for human rights, anti-corruption and bribery, diversity on company boards, and how these matters affect the development, performance and position of the company.[20] Companies are required to use a standard reporting format for their annual report, including the sustainability information that they have to disclose.[21] To enable such reporting, the CSRD introduces a requirement to report in more detail according to mandatory sustainability reporting standards.[22] On 31 July 2023, the *European Sustainability Reporting Standards*[23] were adopted, covering the data points (or KPIs) on which companies need to report pursuant to the CSRD. Moreover, these standards are relevant for the *Taxonomy Regulation*, the *Proposal for the Directive on Corporate Sustainability Due Diligence*,[24] and the obligations regarding sustainability disclosures that investors need to comply with under the SFDR. The reform should be seen in the context of other international initiatives, frameworks and standards for non-financial disclosure and reporting being developed and refined as discussed in this book.

While the NFRD already requires the auditor to check whether a non-financial statement is provided,[25] the CSRD further stipulates that a limited level of assurance has to be provided. This means that:

- the auditing process must conform with the requirements of the *Taxonomy Regulation*
- the involvement of a key audit partner is required
- the auditor must provide an opinion about the company's compliance with the sustainability reporting requirements
- this opinion must be integrated in the auditor's report.[26]

---

18 *Directive 2014/95/EU of the European Parliament and of the Council of 22 October 2014 Amending Directive 2013/34/EU as Regards Disclosure of Non-financial and Diversity Information by Certain Large Undertakings and Groups* (Text with EEA relevance) art 1.

19 KPMG, 'Corporate Sustainability Reporting Directive' <https://home.kpmg/nl/en/home/topics/environmental-social-governance/corporate-sustainability-reporting-directive.html>.

20 *Directive (EU) 2022/2464 of the European Parliament and of the Council of 14 December 2022 Amending Regulation (EU) No 537/2014, Directive 2004/109/EC, Directive 2006/43/EC and Directive 2013/34/EU, as Regards Corporate Sustainability Reporting* (Text with EEA Relevance) art 19a.

21 Ibid art 19d.

22 Ibid art 19b.

23 *Commission Delegated Regulation (EU) 2023/2772 of 31.7.2023 Supplementing Directive 2013/34/EU of the European Parliament and of the Council as Regards Sustainability Reporting Standards.*

24 See Section 12.2.4.5.

25 Articles 19a(5), 20(3), 29a(5) of Directive 2013/34 as amended by Directive 2014/95. See also CSRD Preamble (53).

26 *Directive (EU) 2022/2464 of the European Parliament and of the Council of 14 December 2022 Amending Regulation (EU) No 537/2014, Directive 2004/109/EC, Directive 2006/43/EC and Directive 2013/34/EU, as Regards Corporate Sustainability Reporting* (Text with EEA relevance) Preamble (53) and (55), art 34.

The CSRD is applicable to all large companies[27] and all listed companies including small and medium enterprises ('SMEs'). Micro-enterprises are excluded from application of the law.[28] The CSRD will be in effect for entities already subject to the NFRD from 2025 (for the financial year 2024); for large entities not currently reporting under the NFRD from 2026 (for the financial year 2025); and for SMEs from 2027 (for the financial year 2026), with a possibility to opt out until 2028. In total, 49 000 entities are expected to be subject to the new CSRD.[29]

12.2.4.5 *Corporate Sustainability Due Diligence Directive* ('CSDDD')

On 23 February 2022 the EU Commission presented its *Proposal for the Directive on Corporate Sustainability Due Diligence* ('CSDDD').[30] This Proposal introduces mandatory due diligence requirements and links them to the duties of corporate boards. It requires that the directors of the company consider, in their decision-making processes, any impacts of the decisions on sustainability issues in their international value chains, such as climate and environmental consequences, social responsibility and treatment of employees, respect for human rights, anti-corruption and bribery, and diversity on company boards in the short-, medium- and long-term when acting in the best interests of the company.[31] The Proposal for the CSDDD furthermore stipulates that boards 'are responsible for putting in place and overseeing the company's due diligence [actions] with due consideration of relevant input from stakeholders and civil society organisations'.[32]

Specifically, the Proposal requires of companies to carry out a human rights and environmental due diligence for all their business operations and to adopt a plan in which they indicate how their business model and company's strategy is in line with the sustainability transition and the targets agreed in the *Paris Agreement*.[33]

The human rights and environmental due diligence requires companies to:

(a) integrate due diligence in their policies and to have a due diligence policy in place
(b) identify actual or potential adverse human rights and environmental impacts that arise from their business operations, its subsidiaries and its value chain
(c) prevent or mitigate any potential adverse human rights or environmental impacts

---

27   Large companies are companies that exceed at least two of the following requirements: (a) a balance sheet total of 20 million; (b) a net turnover of 40 million; and (c) an average number of 250 employees.
28   Micro-companies are companies that meet at least two of the following requirements: (1) a balance sheet total of less than €350 000; (2) a net turnover of less than €700 000; and (3) on average less than 10 employees. See art 3(1) of Directive 2013/34.
29   See KPMG, 'Corporate Sustainability Reporting Directive' <https://home.kpmg/nl/en/home/topics/environmental-social-governance/corporate-sustainability-reporting-directive.html>.
30   *Proposal for a Directive of the European Parliament and of the Council on Corporate Sustainability Due Diligence and Amending Directive (EU) 2019/1937* (COM/2022/71 final). At this stage it is uncertain whether the CSDDD will be adopted. The text was adopted by the Council on 15 March 2024. The effectiveness has been downsized to only cover the largest companies. The European Parliament has to vote on it in May 2024.
31   Ibid art 25. On 1 June 2023, the European Parliament adopted its position on the CSDDD in its first reading. For the proposed legislative changes see European Parliament, 'Texts adopted' (1 June 2023) <https://www.europarl.europa.eu/doceo/document/TA-9-2023-0209_EN.html>.
32   *Proposal for a Directive of the European Parliament and of the Council on Corporate Sustainability Due Diligence and Amending Directive (EU) 2019/1937* (COM/2022/71 final) art 26.
33   Ibid art 15.

(d) establish a complaints procedure where stakeholders can file a complaint if they have concerns regarding human rights or environmental impacts

(e) monitor periodically to assess whether the due diligence process is effective; and

(f) communicate about the due diligence process on the company's website every year not later than 30 April.[34]

The human rights and environmental due diligence requirements not only apply to the company's own operations, but also to their subsidiaries and 'established business relationships' throughout the value chain.[35]

With regard to these requirements, the CSDDD will introduce a new civil liability regime. In contrast to the CSRD, which will merely require transparency on due diligence with regard to substainability matters, the CSDDD will introduce a behavioural obligation (that is, an obligation to act) on the company, the board and the employees of the company. This is an obligation to act in particular to 'identify, prevent, mitigate' and end adverse human rights and environmental impacts.[36] Member states will be able to impose fines on companies, or issue orders requiring the company to comply with the due diligence obligation. Victims affected by harm that could have been prevented or mitigated will be able to bring a civil liability claim before the competent national courts. Companies will be liable to pay any damages that are incurred by failing to comply with the mandated due diligence obligations.[37]

The CSDDD will be applicable to companies meeting one of the following thresholds:

(a) having on average 500 employees and a net worldwide turnover of at least EU$150 million

(b) having on average more than 250 employees and a net worldwide turnover of at least EU$40 million of which at least 50 per cent was generated in high-impact sectors, such as the garment sector, agricultural sector or sectors that extract mineral resources

(c) for companies incorporated outside of Europe – a net turnover of more than EU$150 million in the EU in the previous financial year or a net turnover between EU$40–50 million in the EU in the previous financial year of which at least 50 per cent of the turnover was generated in high-impact sectors.[38]

SMEs are excluded from the due diligence obligations. Approximately 13 000 EU companies and 4000 non-EU companies are expected to fall within the scope of this CSDDD.[39]

---

34 Ibid arts 4–11.

35 *Proposal for a Directive of the European Parliament and of the Council on Corporate Sustainability Due Diligence and Amending Directive (EU) 2019/1937* (COM/2022/71 final) art 6 (1).

36 See 'European Commission proposes mandatory corporate sustainability due diligence and climate change plans', *Sullivan and Cromwell LLP* (7 March 2022) <https://www.sullcrom.com/sc-publication-eu-proposes-mandatory-corporate-sustainability-due-diligence-and-climate-change-plans>.

37 *Proposal for a Directive of the European Parliament and of the Council on Corporate Sustainability Due Diligence and Amending Directive (EU) 2019/1937* (COM/2022/71 final) art 22.

38 Ibid art 2(1), (2).

39 See 'European Commission proposes mandatory corporate sustainability due diligence and climate change plans', *Sullivan and Cromwell LLP* (7 March 2022).

12.2.4.6 Gender balance and board diversity

Another area of corporate governance concerns the gender balance in corporate boards. To this end, the EU has proposed a *Gender Balance Directive*.[40] Although the the Directive was initiated in November 2012, it took until June 2022 for the European Parliament and the Council to agree upon its content. The provisional agreement[41] for the Directive stipulates that listed companies are either required to have a representation of 40 per cent of the under-represented gender for non-executive director positions or to have a representation of 33 per cent of the under-represented gender for both executive and non-executive director positions.

These targets must be met by 30 June 2026.[42] If a company fails to meet the target(s), the company has to adjust its selection, appointment and selection process concerning directors. For the selection of directors for positions, companies should use neutral and unambiguous selection criteria in their communication in advance of selecting candidates.[43] If two candidates of the same gender are equally qualified, preference must be given to the candidate of the under-represented sex.[44] If a candidate for a director's position has not been selected, she or he can file a request to the company asking the company to disclose the selection criteria, the objective assessment of the candidates based on the selection criteria as well as the specific considerations for selecting a candidate of the other sex, after which the company must disclose this information.[45]

The *Gender Balance Directive* comes with reporting obligations. Companies must report every year about the gender representation among the executive and non-executive directors, and about the measures they took to meet the gender targets.[46] If the targets are not met, the company must explain its reasons for not meeting the objectives, and highlight what measures have been taken in order to meet the targets in the future.[47] This information must be disclosed on the company's website, in the corporate governance statement and be filed with the competent authorities.[48] It is up to the member states to decide on penalties concerning failure to meet the targets. Penalties may include fines, or nullity of the director's appointment.[49]

12.2.5 Future directions

With the development of the above-mentioned proposals, introduced in the context of the Green Deal, the EU has devised a series of measures that will have significant impact

---

40 *Proposal for a Directive of the European Parliament and of the Council on Improving the Gender Balance among Non-executive Directors of Companies Listed on Stock Exchanges and Related Measures* (COM/2012/614 final). The final adopted text of the Directive was not ready at the time of writing this section – accordingly, this section discusses the provisional agreement.
41 For the provisional agreement on the Directive that was published on 7 June 2022 see ibid Annex E.
42 Proposal for a Directive of the European Parliament and of the Council on Improving the Gender Balance among Non-executive Directors of Companies Listed on Stock Exchanges and Related Measures (COM/2012/614 final) art 4(1).
43 Ibid art 4a(1).
44 Ibid art 4a(2).
45 Ibid art 4a(3).
46 Ibid art 5(2).
47 Ibid art 5(3).
48 Ibid arts 5(2),(4).
49 Ibid art 6(1).

in the areas of (company) law, reporting, and finance, and potentially significant impacts on boards, companies, investors, issuers, banks, insurers and regulators.

Based on our analysis above of the most recent EU directives and their potential impact on the law in member states, we consider three issues particularly relevant. First, the EU framework for sustainable finance and corporate sustainability introduces a significant number of novel concepts with potential impacts in diverse disciplinary domains. For instance, the NFRD introduced the concept of 'double materiality' in reporting standards,[50] which extends notions of audiences and materiality in accounting.[51] This concept underpins not only the CSRD, but also the differentiation of activities in the *Taxonomy Regulation*, the reporting of investment impacts pursuant to the *Sustainable Finance Disclosure Regulation* and the expansion of the concept of due diligence in the CSDDD. The development of these concepts, and their potential impact on the theory and practice of corporate governance, for instance in the area of directors' duties, has recently informed significant academic debates.[52]

Second, there is increasing scrutiny of ESG as a construct.[53] The debate on the quality of this construct, and on the content of reporting standards and the quality of reporting, is likely to intensify in the coming years. Relatedly, the development of the *Taxonomy Regulation* and *European Sustainability Reporting Standards*[54] are likely to significantly inform debates on disclosure and reporting, not only in the EU, but internationally. Future research will track the development of these debates and the extent to which they impact on the implementation and uptake of the Green Deal by EU companies and enterprises affected by these developments. Will the Green Deal impact significantly on 'greenwashing' by EU companies and enterprises, and how will this compare with other international companies and enterprises not falling under the strict EU requirements?

Third, building on the last point, we predict that the proposals of the European Commission are likely to affect standards worldwide. The status of the EU as the world's largest trade bloc and the aim of the European Commission to establish a framework that allows for regulatory coherence are likely to have considerable impact on the development of standards and regulations beyond the EU. The European Commission observed in its Green Deal communication that '[a]s the world's largest single market, the EU can set standards that apply across global value chains'.[55] As mentioned in passing

---

50 As included in the Proposal for a new Corporate Sustainability Reporting Directive, put forward on 21 April 2021: see European Commission, 'Corporate sustainability reporting' <https://ec.europa .eu/info/business-economy-euro/company-reporting-and-auditing/company-reporting/corporate-sustainability-reporting_en>.

51 See J Veldman and A Jansson, 'Planetary boundaries and corporate reporting: The role of the conceptual basis of the corporation' (2020) 10(2) *Accounting, Economics, and Law: A Convivium* <https://doi.org/10.1515/ael-2018-0037>.

52 See MJ Roe et al, *The European Commission's Sustainable Corporate Governance Report: A Critique* (Harvard Business School, 2020).

53 See RG Eccles, 'The topology of hate for ESG', *Forbes* (3 June 2022) <https://www.forbes.com/sites/ bobeccles/2022/06/03/the-topology-of-hate-for-esg/?sh=723120801b0a>.

54 European Commission, 'The Commission adopts the European Sustainability Reporting Standards' <https://finance.ec.europa.eu/news/commission-adopts-european-sustainability-reporting-standards-2023-07-31_en>.

55 *The European Green Deal* (COM/2019/640 final) s 3.

above, beyond implicit pressure through global value chain regulation, it is notable that some aspects of the CSDDD already provide binding legislation for entities domiciled outside the EU.

Finally, it is particularly important to note that many other jurisdictions, including China and the UK, are looking to align their institutional models with (aspects of) the Green Deal.[56] The future is impossible to predict, but one would hope that the fears (as at the last quarter of 2023)[57] of a global recession based on the economic slowdown in the US and the EU, as 'the world's largest single market', will not hamper the exciting and aspirational goals of sustainable development pursued through the EU Green Deal.

12.2.6 Conclusion

The EU has embarked on an ambitious series of changes to the regulatory context for corporate governance. The combination of comprehensive conceptual changes; constructs still under development; a rapid increase of pressures for transparency and assurance; and rapid expansion of the scope of regulation and introduction of sanctionable changes are likely to inform significant debates in academic and practitioner circles. These are interesting times for scholars of corporate governance.

12.3 *G20/OECD Principles of Corporate Governance*

Tineke Lambooy, Jeroen Veldman and Rosalien van 't Foort-Diepeveen

12.3.1 Introduction to and history of the OECD *Principles of Corporate Governance*

The Organisation for Economic Co-operation and Development ('OECD') has 38 member states that share a common mission 'to shape policies that foster prosperity, equality, opportunity and well-being for all'.[58] The OECD develops evidence-based international standards which have become 'global references for capital flows, taxation, anti-bribery and anti-corruption frameworks, responsible business conduct, corporate governance, development assistance, education and, most recently, artificial intelligence'.[59] The 2021 *Vision for the Next Decade* stresses that 'we work towards a strong, sustainable, green, inclusive and resilient growth'.[60] With this mission, the OECD supports OECD members as well as non-OECD members in developing good public governance. By playing this role, it strengthens the global governance architecture and the rules-based international order.[61] Besides public governance, corporate governance is also

56 Pettingale, de Maupeou and Reilly, 'EU taxonomy and the future of reporting', *Harvard Law School Forum on Corporate Governance* (19 December 2023).

57 Philip Carlsson-Szlezak and Paul Swartz, 'Recession or resilience? Here's how the US, Europe, and Asia stacks up', *Fortune* (online, 12 September 2022) <https://fortune.com/2022/09/12/recession-resilience-us-europe-asia-outlook-carlsson-szlezak-swartz/>.

58 See OECD, 'Who we are' <www.oecd.org>.

59 OECD, *Trust for Global Cooperation – The Vision for the Next Decade 2021*, (Meeting of the OECD Council at Ministerial Level, Paris, 5–6 October 2021).

60 Ibid 4.

61 Ibid 4.

considered important by the OECD because of its capacity to 'build an environment of trust, transparency and accountability' necessary for business and investment.[62]

One of the OECD's early projects was to develop a set of principles of corporate governance. The OECD *Principles of Corporate Governance* of 1999 was the first initiative,[63] devised to provide minimum requirements for best practice. The objective was not to promote a single corporate governance model, but rather to promulgate principles that could be applied across OECD and non-OECD countries. These Principles were revised 2004[64] in response to the corporate scandals of the late 1990s and early 2000s. After the 2008 GFC[65] the OECD conducted peer reviews regarding the role of institutional investors (2011), related-party transactions (2012) and board member nominations and elections (2013).[66] Subsequently, a full review process started in 2014. To enhance the global reach of the principles, the G20 countries, the Basel Committee on Banking Supervision ('BCBS'), the Financial Stability Board ('FSB') and the World Bank Group ('WBG') were invited to participate in the review.[67] The process led to the adoption of the *G20/OECD Principles of Corporate Governance* in 2015. These Principles addressed challenges such as the increasing complexity of the investment chain, the changing role of stock exchanges and the emergence of new investors, investment strategies and trading practices. By 2022, 53 jurisdictions adhered to the Principles, including all G20, OECD and FSB members and four other countries (Bulgaria, Croatia, Peru and Romania).[68]

In 2021, the OECD Corporate Governance Committee ('the Committee') started a new review process of the 2015 Principles. After a public consultation was held in 2022, the text of the revised Principles was presented and discussed.[69] While the original focus was to implement insights gained from the COVID-19 crisis, the growing importance of sustainability challenges shifted priorities towards amending the Principles in such a way that corporate governance systems will support the transition to a sustainable and just economy. This aligns with the European approach as set out in Section 12.2. The *G20/OECD Principles of Corporate Governance* (2023) were eventually adopted by the G20 in September 2023. These Principles are also one of the Financial Stability Board's Key Standards for Sound Financial Systems, and form the basis for the World Bank Reports on the Observance of Standards and Codes in the area of corporate governance.[70]

---

62 Ibid 5.
63 OECD, *Principles of Corporate Governance* (1999) <https://one.oecd.org/document/C/MIN(99)6/En/pdf>.
64 OECD, *Principles of Corporate Governance* (2004) <https://www.oecd.org/corporate/ca/corporategovernanceprinciples/31557724.pdf>.
65 See further OECD, *Corporate Governance and the Financial Crisis: Key Findings and Main Messages* (2009) <https://www.oecd.org/daf/ca/corporategovernanceprinciples/43056196.pdf>.
66 See OECD, '2014–15 Review of the OECD Principles of Corporate Governance' <www.oecd.org/daf/ca/2014-review-oecd-corporate-governance-principles.htm>
67 Ibid; *G20/OECD Principles of Corporate Governance* (2015) 3 <https://www.oecd.org/publications/g20-oecd-principles-of-corporate-governance-2015-9789264236882-en.htm>.
68 OECD, *G20/OECD Principles of Corporate Governance* <https://www.oecd.org/corporate/principles-corporate-governance/>.
69 *G20/OECD Principles of Corporate Governance* (2023) ('the Principles'). The Principles are set out in the Appendix to the OECD *Recommendation on Principles of Corporate Governance* (OECD/LEGAL/0413) adopted by the OECD Council on 8 July 2015 and revised on 8 June 2023. The Principles were endorsed by the G20 in September 2023.
70 *G20/OECD Principles of Corporate Governance* (2023) 4.

An interesting source of information about corporate governance frameworks and codes is the *OECD Corporate Governance Factbook*.[71] Issued every two years, it contains information on trends and evolutions in the institutional, legal and regulatory frameworks for corporate governance of listed companies across 49 jurisdictions worldwide. The *Factbook* complements the *G20/OECD Principles of Corporate Governance* as a tool for policymakers to assess and improve their own corporate governance frameworks. The 2023 edition of the *Factbook* includes a focus on new dimensions of the 2023 Principles: namely, corporate sustainability, the use of digital tools for shareholder meetings, and regulatory frameworks for company groups. These new developments reflect changing corporate governance practices and evolving stakeholder expectations with respect to other high-profile issues such as diversity on company boards. They also address oversight of listed companies, and ownership concentration. This is in line with the EU trends and developments discussed in Section 12.2.

12.3.2 Broad aims, structure and drafting process of the *G20/OECD Principles*

The *G20/OECD Principles of Corporate Governance* (2023) ('the *G20/OECD Principles*' or 'the Principles') aim to help governments in their efforts to 'evaluate and improve the legal, regulatory and institutional framework for corporate governance, with a view to supporting market confidence and integrity, economic efficiency, sustainable growth and financial stability'. Furthermore, they provide guidance to stock exchanges, investors and listed companies.[72] The Principles can also support non-listed companies as good governance is important for all companies.[73] As mentioned in Section 1.2, the definition of 'corporate governance' adopted in this book aligns with the definition of 'corporate governance' adopted by the *G20/OECD Principles* and is, therefore, worth repeating:[74]

> a set of relationships between a company's management, board, shareholders and other stakeholders. Corporate governance also provides the structure and systems through which the company is directed and its objectives are set, and the means of attaining those objectives and monitoring performance are determined.

The structure of the Principles is as follows. There are six core Principles that are presented in six chapters:

I) Ensuring the basis for an effective corporate governance framework;

II) The rights and equitable treatment of shareholders and key ownership functions;

III) Institutional investors, stock markets, and other intermediaries;

---

71 *OECD Corporate Governance Factbook 2023* (2023) <https://www.oecd-ilibrary.org/finance-and-investment/oecd-corporate-governance-factbook-2023_6d912314-en>.

72 *G20/OECD Principles of Corporate Governance* (2023) 3.

73 Ibid 7.

74 Ibid 6.

IV) Disclosure and transparency;

V) The responsibilities of the board; and

VI) Sustainability and resilience.[75]

Each chapter is headed by a single Principle that appears in bold italics and is followed by a number of supporting Principles and their sub-Principles in bold. The Principles are supplemented by annotations that provide commentary on the Principles and sub-Principles and are intended to help readers understand their rationale. The annotations may also contain descriptions of dominant or emerging trends and offer alternative implementation methods and examples that may be useful in making the Principles operational.[76]

Review of the Principles is overseen by the OECD Corporate Governance Committee, in which all G20 and FSB jurisdictions have been actively participating since the last time the Principles were reviewed, in 2015, when the G20 endorsed them as the *G20/OECD Principles*. All G20 countries except one now have 'Associate' (voting) status in the Committee; the exception is Saudi Arabia, which continues to participate in the Committee with an 'Invitee' status.[77]

12.3.3 The 2021–23 revision of the *G20/OECD Principles*

12.3.3.1 Topics for review consideration

For the 2021–23 review, the Committee identified various traditional corporate governance topics for consideration. 'Ten priority areas' were mentioned in the *Terms of Reference and Roadmap for the Review of the G20/OECD Principles of Corporate Governance:*[78]

(1) corporate ownership trends and increased concentration

(2) the management of climate change and other environmental, social and governance ('ESG') risks

(3) the role of institutional investors and stewardship

(4) the growth of new digital technologies and emerging opportunities and risks

(5) crisis and risk management

(6) excessive risk-taking in the non-financial corporate sector

(7) the role and rights of debtholders in corporate governance

(8) executive remuneration

(9) the role of board committees

(10) diversity on boards and in senior management.

---

75 Ibid 8.

76 Ibid 8.

77 OECD, *OECD Secretary-General's Second Report to G20 Finance Ministers and Central Bank Governors on the Review of the G20/OECD Principles of Corporate Governance, Indonesia, July 2022* (2022) 5 <www.oecd.org/corporate/oecd-secretary-general-report-G20-FMCBG-review-G20-OECD-principles-corporate-governance-2022.pdf>.

78 OECD, *OECD Secretary-General's Report to G20 Finance Ministers and Central Bank Governors on the Review of the G20/OECD Principles of Corporate Governance, Indonesia, February 2022* (2022) 6–7 <www.oecd.org/corporate/ca/OECD-Secretary-General-First-Report-G20-FMCBG-Review-G20-OECD-Principles-Corporate-Governance-2022.pdf>. See the Annex to this report at 8–13 for the terms of reference and roadmap for the review of the *G20/OECD Principles of Corporate Governance.*

However, during the review process, the members expressed a strong interest in the issue of sustainability and resilience as well as the desire to see the revised *G20/OECD Principles* 'reflect the growing challenges corporations face in managing climate-related impacts and risks', and that the Principles offer guidance in this respect. Hence, besides two progress reports on the review (February and July 2022),[79] another report, entitled *Climate Change and Corporate Governance*,[80] was prepared to inform the review.[81] Other reports that informed the Committee in the review process concerned the use of new digital technologies and emerging opportunities and risks; institutional investors and stewardship; the role of board committees; and the role and rights of debtholders.[82]

The report on climate change discusses the main implications of climate change for corporate governance, focusing on the roles and rights of shareholders, stakeholders, corporate disclosure and the responsibilities of company boards. It appears as an Annex to the July 2022 progress report – that is, the 'Second Report'. An overview of the discussion in the Second Report and the report on climate change, and the adoption of the proposals in these reports in the *G20/OECD Principles*, is provided in the following subsections. The overview is limited to the revisions and innovative approaches taken in the *G20/OECD Principles*.

12.3.3.2 The management of climate change and other ESG risks

The first and main issue discussed in the Second Report concerned 'climate change and corporate governance'.[83] The Committee proposed to include a new chapter on 'Sustainability and resilience' in the revised *G20/OECD Principles* that addresses 'the interconnections between the role of disclosure, shareholders, stakeholders, and the board of directors on sustainability matters'.[84] The new chapter was intended to promote the idea that 'the corporate governance framework should provide incentives for companies to make financing and investment decisions, as well as to manage their risks, in a way that contributes to the sustainability and resilience of the corporation'.[85] The existing Chapter IV of the *G20/OECD Principles* on stakeholders was also proposed to be included in the new chapter, together with some proposed revisions and new recommendations related to stakeholders. The revisions on the issue of sustainability and shareholders aimed at enhancing the 'effective participation of shareholders

---

79 OECD, *OECD Secretary-General's Report to G20 Finance Ministers and Central Bank Governors on the Review of the G20/OECD Principles of Corporate Governance, Indonesia, February 2022* (2022); OECD, *OECD Secretary-General's Second Report to G20 Finance Ministers and Central Bank Governors on the Review of the G20/OECD Principles of Corporate Governance, Indonesia, July 2022* (2022).

80 This report appears as an Annex to OECD, *OECD Secretary-General's Second Report to G20 Finance Ministers and Central Bank Governors on the Review of the G20/OECD Principles of Corporate Governance, Indonesia, July 2022* (2022) at 11–73 (the Annex is renumbered from 1–62).

81 OECD, *OECD Secretary-General's Second Report to G20 Finance Ministers and Central Bank Governors on the Review of the G20/OECD Principles of Corporate Governance, Indonesia, July 2022* ('Second Report') (2022) 5–6.

82 Ibid 5.

83 Ibid 7 and the Annex thereto.

84 Ibid 7.

85 Ibid.

in key corporate governance decisions, including on sustainability matters', which may include deciding about service providers' conflicts of interest.[86] Also, in the other existing chapters, revisions on sustainability were proposed to ensure consistency; for example, they addressed 'disclosure of financial and non-financial information; the use of high-quality international standards; and the external auditing and assurance of sustainability disclosure'. Furthermore, 'the issue of sustainability and boards was addressed in a new sub-Principle on the business judgement rule and through revisions concerning the integrity of the [company's] accounting and reporting systems for financial and sustainability disclosure'.[87]

12.3.3.3 New 'Principle VI. Sustainability and resilience'

A new principle on corporate social responsibility ('CSR'), referred to in the Principles as 'responsible business conduct' ('RBC'), is elaborated in a new chapter of the *G20/OECD Principles*: 'Principle VI. Sustainability and resilience'.[88] The new chapter provides for multiple references to (material sustainability) risks, including climate-related physical and transition risks.[89] It emphasises therein that the competitiveness and ultimate success of a corporation depends on the 'contributions from a range of different resource providers including investors, the workforce, creditors, customers, affected communities, suppliers and other stakeholders'.[90] In Chapter VI, the Principle prescribes that the corporate governance framework must 'consider the rights, roles and interests of stakeholders and encourage active co-operation between companies, shareholders and stakeholders in creating value, quality jobs, and sustainable and resilient companies'.[91] Also, corporations should 'foster value-creating co-operation among stakeholders'.[92] One group of stakeholders anticipated by the new Principle VI is employees. Chapter VI states that 'mechanisms for employee participation should be permitted to develop'.[93] Where stakeholders participate in the corporate governance process, all of them should have access to relevant, sufficient and reliable information on a timely and regular basis.[94] Moreover, all stakeholders, including individual workers and their representative bodies, 'should be able to freely communicate their concerns about illegal or unethical practices to the board and/or to the competent public authorities, and their rights should not be compromised for doing this'.[95]

Principle VI and its sub-Principles require that the rights of stakeholders established by law or through mutual agreements are to be respected. For example, in some jurisdictions, companies must carry out human rights and/or environmental due diligence. As well as fulfilling their legal obligations, companies are encouraged to use

---

86 Ibid.
87 Ibid.
88 *G20/OECD Principles of Corporate Governance* (2023) 44–50.
89 Ibid 7–8.
90 Ibid 48.
91 Ibid.
92 Ibid.
93 Ibid.
94 Ibid 49.
95 Ibid.

'the *OECD Guidelines for Multinational Enterprises* and associated due diligence standards for risk-based due diligence to identify, prevent and mitigate actual and potential adverse impacts of their business, and account for how these impacts are addressed'.[96]

It is fair to say that Chapter VI does not provide much guidance to companies in terms of specifying *how* they must deal with environmental, anti-corruption or ethical concerns that are deemed relevant to a company's decision-making processes. Hence, companies will have to examine and follow the CSR norms and procedures that are incorporated more explicitly in other instruments which are referenced in the *G20/OECD Principles*, such as the *OECD Guidelines for Multinational Enterprises on Responsible Business Conduct* (2023), the OECD *Convention on Combating Bribery of Foreign Public Officials in International Business Transactions*, the United Nations *Guiding Principles on Business and Human Rights*, and the ILO [International Labor Organization] *Declaration on Fundamental Principles and Rights at Work*.[97]

In relation to executive remuneration schemes, the revisions embodied in Chapter VI recommend, among other things, the disclosure of the use of sustainability indicators in compensation.[98] Another issue concerns how board committees (for example, audit, risk, nomination and remuneration committees) can be effectively used to deal with the increasingly complex responsibilities regarding risk management faced by boards. Chapter VI promotes a corporate governance framework within which boards adequately consider material sustainability risks and opportunities when fulfilling their key functions in reviewing, monitoring and guiding governance practices, disclosure, strategy, risk management and internal control systems, including with respect to climate-related physical and transition risks.[99] Boards are also to ensure that companies' lobbying activities are coherent with their sustainability-related goals and targets.[100]

12.3.3.4 The revised Principles and disclosure and transparency

Chapter IV of the Principles stipulates that disclosure of sustainability matters, financial reporting and other corporate information be connected.[101] Clearly, we see here a strong connection to 'Principle IV. Disclosure and transparency'. This Principle stipulates that the corporate governance framework 'ensure[s] that timely and accurate disclosure is made on all material matters regarding the corporation, including the financial situation, performance, sustainability, ownership, and governance of the company'.[102] The OECD considers the implementation of this Principle key, because a strong disclosure regime promotes transparency, ensures effective monitoring of companies and is central to shareholders' and stakeholders' ability to exercise their rights on an informed basis.[103] By contrast, 'weak disclosure and non-transparent practices can contribute to unethical behaviour and to a loss of market integrity at great cost, not just to the company and its shareholders but also

---

96 Ibid 48.
97 Ibid 7.
98 Ibid 47.
99 Ibid. According to the CSRD (see Section 12.2.4.4 above), companies also must disclose information about their lobby activities.
100 Ibid.
101 Ibid 46.
102 Ibid 27.
103 Ibid.

to the economy as a whole'.[104] While corporate disclosure should focus on what is material to investors' decisions and may include an assessment of a company's value, it may also help improve public understanding of the structure and activities of companies, corporate policies and performance with respect to environmental, social and governance matters.[105] Chapter IV provides specific ways of ensuring the implementation of this Principle.[106]

Just like corporate governance norms in the EU (see Section 12.2.4.6), the revised *G20/OECD Principles* push for gender diversity on boards and in senior management. To that end, Chapter IV stipulates that corporate governance frameworks require companies to provide information on the gender of board members, talent development and succession planning, board nomination and election processes, and board evaluation.[107]

12.3.3.5 The growth of new digital technologies and emerging opportunities and risks

The Second Report highlighted how the COVID-19 pandemic and new digital technologies allowed companies to strengthen corporate governance practices and monitoring through the use of digital tools.[108] A new sub-Principle was proposed requiring that companies explain 'framework-related issues for the use of digitalisation in the supervision and promotion of good corporate governance practices'.[109] This proposal has been adopted in 'Chapter I. Ensuring the basis for an effective corporate governance framework' of the *G20/OCED Principles*. This Chapter addresses the ability of digital technologies to enhance the efficiency and effectiveness of supervisory and enforcement processes related to corporate governance. Benefits can be seen in, for example, market integrity. The regulatory burden on regulated entities can be alleviated by digital tools in order to lower compliance costs and to enhance risk management capabilities. However, it is recommended that supervisory and regulatory authorities give due attention to the management of associated risks:[110]

> Adopting digital solutions in regulatory and supervisory processes also comes with challenges and risks. Important considerations include ensuring the quality of data; ensuring that staff have proper technical competence; considering interoperability between systems in the development of reporting formats; and managing third-party dependencies and digital security risks. When artificial intelligence and algorithmic decision-making are used in supervisory processes, it is critical to maintain a human element in place to mitigate against risks of incorporating existing biases in algorithmic models and the risks from an overreliance on models and digital technologies. At the same time, regulators in most jurisdictions espouse the value of a technology-neutral approach that does not discourage innovation and the adoption of alternative technological solutions. As technologies evolve and may serve to strengthen corporate

---

104 Ibid.
105 Ibid.
106 Ibid 5, 9.
107 Ibid 29.
108 Second Report (2022) 8.
109 Ibid 8.
110 *G20/OECD Principles of Corporate Governance* (2023) 12.

governance practices, the regulatory framework may require review and adjustments to facilitate their use.

Other revisions proposed in the Second Report included creating the option to hold virtual and hybrid shareholder meetings and addressing digital security risks and board responsibilities to that end.[111] The option of hybrid shareholder meetings has been included in 'Chapter II. The rights and equitable treatment of shareholders and key ownership functions' of the *G20/OECD Principles*:

> General shareholder meetings allowing for remote shareholder participation should be permitted by jurisdictions as a means to facilitate and reduce the costs to shareholders of participation and engagement. Such meetings should be conducted in a manner that ensures equal access to information and opportunities for participation of all shareholders.[112]

12.3.3.6 Corporate ownership trends and increased concentration

In the Second Report, the proposed revisions on corporate ownership trends and increased concentration highlighted two main issues: complex group structures and related-party transactions. It was proposed that disclosures include:[113] capital structures, group structures and their control arrangements; minority shareholder protection from abusive actions; the integrity of corporate disclosure and reporting on large or complex risks related to company groups; access to information for company groups; and related-party transactions. Other revisions pertained to the role of both passive and active investment strategies in price discovery.[114] The revisions proposed in the Second Report have found their way into 'Chapter II. The rights and equitable treatment of shareholders and key ownership functions', which addresses some of these issues,[115] and 'Chapter IV. Disclosure and transparency', which deals with the others.[116]

12.3.3.7 Institutional investors and stewardship

In the Second Report, revisions were proposed to address the growing importance of institutional investors in global markets, their increasing engagement with portfolio companies, and the increased importance of stewardship codes as a tool to support shareholder engagement.[117] Furthermore, in the same report, the increased use of indexing, ESG indices, data, and ratings by institutional investors were evaluated as indirect engagement tools. The revisions proposed in the Second Report have been elaborated in 'Chapter II. The rights and equitable treatment of shareholders and key ownership functions' and 'Chapter III. Institutional investors, stock markets, and other intermediaries'.[118]

----

111 Second Report (2023) 8.
112 *G20/OECD Principles of Corporate Governance* (2023) 16.
113 Second Report (2023) 8.
114 Ibid 8.
115 *G20/OECD Principles of Corporate Governance* (2023) 16.
116 Ibid 28, 30.
117 Second Report (2023) 9.
118 *G20/OECD Principles of Corporate Governance* (2023) 14–26.

12.3.4 Conclusions on the *G20/OECD Principles* and the 2021–23 update

A unique aspect of the *G20/OECD Principles* (2023) is that they operate across borders and without preferencing any corporate law system or board structure.[119] The Principles emphasise that a corporate governance framework 'typically comprises elements of legislation, regulation, self-regulatory arrangements, voluntary commitments and business practices that are the result of a country's specific circumstances, history and tradition'.[120] Since there are often overlapping public and private enforcement mechanisms, effective enforcement requires 'that the allocation of responsibilities for supervision, implementation and enforcement among different authorities is clearly defined and formalised so that the competencies of complementary bodies and agencies are respected and used most effectively'.[121] As part of the 2021–23 revision process of the *G20/OECD Principles*, the scope of the Principles has been widened towards how companies and investors can add value to society. The concern is whether they are effectively dealing with climate change and other global environmental challenges in combination with avoiding corruption and complying with human rights and social norms.

12.4 Germany

Alexander Scheuch

12.4.1 Overview

In the international corporate governance landscape Germany stands out mainly due to its mandatory two-tier board system (management board and supervisory board) and the strong support for co-determination by employees.[122] In recent years corporate social responsibility ('CSR') has been the main addition to the debate about corporate governance in Germany,[123] primarily driven by the recent expectations of corporations to move away from short-term shareholder value to long-term stakeholder value.[124]

---

119 Ibid 6.
120 Ibid 9.
121 Ibid 11.
122 Axel von Werder in Thomas Kremer et al (eds), *Deutscher Corporate Governance Kodex* (CH Beck, 8th ed, 2021) pt 3 *Preambule* [31]; cf also Jean J du Plessis et al, *German Corporate Governance in International and European Context* (Springer, 3rd ed, 2017) 2. For a more comprehensive discussion, in English, of several other issues related to the German corporate governance model, the book by Jean J du Plessis et al (ibid) will provide a good starting point.
123 Cf Alexander Scheuch, 'Soft law requirements with hard law effects? The influence of CSR on corporate law from a German perspective' in Jean J du Plessis et al (eds), *Globalisation of Corporate Social Responsibility and its Impact on Corporate Governance* (Springer, 2017) 203.
124 US Business Roundtable, *Statement on the Purpose of a Corporation* (Statement, 19 August 2019) <https://s3.amazonaws.com/brt.org/2022.08.01-BRTStatementonthePurposeofa CorporationwithSignatures-Compressed.pdf>; European Union, European Commission, *Inception Impact Assessment: Sustainable Corporate Governance* (Doc No Ares [2020] 4034032, 30 July 2020); Birgit Spießhöfer, 'Sustainable corporate governance' (2022) 10 *Neue Zeitschrift für Gesellschaftsrecht* 435, 436.

12.4.2 Regulatory environment

The sources for corporate governance in Germany are spread out over a variety of hard and soft laws.[125] Germany has long embraced the general principles of responsible corporate management and good corporate control structures.[126] With the rise of globalisation, the English term 'corporate governance' became well-known in Germany as well.[127] German enterprises sought international investors that were familiar with corporate governance codes, which had gained prominence after the release of the Cadbury Report in the UK in 1992.[128] After the stock market crash of the *Neue Markt* segment in the early 2000s, corporate governance became a high priority on Germany's corporate law agenda with the aims to regain (international) investors' trust and keep the financial marketplace competitive.[129]

Private initiatives initially created drafts for a corporate governance code in Germany. After their positive reception,[130] the German government formed the Baums Commission which ultimately recommended the adoption of a corporate governance code.[131] This task was referred to the newly established German Corporate Governance Commission (*Regierungskommission Deutscher Corporate Governance Kodex*). In June 2002 the *Deutscher Corporate Governance Kodex* (German Corporate Governance Code ['GCGC']) came into effect.[132] The Commission, which consists of board members of German listed companies and stakeholders, remains active to this day. Though appointed by the Minister of Justice, the Commission operates independently from the government in its work and financing structure.[133] Its primary responsibility is to regularly review the GCGC, resulting in almost annual updates.[134] The current version of the Code came into effect on 27 June 2022.[135]

---

125 Rainer Wernsmann and Ulrich Gatzka, 'Der Deutsche Corporate Governance Kodex und die Entsprechenserklärung nach § 161 Akt' (2011) 26 *Neue Zeitschrift für Gesellschaftsrecht* 1001, 1002. For more details on the governing legislation for corporations, see Section 12.4.3.

126 The German discussion about these principles can be traced back to the 1950s: Philipp Hanfland, *Haftungsrisiken im Zusammenhang mit § 161 AktG und dem Deutschen Corporate Governance Kodex* (Nomos, 2006) 19, 32.

127 For the development of the usage of the term 'corporate governance' in Germany, see Carsten Berrar, *Die Entwicklung der Corporate Governance in Deutschland im internationalen Vergleich* (Nomos, 2001) 24.

128 Klaus J Hopt, 'Law and corporate governance: Germany within Europe' (2015) 27(4) *Journal of Applied Corporate Finance* 8, 13; Wernsmann and Gatzka, 'Der Deutsche Corporate Governance Kodex und die Entsprechenserklärung nach § 161 Akt' (2011) 26 *Neue Zeitschrift für Gesellschaftsrecht* 1001, 1002.

129 Marc Steffen Rapp and Christian Strenger, 'Corporate governance in Germany: Recent developments and challenges' (2015) 27(4) *Journal of Applied Finance* 16. For more details on the historical development, cf Du Plessis et al, *German Corporate Governance in International and European Context* (2017) 17.

130 Hanfland, *Haftungsrisiken im Zusammenhang mit § 161 AktG und dem Deutschen Corporate Governance Kodex* (2006) 22.

131 Marcus Lutter, 'Corporate governance in Germany: The big leap' (2010) 22(1/2) *Journal of Interdisciplinary Economics* 17, 20.

132 Ibid.

133 Gregor Bachmann in Kremer et al (eds), *Deutscher Corporate Governance Kodex* (2021) pt 2 [62].

134 Ibid [8], [14].

135 See Regierungskommission, 'Deutscher Corporate Governance Kodex' <https://www.dcgk.de/en/home.html>.

12.4.3 Legislation and regulators

The governing legislation for enterprises in Germany is mainly based on statutes (albeit supplemented by case law), most importantly the *Stock Corporation Act* (*Aktiengesetz* ['*AktG*']), the *Commercial Code* (*Handelsgesetzbuch* ['*HGB*']), the *Co-Determination Act* (*Mitbestimmungsgesetz* ['*MitbestG*']) and the *One Third Participation Act* (*Drittelbeteiligungsgesetz* ['*DrittelbG*']). The *AktG* mandates the application of the two-tier board system, consisting of a management board (*Vorstand*) and a supervisory board (*Aufsichtsrat*).

The management board derives its exclusive powers to manage the business of the enterprise from s 76[1] of the *AktG* and is not subject to instructions by the general meeting (*Hauptversammlung*) or the supervisory board. Deviations from this governance structure are permissible in corporate groups (*Konzern*), a salient feature of German corporate law being that the *AktG* contains explicit provisions on groups, employing a unique concept.[136] Section 93[1] of the *AktG* requires management board members to exercise the 'due care of a prudent manager faithfully complying with their duties'. Failure to do so will result in liability to the company according to s 93[2] of the *AktG*. The 'business judgment rule' has been codified in s 93[1] sentence 2 of the *AktG*.

The supervisory board was introduced to German corporate law in 1870, replacing the previous state licensing and control system.[137] A regulatory authority with similar powers to, for instance, the Australian Securities and Investments Commission ('ASIC') does not exist in Germany.[138] Authorities were only established for specific sectors and issues, most notably the Federal Financial Supervisory Authority (*Bundesanstalt für Finanzdienstleistungsaufsicht* ['*BaFin*']), tasked with ensuring the proper functioning, stability and integrity of the German financial system and its companies.

The supervisory board, separated from the management board through strict incompatibility rules, has statutory powers to appoint, supervise and dismiss management board members. While day-to-day management lies strictly with the management board, the supervisory board shares responsibility for fundamental decisions and acts (for example, those concerning the annual report).[139] Transactions of fundamental importance require approval of the supervisory board.[140] It also represents the company vis-à-vis the management board.[141] However, as management failures can at times also be perceived as supervisory failures, supervisory boards were often reluctant to pursue liability claims

---

136 For a detailed overview, see Alexander Scheuch, 'Konzernrecht: An overview of the German regulation of corporate groups and resulting liability issues' (2016) 13(5) *European Company Law* 191.

137 Klaus J Hopt, 'The German two-tier board (Aufsichtsrat): A German view on corporate governance' in Klaus J Hopt et al (eds), *Comparative Corporate Governance: Essays and Materials* (de Gruyter, 1997) 3, 6.

138 For an evaluation of ASIC from a German perspective, see Thilo Kuntz, 'Regulierungsstrategien zur Durchsetzung von Gemeinwohlinteressen im Aktienrecht' in Stefan Grundmann et al (eds), *Festschrift für Klaus J Hopt zum 80 Geburtstag* (C H Beck, 2020) 653, 664; cf also Jean J du Plessis and Niklas Cordes, 'Claiming damages from members of management boards in Germany: Time for a radical rethink and possible lessons from Down Under?' (2015) 36(11) *Company Lawyer* 339.

139 *AktG* s 171.

140 *AktG* s 111[4] cl 2. See in particular Mathias Habersack, *Münchener Kommentar zum Aktiengesetz*, ed Wulf Goette, Mathias Habersack and Susanne Kalss (CH Beck, 6th ed, 2023) vol 2, § 111 AktG [120].

141 *AktG* s 112.

of the company against the management board.[142] That changed with the landmark *ARAG/Garmenbeck* decision by the German Federal Court of Justice (*Bundesgerichtshof* ['*BGH*']), which emphasised the supervisory board's obligation to pursue such claims.[143]

In principle, the supervisory board is elected by the general meeting,[144] which also sets the remuneration for the supervisory board and votes on the proposed remuneration scheme for the management board.[145] The general meeting holds further competences, including amendments to the articles of association and decisions on other fundamental issues.[146] Section 147 of the *AktG* grants the general meeting the right to pursue claims against the company's bodies (management as well as supervisory board) and to appoint a special representative tasked with pursuing these claims.[147] The use of this instrument has increased in recent years.[148] Germany also recognises a statutory derivative action by minority shareholders.[149] However, due to the high threshold (one percent or EUR 100 000 of the company's share capital), the lack of incentive (a collective action problem) and the possibility of the supervisory board to take over the proceeding, derivative lawsuits hardly occur in practice.[150]

A special feature of German law has a fundamental influence on the governance structure of large German corporations: half of the seats of the supervisory board (under the *MitbestG*) or one-third of seats (under the *DrittelbG*) are allocated to employee representatives, including labour unions, as per s 7[2] cl 1 of the *MitbestG*. The former applies once the threshold of 2000 employees (also counting those of subsidiaries within a corporate group) has been passed, with a number of 500 employees[151] sufficing for the application of the latter.[152]

Public companies subject to the *MitbestG* are required by law to meet binding gender quotas for their respective boards.[153] The management board must include at least one male and one female member, if it has more than three members.[154] On the

---

142 Cf Jens Koch, 'Die Überwachung des Aufsichtsrats durch den Vorstand' (2016) 180 *Zeitschrift für das gesamte Handels und Wirtschaftsrecht* 578, 584.

143 Bundesgerichtshof [German Federal Court of Justice], II ZR 175/95, 21.04.1997 reported in (1997) 135 BGHZ 244.

144 *AktG* s 101.

145 Cf Section 12.4.4.3, which deals with remuneration.

146 In *AktG* s 119, an enumerative list is provided. Jurisprudence has, however, developed principles under which the general meeting can also decide on other fundamental questions, referred to as the *Holzmüller* and *Gelatine* doctrine. For details, see Jens Koch, *Aktiengesetz* (CH Beck, 17th ed, 2023) § 119 [16].

147 For that, the representative is equipped with the right of information and examination vis-à-vis both boards and employees insofar as this is not exercised in an obviously improper manner and is related to the prosecution of the claim; for more details see Sebastian Mock, *Aktienrecht*, ed Gerald Spindler and Eberhard Stilz (CH Beck, 5th ed, 2022) § 147 AktG [190].

148 Ibid [12].

149 *AktG* s 148.

150 Du Plessis and Cordes, 'Claiming damages from members of management boards in Germany' (2015) 36(11) *Company Lawyer* 339.

151 For the calculation in corporate groups, cf Mathias Habersack, *Mitbestimmungsrecht*, ed Mathias Habersack and Martin Henssler (CH Beck, 4th ed, 2018) § 2 DrittelbG [13].

152 Georg Annuß (n 19), vol 2 § 1 DrittelbG [3], § 4 DrittelbG [1], § 1 MitbestG [9], § 7 MitbestG [1].

153 For a comparison with the Norwegian arrangement, see Jean J du Plessis, Ingo Saenger and Richard Foster, 'Board diversity or gender diversity? Perspectives from Europe, Australia and South Africa' (2012) 17(2) *Deakin Law Review* 207, 209–10.

154 *AktG* s 76[3a].

supervisory board each gender must make up at least 30 per cent of the members.[155] Additionally, listed companies, or those subject to the *MitbestG*, must set target values for female board representation.[156] If the company fails to meet the target values an obligation to explain is triggered.[157] The existing German rules on gender quotas already meet the requirements set forth by the newly enacted *European Gender Balance Directive*.[158]

The *AktG* and the *HGB* mandate an annual resolution on a financial statement by the management board, followed by approval of the supervisory board after an independent audit. Larger companies are also required to annually disclose a CSR report,[159] an obligation stemming from EU directives.[160] German law has implemented a 'comply or explain' mechanism regarding the use of a national, EU-based or international framework such as the Global Reporting Initiative ('GRI')[161] for the CSR report.[162] The EU's latest reporting directive, yet to be implemented in the member states,[163] states the goal of creating uniform standards, avoiding the fragmentation of standards.[164]

12.4.4 Codes of practice

The GCGC, which is also available in an English version,[165] contains non–legally binding provisions, characterised as 'soft law'[166] as in most other jurisdictions where such corporate governance codes are in place.

12.4.4.1 Types of provisions and enforcement of the GCGC

The Code's provisions are divided into principles (*Grundsätze*), recommendations (*Empfehlungen*) and suggestions (*Anregungen*).[167]

The Principles consolidate key concepts of German corporate legislation. Recommendations, denoted by '*soll*'(shall), make up the majority of the GCGC and represent generally accepted guidelines of good and responsible corporate governance. Compliance with and departures from these recommendations need to be disclosed annually,

---

155 *AktG*,s 96[2]. For more details, see Koch, *Aktiengesetz* (2023) § 96 [13].
156 *AktG* s 111[5], s 76[4].
157 Koch, *Aktiengesetz* (2023) § 76 [83].
158 Jessica Schmidt, 'BB-Gesetzgebungs- und Rechtsprechungsreport zum Europäischen Unternehmensrecht 2022/2023' (2023) 33–34 *Betriebs-Berater* 1859, 1860.
159 *HGB* s 289c.
160 For a detailed overview, see Scheuch, 'Soft law requirements with hard law effects?' in Du Plessis et al (eds), *Globalisation of Corporate Social Responsibility and Its Impact on Corporate Governance* (2017) 203.
161 GRI (Web Page) <https://www.globalreporting.org>.
162 *HGB* s 289d cl 1. For more details, see Peter Kajüter '*Münchener Kommentar zum Handelsgesetzbuch*' in Karsten Schmidt and Werner F Ebke (eds) (CH Beck, 4th ed, 2020) §§ 289b–289e [58].
163 For an assessment from a German perspective see Jens Ekkenga, 'Externe Nachhaltigkeitsberichterstattung nach der neuen CSRD' (2023) (187)*Zeitschrift für das gesamte Handelsrecht und Wirtschaftsrecht* 228.
164 *Directive (EU) 2022/2464 of the European Parliament and of the Council of 14 December 2022 Amending Regulation (EU) No 537/2014, Directive 2004/109/EC, Directive 2006/43/EC and Directive 2013/34/EU, as Regards Corporate Sustainability* (Text with EEA Relevance) recital 37 <http://data.europa.eu/eli/dir/2022/2464/oj>.
165 For its background and evolution, see Section 12.4.2.
166 Lambertus Fuhrmann, Markus Linnerz and Andreas Pohlmann, *Deutscher Corporate Governance Kodex*, ed David Barst et al (Recht und Wirtschaft, 2016) ch 1 [4].
167 For more details on their contents, see Section 12.4.4.3.

and departures must be explained. This 'comply or explain' mechanism is stipulated in s 161 of the *AktG*. Though departures and non-disclosure do not have any direct legal consequences,[168] non-compliance may negatively impact the company's market price, creating pressure to disclose an explanation and to comply with the recommendations of the GCGC.[169] In light of this mechanism, the Code's lack of democratic legitimacy has been criticised.[170] However, it should be kept in mind that it is assumed that EU law[171] requires each member state to adopt the 'comply or explain principle', which in turn implies the adoption of a corporate governance code in which the principle is embedded.[172] Despite this debate, the GCGC has been widely accepted by companies and courts[173] and mostly followed in practice.[174]

The Code's suggestions, marked by '*sollte*' (should), are not part of the 'comply or explain' regime as they are deemed to represent good corporate governance, but have yet to gain widespread adoption.[175]

12.4.4.2 Foreword – key principles and structure

The GCGC's foreword (*Präambel*) provides an overview of the guiding principles for corporate governance within Germany's two-tier board system and explains the Code's structure.[176] It includes the 'reputable businessman concept' (*Leitbild des ehrbaren Kaufmanns*), promoting ethical and responsible behaviour. Emphasis is further placed on CSR, encouraging enterprises to also consider the interests of stakeholders as well as those of shareholders. Both boards (supervisory and management) are expected to consider the impact their company has on people and the environment, affirming a deeply embedded stakeholder approach towards corporate governance in Germany.[177] Addressing the shareholders' role, the foreword encourages active and responsible exercise of ownership rights in alignment with transparent principles, respecting sustainability. This aims at fostering good corporate governance for German enterprises governed by the GCGC.[178]

---

168 Koch, *Aktiengesetz* (2023) § 161 [25].

169 Thomas Schmeing in Nima Ghassemi-Tabar (ed), *Deutscher Corporate Governance Kodex* (CH Beck, 2nd ed, 2023) § 161 AktG [2].

170 See Gerald Spindler, 'Zur Zukunft der Corporate Governance Kommission und des § 161 AktG' (2011) 26 *Neue Zeitschrift für Gesellschaftsrecht* 1007, 1008 with further references. For a more recent critique, see Jens Koch, '20 Jahre Deutscher Corporate Governance Kodex' (2022) 1 *Die Aktiengesellschaft* 1, 2.

171 *Directive 2006/46/EC of the European Parliament and of the Council of 14 June 2006* ([2006] OJ L 224/1) art 7(2).

172 Christoph Seibt and Jean Mohamed, 'Das Konzept des Deutschen Corporate Governance Kodex' (2022) 10 *Die Aktiengesellschaft* 357, 359.

173 Fuhrmann, Linnerz and Pohlmann, *Deutscher Corporate Governance Kodex* (2016) Preamble [4] with further references.

174 Cf Center for Research in Financial Communication, *Entsprechenserklärungen 2020/2021 zum Deutschen Corporate Governance Kodex: Eine Analyse der Einflussfaktoren und Abweichungsbegründungen* (Report, July 2021) <https://www.financialcommunication.org/fileadmin/webcontent_crifc/Studien/CRiFC-Kurzstudie_Entsprechenserkla__rungen_zum_DCGK.pdf>.

175 Von Werder, *Deutscher Corporate Governance Kodex* (2021) Preamble [51].

176 Schmeing, *Deutscher Corporate Governance Kodex* (2023) Preamble [1].

177 Jakob C Timmel, 'Der Entwurf zum DCGK 2022 – Nachhaltigkeit im Fokus' (2022) 3 *Zeitschrift für Rechtspolitik* 70, 71.

178 Schmeing, *Deutscher Corporate Governance Kodex* (2023) Preamble [15].

12.4.4.3 Principles, recommendations and suggestions

The provisions of the GCGC are organised by topic. The principles on each topic are listed first, followed by the corresponding recommendations and, if applicable, further suggestions.

Section A: Management and supervision

The GCGC's first section outlines the main functions of the managing and supervisory boards as well as the general meeting.

The management board is accountable for managing the enterprise in its best interest, ensuring compliance with legal provisions, developing an enterprise strategy, and implementing a risk management and controlling system. The management board is advised to comment on the system's effectiveness and appropriateness in its management report. The GCGC's recommendations regarding sustainability are discussed under Section 12.4.5.

The principles on the supervisory board summarise the legal functions described in Section 12.4.3, additionally emphasising the obligation to advise the management board, especially on sustainability issues. It is suggested that the chairperson may be available to discuss supervisory board related issues with investors, acknowledging the chair's competence in investor relations.[179]

While the GCGC acknowledges the potential corporate governance role of shareholders in its foreword, it has so far not elaborated on it in its section on the general meeting. For the general meeting's potential role regarding sustainability issues, see Section 12.4.5.

Section B: Appointment of the management board

The Code's second section covers the appointment of management board members. The relevant principle states that the qualifications of the candidates, as well as gender target values,[180] are to be considered. It is recommended that the supervisory board takes diversity into account, plans for long-term success and establishes an age limit for board members. German law allows for management board members to be appointed for up to five years – a maximum period prescribed by statute – with the dismissal by the supervisory board only being possible under special circumstances.[181] The risk of tying an unsuitable candidate to the company for an extended period is recognised by German law to some extent, only allowing for the reappointment of management board members in the last year of the appointment period.[182] This, however, can be bypassed by mutually agreeing on the dismissal and immediate reappointment.[183] To mitigate risks, the GCGC

---

179 For the discussion of this point, cf Jens Koch, 'Investorengespräche des Aufsichtsrats' (2017) 5 *Die Aktiengesellschaft* 129.

180 See Section 12.4.3.

181 *AktG* s 84[1] cl 4. For discussion on changes regarding the dismissal of board members, see Julia Redenius-Hövermann, 'Die Abberufung von Organmitgliedern als Instrument guter Corporate Governance: ein Werkstattbericht' (2022) 17 *Zeitschrift für Wirtschaftsrecht* 817.

182 *AktG* s 84[1] cl 3.

183 Bundesgerichtshof [German Federal Court of Justice], II ZR 55/11, 17.07.2012 reported in (2012) *Neue Zeitschrift für Gesellschaftsrecht* 1027.

suggests appointing first-time board members for a maximum of three years and using the bypass cautiously.[184]

Section C: Composition of the supervisory board

The GCGC's third section covers the composition of the supervisory board, reiterating the legislative framework described in Section 12.4.3. The general meeting should consider personal qualifications and gender quotas when electing supervisory board members. Correspondingly, it is recommended for the supervisory board to set out a skill and expertise profile for the entire board,[185] taking sustainability into account, and to set an age limit. While a broad expertise profile is beneficial, the necessity to consider a large number of criteria may dilute the quality and hinder finding suitable candidates.[186] It was proposed to instead add more transparency to the proposals regarding new board members, empowering the shareholders to make more informed decisions.[187] To address 'overboarding', the GCGC recommends limiting the number of simultaneous external (that is, outside of the corporate group) mandates in supervisory boards to two for management board members of a listed company and to five for others.[188]

The GCGC's recommendations also aim to ensure independence of shareholder representatives on the supervisory board[189] through various measures, including quotas for board members independent from the company, its management and controlling shareholders. It is assumed that independent members can monitor the management board more efficiently and are better suited to challenge business decisions.[190] It is further recommended for the supervisory board to disclose the candidates' relationships with the company, its corporate bodies and significant shareholders when proposing new shareholder representatives for election by the general meeting and to individually vote on the election of each candidate.

Section D: Supervisory board procedures

The fourth section of the GCGC aims to ensure effective and efficient procedures of the supervisory board,[191] stressing the need for cooperation with the management board.

---

184 Dirk Busch and Simon Patrick Link in Ghassemi-Tabar (ed), *Deutscher Corporate Governance Kodex* (2023) B.3 [2].

185 *AktG* s 100[5] requires supervisory boards of companies of public interest (banks, insurance companies, and publicly listed companies) to have only members that are familiar with the company's sector and to have at least one member with experience in accounting and one member with experience in auditing.

186 Gesellschaftsrechtliche Vereinigung, 'Stellungnahme zu dem Entwurf des Deutschen Corporate Governance Kodex 2022 vom 21.1.2022' (2022) 7 *Die Aktiengesellschaft* [42].

187 Ibid.

188 Hans-Ulrich Wilsing and Luise Winkler, 'Deutscher Corporate Governance Kodex 2019: Ein Überblick' (2019) 28–29 *Betriebs-Berater* 1603, 1607.

189 Supervisory board shareholder representatives are independent if they have no business or personal relationship to the company, the management board and its controlling shareholder; for more details see C.6 GCGC. The independence requirement is only stipulated for shareholder representatives as the supervisory board, acting through its shareholder side, only submits the election proposals for supervisory board members from the shareholder side to the annual general meeting in accordance with *AktG* s 124[3] cls 1, 5. The supervisory board has no influence on the composition of the employee representatives in accordance with the co-determination laws.

190 Jan Lieder, 'The German supervisory board on its way to professionalism' (2010) 11(2) *German Law Journal* 115, 131.

191 Schmeing, *Deutscher Corporate Governance Kodex* (2023) § 161 AktG [2].

Committees, including an audit committee with the support of external auditors, must be formed by the supervisory board. Its members are reminded of their responsibility to undertake the training necessary to fulfil their duties. Regular meetings and self-assessment of the supervisory board are recommended.

Section E: Conflicts of interest

The GCGC's principle on conflicts of interest emphasises that board members must act in the company's best interest. Management board members are subject to a non-compete clause for the duration of their appointment. To avoid conflicts, supervisory board members should disclose any potential conflict[192] and terminate their mandate if a non-temporary conflict arises. Management board members should disclose conflicts of interests to the chairs of both boards and seek supervisory board approval for sideline activities, including supervisory board mandates in other enterprises.

Section F: Transparency and external reporting

The Code's sixth section, covering transparency and external reporting, intends to mitigate information asymmetries and prevent opportunistic behaviour. At the same time transparency aims to strengthen the stakeholders' and third parties' trust in the company.[193] It is emphasised that shareholders need to be informed equally and that certain statements and reports (including the corporate governance report dealing with code compliance) must be provided. It is recommended to disclose to shareholders' information made available to financial analysts and to prevent any undue delays in the publication of relevant information, with time limits being set.

Section G: Remuneration

The GCGC's final section addresses the remuneration of board members, aiming for a clear, comprehensible and socially acceptable system that provides sufficient incentives and adequate compensation.[194] Whereas the supervisory board's remuneration is set directly by the general meeting, the supervisory board must draft and present a system for management remuneration to the general meeting. Although approval or disapproval by the shareholders ('Say on Pay') does not have any direct legal effect, disapproval regularly causes a significant loss of trust.[195]

Various recommendations and suggestions in the GCGC cover technicalities on the parameters to be used for the remuneration system such as the structuring of fixed and variable remuneration.[196]

---

192 Cf also *AktG* s 171[2]; Busch and Link in Ghassemi-Tabar (ed), *Deutscher Corporate Governance Kodex* (2023) E.1 [23].

193 Von Werder in Kremer et al (eds), *Deutscher Corporate Governance Kodex* (2021) G20 [2].

194 Dermot Fleischmann in Ghassemi-Tabar (ed), *Deutscher Corporate Governance Kodex* (2023) Grds 24 [1].

195 Matthias Gärtner and Elena Himmelmann, 'Beschlüsse der Hauptversammlung zur Vorstandsvergütung nach ARUG II' (2021) 7 *Die Aktiengesellschaft* 259.

196 Remuneration systems are based on European law. For more details, see Section 12.2. For more details on the regulatory framework of the 'Say on Pay' mechanism, see ibid.

12.4.5 Sustainability

Attempts to strengthen sustainability through corporate law and to promote CSR in Germany mostly find their roots in EU law (see Section 12.2).[197]

On the national level, the German Government adopted a 'National Plan of Action for the Economy and Human Rights' (*Nationaler Aktionsplan für Wirtschaft und Menschenrechte*, or 'NAP') in 2016. As a result, on 22 July 2021, the 'Act on Corporate Due Diligence Obligations for the Prevention of Human Rights Violations in Supply Chains' (*Lieferkettensorgfaltspflichtengesetz* ['*LkSG*']) was adopted. It obliges enterprises to take preventive measures to protect humans and have regard to environmental issues within their supply chain.[198] Enterprises must disclose the measures in an annual report.[199] While the *LkSG* itself does not impose a civil liability,[200] enterprises can be fined for not meeting its requirements.[201]

The GCGC deals with questions of sustainability in an increasing number of recommendations. The Code recommends that the management board include ecological and social objectives in the enterprise's strategy and that it systemically identify and assess corresponding risks and opportunities as well as the ecological and social impact of the company's activities. It is further recommended to incorporate sustainability-related objectives in the risk management and controlling system. The GCGS's foreword also provides that these factors must be taken into account by both the supervisory and the management board within the enterprise's best interest.[202]

There is currently a lively debate in Germany about the increasingly active role of the general meeting (that is, shareholder activism) regarding sustainability. For instance, the 'say on climate' initiative, supported by many institutional investors, proxy voters and NGOs, demands an annual disclosure of emissions, a plan on handlings these emissions, and shareholder voting rights on the appropriateness of measures.[203] Given the debate on questions such as to what extent and by which means shareholders' 'say on climate' should be implemented,[204] it is disappointing that aspects of this initiative have not been included in the current version of the GCGC, at least as mere suggestions.[205]

12.4.6 Future directions

Regulation of CSR and sustainability-related issues is further shifting to the supranational level. For instance, responsibility for supply chains – including civil liability – will be at

---

197 For instance, one of the more recent regulations on corporate governance, the *Whistleblower Protection Act (Hinweisgeberschutzgesetz)*, adopted on 31 May 2023, was based on *Directive (EU) 2019/1937 of the European Parliament and of the Council of 23 October 2019 on the Protection of Persons Who Report Breaches of Union Law*.

198 Eric Wagner and Marc Ruttloff, 'Das Lieferkettensorgfaltspflichtengesetz – eine erste Einordnung' (2021) 30 *Neue Juristische Wochenschrift* 2145 [8].

199 *LkSG* s 10[2].

200 *LkSG* s 3[3] cl 1. See further Deutscher Bundestag [German National Parliament], *Beschlussempfehlung und Bericht des Ausschusses für Arbeit und Soziales* (Doc No 19/30505, 39, 9 June 2021).

201 *LkSG* s 24.

202 Vereinigung, 'Stellungnahme zu dem Entwurf des Deutschen Corporate Governance Kodex 2022 vom 21.1.2022' (2022) 7 *Die Aktiengesellschaft* [6].

203 For more information, see *Say on Climate* (Web Page) <https://sayonclimate.org>.

204 Rafael Harnos and Maximilian Holle, 'Say on climate' (2021) 23 *Die Aktiengesellschaft* [17 et seq].

205 Vereinigung, 'Stellungnahme zu dem Entwurf des Deutschen Corporate Governance Kodex 2022 vom 21.1.2022' (2022) 7 *Die Aktiengesellschaft* [36].

the centre of a new EU directive.[206] On the national level, corporate governance discussions will continue to revolve around GCGC. Traditionally, each new version sparks lively debates on proposed amendments. One central point of discussion is whether the GCGC should incorporate elements from international CSR frameworks, given the multitude of existing regulations.[207] Apart from the debate on shareholder activism,[208] another area of discussion that has recently returned to the spotlight is employee co-determination.[209] This hallmark of German corporate law has come under pressure as numerous companies have found ways to avoid co-determination, for example by resorting to foreign forms of companies or European stock corporations (*Societas Europaea*, or 'SE'). The German Government plans to introduce statutory measures to prevent methods used to bypass co-determination.[210] With a decision in the landmark case *Lliuya v RWE*[211] on the horizon, climate change litigation may also play a role in shaping German corporate governance.

12.4.7 Conclusion

Corporate governance in Germany is constantly evolving. It is most prominently characterised by its two-tier board structure and the remarkably strong (but challenged) role of employee co-determination. Recent developments point to sustainability and the role of active shareholders forming the centre of future discussions.[212] It is to be expected that regulations on CSR, and reporting on non-financial issues and matters (including sustainability, as well as environmental, social and governance ('ESG') matters), will continuously be added to the GCGC. As the Chair of the German Corporate Commission put it in 2019, the GCGC 'will cover everything there is on sustainable governance'.[213]

12.5 Japan

Souichirou Kozuka and Luke Nottage

12.5.1 Overview

Japan developed vibrant commercial activity domestically towards the end of the Tokugawa Shogunate era (1603–1867), when it largely closed itself off to the world. As the

---

206 European Union, European Commission, *Proposal for a Directive of the European Parliament and of the Council on Corporate Sustainability Due Diligence and Amending Directive (EU) 2019/1937* (COM/2022/71 final); Schmidt, 'BB-Gesetzgebungs- und Rechtsprechungsreport zum Europäischen Unternehmensrecht 2022/2023' (2023) 33–34 *Betriebs-Berater* 1859, 1860.

207 Spießhöfer, 'Sustainable corporate governance' (2022) 10 *Neue Zeitschrift für Gesellschaftsrecht* 435, 436, 440.

208 See Section 12.4.5.

209 See Section 12.4.3.

210 See Deutsche Bundesregierung [German Federal Government], *Koalitionsvertrag 2021 – 2025 zwischen der Sozialdemokratischen Partei Deutschlands (SPD), BÜNDNIS 90 / DIE GRÜNEN und den Freien Demokraten (FDP)* (Coalition Agreement, 7 December 2021) 71, 134 <https://www.bundesregierung.de/resource/blob/974430/1990812/04221173eef9a6720059cc353d759a2b/2021-12-10-koav2021-data.pdf?download=1>.

211 Ongoing proceedings at the Oberlandesgericht [Higher Regional Court] Hamm filed under 5 U 15/17.

212 For the current government's plans on CSR, cf ibid 35, 111, 170.

213 Rolf Nonnenmacher, 'Zum Stand der Corporate Governance in Deutschland' (Speech, *17 Konferenz Deutscher Corporate Governance Kodex*, 28 November 2019) 7 <https://www.dcgk.de/de/presse/deteilansicht/id-17-konferenz-deutscher-corporate-governance-kodex.html>.

country reopened, and expanded industrialisation during the Meiji Era (1868–1912), it introduced codifications and legal institutions mostly influenced by the European (especially German) civil law tradition.[214] Stock exchanges were established and investment often grew into family-owned companies, resulting in considerable emphasis on (especially controlling) shareholder primacy before World War II.

The Allied Occupation (1946–51) led to some corporate and securities law reforms inspired by United States ('US') law that also enhanced minority shareholder rights, at least in theory. In practice, however, until at least the 1980s Japan became renowned for its wider stakeholder approach to corporate governance. Supporting institutions started to unravel after an asset bubble collapsed and Japan entered a 'lost decade' of economic stagnation from the 1990s. Growing foreign investment into the Japanese stock market also supported a 'gradual transformation' towards more shareholder primacy,[215] including partial shifts towards the 'monitoring' rather than the management board, especially in listed companies (see Section 12.5.2).

The transformation since the 1990s has been reinforced by legislative and regulatory reforms, especially from the early 2000s (see Section 12.5.3). This and related case law show the influence also from the Anglo-Commonwealth approach to corporate governance, not just US approaches, as do the more recent 'soft law' ('comply or explain') codes for corporate governance and engagement or stewardship by institutional investors (see Section 12.5.4).

Much discussion has emerged recently also around environmental, social and governance ('ESG') for investors and managers in Japan, as in many other jurisdictions with large securities markets (see Section 12.5.5). A key question is whether this means even greater shareholder primacy, as foreign institutional investors in particular have pushed for more ESG initiatives from Japanese firms, or whether it marks the return of Japanese firms towards more stakeholder-based corporate governance as in years gone by. The answer is important for predicting likely future directions in Japan (see Section 12.5.6).

12.5.2 Historical trajectory

When Japan reopened fully to the world in 1868, to renegotiate 'unequal treaties' with the US and European imperial powers, the Meiji Government enacted comprehensive codifications along European lines, including a commercial code containing corporate law provisions to support both smaller enterprises and large-scale industrialisation.[216] The German law-inspired *Commercial Code* of 1899 was enacted, which included 1884 legislation on stock companies. Key terms and mechanisms were introduced such as

---

214 Luke Nottage, 'The development of comparative law in Japan' in Mathias Reimann and Reinhard Zimmermann (eds), *The Oxford Handbook of Comparative Law* (Oxford University Press, 2nd ed, 2019) 201.

215 Luke Nottage et al (eds), *Corporate Governance in the 21st Century: Japan's Gradual Transformation* (Edward Elgar, 2008).

216 For more details, see the much lengthier and extensively footnoted 2018 edition of this subsection by Kozuka and Nottage (https://www.cambridge.org/engage/coe/article-details/624e0db254b5d9173dec691a). We thank Adj Prof Bruce Aronson for helpful comments on an earlier draft of this edition's section.

sokai (general shareholders' meeting), *torishimariyaku* (directors) and *kansayaku* (statutory auditors, tasked with ensuring directors complied with the law). A comprehensive reform to the Code was made in 1938, again largely based on Germany's *Stock Corporation Act 1937*, with both countries attempting to address the emerging separation of ownership and control. At the same time, Japan belatedly enacted separate legislation for a private limited liability company (*yugen kaisha* or 'YK'), similar to the *Gesellschaft mit beschränkter Haftung* ('GmbH') already found in the 1937 German code. By the end of World War II, there were nearly half as many YKs as KKs (*kabushiki kaisha*), although many closely held companies persisted in incorporating as KKs mainly for perceived prestige.

The US-led Occupation inaugurated securities regulation and anti-monopoly law, and also significant reforms to the *Commercial Code*, all based this time on US law. The Code amendments aimed to redistribute corporate powers. The *sokai*'s jurisdiction was limited to matters set in law or articles of incorporation, ushering in the institution of the board of directors to collectively hold and exercise powers and managerial functions. Amendments also added fiduciary duties of directors.

The ensuing four decades, through to the collapse of Japan's 'bubble economy' in 1990, witnessed the emergence of a new hybrid corporate governance regime, intertwined with other post-war economic institutions. One central pillar was the 'main bank', the largest lender as well as a significant shareholder (albeit subject to a statutory five per cent cap). Main banks provided diverse financing, monitoring, and information and management support. Cross-shareholding was a second feature, with about two-thirds of listed company shares held by 'stable' shareholders in the early 1990s. The epitome were the *keiretsu*, 'historically derived clusters of affiliated firms held together by stable cross-share ownership, interlocking directorates, extensive product market exchanges, and other linkages that enhance group identity and facilitate information exchange'.[217] Six major post-war 'horizontal' *keiretsu* were centred on main banks; 'vertical' *keiretsu* brought together groups of production and investment chains. A third significant practice in larger firms (and an ideal for many others) was 'lifetime employment', whereby workers implicitly traded initially below-market wages for continuous employment and above-market wages in the second half of his or (to a lesser extent) her career.

In addition, government–business relations involved considerable 'administrative guidance' (informal enforcement of regulatory objectives), with bureaucrats – and the long-reigning Liberal Democratic Party ('LDP') – promoting consensus-based policy-making through repeated informal contacts with firms and industry associations. All this reduced the need for the active board monitoring function promoted by post-war Occupation reformers and, indeed, for the disciplinary effect of hostile takeovers.

This post-war system was never universal or completely stable, and it began to fray from the 1980s when larger firms turned increasingly from being bank-financed to shareholder-financed. Bigger challenges came from the collapse of asset prices in 1990 and Japan's consequent 'lost decade' of economic stagnation, including failures of major financial institutions and 'Big Bang' deregulation of financial markets from 1997.

---

217 Curtis Milhaupt and Mark West, *Economic Organizations and Corporate Governance in Japan* (Oxford University Press, 2004) 14.

The direct consequence of the latter was diminished cross-shareholdings, first motivated by banks improving their balance sheets, then accelerated by new controls over banks holding other companies' assets. Aggregate listed shares held by 'insider shareholders' (banks, insurers and other non-financial business corporations), which may be approximated to crossly-held shares, decreased from the peak of 61.8 per cent in 1986 to 31.2 per cent in 2012. Most of the shares that insider shareholders released were picked up by 'outside shareholders' comprising individuals, foreigners and trust banks (collectively holding 65.9 per cent of all shares in 2012). This shift in shareholding, however, occurred unevenly among listed companies: more conspicuous in large, globally well-known companies than smaller, domestically focused companies. The former firms therefore gradually faced pressures from outside shareholders, in particular foreign and institutional investors, demanding more disciplined corporate governance. This pressure came not only from foreign investors, but also from the Japan Pension Fund Association ('PFA') and others. The PFA encouraged developments towards the monitoring model by publishing principles calling for greater independence, and other calls came from individual investors in Japan as well as institutional investors from abroad.

Japan's apparent failure to restore a vibrant economy and the changes in shareholding structure drove domestic policy-making elites to embark on major reforms to commercial regulation generally, and corporate law in particular. Their main objectives, long sought also by Anglo-American investors and governments, included greater flexibility in corporate law rules – moving away from the German tradition of detailed mandatory provisions – and greater focus on the interests of shareholders vis-à-vis other stakeholders (such as core employees, trading partners and main banks). The amendments were first made in a piecemeal manner and then consolidated into the *Companies Act 2005* (Japan) ('JCA 2005'), followed by significant amendments in 2014 (see Section 12.5.3).

Stakeholders simultaneously developed the Japanese *Corporate Governance Code* ('2015 JCGC'), implemented from 2015 by all stock exchanges. Albeit a 'comply or explain' instrument, it sometimes introduced more radical corporate governance changes than the JCA 2005, including requirements regarding independent directors.[218] The 2015 JCGC was then revised ('2021 JCGC').[219] Japan introduced the 2014 *Stewardship Code* ('2014 JSC'), aiming to change the attitude of (especially) domestic institutional investors to actively promote shareholder interests. Although inspired by the *UK Corporate Governance Code*, its aim is different from the latter, which instead sought to restrain excessive risk-taking and short-termism by making institutional investors more responsible to the wider public (see Section 12.5.4).[220] The 2014 JSC has also been revised twice before the current version ('2020 JSC').[221]

218 Gen Goto, Manabu Matsunaka and Souichirou Kozuka, 'Japan's gradual reception of independent directors: An empirical and political-economic analysis' in Dan Puchniak, Harald Baum and Luke Nottage (eds), *Independent Directors in Asia* (Cambridge University Press, 2017) 135.

219 See JPX Tokyo Stock Exchange, *Japan's Corporate Governance Code* (11 June 2021) <https://www.jpx .co.jp/english/news/1020/b5b4pj0000046kxj-att/b5b4pj0000046l0c.pdf>.

220 Gen Goto, 'The logic and limits of stewardship codes: The case of Japan' (2019) 15 *Berkeley Business Law Journal* 365.

221 See JPX Tokyo Stock Exchange, *Japan's Corporate Governance Code* (2021).

12.5.3 Legislation and regulators

12.5.3.1 An overview

The Ministry of Justice ('MoJ') traditionally promoted corporate law reforms, but the role of the Ministry of Economy Trade and Industry ('METI'), and even private members' Bills, became more important as economic stagnation persisted from the 1990s. The Japanese Financial Services Agency ('JFSA') has jurisdiction over the securities exchanges, so both METI and JFSA also are important for securities law reform and the development of the soft law codes issued and revised since 2015. The public prosecutors (also connected to the MoJ), the Securities and Exchange Surveillance Commission and securities exchange now also have important regulatory enforcement roles in Japan.

As in other mature economies, Japan's law and policy-makers must address a variety of company forms, from small startups and family-owned companies to large, public listed companies attracting global investors. From 1 April 2022, the Tokyo Stock Exchange ('TSE') (now under the Japan Exchange Group) has restructured into Prime, Standard and Growth Sections. The idea was to select only the most globally active and/or attractive Japanese companies for the Prime Section and to list smaller companies, mostly with domestic shareholders, on the Standard Section, but 1839 companies chose the Prime Section – most probably based on the perceived prestige associated with the Prime Section. The Growth Section is for companies who make an initial public offering for the first time.

For startups, the entrepreneur usually chooses to incorporate either a KK or *godo kaisha* ('GK'). Incorporating a KK has become easy, with minimum paid-up capital abolished in 2005, and necessary procedures including registration recently available online. A KK may issue different classes of shares,[222] ensuring that the different types of shareholding are easily identifiable in the corporate structure. The GK is the Japanese equivalent of limited liability company ('LLC') in common law jurisdictions and may be flexibly designed through arrangements of entrepreneurs and investors subject to minimal mandatory JCA 2005 rules.[223] GKs are also used by non-Japanese companies to set up simple subsidiaries in Japan. Since GKs were provided under the JCA 2005, new YKs cannot be established, while existing YKs are deemed to be a KK without a board.

As opposed to large public companies, for which the 2015 JCGC (see Section 12.5.4) as well as the *Financial Instruments and Exchange Act 1948* ('FIEA 1948') are more relevant, the JCA 2005 is the main legislative source for smaller KKs.[224] Most small companies restrict share transferability through the articles of association. Gaps tend to arise between the 'law in the books' and the 'law in action', due to the controlling shareholders at times ignoring statutory rules. In family-owned companies, disputes over management can arise from family problems, and pointing to non-compliance with corporate law regulations (which the relevant parties have ignored until the dispute arises) may

---

222 JCA 2005 ss 107, 108.
223 JCA 2005 s 575 *et seq.*
224 Bruce Aronson, Souichirou Kozuka and Luke Nottage, 'Corporate legislation in Japan' in Parissa Haghirian (ed), *Routledge Handbook of Japanese Business and Management* (Routledge, 2016) 103.

appear as an abusive claim. Japanese judges tend to avoid literally enforcing the JCA 2005 rules, considering such background facts to reach a balanced conclusion.

Several court cases also deal with conflicts between the controlling shareholder and minority shareholders in public companies. They normally arise when managers decide to go private and launch management buyouts ('MBOs'), or when the parent company acquires the floating shares of its listed subsidiary. The *J:COM* Supreme Court judgment (1 July 2016) held that a fair procedure must be followed to solve conflict of interests with an MBO under a two-tier tender offer. This case resulted in METI issuing the *Fair M&A Guidelines* in 2019, which focused on the enhancement of corporate value through mergers and acquisitions. These require that some 'fairness ensuring measures' must be taken when conflicts of interests exist between the controlling shareholders or managers and minority shareholders.

12.5.3.2 Directors' duties and derivative actions

Section 355 of the JCA 2005 requires directors to comply with all laws, articles of association and resolutions of general shareholders' meetings. A Supreme Court decision in 1970 (*Yawata Iron & Steel*) on s 254(3) of the *Commercial Code*, now s 330 of the JCA 2005, followed German law to incorporate the *Civil Code*'s high standard for directors' duty of care. Their duty to establish systems for internal control is now required under the FIEA 1948 (J-SOX regulation),[225] as well as under JCA 2005 provisions, dealing with the board's mandate for internal control systems. A KK director is also obliged to request board approval before engaging in transactions to deprive corporate opportunity or dealing with the company.[226] JCA 2005 liability arising from unapproved self-dealing is negligence-based, rather than strict,[227] like liability regarding illegal distributions.[228]

The US-style derivative suit litigation by shareholders, introduced in 1950, had long been dormant but increased after the then *Commercial Code* was amended in mid-1993,[229] fixing the court filing fee uniformly at 8200 yen, instead of proportionately to damages claimed.[230] The issue was highlighted by the Y$80 billion awarded by the court of first instance in the Daiwa Bank case, although a Y$250 million settlement was reached during the appeal.[231] A Supreme Court judgment (*Apaman Shop*, 15 July 2010[232]) affirmed a version of the business judgment rule, denying the liability of directors for corporate group restructuring after finding that the procedure for decision-making involved nothing inappropriate and that the decision itself was not grossly unreasonable.

225 This part of the FIEA 1948 is known as 'J-SOX regulation', as Japan introduced it by referring to the *Sarbanes-Oxley Act of 2002* ('SOX') in the United States.
226 JCA 2005 s 365.
227 Ibid s 423(3).
228 Ibid s 462.
229 Currently provided for in ibid s 847(6).
230 Tomotaka Fujita, 'Transformation of the management liability regime in Japan in the wake of the 1993 revision' in Hideki Kanda et al (eds), *Transforming Corporate Governance in East Asia* (Routledge, 2008) 17.
231 Bruce Aronson, 'Reconsidering the importance of law in Japanese corporate governance: Evidence from the Daiwa Bank shareholder derivative case' (2003) 36(1) *Cornell International Law Journal* 11.
232 *Apamanshop Case* (Supreme Court, 15 July 1970 – Case No 2009 ju 183).

12.5.3.3 Boards and choices in governance structures[233]

For public companies, the focus of corporate governance reform during the last two decades has been the board of directors. The legislative amendment in 2002 created the option of substituting a (more Anglo-American) 'company with committees', now named 'company with nomination and other committees' for the (German) statutory auditor board structure. Such 'elective corporate governance reform' partly reflected a compromise among Japan's major corporate law reform institutions.[234] The amendments of 2014 further allowed, as a third option, a 'company with audit and supervisory committee'.

If the company chooses the committee structure, the board of directors establishes three committees (nomination committee, audit committee and remuneration committee),[235] each having three or more members with the outside directors occupying the majority.[236] No statutory auditor is appointed. The board of directors in this type of company can (but need not) abstain from executive decisions and delegate them to the executive officers (*shikkoyaku*).[237] Soon after 2002, this option proved to be extremely unpopular. Many Japanese companies were hesitant about its monitoring board, in contrast to their support for the traditional decision-making board, with the latter perhaps intertwined with the 'company community' culture.[238]

The third 'company with audit and supervisory committee' option since 2014 is much more popular, chosen by 1106 companies or 30.1 per cent of all TSE listed companies. Only 76 companies (2.1 per cent) have opted to be companies with nomination and other committees, while 2495 companies (67.9 per cent) have remained as traditional companies with statutory auditors.[239] This third type must have only one audit and supervisory committee, dominated by outside directors. Thus, nominating top management and assessing managers' performance through remuneration can remain in the hands of (board) insiders. The legislature seems to have adopted a 'hybrid approach', argued for before the amendments.[240]

12.5.3.4 Takeovers regulation

A few hostile takeovers and defensive measures emerged around 2005, but have receded. Court judgments, METI/MoJ Guidelines and the 2021 JCGC allowed defensive

233 For another explanation of the different Japanese corporate law and corporate governance models, see the explanation, based on the work of Kozuka and Nottage, in Jean Jacques du Plessis, 'Board composition: Between independent directors, minority representatives and employee representatives' in Afra Afsharipour and Martin Gelter (eds), *Comparative Corporate Governance* (Edward Elgar, 2021) 144, 164–6.
234 Ronald Gilson and Curtis Milhaupt, 'Choice as regulatory reform: The case of Japanese corporate governance' (2005) 53(2) *American Journal of Comparative Law* 243, 353–4.
235 JCA 2005 s 404.
236 Ibid s 400.
237 Ibid s 416.
238 Kenichi Osugi, 'Stagnant Japan? – why outside (independent) directors have been rare in Japanese companies' in Zenichi Shishido (ed), *Enterprise Law: Contracts, Markets and Laws in the US and Japan* (Edward Elgar, 2014) 252.
239 Tokyo Stock Exchange, *TSE-Listed Companies White Paper on Corporate Governance 2021* (2021) 105 <https://www.jpx.co.jp/english/equities/listing/cg/tvdivq0000008jb0-att/b5b4pj0000049wa0.pdf>.
240 Bruce Aronson, 'The Olympus scandal and corporate governance reform: Can Japan find a middle ground between the board monitoring model and management model?' (2012) 30(1) *Pacific Basin Law Journal* 93.

measures with more emphasis on shareholder approval or value than Delaware case law on poison pills.[241]

12.5.4 Codes of practice

For large public KKs, the JCA 2005 provisions seem insufficient to satisfy current expectations of investors in these large Japanese corporations. The 2015 JCGC sets higher standards, although leaving room for companies not to 'comply' but 'explain'. This is especially the case with traditional companies with statutory auditors. While the JCA 2005 assumes that the directors of such companies comprise a management board, the 2021 JCGC urges the board to strengthen monitoring of management. The 2021 JCGC therefore requires that all listed companies appoint at least two independent directors, while the JCA 2005 obligation is only that all the listed companies have at least one outside director.[242] The 2021 JCGC requires at least one-third of all the directors for Prime Section companies to be 'independent'. Furthermore, it suggests that committees for nomination and succession of top management, as well as their remuneration, be organised under the board and led by independent directors, despite such committees being mandated under the JCA 2005 only in companies with nomination and other committees. For statutory auditors, traditionally monitoring compliance, the 2021 JCGC warns that their role should not be narrowly defined and urges them to voice their views when appropriate.

While the 2021 JCGC (and predecessors) urges the corporate managers to take demands from the capital market seriously, it does not focus strictly on shareholder primacy. Rather, it mentions that 'a range of stakeholders, including the employees, customers, business partners, creditors and local communities' support the company's sustainable growth and mid to long-term creation of corporate value, emphasising the need to collaborate with such stakeholders. This illustrates that Japan also has a widening gap between the law as reflected in corporations legislation and contemporary expectations of investors and non-shareholder stakeholders, as reflected in corporate governance codes world-wide.

12.5.5 Sustainability

12.5.5.1 Sustainability requirements under the corporate governance and stewardship codes

A striking development has been the rapid uptake of ESG considerations among listed companies and institutional investors in Japan, particularly compared to other parts of Asia. By early 2021, globally, Japan had the most listed companies already following recommendations of the Taskforce on Climate-related Financial Disclosures ('TCFD').[243] However, Japanese firms may have been strongest on the 'E' (environment), middling

241 Kenichi Osugi, 'Transplanting poison pills in foreign soil: Japan's experiment' in Curtis Milhaupt et al (eds), *Transforming Corporate Governance in East Asia* (Routledge, 2008) 36.
242 JCA 2005 s 327-2.
243 Cited in Souichirou Kozuka, 'introducing sustainability into Japanese corporate governance: Shift to 'new capitalism' or a continued gradual transformation?' (2022) 54 *Journal of Japanese Law* 63. The key points summarised in this subsection derive from that detailed study, unless otherwise footnoted below.

on the 'S' (social factors, like care for employees or suppliers or customers) and weak on the 'G' (governance – for example, by failing to utilise a supposedly more effective monitoring-style board with many independent directors).[244]

Very soon after the United Nations declared the 17 Sustainable Development Goals ('SDGs') in 2015,[245] and the TCFD recommendations were issued in 2017, the 2014 JSC was revised, resulting in the *Stewardship Code* of 2017 ('2017 JSC'). The 2017 JSC now included ESG as a risk factor for signatory institutional investors.[246] The 2020 JSC further required institutional investors to dialogue with investee firms, considering their medium to long-term sustainability, including ESG factors. The 2021 JCGC also urges all listed companies to collaborate with diverse stakeholders to aim for sustainable growth and address ESG-related sustainability issues. Prime Section companies must further disclose climate risks and opportunities under the TCFD or equivalent framework. The 2020 JSC and the 2021 JCGC only apply on a 'comply or explain' basis, but Japan's experience parallels other jurisdictions showing ever-growing compliance generally.

12.5.5.2 Prospects for statutory reform on climate-related disclosures

Such 'soft law' may harden into some legislative requirements, as seen with independent director requirements for listed company boards. In late 2021, the JFSA added ESG-related recommendations to its annual 'Good Practices in the Disclosure of Descriptive Information' and added the topic to its Disclosure Working Group deliberations. Mandating such disclosures mandatory under the FIEA 1948 could be controversial because they will tend to involve qualitative information, yet potentially attract criminal sanctions if later found insufficient, and because this securities legislation is applicable to over 4000 companies. Nonetheless, during 2022 little opposition was expressed even by industry representatives on the Working Group towards the idea of mandatory requirements, so more forms of mandatory disclosure for Japanese corporations are likely to be legislated. The JFSA, like counterpart securities regulators abroad, is also keen to address greenwashing (see discussion in Section 3.4.4) regarding the ballooning market for ESG bond issuance and investment funds.

Thus, recent developments in Japan reflect almost identical international developments in several jurisdictions, discussed in greater detail in Chapters 11 and the present chapter of this book. By contrast, focusing on sustainability does not mean a turn from Japan's shareholder-centrism corporate governance reform. Rather, it is a continuation of Japan's efforts to rely on corporate governance reform as the driver for economic growth by being responsive to the demands from the capital market. This is true concerning the motivation, modality and result of the reform, as the following shows. First, institutional investors, both from abroad and in Japan, especially the Government Pension

---

244 Bruce Aronson and Yumiko Miwa, 'The rapid growth of ESG in Japan through public-private partnership' (2022) 2 *USALI East-West Studies* <https://usali.org/asia-pacific-symposium-essays/the-rapid-growth-of-esg-in-japan-through-public-private-partnership>.
245 See United Nations, Department of Economic and Social Affairs, 'Sustainable development – the 17 Goals' <https://sdgs.un.org/goals>.
246 See Sustainable Stock Exchanges Initiative, 'Japan – Japanese Stewardship Code' <https://sseinitiative.org/securities-regulator/japanese-stewardship-code-2017/#:~:text=The%20Japanese%20Stewardship%20Code%20states,sustainable%20growth%20of%20the%20companies>.

Investment Fund ('GPIF') since it started TCFD-recommended climate disclosures for its huge portfolio from 2019, are encouraging firms to also explain and address ESG factors. Because Japanese shareholdings are still relatively dispersed, unlike other parts of Asia (with more family- and government-linked companies),[247] institutional shareholder influence is an important factor that reinforces the shift towards shareholder primacy in Japanese listed companies. It implies that the major impetus for reform comes from the capital markets, just as was the case with introducing independent directors.

Second, this institutional investor pressure is reinforced by an emerging tendency to find ESG-related shareholder activism in general meetings. Shareholders holding 300 (for at least six months) or one per cent or more voting rights can submit proposals. They did so for climate-related matters in 2021 meetings for Mitsubishi UFJ bank and (with proxy advisors) Sumitomo Corporation – despite both companies already making TCFD disclosures and taking other ESG initiatives. Although voted down, these and other companies are expected to continue down that line to minimise adverse publicity from further such proposals. However, rather like the derivative suits brought by the Shareholder Ombudsman group or other activist shareholders, this is a somewhat curious promotion of shareholder primacy as going to this trouble is not necessarily in the financial interests of the activists or indeed (demonstrably) for most shareholders.

Third, there is close collaboration between business groups and the government in pushing for ESG, especially METI, the Ministry of Environment and the JFSA (plus the TSE under its jurisdiction). Examples include a TCFD consortium that has issued two climate-related guidelines since 2019, and a 2020 handbook on ESG disclosures issued from the TSE and its parent.

Fourth, the political initiative comes from the centre-right LDP-led coalition government that has led Japan for most of the post–World War II period, like it did earlier for the more gradual adoption of independent director requirements.[248] This may seem curious compared to other countries, where the push, say, for more climate-related initiatives comes more from centre-left parties. Yet the common theme is that the government (including via the GPIF) emphasises the growth potential for local firms adjusting to a decarbonising world. Unlike reform debates around independent director requirements for boards, however, there has been less discussion so far about the nuances of such empirical arguments.[249] Nor has there been much discussion, along the lines of public choice theory or regulatory capture for example, about the high compliance costs for climate disclosures or other ESG factors being promoted by larger firms to gain an artificial competitive advantage over smaller firms.

Fifth, a Japanese hybrid approach to corporate governance is developing in this field. Several prominent companies (such as Asahi Holdings) have voluntarily established

---

247 Cf Dan Puchniak, 'The false hope of stewardship in the context of controlling shareholders: Making sense out of the global transplant of a legal misfit' (Law Working Paper No 589/2021, European Corporate Governance Institute, June 2021).

248 See generally Manabu Matsunaka, 'Politics of Japanese corporate governance reform: Politicians do matter' (2018) 15(1) *Berkeley Business Law Journal* 154.

249 Cf Gen Goto, Manabu Matsunaka and Souichirou Kozuka, 'Japan's gradual reception of independent directors: An empirical and political-economic analysis' in Dan Puchniak, Harald Baum and Luke Nottage (eds), *Independent Directors in Asia* (Cambridge University Press, 2017) 135, 151–60.

a sustainability committee, but led by executives rather than independent directors. Kao added a separate advisory board including some women and non-Japanese members, but none are non-executive directors and the members merely advise Kao's ESG Committee. This is reminiscent of the outcome for most listed company boards, which have started to appoint independent directors over the last decade but use them mainly in advisory (and compliance) roles rather than more strategic monitoring roles vis-à-vis top executives. An example is reflected in the popularity of a corporate form introduced that allows a single committee for 'audit and supervision' (including one or more independent directors), sometimes supplemented by a voluntary nomination and/or remuneration committee (not necessarily with independent directors). Other Japanese firms have experimented with further hybrid forms.[250] By contrast, the corporate form replacing *kansayaku* (statutory auditors) with nomination, remuneration and audit committees (each with independent directors) has remained unpopular since 2004, arguably because this structure will usually make the independent directors more than mere advisors and potentially therefore more threatening to the executives.

12.5.6 Future directions and conclusions

These trends allow us to draw a number of conclusions. The first is that Japanese (listed) companies have shifted partly towards more shareholder primacy since the 1990s, in the law as well as practice, due to capital market pressures, but interactions with key stakeholders remain important. More falteringly, companies have also moved towards a more monitoring-style board, but the independent directors supposedly central to such a board still tend to be mainly advisors to the (typically more numerous) executive directors and top management. It remains unclear whether this is an economically suboptimal outcome and therefore more likely to change, or it is due to path dependence and thus likely to remain firmly in place as a new type of equilibrium.

Second, Japan is likely to see continued influence from emerging global standards, reflecting the influence of liberalised capital markets, but filtered through many law reform and other policy-making committees. An emerging new feature is the influence on reformers and thought-leaders from major Australasian securities markets, not just European and US markets.

Third, however, we are unlikely to see much 'export' of the evolving Japanese model of corporate governance, even in the Asian region where Official Development Assistance has been extensive and quite influential in helping law reform in some developing economies (such as private law in Cambodia, or competition law in Vietnam). The latter initiatives have sometimes been marketed as better suited to Asian legal systems than legal transplants from Western countries, as Japan has already had to adjust its own transplants to local circumstances and undertake extensive comparative law research. The same argument has not been disseminated to promote Japanese corporate law as a model for law reform in Asia, although it had some influence, for example in Myanmar. One reason may be that each jurisdiction's corporate governance regime is

---

250 Bruce Aronson, 'Case studies of independent directors in Asia' in Dan Puchniak, Harald Baum and Luke Nottage (eds), *Independent Directors in Asia* (Cambridge University Press, 2017) 431, 438–50.

deeply intertwined with different socioeconomic and institutional contexts. For Japan these include core practices such as lifelong employment, and comparatively tight relationships with key suppliers and banks, with limited opportunities to recreate such practices alongside new legal regimes, even in nearby countries in Asia. A second reason is that Japan's corporate law itself, as highlighted even succinctly above, has become increasingly complex, making it difficult to export abroad.

Ultimately, however, there is no doubt that contemporary international developments in the area of corporate governance have left clear fingerprints all over the Japanese corporate governance model. Examples include a Japanese corporate governance code, a Japanese stewardship code, independent director requirements, and ESG initiatives.

12.6 China

Chao Xi

12.6.1 Overview

China's corporate governance regime is shaped by a number of structural factors characterising its listed sector: most notably, dominance of state ownership and control, concentrated ownership, and the prevalence of business groups. Hence, the predominant form of agency problem in Chinese listed companies are the conflicts between controlling and non-controlling shareholders. The sweeping Chinese corporate governance reforms of the past two decades have concerned themselves primarily with curbing rent extraction and expropriation by controllers.

The Chinese legislative framework for corporate governance has come under the influence of its own civil tradition. It features an allocation of decision-making that tilts toward the shareholders' meeting (as opposed to the board of directors), a dual-board structure (with an organisational separation between the board of directors and the supervisory board) and workers' co-determination. However, elements of international best practice, many of which find inspiration in common law jurisdictions, have made their way into Chinese legal and regulatory reforms purported to rein in controller opportunism. An increasingly sophisticated body of governance strategies and tactics have ensued. These include the minority appointment right (for example, cumulative voting in board elections), minority shareholder decision rights (for example, derivative actions, super-majority voting and the majority-of-the-minority rule) and the trustee strategy (for example, independent directors, directors' fiduciary duty, and imposition of fiduciary duty on the controlling shareholder).

The Chinese *Code of Corporate Governance of Listed Companies* ('CCGLC') is semi-mandatory, as opposed to 'comply or explain', in nature. It emphasises constraining the controlling shareholder's opportunistic behaviour, while assigning an important governance role to institutional investors and asset managers. The notion of corporate sustainability has recently gained prominence in Chinese corporate governance. Rules enacted by China's official stock exchanges adopt an all-encompassing conceptualisation of sustainability.

12.6.2 Regulatory environment

A defining characteristic of the broader Chinese approach to economic governance is the intensive and close involvement of the state in the country's economy, including its listed sector. The Chinese state is loosely understood here to encompass its central and local governments, as well as departments and agencies. Thus, one of the key features of the Chinese listed sector is a high degree of state ownership and control. In 2014, for instance, state-owned listed firms contributed to close to 65 per cent of the market capitalisation of China's listed sector.[251] The dominance of state ownership is best understood in the historical evolution of the broader Chinese enterprise sector.[252] China's nationalisation campaign in the 1950s resulted in an end to private ownership in Chinese industries and an economy almost monopolised by state-owned enterprises ('SOEs'). However, the post-1978 economic reforms reopened the Chinese economy to foreign investment and revived private entrepreneurship.[253] In their competition with foreign investment enterprises and privately-owned firms, SOEs were outperformed in terms of efficiency and productivity, leaving them in such a state of financial stress that at one stage they even threatened to 'drag down the nation's entire economy with it'.[254] To salvage the ailing SOE sector, various reforms were rolled out, including one that 'incorporatised' SOEs into state-owned corporations.[255] The corporate form was of crucial importance as it enabled SOEs to be publicly listed, thereby raising capital from China's household sector. Indeed, the revival of the Chinese securities markets in the early 1990s served the primary purpose of channeling massive Chinese household savings to the SOEs that enabled their survival and subsequent revitalisation. The listing process ensuing from the SOE corporatisation campaign was largely guided by that purpose, particularly in the formative years of Chinese securities markets. The state hand-picked firms for the 'privilege' of public listing, strongly favoring incorporatised SOEs over privately owned firms.

The state also strived to maintain its control over listed state-owned firms, typically by holding a controlling equity stake in them. To be sure, privately owned firmed have in recent years crowded the Chinese listing landscape, and indeed aggregately outnumbered listed state-owned firms. However, the dominance of state ownership has remained, as measured by its outsize share in market capitalisation. Even measured on a global scale, Chinese state ownership is prominent, accounting for as much as 57 per cent of total public sector ownership in global equity markets.[256]

A closely related feature of the Chinese listed sector is its high level of ownership concentration, relative to the dispersed ownership patterns seen in the United States

251 TJ Wong, 'Corporate governance research on listed firms in China: Institutions, governance and accountability' (2014) 9(4) *Foundations and Trends in Accounting* 259, 272.
252 See generally Chao Xi, *Corporate Governance and Legal Reform in China* (Wildy, Simmonds and Hill Publishing, 2009) 6–35.
253 Vivienne Bath, 'The Company Law and foreign investment enterprises in the PRC – parallel systems of Chinese-foreign regulation' (2007) 30(3) *University of New South Wales Law Journal* 774.
254 Edward S Steinfeld, *Forging Reform in China: The Fate of State-Owned Industry* (Cambridge University Press, 1998) 3.
255 Fang Liufang, 'China's corporatization experiment' (1995) 5(2) *Duke Journal of Comparative and International Law* 149. These incorporatised SOEs are referred to as 'state-owned firms' below.
256 De La Cruz, AA Medina and Y Tang, *Owners of the World's Listed Companies* (OECD Capital Market Series, October 2019) 9.

('US') and United Kingdom ('UK'), for instance. As a matter of fact, ownership concentration in China is not dissimilar to that featuring many continental European economies. An OECD report surveying ownership concentration in global securities markets places China next to Germany both at market and company levels.[257] Another recent empirical assessment of corporate control around the world shows that China (72.2 per cent) leads Germany (68.7 per cent) and France (68.0 per cent) in respect of the share of controlled firms in the listed sectors.[258] In tandem with concentrated ownership is the prevalence of business groups. Often times a Chinese listed company is a member firm in a business group bound typically by common ownership (that is, a common controller), while actively engaging in transactions with affiliated firms in the same group. The prevalent presence of business groups is a defining feature of many state-controlled national champions of China Inc[259] and also more generally.[260]

Concentrated ownership and the prevalence of business groups in China's listed sector set the scene for the primary form of conflicts of interest that its corporate governance regime attempts to address. Among the three generic conflicts of interest – conflicts between controlling and non-controlling shareholders, conflicts between shareholders and managers, and conflicts between shareholders and the company's other stakeholders[261] – the controller-non-controller conflicts is generally seen as the most pressing principal–agent problem in Chinese listed companies.[262] In the absence of adequate checks, the controllers can – and they do – engage in 'tunnelling', diverting corporate wealth to themselves at the expense of non-controlling shareholders.[263]

12.6.3 Legislation and regulators

12.6.3.1 Legislative and institutional framework

China is featured by a unitary (as opposed to a federal) government system, with the national authorities assuming the highest authority. The corporate law and corporate governance framework depicted below is mostly developed by China's national legislative, governmental and regulatory bodies. It is applicable to all Chinese listed companies, both state-owned and non-state-owned.

The framework is broadly composed of four hierarchical tiers. The top tier consists of national primary legislation, most notably the *Company Law of the People's Republic of China* ('CLPRC') enacted by the PRC's national legislature, the National People's Congress Standing Committee ('NPCSC'). The CLPRC is what would be called

---

257 Ibid 18–19.
258 Gur Aminadav and Elias Papaioannou, 'Corporate control around the world' (2020) 75(4) *Journal of Finance* 1191.
259 Li-Wen Lin and Curtis J Milhaupt, 'We are the (national) champions: Understanding the mechanisms of state capitalism in China' (2013) 65(4) *Stanford Law Review* 697.
260 Jia He et al, 'Business groups in China' (2013) 22 *Journal of Corporate Finance* 166.
261 John Armour et al, 'What is corporate law' in Reinier Kraakman et al (eds), *The Anatomy of Corporate Law: A Comparative and Functional Approach* (Oxford University Press, 3rd ed, 2017) 2.
262 Fuxiu Jiang and Kenneth A Kim, 'Corporate governance in China: A survey' (2020) 24(4) *Review of Finance* 733.
263 Guohua Jiang, Charles MC Lee and Heng Yue, 'Tunneling through intercorporate loans: The China experience' (2010) 98(1) *Journal of Financial Economics* 1.

the overarching 'Companies, Corporations or Business Corporations Act' in other jurisdictions. Promulgated in 2005, the current CLPRC came into force in 2006 and was
amended in 2013 and 2018. It is currently undergoing a major overhaul. Another important source of primary legislation on corporate governance of listed companies is the
Securities Law of the People's Republic of China ('SLPRC'), also enacted by the NPCSC. The
current SLPRC has been in effect since 2020. The second tier of corporate governance
laws are enacted by the State Council, China's central government. They often contain
policy pronouncements and statements that are broad and general in nature. However,
they also typically herald specific corporate governance rules to be introduced by the
State Council's departments and agencies, most notably the China Securities Regulatory
Commission ('CSRC'), the sector regulator for China's securities markets. These rules are
wide-ranging, regulating issues ranging from disclosure to liability, and from enforcement actions to the CCGLC. They comprise the third tier of China's corporate governance
regime. Finally, there is a fourth tier comprised of rules made by China's three official,
national stock exchanges – the Beijing, Shanghai and Shenzhen Stock Exchanges – and
other semi-regulatory/public bodies. These rules are self-regulatory in nature, but can be
consequential for their violators.[264]

The primary public enforcer of China's corporate governance laws is the CSRC. It
is vested under the SLPRC with the authority to investigate possible violations of securities laws and regulations and to discipline culpable firms and individuals. Its headquarters in Beijing focuses its efforts on the core areas of regulatory concern, and has
jurisdiction over cases that are otherwise 'complex, sensitive, or of a unique character'. Its local offices pursue primarily matters occurring within their respective territo-
rial boundaries.[265] The official stock exchanges have in recent years become primary
front-line enforcers against securities violations. During the period of 2004–16, close to
7000 enforcement actions were taken by the CSRC, its local offices, as well as the stock
exchanges, which were empirically shown to have helped to deter violations.[266]

Chinese courts have emerged as an active player in the private enforcement of corporate governance laws. The courts have enforced corporate and securities laws on, among
other things, directors' fiduciary duties and derivative actions. The courts' enforcement
role has more recently been enhanced by the introduction in China of class actions. In
late 2021 a court, for the first time based on a class action, made an award of approximately US$384 million to 55 326 defrauded investors.[267] Chinese courts also actively
engage in judicial rule-making that helps to shape the private enforcement landscape.
This is done primarily by the Supreme People's Court ('SPC'), China's highest-level court,

264 Benjamin L Liebman and Curtis J Milhaupt, 'Reputational sanctions in China's securities market'
   (2008) 108(4) *Columbia Law Review* 929.
265 Wenming Xu and Guangdong Xu, 'Understanding public enforcement of securities law in China:
   An empirical analysis of the enforcement actions of the CSRC and its regional offices against
   informational misconduct' (2020) 61 *International Review of Law and Economics* 105877.
266 Ning Cao, Paul B Mcguinness and Chao Xi, 'Does securities enforcement improve disclosure quality?
   An examination of Chinese listed companies' restatement activities' (2021) 67 *Journal of Corporate
   Finance* 101877.
267 Reuters, 'Chinese court rules against Kangmei in "Milestone" case' (13 November 2021) <https://
   www.reuters.com/business/healthcare-pharmaceuticals/chinese-court-rules-against-kangmei-
   milestone-case-2021-11-12/>.

which has been enacting a growing body of legally binding 'interpretations' of statutes on how private litigants bring actions against breaches and violations of corporate law and governance rules. Another noteworthy aspect is the judicial creativity exhibited by sub-national courts in developing novel judicial rules that serve to render vaguely worded company statutory provisions judicially enforceable.[268]

12.6.3.2 Legal framework for corporate governance

The shareholders' meeting as the most important company organ

Chinese company law takes a mandatory approach to the allocation of decision-making between shareholders and the board. Under Chinese company law, the gravity of corporate decision-making rests with the shareholders' meeting. Shareholders are vested with powers and authority over a wide range of corporate matters.[269] These matters include fundamental changes (such as the increase or reduction of the capital, and the amendment of the articles of association), as well as the election and remuneration of (dual) board members. The Chinese shareholders' meeting is also conferred with powers over matters, such as the making of business policies and investment plans, which are typically reserved for the board in many common law jurisdictions.

The (management) board and the supervisory board

Under Chinese corporate law a dual board structure is required for listed companies. Although the way in which the boards are appointed and what power they have are different from the German two-tier board system (see Section 12.4), it can broadly be described under Chinese corporate law as a management board and a supervisory board. Both boards are formed by the election of their members by the shareholders in general meeting. Both boards are also accountable directly to the shareholders. The (management) board is in effect the executive arm of the shareholders' meeting. It makes business and managerial decisions within the powers conferred upon it by law and the authority delegated to them, from time to time, by the shareholders by way of provisions in the corporation's articles of association. The power to appoint and to remunerate executives are also powers vested in the (management) board.[270] The supervisory board is assigned a monitoring role, providing supervision over members of the (management) board and over executives. The supervisory board is entitled to bring derivative actions against directors and executives for a breach of their duties.[271]

Worker participation at the supervisory board is mandatory for all companies, and at least one-third of the supervisory board must be composed of 'worker representatives' duly elected by workers.[272] Co-determination on the (management) board is generally required for state-owned companies,[273] although no minimum threshold for worker representatives is specified in the CLPRC. Presumably, the presence of one worker

---

268 Chao Xi, 'Local courts as legislators? Judicial lawmaking by sub-national courts in China' (2012) 33(1) *Statute Law Review* 39.
269 *Company Law of the People's Republic of China*, as amended in 2018 ('2018 CLPRC') art 37.
270 Ibid s 46.
271 Ibid s 53.
272 Ibid ss 51, 70, 117.
273 Ibid ss 44, 67.

representative will suffice the statutory requirement for co-determination on the (management) board. It is worth noting that these co-determination requirements apply universally to Chinese companies, regardless of their sizes and legal types. More generally, companies are obliged to consult their trade unions and workers' congresses during the decision-making process concerning major corporate matters.[274]

12.6.3.3 Legal strategies for mitigating the conflicts between controlling and non-controlling shareholders

As noted above, the Chinese regime of corporate governance concerns itself primarily with mitigating the conflicts of interest between the controlling and non-controlling shareholders. The sweeping Chinese corporate governance reforms of the past two decades have resulted in an array of strategies and tactics aimed at protecting minority shareholders from controller expropriation and 'tunneling'.[275]

Enhanced voting rights for minority shareholders

Minority shareholders can be protected by legal rules that override their votes in the election of directors. This approach is exemplified under Chinese corporate law by the use of what is known as 'cumulative voting' in the election of the dual boards. Originating in US corporate law, cumulative voting is an arrangement under which shareholders are allowed to cast multiple votes for a single candidate, thereby enhancing the (large) minority shareholders' chance to elect their representatives to the board. It is a deviation from the 'one share, one vote' principle.[276] The Chinese statutory rules on cumulative voting are permissive, as opposed to mandatory, in nature.[277] However, the CSRC-enacted regulatory rules require adoption of cumulative voting by the listed company where a shareholder controls more than 30 per cent of the company's shares. By contrast, cumulative voting is only elective for listed companies with no shareholders crossing the 30 per cent mark. Earlier empirical work shows that many Chinese firms voluntarily adopted cumulative voting.[278] More recent empirical studies suggest that Chinese (large) minority shareholders have successfully utilised cumulative voting to elect their representatives onto the board.[279]

Enhanced decision rights for minority shareholders

Minority shareholders can also be protected by having rights to directly make corporate decisions – a corporate law strategy known as 'minority shareholder decision rights'.

274 Ibid s 18.
275 The ensuing analysis borrows the analytical framework developed in Luca Enriques et al, 'The basic governance structure: Minority shareholders and non-shareholder constituencies' in Reinier Kraakman et al (eds), *The Anatomy of Corporate Law: A Comparative and Functional Approach* (Oxford University Press, 3rd ed, 2017) 79.
276 China has also recently relaxed the 'one share one vote' rule for companies listed on its newly created Sci-Tech Innovation Board.
277 2018 CLPRC s 105.
278 Chao Xi and Yugang Chen, 'Does cumulative voting matter? The case of China: An empirical assessment' (2014) 15 *European Business Organization Law Review* 585.
279 Yinghui Chen and Julan Du, 'Does regulatory reform of cumulative voting promote a more balanced power distribution in the boardroom?' (2020) 64 *Journal of Corporate Finance* 101655.

Such rights occupy a central part in the Chinese system of corporate governance. Most notably, Chinese company law allows individual shareholders meeting the standing requirements to bring derivative suits in the company's name against members of the board of directors and senior executives against whom the company may have a cause of action.[280] For listed companies, to meet the standing requirement the shareholder(s) must hold more than one per cent of the company's shares, either singularly or aggregately, for a minimum consecutive period of 180 days. A recent analysis of the 380 publicly accessible Chinese derivation action cases brought between 2006 and 2019 suggests an under-utility by shareholders of this decision right, particularly in listed companies.[281]

Another example of the minority decision right is the requirements for 'majority of the minority' ('MOM') approval of the transactions in which listed companies self-deal with its controlling shareholders or other related parties, or related-party transactions ('RPTs').[282] Seen also in the corporate law regimes of the UK, Italy, Israel and India, to name a few, the MOM rule in effect vests decision-making authority over the transaction tainted with conflicts in non-conflicted shareholders, and subjects it to approval by a majority of the disinterested votes cast. A recent empirical assessment of the Chinese MOM rule finds that it can thwart potentially inefficient RPTs: among the 31 649 controller RPT resolutions voted on in Chinese mainboard listed companies during the period of 2015–19, 747 (or 2.4 per cent) were vetoed by the disinterested minority votes.[283]

Minority decision rights are also vested in the hands of non-controlling shareholders over fundamental company matters via supermajority approval requirements. These matters include the amendment of the articles of association, increase or reduction in the company's capital, as well as mergers, splits and dissolution of the company.[284] In the case of the listed company, they also include very substantial acquisition or disposal of assets, as well as the company's guarantee in favour of a third party.[285] These all require the approval of two-thirds of the votes present and cast at the shareholders' meeting.

The role of independent directors

Another device of minority shareholder protection in the Chinese corporate governance regime is the role of independent directors. The CLPRC has general provisions on the appointment of independent directors in the listed company.[286] CSRC-enacted regulatory rules further require that at least one-third of the board of directors meet independent requirements. The board's audit, nomination, remuneration and appraisal committees must each be composed, by majority, of independent directors, and chaired

---

280 2018 CLPRC s 151, and also a set of SPC judicial interpretations.
281 Jingchen Zhao and Chuyi Wei, 'Shareholder remedies in China – developments towards a more effective, more accessible and fairer derivative action mechanism' (2021) 16(4) *Capital Markets Law Journal* 445.
282 2018 CLPRC s 16, and also a body of CSRC-enacted regulatory rules applicable to listed companies.
283 Chao Xi, 'Related party transactions and the majority-of-the-minority rule: Data-driven evidence from China and implications for Europe' (2023) (4) *Journal of Business Law* 309.
284 2018 CLPRC ss 43, 103.
285 Ibid s 121.
286 Ibid s 122.

by an independent director.[287] Independent directors are assigned gatekeepers roles in the approval of material RPTs, the appointment (and removal) of the company's accountant, and so on. They are also empowered to play governance roles by being allowed to solicit proxy votes of other shareholders, and engaging external auditors to examine the company's affairs.[288] Scepticism has long been expressed as to the 'fit' between independent directors and China's institutional environment (particularly the legal environment).[289] Recent empirical studies have, however, offered some evidence that independent director dissension improves corporate governance[290] and, more generally, that board independence helps to induce improvement in firm performance in Chinese listed companies.[291]

Fiduciary duties of directors and controlling shareholders

Other important legal constraints on controlling shareholders' expropriation of minority shareholders include fiduciary duties. The doctrine of the director's fiduciary duty has gained a footing in the Chinese company statute since 2006.[292] An analysis of fiduciary case law reveals the Chinese courts' reluctance to enforce fiduciary duties in relation to directors of listed companies. Yet, the CSRC has developed through its enforcement actions a jurisprudence on directorial fiduciary duties, offering greater clarity on what directors' duties entail.[293] Interestingly, the CSRC has also advocated the notion that a controlling shareholder in the Chinese listed company owes fiduciary duties to the minority shareholders and to the company. The imposition of fiduciary duties on the controlling shareholders is now 'codified' in the CSRC-enacted Model Articles of Association, which are generally followed by Chinese listed companies.[294]

12.6.4 Chinese corporate governance code

China's current corporate governance code, the CCGC, was enacted by the CSRC in 2002, and it applies to all companies listed on China's official stock exchanges.[295] The original Code was amended in 2018. Different from most other jurisdictions where there is a corporate governance code, the CCGLC does not adopt the 'comply or explain' approach. Rather, it is semi-mandatory in nature. Deviations from the Code can attract

287 *CSRC Measures on Independent Directors of Listed Companies* (2022) art 4.
288 Ibid art 32.
289 Donald C Clarke, 'The independent director in Chinese corporate governance' (2006) 31(1) *Delaware Journal of Corporate Law* 125.
290 Wei Jiang, Hualin Wan and Shan Zhao, 'Reputation concerns of independent directors: Evidence from individual director voting' (2016) 29(3) *Review of Financial Studies* 655.
291 Yu Liu et al, 'Board independence and firm performance in China' (2015) 30 *Journal of Corporate Finance* 223.
292 2018 CLPRC s 147. The director's fiduciary duty had been recognised by Chinese courts prior to its codification. See Nicholas Calcina Howson, 'The doctrine that dared not speak its name: Anglo-American fiduciary duties in China's 2005 company law and case law intimations of prior convergence' in Curtis Milhaupt, Kon-Sik Kim and Hideki Kanda (eds), *Transforming Corporate Governance in East Asia* (Routledge, 2008) 193.
293 Guangdong Xu et al, 'Directors' duties in China' (2013) 14(1) *European Business Organization Law Review* 57.
294 Yu-Hsin Lin and Yun-chien Chang, 'An empirical study of corporate default rules and menus in China, Hong Kong, and Taiwan' (2018) 15(4) *Journal of Empirical Legal Studies* 875.
295 *Code of Corporate Governance of Listed Companies* (amended in 2018) ('2018 CCGC') art 2.

interventions from the CSRC and its local apparatuses, as well self-regulatory bodies (such as the stock exchanges); enforcement actions may ensue where deviations are considered material.[296]

The CCGLC primarily addresses eight governance areas, each attracting a dedicated chapter. These areas are: shareholders and the shareholders' meeting (arts 7–17); directors and the board of directors (arts 18–43); supervisors and the supervisory board (arts 44–50); senior executives, and their incentives and constraints (arts 51–62); controlling shareholders and related parties (arts 63–77); institutional investors and gatekeepers (arts 78–82); stakeholders and environmental, social and governance ('ESG') issues (arts 83–87); and information disclosures (arts 88–96). The Code combines elements of international best practice and selected governance measures that have been locally developed to suit distinctive Chinese corporate law and corporate governance approaches.

It is worth noting the CCGLC's emphasis on constraining the controlling shareholder's opportunistic behaviour. The Code reiterates the fiduciary duties that a controlling shareholder owes to the listed company and to non-controlling shareholders. The controller shall not abuse its control over the listed company and must not exploit its control to pursue illicit gains;[297] nor can the controlling shareholder take the place of the shareholders' meeting and the board of directors in corporate decision-making.[298] Diversion of the listed company's assets to its controller is yet another abuse that the CCGLC seeks to categorically prevent.[299] In addition to these declaratory, general provisions, the CCGLC also addresses two specific practices where the controller–non-controller conflicts are known to be acute in the Chinese listed sector: voluntary undertakings given by the controlling shareholder; and change of corporate control, by imposing heightened duties upon the controlling shareholder.[300]

Another distinctive aspect to note is that the CCGLC assigns a governance role to institutional investors. Institutional investors and asset managers of all sorts are generally encouraged to take part in corporate governance by exercising their shareholders' rights, such as the right to vote, the right to inquiry and the right to make shareholder proposals.[301] The CCGLC further specifies some possible activist steps that Chinese institutions can consider taking, such as taking part in the decision-making on fundamental corporate matters; nominating candidates to become directors and supervisors; and overseeing performance of directors and supervisors.[302] The CCGLC also calls on institutional investors and asset managers to enhance transparency in respect of their

---

296 Ibid art 6.
297 Ibid art 63.
298 Ibid art 65.
299 Ibid art 70.
300 Ibid arts 66, 67. Chinese controlling shareholders from time to time give undertakings to, for instance, take remedial steps mitigating critical corporate governance weaknesses, in their attempts to address concerns by public investors and regulators. There are reported occasions in which some of these undertakings failed to follow through, plunging share prices and saddling investors with heavy losses.
301 Ibid art 78.
302 Ibid art 79.

engagement strategies by disclosing the objectives and principles of their engagement; their voting strategies; how they exercise their shareholder rights; and what is hoped to be achieved by these measures.[303] The CCGLC seems to have placed considerable faith in institutional investor activism, notwithstanding the legal and institutional constraints that can limit its potential of constraining majority shareholders' expropriation of minority investors.[304] Recent studies point to evidence of Chinese institutional investors playing an increasingly important corporate governance role.[305]

Other governance improvements that the CCGLC seeks to promote include: increased shareholders' participation in corporate governance (for example, remote attendance of the shareholders' meeting, electronic voting, and proxy solicitation); greater board diversity; enhanced duties imposed on independent directors; greater governance roles assigned to the board's committees; executive incentive programs and 'Say on Pay'; enhanced internal control over disclosure; and a greater stakeholder-focus through ESG reporting.

12.6.5 Sustainability

The notion of corporate sustainability has been recognised as a principle under the current CLPRC since it came into effect in 2006. The statutory provision on sustainability itself contains only a bare-bone requirement that Chinese companies should 'undertake social responsibility'.[306] Legislative materials suggest that Chinese legislature's conceptualisation of sustainability places considerable emphasis on two particular dimensions, namely the environment and employees, and not much beyond.[307]

Notwithstanding a relatively weak focus on sustainability-related issues in the CLPRC, state-centric 'corporate social responsibility' ('CSR') initiatives have been promoted in China recently.[308] Chinese courts have also played a role by innovatively implementing and promoting CSR approaches.[309] It should also be noted the two official exchanges, the Shenzhen and Shanghai Stock Exchanges, have been promoting and developing a CSR-focused approach for corporations listed on these exchanges. An illustration of this is the Shenzhen Stock Exchange's *Guide on Social Responsibility of Listed Companies* ('Shenzhen CSR Guide'),[310] which came into effect on 25 September 2006, particularly its ss 1–3.

303 Ibid art 80.
304 Chao Xi, 'Institutional shareholder activism in China: Law and practice' (2006) 17(10) *International Company and Commercial Law Review* 251.
305 Lin Lin and Dan W Puchniak, 'Institutional investors in China: Corporate governance and policy channeling in the market within the state' (2022) 35(1) *Columbia Journal of Asian Law* 74.
306 2018 CLPRC s 5.
307 This and the following two subsections are drawn largely from Chao Xi, 'Shareholder voting and corporate sustainability in China' in Beate Sjåfjell and Christopher Bruner (eds), *Cambridge Handbook of Corporate Law, Corporate Governance and Sustainability* (Cambridge University Press, 2019) 431, 433.
308 Virginia Harper Ho, 'Beyond regulation: A comparative look at state-centric corporate social responsibility and the law in China' (2013) 46 *Vanderbilt Journal of Transnational Law* 375.
309 Li-Wen Lin, 'Mandatory corporate social responsibility? Legislative innovation and judicial application in China' (2020) 68(3) *American Journal of Comparative Law* 576.
310 For an informal translation of the Guide, see Shenzen Stock Exchange, *Shenzhen Stock Exchange Social Responsibility: Instructions to Listed Companies* (2006) <https://www.szse.cn/English/rules/siteRule/t20070604_559475.html>.

The Chinese stock exchanges' conceptualisation of CSR is considerably broader than the legislature's restricted focus. For instance, the Shenzhen CSR Guide stipulates that the company bears responsibilities toward 'the holistic development of the country and society, to natural environment and resources, and to stakeholders including shareholders, creditors, employees, customers, consumers, suppliers, as well as the community'.[311] Hence, the economic function of Chinese listed firms goes hand-in-hand with their other responsibilities, with the ultimate aim of achieving 'coherent and harmonious' co-development with society.[312] Of particular note is the Shenzhen CSR Guide's focus on environmental protection and sustainable development, to which its Chapter V is exclusively dedicated.

China's CSR disclosure regime is based on two different arrangements. CSR reporting is màndatory for certain groups of listed firms, and largely voluntary for others. CSRC-enacted rules generally encourage listed firms to disclose the steps they have taken to fulfil their social responsibilities. The exception to the voluntariness principle pertains to heavy polluters,[313] which are required to provide pollution-related information in their annual reports. Exchanges-made rules add an important layer. While CSR reporting is voluntary in general, it is mandatory for three types of Shanghai Stock Exchange–listed firms – the constituent firms of the SHSE Corporate Governance Index, dual-listed firms and financial services firms – and for one type of Shenzhen Stock Exchange-listed firm, the constituent firms of the SZSE100 Index.[314]

12.6.6 Future directions

A major overhaul of Chinese corporate law and governance is under way at the time of writing (August 2023). The NPCSC, China's national legislature, deliberated an amendment bill of the CLPRC in December 2021.[315]

The Bill proposes a number of significant changes to China's corporate governance regime. These include a reallocation of corporate decision-making by vesting the 'residual' power to the board of directors, therefore marking a broad shift towards a board-centred approach. The Bill also relaxes the mandatory dual-board structure, allowing Chinese companies to opt between the traditional dual board and the to-be-introduced one-tier board. The monitoring role in the company opting for the one-tier board structure is required to be assumed by an audit committee, composed by majority of non-executive directors. Also proposed by the Bill is a liability rule holding the controlling holder liable for any losses incurred to the company and shareholders that result from its abuse of control.[316]

---

311 Shenzhen Stock Exchange, *Guide on Social Responsibility of Listed Companies* (2006) art 2.
312 Ibid art 3.
313 Lists of local heavy polluters are maintained and regularly updated by the environmental protection departments of Chinese local governments.
314 Chao Xi, 'Shareholder voting and corporate sustainability in China' in Sjåfjell and Bruner (eds), *Cambridge Handbook of Corporate Law, Corporate Governance and Sustainability* (2019) 431, 436–7.
315 'Chinese lawmakers review legal amendments to improve corporate governance' <http://www.npc .gov.cn/englishnpc/c23934/202112/4d5edbca9eb94162b65239585cd5c77a.shtml>.
316 See, eg, Simon Li and Linda Gao, 'China set to revise its company law', *China Law Vision* (24 April 2022) <https://www.chinalawvision.com/2022/04/company-law/china-set-to-revise-its-company-law/>.

12.6.7 Conclusion

China's corporate governance reforms in the past two decades have been a fertile ground for elements of international best practice to be combined and fused with locally developed rules to suit distinctive Chinese corporate law and corporate governance approaches. The ensuing array of governance strategies and tactics have been primarily aimed at curbing controller extraction of private benefits at the expense of minority shareholders, a practice that has plagued the Chinese listed sector for the past two decades. It should, however, be pointed out that empirical evidence has produced mixed conclusions as to how effective these corporate governance reforms have been. It remains to be seen how future corporate governance developments in China will help to offer fresh comparative perspectives on how best to address the conflicts of interest between controlling and non-controlling shareholders.

INDEX

Printed in the United States
by Baker & Taylor Publisher Services